THE NEW TESTAMENT

OF OUR LORD AND SAVIOR JESUS CHRIST

Revised Standard Version

With Pictures

To Floyd and Opal,
October, 1964

Wishing you happy reading and enjoyment of the authentic pictures taken in Bible Lands. They were taken by American Bible Society people years before World Wars destroyed many of the views which remain only on the negatives or plates in the keeping of the Bible Society.

John & Gay.

AMERICAN BIBLE SOCIETY

NEW YORK

CONTENTS

I. THE LIGHT OF THE WORLD   PAGES

    Matthew . . . . 3 — 31

II. SOWING THE SEED

    Mark . . . . 35 — 63

III. THE GOOD NEWS

    Luke . . . . 67 — 95

IV. HE GAVE HIS ONLY SON

    John . . . . 99 — 127

V. INTO ALL THE WORLD

    The Acts of the Apostles . . . . 131 — 158

VI. MORE THAN CONQUERORS

    Romans . . . . 163 — 174

    1 Corinthians . . . . 175 — 186

    2 Corinthians . . . . 187 — 191

VII. A CLOUD OF WITNESSES

    Galatians . . . . 195 — 199

    Ephesians . . . . 199 — 202

    Philippians . . . . 203 — 204

    Colossians . . . . 205 — 207

    1 & 2 Thessalonians . . . . 207 — 210

    1 & 2 Timothy . . . . 211 — 214

    Titus 215

    Philemon 216

    Hebrews . . . . 217 — 223

VIII. OUT OF DEATH INTO LIFE

    James . . . . 227 — 229

    1 & 2 Peter . . . . 230 — 234

    1, 2 & 3 John . . . . 234 — 237

    Jude 237

    Revelation . . . . 238 — 255

THE NEW TESTAMENT RS250 IL
ABS—1963—50M—D

The Light of the World

EARLY MORNING ON THE SEA OF GALILEE

THE GOSPEL ACCORDING TO MATTHEW

REVISED STANDARD VERSION

PALESTINE AND NEIGHBORING LANDS

Frequent mention is made in the Gospel according to Matthew of lands and cities located in the area surrounding the land of Palestine, as well as to cities and villages in Palestine itself.

Egypt. In Matthew 2:13–15 it is related that Joseph and Mary fled with Jesus to Egypt. Travel between Palestine and Egypt was common from the time of Abraham (Genesis 12:10). The most frequently traveled route ran down along the coast all the way to Egypt. Another way went past wells at Beersheba and Rehoboth and on across the wilderness of Shur to Egypt.

Sheba. In Matthew 12:42 Jesus speaks of "the queen of the South," meaning the queen of Sheba, who came to hear the wisdom of Solomon (1 Kings 10:1). The land of Sheba, or Saba, was in the southwestern corner of Arabia, with its capital at Marib, site of a famous irrigation dam.

Syria. In Matthew 4:24 the fame of Jesus is said to have spread throughout all Syria. Geographically speaking, the name Syria was applied to the entire tract of fertile land at the eastern end of the Mediterranean Sea, including Palestine. Politically, however, Palestine was often separate, while the name Syria was used to designate the kingdom or province to the north. Under Roman administration its limits reached down the coast to include Phoenicia and Mount Carmel, with oversight over Palestine. The end of the rule of Pontius Pilate as procurator of Judea, Samaria and Idumea came when he was deposed by the Syrian governor Vitellius.

Tyre and Sidon. The most famous cities of Phoenicia, Tyre and Sidon, are referred to on two different occasions in the Gospel of Matthew. In Matthew 11:20–24 Jesus declares that it will be more tolerable for Tyre and Sidon on the day of judgment than for those cities of Galilee where he had performed his mighty works. Again, in Matthew 15:21, it is related that Jesus withdrew to the district of Tyre and Sidon, where he healed the daughter of a woman from that region.

Tyre was situated on an island south of the port of Sidon. In the time of Solomon, Tyre was ruled by King Hiram, who supplied timber for the construction of the Temple in Jerusalem (1 Kings 5:1–12). Alexander the Great conquered it by building a causeway from the shore to the island; afterward this silted up to form the arm of land by which the city is now connected with the mainland. Sidon, unlike Tyre, submitted to Alexander the Great without a struggle and escaped the destruction which he visited on the sister city. At both Tyre and Sidon fine buildings were erected by Herod the Great.

Nineveh. In Matthew 12:41 Jesus refers to the preaching of Jonah in the city of Nineveh. This was the magnificent capital of ancient Assyria, whose king Sargon II (Isaiah 20:1) captured Samaria and put an end to the northern kingdom of Israel in 722–1 B.C. (2 Kings 17:6). His son and successor, Sennacherib (705–681 B.C.), invaded Judah in the days of Hezekiah (2 Kings 18:13).

The East. In the second chapter of Matthew there is related the story of the coming of the wise men, or Magi, from the East to Jerusalem to worship the new-born king of the Jews. The Magi were a priestly caste who may have come originally from Media. They were considered to have superior knowledge and held an important position in the eastern empires of Babylonia, Media and Persia (Daniel 2:2). This whole territory east of the Euphrates was conquered by the Parthians in the second century B.C. and later formed the eastern boundary of the Roman Empire. The traditional view has been that the wise men who presented their gifts to the infant Jesus were from Persia, the area now known as Iran.

Bethlehem, 5 miles south of Jerusalem, figures prominently in the account of the birth of Christ and the visit of the wise men (ch. 2:1–18). It was the native city of David (1 Samuel 16:1) and the town from which the prophet Micah foretold that a wonderful ruler would come forth (Micah 5:2).

Jerome went to Bethlehem in A.D. 385 and stayed most of the remaining years of his life, devoting himself to his scholarly translation of the Bible. The church marking the traditional place of the birth of Christ was built by Helena, mother of the Emperor Constantine. This venerable lady made a pilgrimage to Palestine at the age of eighty and before she died in A.D. 327 dedicated a church "at the grotto which had been the scene of the Savior's birth," as Eusebius relates. Portions of the original basilica have been found underneath the present Church of the Nativity, which is a larger structure built in the sixth century by Justinian.

The Decapolis ("Ten Cities") spoken of in Matthew 4:25 as being one of the localities from which great crowds followed Jesus, was a federation lying mostly east of the Jordan River. The ten cities as listed by Pliny, a Roman consul of Pontus and Bithynia in the second century

A.D., were as follows: Damascus, Philadelphia, Raphana, Scythopolis, Gadara, Hippos, Dion, Pella, Gerasa and Canatha. Other writers substitute other names, showing that the federation varied in extent from time to time. As its Greek name suggests, these cities were strongly Hellenistic in culture, with colonnaded streets, temples and theaters.

Caesarea Philippi. According to Matthew 16:13–20 it was in the district of Caesarea Philippi that Peter made his great confession, "You are the Christ, the Son of the living God." Caesarea Philippi lay near the foot of snow-capped Mount Hermon, by one of the main sources of the Jordan River. A place of rare beauty, the city had formerly been known as Paneas in honor of Pan, the god of fertility. A marble temple for the worship of Pan was built there by Herod the Great. Philip the tetrarch later enlarged and adorned the town and changed its name to Caesarea in honor of the Roman emperor Tiberius Caesar. It is known as Caesarea Philippi, or Caesarea of Philip, to distinguish it from the Caesarea located on the coast of Palestine.

THE HERODS

Herod the Great was the son of Antipater. Through his friendship with Mark Anthony, Herod secured from the Roman Senate the title King of Judea, occupied Jerusalem in 37 B.C. and reigned until 4 B.C. He rebuilt and beautified the second Temple in Jerusalem. His family life was full of trouble. He had ten wives in all, of whom Mariamne seems to have been his favorite. Later, in jealous rage he murdered her and her two sons on the suspicion that they were seeking his throne. It was this same Herod who also ordered the massacre of all the babies in Bethlehem (Matthew 2:16).

On the death of Herod the Great in 4 B.C. (Matthew 2:19) his kingdom was divided among his sons Archelaus, Herod Antipas and Philip. Archelaus, whose succession to the throne in Judea encouraged Joseph to return with his family to Nazareth (Matthew 2:22), was deposed by the Emperor Augustus on complaints by the Jews in A.D. 6. Herod Antipas, who became the tetrarch of Galilee and Perea, was the Herod who executed John the Baptist (Matthew 14:10) and who was reigning at Jesus' death. He repudiated his wife to marry Herodias, the wife of one of his half-brothers, for which he was rebuked by John the Baptist (Matthew 14:3, 4). The Emperor Caligula finally banished him in A.D. 39. Herod the Great's son Philip, mentioned in the New Testament only in Luke 3:1, was the tetrarch of the region east of Galilee.

(For additional geographical and historical material see other illustrated portions of the New Testament books of this series.)

Hebron, city of Hebrew patriarchs Abraham, Isaac and Jacob. The lower part of the construction of the mosque seen in the middle center dates from the original memorial building constructed over the Cave of Machpelah in the time of Herod the Great. In the 6th century A.D. Justinian turned it into a church, which was rebuilt as a mosque in later times

Matson Photo Service

THE LIGHT
OF THE WORLD

The Gospel according to MATTHEW

Matson Photo Service

Herodian wall at Hebron. These beautifully drafted stones are exactly like those in Herod's Temple in Jerusalem

Mosque at Hebron. The Herodian drafted stones supply the base of the wall at the left of the picture

Matson Photo Service

The Genealogy of Jesus Christ

[Matthew 1:1–17]

THE book of the genealogy of Jesus Christ, the son of David, the son of Abraham.

Abraham was the father of Isaac, and Isaac the father of Jacob, and Jacob the father of Judah and his brothers, and Judah the father of Perez and Zerah by Tamar, and Perez the father of Hezron, and Hezron the father of Ram,ᵃ and Ramᵃ the father of Ammin'adab, and Ammin'adab the father of Nahshon, and Nahshon the father of Salmon, and Salmon the father of Boaz by Rahab, and Boaz the father of Obed by Ruth, and Obed the father of Jesse, and Jesse the father of David the king.

And David was the father of Solomon by the wife of Uri'ah, and Solomon the father of Rehobo'am, and Rehobo'am the father of Abi'jah, and Abi'jah the father of Asa,ᵇ and Asaᵇ the father of Jehosh'aphat, and Jehosh'aphat the father of Joram, and Joram the father of Uzzi'ah, and Uzzi'ah the father of Jotham, and Jotham the father of Ahaz, and Ahaz the father of Hezeki'ah, and Hezeki'ah the father of Manas'seh, and Manas'seh the father of Amos,ᶜ and Amosᶜ the father of Josi'ah, and Josi'ah the father of Jechoni'ah and his brothers, at the time of the deportation to Babylon.

And after the deportation to Babylon: Jechoni'ah was the father of She-al'ti-el,ᵈ and She-al'ti-elᵈ the father of Zerub'babel, and Zerub'babel the father of Abi'ud, and Abi'ud the father of Eli'akim, and Eli'akim the father of Azor, and Azor the father of Zadok, and Zadok the father of Achim, and Achim the father of Eli'ud, and Eli'ud the father of Elea'zar, and Elea'zar the father of Matthan, and Matthan the father of Jacob, and Jacob the father of Joseph the husband of Mary, of whom Jesus was born, who is called Christ.

So all the generations from Abraham to David were fourteen generations, and from David to the deportation to Babylon fourteen generations, and from the deportation to Babylon to the Christ fourteen generations.

ᶜOther authorities read *Amon*
ᵈGreek *Salathiel*

ᵃGreek *Aram*
ᵇGreek *Asaph*

3

Nazareth, where Joseph and Mary lived

Entrance to the Church of the Nativity in Bethlehem, showing walled-in arch from the time of the Crusades

Matson Photo Service

The Birth of Jesus [1:18–25]

Now the birth of Jesus Christ[f] took place in this way. When his mother Mary had been betrothed to Joseph, before they came together she was found to be with child of the Holy Spirit; and her husband Joseph, being a just man and unwilling to put her to shame, resolved to divorce her quietly. But as he considered this, behold, an angel of the Lord appeared to him in a dream, saying, "Joseph, son of David, do not fear to take Mary your wife, for that which is conceived in her is of the Holy Spirit; she will bear a son, and you shall call his name Jesus, for he will save his people from their sins." All this took place to fulfil what the Lord had spoken by the prophet:

"Behold, a virgin shall conceive and bear
    a son,
    and his name shall be called Emman'u-
        el"[1]

(which means, God with us). When Joseph woke from sleep, he did as the angel of the

[f]Other ancient authorities read *of the Christ*
[1]Isaiah 7:14

4

Bethlehem, where Jesus was born

The Church of the Nativity at Bethlehem, built by Constantine in the 4th century, built anew by Justinian in the 6th century, often repaired in later times

Lord commanded him; he took his wife, but knew her not until she had borne a son; and he called his name Jesus.

The Visit of the Wise Men

[Matthew 2:1–6]

NOW when Jesus was born in Beth'lehem of Jude'a in the days of Herod the king, behold, wise men from the East came to Jerusalem, saying, "Where is he who has been born king of the Jews? For we have seen his star in the East, and have come to worship him." When Herod the king heard this, he was troubled, and all Jerusalem with him; and assembling all the chief priests and scribes of the people, he inquired of them where the Christ was to be born. They told him, "In Beth'lehem of Jude'a; for so it is written by the prophet:

'And you, O Beth'lehem, in the land of Judah,
    are by no means least among the rulers of Judah;
for from you shall come a ruler
    who will govern my people Israel.' "[2]

[2]Micah 5:2

5

L. Kofod

On the road to Bethlehem

Paul's Photos

Not far from the ancient city of Heliopolis in Egypt is the little village of Matariyeh. This ancient sycamore tree has been pointed out since the 17th century as a spot where Mary and Jesus rested on their flight to Egypt

L. A. Fereday

Palestinian inn of the Middle Ages, with dwelling rooms on the second floor and stables on the ground floor

The Wise Men Worship Jesus [2:7–12]

Then Herod summoned the wise men secretly and ascertained from them what time the star appeared; and he sent them to Beth'lehem, saying, "Go and search diligently for the child, and when you have found him bring me word, that I too may come and worship him." When they had heard the king they went their way; and lo, the star which they had seen in the East went before them, till it came to rest over the place where the child was. When they saw the star, they rejoiced exceedingly with great joy; and going into the house they saw the child with Mary his mother, and they fell down and worshiped him. Then, opening their treasures, they offered him gifts, gold and frankincense and myrrh.

And being warned in a dream not to return to Herod, they departed to their own country by another way.

The Flight to Egypt [2:13–15]

Now when they had departed, behold, an angel of the Lord appeared to Joseph in a dream and said, "Rise, take the child and his mother, and flee to Egypt, and remain there till I tell you; for Herod is about to search for the child, to destroy him." And he rose and took the child and his mother by night, and departed to Egypt, and remained there until the death of Herod. This was to fulfil what the Lord had spoken by the prophet, "Out of Egypt have I called my son."[3]

[3]*Hosea* 11:1

View in the Nile Delta area, Egypt

J. Lane Miller from Ewing Galloway, N.Y.

Bethlehem from the Shepherds' Fields.—Herod the Great, who killed all the male children in Bethlehem, had been made King of Judea by the Roman Senate through his friendship with Mark Anthony. He rebuilt and beautified the Temple in Jerusalem and constructed many other important buildings. He had ten wives in all, of whom Mariamne seems to have been his favorite; but he murdered her and her two sons on the suspicion that they were seeking his throne

The Male Children Killed [2:16-18]

Then Herod, when he saw that he had been tricked by the wise men, was in a furious rage, and he sent and killed all the male children in Beth'lehem and in all that region who were two years old or under, according to the time which he had ascertained from the wise men. Then was fulfilled what was spoken by the prophet Jeremi'ah:

"A voice was heard in Ramah,
  wailing and loud lamentation,
Rachel weeping for her children;
  she refused to be consoled,
because they were no more."[4]

[4]*Jeremiah 31:15*

The Return to Nazareth [2:19-23]

But when Herod died, behold, an angel of the Lord appeared in a dream to Joseph in Egypt, saying, "Rise, take the child and his mother, and go to the land of Israel, for those who sought the child's life are dead." And he rose and took the child and his mother, and went to the land of Israel. But when he heard that Archela'us reigned over Jude'a in place of his father Herod, he was afraid to go there, and being warned in a dream he withdrew to the district of Gal'ilee. And he went and dwelt in a city called Naz'areth, that what was spoken by the prophets might be fulfilled, "He shall be called a Naz'arene."

When Herod the Great died he was buried at one of his castles on a conical, artificially heightened hill south of Bethlehem. The hill, on the summit of which are the ruins of Herod's building, is now known as the Herodium or as Frank Mountain

View of Nazareth.—On the death of Herod the Great (Matt. 2:19) his kingdom was divided among his sons Archelaus, Herod Antipas and Philip. Archelaus, whose succession to the throne in Judea encouraged Joseph to return with his family to Nazareth (Matt. 2:22), was deposed by the Emperor Augustus on complaints by the Jews in A.D. 6. Herod Antipas, who became the tetrarch of Galilee and Perea, was the Herod who executed John the Baptist (Matt. 14:10) and who was reigning at Jesus' death. He repudiated his wife to marry Herodias, the wife of one of his half-brothers, for which he was rebuked by John the Baptist (Matt. 14:3-4). The Emperor Caligula finally banished him in A.D. 39. Herod the Great's son Philip, mentioned in the New Testament only in Luke 3:1, was the tetrarch of the region east of Galilee

Wilderness of Judea between Jerusalem and the Dead Sea

Harvest time at Bethlehem. The chaff and grain are thrown into the wind. The chaff is blown away but the heavy grain falls into a heap

The Preaching of John the Baptist

[Matthew 3:1–6]

IN those days came John the Baptist, preaching in the wilderness of Jude'a, "Repent, for the kingdom of heaven is at hand." For this is he who was spoken of by the prophet Isai'ah when he said,

"The voice of one crying in the wilderness:
Prepare the way of the Lord,
make his paths straight."⁵

Now John wore a garment of camel's hair, and a leather girdle around his waist; and his food was locusts and wild honey. Then went out to him Jerusalem and all Judea and all the region about the Jordan, and they were baptized by him in the river Jordan, confessing their sins.

⁵Isaiah 40:3

Pharisees and Sadducees Rebuked

[3:7–12]

But when he saw many of the Phar'isees and Sad'ducees coming for baptism, he said to them, "You brood of vipers! Who warned you to flee from the wrath to come? Bear fruit that befits repentance, and do not presume to say to yourselves, 'We have Abraham as our father'; for I tell you, God is able from these stones to raise up children to Abraham. Even now the axe is laid to the root of the trees; every tree therefore that does not bear good fruit is cut down and thrown into the fire.

"I baptize you with water for repentance, but he who is coming after me is mightier than I, whose sandals I am not worthy to carry; he will baptize you with the Holy Spirit and with fire. His winnowing fork is in his hand, and he will clear his threshing floor and gather his wheat into the granary, but the chaff he will burn with unquenchable fire."

The Baptism of Jesus [3:13–17]

Then Jesus came from Gal'ilee to the Jordan to John, to be baptized by him. John would have prevented him, saying, "I need to be baptized by you, and do you come to me?" But Jesus answered him, "Let it be so now; for thus it is fitting for us to fulfil all righteousness." Then he consented. And when Jesus was baptized, he went up immediately from the water, and behold, the heavens were opened*g* and he saw the Spirit of God descending like a dove, and alighting on him; and lo, a voice from heaven, saying, "This is my beloved Son,*h* with whom I am well pleased."⁶

*g*Other ancient authorities add *to him*
*h*Or *my Son, my* (or *the*) *Beloved*
⁶Psalm 2:7; Isaiah 42:1

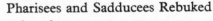

The Jordan River and the surrounding valley near Jericho, most of which is wilderness. The Jordan runs from the foothills of Mount Hermon through the Sea of Galilee, then meanders over 100 miles to the Dead Sea. For nearly all of its course it runs below sea level

8

The Temptation of Jesus [Matthew 4:1-11]

THEN Jesus was led up by the Spirit into the wilderness to be tempted by the devil. And he fasted forty days and forty nights, and afterward he was hungry. And the tempter came and said to him, "If you are the Son of God, command these stones to become loaves of bread." But he answered, "It is written,

'Man shall not live by bread alone,
but by every word that proceeds from the mouth of God.' "[7]

Then the devil took him to the holy city, and set him on the pinnacle of the temple, and said to him, "If you are the Son of God, throw yourself down; for it is written,

'He will give his angels charge of you,'[8]
and
'On their hands they will bear you up, lest you strike your foot against a stone.' "[8]

Jesus said to him, "Again it is written, 'You shall not tempt the Lord your God.' "[9] Again, the devil took him to a very high mountain, and showed him all the kingdoms of the world and the glory of them; and he said to him, "All these I will give you, if you will fall down and worship me." Then Jesus said to him, "Begone, Satan! for it is written,

'You shall worship the Lord your God and him only shall you serve.' "[10]

Then the devil left him, and behold, angels came and ministered to him.

Jesus Begins His Ministry [4:12-17]

Now when he heard that John had been arrested, he withdrew into Gal'ilee; and leaving Naz'areth he went and dwelt in Caper'na-um by the sea, in the territory of Zeb'ulun and Naph'tali, that what was spoken by the prophet Isai'ah might be fulfilled:

"The land of Zeb'ulun and the land of Naph'tali,
toward the sea, across the Jordan,
Gal'ilee of the Gentiles—
the people who sat in darkness
have seen a great light,
and for those who sat in the region and shadow of death
light has dawned."[11]

From that time Jesus began to preach, saying, "Repent, for the kingdom of heaven is at hand."

Jesus Calls Four Fishermen [4:18-22]

As he walked by the Sea of Gal'ilee, he saw two brothers, Simon who is called Peter and Andrew his brother, casting a net into the sea; for they were fishermen. And he said to them, "Follow me, and I will make you fishers of men." Immediately they left their nets and followed him. And going on from there he saw two other brothers, James the son of Zeb'edee and John his brother, in the boat with Zeb'edee their father, mending their nets, and he called them. Immediately they left the boat and their father, and followed him.

[7]Deuteronomy 8:3
[8]Psalms 91:11-12
[9]Deuteronomy 6:16
[10]Deuteronomy 6:13
[11]Isaiah 9:1-2

Religious News Service

Matson Photo Service

Approaching Jebel Qarantal, traditional Mount of Temptation

The pinnacle of the Temple may have been near the corner of the original temple enclosure, 170 feet above the gorge of the Kidron, where, as Josephus said, "one who looked down grew dizzy" →

The ruins of the synagogue at Capernaum on the shore of Galilee, probably built over site of older synagogue about 200 A.D.

Three Lions

Teaching, Preaching and Healing in Galilee [4:23-25]

And he went about all Gal'ilee, teaching in their synagogues and preaching the gospel of the kingdom and healing every disease and every infirmity among the people. So his fame spread throughout all Syria, and they brought him all the sick, those afflicted with various diseases and pains, demoniacs, epileptics, and paralytics, and he healed them. And great crowds followed him from Gal'ilee and the Decap'olis and Jerusalem and Jude'a and from beyond the Jordan.

The Sermon on the Mount [Matthew 5:1-2]

SEEING the crowds, he went up on the mountain, and when he sat down his disciples came to him. And he opened his mouth and taught them, saying:

The Beatitudes [5:3-12]

"Blessed are the poor in spirit, for theirs is the kingdom of heaven.

"Blessed are those who mourn, for they shall be comforted.

"Blessed are the meek, for they shall inherit the earth.

"Blessed are those who hunger and thirst for righteousness, for they shall be satisfied.

"Blessed are the merciful, for they shall obtain mercy.

"Blessed are the pure in heart, for they shall see God.

"Blessed are the peacemakers, for they shall be called sons of God.

"Blessed are those who are persecuted for righteousness' sake, for theirs is the kingdom of heaven.

"Blessed are you when men revile you and persecute you and utter all kinds of evil against you falsely on my account. Rejoice and be glad, for your reward is great in heaven, for so men persecuted the prophets who were before you.

The Salt of the Earth [5:13]

"You are the salt of the earth; but if salt has lost its taste, how shall its saltness be restored? It is no longer good for anything except to be thrown out and trodden under foot by men.

Selling salt

Oriental Institute, University of Chicago

Three Lions

The Horns of Hattin, a rocky hill near the Sea of Galilee, traditionally connected with the Sermon on the Mount

The Light of the World [5:14-16]

"You are the light of the world. A city set on a hill cannot be hid. Nor do men light a lamp and put it under a bushel, but on a stand, and it gives light to all in the house. Let your light so shine before men, that they may see your good works and give glory to your Father who is in heaven.

The Law and the Prophets [5:17-20]

"Think not that I have come to abolish the law and the prophets; I have come not to abolish them but to fulfil them. For truly, I say to you, till heaven and earth pass away, not an iota, not a dot, will pass from the law until all is accomplished. Whoever then relaxes one of the least of these commandments and teaches men so, shall be called least in the kingdom of heaven; but he who does them and teaches them shall be called great in the kingdom of heaven. For I tell you, unless your righteousness exceeds that of the scribes and Phar'isees, you will never enter the kingdom of heaven.

Anger and Judgment [5:21-26]

"You have heard that it was said to the men of old, 'You shall not kill; and whoever kills shall be liable to judgment.'[12] But I say to you that every one who is angry with his brother[i] shall be liable to judgment; whoever insults[j] his brother shall be liable to the council, and whoever says, 'You fool!' shall be liable to the hell[k] of fire. So if you are offering your gift at the altar, and there remember that your brother has something against you, leave your gift there before the altar and go; first be reconciled to your brother, and then come and offer your gift. Make friends quickly with your accuser, while you are going with him to court, lest your accuser hand you over to the judge, and the judge to the guard, and you be put in prison; truly, I say to you, you will never get out till you have paid the last penny.

Adultery [5:27-30]

"You have heard that it was said, 'You shall not commit adultery.'[13] But I say to you that every one who looks at a woman lustfully has already committed adultery with her in his heart. If your right eye causes you to sin, pluck it out and throw it away; it is better that you lose one of your members than that your whole body be thrown into hell.[k] And if your right hand causes you to sin, cut it off and throw it away; it is better that you lose one of your members than that your whole body go into hell.[k]

[13]*Exodus* 20:14; *Deuteronomy* 5:18

American University Museum, Beirut

Lamp dating from period between 1st and 3rd centuries A.D.

Blowing the shofar, traditional Jewish horn

[i]Other ancient authorities insert *without cause*
[j]Greek *says Raca to* (an obscure term of abuse)
[k]Greek *Gehenna*
[12]*Exodus* 20:13; *Deuteronomy* 5:17

Divorce [5:31-32]

"It was also said, 'Whoever divorces his wife, let him give her a certificate of divorce.'[14] But I say to you that every one who divorces his wife, except on the ground of unchastity, makes her an adulteress; and whoever marries a divorced woman commits adultery.

Oaths [5:33-37]

"Again you have heard that it was said to the men of old, 'You shall not swear falsely, but shall perform to the Lord what you have sworn.'[15] But I say to you, Do not swear at all, either by heaven, for it is the throne of God, or by the earth, for it is his footstool, or by Jerusalem, for it is the city of the great King. And do not swear by your head, for you cannot make one hair white or black. Let what you say be simply 'Yes' or 'No'; anything more than this comes from evil.[j]

Retaliation [5:38-42]

"You have heard that it was said, 'An eye for an eye and a tooth for a tooth.'[16] But I say to you, Do not resist one who is evil. But if any one strikes you on the right cheek, turn to him the other also; and if any one would sue you and take your coat, let him have your cloak as well; and if any one forces you to go one mile, go with him two miles. Give to him who begs from you, and do not refuse him who would borrow from you.

"Love Your Enemies" [5:43-48]

"You have heard that it was said, 'You shall love your neighbor and hate your enemy.'[17] But I say to you, Love your enemies and pray for those who persecute you, so that you may be sons of your Father who is in heaven; for he makes his sun rise on the evil and on the good, and sends rain on the just and on the unjust. For if you love those who love you, what reward have you? Do not even the tax collectors do the same? And if you salute only your brethren, what more are you doing than others? Do not even the Gentiles do the same? You, therefore, must be perfect, as your heavenly Father is perfect.

A Warning Against Hypocrisy

[Matthew 6:1]

"BEWARE of practicing your piety before men in order to be seen by them; for then you will have no reward from your Father who is in heaven.

Almsgiving [6:2-4]

"Thus, when you give alms, sound no trumpet before you, as the hypocrites do in the synagogues and in the streets, that they may be praised by men. Truly, I say to you, they have their reward. But when you give alms, do not let your left hand know what your right hand is doing, so that your alms may be in secret; and your Father who sees in secret will reward you.

[j]Or the evil one
[14]Deuteronomy 24:1-4
[15]Leviticus 19:12; Numbers 30:2; Deuteronomy 23:21
[16]Exodus 21:24; Leviticus 24:20; Deuteronomy 19:21
[17]Leviticus 19:18

Pray in Secret [6:5-6]

"And when you pray, you must not be like the hypocrites; for they love to stand and pray in the synagogues and at the street corners, that they may be seen by men. Truly, I say to you, they have their reward. But when you pray, go into your room and shut the door and pray to your Father who is in secret; and your Father who sees in secret will reward you.

The Lord's Prayer [6:7-15]

"And in praying do not heap up empty phrases as the Gentiles do; for they think that they will be heard for their many words. Do not be like them, for your Father knows what you need before you ask him. Pray then like this:
Our Father who art in heaven,
Hallowed be thy name.
Thy kingdom come,
Thy will be done,
On earth as it is in heaven.
Give us this day our daily bread;[m]
And forgive us our debts,
As we also have forgiven our debtors;
And lead us not into temptation,
But deliver us from evil.[n]

According to late tradition the place where Christ taught his disciples the Lord's Prayer was located on the Mount of Olives. The Church of the Pater Noster stands there, with tablets inscribed with the Lord's Prayer in many different languages

Matson Photo Service

For if you forgive men their trespasses, your heavenly Father also will forgive you; but if you do not forgive men their trespasses, neither will your Father forgive your trespasses.

Fasting before the Father [6:16-18]

"And when you fast, do not look dismal, like the hypocrites, for they disfigure their faces that their fasting may be seen by men. Truly, I say to you, they have their reward. But when you fast, anoint your head and wash your face, that your fasting may not be seen by men but by your Father who is in secret; and your Father who sees in secret will reward you.

Possessions [6:19-21]

"Do not lay up for yourselves treasures on earth, where moth and rust[o] consume

[m]Or our bread for the morrow
[n]Or the evil one. Other authorities, some ancient, add, in some form, For thine is the kingdom and the power and the glory, for ever. Amen.
[o]Or worm

and where thieves break in and steal, but lay up for yourselves treasures in heaven, where neither moth nor rust[o] consumes and where thieves do not break in and steal. For where your treasure is, there will your heart be also.

The Parable of the Sound Eye [6:22-23]

"The eye is the lamp of the body. So, if your eye is sound, your whole body will be full of light; but if your eye is not sound, your whole body will be full of darkness. If then the light in you is darkness, how great is the darkness!

Serving Two Masters [6:24]

"No one can serve two masters; for either he will hate the one and love the other, or he will be devoted to the one and despise the other. You cannot serve God and mammon.

Anxiety [6:25-34]

"Therefore I tell you, do not be anxious about your life, what you shall eat or what you shall drink, nor about your body, what you shall put on. Is not life more than food, and the body more than clothing? Look at the birds of the air: they neither sow nor reap nor gather into barns, and yet your heavenly Father feeds them. Are you not of more value than they? And which of you by being anxious can add one cubit to his span of life?[p] And why are you anxious about clothing? Consider the lilies of the field, how they grow; they neither toil nor spin; yet I tell you, even Solomon in all his glory was not arrayed like one of these. But if God so clothes the grass of the field, which today is alive and tomorrow is thrown into the oven, will he not much more clothe you, O men of little faith? Therefore do not be anxious, saying, 'What shall we eat?' or 'What shall we drink?' or 'What shall we wear?' For the Gentiles seek all these things; and your heavenly Father knows that you need them all. But seek first his kingdom and his righteousness, and all these things shall be yours as well.

"Therefore do not be anxious about tomorrow, for tomorrow will be anxious for itself. Let the day's own trouble be sufficient for the day.

[p]Or to his stature

The "lily of the field" may have been the anemone coronaria, as shown in this picture

Palestine Institute

Modern grape picker in Palestine

Flowers in a small valley in Palestine

Palestine Institute

Judging Others [Matthew 7:1–6]

"JUDGE not, that you be not judged. For with the judgment you pronounce you will be judged, and the measure you give will be the measure you get. Why do you see the speck that is in your brother's eye, but do not notice the log that is in your own eye? Or how can you say to your brother, 'Let me take the speck out of your eye,' when there is the log in your own eye? You hypocrite, first take the log out of your own eye, and then you will see clearly to take the speck out of your brother's eye.

"Do not give dogs what is holy; and do not throw your pearls before swine, lest they trample them under foot and turn to attack you.

Ask, Seek, Knock [7:7–12]

"Ask, and it will be given you; seek, and you will find; knock, and it will be opened to you. For every one who asks receives, and he who seeks finds, and to him who knocks it will be opened. Or what man of you, if his son asks him for bread, will give him a stone? Or if he asks for a fish, will give him a serpent? If you then, who are evil, know how to give good gifts to your children, how much more will your Father who is in heaven give good things to those who ask him! So whatever you wish that men would do to you, do so to them; for this is the law and the prophets.

The Parable of the Narrow Gate [7:13–14]

"Enter by the narrow gate; for the gate is wide and the way is easy,*q* that leads to destruction, and those who enter by it are many. For the gate is narrow and the way is hard, that leads to life, and those who find it are few.

The Parable of the Fruit Tree [7:15–20]

"Beware of false prophets, who come to you in sheep's clothing but inwardly are ravenous wolves. You will know them by their fruits. Are grapes gathered from thorns, or figs from thistles? So, every sound tree bears good fruit, but the bad tree bears evil fruit. A sound tree cannot bear evil fruit, nor can a bad tree bear good fruit. Every tree that does not bear good fruit is cut down and thrown into the fire. Thus you will know them by their fruits.

"I Never Knew You" [7:21–23]

"Not every one who says to me, 'Lord, Lord,' shall enter the kingdom of heaven, but he who does the will of my Father who is in heaven. On that day many will say to me, 'Lord, Lord, did we not prophesy in your name, and cast out demons in your name, and do many mighty works in your name?' And then will I declare to them, 'I never knew you; depart from me, you evil-doers.'

The Two Foundations [7:24–29]

"Every one then who hears these words of mine and does them will be like a wise man who built his house upon the rock; and the rain fell, and the floods came, and the winds blew and beat upon that house,

but it did not fall, because it had been founded on the rock. And every one who hears these words of mine and does not do them will be like a foolish man who built his house upon the sand; and the rain fell, and the floods came, and the winds blew and beat against that house, and it fell; and great was the fall of it."

And when Jesus finished these sayings, the crowds were astonished at his teaching, for he taught them as one who had authority, and not as their scribes.

Jesus Cleanses a Leper [Matthew 8:1–4]

WHEN he came down from the mountain, great crowds followed him; and behold, a leper came to him and knelt before him, saying, "Lord, if you will, you can make me clean." And he stretched out his hand and touched him, saying, "I will; be clean." And immediately his leprosy was cleansed. And Jesus said to him, "See that you say nothing to any one; but go, show yourself to the priest, and offer the gift that Moses commanded, for a proof to the people."*r*

A Centurion's Servant Healed [8:5–13]

As he entered Caper'na-um, a centurion came forward to him, beseeching him and saying, "Lord, my servant is lying paralyzed at home, in terrible distress." And he said to him, "I will come and heal him." But the centurion answered him, "Lord, I am not worthy to have you come under my roof; but only say the word, and my servant will be healed. For I am a man under authority, with soldiers under me; and I say to one, 'Go,' and he goes, and to another, 'Come,' and he comes, and to my slave, 'Do this,' and he does it." When Jesus heard him, he marveled, and said to those who followed him, "Truly, I say to you, not even*s* in Israel have I found such faith. I tell you, many will come from east and west and sit at table with Abraham, Isaac, and Jacob in the kingdom of heaven, while the sons of the kingdom will be thrown into the outer darkness; there men will weep and gnash their teeth." And to the centurion Jesus said, "Go; be it done for you as you have believed." And the servant was healed at that very moment.

Jesus Heals Peter's Mother-in-law [8:14–17]

And when Jesus entered Peter's house, he saw his mother-in-law lying sick with a fever; he touched her hand, and the fever left her, and she rose and served him. That evening they brought to him many who were possessed with demons; and he cast out the spirits with a word, and healed all who were sick. This was to fulfil what was spoken by the prophet Isai'ah, "He took our infirmities and bore our diseases."[18]

The Would-be Followers of Jesus [8:18–22]

Now when Jesus saw great crowds around him, he gave orders to go over to the other side. And a scribe came up and said to him, "Teacher, I will follow you

*r*Greek *to them*
*s*Other ancient authorities read *with no one*
[18]Isaiah 53:4

*q*Other ancient authorities read *for the way is wide and easy*

wherever you go." And Jesus said to him, "Foxes have holes, and birds of the air have nests; but the Son of man has nowhere to lay his head." Another of the disciples said to him, "Lord, let me first go and bury my father." But Jesus said to him, "Follow me, and leave the dead to bury their own dead."

Jesus Calms a Storm [8:23–27]

And when he got into the boat, his disciples followed him. And behold, there arose a great storm on the sea, so that the boat was being swamped by the waves; but he was asleep. And they went and woke him, saying, "Save, Lord; we are perishing." And he said to them, "Why are you afraid, O men of little faith?" Then he rose and rebuked the winds and the sea; and there was a great calm. And the men marveled, saying, "What sort of man is this, that even winds and sea obey him?"

The Gadarene Demoniacs Healed
[8:28–34]

And when he came to the other side, to the country of the Gadarenes, two demoniacs met him, coming out of the tombs, so fierce that no one could pass that way. And behold, they cried out, "What have you to do with us, O Son of God? Have you come here to torment us before the time?" Now a herd of many swine was feeding at some distance from them. And the demons begged him, "If you cast us out, send us away into the herd of swine." And he said to them, "Go." So they came out and went into the swine; and behold, the whole herd rushed down the steep bank into the sea, and perished in the waters. The herdsmen fled, and going into the city they told everything, and what had happened to the demoniacs. And behold, all the city came out to meet Jesus; and when they saw him, they begged him to leave their neighborhood.

Jesus Heals a Paralytic [Matthew 9:1–8]

AND getting into a boat he crossed over and came to his own city. And behold, they brought to him a paralytic, lying on his bed; and when Jesus saw their faith he said to the paralytic, "Take heart, my son; your sins are forgiven." And behold, some of the scribes said to themselves, "This man is blaspheming." But Jesus, knowing[u] their thoughts, said, "Why do you think evil in your hearts? For which is easier, to say, 'Your sins are forgiven,' or to say, 'Rise and walk'? But that you may know that the Son of man has authority on earth to for-

[t]Other ancient authorities read *Gergesenes;* some, *Gerasenes*
[u]Other ancient authorities read *seeing*

give sins"—he then said to the paralytic— "Rise, take up your bed and go home." And he rose and went home. When the crowds saw it, they were afraid, and they glorified God, who had given such authority to men.

The Call of Matthew [9:9]

As Jesus passed on from there, he saw a man called Matthew sitting at the tax office; and he said to him, "Follow me." And he rose and followed him.

Jesus Eats with Sinners [9:10–13]

And as he sat at table[v] in the house, behold, many tax collectors and sinners came and sat down with Jesus and his disciples. And when the Phar'isees saw this, they said to his disciples, "Why does your teacher eat with tax collectors and sinners?" But when he heard it, he said, "Those who are well have no need of a physician, but those who are sick. Go and learn what this means, 'I desire mercy, and not sacrifice.'[19] For I came not to call the righteous, but sinners.'

The Question about Fasting [9:14–17]

Then the disciples of John came to him, saying, "Why do we and the Phar'isees fast,[w] but your disciples do not fast?"

And Jesus said to them, "Can the wedding guests mourn as long as the bridegroom is with them? The days will come, when the bridegroom is taken away from them, and then they will fast. And no one puts a piece of unshrunk cloth on an old garment, for the patch tears away from the garment, and a worse tear is made. Neither is new wine put into old wineskins; if it is, the skins burst, and the wine is spilled, and the skins are destroyed; but new wine is put into fresh wineskins, and so both are preserved."

A Ruler's Daughter Raised [9:18–26]

While he was thus speaking to them, behold, a ruler came in and knelt before him, saying, "My daughter has just died; but come and lay your hand on her, and she will live." And Jesus rose and followed him, with his disciples. And behold, a woman who had suffered from a hemorrhage for twelve years came up behind him and touched the fringe of his garment; for she said to herself, "If I only touch his garment, I shall be made well." Jesus turned, and seeing her he said, "Take heart, daughter; your faith has made you well."

[v]Greek *reclined*
[w]Other ancient authorities add *much* or *often*
[19]*Hosea* 6:6

And instantly the woman was made well. And when Jesus came to the ruler's house, and saw the flute players, and the crowd making a tumult, he said, "Depart; for the girl is not dead but sleeping." And they laughed at him. But when the crowd had been put outside, he went in and took her by the hand, and the girl arose. And the report of this went through all that district.

Two Blind Men Receive Sight [9:27–31]

And as Jesus passed on from there, two blind men followed him, crying aloud, "Have mercy on us, Son of David." When he entered the house, the blind men came to him; and Jesus said to them, "Do you believe that I am able to do this?" They said to him, "Yes, Lord." Then he touched their eyes, saying, "According to your faith be it done to you." And their eyes were opened. And Jesus sternly charged them, "See that no one knows it." But they went away and spread his fame through all that district.

A Dumb Man Speaks [9:32–34]

As they were going away, behold, a dumb demoniac was brought to him. And when the demon had been cast out, the dumb man spoke; and the crowds marveled, saying, "Never was anything like this seen in Israel." But the Phar'isees said, "He casts out demons by the prince of demons."

"The Harvest Is Plentiful" [9:35–38]

And Jesus went about all the cities and villages, teaching in their synagogues and preaching the gospel of the kingdom, and healing every disease and every infirmity. When he saw the crowds, he had compassion for them, because they were harassed and helpless, like sheep without a shepherd. Then he said to his disciples, "The harvest is plentiful, but the laborers are few; pray therefore the Lord of the harvest to send out laborers into his harvest."

Jesus Chooses the Twelve [Matthew 10:1–4]

AND he called to him his twelve disciples and gave them authority over unclean spirits, to cast them out, and to heal every disease and every infirmity. The names of the twelve apostles are these: first, Simon, who is called Peter, and Andrew his brother; James the son of Zeb'edee and John his brother; Philip and Barthol'omew; Thomas and Matthew the tax collector; James the son of Alphae'us, and Thad'-daeus;[x] Simon the Cananae'an, and Judas Iscar'iot, who betrayed him.

[x]Other ancient authorities read *Lebbaeus or Lebbaeus called Thaddaeus*

Swine on Arab farm in Palestine
L. Kofod

"The harvest is plentiful, but the laborers are few"
L. A. Fereday

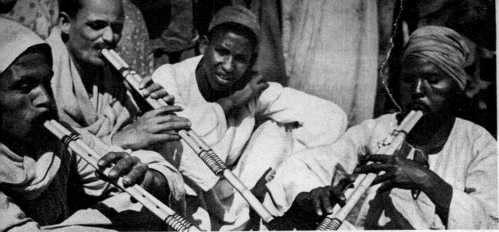

"We piped to you, and you did not dance"

The Mission of the Twelve
[10:5-15]

These twelve Jesus sent out, charging them, "Go nowhere among the Gentiles, and enter no town of the Samar'itans, but go rather to the lost sheep of the house of Israel. And preach as you go, saying, 'The kingdom of heaven is at hand.' Heal the sick, raise the dead, cleanse lepers, cast out demons. You received without pay, give without pay. Take no gold, nor silver, nor copper in your belts, no bag for your journey, nor two tunics, nor sandals, nor a staff; for the laborer deserves his food. And whatever town, or village you enter, find out who is worthy in it, and stay with him until you depart. As you enter the house, salute it. And if the house is worthy, let your peace come upon it; but if it is not worthy, let your peace return to you. And if any one will not receive you or listen to your words, shake off the dust from your feet as you leave that house or town. Truly, I say to you, it shall be more tolerable on the day of judgment for the land of Sodom and Gomor'rah than for that town.

Coming Persecutions [10:16-25]

"Behold, I send you out as sheep in the midst of wolves; so be wise as serpents and innocent as doves. Beware of men; for they will deliver you up to councils, and flog you in their synagogues, and you will be dragged before governors and kings for my sake, to bear testimony before them and the Gentiles. When they deliver you up, do not be anxious how you are to speak or what you are to say; for what you are to say will be given to you in that hour; for it is not you who speak, but the Spirit of your Father speaking through you. Brother will deliver up brother to death, and the father his child, and children will rise against parents and have them put to death; and you will be hated by all for my name's sake. But he who endures to the end will be saved. When they persecute you in one town, flee to the next; for truly, I say to you, you will not have gone through all the towns of Israel, before the Son of man comes.

"A disciple is not above his teacher, nor a servant[y] above his master; it is enough for the disciple to be like his teacher, and the servant[y] like his master. If they have called the master of the house Be-el'zebul, how much more will they malign those of his household.

[y]Or *slave*

Acknowledging Jesus before Men
[10:26-33]

"So have no fear of them; for nothing is covered that will not be revealed, or hidden that will not be known. What I tell you in the dark, utter in the light; and what you hear whispered, proclaim upon the housetops. And do not fear those who kill the body but cannot kill the soul; rather fear him who can destroy both soul and body in hell.[z] Are not two sparrows sold for a penny? And not one of them will fall to the ground without your Father's will. But even the hairs of your head are all numbered. Fear not, therefore; you are of more value than many sparrows. So every one who acknowledges me before men, I also will acknowledge before my Father who is in heaven; but whoever denies me before men, I also will deny before my Father who is in heaven.

Not Peace, but a Sword [10:34-39]

"Do not think that I have come to bring peace on earth; I have not come to bring peace, but a sword. For I have come to set a man against his father, and a daughter against her mother, and a daughter-in-law against her mother-in-law; and a man's foes will be those of his own household. He who loves father or mother more than me is not worthy of me; and he who loves son or daughter more than me is not worthy of me; and he who does not take his cross and follow me is not worthy of me. He who finds his life will lose it, and he who loses his life for my sake will find it.

Rewards [10:40-42]

"He who receives you receives me, and he who receives me receives him who sent me. He who receives a prophet because he is a prophet shall receive a prophet's reward, and he who receives a righteous man because he is a righteous man shall receive a righteous man's reward. And whoever gives to one of these little ones even a cup of cold water because he is a disciple, truly I say to you, he shall not lose his reward."

The Messengers from John the Baptist

[Matthew 11:1-6]

AND when Jesus had finished instructing his twelve disciples, he went on from there to teach and preach in their cities.

[z]Greek *Gehenna*

Now when John heard in prison about the deeds of the Christ, he sent word by his disciples and said to him, "Are you he who is to come, or shall we look for another?" And Jesus answered them, "Go and tell John what you hear and see: the blind receive their sight and the lame walk, lepers are cleansed and the deaf hear, and the dead are raised up, and the poor have good news preached to them. And blessed is he who takes no offense at me."

Jesus' Testimony to John the Baptist
[11:7-15]

As they went away, Jesus began to speak to the crowds concerning John: "What did you go out into the wilderness to behold? A reed shaken by the wind? Why then did you go out? To see a man[a] clothed in soft raiment? Behold, those who wear soft raiment are in kings' houses. Why then did you go out? To see a prophet?[b] Yes, I tell you, and more than a prophet. This is he of whom it is written,
'Behold, I send my messenger before thy face,
who shall prepare thy way before thee.'[20]
Truly, I say to you, among those born of women there has risen no one greater than John the Baptist; yet he who is least in the kingdom of heaven is greater than he. From the days of John the Baptist until now the kingdom of heaven has suffered violence,[c] and men of violence take it by force. For all the prophets and the law prophesied until John; and if you are willing to accept it, he is Eli'jah who is to come. He who has ears to hear,[d] let him hear.

What This Generation Is Like [11:16-19]

"But to what shall I compare this generation? It is like children sitting in the market places and calling to their playmates,
'We piped to you, and you did not dance;
we wailed, and you did not mourn.'
For John came neither eating nor drinking, and they say, 'He has a demon'; the Son of man came eating and drinking, and they say, 'Behold, a glutton and a drunkard, a friend of tax collectors and sinners!' Yet wisdom is justified by her deeds."[e]

Woes to Unrepentant Cities [11:20-24]

Then he began to upbraid the cities where most of his mighty works had been done, because they did not repent. "Woe to you, Chora'zin! woe to you, Beth-sa'ida! for if the mighty works done in you had been done in Tyre and Sidon, they would have repented long ago in sackcloth and ashes. But I tell you, it shall be more tolerable on the day of judgment for Tyre and Sidon than for you. And you, Caper'na-um, will you be exalted to heaven? You shall be brought down to Hades. For if the mighty works done in you, had been done in Sodom, it would have remained until this day. But I tell you that it shall be more tolerable on the day of judgment for the land of Sodom than for you."

[a]Or *What then did you go out to see? A man . . .*
[b]Other ancient authorities read *What then did you go out to see? A prophet?*
[c]Or *has been coming violently*
[d]Other ancient authorities omit *to hear*
[e]Other ancient authorities read *children* (Luke 7:35)
[20]*Malachi* 3:1

"Come to Me and Rest" [11:25-30]

At that time Jesus declared, "I thank thee, Father, Lord of heaven and earth, that thou hast hidden these things from the wise and understanding and revealed them to babes; yea, Father, for such was thy gracious will.' All things have been delivered to me by my Father; and no one knows the Son except the Father, and no one knows the Father except the Son and any one to whom the Son chooses to reveal him. Come to me, all who labor and are heavy laden, and I will give you rest. Take my yoke upon you, and learn from me; for I am gentle and lowly in heart, and you will find rest for your souls. For my yoke is easy, and my burden is light."

The Lord of the Sabbath

[Matthew 12:1-8]

AT that time Jesus went through the grainfields on the Sabbath; his disciples were hungry, and they began to pluck ears of grain and to eat. But when the Phar'isees saw it, they said to him, "Look, your disciples are doing what is not lawful to do on the sabbath." He said to them, "Have you not read what David did, when he was hungry, and those who were with him: how he entered the house of God and ate the bread of the Presence, which it was not lawful for him to eat nor for those who were with him, but only for the priests? Or have you not read in the law how on the sabbath the priests in the temple profane the sabbath, and are guiltless? I tell you, something greater than the temple is here. And if you had known what this means, 'I desire mercy, and not sacrifice,'[21] you would not have condemned the guiltless. For the Son of man is lord of the sabbath."

Jesus Heals on the Sabbath

[12:9-14]

And he went on from there, and entered their synagogue. And behold, there was a man with a withered hand. And they asked him, "Is it lawful to heal on the sabbath?" so that they might accuse him. He said to them, "What man of you, if he has one sheep and it falls into a pit on the sabbath, will not lay hold of it and lift it out? Of how much more value is a man than a sheep! So it is lawful to do good on the sabbath." Then he said to the man, "Stretch out your hand." And the man stretched it out, and it was restored, whole like the other. But the Phar'isees went out and took counsel against him, how to destroy him.

The Chosen Servant [12:15-21]

Jesus, aware of this, withdrew from there. And many followed him, and he healed them all, and ordered them not to make him known. This was to fulfil what was spoken by the prophet Isai'ah:

"Behold, my servant whom I have chosen,
    my beloved with whom my soul is
    well pleased.
I will put my Spirit upon him,
    and he shall proclaim justice to the
    Gentiles.
He will not wrangle or cry aloud,
    nor will any one hear his voice in the
    streets;

'Or so it was well-pleasing before thee

[21]Hosea 6:6

Frank Hurley from Rapho-Guillumette

Drawing water from a well
"Come to me, all who labor and are heavy laden, and I will give you rest"

he will not break a bruised reed
    or quench a smoldering wick,
till he brings justice to victory;
    and in his name will the Gentiles
    hope."[22]

Jesus and Beelzebul

[12:22-32]

Then a blind and dumb demoniac was brought to him, and he healed him, so that the dumb man spoke and saw. And all the people were amazed, and said, "Can this be the Son of David?" But when the Phar'isees heard it they said, "It is only by Be-el'zebul, the prince of demons, that this man casts out demons." Knowing their thoughts, he said to them, "Every kingdom divided against itself is laid waste, and no city or house divided against itself will stand; and if Satan casts out Satan, he is divided against himself; how then will his kingdom stand? And if I cast out demons by Be-el'zebul, by whom do your sons cast them out? Therefore they shall be your judges. But if it is by the Spirit of God that I cast out demons, then the kingdom of God has come upon you. Or how can one enter a strong man's house and plunder his goods, unless he first binds the strong man? Then indeed he may plunder his house. He who is not with me is against me; and he who does not gather with me scatters. Therefore I tell you, every sin and blasphemy will be forgiven men, but the blasphemy against the Spirit will not be forgiven. And whoever says a word against the Son of man will be forgiven; but whoever speaks against the Holy Spirit will not be forgiven, either in this age or in the age to come.

[22]Isaiah 42:1-4

L. A. Fereday

Woman with a cradle going to the fields

A modern Palestinian porter

Matson Photo Service

15

American Foundation for the Study of Man

Peristyle of the Temple of the Moon God in Marib, capital of ancient Sheba in South Arabia. From here the "Queen of the South" went to visit Solomon

American Foundation for the Study of Man

Part of an ancient scroll of the Book of Isaiah, recently discovered in a cave near the Dead Sea with other scrolls dating from before the time of Jesus, showing the passage Is. 6:8–10. Below it is the same passage in modern Hebrew print

American Schools of Oriental Research

עזרך וחמאותיך חצור יאשמע את קול אדני אמר את מי
אשלח ומי ילך לנו ואמרה העני שלחני 9 ויאמר לך ואמרתה
לעם הזה שמעו שמוע ועל תבינו ראו ראו ועל תדעו 10 השם
לב העם הזה ואזניו הכבד ועיניו השע פן יראה בעיניו
5 ובאזניו ישמעו בלבבו יבין ושב ורפא לו 11 ואמרה עד מתי
יהוה ויאמר עד אשר אם שאו ערים מאין יושב ובתים
מאין אדם והאדמה תשאה שממה 12 ורחק יהוה את האדם
ורבה עזובה בקרב הארץ 13 ועוד בה עשריה ושבה והיתה
לבער כאלה וכאלון אשר משלכת מצבת במה זרע הקדש
10 מצבתה

Bronze statue which was standing in the time of Christ in the Temple of the Moon God at Marib ←

"Out of the Abundance of the Heart"

[12:33-37]

"Either make the tree good, and its fruit good; or make the tree bad, and its fruit bad; for the tree is known by its fruit. You brood of vipers! how can you speak good, when you are evil? For out of the abundance of the heart the mouth speaks. The good man out of his good treasure brings forth good, and the evil man out of his evil treasure brings forth evil. I tell you, on the day of judgment men will render account for every careless word they utter; for by your words you will be justified, and by your words you will be condemned."

The Sign of Jonah [12:38-42]

Then some of the scribes and Phar'isees said to him, "Teacher, we wish to see a sign from you." But he answered them, "An evil and adulterous generation seeks for a sign; but no sign shall be given to it except the sign of the prophet Jonah. For as Jonah was three days and three nights in the belly of the whale, so will the Son of man be three days and three nights in the heart of the earth. The men of Nin'eveh will arise at the judgment with this generation and condemn it; for they repented at the preaching of Jonah, and behold, something greater than Jonah is here. The queen of the South will arise at the judgment with this generation and condemn it; for she came from the ends of the earth to hear the wisdom of Solomon, and behold, something greater than Solomon is here.

The Return of the Unclean Spirit

[12:43-45]

"When the unclean spirit has gone out of a man, he passes through waterless places seeking rest, but he finds none. Then he says, 'I will return to my house from which I came.' And when he comes he finds it empty, swept, and put in order. Then he

goes and brings with him seven other spirits more evil than himself, and they enter and dwell there; and the last state of that man becomes worse than the first. So shall it be also with this evil generation."

Jesus' Mother and Brothers [12:46-50]

While he was still speaking to the people, behold, his mother and his brothers stood outside, asking to speak to him.[g] But he replied to the man who told him, "Who is my mother, and who are my brothers?" And stretching out his hand toward his disciples, he said, "Here are my mother and my brothers! For whoever does the will of my Father in heaven is my brother, and sister, and mother."

The Parable of the Sower [Matthew 13:1-9]

THAT same day Jesus went out of the house and sat beside the sea. And great crowds gathered about him, so that he got into a boat and sat there; and the whole crowd stood on the beach. And he told them many things in parables, saying: "A sower went out to sow. And as he sowed, some seeds fell along the path, and the birds came and devoured them. Other seeds fell on rocky ground, where they had not much soil, and immediately they sprang up, since they had no depth of soil, but when the sun rose they were scorched; and since they had no root they withered away. Other seeds fell upon thorns, and the thorns grew up and choked them. Other seeds fell on good soil and brought forth grain, some a hundredfold, some sixty, some thirty. He who has ears,[h] let him hear."

The Purpose of the Parables [13:10-17]

Then the disciples came and said to him, "Why do you speak to them in parables?" And he answered them, "To you it has been given to know the secrets of the kingdom of heaven, but to them it has not been given. For to him who has will more be given, and he will have abundance; but from him who has not, even what he has will be taken away. This is why I speak to them in parables, because seeing they do not see, and hearing they do not hear, nor do they understand. With them indeed is fulfilled the prophecy of Isai'ah which says:

'You shall indeed hear but never understand,
and you shall indeed see but never perceive.
For this people's heart has grown dull,
and their ears are heavy of hearing,
and their eyes they have closed,
lest they should perceive with their eyes,
and hear with their ears,
and understand with their heart,
and turn for me to heal them.'[23]

But blessed are your eyes, for they see, and your ears, for they hear. Truly, I say to you, many prophets and righteous men longed to see what you see, and did not see it, and to hear what you hear, and did not hear it.

[g]Other ancient authorities insert verse 47, *Some one told him, "Your mother and your brothers are standing outside, asking to speak to you"*
[h]Other ancient authorities add here and in verse 43 *to hear*
[23]*Isaiah 6:9–10*

16

Jesus Explains the Parable of the Sower
[13:18-23]

"Hear then the parable of the sower. When any one hears the word of the kingdom and does not understand it, the evil one comes and snatches away what is sown in his heart; this is what was sown along the path. As for what was sown on rocky ground, this is he who hears the word and immediately receives it with joy; yet he has no root in himself, but endures for a while, and when tribulation or persecution arises on account of the word, immediately he falls away.[i] As for what was sown among thorns, this is he who hears the word, but the cares of the world and the delight in riches choke the word, and it proves unfruitful. As for what was sown on good soil, this is he who hears the word and understands it; he indeed bears fruit, and yields, in one case a hundredfold, in another sixty, and in another thirty."

The Parable of the Weeds among the Wheat [13:24-30]

Another parable he put before them, saying, "The kingdom of heaven may be compared to a man who sowed good seed in his field; but while men were sleeping, his enemy came and sowed weeds among the wheat, and went away. So when the plants came up and bore grain, then the weeds appeared also. And the servants[j] of the householder came and said to him, 'Sir, did you not sow good seed in your field? How then has it weeds?' He said to them, 'An enemy has done this.' The servants[j] said to him, 'Then do you want us to go and gather them?' But he said, 'No; lest in gathering the weeds you root up the wheat along with them. Let both grow together until the harvest; and at harvest time I will tell the reapers, Gather the weeds first and bind them in bundles to be burned, but gather the wheat into my barn.' "

The Parable of the Mustard Seed
[13:31-32]

Another parable he put before them, saying, "The kingdom of heaven is like a grain of mustard seed which a man took and sowed in his field; it is the smallest of all seeds, but when it has grown it is the greatest of shrubs and becomes a tree, so that the birds of the air come and make nests in its branches."

The Parable of the Leaven
[13:33]

He told them another parable. "The kingdom of heaven is like leaven which a woman took and hid in three measures of meal, till it was all leavened."

Jesus' Use of Parables
[13:34-35]

All this Jesus said to the crowds in parables; indeed he said nothing to them without a parable. This was to fulfil what was spoken by the prophet:[k]

Matson Photo Service

Gathering weeds from the wheat in a field at Bethel

"I will open my mouth in parables,
I will utter what has been hidden since
the foundation of the world."[24]

Jesus Explains the Parable of the Weeds Among the Wheat [13:36-43]

Then he left the crowds and went into the house. And his disciples came to him, saying, "Explain to us the parable of the weeds of the field." He answered, "He who sows the good seed is the Son of man; the field is the world, and the good seed means the sons of the kingdom; the weeds are the sons of the evil one, and the enemy who sowed them is the devil; the harvest is the close of the age, and the reapers are angels. Just as the weeds are gathered and burned with fire, so will it be at the close of the age. The Son of man will send his angels, and they will gather out of his kingdom all causes of sin and all evildoers, and throw them into the furnace of fire; there men will weep and gnash their teeth. Then the righteous will shine like the sun in the kingdom of their Father. He who has ears, let him hear.

The Parable of the Hidden Treasure
[13:44]

"The kingdom of heaven is like treasure hidden in a field, which a man found and covered up; then in his joy he goes and sells all that he has and buys that field.

The Parable of the Pearl of Great Value [13:45-46]

"Again, the kingdom of heaven is like a merchant in search of fine pearls, who, on finding one pearl of great value, went and sold all that he had and bought it.

White Mustard (Sinapis alba)

New York Botanical Garden

Treasure found in a field at Ras Shamra in Syria, dating from about the end of the 6th century B.C.

C. F. A. Schaeffer

[i]Or *stumbles*

[j]Or *slaves*

[k]Other ancient authorities read *the prophet Isaiah*

[24]Psalms 78:2

17

Casting a net into the Sea of Galilee

L. Kofod

The Parable of the Net [13:47-50]

"Again, the kingdom of heaven is like a net which was thrown into the sea and gathered fish of every kind; when it was full, men drew it ashore and sat down and sorted the good into vessels but threw away the bad. So it will be at the close of the age. The angels will come out and separate the evil from the righteous, and throw them into the furnace of fire; there men will weep and gnash their teeth.

Treasures New and Old [13:51-52]

"Have you understood all this?" They said to him, "Yes." And he said to them, "Therefore every scribe who has been trained for the kingdom of heaven is like a householder who brings out of his treasure what is new and what is old."

Jesus Rejected at Nazareth [13:53-58]

And when Jesus had finished these parables, he went away from there, and coming to his own country he taught them in their synagogue, so that they were astonished, and said, "Where did this man get this wisdom and these mighty works? Is not this the carpenter's son? Is not his mother called Mary? And are not his brothers James and Joseph and Simon and Judas? And are not all his sisters with us?' Where then did this man get all this?" And they took offense at him. But Jesus said to them, "A prophet is not without honor except in his own country and in his own house." And he did not do many mighty works there, because of their unbelief.

The Death of John the Baptist

[Matthew 14:1-12]

AT that time Herod the tetrarch heard about the fame of Jesus; and he said to his servants, "This is John the Baptist, he has been raised from the dead; that is why these powers are at work in him." For Herod had seized John and bound him and put him in prison, for the sake of Hero'dias, his brother Philip's wife;¹ because John said to him, "It is not lawful for you to have her." And though he wanted to put him to death, he feared the people, because they held him to be a prophet. But when Herod's birthday came, the daughter of Hero'di-as danced before the company, and pleased

¹Other ancient authorities read *his brother's wife*

Herod, so that he promised with an oath to give her whatever she might ask. Prompted by her mother, she said, "Give me the head of John the Baptist here on a platter." And the king was sorry; but because of his oaths and his guests he commanded it to be given; he sent and had John beheaded in the prison, and his head was brought on a platter and given to the girl, and she brought it to her mother. And his disciples came and took the body and buried it; and they went and told Jesus.

The Feeding of the Five Thousand

[14:13-21]

Now when Jesus heard this, he withdrew from there in a boat to a lonely place apart. But when the crowds heard it, they followed him on foot from the towns. As he went ashore he saw a great throng; and he had compassion on them, and healed their sick. When it was evening, the disciples came to him and said, "This is a lonely place, and the day is now over; send the crowds away to go into the villages and buy food for themselves." Jesus said, "They need not go away; you give them something to eat." They said to him, "We have only five loaves here and two fish." And he said, "Bring them here to me." Then he ordered the crowds to sit down on the grass; and taking the five loaves and the two fish he looked up to heaven, and blessed, and broke and gave the loaves to the disciples, and the disciples gave them to the crowds. And they all ate and were satisfied. And they took up twelve baskets full of the broken pieces left over. And those who ate were about five thousand men, besides women and children.

Jesus Walks on the Water [14:22-27]

Then he made the disciples get into the boat and go before him to the other side, while he dismissed the crowds. And after he had dismissed the crowds, he went up into the hills by himself to pray. When evening came, he was there alone, but the boat by this time was many furlongs distant from the land,ᵐ beaten by the waves; for the wind was against them. And in the fourth watch of the night he came to them, walking on the sea. But when the disciples saw him walking on the sea, they were terrified, saying, "It is a ghost!" And they cried out for fear. But immediately he spoke to them, saying, "Take heart, it is I; have no fear."

ᵐOther ancient authorities read *was out on the sea*

Peter Walks on the Water [14:28-33]

And Peter answered him, "Lord, if it is you, bid me come to you on the water." He said, "Come." So Peter got out of the boat and walked on the water and came to Jesus; but when he saw the wind,ⁿ he was afraid, and beginning to sink he cried out, "Lord, save me." Jesus immediately reached out his hand and caught him, saying to him, "O man of little faith, why did you doubt?" And when they got into the boat, the wind ceased. And those in the boat worshiped him, saying, "Truly you are the Son of God."

Jesus Heals the Sick in Gennesaret

[14:34-36]

And when they had crossed over, they came to land at Gennes'aret. And when the men of that place recognized him, they sent round to all that region and brought to him all that were sick, and besought him that they might only touch the fringe of his garment; and as many as touched it were made well.

The Tradition of the Elders

[Matthew 15:1-9]

THEN Phar'isees and scribes came to Jesus from Jerusalem and said, "Why do your disciples transgress the tradition of the elders? For they do not wash their hands when they eat." He answered them, "And why do you transgress the commandment of God for the sake of your tradition? For God commanded, 'Honor your father and your mother,' and, 'He who speaks evil of father or mother, let him surely die.'²⁵ But you say, 'If any one tells his father or his mother, What you would have gained from me is given to God,ᵒ he need not honor his father.' So, for the sake of your tradition, you have made void the wordᵖ of God. You hypocrites! Well did Isai'ah prophesy of you, when he said:

'This people honors me with their lips,
 but their heart is far from me;
in vain do they worship me,
 teaching as doctrines the precepts of
  men.' "²⁶

The Things That Defile

[15:10-20]

And he called the people to him and said to them, "Hear and understand: not what goes into the mouth defiles a man, but what comes out of the mouth, this defiles a man." Then the disciples came and said to him, "Do you know that the Phar'isees were offended when they heard this saying?" He answered, "Every plant which my heavenly Father has not planted will be rooted up. Let them alone; they are blind guides. And if a blind man leads a blind man, both will fall into a pit." But Peter said to him, "Explain the parable to us." And he said, "Are you also still without understanding? Do you not see that whatever goes into the mouth passes into

ⁿOther ancient authorities read *strong wind*
ᵒOr *an offering*
ᵖOther ancient authorities read *law*
²⁵*Exodus* 20:12; 21:17; *Deuteronomy* 5:16; *Leviticus* 20:9
²⁶*Isaiah* 29:13

the stomach, and so passes on?[q] But what comes out of the mouth proceeds from the heart, and this defiles a man. For out of the heart come evil thoughts, murder, adultery, fornication, theft, false witness, slander. These are what defile a man; but to eat with unwashed hands does not defile a man."

The Canaanite Woman's Plea

[15:21–28]

And Jesus went away from there and withdrew to the district of Tyre and Sidon. And behold, a Canaanite woman from that region came out and cried. "Have mercy on me, O Lord, Son of David; my daughter is severely possessed by a demon." But he did not answer her a word. And his disciples came and begged him, saying, "Send her away, for she is crying after us." He answered, "I was sent only to the lost sheep of the house of Israel." But she came and knelt before him, saying, "Lord, help me." And he answered, "It is not fair to take the children's bread and throw it to the dogs." She said, "Yes, Lord, yet even the dogs eat the crumbs that fall from their masters' table." Then Jesus answered her, "O woman, great is your faith! Be it done for you as you desire." And her daughter was healed instantly.

Jesus Heals Many People

[15:29–31]

And Jesus went on from there and passed along the Sea of Gal'ilee. And he went up into the hills, and sat down there. And great crowds came to him, bringing with them the lame, the maimed, the blind, the dumb, and many others, and they put them at his feet, and he healed them, so that the throng wondered, when they saw the dumb speaking, the maimed whole, the lame walking, and the blind seeing; and they glorified the God of Israel.

The Feeding of the Four Thousand

[15:32–39]

Then Jesus called his disciples to him and said, "I have compassion on the crowd, because they have been with me now three days, and have nothing to eat; and I am unwilling to send them away hungry, lest they faint on the way." And the disciples said to him, "Where are we to get bread enough in the desert to feed so great a crowd?" And Jesus said to them, "How many loaves have you?" They said, "Seven, and a few small fish." And commanding the crowd to sit down on the ground, he took the seven loaves and the fish, and having given thanks he broke them and gave them to the disciples, and the disciples gave them to the crowds. And they all ate and were satisfied; and they took up seven baskets full of the broken pieces left over. Those who ate were four thousand men, besides women and children. And sending away the crowds, he got into the boat and went to the region of Mag'adan.

The Sign of Jonah

[Matthew 16:1–4]

AND the Phar'isees and Sad'ducees came, and to test him they asked him to show them a sign from heaven. He an-

[q]Or is evacuated

swered them,[r] "When it is evening, you say, 'It will be fair weather; for the sky is red.' And in the morning, 'It will be stormy today, for the sky is red and threatening.' You know how to interpret the appearance of the sky, but you cannot interpret the signs of the times. An evil and adulterous generation seeks for a sign, but no sign shall be given to it except the sign of Jonah." So he left them and departed.

The Leaven of the Pharisees and Sadducees [16:5–12]

When the disciples reached the other side, they had forgotten to bring any bread. Jesus said to them, "Take heed and beware of the leaven of the Phar'isees and Sad'ducees." And they discussed it among themselves, saying, "We brought no bread." But Jesus, aware of this, said, "O men of little faith, why do you discuss among yourselves the fact that you have no bread? Do you not yet perceive? Do you not remember the five loaves of the five thousand, and how many baskets you gathered? Or the seven loaves of the four thousand, and how many baskets you gathered? How is it that you fail to perceive that I did not speak about bread? Beware of the leaven of the Phar'isees and Sad'ducees." Then they understood that he did not tell them to beware of the leaven of bread, but of the teaching of the Phar'isees and Sad'ducees.

Peter's Declaration about Jesus [16:13–20]

Now when Jesus came into the district of Caesare'a Phil'ippi, he asked his disciples, "Who do men say that the Son of man is?" And they said, "Some say John the Baptist, others say Eli'jah, and others Jeremi'ah or one of the prophets." He said to them, "But who do you say that I am?" Simon Peter replied, "You are the Christ, the Son of the living God." And Jesus answered him, "Blessed are you, Simon Bar-Jo'na! For flesh and blood has not revealed this to you, but my Father who is in heaven. And I tell you, you are Peter,[s] and on this rock[t] I will build my church, and the powers of death[u] shall not prevail against it. I will give you the keys of the kingdom of heaven, and whatever you bind on earth shall be bound in heaven, and whatever you loose on earth shall be loosed in heaven." Then he strictly charged the disciples to tell no one that he was the Christ.

Jesus Foretells His Death

[16:21–23]

From that time Jesus began to show his disciples that he must go to Jerusalem and suffer many things from the elders and chief priests and scribes, and be killed, and on the third day be raised. And Peter took him and began to rebuke him, saying, "God forbid, Lord! This shall never happen to you." But he turned and said to Peter, "Get behind me, Satan! You are a hindrance[v] to me; for you are not on the side of God, but of men."

[r]Other ancient authorities omit the following words to the end of verse 3
[s]Greek *Petros*
[t]Greek *petra*
[u]Greek *the gates of Hades*
[v]Greek *stumbling block*

Roman bridge and city gate at Banias, ancient Caesarea Philippi, scene of Peter's confession of faith in Christ

The Way of the Cross [16:24–28]

Then Jesus told his disciples, "If any man would come after me, let him deny himself and take up his cross and follow me. For whoever would save his life will lose it, and whoever loses his life for my sake will find it. For what will it profit a man, if he gains the whole world and forfeits his life? Or what shall a man give in return for his life? For the Son of man is to come with his angels in the glory of his Father, and then he will repay every man for what he has done. Truly, I say to you, there are some standing here who will not taste death before they see the Son of man coming in his kingdom."

The Transfiguration [Matthew 17:1–8]

AND after six days Jesus took with him Peter and James and John his brother, and led them up a high mountain apart. And he was transfigured before them, and his face shone like the sun, and his garments became white as light. And behold, there appeared to them Moses and Eli'jah, talking with him. And Peter said to Jesus, "Lord, it is well that we are here; if you wish, I will make three booths here, one for you and one for Moses and one for Eli'jah." He was still speaking, when lo, a bright cloud overshadowed them, and a voice from the cloud said, "This is my beloved Son,[w] with whom I am well pleased; listen to him." When the disciples heard this, they fell on their faces, and were filled with awe. But Jesus came and touched them, saying, "Rise, and have no fear." And when they lifted up their eyes, they saw no one but Jesus only.

[w]Or *my Son, my* (or *the*) *Beloved*

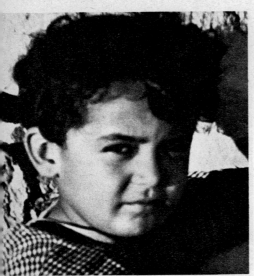

J. Lane Miller

UNICEF

Religious News Service

"Truly, I say to you, unless you turn and become like children, you will never enter the kingdom of heaven"

The Coming of Elijah [17:9-13]

And as they were coming down the mountain, Jesus commanded them, "Tell no one the vision, until the Son of man is raised from the dead." And the disciples asked him, "Then why do the scribes say that first Eli'jah must come?" He replied, "Eli'jah does come, and he is to restore all things; but I tell you that Eli'jah has already come, and they did not know him, but did to him whatever they pleased. So also the Son of man will suffer at their hands." Then the disciples understood that he was speaking to them of John the Baptist.

Jesus Heals an Epileptic Boy [17:14-21]

And when they came to the crowd, a man came up to him and kneeling before him said, "Lord, have mercy on my son, for he is an epileptic and he suffers terribly; for often he falls into the fire, and often into the water. And I brought him to your disciples, and they could not heal him." And Jesus answered, "O faithless and perverse generation, how long am I to be with you? How long am I to bear with you? Bring him here to me." And Jesus rebuked him, and the demon came out of him, and the boy was cured instantly. Then the disciples came to Jesus privately and said, "Why could we not cast it out?" He said to them, "Because of your little faith. For truly, I say to you, if you have faith as a grain of mustard seed, you will say to this mountain, 'Move hence to yonder place,' and it will move; and nothing will be impossible to you."[x]

Jesus again Foretells His Death

[17:22-23]

As they were gathering[y] in Gal'ilee, Jesus said to them, "The Son of man is to be delivered into the hands of men, and they will kill him, and he will be raised on the third day." And they were greatly distressed.

Paying the Temple Tax [17:24-27]

When they came to Caper'na-um, the collectors of the half-shekel tax went up to Peter and said, "Does not your teacher pay the tax?" He said, "Yes." And when he came home, Jesus spoke to him first, saying, "What do you think, Simon? From whom do kings of the earth take toll or tribute? From their sons or from others?" And when he said, "From others," Jesus said to him, "Then the sons are free. However, not to give offense to them, go to the sea and cast a hook, and take the first fish that comes up, and when you open its mouth you will find a shekel; take that and give it to them for me and for yourself."

"Who is the Greatest?"

[Matthew 18:1-4]

AT that time the disciples came to Jesus, saying, "Who is the greatest in the kingdom of heaven?" And calling to him a child, he put him in the midst of them, and said, "Truly, I say to you, unless you turn and become like children, you will never enter the kingdom of heaven. Whoever humbles himself like this child, he is the greatest in the kingdom of heaven.

Temptations to Sin

[18:5-9]

"Whoever receives one such child in my name receives me; but whoever causes one of these little ones who believe in me to sin,[z] it would be better for him to have a great millstone fastened round his neck and to be drowned in the depth of the sea.

"Woe to the world for temptations to sin![a] For it is necessary that temptations come, but woe to the man by whom the temptation comes! And if your hand or your foot causes you to sin,[z] cut it off and throw it from you; it is better for you to enter life maimed or lame than with two hands or two feet to be thrown into the eternal fire. And if your eye causes you to sin,[z] pluck it out and throw it from you; it is better for you to enter life with one eye than with two eyes to be thrown into the hell[b] of fire.

The Parable of the Lost Sheep

[18:10-14]

"See that you do not despise one of these little ones; for I tell you that in heaven their angels always behold the face of my Father who is in heaven.[c] What do you think? If a man has a hundred sheep, and one of them has gone astray, does he not leave the ninety-nine on the hills and go in search of the one that went astray? And if he finds it, truly, I say to you, he rejoices over it more than over the ninety-nine that never went astray. So it is not the will of my[d] Father who is in heaven that one of these little ones should perish.

A Brother Who Sins [18:15-20]

"If your brother sins against you, go and tell him his fault, between you and him alone. If he listens to you, you have gained your brother. But if he does not listen, take one or two others along with you, that every word may be confirmed by the evidence of two or three witnesses. If he refuses to listen to them, tell it to the church; and if he refuses to listen even to the church, let him be to you as a Gentile and a tax collector. Truly, I say to you, whatever you bind on earth shall be bound in heaven, and whatever you loose on earth shall be loosed in heaven. Again I say to you, if two of you agree on earth about anything they ask, it will be done for them by my Father in heaven. For where two or three are gathered in my name, there am I in the midst of them."

The Parable of the Unforgiving Servant [18:21-35]

Then Peter came up and said to him, "Lord, how often shall my brother sin against me, and I forgive him? As many as

---

[z]Greek *causes . . . to stumble*
[a]Greek *stumbling blocks*
[b]Greek *Gehenna*
[c]Other ancient authorities add verse 11, *For the Son of man came to save the lost*
[d]Other ancient authorities read *your*

[x]Other ancient authorities insert verse 21, *"But this kind never comes out except by prayer and fasting"*
[y]Other ancient authorities read *abode*

seven times?" Jesus said to him, "I do not say to you seven times, but seventy times seven.[e]

"Therefore the kingdom of heaven may be compared to a king who wished to settle accounts with his servants. When he began the reckoning, one was brought to him who owed him ten thousand talents;[f] and as he could not pay, his lord ordered him to be sold, with his wife and children and all that he had, and payment to be made. So the servant fell on his knees, imploring him, 'Lord, have patience with me, and I will pay you everything.' And out of pity for him the lord of that servant released him and forgave him the debt. But that same servant, as he went out, came upon one of his fellow servants who owed him a hundred denarii;[g] and seizing him by the throat he said, 'Pay what you owe.' So his fellow servant fell down and besought him, 'Have patience with me, and I will pay you.' He refused and went and put him in prison till he should pay the debt. When his fellow servants saw what had taken place, they were greatly distressed, and they went and reported to their lord all that had taken place. Then his lord summoned him and said to him, 'You wicked servant! I forgave you all that debt because you besought me; and should not you have had mercy on your fellow servant, as I had mercy on you?' And in anger his lord delivered him to the jailers,[h] till he should pay all his debt. So also my heavenly Father will do to every one of you, if you do not forgive your brother from your heart."

Multitudes Follow Jesus

[Matthew 19:1–2]

NOW when Jesus had finished these sayings, he went away from Gal'ilee and entered the region of Jude'a beyond the Jordan; and large crowds followed him, and he healed them there.

Jesus' Teaching about Divorce [19:3–12]

And Phar'isees came up to him and tested him by asking, "Is it lawful to divorce one's wife for any cause?" He answered, "Have you not read that he who made them from the beginning made them male and female, and said, 'For this reason a man shall leave his father and mother and be joined to his wife, and the two shall become one'?[i][27] So they are no longer two but one.[i] What therefore God has joined together, let no man put asunder." They said to him, "Why then did Moses command one to give a certificate of divorce, and to put her away?" He said to them, "For your hardness of heart Moses allowed you to divorce your wives, but from the beginning it was not so. And I say to you: whoever divorces his wife, except for unchastity,[j] and marries another, commits adultery."[k]

The disciples said to him, "If such is the case of a man with his wife, it is not expedient to marry." But he said to them, "Not all men can receive this precept, but only those to whom it is given. For there are eunuchs who have been so from birth, and there are eunuchs who have been made eunuchs by men, and there are eunuchs who have made themselves eunuchs for the sake of the kingdom of heaven. He who is able to receive this, let him receive it."

Jesus Blesses Little Children

[19:13–15]

Then children were brought to him that he might lay his hands on them and pray. The disciples rebuked the people; but Jesus said, "Let the children come to me, and do not hinder them; for to such belongs the kingdom of heaven." And he laid his hands on them and went away.

The Rich Young Man

[19:16–22]

And behold, one came up to him, saying, "Teacher, what good deed must I do, to have eternal life?" And he said to him, "Why do you ask me about what is good? One there is who is good. If you would enter life, keep the commandments." He said to him, "Which?" And Jesus said, "You shall not kill, You shall not commit adultery, You shall not steal, You shall not bear false witness, Honor your father and mother,[28] and, You shall love your neighbor as yourself."[29] The young man said to him, "All these I have observed; what do I still lack?" Jesus said to him, "If you would be perfect, go, sell what you possess and give to the poor, and you will have treasure in heaven; and come, follow me." When the young man heard this he went away sorrowful; for he had great possessions.

The Danger of Riches

[19:23–30]

And Jesus said to his disciples, "Truly, I say to you, it will be hard for a rich man to enter the kingdom of heaven. Again I tell you, it is easier for a camel to go through the eye of a needle than for a rich man to enter the kingdom of God." When the disciples heard this they were greatly astonished, saying, "Who then can be saved?" But Jesus looked at them and said to them, "With men this is impossible, but with God all things are possible." Then Peter said in reply, "Lo, we have left everything and followed you. What then shall we have?" Jesus said to them, "Truly, I say to you, in the new world, when the Son of man shall sit on his glorious throne, you who have followed me will also sit on twelve thrones, judging the twelve tribes of Israel. And every one who has left houses or brothers or sisters or father or mother or children or lands, for my name's sake, will receive a hundredfold,[l] and inherit eternal life. But many that are first will be last, and the last first.

Matson Photo Service

The Jaffa Gate closed, showing at the lower right a smaller opening which some call "the eye of a needle"

L. Kofod

Central part of an ancient rotary millstone for grinding grain

Stone used to measure weight of a talent

L. Kofod

[e]Or *seventy-seven times*
[f]This talent was probably worth about a thousand dollars
[g]The denarius was worth about twenty cents
[h]Greek *torturers*
[i]Greek *one flesh*
[j]Other ancient authorities, after *unchastity*, read *makes her commit adultery*
[k]Other ancient authorities insert *and he who marries a divorced woman commits adultery*
[27]Genesis 2:24

[l]Other ancient authorities read *manifold*
[28]Exodus 20:12–16; Deuteronomy 5:16–20
[29]Leviticus 19:18

21

Watchtower in vineyard in Palestine

An ancient winepress at Ain Karem

Recently excavated colonnade at Jericho, dating from New Testament times

Excavations at Jericho. The curved water basin in front of the terraced garden still holds water as tightly as in the days of Jesus

The Parable of the Laborers in the Vineyard [Matthew 20:1–16]

"FOR the kingdom of heaven is like a householder who went out early in the morning to hire laborers for his vineyard. After agreeing with the laborers for a denarius[m] a day, he sent them into his vineyard. And going out about the third hour he saw others standing idle in the market place; and to them he said, 'You go into the vineyard too, and whatever is right I will give you.' So they went. Going out again about the sixth hour and the ninth hour, he did the same. And about the eleventh hour he went out and found others standing; and he said to them, 'Why do you stand here idle all day?' They said to him, 'Because no one has hired us.' He said to them, 'You go into the vineyard too.' And when evening came, the owner of the vineyard said to his steward, 'Call the laborers and pay them their wages, beginning with the last, up to the first.' And when those hired about the eleventh hour came, each of them received a denarius. Now when the first came, they thought they would receive more; but each of them also received a denarius. And on receiving it they grumbled at the householder, saying, 'These last worked only one hour, and you have made them equal to us who have borne the burden of the day and the scorching heat.' But he replied to one of them, 'Friend, I am doing you no wrong; did you not agree with me for a denarius? Take what belongs to you, and go; I choose to give to this last as I give to you. Am I not allowed to do what I choose with what belongs to me? Or do you begrudge my generosity?'[n] So the last will be first, and the first last."

Jesus Foretells His Death a Third Time

[20:17–19]

And as Jesus was going up to Jerusalem, he took the twelve disciples aside, and on the way he said to them, "Behold, we are

[m]The denarius was worth about twenty cents
[n]Or *is your eye evil because I am good?*

going up to Jerusalem; and the Son of man will be delivered to the chief priests and scribes, and they will condemn him to death, and deliver him to the Gentiles to be mocked and scourged and crucified, and he will be raised on the third day."

The Request of James and John

[20:20–28]

Then the mother of the sons of Zeb'edee came up to him, with her sons, and kneeling before him she asked him for something. And he said to her, "What do you want?" She said to him, "Command that these two sons of mine may sit, one at your right hand and one at your left, in your kingdom." But Jesus answered, "You do not know what you are asking. Are you able to drink the cup that I am to drink?" They said to him, "We are able." He said to them, "You will drink my cup, but to sit at my right hand and at my left is not mine to grant, but it is for those for whom it has been prepared by my Father." And when the ten heard it, they were indignant at the two brothers. But Jesus called them to him and said, "You know that the rulers of the Gentiles lord it over them, and their great men exercise authority over them. It shall not be so among you; but whoever would be great among you must be your servant, and whoever would be first among you must be your slave; even as the Son of man came not to be served but to serve, and to give his life as a ransom for many."

Two Blind Men Receive Sight [20:29–34]

And as they went out of Jer'icho, a great crowd followed him. And behold, two blind men sitting by the roadside, when they heard that Jesus was passing by, cried out,[o] "Have mercy on us, Son of David!" The crowd rebuked them, telling them to be silent; but they cried out the more, "Lord, have mercy on us, Son of David!" And Jesus stopped and called them, saying,

[o]Other ancient authorities insert *Lord*

L. A. Fereday

"And when they drew near to Jerusalem . . . ."

"What do you want me to do for you?" They said to him, "Lord, let our eyes be opened." And Jesus in pity touched their eyes, and immediately they received their sight and followed him.

Triumphal Entry into Jerusalem

[Matthew 21:1–11]

AND when they drew near to Jerusalem and came to Beth'phage, to the Mount of Olives, then Jesus sent two disciples, saying to them, "Go into the village opposite you, and immediately you will find an ass tied, and a colt with her; untie them and bring them to me. If any one says anything to you, you shall say, 'The Lord has need of them,' and he will send them immediately." This took place to fulfil what was spoken by the prophet, saying,

"Tell the daughter of Zion,
Behold, your king is coming to you,
humble, and mounted on an ass,
and on a colt, the foal of an ass."[30]

The disciples went and did as Jesus had directed them; they brought the ass and the colt, and put their garments on them, and he sat thereon. Most of the crowd spread their garments on the road, and others cut branches from the trees and spread them on the road. And the crowds that went before him and that followed him shouted, "Hosanna to the Son of David! Blessed is he who comes in the name of the Lord! Hosanna in the highest!" And when he entered Jerusalem, all the city was stirred, saying, "Who is this?" And the crowds said, "This is the prophet Jesus from Naz'areth of Gal'ilee."

The Cleansing of the Temple [21:12–17]

And Jesus entered the temple of God[p]

and drove out all who sold and bought in the temple, and he overturned the tables of the money-changers and the seats of those who sold pigeons. He said to them, "It is written, 'My house shall be called a house of prayer';[31] but you make it a den of robbers."

And the blind and the lame came to him in the temple, and he healed them. But when the chief priests and the scribes saw the wonderful things that he did, and the children crying out in the temple, "Hosanna to the Son of David!" they were indignant; and they said to him, "Do you hear what these are saying?" And Jesus said to them, "Yes; have you never read,

'Out of the mouth of babes and sucklings
thou hast brought perfect praise'?"[32]

And leaving them, he went out of the city to Beth'any and lodged there.

The Cursing of the Fig Tree

[21:18–22]

In the morning, as he was returning to the city, he was hungry. And seeing a fig tree by the wayside he went to it, and found nothing on it but leaves only. And he said to it, "May no fruit ever come from you again!" And the fig tree withered at once. When the disciples saw it they marveled, saying, "How did the fig tree wither at once?" And Jesus answered them, "Truly, I say to you, if you have faith and never doubt, you will not only do what has been done to the fig tree, but even if you say to this mountain, 'Be taken up and cast into the sea,' it will be done. And whatever you ask in prayer, you will receive, if you have faith."

Matson Photo Service

When Jesus entered Jerusalem it was probably through a gate located approximately where the Golden Gate, now walled up, stands

Branch of fig tree with ripe fruits

Underwood and Underwood

[p]Other ancient authorities omit *of God*
[30]*Isaiah 62:11; Zechariah 9:9*

[31]*Isaiah 56:7*
[32]*Psalms 8:2*

23

Phylacteries, such as this Jewish boy is wearing, are passages of Scripture written on leather strips, enclosed in a small case and bound upon the arm or forehead

Jesus' Authority Questioned [21:23–27]

And when he entered the temple, the chief priests and the elders of the people came up to him as he was teaching, and said, "By what authority are you doing these things, and who gave you this authority?" Jesus answered them, "I also will ask you a question; and if you tell me the answer, then I also will tell you by what authority I do these things. The baptism of John, whence was it? From heaven or from men?" And they argued with one another, "If we say, 'From heaven,' he will say to us, 'Why then did you not believe him?' But if we say, 'From men,' we are afraid of the multitude; for all hold that John was a prophet." So they answered Jesus, "We do not know." And he said to them, "Neither will I tell you by what authority I do these things.

The Parable of the Two Sons [21:28–32]

"What do you think? A man had two sons; and he went to the first and said, 'Son, go and work in the vineyard today.' And he answered, 'I will not'; but afterward he repented and went. And he went to the second and said the same; and he answered, 'I go, sir,' but did not go. Which of the two did the will of his father?" They said, "The first." Jesus said to them, "Truly, I say to you, the tax collectors and the harlots go into the kingdom of God before you. For John came to you in the way of righteousness, and you did not believe him, but the tax collectors and the harlots believed him; and even when you saw it, you did not afterward repent and believe him.

The Parable of the Vineyard and the Tenants [21:33–46]

"Hear another parable. There was a householder who planted a vineyard, and set a hedge around it, and dug a wine press in it, and built a tower, and let it out to tenants, and went into another country. When the season of fruit drew near, he sent his servants to the tenants, to get his fruit; and the tenants took his servants and beat one, killed another, and stoned another. Again he sent other servants, more than the first; and they did the same to them. Afterward he sent his son to them, saying, 'They will respect my son.' But when the tenants saw the son, they said to themselves, 'This is the heir; come, let us

kill him and have his inheritance.' And they took him and cast him out of the vineyard, and killed him. When therefore the owner of the vineyard comes, what will he do to those tenants?" They said to him, "He will put those wretches to a miserable death, and let out the vineyard to other tenants who will give him the fruits in their seasons."

Jesus said to them, "Have you never read in the scriptures:

'The very stone which the builders rejected
has become the head of the corner;
this was the Lord's doing,
and it is marvelous in our eyes'?[33]

Therefore I tell you, the kingdom of God will be taken away from you and given to a nation producing the fruits of it."[q]

When the chief priests and the Phar'isees heard his parables, they perceived that he was speaking about them. But when they tried to arrest him, they feared the multitudes, because they held him to be a prophet.

The Parable of the Marriage Feast

[Matthew 22:1–14]

AND again Jesus spoke to them in parables, saying, "The kingdom of heaven may be compared to a king who gave a marriage feast for his son, and sent his servants to call those who were invited to the marriage feast; but they would not come. Again he sent other servants, saying, 'Tell those who are invited, Behold, I have made ready my dinner, my oxen and my fat calves are killed, and everything is ready; come to the marriage feast.' But they made light of it and went off, one to his farm, another to his business, while the rest seized his servants, treated them shamefully, and killed them. The king was angry, and he sent his troops and destroyed those murderers and burned their city. Then he said to his servants, 'The wedding is ready, but those invited were not worthy. Go therefore to the thoroughfares, and invite to the marriage feast as many as you find.' And those servants went out into the streets and gathered all whom they found, both bad and good; so the wedding hall was filled with guests.

"But when the king came in to look at the guests, he saw there a man who had no wedding garment; and he said to him, 'Friend, how did you get in here without a wedding garment?' And he was speechless. Then the king said to the attendants, 'Bind him hand and foot, and cast him into the outer darkness; there men will weep and gnash their teeth.' For many are called, but few are chosen."

Paying Taxes to Caesar

[22:15–22]

Then the Phar'isees went and took counsel how to entangle him in his talk. And they sent their disciples to him, along with the Hero'di-ans, saying, "Teacher, we know that you are true, and teach the way of God truthfully, and care for no man; for you do not regard the position of men. Tell us, then, what you think. Is it lawful to pay taxes to Caesar, or not?" But Jesus, aware

of their malice, said, "Why put me to the test, you hypocrites? Show me the money for the tax." And they brought him a coin.[r] And Jesus said to them, "Whose likeness and inscription is this?" They said, "Caesar's." Then he said to them, "Render therefore to Caesar the things that are Caesar's, and to God the things that are God's." When they heard it, they marveled; and they left him and went away.

The Question about the Resurrection

[22:23–33]

The same day Sad'ducees came to him, who say that there is no resurrection; and they asked him a question, saying, "Teacher, Moses said, 'If a man dies, having no children, his brother must marry the widow, and raise up children for his brother.'[34] Now there were seven brothers among us; the first married, and died, and having no children left his wife to his brother. So too the second and third, down to the seventh. After them all, the woman died. In the resurrection, therefore, to which of the seven will she be wife? For they all had her."

But Jesus answered them, "You are wrong, because you know neither the scriptures nor the power of God. For in the resurrection they neither marry nor are given in marriage, but are like angels[s] in heaven. And as for the resurrection of the dead, have you not read what was said to you by God, 'I am the God of Abraham, and the God of Isaac, and the God of Jacob'?[35] He is not God of the dead, but of the living." And when the crowd heard it, they were astonished at his teaching.

The Great Commandment

[22:34–40]

But when the Phar'isees heard that he had silenced the Sad'ducees, they came together. And one of them, a lawyer, asked him a question, to test him. "Teacher, which is the great commandment in the law?" And he said to him, "You shall love the Lord your God with all your heart, and with all your soul, and with all your mind.[36] This is the great and first commandment. And a second is like it, You shall love your neighbor as yourself.[37] On these two commandments depend all the law and the prophets."

The Question about the Son of David

[22:41–45]

Now while the Phar'isees were gathered together, Jesus asked them a question, saying, "What do you think of the Christ? Whose son is he?" They said to him, "The son of David." He said to them, "How is it then that David, inspired by the Spirit,[t] calls him Lord, saying,

'The Lord said to my Lord,
Sit at my right hand,
til I put thy enemies under thy feet'?[38]

[r]Greek *a denarius*
[s]Other ancient authorities add *of God*
[t]Or *David in the Spirit*
[34]*Deuteronomy* 25:5
[35]*Exodus* 3:6
[36]*Deuteronomy* 6:5
[37]*Leviticus* 19:18
[38]*Psalms* 110:1

[q]Other ancient authorities add verse 44, "*And he who falls on this stone will be broken to pieces; but when it falls on any one, it will crush him*"
[33]*Psalms* 118:22–23

If David thus calls him Lord, how is he his son?" And no one was able to answer him a word, nor from that day did any one dare to ask him any more questions.

Jesus Denounces the Scribes and Pharisees [Matthew 23:1–36]

THEN said Jesus to the crowds and to his disciples, "The scribes and the Phar'isees sit on Moses' seat; so practice and observe whatever they tell you, but not what they do; for they preach, but do not practice. They bind heavy burdens, hard to bear,[u] and lay them on men's shoulders; but they themselves will not move them with their finger. They do all their deeds to be seen by men; for they make their phylacteries broad and their fringes long, and they love the place of honor at feasts and the best seats in the synagogues, and salutations in the market places, and being called rabbi by men. But you are not to be called rabbi, for you have one teacher, and you are all brethren. And call no man your father on earth, for you have one Father, who is in heaven. Neither be called masters, for you have one master, the Christ. He who is greatest among you shall be your servant; whoever exalts himself will be humbled, and whoever humbles himself will be exalted.

"But woe to you, scribes and Phar'isees, hypocrites! because you shut the kingdom of heaven against men; for you neither enter yourselves, nor allow those who would enter to go in.[v] Woe to you, scribes and Phar'isees, hypocrites! for you traverse sea and land to make a single proselyte, and when he becomes a proselyte, you make him twice as much a child of hell[w] as yourselves.

"Woe to you, blind guides, who say, 'If any one swears by the temple, it is nothing; but if any one swears by the gold of the temple, he is bound by his oath.' You blind fools! For which is greater, the gold or the temple that has made the gold sacred? And you say, 'If any one swears by the altar, it is nothing; but if any one swears by the gift that is on the altar, he is bound by his oath.' You blind men! For which is greater, the gift or the altar that makes the gift sacred? So he who swears by the altar, swears by it and by everything on it; and he who swears by the temple, swears by it and by him who dwells in it; and he who swears by heaven, swears by the throne of God and by him who sits upon it.

"Woe to you, scribes and Phar'isees, hypocrites! for you tithe mint and dill and cummin, and have neglected the weightier matters of the law, justice and mercy and faith; these you ought to have done, without neglecting the others. You blind guides, straining out a gnat and swallowing a camel!

"Woe to you, scribes and Phar'isees, hypocrites! for you cleanse the outside of the cup and of the plate, but inside they are full of extortion and rapacity. You blind Phar'isee! first cleanse the inside of the cup and of the plate, that the outside also may be clean.

"Woe to you, scribes and Phar'isees, hypocrites! for you are like whitewashed tombs, which outwardly appear beautiful, but within they are full of dead men's bones and all uncleanness. So you also outwardly appear righteous to men, but within you are full of hypocrisy and iniquity.

"Woe to you, scribes and Phar'isees, hypocrites! for you build the tombs of the prophets and adorn the monuments of the righteous, saying, 'If we had lived in the days of our fathers, we would not have taken part with them in shedding the blood of the prophets.' Thus you witness against yourselves, that you are sons of those who murdered the prophets. Fill up, then, the measure of your fathers. You serpents, you brood of vipers. how are you to escape being sentenced to hell?[w] Therefore I send you prophets and wise men and scribes, some of whom you will kill and crucify, and some you will scourge in your synagogues and persecute from town to town, that upon you may come all the righteous blood shed on earth, from the blood of innocent Abel to the blood of Zechari'ah the son of Barachi'ah, whom you murdered between the sanctuary and the altar. Truly, I say to you, all this will come upon this generation.

Jesus Laments over Jerusalem

[23:37–39]

"O Jerusalem, Jerusalem, killing the prophets and stoning those who are sent to you! How often would I have gathered your children together as a hen gathers her brood under her wings, and you would not! Behold, your house is forsaken and desolate.[z] For I tell you, you will not see me again, until you say, 'Blessed is he who comes in the name of the Lord.' "

Jesus Foretells the Destruction of the Temple [Matthew 24:1–2]

JESUS left the temple and was going away, when his disciples came to point out to him the buildings of the temple. But he answered them, "You see all these, do you not? Truly, I say to you, there will not be left here one stone upon another, that will not be thrown down."

Signs of Jesus' Coming [24:3–8]

As he sat on the Mount of Olives, the disciples came to him privately, saying, "Tell us, when will this be, and what will be the sign of your coming and of the close of the age?" And Jesus answered them, "Take heed that no one leads you astray. For many will come in my name, saying, 'I am the Christ,' and they will lead many astray. And you will hear of wars and rumors of wars; see that you are not alarmed; for this must take place, but the end is not yet. For nation will rise against nation, and kingdom against kingdom, and there will be famines and earthquakes in various places: all this is but the beginning of the sufferings.

Tribulation Foretold [24:9–14]

"Then they will deliver you up to tribulation, and put you to death; and you will be hated by all nations for my name's sake.

On the western slope of the Mount of Olives are innumerable tombstones and three larger monuments traditionally known as (from left to right) the Tomb of Absalom, the Grotto of St. James and the Pyramid of Zacharias. All date from the time of Christ or immediately before. In recent Christian tradition it is supposed that the Pyramid of Zacharias is a memorial to the Zechariah mentioned in Matthew 23:35

And then many will fall away,[y] and betray one another, and hate one another. And many false prophets will arise and lead many astray. And because wickedness is multiplied, most men's love will grow cold. But he who endures to the end will be saved. And this gospel of the kingdom will be preached throughout the whole world, as a testimony to all nations; and then the end will come.

The Desolating Sacrilege [24:15–28]

"So when you see the desolating sacrilege spoken of by the prophet Daniel, standing in the holy place (let the reader understand), then let those who are in Jude'a flee to the mountains; let him who is on the housetop not go down to take what is in his house; and let him who is in the field not turn back to take his mantle. And alas for those who are with child and for those who give suck in those days! Pray that your flight may not be in winter or on a sabbath. For then there will be great tribulation, such as has not been from the beginning of the world until now, no, and never will be. And if those days had not been shortened, no human being would be saved; but for the sake of the elect those days will be shortened. Then if any one says to you, 'Lo, here is the Christ!' or 'There he is!' do not believe it. For false Christs and false prophets will arise and show great signs and wonders, so as to lead astray, if possible, even the elect. Lo, I have told you beforehand. So, if they say to you, 'Lo, he is in the wilderness,' do not go out; if they say, 'Lo, he is in the inner rooms,' do not believe it. For as the lightning comes from the east and shines as far as the west, so will be the coming of the Son of man. Wherever the body is, there the eagles[z] will be gathered together.

[y]Or stumble
[z]Or vultures

[u]Other ancient authorities omit hard to bear.
[v]Other authorities add here (or after verse 12) verse 14, Woe to you, scribes and Pharisees, hypocrites! for you devour widows' houses and for a pretense you make long prayers; therefore you will receive the greater condemnation
[w]Greek Gehenna

[z]Other ancient authorities omit and desolate

25

The Coming of the Son of Man
[24:29-31]

"Immediately after the tribulation of those days the sun will be darkened, and the moon will not give its light, and the stars will fall from heaven, and the powers of the heavens will be shaken; then will appear the sign of the Son of man in heaven, and then all the tribes of the earth will mourn, and they will see the Son of man coming on the clouds of heaven with power and great glory; and he will send out his angels with a loud trumpet call, and they will gather his elect from the four winds, from one end of heaven to the other.

The Lesson from the Fig Tree [24:32-35]

"From the fig tree learn its lesson: as soon as its branch becomes tender and puts forth its leaves, you know that summer is near. So also, when you see all these things, you know that he is near, at the very gates. Truly, I say to you, this generation will not pass away till all these things take place. Heaven and earth will pass away, but my words will not pass away.

No One Knows the Day and Hour
[24:36-44]

"But of that day and hour no one knows, not even the angels of heaven, nor the Son,[a] but the Father only. As were the days of Noah, so will be the coming of the Son of man. For as in those days before the flood they were eating and drinking, marrying and giving in marriage, until the day when Noah entered the ark, and they did not know until the flood came and swept them all away, so will be the coming of the Son of man. Then two men will be in the field; one is taken and one is left. Two women will be grinding at the mill; one is taken and one is left. Watch therefore, for you do not know on what day your Lord is coming. But know this, that if the householder had known in what part of the night the thief was coming, he would have watched and would not have let his house be broken into. Therefore you also must be ready; for the Son of man is coming at an hour you do not expect.

Faithful and Unfaithful Servants
[24:45-51]

"Who then is the faithful and wise servant, whom his master has set over his household, to give them their food at the proper time? Blessed is that servant whom his master when he comes will find so doing. Truly, I say to you, he will set him over all his possessions. But if that wicked servant says to himself, 'My master is delayed,' and begins to beat his fellow servants, and eats and drinks with the drunken, the master of that servant will come on a day when he does not expect him and at an hour he does not know, and will punish[b] him, and put him with the hypocrites; there men will weep and gnash their teeth.

The Parable of the Ten Maidens
[Matthew 25:1-13]

"THEN the kingdom of heaven shall be compared to ten maidens who took their lamps and went to meet the bridegroom.[c] Five of them were foolish, and five

[a]Other ancient authorities omit *nor the Son*
[b]Or *cut him in pieces*
[c]Other ancient authorities add *and the bride*

Philip Gendreau, N.Y.

This arch was erected in Rome to celebrate the victory of Titus over the Jews. Jesus predicted the destruction of Jerusalem

were wise. For when the foolish took their lamps, they took no oil with them; but the wise took flasks of oil with their lamps. As the bridegroom was delayed, they all slumbered and slept. But at midnight there was a cry, 'Behold, the bridegroom! Come out to meet him.' Then all those maidens rose and trimmed their lamps. And the foolish said to the wise, 'Give us some of your oil, for our lamps are going out.' But the wise replied, 'Perhaps there will not be enough for us and for you; go rather to the dealers and buy for yourselves.' And while they went to buy, the bridegroom came, and those who were ready went in with him to the marriage feast; and the door was shut. Afterward the other maidens came also, saying, 'Lord, lord, open to us.' But he replied, 'Truly, I say to you, I do not know you.' Watch therefore, for you know neither the day nor the hour.

J. Lane Miller

Reddish clay lamp from New Testament times, found at Jericho

The Parable of the Talents [25:14-30]

"For it will be as when a man going on a journey called his servants and entrusted to them his property; to one he gave five talents,[d] to another two, to another one, to each according to his ability. Then he went away. He who had received the five talents went at once and traded with them; and he made five talents more. So also, he who had the two talents made two talents more. But he who had received the one talent went and dug in the ground and hid his master's money. Now after a long time the master of those servants came and settled accounts with them. And he who had received the five talents came forward, bringing five talents more, saying, 'Master, you delivered to me five talents; here I have made five talents more.' His master said to him, 'Well done, good and faithful servant; you have been faithful over a little, I will set you over much; enter into the joy of your master.' And he also who had the two talents came forward, saying, 'Master, you delivered to me two talents; here I have made two talents more.' His master said to him, 'Well done, good and faithful servant; you have been faithful over a little, I will set you over much; enter into the joy of your master.' He also who had received the one talent came forward, saying, 'Master, I knew you to be a hard man, reaping where you did not sow, and gathering where you did not winnow; so I was afraid, and I went and hid your talent in the ground. Here

[d]This talent was probably worth about a thousand dollars

you have what is yours.' But his master answered him, 'You wicked and slothful servant! You knew that I reap where I have not sowed, and gather where I have not winnowed? Then you ought to have invested my money with the bankers, and at my coming I should have received what was my own with interest. So take the talent from him, and give it to him who has the ten talents. For to every one who has will more be given, and he will have abundance; but from him who has not, even what he has will be taken away. And cast the worthless servant into the outer darkness; there men will weep and gnash their teeth.'

The Judgment of the Nations [25:31–46]

"When the Son of man comes in his glory, and all the angels with him, then he will sit on his glorious throne. Before him will be gathered all the nations, and he will separate them one from another as a shepherd separates the sheep from the goats, and he will place the sheep at his right hand, but the goats at the left. Then the King will say to those at his right hand, 'Come, O blessed of my Father, inherit the kingdom prepared for you from the foundation of the world; for I was hungry and you gave me food, I was thirsty and you gave me drink, I was a stranger and you welcomed me, I was naked and you clothed me, I was sick and you visited me, I was in prison and you came to me.' Then the righteous will answer him, 'Lord, when did we see thee hungry and feed thee, or thirsty and give thee drink? And when did we see thee a stranger and welcome thee, or naked and clothe thee? And when did we see thee sick or in prison and visit thee?' And the King will answer them, 'Truly, I say to you, as you did it to one of the least of these my brethren, you did it to me.' Then he will say to those at his left hand, 'Depart from me, you cursed, into the eternal fire prepared for the devil and his angels; for I was hungry and you gave me no food, I was thirsty and you gave me no drink, I was a stranger and you did not welcome me, naked and you did not clothe me, sick and in prison and you did not visit me.' Then they also will answer, 'Lord, when did we see thee hungry or thirsty or a stranger or naked or sick or in prison, and did not minister to thee?' Then he will answer them, 'Truly, I say to you, as you did it not to one of the least of these, you did it not to me.' And they will go away into eternal punishment, but the righteous into eternal life."

Sheep and goats

L. A. Fereday

Woman using grinding stone in Palestine

Palestine Institute

The Leaders Plot against Jesus

[Matthew 26:1–5]

WHEN Jesus had finished all these sayings, he said to his disciples, "You know that after two days the Passover is coming, and the Son of man will be delivered up to be crucified."

Then the chief priests and the elders of the people gathered in the palace of the high priest, who was called Cai'aphas, and took counsel together in order to arrest Jesus by stealth and kill him. But they said, "Not during the feast, lest there be a tumult among the people."

Jesus Anointed at Bethany [26:6–13]

Now when Jesus was at Beth'any in the house of Simon the leper, a woman came up to him with an alabaster jar of very expensive ointment, and she poured it on his head, as he sat at table. But when the disciples saw it, they were indignant, saying, "Why this waste? For this ointment might have been sold for a large sum, and given to the poor." But Jesus, aware of this, said to them, "Why do you trouble the woman? For she has done a beautiful thing to me. For you always have the poor with you, but you will not always have me. In pouring this ointment on my body she has done it to prepare me for burial. Truly, I say to you,

wherever this gospel is preached in the whole world, what she has done will be told in memory of her."

Judas Agrees to Betray Jesus [26:14–16]

Then one of the twelve, who was called Judas Iscar'iot, went to the chief priests and said, "What will you give me if I deliver him to you?" And they paid him thirty pieces of silver. And from that moment he sought an opportunity to betray him.

The Last Supper [26:17–29]

Now on the first day of Unleavened Bread the disciples came to Jesus, saying, "Where will you have us prepare for you to eat the passover?" He said, "Go into the city to such a one, and say to him, 'The Teacher says, My time is at hand; I will keep the passover at your house with my disciples.' " And the disciples did as Jesus had directed them, and they prepared the passover.

When it was evening, he sat at table with the twelve disciples;[e] and as they were eating, he said, "Truly, I say to you, one of you will betray me." And they were very sorrowful, and began to say to him one after another, "Is it I, Lord?" He answered, "He who has dipped his hand in the dish with me, will betray me. The Son of man goes as it is written of him, but woe to that man by whom the Son of man is betrayed! It would have been better for that man if he had not been born." Judas, who betrayed him, said, "Is it I, Master?"[f] He said to him, "You have said so."

Now as they were eating, Jesus took bread, and blessed, and broke it, and gave it to the disciples and said, "Take, eat; this is my body." And he took a cup, and when he had given thanks he gave it to them, saying, "Drink of it, all of you; for this is my blood of the[g] covenant, which is poured out for many for the forgiveness of sins. I tell you I shall not drink again of this fruit of the vine until that day when I drink it new with you in my Father's kingdom."

[e]Other authorities omit *disciples*
[f]Or *Rabbi*
[g]Other ancient authorities insert *new*

27

Jack Finegan

Looking toward the Garden of Gethsemane from the wall of Jerusalem

Peter's Denial Foretold [26:30-35]

And when they had sung a hymn, they went out to the Mount of Olives. Then Jesus said to them, "You will all fall away because of me this night; for it is written, 'I will strike the shepherd, and the sheep of the flock will be scattered.'[39] But after I am raised up, I will go before you to Gal'ilee." Peter declared to him, "Though they all fall away because of you, I will never fall away." Jesus said to him, "Truly, I say to you, this very night, before the cock crows, you will deny me three times." Peter said to him, "Even if I must die with you, I will not deny you." And so said all the disciples.

Jesus Prays in Gethsemane [26:36-46]

Then Jesus went with them to a place called Gethsem'ane, and he said to his disciples, "Sit here, while I go yonder and pray." And taking with him Peter and the two sons of Zeb'edee, he began to be sorrowful and troubled. Then he said to them, "My soul is very sorrowful, even to death; remain here, and watch[h] with me." And going a little farther he fell on his face and prayed, "My Father, if it be possible, let this cup pass from me; nevertheless, not as I will, but as thou wilt." And he came to the disciples and found them sleeping; and he said to Peter, "So, could you not watch[h] with me one hour? Watch[h] and pray that you may not enter into temptation; the spirit indeed is willing, but the flesh is weak." Again, for the second time, he went away and prayed, "My Father, if this cannot pass unless I drink it, thy will be done." And again he came and found them sleeping, for their eyes were heavy. So, leaving them again, he went away and prayed for the third time, saying the same words. Then he came to the disciples and said to them, "Are you still sleeping and taking your rest? Behold, the hour is at hand, and the Son of man is betrayed into the hands of sinners. Rise, let us be going; see, my betrayer is at hand."

The Betrayal and Arrest of Jesus [26:47-56]

While he was still speaking, Judas came, one of the twelve, and with him a great crowd with swords and clubs, from the chief priests and the elders of the people. Now the betrayer had given them a sign, saying, "The one I shall kiss is the man; seize him." And he came up to Jesus at once and said, "Hail, Master!"[i] And he kissed him. Jesus said to him, "Friend, why are you here?"[j] Then they came up and laid hands on Jesus and seized him. And behold, one of those who were with Jesus stretched out his hand and drew his sword, and struck the slave of the high priest, and cut off his ear. Then Jesus said to him, "Put your sword back into its place; for all who take the sword will perish by the sword. Do you think that I cannot appeal to my Father, and he will at once send me more than twelve legions of angels? But how then should the scriptures be fulfilled, that it must be so?" At that hour Jesus said to the crowds, "Have you come out as against a robber, with swords and clubs to capture me? Day after day I sat in the temple teaching, and you did not seize me. But all this has taken place, that the scriptures of the prophets might be fulfilled." Then all the disciples forsook him and fled.

Jesus before the Council [26:57-68]

Then those who had seized Jesus led him to Cai'aphas the high priest, where the scribes and the elders had gathered. But Peter followed him at a distance, as far as the courtyard of the high priest, and going inside he sat with the guards to see the end. Now the chief priests and the whole council sought false testimony against Jesus that they might put him to death, but they found none, though many false witnesses came forward. At last two came forward and said, "This fellow said, 'I am able to destroy the temple of God, and to build it in three days.' " And the high priest stood up and said, "Have you no answer to make? What is it that these men testify against you?" But Jesus was silent. And the high priest said to him, "I adjure you by the living God, tell us if you are the Christ, the Son of God." Jesus said to him, "You have said so. But I tell you, hereafter you will see the Son of man seated at the right hand of Power, and coming on the clouds of heaven." Then the high priest tore his robes, and said, "He has uttered blasphemy. Why do we still need witnesses? You have now heard his blasphemy. What is your judgment?" They answered, "He deserves death." Then they spat in his face, and struck him; and some slapped him, saying, "Prophesy to us, you Christ! Who is it that struck you?"

Peter Denies Jesus [26:69-75]

Now Peter was sitting outside in the courtyard. And a maid came up to him, and said, "You also were with Jesus the Galilee'an." But he denied it before them all, saying, "I do not know what you mean." And when he went out to the porch, another maid saw him, and she said to the bystanders, "This man was with Jesus of Naz'areth." And again he denied it with an oath, "I do not know the man." After a little

---

Matson Photo Service

The traditional site of the House of Caiaphas is not far from the Zion Gate at Jerusalem

[h]Or *keep awake*
[39]*Zechariah* 13:7

[i]Or *Rabbi*
[j]Or *do that for which you have come*

while the bystanders came up and said to Peter, "Certainly you are also one of them, for your accent betrays you." Then he began to invoke a curse on himself and to swear, "I do not know the man." And immediately the cock crowed. And Peter remembered the saying of Jesus, "Before the cock crows, you will deny me three times." And he went out and wept bitterly.

Jesus Brought before Pilate [Matthew 27:1–2]

WHEN morning came, all the chief priests and the elders of the people took counsel against Jesus to put him to death; and they bound him and led him away and delivered him to Pilate the governor.

The Death of Judas [27:3–10]

When Judas, his betrayer, saw that he was condemned, he repented and brought back the thirty pieces of silver to the chief priests and the elders, saying, "I have sinned in betraying innocent blood." They said, "What is that to us? See to it yourself." And throwing down the pieces of silver in the temple, he departed; and he went and hanged himself. But the chief priests, taking the pieces of silver, said, "It is not lawful to put them into the treasury, since they are blood money." So they took counsel, and bought with them the potter's field, to bury strangers in. Therefore that field has been called the Field of Blood to this day. Then was fulfilled what had been spoken by the prophet Jeremi'ah, saying, "And they took the thirty pieces of silver, the price of him on whom a price had been set by some of the sons of Israel, and they gave them for the potter's field, as the Lord directed me."[40]

Pilate Questions Jesus [27:11–14]

Now Jesus stood before the governor; and the governor asked him, "Are you the King of the Jews?" Jesus said to him, "You have said so." But when he was accused by the chief priests and elders, he made no answer. Then Pilate said to him, "Do you not hear how many things they testify against you?" But he gave him no answer, not even to a single charge; so that the governor wondered greatly.

Jesus Sentenced To Die [27:15–26]

Now at the feast the governor was accustomed to release for the crowd any one prisoner whom they wanted. And they had then a notorious prisoner, called Barab'bas.[k] So when they had gathered, Pilate said to them, "Whom do you want me to release for you, Barab'bas or Jesus who is called Christ?" For he knew that it was out of envy that they had delivered him up. Besides, while he was sitting on the judgment seat, his wife sent word to him, "Have nothing to do with that righteous man, for I have suffered much over him today in a dream." Now the chief priests and the elders persuaded the people to ask for Barab'bas and destroy Jesus. The governor again said to them, "Which of the two do you want me to release for you?" And they said, "Barab'bas." Pilate said

The Lithostroton, a Roman pavement of very large flat stones in the court of the Tower of Antonia, has been identified with the Roman Praetorium where Jesus was tried before Pontius Pilate

to them, "Then what shall I do with Jesus who is called Christ?" They all said, "Let him be crucified." And he said, "Why, what evil has he done?" But they shouted all the more, "Let him be crucified."

So when Pilate saw that he was gaining nothing, but rather that a riot was beginning, he took water and washed his hands before the crowd, saying, "I am innocent of this man's blood;[l] see to it yourselves." And all the people answered, "His blood be on us and on our children!" Then he released for them Barab'bas, and having scourged Jesus, delivered him to be crucified.

The Soldiers Mock Jesus [27:27–31]

Then the soldiers of the governor took Jesus into the praetor'ium, and they gathered the whole battalion before him. And they stripped him and put a scarlet robe upon him, and plaiting a crown of thorns they put it on his head, and put a reed in his right hand. And kneeling before him they mocked him, saying, "Hail, King of the Jews!" And they spat upon him, and took the reed and struck him on the head. And when they had mocked him, they stripped him of the robe, and put his own clothes on him, and led him away to crucify him.

Some of the large stones still show the markings of games played by the Roman soldiers stationed at the Fortress Antonia

[k]Other ancient authorities read *Jesus Barabbas*
[40]Zechariah 11:12–13

[l]Other authorities read *this righteous blood* or *this righteous man's blood*

Looking toward the northeast corner of Jerusalem and the Mount of Olives from the northwest. Some locate Calvary in the foreground

The Crucifixion

[27:32–44]

As they were marching out, they came upon a man of Cyre'ne, Simon by name; this man they compelled to carry his cross. And when they came to a place called Gol'gotha (which means the place of a skull), they offered him wine to drink, mingled with gall; but when he tasted it, he would not drink it. And when they had crucified him, they divided his garments among them by casting lots; then they sat down and kept watch over him there. And over his head they put the charge against him, which read, "This is Jesus the King of the Jews." Then two robbers were crucified with him, one on the right and one on the left. And those who passed by derided him, wagging their heads and saying, "You who would destroy the temple and build it in three days, save yourself! If you are the Son of God, come down from the cross." So also the chief priests, with the scribes and elders, mocked him, saying, "He saved others; he cannot save himself. He is the King of Israel; let him come down now from the cross, and we will believe in him. He trusts in God; let God deliver him now, if he desires him; for he said, 'I am the Son of God.' " And the robbers who were crucified with him also reviled him in the same way.

The Death of Jesus

[27:45–50]

Now from the sixth hour there was darkness over all the land[m] until the ninth hour. And about the ninth hour Jesus cried with a loud voice, "Eli, Eli, la'ma sabach-tha'ni?" that is, "My God, my God, why hast thou forsaken me?" And some of the bystanders hearing it said, "This man is calling Eli'jah." And one of them at once ran and took a sponge, filled it with vinegar, and put it on a reed, and gave it to him to drink. But the others said, "Wait, let us see whether Eli'jah will come to save him."[n] And Jesus cried again with a loud voice and yielded up his spirit.

The Tearing of the Temple Curtain

[27:51–56]

And behold, the curtain of the temple was torn in two, from top to bottom; and the earth shook, and the rocks were split;

[m]Or *earth*
[n]Other ancient authorities insert *And another took a spear and pierced his side, and out came water and blood*

the tombs also were opened, and many bodies of the saints who had fallen asleep were raised, and coming out of the tombs after his resurrection they went into the holy city and appeared to many. When the centurion and those who were with him, keeping watch over Jesus, saw the earthquake and what took place, they were filled with awe, and said, "Truly this was the Son[x] of God!"

There were also many women there, looking on from afar, who had followed Jesus from Gal'ilee, ministering to him; among whom were Mary Mag'dalene, and Mary the mother of James and Joseph, and the mother of the sons of Zeb'edee.

The Burial of Jesus [27:57–61]

When it was evening, there came a rich man from Arimathe'a, named Joseph, who also was a disciple of Jesus. He went to Pilate and asked for the body of Jesus. Then Pilate ordered it to be given to him. And Joseph took the body, and wrapped it in a clean linen shroud, and laid it in his own new tomb, which he had hewn in the rock; and he rolled a great stone to the door of the tomb, and departed. Mary Mag'dalene and the other Mary were there, sitting opposite the sepulchre.

[x]Or *a son*

Steps leading up to the Chapel of the Agony, part of the Church of the Holy Sepulchre

Two women going through a street in old Jerusalem

The Guard at the Tomb

[27:62–66]

Next day, that is, after the day of Preparation, the chief priests and the Phar'isees gathered before Pilate and said, "Sir, we remember how that impostor said, while he was still alive, 'After three days I will rise again.' Therefore order the sepulchre to be made secure until the third day, lest his disciples go and steal him away, and tell the people, 'He has risen from the dead,' and the last fraud will be worse than the first." Pilate said to them, "You have a guard[o] of soldiers; go, make it as secure as you can."[p] So they went and made the sepulchre secure by sealing the stone and setting a guard.

The Resurrection [Matthew 28:1–10]

NOW after the sabbath, toward the dawn of the first day of the week, Mary Mag'dalene and the other Mary went to see the sepulchre. And behold, there was a great earthquake; for an angel of the Lord descended from heaven and came and rolled back the stone, and sat upon it. His appearance was like lightning, his raiment white as snow. And for fear of him the guards trembled and became like dead men. But the angel said to the women, "Do not be afraid; for I know that you seek Jesus who was crucified. He is not here; for he has risen, as he said. Come, see the place where he[q] lay. Then go quickly and tell his disciples that he has risen from the dead, and behold, he is going before you to Gal'ilee; there you will see him. Lo, I have told you." So they departed quickly from the tomb with fear and great joy, and ran to tell his disciples. And behold, Jesus met them and said, "Hail!" And they came up and took hold of his feet and worshiped him. Then Jesus said to them, "Do not be afraid; go and tell my brethren to go to Gal'ilee, and there they will see me."

The Report of the Guard [28:11–15]

While they were going, behold, some of the guard went into the city and told the chief priests all that had taken place. And when they had assembled with the elders and taken counsel, they gave a sum of money to the soldiers and said, "Tell people, 'His disciples came by night and stole him away while we were asleep.' And if this comes to the governor's ears, we will satisfy him and keep you out of trouble." So they took the money and did as they were directed; and this story has been spread among the Jews to this day.

Jesus Commissions the Eleven [28:16–20]

Now the eleven disciples went to Gal'ilee, to the mountain to which Jesus had directed them. And when they saw him they worshiped him; but some doubted. And Jesus came and said to them, "All authority in heaven and on earth has been given to me. Go therefore and make disciples of all nations, baptizing them in the name of the Father and of the Son and of the Holy Spirit, teaching them to observe all that I have commanded you; and lo, I am with you always, to the close of the age."

[o]Or *Take a guard*
[p]Greek *know*
[q]Other ancient authorities read *the Lord*

Matson Photo Service

A rock-hewn tomb in a garden north of the walled city of Jerusalem

The entrance to the Church of the Holy Sepulchre, which marks the traditional site of the burial of Christ. The façade dates from the time of the Crusades

Ewing Galloway, N.Y.

THE PEOPLE WHO SAT IN DARKNESS HAVE SEEN A GREAT LIGHT,
AND FOR THOSE WHO SAT IN THE REGION AND SHADOW OF
DEATH LIGHT HAS DAWNED   MATT. 4:16

Safed, a city built on a hill

Matson Photo Service

Roman lamp of first century

Metropolitan Museum

A CITY SET ON A HILL CANNOT BE HID. NOR DO MEN LIGHT A
LAMP AND PUT IT UNDER A BUSHEL, BUT ON A STAND   MATT. 5:14-15

Ancient lampstand found in Jerusalem

L. Kofod

Lampstand from Jewish tombstone in Rome, 2nd or 3rd century A.D.

Jewish Museum

LET YOUR LIGHT SO SHINE BEFORE MEN, THAT THEY MAY SEE YOUR GOOD
WORKS AND GIVE GLORY TO YOUR FATHER WHO IS IN HEAVEN   MATT. 5:16

Sowing The Seed

Matson Photo Service

THE GOSPEL ACCORDING TO MARK

REVISED STANDARD VERSION

GALILEE

Much of the life of Christ as told in the Gospel according to Mark, except for his last week in Jerusalem, was spent in Galilee. Galilee was the name of the northern part of the land of Palestine. Galilee included the large Plain of Esdraelon in the south, the hills and valleys of Lower (Southern) Galilee and the more rugged plateaus and mountains of Upper (Northern) Galilee. On the eastern side all of these zones stop at the deep valley where the Jordan River flows south through the Sea of Galilee, which is the natural focus of the region. In all, Galilee measures some 50 miles from south to north and 30 miles from west to east, and thus has an area of approximately 1,500 square miles. The highest elevation is in the north, where one point is nearly 4,000 feet above sea level; the lowest is the surface of the Sea of Galilee, which is about 685 feet below sea level.

In contrast with the more arid Judea, Galilee has a relative abundance of water. There are springs, wells and perennial streams in addition to the lake, and the land is very fertile. The Sea of Galilee itself is a body of fresh water 13 miles long and, at its broadest point, 8 miles across. Its waves sparkle in the sunshine and its depths teem with fish. Of it the Jewish Rabbis said: "The Lord has created seven seas, but the Sea of Gennesaret is his delight." Gennesaret was but one of several other names which were applied to the Sea of Galilee, for it was also called the Sea of Tiberias and the Lake of Chinnereth. It was beside this sea that Jesus called his first disciples (Mk. 1:16–20); where he taught the multitudes from a boat (Mk. 4:1); near which he healed the demoniac (Mk. 5:1–13) and fed the five thousand (Mk. 6:30–44); whose waters he stilled (Mk. 4:35–41) and upon which he walked (Mk. 6:45–52).

After 733 B.C., when the Assyrian king Tiglath-pileser III invaded Galilee and deported many of its Israelite inhabitants (2 Kings 15:29), Galilee seems to have had a largely foreign population; but by the end of the second century B.C. it was controlled by the Maccabees. In the time of Jesus the population was still mixed, but was predominantly Jewish in the southern portion.

When the kingdom of Herod the Great was divided among his sons, Herod Antipas received Galilee as well as Peraea. He established his capital three miles north of Nazareth at Sepphoris, a city which according to Josephus he made the ornament of all Galilee. Later, a few years before the beginning of the public ministry of Jesus, he built a new capital on the shore of the Sea of Galilee and named it Tiberias in honor of the reigning Roman emperor, Tiberius. Both of these cities were centers of Gentile influence. Because of the Hellenistic civilization which prevailed in Galilee, a knowledge of spoken Greek was almost a business necessity.

Again in contrast with Judea, which was relatively isolated, Galilee was, as George Adam Smith once said, "covered with roads everywhere." The Road of the Sea (Via Maris) ran from Damascus to the Lake of Galilee and went on to the Mediterranean. The great south road passed by the Sea of Galilee and continued to Egypt. The great road of the east crossed lower Galilee to Scythopolis and led to the Decapolis, Peraea and Arabia.

Nazareth is the city from which Jesus came when he was baptized by John (Mk. 1:9). It is situated in Lower Galilee and occupies a sort of natural amphitheater on the southern slope of a mountain known as Jebel es-Sikh. From the summit of the hill above, there is a splendid view east to Mount Tabor (elevation, 1,843 feet) five miles away, south to the Plain of Esdraelon, west to Mount Carmel (1,810 feet) and the Mediterranean, and north to Mount Hermon (9,100 feet). Surrounded by olive trees, fig trees, and today by cactus hedges, and with the white walls of its buildings shining in the sun, the town presents an attractive appearance. A spring running out of the mountain provides water, which is piped down to an enclosure where the women of Nazareth still come to carry water to their homes in large jars or other containers.

Capernaum, where Jesus taught in the synagogue (Mk. 1:21) and visited the home of Simon and Andrew (Mk. 1:29), and where he healed the paralytic (Mk. 2:1–12), is the modern Arabic Tell Hum on the northwestern shore of the Sea of Galilee. The ruins of the ancient town extend for nearly a mile along the lake. Among the ruins a syna-

gogue has been found, excavated and partially restored. It was a rectangular building, constructed of cut blocks of fine white limestone. It faced southward toward the lake and toward Jerusalem, so that those who prayed in it might face the holy city. The interior was seventy feet long and fifty feet wide. There was an upper gallery intended for the women. Some of the tall columns, with their Corinthian capitals, are still there, and many fragments of ornamental stone have been found, with foliage, palm trees, eagles, lions and other figures. Sometimes held to be the ruins of the very synagogue in which Jesus preached, it is probable that these stones come instead from a later rebuilding of the same synagogue, which may have been built on the original site of the older synagogue destroyed by Vespasian in A.D. 67.

Bethsaida, to which Jesus sent his disciples after the feeding of the five thousand (Mk. 6:43) and where he healed a blind man (Mk. 8:22–26), may have been the village of that name of which Josephus tells. He says that it was rebuilt by Herod's son Philip, and renamed Julias, after the daughter of the emperor Augustus. This place seems to have been just east of the Jordan near where that river enters the Sea of Galilee.

(For additional geographical and historical material see other illustrated portions of the New Testament books of this series.)

This view of Jerusalem shows the temple area as it is today. Few of the large Herodian drafted stones in the ancient walls have survived the destruction of the city by Titus in A.D. 70. The smaller stones in the present walls date from the time of Suleiman the Magnificent in 1542. Tradition reports that St. Mark's mother had her home in the old city and that the early disciples visited there. Some believe that the gift of the tongues at Pentecost may have occurred in her house

SOWING THE SEED

as reported in the Gospel according to

MARK

The Preaching of John the Baptist

[Mark 1:1–8] The beginning of the gospel of Jesus Christ, the Son of God.[a]
As it is written in Isai'ah the prophet,[b]
"Behold, I send my messenger before thy face,
who shall prepare thy way;[1]
the voice of one crying in the wilderness:
Prepare the way of the Lord,
make his paths straight—"[2]
John the baptizer appeared[c] in the wilderness, preaching a baptism of repentance for the forgiveness of sins. And there went out to him all the country of Jude'a and all the people of Jerusalem; and they were baptized by him in the river Jordan, confessing their sins. Now John was clothed with camel's hair, and had a leather girdle around his waist, and ate locusts and wild honey. And he preached, saying, "After me comes he who is mightier than I, the thong of whose sandals I am not worthy to stoop down and untie. I have baptized you with water; but he will baptize you with the Holy Spirit."

[a]Other ancient authorities omit *the Son of God*
[b]Other ancient authorities read *in the prophets*
[c]Other ancient authorities read *John was baptizing*

[1]*Malachi* 3:1
[2]*Isaiah* 40:3

Paul's Photos

This is the wilderness country of Judea, between the Dead Sea and Jerusalem. The monastery of Mar Saba, begun in the 5th century A. D., overlooks the Kidron Valley

A view overlooking Nazareth

A modern road from Nazareth

The Baptism of Jesus

[1:9–11]

In those days Jesus came from Naz'-areth of Gal'ilee and was baptized by John in the Jordan. And when he came up out of the water, immediately he saw the heavens opened and the Spirit descending upon him like a dove; and a voice came from heaven, "Thou art my beloved Son;[d] with thee I am well pleased."

[d] Or *my Son, my* (or *the*) *Beloved*

The River Jordan

Keren Hayesod

This is the desolate wilderness traditionally identified as the place of the temptation of Jesus. This mountain, northwest of nearby Jericho, is called Jebel Qarantal, from the name Quarantana, first applied to it by the Crusaders in memory of the forty days of Jesus' fast. A Greek monastery clings to the side of the rock

The Temptation of Jesus [1:12–13]

The Spirit immediately drove him out into the wilderness. And he was in the wilderness forty days, tempted by Satan; and he was with the wild beasts; and the angels ministered to him.

Jesus Begins His Ministry [1:14–15]

Now after John was arrested, Jesus came into Gal'ilee, preaching the gospel of God, and saying, "The time is fulfilled, and the kingdom of God is at hand; repent, and believe in the gospel."

Matson Photo Service

The tortuous course of the Jordan River appears clearly in this air view

These ancient caves, once inhabited by Christian hermits, honeycomb the traditional Mount of the Temptation

Gene Badger from Rapho-Guillumette

Fisherman casting his net into the Sea of Galilee

Fishermen mending their nets on the Sea of Galilee

Jesus Calls Four Fishermen [1:16–20]

And passing along by the Sea of Gal'ilee, he saw Simon and Andrew the brother of Simon casting a net in the sea; for they were fishermen. And Jesus said to them, "Follow me and I will make you become fishers of men." And immediately they left their nets and followed him. And going on a little farther, he saw James the son of Zeb'edee and John his brother, who were in their boat mending the nets. And immediately he called them; and they left their father Zeb'edee in the boat with the hired servants, and followed him.

A Man with an Unclean Spirit
[1:21–28]

And they went into Caper'na-um; and immediately on the sabbath he entered the synagogue and taught. And they were astonished at his teaching, for he taught them as one who had authority, and not as the scribes. And immediately there was in their synagogue a man with an unclean spirit; and he cried out, "What have you to do with us, Jesus of Naz'areth? Have you come to destroy us? I know who you are, the Holy One of God." But Jesus rebuked him, saying, "Be silent, and come out of him!" And the unclean spirit, convulsing him and crying with a loud voice, came out of him. And they were all amazed, so that they questioned among themselves, saying, "What is this? A new teaching! With authority he commands even the unclean spirits, and they obey him." And at once his fame spread everywhere throughout all the surrounding region of Gal'ilee.

Jesus Heals Peter's Mother-in-law
[1:29–31]

And immediately he[e] left the synagogue, and entered the house of Simon and Andrew, with James and John. Now Simon's mother-in-law lay sick with a fever, and immediately they told him of her. And he came and took her by the hand and lifted her up, and the fever left her; and she served them.

Jesus Heals Many at Evening [1:32–34]

That evening, at sundown, they brought to him all who were sick or possessed with demons. And the whole city was gathered together about the door. And he healed many who were sick with various diseases, and cast out many demons; and he would not permit the demons to speak, because they knew him.

Jesus Departs on a Preaching Tour
[1:35–39]

And in the morning, a great while before

[e]Other ancient authorities read *they*

day, he rose and went out to a lonely place, and there he prayed. And Simon and those who were with him followed him, and they found him and said to him, "Every one is searching for you." And he said to them, "Let us go on to the next towns, that I may preach there also; for that is why I came out." And he went throughout all Gal'ilee, preaching in their synagogues and casting out demons.

Jesus Cleanses a Leper [1:40–45]

And a leper came to him beseeching him, and kneeling said to him, "If you will, you can make me clean." Moved with pity, he stretched out his hand and touched him, and said to him, "I will; be clean." And immediately the leprosy left him, and he was made clean. And he sternly charged him, and sent him away at once, and said to him, "See that you say nothing to any one; but go, show yourself to the priest, and offer for your cleansing what Moses commanded, for a proof to the people."*f* But he went out and began to talk freely about it, and to spread the news, so that Jesus*g* could no longer openly enter a town, but was out in the country; and people came to him from every quarter.

Jesus Heals a Paralytic [MARK 2:1–12]

AND when he returned to Caper'na-um after some days, it was reported that he was at home. And many were gathered together, so that there was no longer room for them, not even about the door; and he was preaching the word to them. And they came, bringing to him a paralytic carried by four men. And when they could not get near him because of the crowd, they removed the roof above him; and when they had made an opening, they let down the pallet on which the paralytic lay And when Jesus saw their faith, he said to the paralytic, "My son, your sins are forgiven." Now some of the scribes were sitting there, questioning in their hearts, "Why does this man speak thus? It is blasphemy! Who can forgive sins but God alone?" And immediately Jesus, perceiving in his spirit that they thus questioned within themselves, said to them, "Why do you question thus in your hearts? Which is easier, to say to the paralytic, 'Your sins are forgiven,' or to say, 'Rise, take up your pallet and walk'? But that you may know that the Son of man has authority on earth to forgive sins"—he said to the paralytic—"I say to you, rise, take up your pallet and go home." And he rose, and immediately took up the pallet and went out before them all; so that they were all amazed and glorified God, saying, "We never saw anything like this!"

f Greek *to them*   *g* Greek *he*

This painting of the Healing of the Paralytic was found on the wall of an early Christian chapel at Dura-Europos dating from the early 3rd century A.D.

The Synagogue at Capernaum, probably built on site of earlier synagogue from the time of Christ

Goatskins are still used to carry liquids in Bible countries, sometimes holding them for weeks

Cloth market at Lydda

The Call of Levi [2:13–14]

He went out again beside the sea; and all the crowd gathered about him, and he taught them. And as he passed on, he saw Levi the son of Alphae'us sitting at the tax office, and he said to him, "Follow me." And he rose and followed him.

Jesus Eats with Sinners [2:15–17]

And as he sat at table in his house, many tax collectors and sinners were sitting with Jesus and his disciples; for there were many who followed him. And the scribes of [h] the Phar'isees, when they saw that he was eating with sinners and tax collectors, said to his disciples, "Why does he eat [i] with tax collectors and sinners?" And when Jesus heard it, he said to them, "Those who are well have no need of a physician, but those who are sick; I came not to call the righteous, but sinners."

The Question about Fasting [2:18–22]

Now John's disciples and the Phar'isees were fasting; and people came and said to him, "Why do John's disciples and the disciples of the Phar'isees fast, but your disciples do not fast?" And Jesus said to them, "Can the wedding guests fast while the bridegroom is with them? As long as they have the bridegroom with them, they cannot fast. The days will come, when the bridegroom is taken away from them, and then they will fast in that day. No one sews a piece of unshrunk cloth on an old garment; if he does, the patch tears away from it, the new from the old, and a worse tear is made. And no one puts new wine into old wineskins; if he does, the wine will burst the skins, and the wine is lost, and so are the skins; but new wine is for fresh skins." [j]

The Lord of the Sabbath [2:23–28]

One sabbath he was going through the grainfields; and as they made their way his disciples began to pluck ears of grain. And the Phar'isees said to him, "Look, why are they doing what is not lawful on the sabbath?" And he said to them, "Have you never read what David did, when he was in need and was hungry, he and those who were with him: how he entered the house of God, when Abi'athar was high priest, and ate the bread of the Presence, which it is not lawful for any but the priests to eat, and also gave it to those who were with him?" And he said to them, "The sabbath was made for man, not man for the sabbath; so the Son of man is lord even of the sabbath."

[h]Other ancient authorities read *and*
[i]Other ancient authorities add *and drink*
[j]Other ancient authorities omit *but new wine is for fresh skins*

Jesus Heals on the Sabbath

[Mark 3:1–6]

AGAIN he entered the synagogue, and a man was there who had a withered hand. And they watched him, to see whether he would heal him on the sabbath, so that they might accuse him. And he said to the man who had the withered hand, "Come here." And he said to them, "Is it lawful on the sabbath to do good or to do harm, to save life or to kill?" But they were silent. And he looked around at them with anger, grieved at their hardness of heart, and said to the man, "Stretch out your hand." He stretched it out, and his hand was restored. The Phar'isees went out, and immediately held counsel with the Hero'di-ans against him, how to destroy him.

A Multitude at the Seaside [3:7–12]

Jesus withdrew with his disciples to the sea, and a great multitude from Gal'ilee followed; also from Jude'a and Jerusalem and Idume'a and from beyond the Jordan and from about Tyre and Sidon a great multitude, hearing all that he did, came to him. And he told his disciples to have a boat ready for him because of the crowd, lest they should crush him; for he had healed many, so that all who had diseases pressed upon him to touch him. And whenever the unclean spirits beheld him, they fell down before him and cried out, "You are the Son of God." And he strictly ordered them not to make him known.

Jesus Chooses the Twelve [3:13–19]

And he went up into the hills, and called to him those whom he desired; and they came to him. And he appointed twelve,[k] to be with him, and to be sent out to preach and have authority to cast out demons: Simon whom he surnamed Peter; James the son of Zeb'edee and John the brother of James, whom he surnamed Bo-aner'ges, that is, sons of thunder; Andrew, and Philip, and Barthol'omew, and Matthew, and Thomas, and James the son of Alphae'us and Thad'daeus, and Simon the Cananae'an, and Judas Iscar'iot, who betrayed him.

Jesus and Beelzebul [3:20–30]

Then he went home; and the crowd came together again, so that they could not even eat. And when his friends heard it, they went out to seize him, for they said, "He is beside himself." And the scribes who came down from Jerusalem said, "He is possessed by Be-el'zebul, and by the prince of demons he casts out the demons." And he called them to him, and said to them in parables, "How can Satan cast out Satan? If a kingdom is divided against itself, that kingdom cannot stand. And if a house is

[k]Other ancient authorities add *whom also he named apostles*

Matson Photo Service

Tyre, situated on an island about 20 miles south of the port of Sidon, resisted Nebuchadnezzar for 13 years but was conquered by Alexander the Great, who built a causeway from the mainland in 332 B.C.

divided against itself, that house will not be able to stand. And if Satan has risen up against himself and is divided, he cannot stand, but is coming to an end. But no one can enter a strong man's house and plunder his goods, unless he first binds the strong man; then indeed he may plunder his house.

"Truly, I say to you, all sins will be forgiven the sons of men, and whatever blasphemies they utter; but whoever blasphemes against the Holy Spirit never has forgiveness, but is guilty of an eternal sin" —for they had said, "He has an unclean spirit."

Jesus' Mother and Brothers

[3:31–35]

And his mother and his brothers came; and standing outside they sent to him and called him. And a crowd was sitting about him; and they said to him, "Your mother and your brothers[l] are outside, asking for you." And he replied, "Who are my mother and my brothers?" And looking around on those who sat about him, he said, "Here are my mother and my brothers! Whoever does the will of God is my brother, and sister, and mother."

[l]Other early authorities add *and your sisters*

Sidon submitted to Alexander the Great without a struggle and escaped destruction. Herod the Great erected fine buildings in both Tyre and Sidon

Matson Photo Service

Palestine Foundation Fund

Arab using hand-made wooden plow in Palestine

scorched, and since it had no root it withered away. Other seed fell among thorns and the thorns grew up and choked it, and it yielded no grain. And other seeds fell into good soil and brought forth grain, growing up and increasing, and yielding thirtyfold and sixtyfold and a hundredfold." And he said, "He who has ears to hear, let him hear."

Jesus Explains the Parable of the Sower
[4:10–20]

And when he was alone, those who were about him with the twelve asked him concerning the parables. And he said to them, "To you has been given the secret of the kingdom of God, but for those outside everything is in parables; so that they may indeed see but not perceive, and may indeed hear but not understand; lest they should turn again, and be forgiven." And he said to them, "Do you not understand this parable? How then will you understand all the parables? The sower sows the word. And these are the ones along the path, where the word is sown; when they hear, Satan immediately comes and takes away the word which is sown in them. And these in like manner are the ones sown upon rocky ground, who, when they hear the word, immediately receive it with joy; and they have no root in themselves, but endure for a while; then, when tribulation or persecution arises on account of the word, immediately they fall away.[m] And others are the ones sown among thorns; they are those who hear the word, but the cares of the world, and the delight in riches, and the desire for other things, enter in and choke the word, and it proves unfruitful. But those that were sown upon the good soil are the ones who hear the word and accept it and bear fruit, thirtyfold and sixtyfold and a hundredfold."

[m]Or *stumble*

The Parable of the Sower
[Mark 4:1–9]

AGAIN he began to teach beside the sea. And a very large crowd gathered about him, so that he got into a boat and sat in it on the sea; and the whole crowd was beside the sea on the land. And he taught them many things in parables, and in his teaching he said to them: "Listen! A sower went out to sow. And as he sowed, some seed fell along the path, and the birds came and devoured it. Other seed fell on rocky ground, where it had not much soil, and immediately it sprang up, since it had no depth of soil; and when the sun rose it was

Palestinian thorn bush

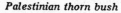

E. A. Nida

L. A. Fereday

"A sower went out to sow"

The Parable of the Hidden Lamp

[4:21–25]

And he said to them, "Is a lamp brought in to be put under a bushel, or under a bed, and not on a stand? For there is nothing hid, except to be made manifest; nor is anything secret, except to come to light. If any man has ears to hear, let him hear." And he said to them, "Take heed what you hear; the measure you give will be the measure you get, and still more will be given you. For to him who has will more be given; and from him who has not, even what he has will be taken away."

The Parable of the Growing Seed

[4:26–29]

And he said, "The kingdom of God is as if a man should scatter seed upon the ground, and should sleep and rise night and day, and the seed should sprout and grow, he knows not how. The earth produces of itself, first the blade, then the ear, then the full grain in the ear. But when the grain is ripe, at once he puts in the sickle, because the harvest has come."

The Parable of the Mustard Seed

[4:30–32]

And he said, "With what can we compare the kingdom of God, or what parable shall we use for it? It is like a grain of mustard seed, which, when sown upon the ground, is the smallest of all the seeds on earth; yet when it is sown it grows up and becomes the greatest of all shrubs, and puts forth large branches, so that the birds of the air can make nests in its shade."

Jesus' Use of Parables [4:33–34]

With many such parables he spoke the word to them, as they were able to hear it; he did not speak to them without a parable, but privately to his own disciples he explained everything.

Jesus Calms a Storm [4:35–41]

On that day, when evening had come, he said to them, "Let us go across to the other side." And leaving the crowd, they took him with them, just as he was, in the boat. And other boats were with him. And a great storm of wind arose, and the waves beat into the boat, so that the boat was already filling. But he was in the stern, asleep on the cushion; and they woke him and said to him, "Teacher, do you not care if we perish?" And he awoke and rebuked the wind, and said to the sea, "Peace! Be still!" And the wind ceased, and there was a great calm. He said to them, "Why are you afraid? Have you no faith?" And they were filled with awe, and said to one another, "Who then is this, that even wind and sea obey him?"

L. A. Fereday

Mustard tree

Storm on the Sea of Galilee

Matson Photo Service

C. C. McCown

The main street of Gerasa, one of the most prominent cities of the Decapolis

The Testimony of the Healed Demoniac [5:14-20]

The herdsmen fled, and told it in the city and in the country. And people came to see what it was that had happened. And they came to Jesus, and saw the demoniac sitting there, clothed and in his right mind, the man who had had the legion; and they were afraid. And those who had seen it told what had happened to the demoniac and to the swine. And they began to beg Jesus[p] to depart from their neighborhood. And as he was getting into the boat, the man who had been possessed with demons begged him that he might be with him. But he refused, and said to him, "Go home to your friends, and tell them how much the Lord has done for you, and how he has had mercy on you." And he went away and began to proclaim in the Decap'olis how much Jesus had done for him; and all men marveled.

Jairus Pleads for His Daughter
[5:21-24]

And when Jesus had crossed again in the boat to the other side, a great crowd gathered about him; and he was beside the sea. Then came one of the rulers of the synagogue, Jairus by name; and seeing him, he fell at his feet, and besought him, saying, "My little daughter is at the point of death. Come and lay your hands on her, so that she may be made well, and live." And he went with him.

The Woman Who Touched Jesus' Garment [5:25-34]

And a great crowd followed him and thronged about him. And there was a woman who had had a flow of blood for twelve years, and who had suffered much under many physicians, and had spent all that she had, and was no better but rather grew worse. She had heard the reports about Jesus, and came up behind him in the crowd and touched his garment. For she said, "If I touch even his garments, I shall be made well." And immediately the hemorrhage ceased; and she felt in her body that she was healed of her disease. And Jesus, perceiving in himself that power had gone forth from him, immediately turned about in the crowd, and said, "Who touched my garments?" And his disciples said to him, "You see the crowd pressing around you, and yet you say, 'Who touched me?'" And he looked around to see who had done it. But the woman, knowing what had been done to her, came in fear and trembling and fell down before him, and told him the whole truth. And he said to her, "Daughter, your faith has made you well; go in peace, and be healed of your disease."

The Gerasene Demoniac Healed
[Mark 5:1-13]

THEY came to the other side of the sea, to the country of the Ger'asenes.[n] And when he had come out of the boat, there met him out of the tombs a man with an unclean spirit, who lived among the tombs; and no one could bind him any more, even with a chain; for he had often been bound with fetters and chains, but the chains he wrenched apart, and the fetters he broke in pieces; and no one had the strength to subdue him. Night and day among the tombs and on the mountains he was always crying out, and bruising himself with stones. And when he saw Jesus from afar, he ran and worshiped him; and crying out with a loud voice, he said, "What have you to do with me, Jesus, Son of the Most High God? I adjure you by God, do not torment me." For he had said to him, "Come out of the man, you unclean spirit!" And Jesus[o] asked him, "What is your name?" He replied, "My name is Legion; for we are many." And he begged him eagerly not to send them out of the country. Now a great herd of swine was feeding there on the hillside; and they begged him, "Send us to the swine, let us enter them." So he gave them leave. And the unclean spirits came out, and entered the swine; and the herd, numbering about two thousand, rushed down the steep bank into the sea, and were drowned in the sea.

[n]Other ancient authorities read *Gergesenes*, some *Gadarenes*
[o]Greek *he*
[p]Greek *him*

Three Lions

A carpenter shop in Nazareth

44

Jairus' Daughter Raised

[5:35-43]

While he was still speaking, there came from the ruler's house some who said, "Your daughter is dead. Why trouble the Teacher any further?" But ignoring[q] what they said, Jesus said to the ruler of the synagogue, "Do not fear, only believe." And he allowed no one to follow him except Peter and James and John the brother of James. When they came to the house of the ruler of the synagogue, he saw a tumult, and people weeping and wailing loudly. And when he had entered, he said to them, "Why do you make a tumult and weep? The child is not dead but sleeping." And they laughed at him. But he put them all outside, and took the child's father and mother and those who were with him, and went in where the child was. Taking her by the hand he said to her, "Tali'tha cu'mi"; which means, "Little girl, I say to you, arise." And immediately the girl got up and walked; for she was twelve years old. And immediately they were overcome with amazement. And he strictly charged them that no one should know this, and told them to give her something to eat.

Jesus Rejected in Nazareth

[Mark 6:1-6]

HE went away from there and came to his own country; and his disciples followed him. And on the sabbath he began to teach in the synagogue; and many who heard him were astonished, saying, "Where did this man get all this? What is the wisdom given to him? What mighty works are wrought by his hands! Is not this the carpenter, the son of Mary and brother of James and Joses and Judas and Simon, and are not his sisters here with us?" And they took offense[r] at him. And Jesus said to them, "A prophet is not without honor, except in his own country, and among his own kin, and in his own house." And he could do no mighty work there, except that he laid his hands upon a few sick people and healed them. And he marveled because of their unbelief.

And he went about among the villages teaching.

The Mission of the Twelve

[6:7-13]

And he called to him the twelve, and began to send them out two by two, and gave them authority over the unclean spirits. He charged them to take nothing for their journey except a staff; no bread, no bag, no money in their belts; but to wear sandals and not put on two tunics. And he said to

[q]Or *overhearing.* Other ancient authorities read *hearing*

[r]Or *stumbled*

Matson Photo Service

Machaerus—ancient remains on Castle Hill, where John the Baptist was imprisoned

them, "Where you enter a house, stay there until you leave the place. And if any place will not receive you and they refuse to hear you, when you leave, shake off the dust that is on your feet for a testimony against them." So they went out and preached that men should repent. And they cast out many demons, and anointed with oil many that were sick and healed them.

The Death of John the Baptist

[6:14-29]

King Herod heard of it; for Jesus's[s] name had become known. Some[t] said, "John the baptizer has been raised from the dead; that is why these powers are at work in him." But others said, "It is Eli'jah." And others said, "It is a prophet, like one of the prophets of old." But when Herod heard of it he said, "John, whom I beheaded, has been raised." For Herod had sent and seized John, and bound him in prison for the sake of Hero'di-as, his brother Philip's wife; because he had married her. For John said to Herod, "It is not lawful for you to have your brother's wife." And Hero'di-as had a grudge against him, and wanted to

[s]Greek *his*

[t]Other ancient authorities read *he*

kill him. But she could not, for Herod feared John, knowing that he was a righteous and holy man, and kept him safe. When he heard him, he was much perplexed; and yet he heard him gladly. But an opportunity came when Herod on his birthday gave a banquet for his courtiers and officers and the leading men of Gal'ilee. For when Hero'di-as' daughter came in and danced, she pleased Herod and his guests; and the king said to the girl, "Ask me for whatever you wish, and I will grant it." And he vowed to her, "Whatever you ask me, I will give you, even half of my kingdom." And she went out, and said to her mother, "What shall I ask?" And she said, "The head of John the baptizer." And she came in immediately with haste to the king, and asked, saying, "I want you to give me at once the head of John the Baptist on a platter." And the king was exceedingly sorry; but because of his oaths and his guests he did not want to break his word to her. And immediately the king sent a soldier of the guard and gave orders to bring his head. He went and beheaded him in the prison, and brought his head on a platter, and gave it to the girl; and the girl gave it to her mother. When his disciples heard of it, they came and took his body, and laid it in a tomb.

The Sea of Galilee

The Feeding of the Five Thousand
[6:30-44]

The apostles returned to Jesus, and told him all that they had done and taught. And he said to them, "Come away by yourselves to a lonely place, and rest a while." For many were coming and going, and they had no leisure even to eat. And they went away in the boat to a lonely place by themselves. Now many saw them going, and knew them, and they ran there on foot from all the towns, and got there ahead of them. As he landed he saw a great throng, and he had compassion on them, because they were like sheep without a shepherd; and he began to teach them many things. And when it grew late, his disciples came to him and said, "This is a lonely place, and the hour is now late; send them away, to go into the country and villages round about and buy themselves something to eat." But he answered them, "You give them something to eat." And they said to him, "Shall we go and buy two hundred denarii[u] worth of bread, and give it to them to eat?" And he said to them, "How many loaves have you? Go and see." And when they had found out, they said, "Five, and two fish."

[u]The denarius was worth about twenty cents

Sea of Galilee at Tabgha, on the northwestern shore, near traditional site of the feeding of the five thousand

Three Lions

Then he commanded them all to sit down by companies upon the green grass. So they sat down in groups, by hundreds and by fifties. And taking the five loaves and the two fish he looked up to heaven, and blessed, and broke the loaves, and gave them to the disciples to set before the people; and he divided the two fish among them all. And they all ate and were satisfied. And they took up twelve baskets full of broken pieces and of the fish. And those who ate the loaves were five thousand men.

Jesus Walks on the Sea
[6:45-52]

Immediately he made his disciples get into the boat and go before him to the other side, to Beth-sa'ida, while he dismissed the crowd. And after he had taken leave of them, he went into the hills to pray. And when evening came, the boat was out on the sea, and he was alone on the land. And he saw that they were distressed in rowing, for the wind was against them. And about the fourth watch of the night he came to them, walking on the sea. He meant to pass by them, but when they saw him walking on the sea they thought it was a ghost, and cried out; for they all saw him, and were terrified. But immediately he spoke to them and said, "Take heart, it is I; have no fear." And he got into the boat with them and the wind ceased. And they were utterly astounded, for they did not understand about the loaves, but their hearts were hardened.

Jesus Heals the Sick in Gennesaret
[6:53-56]

And when they had crossed over, they came to land at Gennes'aret, and moored to the shore. And when they got out of the boat, immediately the people recognized him, and ran about the whole neighborhood and began to bring sick people on their pallets to any place where they heard he was. And wherever he came, in villages, cities, or country, they laid the sick in the market places, and besought him that they might touch even the fringe of his garment; and as many as touched it were made well.

The Tradition of the Elders
[Mark 7:1-8]

NOW when the Phar'isees gathered together to him, with some of the scribes, who had come from Jerusalem, they saw that some of his disciples ate with hands defiled, that is, unwashed. (For the Phar'isees, and all the Jews, do not eat unless they wash their hands,[v] observing the tradition of the elders; and when they come from the market place, they do not

[v]One Greek word is of uncertain meaning and is not translated

46

eat unless they purify[w] themselves; and there are many other traditions which they observe, the washing of cups and pots and vessels of bronze.[x]) And the Phar′isees and the scribes asked him, "Why do your disciples not live[y] according to the tradition of the elders, but eat with hands defiled?" And he said to them, "Well did Isai′ah prophesy of you hypocrites, as it is written,

'This people honors me with their lips,
  but their heart is far from me;
in vain do they worship me,
  teaching as doctrines the precepts of men.'[3]

You leave the commandment of God, and hold fast the tradition of men."

Rejecting the Commandment of God
[7:9–13]

And he said to them, "You have a fine way of rejecting the commandment of God, in order to keep your tradition! For Moses said, 'Honor your father and your mother'; and, 'He who speaks evil of father or mother, let him surely die';[4] but you say, 'If a man tells his father or his mother, What you would have gained from me is Corban' (that is, given to God)[z]—then you no longer permit him to do anything for his father or mother, thus making void the word of God through your tradition which you hand on. And many such things you do."

The Things that Defile
[7:14–23]

And he called the people to him again, and said to them, "Hear me, all of you, and understand: there is nothing outside a man which by going into him can defile him; but the things which come out of a man are what defile him."[a] And when he had entered the house, and left the people, his disciples asked him about the parable. And he said to them, "Then are you also without understanding? Do you not see that whatever goes into a man from outside cannot defile him, since it enters, not his heart but his stomach, and so passes on[b]?" (Thus he declared all foods clean.) And he said, "What comes out of a man is what defiles a man. For from within, out of the heart of man, come evil thoughts, fornication, theft, murder, adultery, coveting, wickedness, deceit, licentiousness, envy, slander, pride, foolishness. All these evil things come from within, and they defile a man."

[w]Other ancient authorities read *baptize*
[x]Other ancient authorities add *and beds*
[y]Greek *walk*
[z]Or *an offering*
[a]Other ancient authorities add verse 16, "*If any man has ears to hear, let him hear*"
[b]Or *is evacuated*
[3]Isaiah 29:13
[4]Exodus 20:12; 21:17; Deuteronomy 5:16; Leviticus 20:9

Three Lions

The Sea of Galilee and the Plain of Gennesaret

The Syrophoenician Woman's Faith
[7:24–30]

And from there he arose and went away to the region of Tyre and Sidon.[c] And he entered a house, and would not have any one know it; yet he could not be hid. But immediately a woman, whose little daughter was possessed by an unclean spirit, heard of him, and came and fell down at his feet. Now the woman was a Greek, a Syro-

[c]Other ancient authorities omit *and Sidon*

phoeni′cian by birth. And she begged him to cast the demon out of her daughter. And he said to her, "Let the children first be fed, for it is not right to take the children's bread and throw it to the dogs." But she answered him, "Yes, Lord; yet even the dogs under the table eat the children's crumbs." And he said to her, "For this saying you may go your way; the demon has left your daughter." And she went home, and found the child lying in bed, and the demon gone.

A market place in Jaffa

Underwood and Underwood

Gideon W. Bachmann

One of the sources of the Jordan, near Mt. Hermon and Caesarea Philippi

Jesus Heals a Deaf and Dumb Man
[7:31–37]

Then he returned from the region of Tyre, and went through Sidon to the Sea of Gal'ilee, through the region of the Decap'o-lis. And they brought to him a man who was deaf and had an impediment in his speech; and they besought him to lay his hand upon him. And taking him aside from the multitude privately, he put his fingers into his ears, and he spat and touched his tongue; and looking up to heaven, he sighed, and said to him, "Eph'phatha," that is, "Be opened." And his ears were opened, his tongue was released, and he spoke plainly. And he charged them to tell no one; but the more he charged them, the more zealously they proclaimed it. And they were astonished beyond measure, saying, "He has done all things well; he even makes the deaf hear and the dumb speak."

The Plain of Gennesaret

L. A. Fereday

The Feeding of the Four Thousand
[Mark 8:1–10]

IN those days, when again a great crowd had gathered, and they had nothing to eat, he called his disciples to him, and said to them, "I have compassion on the crowd, because they have been with me now three days, and have nothing to eat; and if I send them away hungry to their homes, they will faint on the way; and some of them have come a long way." And his disciples answered him, "How can one feed these men with bread here in the desert?" And he asked them, "How many loaves have you?" They said, "Seven." And he commanded the crowd to sit down on the ground; and he took the seven loaves, and having given thanks he broke them and gave them to his disciples to set before the people; and they set them before the crowd. And they had a few small fish; and having blessed them, he commanded that these also should be set before them. And they ate, and were satisfied; and they took up the broken pieces left over, seven baskets full. And there were about four thousand people. And he sent them away; and immediately he got into the boat with his disciples, and went to the district of Dalmanu'tha.[d]

The Demand for a Sign [8:11–13]

The Phar'isees came and began to argue with him, seeking from him a sign from heaven, to test him. And he sighed deeply in his spirit, and said, "Why does this generation seek a sign? Truly, I say to you, no sign shall be given to this generation." And he left them, and getting into the boat again he departed to the other side.

The Leaven of the Pharisees and of Herod [8:14–21]

Now they had forgotten to bring bread; and they had only one loaf with them in the boat. And he cautioned them, saying, "Take heed, beware of the leaven of the Phar'isees and the leaven of Herod."[e] And they discussed it with one another, saying, "We have no bread." And being aware of it, Jesus said to them, "Why do you discuss the fact that you have no bread? Do you not yet perceive or understand? Are your hearts hardened? Having eyes do you not see, and having ears do you not hear? And do you not remember? When I broke the five loaves for the five thousand, how many baskets full of broken pieces did you take up?" They said to him, "Twelve." "And the seven for the four thousand, how many baskets full of broken pieces did you take up?" And they said to him, "Seven." And he said to them, "Do you not yet understand?"

[d]Other ancient authorities read *Magadan* or *Magdala*
[e]Other ancient authorities read *the Herodians*

A Blind Man Healed at Bethsaida
[8:22–26]

And they came to Beth-sa'ida. And some people brought to him a blind man, and begged him to touch him. And he took the blind man by the hand, and led him out of the village; and when he had spit on his eyes and laid his hands upon him, he asked him, "Do you see anything?" And he looked up and said, "I see men; but they look like trees, walking." Then again he laid his hands upon his eyes; and he looked intently and was restored, and saw everything clearly. And he sent him away to his home, saying, "Do not even enter the village."

Peter's Declaration about Jesus [8:27–30]

And Jesus went on with his disciples, to the villages of Caesare'a Phil'ippi; and on the way he asked his disciples, "Who do men say that I am?" And they told him, "John the Baptist; and others say, Eli'jah; and others one of the prophets." And he asked them, "But who do you say that I am?" Peter answered him, "You are the Christ." And he charged them to tell no one about him.

Jesus Foretells His Death
[8:31–33]

And he began to teach them that the Son of man must suffer many things, and be rejected by the elders and the chief priests and the scribes, and be killed, and after three days rise again. And he said this plainly. And Peter took him, and began to rebuke him. But turning and seeing his disciples, he rebuked Peter, and said, "Get behind me, Satan! For you are not on the side of God, but of men."

The Way of the Cross
[8:34—9:1]

And he called to him the multitude with his disciples, and said to them, "If any man would come after me, let him deny himself and take up his cross and follow me. For whoever would save his life will lose it; and whoever loses his life for my sake and the gospel's will save it. For what does it profit a man, to gain the whole world and forfeit his life? For what can a man give in return for his life? For whoever is ashamed of me and of my words in this adulterous and sinful generation, of him will the Son of man also be ashamed, when he comes in the glory of his Father with the holy angels." And he said to them, "Truly, I say to you, there are some standing here who will not taste death before they see the kingdom of God come with power."

Underwood and Underwood

Mt. Tabor is the traditional site of the Transfiguration from very ancient times

The Transfiguration [Mark 9:2–8]

AND after six days Jesus took with him Peter and James and John, and led them up a high mountain apart by themselves; and he was transfigured before them, and his garments became glistening, intensely white, as no fuller on earth could bleach them. And there appeared to them Eli'jah with Moses; and they were talking to Jesus. And Peter said to Jesus, "Master,*ƒ* it is well that we are here; let us make three booths, one for you and one for Moses and one for Eli'jah." For he did not know what to say, for they were exceedingly afraid. And a cloud overshadowed them, and a voice came out of the cloud, "This is my beloved Son;*ᵍ* listen to him." And suddenly looking around they no longer saw any one with them but Jesus only.

ƒ Or *Rabbi*
ᵍ Or *my Son, my* (or *the*) *Beloved*

Mt. Hermon, altitude 9,100 feet, is near Caesarea Philippi

The upper millstone is rotated upon the lower millstone to grind the grain

Three Lions

The Coming of Elijah [9:9–13]

And as they were coming down the mountain, he charged them to tell no one what they had seen, until the Son of man should have risen from the dead. So they kept the matter to themselves, questioning what the rising from the dead meant. And they asked him, "Why do the scribes say that first Eli'jah must come?" And he said to them, "Eli'jah does come first to restore all things; and how is it written of the Son of man, that he should suffer many things and be treated with contempt? But I tell you that Eli'jah has come, and they did to him whatever they pleased, as it is written of him."

Jesus Heals an Epileptic Boy [9:14–29]

And when they came to the disciples, they saw a great crowd about them, and scribes arguing with them. And immediately all the crowd, when they saw him, were greatly amazed, and ran up to him and greeted him. And he asked them, "What are you discussing with them?" And one of the crowd answered him, "Teacher, I brought my son to you, for he has a dumb spirit; and wherever it seizes him, it dashes him down; and he foams and grinds his teeth and becomes rigid; and I asked your disciples to cast it out, and they were not able." And he answered them, "O faithless generation, how long am I to be with you? How long am I to bear with you? Bring him to me." And they brought the boy to him; and when the spirit saw him, immediately it convulsed the boy, and he fell on the ground and rolled about, foaming at the mouth. And Jesus[h] asked his father, "How long has he had this?" And he said, "From childhood. And it has often cast him into the fire and into the water, to destroy him;

[h]Greek *he*

but if you can do anything, have pity on us and help us." And Jesus said to him, "If you can! All things are possible to him who believes." Immediately the father of the child cried out[i] and said, "I believe; help my unbelief!" And when Jesus saw that a crowd came running together, he rebuked the unclean spirit, saying to it, "You dumb and deaf spirit, I command you, come out of him, and never enter him again." And after crying out and convulsing him terribly, it came out, and the boy was like a corpse; so that most of them said, "He is dead." But Jesus took him by the hand and lifted him up, and he arose. And when he had entered the house, his disciples asked him privately, "Why could we not cast it out?" And he said to them, "This kind cannot be driven out by anything but prayer."[j]

Jesus again Foretells His Death [9:30–32]

They went on from there and passed through Gal'ilee. And he would not have any one know it; for he was teaching his disciples, saying to them, "The Son of man will be delivered into the hands of men, and they will kill him; and when he is killed, after three days he will rise." But they did not understand the saying, and they were afraid to ask him.

"Who Is the Greatest?" [9:33–37]

And they came to Caper'na-um; and when he was in the house he asked them, "What were you discussing on the way?" But they were silent; for on the way they had discussed with one another who was the greatest. And he sat down and called the twelve; and he said to them, "If any one would be first, he must be last of all and servant of all." And he took a child, and put him in the midst of them; and taking him in his arms, he said to them, "Whoever receives one such child in my name receives me; and whoever receives me, receives not me but him who sent me."

"He That Is Not against Us Is for Us" [9:38–41]

John said to him, "Teacher, we saw a man casting out demons in your name,[k] and we forbade him, because he was not following us." But Jesus said, "Do not forbid him; for no one who does a mighty work in my name will be able soon after to speak evil of me. For he that is not against us is for us. For truly, I say to you, whoever gives you a cup of water to drink because you bear the name of Christ, will by no means lose his reward.

[i]Other ancient authorities add *with tears*
[j]Other ancient authorities add *and fasting*
[k]Other ancient authorities add *who does not follow us*

Temptations To Sin

[9:42–50]

"Whoever causes one of these little ones who believe in me to sin,[l] it would be better for him if a great millstone were hung round his neck and he were thrown into the sea. And if your hand causes you to sin,[l] cut if off; it is better for you to enter life maimed than with two hands to go to hell,[m] to the unquenchable fire.[n] And if your foot causes you to sin,[l] cut it off; it is better for you to enter life lame than with two feet to be thrown into hell.[m, n] And if your eye causes you to sin,[l] pluck it out; it is better for you to enter the kingdom of God with one eye than with two eyes to be thrown into hell,[m] where their worm does not die, and the fire is not quenched. For every one will be salted with fire.[o] Salt is good; but if the salt has lost its saltness, how will you season it? Have salt in yourselves, and be at peace with one another."

Jesus' Teaching about Divorce

[Mark 10:1–12]

AND he left there and went to the region of Jude'a and beyond the Jordan, and crowds gathered to him again; and again, as his custom was, he taught them.

And Phar'isees came up and in order to test him asked, "Is it lawful for a man to divorce his wife?" He answered them, "What did Moses command you?" They said, "Moses allowed a man to write a certificate of divorce, and to put her away." But Jesus said to them, "For your hardness of heart he wrote you this commandment. But from the beginning of creation, 'God made them male and female.'[5] 'For this reason a man shall leave his father and mother and be joined to his wife,[p] and the two shall become one.'[q 6] So they are no longer two but one.[q] What therefore God has joined together, let not man put asunder."

And in the house the disciples asked him again about this matter. And he said to them, "Whoever divorces his wife and marries another, commits adultery against her; and if she divorces her husband and marries another, she commits adultery."

[l]Greek *stumble*

[m]Greek *Gehenna*

[n]Verses 44 and 46 (which are identical with verse 48) are omitted by the best ancient authorities

[o]Other ancient authorities add *and every sacrifice will be salted with salt*

[p]Other ancient authorities omit *and be joined to his wife*

[q]Greek *one flesh*

[5]*Genesis* 1:27; 5:2

[6]*Genesis* 2:24

Jesus Blesses Little Children

[10:13–16]

And they were bringing children to him, that he might touch them; and the disciples rebuked them. But when Jesus saw it he was indignant, and said to them, "Let the children come to me, do not hinder them; for to such belongs the kingdom of God. Truly, I say to you, whoever does not receive the kingdom of God like a child shall not enter it." And he took them in his arms and blessed them, laying his hands upon them.

The Rich Young Man [10:17–22]

And as he was setting out on his journey, a man ran up and knelt before him, and asked him, "Good Teacher, what must I do to inherit eternal life?" And Jesus said to him, "Why do you call me good? No one is good but God alone. You know the commandments: 'Do not kill, Do not commit adultery, Do not steal, Do not bear false witness, Do not defraud, Honor your father and mother.' "[7] And he said to him, "Teacher, all these I have observed from my youth." And Jesus looking upon him loved him, and said to him, "You lack one thing; go, sell what you have, and give to the poor, and you will have treasure in heaven; and come, follow me." At that saying his countenance fell, and he went away sorrowful; for he had great possessions.

The Danger of Riches [10:23–31]

And Jesus looked around and said to his disciples, "How hard it will be for those who have riches to enter the kingdom of God!" And the disciples were amazed at his words. But Jesus said to them again, "Children, how hard it is[r] to enter the kingdom of God! It is easier for a camel to go through the eye of a needle than for a rich man to enter the kingdom of God." And they were exceedingly astonished, and said to him,[s] "Then who can be saved?" Jesus looked at them and said, "With men it is impossible, but not with God; for all things are possible with God." Peter began to say to him, "Lo, we have left everything and followed you." Jesus said, "Truly, I say to you, there is no one who has left house or brothers or sisters or mother or father or children or lands, for my sake and for the gospel, who will not receive a hundred-fold now in this time, houses and brothers and sisters and mothers and children and lands, with persecutions, and in the age to come eternal life. But many that are first will be last, and the last first."

[r]Other ancient authorities add *for those who trust in riches*
[s]Other ancient authorities read *to one another*
[7]*Exodus* 20:12–16; *Deuteronomy* 5:16–20

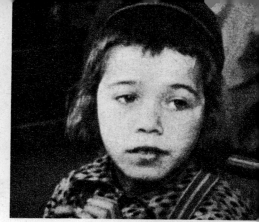

UNICEF

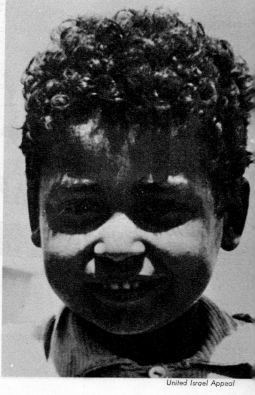

United Israel Appeal

"Let the children come to me, do not hinder them; for to such belongs the kingdom of God"

L. Kofod

J. L. Kelso

A close-up of the excavations at New Testament Jericho. The background is dominated by a mountain, which was crowned by a fortress in Jesus' time

Philip Gendreau, N.Y.

An Arab at Jericho

Jesus Foretells His Death a Third Time

[10:32–34]

And they were on the road, going up to Jerusalem, and Jesus was walking ahead of them; and they were amazed, and those who followed were afraid. And taking the twelve again, he began to tell them what was to happen to him, saying, "Behold, we are going up to Jerusalem; and the Son of man will be delivered to the chief priests and the scribes, and they will condemn him to death, and deliver him to the Gentiles; and they will mock him, and spit upon him, and scourge him, and kill him; and after three days he will rise."

The Request of James and John

[10:35–45]

And James and John, the sons of Zeb'e-dee, came forward to him, and said to him, "Teacher, we want you to do for us whatever we ask of you." And he said to them, "What do you want me to do for you?" And they said to him, "Grant us to sit, one at your right hand and one at your left, in your glory." But Jesus said to them, "You do not know what you are asking. Are you able to drink the cup that I drink, or to be baptized with the baptism with which I am baptized?" And they said to him, "We are able." And Jesus said to them, "The cup that I drink you will drink; and with the baptism with which I am baptized, you will be baptized; but to sit at my right hand or at my left is not mine to grant, but it is for those for whom it has been prepared." And when the ten heard it, they began to be indignant at James and John. And Jesus called them to him and said to them, "You know that those who are supposed to rule over the Gentiles lord it over them, and their great men exercise authority over them. But it shall not be so among you; but whoever would be great among you must be your servant, and whoever would be first among you must be slave of all. For the Son of man also came not to be served but to serve, and to give his life as a ransom for many."

The road from the upper right skirts the Mount of Olives, goes past the traditional Garden of Gethsemane and swings up the Kidron Valley to the city of Jerusalem

An infrared photograph from the Mount of Olives showing Bethphage in the foreground and the Dead Sea in the distance

Blind Bartimaeus Receives Sight

[10:46–52]

And they came to Jer'icho; and as he was leaving Jer'icho with his disciples and a great multitude, Bartimae'us, a blind beggar, the son of Timae'us, was sitting by the roadside. And when he heard that it was Jesus of Naz'areth, he began to cry out and say, "Jesus, Son of David, have mercy on me!" And many rebuked him, telling him to be silent; but he cried out all the more, "Son of David, have mercy on me!" And Jesus stopped and said, "Call him." And they called the blind man, saying to him, "Take heart; rise, he is calling you." And throwing off his mantle he sprang up and came to Jesus. And Jesus said to him, "What do you want me to do for you?" And the blind man said to him, "Master,[t] let me receive my sight." And Jesus said to him, "Go your way; your faith has made you well." And immediately he received his sight and followed him on the way.

[t]Or *Rabbi*

Triumphal Entry into Jerusalem

[Mark 11:1–11]

AND when they drew near to Jerusalem, to Beth'phage and Beth'any, at the Mount of Olives, he sent two of his disciples, and said to them, "Go into the village opposite you, and immediately as you enter it you will find a colt tied, on which no one has ever sat; untie it and bring it. If any one says to you, 'Why are you doing this?' say, 'The Lord has need of it and will send it back here immediately.' " And they went away, and found a colt tied at the door out in the open street; and they untied it. And those who stood there said to them, "What are you doing, untying the colt?" And they told them what Jesus had said; and they let them go. And they brought the colt to Jesus, and threw their garments on it; and he sat upon it. And many spread their garments on the road, and others spread leafy branches which they had cut from the fields. And those who went before and those who followed cried out, "Hosanna! Blessed is he who comes in the name of the Lord! Blessed is the kingdom of our father David that is coming! Hosanna in the highest!"

The ancient Temple area in Jerusalem is known today as the Haram esh-Sherif. It is entered from the city by seven gates. Counting from the south, this is the second, the Gate of the Chain, at the end of David Street

Modern Damascus Gate of Jerusalem from inside the city

Three Lions

The Dome of the Rock, marking the site of the ancient Jewish Temple, as seen from the Aqsa Mosque at the south side of the Haram esh-Sherif

The Cursing of the Fig Tree [11:12–14]

And he entered Jerusalem, and went into the temple; and when he had looked round at everything, as it was already late, he went out to Beth'any with the twelve.

On the following day, when they came from Beth'any, he was hungry. And seeing in the distance a fig tree in leaf, he went to see if he could find anything on it. When he came to it, he found nothing but leaves, for it was not the season for figs. And he said to it. "May no one ever eat fruit from you again." And his disciples heard it.

The Cleansing of the Temple

[11:15–19]

And they came to Jerusalem. And he entered the temple and began to drive out those who sold and those who bought in the

Matson Photo Service

The early fig usually ripens in June, the summer fig in August, while a winter fig sometimes hangs on the tree until the following spring. The first and second figs are shown here. The fig buds appear almost as soon as the young leaves

temple, and he overturned the tables of the money-changers and the seats of those who sold pigeons; and he would not allow any one to carry anything through the temple. And he taught, and said to them, "Is it not written, 'My house shall be called a house of prayer for all the nations'? But you have made it a den of robbers.'"[8] And the chief priests and the scribes heard it and sought a way to destroy him; for they feared him, because all the multitude was astonished at his teaching. And when evening came they[u] went out of the city.

The Lesson from the Withered Fig Tree [11:20–26]

As they passed by in the morning, they saw the fig tree withered away to its roots. And Peter remembered and said to him,

[u]Other ancient authorities read *he*
[8]*Isaiah 56:7*

"Master,[v] look! The fig tree which you cursed has withered." And Jesus answered them, "Have faith in God. Truly, I say to you, whoever says to this mountain, 'Be taken up and cast into the sea,' and does not doubt in his heart, but believes that what he says will come to pass, it will be done for him. Therefore I tell you, whatever you ask in prayer, believe that you receive it, and you will. And whenever you stand praying, forgive, if you have anything against any one; so that your Father also who is in heaven may forgive you your trespasses."[w]

Jesus' Authority Questioned [11:27–33]

And they came again to Jerusalem. And as he was walking in the temple, the chief priests and the scribes and the elders came to him, and they said to him, "By what authority are you doing these things, or who gave you this authority to do them?" Jesus said to them, "I will ask you a question; answer me, and I will tell you by what authority I do these things. Was the baptism of John from heaven or from men? Answer me." And they argued with one another, "If we say, 'From heaven,' he will say, 'Why then did you not believe him?' But shall we say, 'From men'?"—they were afraid of the people, for all held that John was a real prophet. So they answered Jesus, "We do not know." And Jesus said to them, "Neither will I tell you by what authority I do these things."

The Parable of the Vineyard and the Tenants [Mark 12:1–12]

AND he began to speak to them in parables. "A man planted a vineyard, and set a hedge around it, and dug a pit for the wine press, and built a tower, and let it out to tenants, and went into another country. When the time came, he sent a servant to the tenants, to get from them some of the fruit of the vineyard. And they took him and beat him, and sent him away empty-handed. Again he sent to them another servant, and they wounded him in the head, and treated him shamefully. And he sent another, and him they killed; and so with many others, some they beat and some they killed. He had still one other, a beloved son; finally he sent him to them, saying, 'They will respect my son.' But those tenants said to one another, 'This is the heir; come, let us kill him, and the inheritance will be ours.' And they took him and killed him, and cast him out of the vineyard. What will the owner of the vineyard do? He will come and destroy the tenants, and give the vineyard to others.

[v]Or *Rabbi*.
[w]Other ancient authorities add verse 26, "*But if you do not forgive, neither will your Father who is in heaven forgive your trespasses.*"

Have you not read this scripture:
'The very stone which the builders rejected
has become the head of the corner;
this was the Lord's doing,
and it is marvelous in our eyes'?"[9]
And they tried to arrest him, but feared the multitude, for they perceived that he had told the parable against them; so they left him and went away.

Paying Taxes to Caesar [12:13-17]

And they sent to him some of the Phar'isees and some of the Hero'di-ans, to entrap him in his talk. And they came and said to him, "Teacher, we know that you are true, and care for no man; for you do not regard the position of men, but truly teach the way of God. Is it lawful to pay taxes to Caesar, or not? Should we pay them, or should we not?" But knowing their hypocrisy, he said to them, "Why put me to the test? Bring me a coin,[x] and let me look at it." And they brought one. And he said to them, "Whose likeness and inscription is this?" They said to him, "Caesar's." Jesus said to them, "Render to Caesar the things that are Caesar's, and to God the things that are God's." And they were amazed at him.

The Question about the Resurrection [12:18-27]

And Sad'ducees came to him, who say that there is no resurrection; and they asked him a question, saying, "Teacher, Moses wrote for us that if a man's brother dies and leaves a wife, but leaves no child, the man[y] must take the wife, and raise up children for his brother. There were seven brothers; the first took a wife, and when he died left no children; and the second took her, and died, leaving no children; and the third likewise; and the seven left no children. Last of all the woman also died. In the resurrection whose wife will she be? For the seven had her as wife."

Jesus said to them, "Is not this why you are wrong, that you know neither the scriptures nor the power of God? For when they rise from the dead, they neither marry nor are given in marriage, but are like angels in heaven. And as for the dead being raised, have you not read in the book of Moses, in the passage about the bush, how God said to him, 'I am the God of Abraham, and the God of Isaac, and the God of Jacob'?[10] He is not God of the dead, but of the living; you are quite wrong."

The First Commandment of All [12:28-34]

And one of the scribes came up and heard them disputing with one another, and

A vineyard in Palestine in summer

Matson Photo Service

seeing that he answered them well, asked him, "Which commandment is the first of all?" Jesus answered, "The first is, 'Hear, O Israel: The Lord our God, the Lord is one; and you shall love the Lord your God with all your heart, and with all your soul, and with all your mind, and with all your strength.'[11] The second is this, 'You shall love your neighbor as yourself.'[12] There is no other commandment greater than these." And the scribe said to him, "You are right, Teacher; you have truly said that he is one and there is no other but he; and to love him with all the heart, and with all the understanding, and with all the strength, and to love one's neighbor as oneself, is much more than all whole burnt offerings and sacrifices." And when Jesus saw that he answered wisely, he said to him, "You are not far from the kingdom of God." And after that no one dared to ask him any question.

The Question about the Son of David [12:35-37]

And as Jesus taught in the temple, he said, "How can the scribes say that the Christ is the son of David? David himself, inspired by[z] the Holy Spirit, declared,
'The Lord said to my Lord,
Sit at my right hand,
till I put thy enemies under thy feet.'[13]
David himself calls him Lord; so how is he his son?" And the great throng heard him gladly.

Jesus Denounces the Scribes [12:38-40]

And in his teaching he said, "Beware of the scribes, who like to go about in long robes, and to have salutations in the market places and the best seats in the synagogues and the places of honor at feasts, who devour widows' houses and for a pretense make long prayers. They will receive the greater condemnation."

The name of David is preserved in this street of old Jerusalem

Paul's Photos

[x]Greek *a denarius*
[y]Greek *his brother*
[9] Psalms 118:22-23
[10]Exodus 3:6

[z]Or *himself, in*

[11]Deuteronomy 6:4-5
[12]Leviticus 19:18
[13]Psalms 110:1

Philip Gendreau, N.Y.

The destruction of Jerusalem predicted by Jesus was fulfilled by Titus, A.D. 70. On the Arch of Titus in Rome the conqueror is shown, riding in triumph

"Look, what wonderful stones!" These huge stones, standing above ground, are part of the wall which Herod the Great built around the Temple area

Philip Gendreau, N.Y.

The Widow's Offering
[12:41–44]

And he sat down opposite the treasury, and watched the multitude putting money into the treasury. Many rich people put in large sums. And a poor widow came, and put in two copper coins, which make a penny. And he called his disciples to him, and said to them, "Truly, I say to you, this poor widow has put in more than all those who are contributing to the treasury. For they all contributed out of their abundance; but she out of her poverty has put in everything she had, her whole living."

Jesus Foretells the Destruction of the Temple [Mark 13:1–2]

AND as he came out of the temple, one of his disciples said to him, "Look, Teacher, what wonderful stones and what wonderful buildings!" And Jesus said to him, "Do you see these great buildings? There will not be left here one stone upon another, that will not be thrown down."

Signs before the End
[13:3–8]

And as he sat on the Mount of Olives opposite the temple, Peter and James and John and Andrew asked him privately, "Tell us, when will this be, and what will be the sign when these things are all to be accomplished?" And Jesus began to say to them, "Take heed that no one leads you astray. Many will come in my name, saying, 'I am he!' and they will lead many astray. And when you hear of wars and rumors of wars, do not be alarmed; this must take place, but the end is not yet. For nation will rise against nation, and kingdom against kingdom; there will be earthquakes in various places, there will be famines; this is but the beginning of the sufferings.

Persecution Foretold
[13:9–13]

"But take heed to yourselves; for they will deliver you up to councils; and you will be beaten in synagogues; and you will stand before governors and kings for my sake, to bear testimony before them. And the gospel must first be preached to all nations. And when they bring you to trial and deliver you up, do not be anxious beforehand what you are to say; but say whatever is given you in that hour, for it is not you who speak, but the Holy Spirit. And brother will deliver up brother to death, and the father his child, and children will rise against parents and have them put to death; and you will be hated by all for my name's sake. But he who endures to the end will be saved.

56

The Desolating Sacrilege [13:14–23]

"But when you see the desolating sacrilege set up where it ought not to be (let the reader understand), then let those who are in Jude'a flee to the mountains; let him who is on the housetop not go down, nor enter his house, to take anything away; and let him who is in the field not turn back to take his mantle. And alas for those who are with child and for those who give suck in those days! Pray that it may not happen in winter. For in those days there will be such tribulation as has not been from the beginning of the creation which God created until now, and never will be. And if the Lord had not shortened the days, no human being would be saved; but for the sake of the elect, whom he chose, he shortened the days. And then if any one says to you, 'Look, here is the Christ!' or 'Look, there he is!' do not believe it. False Christs and false prophets will arise and show signs and wonders, to lead astray, if possible, the elect. But take heed; I have told you all things beforehand.

The Coming of the Son of Man
[13:24–27]

"But in those days, after that tribulation, the sun will be darkened, and the moon will not give its light, and the stars will be falling from heaven, and the powers in the heavens will be shaken. And then they will see the Son of man coming in clouds with great power and glory. And then he will send out the angels, and gather his elect from the four winds, from the ends of the earth to the ends of heaven.

The Lesson from the Fig Tree [13:28–31]

"From the fig tree learn its lesson: as soon as its branch becomes tender and puts forth its leaves, you know that summer is near. So also, when you see these things taking place, you know that he is near, at the very gates. Truly, I say to you, this generation will not pass away before all these things take place. Heaven and earth will pass away, but my words will not pass away.

No One Knows the Day and Hour
[13:32–37]

"But of that day or that hour no one knows, not even the angels in heaven, nor the Son, but only the Father. Take heed, watch;[a] for you do not know when the time will come. It is like a man going on a journey, when he leaves home and puts his servants in charge, each with his work, and commands the doorkeeper to be on the watch. Watch therefore—for you do not know when the master of the house will come, in the evening, or at midnight, or at cockcrow, or in the morning—lest he come suddenly and find you asleep. And what I say to you I say to all: Watch."

[a]Other ancient authorities add *and pray*

Matson Photo Service

Air view of the southeast section of the old city of Jerusalem, showing the Temple area and the Kidron Valley

Air view of the central part of the old city of Jerusalem, around the Church of the Holy Sepulchre

Matson Photo Service

The Leaders Plot against Jesus
[Mark 14:1-2]

IT was now two days before the Passover and the feast of Unleavened Bread. And the chief priests and the scribes were seeking how to arrest him by stealth, and kill him; for they said, "Not during the feast, lest there be a tumult of the people."

Jesus Anointed at Bethany
[14:3-9]

And while he was at Beth'any in the house of Simon the leper, as he sat at table, a woman came with an alabaster jar of ointment of pure nard, very costly, and she broke the jar and poured it over his head. But there were some who said to themselves indignantly, "Why was the ointment thus wasted? For this ointment might have been sold for more than three hundred denarii,[b] and given to the poor." And they reproached her. But Jesus said, "Let her alone; why do you trouble her? She has done a beautiful thing to me. For you always have the poor with you, and whenever you will, you can do good to them; but you will not always have me. She has done what she could; she has anointed my body beforehand for burying. And truly, I say to you, wherever the gospel is preached in the whole world, what she has done will be told in memory of her."

Matson Photo Service

Bethany

[b]The denarius was worth about twenty cents

Judas Agrees to Betray Jesus [14:10-11]

Then Judas Iscar'iot, who was one of the twelve, went to the chief priests in order to betray him to them. And when they heard it they were glad, and promised to give him money. And he sought an opportunity to betray him.

The Last Supper [14:12-25]

And on the first day of Unleavened Bread, when they sacrificed the passover lamb, his disciples said to him, "Where will you have us go and prepare for you to eat the passover?" And he sent two of his disciples, and said to them, "Go into the city, and a man carrying a jar of water will meet you; follow him, and wherever he enters, say to the householder, 'The Teacher says, Where is my guest room, where I am to eat the passover with my disciples?' And he will show you a large upper room furnished and ready; there prepare for us." And the disciples set out and went to the city, and found it as he had told them; and they prepared the passover.

And when it was evening he came with the twelve. And as they were at table eating, Jesus said, "Truly, I say to you, one of you will betray me, one who is eating with me." They began to be sorrowful, and to say to him one after another, "Is it I?" He said to them, "It is one of the twelve, one who is dipping bread in the same dish with me. For the Son of man goes as it is

The Mount of Olives. The traditional site of the Garden of Gethsemane is marked by the churches and enclosed area in the central foreground

Ewing Galloway, N.Y.

written of him, but woe to that man by whom the Son of man is betrayed! It would have been better for that man if he had not been born."

And as they were eating, he took bread, and blessed, and broke it, and gave it to them, and said, "Take; this is my body." And he took a cup, and when he had given thanks he gave it to them, and they all drank of it. And he said to them, "This is my blood of the[c] covenant, which is poured out for many. Truly, I say to you, I shall not drink again of the fruit of the vine until that day when I drink it new in the kingdom of God."

Peter's Denial Foretold [14:26–31]

And when they had sung a hymn, they went out to the Mount of Olives. And Jesus said to them, "You will all fall away; for it is written, 'I will strike the shepherd, and the sheep will be scattered.'[14] But after I am raised up, I will go before you to Gal'ilee." Peter said to him, "Even though they all fall away, I will not." And Jesus said to him, "Truly, I say to you, this very night, before the cock crows twice, you will deny me three times." But he said vehemently, "If I must die with you, I will not deny you." And they all said the same.

Jesus Prays in Gethsemane [14:32–42]

And they went to a place which was called Gethsem'ane; and he said to his disciples, "Sit here, while I pray." And he took with him Peter and James and John, and began to be greatly distressed and troubled. And he said to them, "My soul is very sorrowful, even to death; remain here, and watch."[d] And going a little farther, he fell on the ground and prayed that, if it were possible, the hour might pass from him. And he said, "Abba, Father, all things are possible to thee; remove this cup from me; yet not what I will, but what thou wilt." And he came and found them sleeping, and he said to Peter, "Simon, are you asleep? Could you not watch[d] one hour? Watch[d] and pray that you may not enter into temptation; the spirit indeed is willing, but the flesh is weak." And again he went away and prayed, saying the same words. And again he came and found them sleeping, for their eyes were very heavy; and they did not know what to answer him. And he came the third time, and said to them, "Are you still sleeping and taking your rest? It is enough; the hour has come; the Son of man is betrayed into the hands of sinners. Rise, let us be going; see, my betrayer is at hand."

[c]Other ancient authorities insert *new*
[d]Or *keep awake*

[14]*Zechariah* 13:7

Matson Photo Service

The Cenaculum is a room in an old church built on the traditionally accepted site of the house where the Last Supper was held

Old olive tree, believed to be over 2,000 years old, in the Garden of Gethsemane

Jack Finegan

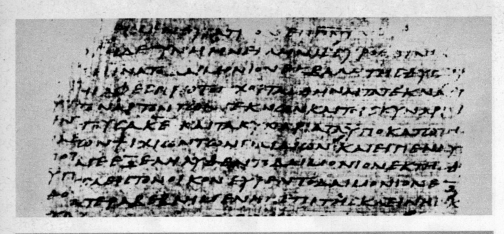

```
                    ... ΑΔΔ[Α] ΕΤΩΤΣ ΑΚΟΤΣΑΣΑ ΓΤΝΗ ΠΕΡΙ ΑΤΤΟΤ
    ΗΣ ΕΙΧΕΝ ΘΤΓΑΤΡΙΟΝ ΕΝ ΠΝΙ ΑΚΑΘΑΡΤΩΙ ΠΡΟΣΕΠΕΣΕΝ ΠΡΟΣ ΤΟΤΣ ΠΟΔΑΣ
    ΑΤΤΟΤ Η ΔΕ ΓΤΝΗ ΗΝ ΕΛΛΗΝΙΣ ΣΤΡΟΦΟΙΝΙΚΙΣΣΑ ΤΩΙ ΓΕΝΕΙ ΚΑΙ ΗΡΩΤΑ
    ΑΤΤΟΝ ΙΝΑ ΤΟ ΔΑΙΜΟΝΙΟΝ ΕΚΒΑΛΗ[Ι] ΤΗΣ ΘΤΓΑΤΡΟΣ ΑΤΤΗΣ ΚΑΙ ΕΛΕΓΕΝ
    ΑΤΤΗΙ ΑΦΕΣ ΠΡΩΤΟΝ ΧΟΡΤΑΣΘΗΝΑΙ ΤΑ ΤΕΚΝΑ ΟΤ ΓΑΡ ΕΣΤΙΝ ΚΑΛΟΝ
    ΛΑΒΕΙΝ ΤΟΝ ΑΡΤΟΝ ΤΩΝ ΤΕΚΝΩΝ ΚΑΙ ΤΟΙΣ ΚΤΝΑΡΙΟΙΣ ΒΑΛΕΙΝ Η ΔΕ ΑΠΕΚΡΙΘΗ
    ΛΕΓΟΤΣΑ ΚΕ ΚΑΙ ΤΑ ΚΤΝΑΡΙΑ ΤΠΟΚΑΤΩ ΤΗΣ ΤΡΑΠΕΖΗΣ ΕΣΘΙΟΤΣΙΝ
    ΑΠΟ ΤΩΝ ΨΙΧΩΝ ΤΩΝ ΠΑΙΔΙΩΝ ΚΑΙ ΕΙΠΕΝ ΑΤΤΗΙ ΔΙΑ ΤΟΤΤΟΝ ΤΟΝ ΛΟΓΟΝ
    ΤΠΑΓΕ ΕΞΕΛΗΛΤΘΕΝ ΤΟ ΔΑΙΜΟΝΙΟΝ ΕΚ ΤΗΣ ΘΤΓΑΤΡΟΣ ΣΟΤ ΚΑΙ
    ΑΠΕΛΘΟΤΣΑ ΕΙΣ ΤΟΝ ΟΙΚΟΝ ΕΤΡΕΝ ΤΟ ΔΑΙΜΟΝΙΟΝ ΕΞΕΛΗΛΤΘΟΣ ΚΑΙ ΤΗΝ
    ΘΤΓΑΤΕΡΑ ΒΕΒΛΗΜΕΝΗΝ ΕΠΙ ΤΗΣ ΚΛΕΙΝΗΣ ΚΑΙ ΠΑΛΙΝ ΕΞΕΛΘΩΝ ...
```

Emery Walker Ltd. London

Upper ten lines of Chester Beatty papyrus of Mark 7:25—8:1, dating from the 3rd century. Below is a reconstruction of the Greek text

Matson Photo Service

Memorial inscription of the 10th Roman Legion, which was stationed at Jerusalem after its destruction by Titus in 70 A.D.

The Betrayal and Arrest of Jesus [14:43-52]

And immediately, while he was still speaking, Judas came, one of the twelve, and with him a crowd with swords and clubs, from the chief priests and the scribes and the elders. Now the betrayer had given them a sign, saying, "The one I shall kiss is the man; seize him and lead him away safely." And when he came, he went up to him at once, and said, "Master!"[e] And he kissed him. And they laid hands on him and seized him. But one of those who stood by drew his sword, and struck the slave of the high priest and cut off his ear. And Jesus said to them, "Have you come out as against a robber, with swords and clubs to capture me? Day after day I was with you in the temple teaching, and you did not seize me. But let the scriptures be fulfilled." And they all forsook him, and fled.

And a young man followed him, with nothing but a linen cloth about his body; and they seized him, but he left the linen cloth and ran away naked.

Jesus before the Council [14:53-65]

And they led Jesus to the high priest; and all the chief priests and the elders and the scribes were assembled. And Peter had followed him at a distance, right into the courtyard of the high priest; and he was sitting with the guards, and warming himself at the fire. Now the chief priests and the whole council sought testimony against

[e] Or *Rabbi*

Jesus to put him to death; but they found none. For many bore false witness against him, and their witness did not agree. And some stood up and bore false witness against him, saying, "We heard him say, 'I will destroy this temple that is made with hands, and in three days I will build another, not made with hands.'" Yet not even so did their testimony agree. And the high priest stood up in the midst, and asked Jesus, "Have you no answer to make? What is it that these men testify against you?" But he was silent and made no answer. Again the high priest asked him, "Are you the Christ, the Son of the Blessed?" And Jesus said, "I am; and you will see the Son of man sitting at the right hand of Power, and coming with the clouds of heaven." And the high priest tore his mantle, and said, "Why do we still need witnesses? You have heard his blasphemy. What is your decision?" And they all condemned him as deserving death. And some began to spit on him, and to cover his face, and to strike him, saying to him, "Prophesy!" And the guards received him with blows.

Peter Denies Jesus [14:66-72]

And as Peter was below in the courtyard, one of the maids of the high priest came; and seeing Peter warming himself, she looked at him, and said, "You also were with the Naz'arene, Jesus." But he denied it, saying, "I neither know nor understand what you mean." And he went out into the gateway.[f] And the maid saw him, and began again to say to the bystanders, "This man is one of them." But again he denied it. And after a little while again the bystanders said to Peter, "Certainly you are one of them; for you are a Galile'an." But he began to invoke a curse on himself and to swear, "I do not know this man of whom you speak." And immediately the cock crowed a second time. And Peter remembered how Jesus had said to him, "Before the cock crows twice, you will deny me three times." And he broke down and wept.

Jesus before Pilate

[Mark 15:1-5]

AND as soon as it was morning the chief priests, with the elders and scribes, and the whole council held a consultation; and they bound Jesus and led him away and delivered him to Pilate. And Pilate asked him, "Are you the King of the Jews?" And he answered him, "You have said so." And the chief priests accused him of many things. And Pilate again asked him, "Have you no answer to make? See how many charges they bring against you." But Jesus made no further answer, so that Pilate wondered.

[f] Or *fore-court*. Other ancient authorities add *and the cock crowed*

Southeast corner of Jerusalem from the Jericho Road

Jesus Sentenced To Die [15:6-15]

Now at the feast he used to release for them one prisoner whom they asked. And among the rebels in prison, who had committed murder in the insurrection, there was a man called Barab'bas. And the crowd came up and began to ask Pilate to do as he was wont to do for them. And he answered them, "Do you want me to release for you the King of the Jews?" For he perceived that it was out of envy that the chief priests had delivered him up. But the chief priests stirred up the crowd to have him release for them Barab'bas instead. And Pilate again said to them, "Then what shall I do with the man whom you call the King of the Jews?" And they cried out again, "Crucify him." And Pilate said to them, "Why, what evil has he done?" But they shouted all the more, "Crucify him." So Pilate, wishing to satisfy the crowd, released for them Barab'bas; and having scourged Jesus, he delivered him to be crucified.

The Soldiers Mock Jesus
[15:16-20]

And the soldiers led him away inside the palace (that is, the praetor'ium); and they called together the whole battalion. And they clothed him in a purple cloak, and plaiting a crown of thorns they put it on him. And they began to salute him, "Hail, King of the Jews!" And they struck his head with a reed, and spat upon him, and they knelt down in homage to him. And when they had mocked him, they stripped him of the purple cloak, and put his own clothes on him. And they led him out to crucify him.

Part of the Lithostroton, or large pavement of the Roman Praetorium, where Jesus was judged by Pontius Pilate and mocked by the Roman soldiers. The picture shows a part of the first step of the staircase leading from the court to the quarters of the Roman cohort stationed at the Fortress Antonia, of which the Praetorium was a part

61

The Sacred Rock, photographed from the dome of the large mosque now standing on the site of Solomon's Temple in Jerusalem

An ancient rock-hewn tomb outside the present wall of Jerusalem

The Crucifixion [15:21–32]

And they compelled a passer-by, Simon of Cyre'ne, who was coming in from the country, the father of Alexander and Rufus, to carry his cross. And they brought him to the place called Gol'gotha (which means the place of a skull). And they offered him wine mingled with myrrh; but he did not take it. And they crucified him, and divided his garments among them, casting lots for them, to decide what each should take. And it was the third hour, when they crucified him. And the inscription of the charge against him read, "The King of the Jews." And with him they crucified two robbers, one on his right and one on his left.[g] And those who passed by derided him, wagging their heads, and saying, "Aha! You who would destroy the temple and build it in three days, save yourself, and come down from the cross!" So also the chief priests mocked him to one another with the scribes, saying, "He saved others; he cannot save himself. Let the Christ, the King of Israel, come down now from the cross, that we may see and believe." Those who were crucified with him also reviled him.

The Death of Jesus [15:33–41]

And when the sixth hour had come, there was darkness over the whole land[h] until the ninth hour. And at the ninth hour Jesus cried with a loud voice, "E'lo-i, E'lo-i, la'ma sabach-tha'ni?" which means, "My God, my God, why hast thou forsaken me?" And some of the bystanders hearing it said, "Behold, he is calling Eli'jah." And one ran and, filling a sponge full of vinegar, put it on a reed and gave it to him to drink, saying, "Wait, let us see whether Eli'jah will come to take him down." And Jesus uttered a loud cry, and breathed his last. And the curtain of the temple was torn in two, from top to bottom. And when the centurion, who stood facing him, saw that he thus[i] breathed his last, he said, "Truly this man was the Son[z] of God!"

There were also women looking on from afar, among whom were Mary Mag'dalene, and Mary the mother of James the younger and of Joses, and Salo'me, who, when he was in Gal'ilee, followed him, and ministered to him; and also many other women who came up with him to Jerusalem.

The Burial of Jesus [15:42–47]

And when evening had come, since it was the day of Preparation, that is, the day before the sabbath, Joseph of Arimathe'a,

[g]Other ancient authorities insert verse 28, *And the scripture was fulfilled which says, "He was reckoned with the transgressors"*
[h]Or *earth*
[i]Other ancient authorities insert *cried out and*
[z]Or *a son*

a respected member of the council, who was also himself looking for the kingdom of God, took courage and went to Pilate, and asked for the body of Jesus. And Pilate wondered if he were already dead; and summoning the centurion, he asked him whether he was already dead.[j] And when he learned from the centurion that he was dead, he granted the body to Joseph. And he bought a linen shroud, and taking him down, wrapped him in the linen shroud, and laid him in a tomb which had been hewn out of the rock; and he rolled a stone against the door of the tomb. Mary Mag'dalene and Mary the mother of Joses saw where he was laid.

The Resurrection [MARK 16:1–8]

AND when the sabbath was past, Mary Mag'dalene, and Mary the mother of James, and Sa lo'me, bought spices, so that they might go and anoint him. And very early on the first day of the week they went to the tomb when the sun had risen. And they were saying to one another, "Who will roll away the stone for us from the door of the tomb?" And looking up, they saw that the stone was rolled back; for it was very large. And entering the tomb, they saw a young man sitting on the right side, dressed in a white robe; and they were amazed. And he said to them, "Do not be amazed; you seek Jesus of Naz'areth, who was crucified. He has risen, he is not here; see the place where they laid him. But go, tell his disciples and Peter that he is going before you to Gal'ilee; there you will see him, as he told you." And they went out and fled from the tomb; for trembling and astonishment had come upon them; and they said nothing to any one, for they were afraid.[k]

Matson Photo Service

Outside the city of Jerusalem, some distance to the north, is a rock-hewn site popularly known as the Tombs of the Kings. It was originally prepared about 60 A.D. as the tomb of Queen Helena of Adiabene, mentioned by Josephus. At the entrance of the tomb proper is a movable rolling stone by which the entrance could be closed

Entrance to the Church of the Holy Sepulchre in Jerusalem, traditional site of the tomb of Christ. The façade dates from the time of the Crusades

Paul's Photos

[j]Other ancient authorities read *whether he had been some time dead*

[k]Other texts and versions add as 16:9-20 the following passage:

Now when he rose early on the first day of the week, he appeared first to Mary Magdalene, from whom he had cast out seven demons. She went and told those who had been with him, as they mourned and wept. But when they heard that he was alive and had been seen by her, they would not believe it.

After this he appeared in another form to two of them, as they were walking into the country. And they went back and told the rest, but they did not believe them.

Afterward he appeared to the eleven themselves as they sat at table; and he upbraided them for their unbelief and hardness of heart, because they had not believed those who saw him after he had risen. And he said to them, "Go into all the world and preach the gospel to the whole creation. He who believes and is baptized will be saved; but he who does not believe will be condemned. And these signs will accompany those who believe; in my name they will cast out demons; they will speak in new tongues; they will pick up serpents, and if they drink any deadly thing, it will not hurt them; they will lay their hands on the sick, and they will recover."

So then the Lord Jesus, after he had spoken to them, was taken up into heaven, and sat down at the right hand of God. And they went forth and preached everywhere, while the Lord worked with them and confirmed the message by the signs that attended it. Amen.

Other ancient authorities add after verse 8 the following:

But they reported briefly to Peter and those with him all that they had been told. And after this, Jesus himself sent out by means of them, from east to west, the sacred and imperishable proclamation of eternal salvation.

LISTEN! A SOWER WENT OUT TO SOW

SOME SEED FELL ALONG THE PATH

OTHER SEED FELL ON ROCKY GROUND

OTHER SEED FELL AMONG THORNS

AND OTHER SEEDS FELL INTO GOOD SOIL

THE FIELD IS THE WORLD MATT. 13:38

THE SEED IS THE WORD OF GOD LUKE 8:11

The Good News

THE SEA OF GALILEE

THE GOSPEL ACCORDING TO LUKE

REVISED STANDARD VERSION

PALESTINE IN THE TIME OF OUR LORD

Palestine, the country where Jesus lived, contains about 10,000 square miles and is a little larger than the State of Vermont. Although so small in area, its influence on human history has been very great because of the events which took place there. Without adequate water supply or rainfall, it has always challenged the resourcefulness and initiative of its inhabitants. Standing on the edge of the desert that separates Asia from Africa and open to European influence from the Mediterranean seacoast, Palestine has been the meeting place and battle-ground of many races and civilizations from Africa, Asia and Europe, although in itself never united as a single country or inhabited by a single race.

It is a land of sharp contrasts. From the snow-capped top of Mount Hermon, 9,100 feet above sea level, to the surface of the Sea of Galilee, 685 feet below sea level, and to the Dead Sea, 1,275 feet below sea level, there are great variations in altitude, temperature and other climatic conditions. Located in the northern part of one of the most remarkable depressions of the earth's surface, this great rift valley stretches from between Mount Lebanon and Mount Hermon on the north, southward through the Dead Sea, the Gulf of Akaba, the Red Sea and into East Africa. It is still subject to earthquakes and shows many traces of volcanic action.

For two thirds of its length the River Jordan flows below sea level. Running from north to south through this great rift valley, it carries the snow waters from Mount Hermon in a rapid descent to the Sea of Galilee. Then, in a more leisurely manner, it meanders slowly for 200 miles to the Dead Sea, which, in a straight line, is only 65 miles distant. Except in January and February, when it overflows its banks, the river twists and turns erratically through its narrow bed or Zor, drawing a green line of vegetation through the desolate and barren hills.

Most of the events in this Gospel took place in the Roman province of Western Palestine, which lies between the Jordan valley and the narrow lowland along the coast and consists of the three districts of Galilee, Samaria and Judea. Galilee is the best watered and least hilly of these three. It abounds in streams and springs and is famous for olives, grapes, wheat, barley, fruit and cattle. A rolling country of alternating hills and cultivated valleys, it was the scene of Jesus' boyhood and early ministry and was the home of most of the Twelve Apostles.

JERUSALEM

Jerusalem is about 2,600 feet above sea level and 3,875 feet above the surface of the Dead Sea, only fifteen miles away. A Holy City to Jews, Christians and Moslems, its name is thought to mean "City of Peace," yet it has been a frequent battle-ground of nations and of religions. At least nine times since Jesus foretold its destruction its control has passed from one religion to another. Enduring at least twenty sieges and blockades during the past 3,000 years, it has gone through almost as many reconstructions. For two periods, at least, it was completely desolate—first after its destruction by Nebuchadnezzar II about 586 B.C. and later after its capture by Hadrian about A.D. 132.

It is not possible today to reconstruct either the City of Jerusalem or the Temple of Jesus' time completely, for since then Jerusalem's valleys have been filled, her hills leveled and her streets and buildings destroyed by hostile hands. Jesus' prophecy of the destruction of the Temple was fulfilled in A.D. 70 when the city was conquered by Titus and the Temple and its fortifications were destroyed.

After the unsuccessful rebellion under Bar Kochba about A.D. 132, the Roman Emperor Hadrian devastated the city even more completely. The site itself was plowed under and a new pagan city, Aelia Capitolina, with pagan temples and shrines, was built over the ruins.

For two centuries after this, little is heard about Jerusalem, until in A.D. 326 Constantine ordered Bishop Macarius of the Greek Church to recover the sites of the crucifixion and of the burial of Jesus. Two great churches were built, one of which, the Church of the Holy

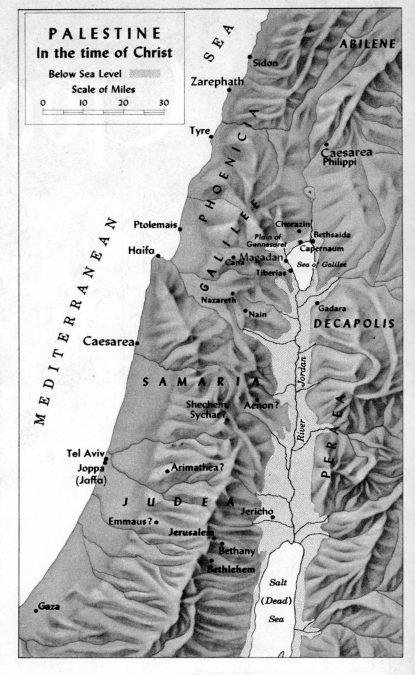

Sepulchre, stood where its present namesake now stands; of the Basilica of the Cross no trace remains.

Conquered by the Persians in 614, reconquered by Heraclius in 629, eight years later it was seized and held by the Mohammedans until the Crusaders occupied it for eighty-eight years before losing it to Saladin in 1187. After the First World War the League of Nations made Palestine a British Mandate. This mandate ended in 1949, and Jerusalem is now occupied partly by Arabs and partly by Jews.

The present walls that enclose the old city were erected by Suleiman the Magnificent in 1542. Prior to 1858 Jerusalem lay wholly within its 16th-century walls. Now the new city without the walls covers a much larger area than that within. Since A.D. 691 the famous rock that is believed to have been part of Solomon's Temple and of the second Temple of Ezra and Nehemiah has been enclosed by the Moslem sanctuary called the "Dome of the Rock," first erected by Abd el Malik in A.D. 691, with subsequent additions. The battered and broken stones in Jerusalem's rebuilt walls cry out today, as they did to Jesus nineteen centuries ago, that Jerusalem, City of Peace, has not yet learned the things that belong unto its peace.

PICTORIAL GOSPEL OF LUKE (RS550P), COPYRIGHT 1963, AMERICAN BIBLE SOCIETY, NEW YORK, N.Y.
REVISED STANDARD VERSION, COPYRIGHT 1946 BY THE DIVISION OF CHRISTIAN EDUCATION, NATIONAL COUNCIL OF CHURCHES, U. S. A.

Matson Photo Service

AIR VIEW OF MODERN JERUSALEM, LOOKING NORTH

Half way up on the extreme right is the Garden of Gethsemane and the base of the Mount of Olives. The famous Temple in which Zechariah served and where Jesus preached and taught no longer exists. Adorned and beautified by Herod the Great with "noble stones and offerings," it was later destroyed by the Romans in A.D. 70, as Jesus pre- *dicted. In its place, in the center of the walled-in area, is the holiest sanctuary of the Mohammedans after Mecca and Medina. In the background, behind the newer part of Jerusalem, is visible part of the hill country of Judea. The foundations of the present walled-in Temple area go back to Herod the Great*

THE GOOD NEWS

as reported in the Gospel according to

LUKE

[Luke 1:1-4] Inasmuch as many have undertaken to compile a narrative of the things which have been accomplished among us, just as they were delivered to us by those who from the beginning were eyewitnesses and ministers of the word, it seemed good to me also, having followed all things closely[a] for some time past, to write an orderly account for you, most excellent Theoph'ilus, that you may know the truth concerning the things of which you have been informed.

The Birth of John the Baptist Foretold [1:5-13]

In the days of Herod, king of Jude'a, there was a priest named Zechari'ah,[b] of the division of Abi'jah; and he had a wife of the daughters of Aaron, and her name was Elizabeth. And they were both righteous before God, walking in all the commandments and ordinances of the Lord blameless. But they had no child, because Elizabeth was barren, and both were advanced in years.

Now while he was serving as priest before God when his division was on duty, according to the custom of the priesthood, it fell to him by lot to enter the temple of the Lord and burn incense. And the whole multitude of the people were praying outside at the hour of incense. And there appeared to him an angel of the Lord standing on the right side of the altar of incense. And Zechari'ah was troubled when he saw him, and fear fell upon him. But the angel said to him, "Do not be afraid, Zechari'ah, for your prayer is heard, and your wife Eliza-

beth will bear you a son, and you shall call his name John.

The Song to Zechariah [1:14-25]

And you will have joy and gladness,
and many will rejoice at his birth;
for he will be great before the Lord,
and he shall drink no wine nor strong drink,
and he will be filled with the Holy Spirit,
even from his mother's womb.
And he will turn many of the sons of Israel to the Lord their God,
and he will go before him in the spirit and power of Eli'jah,
to turn the hearts of the fathers to the children,
and the disobedient to the wisdom of the just,
to make ready for the Lord a people prepared."

And Zechari'ah said to the angel, "How shall I know this? For I am an old man, and my wife is advanced in years." And the angel answered him, "I am Gabriel, who stand in the presence of God; and I was sent to speak to you, and to bring you this good news. And behold, you will be silent and unable to speak until the day that these things come to pass, because you did not believe my words, which will be fulfilled in their time." And the people were waiting for Zechari'ah, and they wondered at his delay in the temple. And when he came out, he could not speak to them, and they per-

[a] Or *accurately*
[b] Greek *Zacharias*

67

Matson Photo Service

Palestinian shepherd keeping watch over his sheep

Religious News Service

Street scene in Bethlehem

Children on stairway to their Bethlehem home

J. Lane Miller

Shepherds' Fields at Bethlehem

J. Lane Miller

ceived that he had seen a vision in the temple; and he made signs to them and remained dumb. And when his time of service was ended, he went to his home.

After these days his wife Elizabeth conceived, and for five months she hid herself, saying, "Thus the Lord has done to me in the days when he looked on me, to take away my reproach among men."

Jesus' Birth Foretold [1:26–38]

In the sixth month the angel Gabriel was sent from God to a city of Gal'ilee named Naz'areth, to a virgin betrothed to a man whose name was Joseph, of the house of David; and the virgin's name was Mary. And he came to her and said, "Hail, O favored one, the Lord is with you!"[c] But she was greatly troubled at the saying, and considered in her mind what sort of greeting this might be. And the angel said to her, "Do not be afraid, Mary, for you have found favor with God. And behold, you will conceive in your womb and bear a son, and you shall call his name Jesus.
He will be great, and will be called the Son of the Most High;
and the Lord God will give to him the throne of his father David,
and he will reign over the house of Jacob for ever;
and of his kingdom there will be no end."
And Mary said to the angel, "How can this be, since I have no husband?" And the angel said to her,
"The Holy Spirit will come upon you,
and the power of the Most High will overshadow you;
therefore the child to be born[d] will be called holy,
the Son of God.
And behold, your kinswoman Elizabeth in her old age has also conceived a son; and this is the sixth month with her who was called barren. For with God nothing will be impossible." And Mary said, "Behold, I am the handmaid of the Lord; let it be to me according to your word." And the angel departed from her.

[c]Other ancient authorities add *"Blessed are you among women!"*
[d]Other ancient authorities add *of you*

Mary Visits Elizabeth [1:39–45]

In those days Mary arose and went with haste into the hill country, to a city of Judah, and she entered the house of Zechari'ah and greeted Elizabeth. And when Elizabeth heard the greeting of Mary, the babe leaped in her womb; and Elizabeth was filled with the Holy Spirit and she exclaimed with a loud cry, "Blessed are you among women, and blessed is the fruit of your womb! And why is this granted me, that the mother of my Lord should come to me? For behold, when the voice of your greeting came to my ears, the babe in my womb leaped for joy. And blessed is she who believed that there would be[e] fulfilment of what was spoken to her from the Lord."

Mary's Song of Praise [1:46–56]

And Mary said,
"My soul magnifies the Lord,
and my spirit rejoices in God my Savior,
for he has regarded the low estate of his handmaiden.
For behold, henceforth all generations will call me blessed;
for he who is mighty has done great things for me,
and holy is his name.
And his mercy is on those who fear him from generation to generation.
He has shown strength with his arm,
he has scattered the proud in the imagination of their hearts,
he has put down the mighty from their thrones,
and exalted those of low degree;
he has filled the hungry with good things,
and the rich he has sent empty away.
He has helped his servant Israel,
in remembrance of his mercy,
as he spoke to our fathers,
to Abraham and to his posterity for ever."
And Mary remained with her about three months, and returned to her home.

The Birth of John the Baptist [1:57–66]

Now the time came for Elizabeth to be delivered, and she gave birth to a son. And her neighbors and kinsfolk heard that the

[e]Or *believed, for there will be*

On market days Bethlehem is again crowded, and there is often no room at the inn

Street scene in old Bethlehem near Manger Square

Lord had shown great mercy to her, and they rejoiced with her. And on the eighth day they came to circumcise the child; and they would have named him Zechari'ah after his father, but his mother said, "Not so; he shall be called John." And they said to her, "None of your kindred is called by this name." And they made signs to his father, inquiring what he would have him called. And he asked for a writing tablet, and wrote, "His name is John." And they all marveled. And immediately his mouth was opened and his tongue loosed, and he spoke, blessing God. And fear came on all their neighbors. And all these things were talked about through all the hill country of Jude'a; and all who heard them laid them up in their hearts, saying, "What then will this child be?" For the hand of the Lord was with him.

Zechariah's Prophecy [1:67–80]

And his father Zechari'ah was filled with the Holy Spirit, and prophesied, saying,
"Blessed be the Lord God of Israel,
for he has visited and redeemed his people,
and has raised up a horn of salvation for us
in the house of his servant David,
as he spoke by the mouth of his holy prophets from of old,
that we should be saved from our enemies,
and from the hand of all who hate us;
to perform the mercy promised to our fathers,
and to remember his holy covenant,
the oath which he swore to our father Abraham, to grant us
that we, being delivered from the hand of our enemies,
might serve him without fear,
in holiness and righteousness before him all the days of our life.
And you, child, will be called the prophet of the Most High;
for you will go before the Lord to prepare his ways,
to give knowledge of salvation to his people
in the forgiveness of their sins,
through the tender mercy of our God,
when the day shall dawn upon[f] us from on high
to give light to those who sit in darkness and in the shadow of death,
to guide our feet into the way of peace."
And the child grew and became strong in spirit, and he was in the wilderness till the day of his manifestation to Israel.

The Birth of Jesus [Luke 2:1–7]

IN those days a decree went out from Caesar Augus'tus that all the world should be enrolled. This was the first enrollment, when Quirin'i-us was governor of Syria. And all went to be enrolled, each to his own city. And Joseph also went up from Gal'ilee, from the city of Naz'areth, to Jude'a, to the city of David, which is called Beth'lehem, because he was of the house and lineage of David, to be enrolled with Mary, his betrothed, who was with child. And while they were there, the time came for her to be delivered. And she gave birth to her first-born son and wrapped him in swaddling cloths, and laid him in a manger, because there was no place for them in the inn.

The Shepherds and the Angels [2:8–20]

And in that region there were shepherds out in the field, keeping watch over their flock by night. And an angel of the Lord appeared to them, and the glory of the Lord shone around them, and they were filled with fear. And the angel said to them, "Be not afraid; for behold, I bring you good news of a great joy which will come to all the people; for to you is born this day in the city of David a Savior, who is Christ the Lord. And this will be a sign for you: you will find a babe wrapped in swaddling cloths and lying in a manger." And suddenly there was with the angel a multitude of the heavenly host praising God and saying,
"Glory to God in the highest,
and on earth peace among men with whom he is pleased!"[g]

[f]Or *whereby the dayspring will visit.* Other ancient authorities read *since the dayspring has visited*

[g]Other ancient authorities read *peace, good will among men*

Church of the Nativity, standing on site of original church built for the Roman Emperor Constantine about 325 A.D.

Note small size of entrance to Church of Nativity

General view of Nazareth

Three Lions

This spring is the only one in Nazareth. Jesus and Mary must have visited it many times

When the angels went away from them into heaven, the shepherds said to one another, "Let us go over to Beth'lehem and see this thing that has happened, which the Lord has made known to us." And they went with haste, and found Mary and Joseph, and the babe lying in a manger. And when they saw it they made known the saying which had been told them concerning this child; and all who heard it wondered at what the shepherds told them.

Ewing Galloway.

But Mary kept all these things, pondering them in her heart. And the shepherds returned, glorifying and praising God for all they had heard and seen, as it had been told them.

The Circumcision of Jesus [2:21]

And at the end of eight days, when he was circumcised, he was called Jesus, the name given by the angel before he was conceived in the womb.

The Presentation of Jesus in the Temple [2:22–38]

And when the time came for their purification according to the law of Moses, they brought him up to Jerusalem to present him to the Lord (as it is written in the law of the Lord, "Every male that opens the womb shall be called holy to the Lord") and to offer a sacrifice according to what is said in the law of the Lord, "a pair of turtle-doves, or two young pigeons." Now there was a man in Jerusalem, whose name was Sim'eon, and this man was righteous and devout, looking for the consolation of Israel, and the Holy Spirit was upon him. And it had been revealed to him by the Holy Spirit that he should not see death before he had seen the Lord's Christ. And inspired by the Spirit[h] he came into the temple; and when the parents brought in the child Jesus, to do for him according to the custom of the law, he took him up in his arms and blessed God and said,
"Lord, now lettest thou thy servant depart in peace,
according to thy word;
for mine eyes have seen thy salvation
which thou hast prepared in the presence of all peoples,
a light for revelation to the Gentiles,
and for glory to thy people Israel."
And his father and his mother marveled at what was said about him; and Sim'eon blessed them and said to Mary his mother,
"Behold, this child is set for the fall and rising of many in Israel,
and for a sign that is spoken against (and a sword will pierce through your own soul also),
that thoughts out of many hearts may be revealed."
And there was a prophetess, Anna, the daughter of Phan'u-el, of the tribe of Asher; she was of a great age, having lived with her husband seven years from her virginity, and as a widow till she was eighty-four. She did not depart from the temple, worshiping with fasting and prayer night and day. And coming up at that very hour she gave thanks to God, and spoke of him to all who were looking for the redemption of Jerusalem.

The Return to Nazareth [2:39–40]

And when they had performed everything according to the law of the Lord, they returned into Gal'ilee, to their own city, Naz'areth. And the child grew and became strong, filled with wisdom; and the favor of God was upon him.

The Boy Jesus in the Temple [2:41–52]

Now his parents went to Jerusalem every year at the feast of the Passover. And when he was twelve years old, they went up according to custom; and when the feast was ended, as they were returning, the boy

[h]Or *in the Spirit*

Jesus stayed behind in Jerusalem. His parents did not know it, but supposing him to be in the company they went a day's journey, and they sought him among their kinsfolk and acquaintances; and when they did not find him, they returned to Jerusalem, seeking him. After three days they found him in the temple, sitting among the teachers, listening to them and asking them questions; and all who heard him were amazed at his understanding and his answers. And when they saw him they were astonished; and his mother said to him, "Son, why have you treated us so? Behold, your father and I have been looking for you anxiously." And he said to them, "How is it that you sought me? Did you not know that I must be in my Father's house?" And they did not understand the saying which he spoke to them. And he went down with them and came to Naz'areth, and was obedient to them; and his mother kept all these things in her heart.

And Jesus increased in wisdom and in stature,[i] and in favor with God and man.

The Preaching of John the Baptist

[Luke 3:1–20]

IN the fifteenth year of the reign of Tiber'i-us Caesar, Pontius Pilate being governor of Jude'a, and Herod being tetrarch of Gal'ilee, and his brother Philip tetrarch of the region of Iturae'a and Trachoni'tis, and Lysa'ni-as tetrarch of Abile'ne, in the high-priesthood of Annas and Cai'aphas, the word of God came to John the son of Zechari'ah in the wilderness; and he went into all the region about the Jordan, preaching a baptism of repentance for the forgiveness of sins. As it is written in the book of the words of Isai'ah the prophet,

"The voice of one crying in the wilderness:
Prepare the way of the Lord,
make his paths straight.
Every valley shall be filled,
and every mountain and hill shall be brought low,
and the crooked shall be made straight,
and the rough ways shall be made smooth;
and all flesh shall see the salvation of God."[1]

He said therefore to the multitudes that came out to be baptized by him, "You brood of vipers! Who warned you to flee from the wrath to come? Bear fruits that befit repentance, and do not begin to say to yourselves, 'We have Abraham as our father'; for I tell you, God is able from these stones to raise up children to Abraham. Even now the axe is laid to the root of the trees; every tree therefore that does not bear good fruit is cut down and thrown into the fire."

And the multitudes asked him, "What then shall we do?" And he answered them, "He who has two coats, let him share with him who has none; and he who has food, let him do likewise." Tax collectors also came to be baptized, and said to him, "Teacher, what shall we do?" And he said to them, "Collect no more than is appointed you." Soldiers also asked him, "And we, what shall we do?" And he said to them, "Rob no one by violence or by false accusation, and be content with your wages."

As the people were in expectation, and all men questioned in their hearts concern-

[i]Or *years*
[1]*Isaiah* 40:3–5

Underwood & Underwood

View of the Jordan River, possibly near the place where Jesus was baptized

Air view of the Jordan meandering below sea level on its way to the Dead Sea

Keren Hayesod

71

Traditional Mount of Temptation as seen from the Jericho Plain

Ewing Galloway

ing John, whether perhaps he were the Christ, John answered them all, "I baptize you with water; but he who is mightier than I is coming, the thong of whose sandals I am not worthy to untie; he will baptize you with the Holy Spirit and with fire. His winnowing fork is in his hand, to clear his threshing floor, and to gather the wheat into his granary, but the chaff he will burn with unquenchable fire."

So, with many other exhortations, he preached good news to the people. But Herod the tetrarch, who had been reproved by him for Hero'di-as, his brother's wife, and for all the evil things that Herod had done, added this to them all, that he shut up John in prison.

The Baptism of Jesus [3:21–22]

Now when all the people were baptized, and when Jesus also had been baptized and was praying, the heaven was opened, and the Holy Spirit descended upon him in bodily form, as a dove, and a voice came from heaven, "Thou art my beloved Son;[j] with thee I am well pleased."[k]

[j]Or *my Son, my* (or *the*) *Beloved*
[k]Other ancient authorities read *today I have begotten thee*

The Genealogy of Jesus [3:23–38]

Jesus, when he began his ministry, was about thirty years of age, being the son (as was supposed) of Joseph, the son of Heli, the son of Matthat, the son of Levi, the son of Melchi, the son of Jan'na-i, the son of Joseph, the son of Mattathi'as, the son of Amos, the son of Nahum, the son of Esli, the son of Nag'ga-i, the son of Ma'ath, the son of Mattathi'as, the son of Sem'e-in, the son of Josech', the son of Joda, the son of Jo-anan, the son of Rhesa, the son of Zerub'babel, the son of She-al'ti-el,[l] the son of Neri, the son of Melchi, the son of Addi, the son of Cosam, the son of Elma'dam, the son of Er, the son of Joshua, the son of Elie'zer, the son of Jorim, the son of Matthat, the son of Levi, the son of Sim'eon, the son of Judah, the son of Joseph, the son of Jonam, the son of Eli'akim, the son of Me'le-a, the son of Menna, the son of Mat'tatha, the son of Nathan, the son of David, the son of Jesse, the son of Obed, the son of Boaz, the son of Sala, the son of Nahshon, the son of Ammin'adab, the son of Admin, the son of Arni, the son of Hezron, the son of Perez, the son of Judah, the son of Jacob,

[l]Greek *Salathiel*

Ancient scroll of Book of Isaiah, recently discovered in a cave above the Dead Sea with other scrolls dating from before Jesus' birth

J. C. Trever

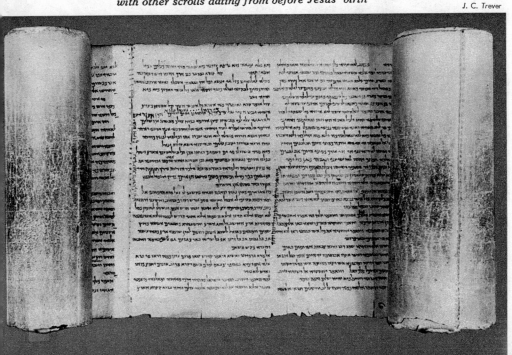

the son of Isaac, the son of Abraham, the son of Terah, the son of Nahor, the son of Serug, the son of Re'u, the son of Peleg, the son of E'ber, the son of Shelah, the son of Ca'inan, the son of Arpha'xad, the son of Shem, the son of Noah, the son of Lamech, the son of Methu'selah, the son of Enoch, the son of Jared, the son of Maha'lale-el, the son of Ca'inan, the son of Enos, the son of Seth, the son of Adam, the son of God.

The Temptation of Jesus [Luke 4:1–13]

AND Jesus, full of the Holy Spirit, returned from the Jordan, and was led by the Spirit for forty days in the wilderness, tempted by the devil. And he ate nothing in those days; and when they were ended, he was hungry. The devil said to him, "If you are the Son of God, command this stone to become bread." And Jesus answered him, "It is written, 'Man shall not live by bread alone.'"[2] And the devil took him up, and showed him all the kingdoms of the world in a moment of time, and said to him, "To you I will give all this authority and their glory; for it has been delivered to me, and I give it to whom I will. If you, then, will worship me, it shall all be yours." And Jesus answered him, "It is written,

'You shall worship the Lord your God,
 and him only shall you serve.'"[3]
And he took him to Jerusalem, and set him on the pinnacle of the temple, and said to him, "If you are the Son of God, throw yourself down from here; for it is written,

'He will give his angels charge of you,
  to guard you,'
and

'On their hands they will bear you up,
 lest you strike your foot against a
  stone.'"[4]
And Jesus answered him, "It is said, 'You shall not tempt the Lord your God.'"[5] And when the devil had ended every temptation, he departed from him until an opportune time.

Jesus Begins His Ministry [4:14–15]

And Jesus returned in the power of the Spirit into Gal'ilee, and a report concerning him went out through all the surrounding country. And he taught in their synagogues, being glorified by all.

Jesus Rejected at Nazareth [4:16–30]

And he came to Naz'areth, where he had been brought up; and he went to the synagogue, as his custom was, on the sabbath day. And he stood up to read; and there was given to him the book of the prophet Isai'ah. He opened the book and found the place where it was written,

"The Spirit of the Lord is upon me,
 because he has anointed me to preach
  good news to the poor.
He has sent me to proclaim release to
  the captives
and recovering of sight to the blind,
 to set at liberty those who are oppressed,
 to proclaim the acceptable year of the
  Lord."[6]
And he closed the book, and gave it back to the attendant, and sat down; and the eyes of all in the synagogue were fixed on him. And he began to say to them, "Today this scripture has been fulfilled in your hearing." And all spoke well of him, and

[2]*Deuteronomy* 8:3
[3]*Deuteronomy* 6:13–14
[4]*Psalms* 91:11–12
[5]*Deuteronomy* 6:16
[6]*Isaiah* 61:1–2

wondered at the gracious words which proceeded out of his mouth; and they said, "Is not this Joseph's son?" And he said to them, "Doubtless you will quote to me this proverb, 'Physician, heal yourself; what we heard you did at Caper'na-um, do here also in your own country.'" And he said, "Truly, I say to you, no prophet is acceptable in his own country. But in truth, I tell you, there were many widows in Israel in the days of Eli'jah, when the heaven was shut up three years and six months, when there came a great famine over all the land; and Eli'jah was sent to none of them but only to Zar'ephath, in the land of Sidon, to a woman who was a widow. And there were many lepers in Israel in the time of the prophet Eli'sha; and none of them was cleansed, but only Na'aman the Syrian." When they heard this, all in the synagogue were filled with wrath. And they rose up and put him out of the city, and led him to the brow of the hill on which their city was built, that they might throw him down headlong. But passing through the midst of them he went away.

A Man with an Unclean Spirit [4:31-37]

And then he went down to Caper'na-um, a city of Gal'ilee. And he was teaching them on the sabbath; and they were astonished at his teaching, for his word was with authority. And in the synagogue there was a man who had the spirit of an unclean demon; and he cried out with a loud voice, "Ah![m] What have you to do with us, Jesus of Naz'areth? Have you come to destroy us? I know who you are, the Holy One of God." But Jesus rebuked him, saying, "Be silent, and come out of him!" And when the demon had thrown him down in the midst, he came out of him, having done him no harm. And they were all amazed and said to one another, "What is this word? For with authority and power he commands the unclean spirits, and they come out." And reports of him went out into every place in the surrounding region.

Jesus Heals Peter's Mother-in-law

[4:38-39]

And he arose and left the synagogue, and entered Simon's house. Now Simon's mother-in-law was ill with a high fever, and they besought him for her. And he stood over her and rebuked the fever, and it left her; and immediately she rose and served them.

Jesus Heals Many at Evening [4:40-41]

Now when the sun was setting, all those who had any that were sick with various diseases brought them to him; and he laid his hands on every one of them and healed them. And demons also came out of many, crying, "You are the Son of God!" But he rebuked them, and would not allow them to speak, because they knew that he was the Christ.

Jesus Departs on a Preaching Tour

[4:42-44]

And when it was day he departed and went into a lonely place. And the people sought him and came to him, and would have kept him from leaving them; but he said to them, "I must preach the good news of the kingdom of God to the other cities

[m]Or Let us alone

Religious News Service

Fishermen on the Sea of Galilee

also; for I was sent for this purpose." And he was preaching in the synagogues of Jude'a.[n]

The Great Catch of Fish [Luke 5:1-11]

WHILE the people pressed upon him to hear the word of God, he was standing by the lake of Gennes'aret. And he saw two boats by the lake; but the fishermen had gone out of them and were washing their nets. Getting into one of the boats, which was Simon's, he asked him to put out a little from the land. And he sat down and taught the people from the boat. And when he had ceased speaking, he said to Simon, "Put out into the deep and let down your nets for a catch." And Simon answered, "Master, we toiled all night and took nothing! But at your word I will let down the nets." And when they had done

[n]Other ancient authorities read *Galilee*

this, they enclosed a great shoal of fish; and as their nets were breaking, they beckoned to their partners in the other boat to come and help them. And they came and filled both the boats, so that they began to sink. But when Simon Peter saw it, he fell down at Jesus' knees, saying, "Depart from me, for I am a sinful man, O Lord." For he was astonished, and all that were with him, at the catch of fish which they had taken; and so also were James and John, sons of Zeb'edee, who were partners with Simon. And Jesus said to Simon, "Do not be afraid; henceforth you will be catching men." And when they had brought their boats to land, they left everything and followed him.

Jesus Cleanses a Leper [5:12-16]

While he was in one of the cities, there came a man full of leprosy; and when he saw Jesus, he fell on his face and besought him, "Lord, if you will, you can make me

Skin bottles are still used to carry water from the ancient cistern in the Temple area of Jerusalem. In Jesus' day they were also used to hold wine

Underwood & Underwood

clean." And he stretched out his hand, and touched him, saying, "I will; be clean." And immediately the leprosy left him. And he charged him to tell no one; but "go and show yourself to the priest, and make an offering for your cleansing, as Moses commanded, for a proof to the people."[o] But so much the more the report went abroad concerning him; and great multitudes gathered to hear and to be healed of their infirmities. But he withdrew to the wilderness and prayed.

Jesus Heals a Paralytic [5:17-26]

On one of those days, as he was teaching, there were Phar′isees and teachers of the law sitting by, who had come from every village of Gal′ilee and Jude′a and from Jerusalem; and the power of the Lord was with him to heal.[p] And behold, men were bringing on a bed a man who was paralyzed, and they sought to bring him in and lay him before Jesus;[q] but finding no way to bring him in, because of the crowd, they went up on the roof and let him down with his bed through the tiles into the midst before Jesus. And when he saw their faith he said, "Man, your sins are forgiven you." And the scribes and the Phar′isees began to question, saying, "Who is this that speaks blasphemies? Who can forgive sins but God only?" When Jesus perceived their questionings, he answered them, "Why do you question in your hearts? Which is easier, to say, 'Your sins are forgiven you,' or to say, 'Rise and walk'? But that you may know that the Son of man has authority on earth to forgive sins"—he said to the man who was paralyzed—"I say to you, rise, take up your bed and go home." And immediately he rose before them, and took up that on which he lay, and went home, glorifying God. And amazement seized them all, and they glorified God and were filled with awe, saying, "We have seen strange things today."

[o]Greek to them
[p]Other ancient authorities read was present to heal them
[q]Greek him

The Call of Levi [5:27-32]

After this he went out, and saw a tax collector, named Levi, sitting at the tax office; and he said to him, "Follow me." And he left everything, and rose and followed him.

And Levi made him a great feast in his house; and there was a large company of tax collectors and others sitting at table[r] with them. And the Phar′isees and their scribes murmured against his disciples, saying, "Why do you eat and drink with tax collectors and sinners?" And Jesus answered them, "Those who are well have no need of a physician, but those who are sick; I have not come to call the righteous, but sinners to repentance."

The Question about Fasting [5:33-39]

And they said to him, "The disciples of John fast often and offer prayers, and so do the disciples of the Phar′isees, but yours eat and drink." And Jesus said to them, "Can you make wedding guests fast while the bridegroom is with them? The days will come, when the bridegroom is taken away from them, and then they will fast in those days." He told them a parable also: "No one tears a piece from a new garment and puts it upon an old garment; if he does, he will tear the new, and the piece from the new will not match the old. And no one puts new wine into old wineskins; if he does, the new wine will burst the skins and it will be spilled, and the skins will be destroyed. But new wine must be put into fresh wineskins. And no one after drinking old wine desires new; for he says, 'The old is good.' "[s]

The Lord of the Sabbath [Luke 6:1-5]

ON a sabbath,[t] while he was going through the grainfields, his disciples plucked and ate some ears of grain, rubbing

[r]Greek reclining
[s]Other ancient authorities read better
[t]Other ancient authorities read On the second first sabbath (on the second sabbath after the first)

them in their hands. But some of the Phar′isees said, "Why are you doing what is not lawful to do on the sabbath?" And Jesus answered, "Have you not read what David did when he was hungry, he and those who were with him: how he entered the house of God, and took and ate the bread of the Presence, which it is not lawful for any but the priests to eat, and also gave it to those with him?" And he said to them, "The Son of man is lord of the sabbath."

Jesus Heals on the Sabbath [6:6-11]

On another sabbath, when he entered the synagogue and taught, a man was there whose right hand was withered. And the scribes and the Phar′isees watched him, to see whether he would heal on the sabbath, so that they might find an accusation against him. But he knew their thoughts, and he said to the man who had the withered hand, "Come and stand here." And he rose and stood there. And Jesus said to them, "I ask you, is it lawful on the sabbath to do good or to do harm, to save life or to destroy it?" And he looked around on them all, and said to him, "Stretch out your hand." And he did so, and his hand was restored. But they were filled with fury and discussed with one another what they might do to Jesus.

Jesus Chooses the Twelve [6:12-16]

In these days he went out into the hills to pray; and all night he continued in prayer to God. And when it was day, he called his disciples, and chose from them twelve, whom he named apostles; Simon, whom he named Peter, and Andrew his brother, and James and John, and Philip, and Barthol′omew, and Matthew, and Thomas, and James the son of Alphae′us, and Simon who was called the Zealot, and Judas the son of James, and Judas Iscar′-iot, who became a traitor.

The Sermon on the Plain [6:17-19]

And he came down with them and stood on a level place, with a great crowd of his disciples and a great multitude of people from all Jude′a and Jerusalem and the seacoast of Tyre and Sidon, who came to hear him and to be healed of their diseases; and those who were troubled with unclean spirits were cured. And all the crowd sought to touch him, for power came forth from him and healed them all.

Beatitudes and Woes [6:20-26]

And he lifted up his eyes on his disciples, and said:

"Blessed are you poor, for yours is the kingdom of God.

"Blessed are you that hunger now, for you shall be satisfied.

"Blessed are you that weep now, for you shall laugh.

"Blessed are you when men hate you, and when they exclude you and revile you, and cast out your name as evil, on account of the Son of man! Rejoice in that day, and leap for joy, for behold, your reward is great in heaven; for so their fathers did to the prophets.

"But woe to you that are rich, for you have received your consolation.

"Woe to you that are full now, for you shall hunger.

"Woe to you that laugh now, for you shall mourn and weep.

The Horns of Hattin, traditional site of the Sermon on the Mount, as seen from the Plain of Gennesaret

Three Lions

74

"Woe to you, when all men speak well of you, for so their fathers did to the false prophets.

"Love Your Enemies" [6:27–36]

"But I say to you that hear, Love your enemies, do good to those who hate you, bless those who curse you, pray for those who abuse you. To him who strikes you on the cheek, offer the other also; and from him who takes away your cloak do not withhold your coat as well. Give to every one who begs from you; and of him who takes away your goods do not ask them again. And as you wish that men would do to you, do so to them.

"If you love those who love you, what credit is that to you? For even sinners love those who love them. And if you do good to those who do good to you, what credit is that to you? For even sinners do the same. And if you lend to those from whom you hope to receive, what credit is that to you? Even sinners lend to sinners, to receive as much again. But love your enemies, and do good, and lend, expecting nothing in return;[v] and your reward will be great, and you will be sons of the Most High; for he is kind to the ungrateful and the selfish. Be merciful, even as your Father is merciful.

Judging Others [6:37–42]

"Judge not, and you will not be judged; condemn not, and you will not be condemned; forgive, and you will be forgiven; give, and it will be given to you; good measure, pressed down, shaken together, running over, will be put into your lap. For the measure you give will be the measure you get back."

He also told them a parable: "Can a blind man lead a blind man? Will they not both fall into a pit? A disciple is not above his teacher, but every one when he is fully taught will be like his teacher. Why do you see the speck that is in your brother's eye, but do not notice the log that is in your own eye? Or how can you say to your brother, 'Brother, let me take out the speck that is in your eye,' when you yourself do not see the log that is in your own eye? You hypocrite, first take the log out of your own eye, and then you will see clearly to take out the speck that is in your brother's eye.

"Out of the Abundance of the Heart"
[6:43–45]

"For no good tree bears bad fruit, nor again does a bad tree bear good fruit; for each tree is known by its own fruit. For figs are not gathered from thorns, nor are grapes picked from a bramble bush. The good man out of the good treasure of his heart produces good, and the evil man out of his evil treasure produces evil; for out of the abundance of the heart his mouth speaks.

The Parable of the Two Builders
[6:46–49]

"Why do you call me 'Lord, Lord,' and not do what I tell you? Every one who comes to me and hears my words and does them, I will show you what he is like: he is like a man building a house, who dug deep, and laid the foundation upon rock; and when a flood arose, the stream broke

[v]Other ancient authorities read *despairing of no man*

against that house, and could not shake it, because it had been well built.[w] But he who hears and does not do them is like a man who built a house on the ground without a foundation; against which the stream broke, and immediately it fell, and the ruin of that house was great."

Jesus Heals a Centurion's Servant
[Luke 7:1–10]

AFTER he had ended all his sayings in the hearing of the people he entered Caper'na-um. Now a centurion had a slave who was dear[z] to him, who was sick and at the point of death. When he heard of Jesus, he sent to him elders of the Jews, asking him to come and heal his slave. And when they came to Jesus, they besought him earnestly, saying, "He is worthy to have you do this for him, for he loves our nation, and he built us our synagogue." And Jesus went with them. When he was not far from the house, the centurion sent friends to him, saying to him, "Lord, do not trouble yourself, for I am not worthy to have you come under my roof; therefore I did not presume to come to you. But say the word, and let my servant be healed. For I am a man set under authority, with soldiers under me: and I say to one, 'Go,' and he goes; and to another, 'Come,' and he comes; and to my slave, 'Do this,' and he does it." When Jesus heard this he marveled at him, and turned and said to the multitude that followed him, "I tell you, not even in Israel have I found such faith." And when those who had been sent returned to the house, they found the slave well.

Jesus Raises the Widow's Son at Nain
[7:11–17]

Soon afterward[y] he went to a city called Na'in, and his disciples and a great crowd went with him. As he drew near to the gate of the city, behold, a man who had died was being carried out, the only son of his mother, and she was a widow; and a large crowd from the city was with her. And when the Lord saw her, he had compassion on her and said to her, "Do not weep." And he came and touched the bier, and the bearers stood still. And he said, "Young man, I say to you, arise." And the dead man sat up, and began to speak. And he gave him to his mother. Fear seized them all; and they glorified God, saying, "A great prophet has arisen among us!" and "God has visited his people!" And this report concerning him spread through the whole of Jude'a and all the surrounding country.

The Messengers from John the Baptist
[7:18–35]

The disciples of John told him of all these things. And John, calling to him two of his disciples, sent them to the Lord, saying, "Are you he who is to come, or shall we look for another?" And when the men had come to him, they said, "John the Baptist has sent us to you, saying, 'Are you he who is to come, or shall we look for another?'" In that hour he cured many of diseases and plagues and evil spirits, and on many that

[w]Other ancient authorities read *founded upon the rock*
[z]Or *valuable*
[y]Other ancient authorities read *Next day*

Atlas Photo

Air view of the Capernaum Synagogue (ca. 200 A.D.). Believed to be built on the site of the synagogue in which Jesus preached and taught

were blind he bestowed sight. And he answered them, "Go and tell John what you have seen and heard: the blind receive their sight, the lame walk, lepers are cleansed, and the deaf hear, the dead are raised up, the poor have good news preached to them. And blessed is he who takes no offense at me."

When the messengers of John had gone, he began to speak to the crowds concerning John: "What did you go out into the wilderness to behold? A reed shaken by the wind? What then did you go out to see? A man

"We piped to you, and you did not dance."

Matson Photo Service

Mt. Hermon, altitude 9,100 ft., covered with perpetual snow, is visible to the north of the Sea of Galilee, which is 685 ft. below sea level

clothed in soft raiment? Behold, those who are gorgeously appareled and live in luxury are in kings' courts. What then did you go out to see? A prophet? Yes, I tell you, and more than a prophet. This is he of whom it is written,

'Behold, I send my messenger before thy face,
who shall prepare thy way before thee.'[7]

I tell you, among those born of women none is greater than John; yet he who is least in the kingdom of God is greater than he." (When they heard this all the people and the tax collectors justified God, having been baptized with the baptism of John; but the Phar'isees and the lawyers rejected the purpose of God for themselves, not having been baptized by him.)

[7]*Malachi* 3:1

"A sower went out to sow his seed"

"To what then shall I compare the men of this generation, and what are they like? They are like children sitting in the market place and calling to one another,

'We piped to you, and you did not dance;
we wailed, and you did not weep.'

For John the Baptist has come eating no bread and drinking no wine; and you say, 'He has a demon.' The Son of man has come eating and drinking; and you say, 'Behold, a glutton and a drunkard, a friend of tax collectors and sinners!' Yet wisdom is justified by all her children."

Jesus at the Home of Simon the Pharisee [7:36–50]

One of the Phar'isees asked him to eat with him, and he went into the Phar'isee's house, and sat at table. And behold, a woman of the city, who was a sinner, when she learned that he was sitting at table in the Phar'isee's house, brought an alabaster flask of ointment, and standing behind him at his feet, weeping, she began to wet his feet with her tears, and wiped them with the hair of her head, and kissed his feet, and anointed them with the ointment. Now when the Phar'isee who had invited him saw it, he said to himself, "If this man were a prophet, he would have known who and what sort of woman this is who is touching him, for she is a sinner." And Jesus answering said to him, "Simon, I have something to say to you." And he answered, "What is it, Teacher?" "A certain creditor had two debtors; one owed five hundred denarii, and the other fifty. When they could not pay, he forgave them both. Now which of them will love him more?" Simon answered, "The one, I suppose, to whom he forgave more." And he said to him, "You have judged rightly." Then, turning toward the woman he said to Simon, "Do you see this woman? I entered your house, you gave me no water for my feet, but she has wet my feet with her tears and wiped them with her hair. You gave me no kiss, but from the time I came in she has not ceased to kiss my feet. You did not anoint my head with oil, but she has anointed my feet with ointment. Therefore I tell you, her sins, which are many, are forgiven, for she loved much; but he who is forgiven little, loves little." And he said to her, "Your sins are forgiven." Then those who were at table with him began to say among themselves, "Who is this, who even forgives sins?" And he said to the woman, "Your faith has saved you; go in peace."

Some Women Accompany Jesus
[Luke 8:1–3]

SOON afterward he went on through cities and villages, preaching and bringing the good news of the kingdom of God. And the twelve were with him, and also some women who had been healed of evil spirits and infirmities: Mary, called Mag'dalene, from whom seven demons had gone out, and Jo-an'na, the wife of Chuza, Herod's steward, and Susanna, and many others, who provided for them[2] out of their means.

The Parable of the Sower [8:4–8]

And when a great crowd came together and people from town after town came to him, he said in a parable: "A sower went out to sow his seed; and as he sowed, some fell along the path, and was trodden under foot, and the birds of the air devoured it. And some fell on the rock; and as it grew up, it withered away, because it had no moisture. And some fell among thorns; and the thorns grew with it and choked it. And some fell into good soil and grew, and yielded a hundredfold." As he said this, he called out, "He who has ears to hear, let him hear."

Jesus Explains the Parable of the Sower [8:9–15]

And when his disciples asked him what this parable meant, he said, "To you it has been given to know the secrets of the kingdom of God; but for others they are in parables, so that seeing they may not see, and

[2]Other ancient authorities read *him*

hearing they may not understand. Now the parable is this: The seed is the word of God. The ones along the path are those who have heard; then the devil comes and takes away the word from their hearts, that they may not believe and be saved. And the ones on the rock are those who, when they hear the word, receive it with joy; but these have no root, they believe for a while and in time of temptation fall away. And as for what fell among the thorns, they are those who hear, but as they go on their way they are choked by the cares and riches and pleasures of life, and their fruit does not mature. And as for that in the good soil, they are those who, hearing the word, hold it fast in an honest and good heart, and bring forth fruit with patience.

The Parable of the Hidden Lamp
[8:16–18]

"No one after lighting a lamp covers it with a vessel, or puts it under a bed, but puts it on a stand, that those who enter may see the light. For nothing is hid that shall not be made manifest, nor anything secret that shall not be known and come to light. Take heed then how you hear; for to him who has will more be given, and from him who has not, even what he thinks that he has will be taken away."

Jesus' Mother and Brothers [8:19–21]

Then his mother and his brothers came to him, but they could not reach him for the crowd. And he was told, "Your mother and your brothers are standing outside, desiring to see you." But he said to them, "My mother and my brothers are those who hear the word of God and do it."

Jesus Calms a Storm [8:22–25]

One day he got into a boat with his disciples, and he said to them, "Let us go across to the other side of the lake." So they set out, and as they sailed he fell asleep. And a storm of wind came down on the lake, and they were filling with water, and were in danger. And they went and woke him, saying, "Master, Master, we are perishing!" And he awoke and rebuked the wind and the raging waves; and they ceased, and there was a calm. He said to them, "Where is your faith?" And they were afraid, and they marveled, saying to one another, "Who then is this, that he commands even wind and water, and they obey him?"

The Gerasene Demoniac Healed
[8:26–39]

Then they arrived at the country of the Ger'asenes,[a] which is opposite Gal'ilee. And as he stepped out on land, there met him a man from the city who had demons; for a long time he had worn no clothes, and he lived not in a house but among the tombs. When he saw Jesus, he cried out and fell down before him, and said with a loud voice, "What have you to do with me, Jesus, Son of the Most High God? I beseech you, do not torment me." For he had commanded the unclean spirit to come out of the man. (For many a time it had seized him; he was kept under guard, and bound with chains and fetters, but he broke the bonds and was driven by the demon into the desert.) Jesus then asked

[a]Other ancient authorities read *Gadarenes*, others *Gergesenes*

"Storm on the Sea of Galilee"
Ewing Galloway

him, "What is your name?" And he said, "Legion"; for many demons had entered him. And they begged him not to command them to depart into the abyss. Now a large herd of swine was feeding there on the hillside; and they begged him to let them enter these. So he gave them leave. Then the demons came out of the man and entered the swine, and the herd rushed down the steep bank into the lake and were drowned. When the herdsmen saw what had happened, they fled, and told it in the city and in the country. Then people went out to see what had happened, and they came to Jesus, and found the man from whom the demons had gone, sitting at the feet of Jesus, clothed and in his right mind; and they were afraid. And those who had seen it told them how he who had been possessed with demons was healed. Then all the people of the surrounding country of the Ger'asenes[a] asked him to depart from them; for they were seized with great fear; so he got into the boat and returned. The man from whom the demons had gone begged that he might be with him; but he sent him away, saying, "Return to your home, and declare how much God has done for you." And he went away, proclaiming throughout the whole city how much Jesus had done for him.

Jairus Pleads for His Daughter [8:40–42a]

Now when Jesus returned, the crowd welcomed him, for they were all waiting for him. And there came a man named Jairus, who was a ruler of the synagogue; and falling at Jesus' feet he besought him

to come to his house, for he had an only daughter, about twelve years of age, and she was dying.

The Woman Who Touched Jesus' Garment [8:42b–48]

As he went, the people pressed round him. And a woman who had had a flow of

Fishermen repairing their nets

Three Lions

77

Bethsaida, the home of Philip, Andrew and Peter, was located on the eastern side of the Jordan near where it flows into the Sea of Galilee

blood for twelve years[b] and could not be healed by any one, came up behind him, and touched the fringe of his garment; and immediately her flow of blood ceased. And Jesus said, "Who was it that touched me?" When all denied it, Peter[c] said, "Master, the multitudes surround you and press upon you!" But Jesus said, "Some one touched me; for I perceive that power has gone forth from me." And when the woman saw that she was not hidden, she came trembling, and falling down before him declared in the presence of all the people why she had touched him, and how she had been immediately healed. And he said to her, "Daughter, your faith has made you well; go in peace."

Jairus' Daughter Raised [8:49-56]

While he was still speaking, a man from the ruler's house came and said, "Your daughter is dead; do not trouble the Teacher any more." But Jesus on hearing this answered him, "Do not fear; only believe, and she shall be well." And when he came to the house, he permitted no one to enter with him, except Peter and John and James, and the father and mother of the child. And all were weeping and bewailing her; but he said, "Do not weep; for she is not dead but sleeping." And they laughed at him, knowing that she was dead. But taking her by the hand he called, saying, "Child, arise." And her spirit returned, and she got up at once; and he directed that something should be given her to eat. And her parents were amazed; but he charged them to tell no one what had happened.

The Mission of the Twelve [Luke 9:1-6]

AND he called the twelve together and gave them power and authority over all demons and to cure diseases, and he sent them out to preach the kingdom of God and to heal. And he said to them, "Take nothing for your journey, no staff, nor bag, nor bread, nor money; and do not have two tunics. And whatever house you enter, stay there, and from there depart. And wherever they do not receive you, when you leave that town shake off the dust from your feet as a testimony against them." And they departed and went through the villages, preaching the gospel and healing everywhere.

The Death of John the Baptist [9:7-9]

Now Herod the tetrarch heard of all that was done, and he was perplexed, because it was said by some that John had been raised from the dead, by some that Eli'jah had appeared, and by others that one of the old prophets had risen. Herod said, "John I beheaded; but who is this about whom I hear such things?" And he sought to see him.

The Feeding of the Five Thousand

[9:10-17]

On their return the apostles told him what they had done. And he took them and withdrew apart to a city called Beth-sa'-ida. When the crowds learned it, they followed him; and he welcomed them and spoke to them of the kingdom of God, and cured those who had need of healing. Now the day began to wear away; and the twelve came and said to him, "Send the crowd away, to go into the villages and country round about, to lodge and get provisions; for we are here in a lonely place." But he said to them, "You give them something to eat." They said, "We have no more than five loaves and two fish—unless we are to go and buy food for all these people." For there were about five thousand men. And he said to his disciples, "Make them sit down in companies, about fifty each." And they did so, and made them all sit down.

And taking the five loaves and the two fish he looked up to heaven, and blessed and broke them, and gave them to the disciples to set before the crowd. And all ate and were satisfied. And they took up what was left over, twelve baskets of broken pieces.

Peter's Declaration about Jesus [9:18-20]

Now it happened that as he was praying alone the disciples were with him; and he asked them, "Who do the people say that I am?" And they answered, "John the Baptist; but others say, Eli'jah; and others, that one of the old prophets has risen." And he said to them, "But who do you say that I am?" And Peter answered, "The Christ of God."

Jesus Foretells His Death [9:21-27]

But he charged and commanded them to tell this to no one, saying, "The Son of man must suffer many things, and be rejected by the elders and chief priests and scribes, and be killed, and on the third day be raised."

And he said to all, "If any man would come after me, let him deny himself and take up his cross daily and follow me. For whoever would save his life will lose it; and whoever loses his life for my sake, he will save it. For what does it profit a man if he gains the whole world and loses or forfeits himself? For whoever is ashamed of me and of my words, of him will the Son of man be ashamed when he comes in his glory and the glory of the Father and of the holy angels. But I tell you truly, there are some standing here who will not taste death before they see the kingdom of God."

The Transfiguration [9:28-36]

Now about eight days after these sayings he took with him Peter and John and James, and went up on the mountain to pray. And as he was praying, the appearance of his countenance was altered, and his raiment became dazzling white. And behold, two men talked with him, Moses and Eli'jah, who appeared in glory and spoke of his departure, which he was to accomplish at Jerusalem. Now Peter and those who were with him were heavy with sleep but kept awake, and they saw his glory and the two men who stood with him. And as the men were parting from him, Peter said to Jesus, "Master, it is well that we are here; let us make three booths, one for you and one for Moses and one for Eli'jah"—not knowing what he said. As he said this, a cloud came and overshadowed them; and they were afraid as they entered the cloud. And a voice came out of the cloud, saying, "This is my Son, my Chosen;[d] listen to him!" And when the voice had spoken, Jesus was found alone. And they kept silence and told no one in those days anything of what they had seen.

Jesus Heals a Boy with an Unclean Spirit [9:37-43]

On the next day, when they had come down from the mountain, a great crowd met him. And behold, a man from the crowd cried, "Teacher, I beg you to look upon my son, for he is my only child; and behold, a spirit seizes him, and he suddenly cries out; it convulses him till he foams, and shatters him, and will hardly leave him. And I begged your disciples to cast

[b]Other ancient authorities add *and had spent all her living upon physicians*
[c]Other ancient authorities add *and those who were with him*

[d]Other ancient authorities read *my Beloved*

it out, but they could not." Jesus answered, "O faithless and perverse generation, how long am I to be with you and bear with you? Bring your son here." While he was coming, the demon tore him and convulsed him. But Jesus rebuked the unclean spirit, and healed the boy, and gave him back to his father. And all were astonished at the majesty of God.

Jesus again Foretells His Death [9:44-45]

But while they were all marveling at everything he did, he said to his disciples, "Let these words sink into your ears; for the Son of man is to be delivered into the hands of men." But they did not understand this saying, and it was concealed from them, that they should not perceive it; and they were afraid to ask him about this saying.

"Who Is the Greatest?" [9:46-48]

And an argument arose among them as to which of them was the greatest. But when Jesus perceived the thought of their hearts, he took a child and put him by his side, and said to them, "Whoever receives this child in my name receives me, and whoever receives me receives him who sent me; for he who is least among you all is the one who is great."

"He That Is Not against You Is for You" [9:49-50]

John answered, "Master, we saw a man casting out demons in your name, and we forbade him, because he does not follow with us." But Jesus said to him, "Do not forbid him; for he that is not against you is for you."

A Samaritan Village Refuses To Receive Jesus [9:51-56]

When the days drew near for him to be received up, he set his face to go to Jerusalem. And he sent messengers ahead of him, who went and entered a village of the Samar'itans, to make ready for him; but the people would not receive him, because his face was set toward Jerusalem. And when his disciples James and John saw it, they said, "Lord, do you want us to bid fire come down from heaven and consume them?"*e* But he turned and rebuked them.*f* And they went on to another village.

The Would-be Followers of Jesus [9:57-62]

As they were going along the road, a man said to him, "I will follow you wherever you go." And Jesus said to him, "Foxes have holes, and birds of the air have nests; but the Son of man has nowhere to lay his head." To another he said, "Follow me." But he said, "Lord, let me first go and bury my father." But he said to him, "Leave the dead to bury their own dead; but as for you, go and proclaim the kingdom of God." Another said, "I will follow you, Lord; but let me first say farewell to those at my home." Jesus said to him, "No one who puts his hand to the plow and looks back is fit for the kingdom of God."

*e*Other ancient authorities add *as Elijah did*
*f*Other ancient authorities add *and he said, "You do not know what manner of spirit you are of; for the Son of man came not to destroy men's lives but to save them"*

Three Lions

View across the housetops of Nain, with Mt. Tabor, the traditional site of the Transfiguration, in the background

The Mission of the Seventy [Luke 10:1-12]

AFTER this the Lord appointed seventy*g* others, and sent them on ahead of him, two by two, into every town and place where he himself was about to come. And he said to them, "The harvest is plentiful, but the laborers are few; pray therefore the Lord of the harvest to send out laborers into his harvest. Go your way; behold, I send you out as lambs in the midst of wolves. Carry no purse, no bag, no sandals;

*g*Other ancient authorities read *seventy-two*

and salute no one on the road. Whatever house you enter, first say, 'Peace be to this house!' And if a son of peace is there, your peace shall rest upon him; but if not, it shall return to you. And remain in the same house, eating and drinking what they provide, for the laborer deserves his wages; do not go from house to house. Whenever you enter a town and they receive you, eat what is set before you; heal the sick in it and say to them, 'The kingdom of God has come near to you.' But whenever you enter a town and they do not receive you, go into its

"No one who puts his hand to the plow and looks back is fit for the kingdom of God"

Keystone View

streets and say, 'Even the dust of your town that clings to our feet, we wipe off against you; nevertheless know this, that the kingdom of God has come near.' I tell you, it shall be more tolerable on that day for Sodom than for that town.

Woes to Unrepentant Cities [10:13-16]

"Woe to you, Chora'zin! woe to you, Beth-sa'ida! for if the mighty works done in you had been done in Tyre and Sidon, they would have repented long ago, sitting in sackcloth and ashes. But it shall be more tolerable in the judgment for Tyre and Sidon than for you. And you, Caper'na-um, will you be exalted to heaven? You shall be brought down to Hades.

"He who hears you hears me, and he who rejects you rejects me, and he who rejects me rejects him who sent me."

The Return of the Seventy [10:17-24]

The seventy*g* returned with joy, saying, "Lord, even the demons are subject to us in your name!" And he said to them, "I saw Satan fall like lightning from heaven. Behold, I have given you authority to tread upon serpents and scorpions, and over all the power of the enemy; and nothing shall hurt you. Nevertheless do not rejoice in this, that the spirits are subject to you; but rejoice that your names are written in heaven."

In that same hour he rejoiced in the Holy Spirit and said, "I thank thee, Father, Lord of heaven and earth, that thou hast hidden these things from the wise and understanding and revealed them to babes; yea, Father, for such was thy gracious will.*h* All

*g*Other ancient authorities read *seventy-two*
*h*Or *so it was well-pleasing before thee*

"What father among you, if his son asks for bread, will give him a stone?"

Rapho

things have been delivered to me by my Father; and no one knows who the Son is except the Father, or who the Father is except the Son and any one to whom the Son chooses to reveal him."

Then turning to the disciples he said privately, "Blessed are the eyes which see what you see! For I tell you that many prophets and kings desired to see what you see, and did not see it, and to hear what you hear, and did not hear it."

The Good Samaritan [10:25-37]

And behold, a lawyer stood up to put him to the test, saying, "Teacher, what shall I do to inherit eternal life?" He said to him, "What is written in the law? How do you read?" And he answered, "You shall love the Lord your God with all your heart, and with all your soul, and with all your strength, and with all your mind; and your neighbor as yourself."*8* And he said to him, "You have answered right; do this, and you will live."

But he, desiring to justify himself, said to Jesus, "And who is my neighbor?" Jesus replied, "A man was going down from Jerusalem to Jer'icho, and he fell among robbers, who stripped him and beat him, and departed, leaving him half dead. Now by chance a priest was going down that road; and when he saw him he passed by on the other side. So likewise a Levite, when he came to the place and saw him, passed by on the other side. But a Samar'-itan, as he journeyed, came to where he was; and when he saw him, he had compassion, and went to him and bound up his wounds, pouring on oil and wine; then he set him on his own beast and brought him to an inn, and took care of him. And the next day he took out two denarii*i* and gave them to the innkeeper, saying, 'Take care of him; and whatever more you spend, I will repay you when I come back.' Which of these three, do you think, proved neighbor to the man who fell among the robbers?" He said, "The one who showed mercy on

*i*The denarius was worth about twenty cents
*8*Deuteronomy 6:5; Leviticus 19:18

him." And Jesus said to him, "Go and do likewise."

Jesus Visits Mary and Martha [10:38-42]

Now as they went on their way, he entered a village; and a woman named Martha received him into her house. And she had a sister called Mary, who sat at the Lord's feet and listened to his teaching. But Martha was distracted with much serving; and she went to him and said, "Lord, do you not care that my sister has left me to serve alone? Tell her then to help me." But the Lord answered her, "Martha, Martha, you are anxious and troubled about many things; one thing is needful.*j* Mary has chosen the good portion, which shall not be taken away from her."

The Lord's Prayer [Luke 11:1-4]

HE was praying in a certain place, and when he ceased, one of his disciples said to him, "Lord, teach us to pray, as John taught his disciples." And he said to them, "When you pray, say:

"Father, hallowed be thy name. Thy kingdom come. Give us each day our daily bread;*k* and forgive us our sins, for we ourselves forgive every one who is indebted to us; and lead us not into temptation."

Ask, Seek, Knock [11:5-13]

And he said to them, "Which of you who has a friend will go to him at midnight and say to him, 'Friend, lend me three loaves; for a friend of mine has arrived on a journey, and I have nothing to set before him'; and he will answer from within, 'Do not bother me; the door is now shut, and my children are with me in bed; I cannot get up and give you anything'? I tell you, though he will not get up and give him anything because he is his friend, yet because of his importunity he will rise and give him whatever he needs. And I tell you, Ask, and it will be given you; seek, and you will find; knock,

*i*Other ancient authorities read *few things are needful, or only one*
*k*Or *our bread for the morrow*

Ewing Galloway

The road from Jerusalem, 2,600 ft. above sea level, going down to Jericho nearly 700 ft. below sea level, passes through desolate and deserted country

This sign on the Jerusalem-Jericho road reads literally in Arabic, "Roof of the Sea," and in Hebrew, "Face of the Sea"

generation. The queen of the South will arise at the judgment with the men of this generation and condemn them; for she came from the ends of the earth to hear the wisdom of Solomon, and behold, something greater than Solomon is here. The men of Nin'eveh will arise at the judgment with this generation and condemn it; for they repented at the preaching of Jonah, and behold, something greater than Jonah is here.

The Parable of the Sound Eye [11:33–36]

"No one after lighting a lamp puts it in a cellar or under a bushel, but on a stand, that those who enter may see the light. Your eye is the lamp of your body; when your eye is sound, your whole body is full of light; but when it is not sound, your body is full of darkness. Therefore be careful lest the light in you be darkness. If then your whole body is full of light, having no part dark, it will be wholly bright, as when a lamp with its rays gives you light."

Jesus Denounces the Pharisees and Lawyers [11:37–54]

While he was speaking, a Phar'isee asked him to dine with him; so he went in and sat at table. The Phar'isee was astonished to see that he did not first wash before dinner. And the Lord said to him, "Now you Phar'isees cleanse the outside of the cup and of the dish, but inside you are full of extortion and wickedness. You fools! Did not he who made the outside make the inside also? But give for alms those things which are within; and behold, everything is clean for you.

"But woe to you Phar'isees! for you tithe mint and rue and every herb, and neglect justice and the love of God; these you ought to have done, without neglecting the others. Woe to you Phar'isees! for you love the best seat in the synagogues and salutations in the market places. Woe to you! for you are like graves which are not seen, and men walk over them without knowing it."

One of the lawyers answered him, "Teacher, in saying this you reproach us also." And he said, "Woe to you lawyers also! for you load men with burdens hard to

and it will be opened to you. For every one who asks receives, and he who seeks finds, and to him who knocks it will be opened. What father among you, if his son asks for[1] a fish, will instead of a fish give him a serpent; or if he asks for an egg, will give him a scorpion? If you then, who are evil, know how to give good gifts to your children, how much more will the heavenly Father give the Holy Spirit to those who ask him!"

Jesus and Beelzebul [11:14–23]

Now he was casting out a demon that was dumb; when the demon had gone out, the dumb man spoke, and the people marveled. But some of them said, "He casts out demons by Be-el'zebul, the prince of demons"; while others, to test him, sought from him a sign from heaven. But he, knowing their thoughts, said to them, "Every kingdom divided against itself is laid waste, and house falls upon house. And if Satan also is divided against himself, how will his kingdom stand? For you say that I cast out demons by Be-el'zebul. And if I cast out demons by Be-el'zebul, by whom do your sons cast them out? Therefore they shall be your judges. But if it is by the finger of God that I cast out demons, then the kingdom of God has come upon you. When a strong man, fully armed, guards his own palace, his goods are in peace; but when one stronger than he assails him and overcomes him, he takes away his armor in which he trusted, and divides his spoil. He who is not with me is against me, and he who does not gather with me scatters.

The Return of the Unclean Spirit [11:24–26]

"When the unclean spirit has gone out of of a man, he passes through waterless places seeking rest; and finding none he says, 'I will return to my house from which I came.' And when he comes he finds it

[1] Other ancient authorities insert *bread, will give him a stone; or if he asks for*

swept and put in order. Then he goes and brings seven other spirits more evil than himself, and they enter and dwell there; and the last state of that man becomes worse than the first."

True Blessedness [11:27–28]

As he said this, a woman in the crowd raised her voice and said to him, "Blessed is the womb that bore you, and the breasts that you sucked!" But he said, "Blessed rather are those who hear the word of God and keep it!"

The Sign of Jonah [11:29–32]

When the crowds were increasing, he began to say, "This generation is an evil generation; it seeks a sign, but no sign shall be given to it except the sign of Jonah. For as Jonah became a sign to the men of Nin'eveh, so will the Son of man be to this

The tall Jewish sepulchre was standing in the time of Christ

Wide World

bear, and you yourselves do not touch the burdens with one of your fingers. Woe to you! for you build the tombs of the prophets whom your fathers killed. So you are witnesses and consent to the deeds of your fathers; for they killed them, and you build their tombs. Therefore also the Wisdom of God said, 'I will send them prophets and apostles, some of whom they will kill and persecute,' that the blood of all the prophets, shed from the foundation of the world, may be required of this generation, from the blood of Abel to the blood of Zechari'ah, who perished between the altar and the sanctuary. Yes, I tell you, it shall be required of this generation. Woe to you lawyers! for you have taken away the key of knowledge; you did not enter yourselves, and you hindered those who were entering."

As he went away from there, the scribes and the Phar'isees began to press him hard, and to provoke him to speak of many things, lying in wait for him, to catch at something he might say.

Underwood & Underwood

"Fear not little flock"

A Warning against Hypocrisy [Luke 12:1–3]

IN the meantime, when so many thousands of the multitude had gathered together that they trod upon one another, he began to say to his disciples first, "Beware of the leaven of the Phar'isees, which is hypocrisy. Nothing is covered up that will not be revealed, or hidden that will not be known. Whatever you have said in the dark shall be heard in the light, and what you have whispered in private rooms shall be proclaimed upon the housetops.

Acknowledging Jesus before Men
[12:4–12]

"I tell you, my friends, do not fear those who kill the body, and after that have no more than they can do. But I will warn you whom to fear: fear him who, after he has killed, has power to cast into hell;[m] yes, I tell you, fear him! Are not five sparrows sold for two pennies? And not one of them is forgotten before God. Why, even the

[m] Greek *Gehenna*

hairs of your head are all numbered. Fear not; you are of more value than many sparrows.

"And I tell you, every one who acknowledges me before men, the Son of man also will acknowledge before the angels of God; but he who denies me before men will be denied before the angels of God. And every one who speaks a word against the Son of man will be forgiven; but he who blasphemes against the Holy Spirit will not be forgiven. And when they bring you before the synagogues and the rulers and the authorities, do not be anxious how or what you are to answer or what you are to say; for the Holy Spirit will teach you in that very hour what you ought to say."

The Parable of the Rich Fool [12:13–21]

One of the multitude said to him, "Teacher, bid my brother divide the inheritance with me." But he said to him,

"Consider the lilies, how they grow"

Matson Photo Service

"Man, who made me a judge or divider over you?" And he said to them, "Take heed, and beware of all covetousness; for a man's life does not consist in the abundance of his possessions." And he told them a parable, saying, "The land of a rich man brought forth plentifully; and he thought to himself, 'What shall I do, for I have nowhere to store my crops?' And he said, 'I will do this: I will pull down my barns, and build larger ones; and there I will store all my grain and my goods. And I will say to my soul, Soul, you have ample goods laid up for many years; take your ease, eat, drink, be merry.' But God said to him, 'Fool! This night your soul is required of you; and the things you have prepared, whose will they be?' So is he who lays up treasure for himself, and is not rich toward God."

Anxiety [12:22–31]

And he said to his disciples, "Therefore I tell you, do not be anxious about your life, what you shall eat, nor about your body, what you shall put on. For life is more than food, and the body more than clothing. Consider the ravens: they neither sow nor reap, they have neither storehouse nor barn, and yet God feeds them. Of how much more value are you than the birds! And which of you by being anxious can add a cubit to his span of life?[n] If then you are not able to do as small a thing as that, why are you anxious about the rest? Consider the lilies, how they grow; they neither toil nor spin;[o] yet I tell you, even Solomon in all his glory was not arrayed like one of these. But if God so clothes the grass which is alive in the field today and tomorrow is thrown into the oven, how much more will he clothe you, O men of little faith! And do not seek what you are to eat and what you are to drink, nor be of anxious mind. For all the nations of the world seek these things; and your Father knows that you need them. Instead, seek his[p] kingdom, and these things shall be yours as well.

[n] Or *to his stature*
[o] Other ancient authorities read *Consider the lilies; they neither spin nor weave*
[p] Other ancient authorities read *God's*

82

Possessions [12:32-34]

"Fear not, little flock, for it is your Father's good pleasure to give you the kingdom. Sell your possessions, and give alms; provide yourselves with purses that do not grow old, with a treasure in the heavens that does not fail, where no thief approaches and no moth destroys. For where your treasure is, there will your heart be also.

Watchful Servants [12:35-40]

"Let your loins be girded and your lamps burning, and be like men who are waiting for their master to come home from the marriage feast, so that they may open to him at once when he comes and knocks. Blessed are those servants whom the master finds awake when he comes; truly, I say to you, he will gird himself and have them sit at table, and he will come and serve them. If he comes in the second watch, or in the third, and finds them so, blessed are those servants! But know this, that if the householder had known at what hour the thief was coming, he would have been awake andᵃ would not have left his house to be broken into. You also must be ready; for the Son of man is coming at an hour you do not expect."

Faithful and Unfaithful Servants
[12:41-48]

Peter said, "Lord, are you telling this parable for us or for all?" And the Lord said, "Who then is the faithful and wise steward, whom his master will set over his household, to give them their portion of

ᵃOther ancient authorities omit *would have been awake and*

food at the proper time? Blessed is that servant whom his master when he comes will find so doing. Truly I tell you, he will set him over all his possessions. But if that servant says to himself, 'My master is delayed in coming,' and begins to beat the menservants and the maidservants, and to eat and drink and get drunk, the master of that servant will come on a day when he does not expect him and at an hour he does not know, and will punishʳ him, and put him with the unfaithful. And that servant who knew his master's will, but did not make ready or act according to his will, shall receive a severe beating. But he who did not know, and did what deserved a beating, shall receive a light beating. Every one to whom much is given, of him will much be required; and of him to whom men commit much they will demand the more.

Jesus the Divider [12:49-53]

"I came to cast fire upon the earth; and would that it were already kindled! I have a baptism to be baptized with; and how I am constrained until it is accomplished! Do you think that I have come to give peace on earth? No, I tell you, but rather division; for henceforth in one house there will be five divided, three against two and two against three; they will be divided, father against son and son against father, mother against daughter and daughter against her mother, mother-in-law against her daughter-in-law and daughter-in-law against her mother-in-law."

Interpreting the Present Time [12:54-56]

He also said to the multitudes, "When you see a cloud rising in the west, you say

ʳOr *cut him in pieces*

at once, 'A shower is coming'; and so it happens. And when you see the south wind blowing, you say, 'There will be scorching heat'; and it happens. You hypocrites! You know how to interpret the appearance of earth and sky; but why do you not know how to interpret the present time?

Settling with an Accuser [12:57-59]

"And why do you not judge for yourselves what is right? As you go with your accuser before the magistrate, make an effort to settle with him on the way, lest he drag you to the judge, and the judge hand you over to the officer, and the officer put you in prison. I tell you, you will never get out till you have paid the very last copper."

Jesus' Call to Repentance [Luke 13:1-5]

THERE were some present at that very time who told him of the Galile'ans whose blood Pilate had mingled with their sacrifices. And he answered them, "Do you think that these Galile'ans were worse sinners than all the other Galile'ans, because they suffered thus? I tell you, No; but unless you repent you will all likewise perish. Or those eighteen upon whom the tower in Silo'am fell and killed them, do you think that they were worse offenders than all the others who dwelt in Jerusalem? I tell you, No; but unless you repent you will all likewise perish."

The Parable of the Fruitless Fig Tree
[13:6-9]

And he told this parable: "A man had a fig tree planted in his vineyard; and he came seeking fruit on it and found none. And he said to the vinedresser, 'Lo, these

Water still flows from Hezekiah's tunnel through the modern Pool of Siloam, just as in the time of Christ.

Religious News Service

The fig tree is still an important source of food in Palestine.

Three Lions

View of modern Jerusalem as seen from the Mount of Olives

three years I have come seeking fruit on this fig tree, and I find none. Cut it down; why should it use up the ground?' And he answered him, 'Let it alone, sir, this year also, till I dig about it and put on manure. And if it bears fruit next year, well and good; but if not, you can cut it down.' "

A Crippled Woman Healed on the Sabbath [13:10–17]

Now he was teaching in one of the synagogues on the sabbath. And there was a woman who had had a spirit of infirmity for eighteen years; she was bent over and could not fully straighten herself. And when Jesus saw her, he called her and said to her, "Woman, you are freed from your infirmity." And he laid his hands upon her, and immediately she was made straight, and she praised God. But the ruler of the synagogue, indignant because Jesus had healed on the sabbath, said to the people, "There are six days on which work ought to be done; come on those days and be healed, and not on the sabbath day." Then the Lord answered him, "You hypocrites! Does not each of you on the sabbath untie his ox or his ass from the manger, and lead it away to water it? And ought not this woman, a daughter of Abraham whom Satan bound for eighteen years, be loosed from this bond on the sabbath day?" As he said this, all his adversaries were put to shame; and all the people rejoiced at all the glorious things that were done by him.

The Parable of the Mustard Seed
[13:18–19]

He said therefore, "What is the kingdom of God like? And to what shall I compare it? It is like a grain of mustard seed which a man took and sowed in his garden; and it grew and became a tree, and the birds of the air made nests in its branches."

The Parable of the Leaven [13:20–21]

And again he said, "To what shall I compare the kingdom of God? It is like leaven which a woman took and hid in three measures of meal, till it was all leavened."

The Parable of the Narrow Door
[13:22–30]

He went on his way through towns and villages, teaching, and journeying toward Jerusalem. And some one said to him, "Lord, will those who are saved be few?" And he said to them, "Strive to enter by the narrow door; for many, I tell you, will seek to enter and will not be able. When once the householder has risen up and shut the door, you will begin to stand outside and to knock at the door, saying, 'Lord, open to us.' He will answer you, 'I do not know where you come from.' Then you will begin to say, 'We ate and drank in your presence, and you taught in our streets.' But he will say, 'I tell you, I do not know where you come from; depart from me, all you workers of iniquity!' There you will weep and gnash your teeth, when you see Abraham and Isaac and Jacob and all the prophets in the kingdom of God and you yourselves thrust out. And men will come from east and west, and from north and south, and sit at table in the kingdom of God. And behold, some are last who will be first, and some are first who will be last."

Jesus Laments over Jerusalem [13:31–35]

At that very hour some Phar'isees came, and said to him, "Get away from here, for Herod wants to kill you." And he said to them, "Go and tell that fox, 'Behold, I cast out demons and perform cures today and tomorrow, and the third day I finish my course. Nevertheless I must go on my way today and tomorrow and the day following; for it cannot be that a prophet should perish away from Jerusalem.' O Jerusalem, Jerusalem, killing the prophets and stoning those who are sent to you! How often would I have gathered your children together as a hen gathers her brood under her wings, and you would not! Behold, your house is forsaken. And I tell you, you will not see me until you say, 'Blessed is he who comes in the name of the Lord!' "[9]

Jesus Heals on the Sabbath [Luke 14:1–6]

ONE sabbath when he went to dine at the house of a ruler who belonged to the Phar'isees, they were watching him. And behold, there was a man before him who had dropsy. And Jesus spoke to the lawyers and Phar'isees, saying, "Is it lawful to heal on the sabbath, or not?" But they were silent. Then he took him and healed him, and let him go. And he said to them, "Which of you, having an ass[s] or an ox that has fallen into a well, will not immediately pull him out on a sabbath day?" And they could not reply to this.

Jesus' Teaching about Humility [14:7–14]

Now he told a parable to those who were invited, when he marked how they chose the places of honor, saying to them, "When you are invited by any one to a marriage feast, do not sit down in a place of honor, lest a more eminent man than you be invited by him; and he who invited you both will come and say to you, 'Give place to this man,' and then you will begin with shame to take the lowest place. But when you are invited, go and sit in the lowest place, so that when your host comes he may say to you, 'Friend, go up higher'; then you will be honored in the presence of all who sit at table with you. For every one who exalts himself will be humbled, and he who humbles himself will be exalted."

He said also to the man who had invited him, "When you give a dinner or a banquet, do not invite your friends or your brothers or your kinsmen or rich neighbors, lest they also invite you in return, and you be repaid. But when you give a feast, invite the poor, the maimed, the lame, the blind, and you will be blessed, because they cannot repay you. You will be repaid at the resurrection of the just."

The Parable of the Great Banquet
[14:15–24]

When one of those who sat at table with him heard this, he said to him, "Blessed is

[9]*Psalms* 118:26

[s]Other ancient authorities read *a son*

84

he who shall eat bread in the kingdom of God!" But he said to him, "A man once gave a great banquet, and invited many; and at the time for the banquet he sent his servant to say to those who had been invited, 'Come; for all is now ready.' But they all alike began to make excuses. The first said to him, 'I have bought a field, and I must go out and see it; I pray you, have me excused.' And another said, 'I have bought five yoke of oxen, and I go to examine them; I pray you, have me excused.' And another said, 'I have married a wife, and therefore I cannot come.' So the servant came and reported this to his master. Then the householder in anger said to his servant, 'Go out quickly to the streets and lanes of the city, and bring in the poor and maimed and blind and lame.' And the servant said, 'Sir, what you commanded has been done, and still there is room.' And the master said to the servant, 'Go out to the highways and hedges, and compel people to come in, that my house may be filled. For I tell you, none of those men who were invited shall taste my banquet.' "

The Cost of Discipleship [14:25–33]

Now great multitudes accompanied him; and he turned and said to them, "If any one comes to me and does not hate his own father and mother and wife and children and brothers and sisters, yes, and even his own life, he cannot be my disciple. Whoever does not bear his own cross and come after me, cannot be my disciple. For which of you, desiring to build a tower, does not first sit down and count the cost, whether he has enough to complete it? Otherwise, when he has laid a foundation, and is not able to finish, all who see it begin to mock him, saying, 'This man began to build, and was not able to finish.' Or what king, going to encounter another king in war, will not sit down first and take counsel whether he is able with ten thousand to meet him who comes against him with twenty thousand? And if not, while the other is yet a great way off, he sends an embassy and asks terms of peace. So therefore, whoever of you does not renounce all that he has cannot be my disciple.

The Parable of the Salt [14:34–35]

"Salt is good; but if salt has lost its taste, how shall its saltness be restored? It is fit neither for the land nor for the dunghill; men throw it away. He who has ears to hear, let him hear."

The Parable of the Lost Sheep

[Luke 15:1–7]

NOW the tax collectors and sinners were all drawing near to hear him. And the Phar'isees and the scribes murmured, saying, "This man receives sinners and eats with them."

So he told them this parable: "What man of you, having a hundred sheep, if he has lost one of them, does not leave the ninety-nine in the wilderness, and go after the one which is lost, until he finds it? And when he has found it, he lays it on his shoulders, rejoicing. And when he comes home, he calls together his friends and his neighbors, saying to them, 'Rejoice with me, for I have found my sheep which was lost.' Just so, I tell you, there will be more joy in heaven over one sinner who repents than over ninety-nine righteous persons who need no repentance.

A shepherd leading his flock

Underwood & Underwood

The Parable of the Lost Coin [15:8–10]

"Or what woman, having ten silver coins,[†] if she loses one coin, does not light a lamp and sweep the house and seek diligently until she finds it? And when she has found it, she calls together her friends and neighbors, saying, 'Rejoice with me, for I have found the coin which I had lost.' Just so, I tell you, there is joy before the angels of God over one sinner who repents."

[†]The drachma, rendered here by *silver coin*, was about sixteen cents

The Parable of the Lost Son [15:11–32]

And he said, "There was a man who had two sons; and the younger of them said to his father, 'Father, give me the share of property that falls to me.' And he divided his living between them. Not many days later, the younger son gathered all he had and took his journey into a far country, and there he squandered his property in loose living. And when he had spent everything, a great famine arose in that country, and he began to be in want. So he went and

"I have found my sheep which was lost"

Matson Photo Service

85

Matson Photo Service

A sycamore fig tree

HE also said to the disciples, "There was a rich man who had a steward, and charges were brought to him that this man was wasting his goods. And he called him and said to him, 'What is this that I hear about you? Turn in the account of your stewardship, for you can no longer be steward.' And the steward said to himself, 'What shall I do, since my master is taking the stewardship away from me? I am not strong enough to dig, and I am ashamed to beg. I have decided what to do, so that people may receive me into their houses when I am put out of the stewardship.' So, summoning his master's debtors one by one, he said to the first, 'How much do you owe my master?' He said, 'A hundred measures of oil.' And he said to him, 'Take your bill, and sit down quickly and write fifty.' Then he said to another, 'And how much do you owe?' He said, 'A hundred measures of wheat.' He said to him, 'Take your bill, and write eighty.' The master commended the dishonest steward for his prudence; for the sons of this world[w] are wiser in their own generation than the sons of light. And I tell you, make friends for yourselves by means of unrighteous mammon, so that when it fails they may receive you into the eternal habitations.

"He who is faithful in a very little is faithful also in much; and he who is dishonest in a very little is dishonest also in much. If then you have not been faithful in the unrighteous mammon, who will entrust to you the true riches? And if you have not been faithful in that which is another's, who will give you that which is your own? No servant can serve two masters; for either he will hate the one and love the other, or he will be devoted to the one and despise the other. You cannot serve God and mammon."

The Law and the Kingdom of God

[16:14–17]

The Phar'isees, who were lovers of money, heard all this, and they scoffed at him. But he said to them, "You are those who justify yourselves before men, but God knows your hearts; for what is exalted among men is an abomination in the sight of God.

"The law and the prophets were until John; since then the good news of the kingdom of God is preached, and every one enters it violently. But it is easier for heaven and earth to pass away, than for one dot of the law to become void.

Jesus' Teaching about Divorce [16:18]

"Every one who divorces his wife and marries another commits adultery, and he who marries a woman divorced from her husband commits adultery.

The Parable of the Rich Man and Lazarus [16:19–31]

"There was a rich man, who was clothed in purple and fine linen and who feasted sumptuously every day. And at his gate lay a poor man named Laz'arus, full of sores, who desired to be fed with what fell from the rich man's table; moreover the dogs came and licked his sores. The poor man died and was carried by the angels to Abraham's bosom. The rich man also died and was buried; and in Hades, being in torment, he lifted up his eyes, and saw

[w]Greek *age*

joined himself to one of the citizens of that country, who sent him into his fields to feed swine. And he would gladly have fed on[u] the pods that the swine ate; and no one gave him anything. But when he came to himself he said, 'How many of my father's hired servants have bread enough and to spare, but I perish here with hunger! I will arise and go to my father, and I will say to him, "Father, I have sinned against heaven and before you; I am no longer worthy to be called your son; treat me as one of your hired servants." ' And he arose and came to his father. But while he was yet at a distance, his father saw him and had compassion, and ran and embraced him and kissed him. And the son said to him, 'Father, I have sinned against heaven and before you; I am no longer worthy to be called your son.'[v] But the father said to his servants, 'Bring quickly the best robe, and put it on him; and put a ring on his hand, and

[u]Other ancient authorities read *filled his belly with*
[v]Other ancient authorities add *treat me as one of your hired servants*

shoes on his feet; and bring the fatted calf and kill it, and let us eat and make merry; for this my son was dead, and is alive again; he was lost, and is found.' And they began to make merry.

"Now his elder son was in the field; and as he came and drew near to the house, he heard music and dancing. And he called one of the servants and asked what this meant. And he said to him, 'Your brother has come, and your father has killed the fatted calf, because he has received him safe and sound.' But he was angry and refused to go in. His father came out and entreated him, but he answered his father, 'Lo, these many years I have served you, and I never disobeyed your command; yet you never gave me a kid, that I might make merry with my friends. But when this son of yours came, who has devoured your living with harlots, you killed for him the fatted calf!' And he said to him, 'Son, you are always with me, and all that is mine is yours. It was fitting to make merry and be glad, for this your brother was dead, and is alive; he was lost, and is found.' "

Grain is still threshed in some parts of Palestine, just as it was in ancient times.

Keystone View

Abraham far off and Laz'arus in his bosom. And he called out, 'Father Abraham, have mercy upon me, and send Laz'arus to dip the end of his finger in water and cool my tongue; for I am in anguish in this flame.' But Abraham said, 'Son, remember that you in your lifetime received your good things, and Laz'arus in like manner evil things; but now he is comforted here, and you are in anguish. And besides all this, between us and you a great chasm has been fixed, in order that those who would pass from here to you may not be able, and none may cross from there to us.' And he said, 'Then I beg you, father, to send him to my father's house, for I have five brothers, so that he may warn them, lest they also come into this place of torment.' But Abraham said, 'They have Moses and the prophets; let them hear them.' And he said, 'No, father Abraham; but if some one goes to them from the dead, they will repent.' He said to him, 'If they do not hear Moses and the prophets, neither will they be convinced if some one should rise from the dead.' ''

Jesus' Teaching about Faith and Forgiveness [Luke 17:1–6]

AND he said to his disciples, "Temptations to sin[z] are sure to come; but woe to him by whom they come! It would be better for him if a millstone were hung round his neck and he were cast into the sea, than that he should cause one of these little ones to sin.[v] Take heed to yourselves; if your brother sins, rebuke him, and if he repents, forgive him; and if he sins against you seven times in the day, and turns to you seven times, and says, 'I repent,' you must forgive him."

The apostles said to the Lord, "Increase our faith!" And the Lord said, "If you had faith as a grain of mustard seed, you could say to this sycamine tree, 'Be rooted up, and be planted in the sea,' and it would obey you.

The Servant's Duty [17:7–10]

"Will any one of you, who has a servant plowing or keeping sheep, say to him when he has come in from the field, 'Come at once and sit down at table'? Will he not rather say to him, 'Prepare supper for me, and gird yourself and serve me, till I eat and drink; and afterward you shall eat and drink'? Does he thank the servant because he did what was commanded? So you also, when you have done all that is commanded you, say, 'We are unworthy servants; we have only done what was our duty.' "

Jesus Cleanses Ten Lepers [17:11–19]

On the way to Jerusalem he was passing along between Samar'ia and Gal'ilee. And as he entered a village, he was met by ten lepers, who stood at a distance and lifted up their voices and said, "Jesus, Master, have mercy on us." When he saw them he said to them, "Go and show yourselves to the priests." And as they went they were cleansed. Then one of them, when he saw that he was healed, turned back, praising God with a loud voice; and he fell on his face at Jesus' feet, giving him thanks. Now he was a Samar'itan. Then said Jesus, "Were not ten cleansed? Where are the nine? Was no one found to return and give praise to God except this foreigner?" And he said to him, "Rise and go your way; your faith has made you well."

[z]Greek stumbling blocks
[v]Greek stumble

J. Lane Miller

In warm weather these rooftops are often used as sleeping quarters

The Coming of the Kingdom [17:20–37]

Being asked by the Phar'isees when the kingdom of God was coming, he answered them, "The kingdom of God is not coming with signs to be observed; nor will they say, 'Lo, here it is!' or 'There!' for behold, the kingdom of God is in the midst of you."[z]

And he said to the disciples, "The days are coming when you will desire to see one of the days of the Son of man, and you will not see it. And they will say to you, 'Lo, there!' or 'Lo, here!' Do not go, do not follow them. For as the lightning flashes and lights up the sky from one side to the other, so will the Son of man be in his day.[a] But first he must suffer many things and be rejected by this generation. As it was in the

[z]Or within you
[a]Other ancient authorities omit in his day

days of Noah, so will it be in the days of the Son of man. They ate, they drank, they married, they were given in marriage, until the day when Noah entered the ark, and the flood came and destroyed them all. Likewise as it was in the days of Lot—they ate, they drank, they bought, they sold, they planted, they built, but on the day when Lot went out from Sodom fire and brimstone rained from heaven and destroyed them all—so will it be on the day when the Son of man is revealed. On that day, let him who is on the housetop, with his goods in the house, not come down to take them away; and likewise let him who is in the field not turn back. Remember Lot's wife. Whoever seeks to gain his life will lose it, but whoever loses his life will preserve it. I tell you, in that night there will be two men in one bed; one will be taken and the other left.

"There will be two women grinding together"

Underwood & Underwood

J. Lane Miller

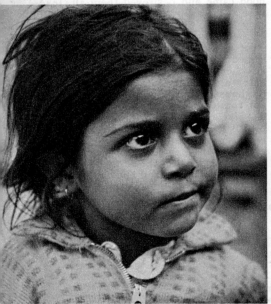

Black Star

There will be two women grinding together; one will be taken and the other left."[b] And they said to him, "Where, Lord?" He said to them, "Where the body is, there the eagles[c] will be gathered together."

The Parable of the Widow and the Judge [Luke 18:1-8]

AND he told them a parable, to the effect that they ought always to pray and not lose heart. He said, "In a certain city there was a judge who neither feared God nor regarded man; and there was a widow in that city who kept coming to him and saying, 'Vindicate me against my adversary.' For a while he refused; but afterward he said to himself, 'Though I neither fear God nor regard man, yet because this widow bothers me, I will vindicate her, or she will wear me out by her continual coming.' " And the Lord said, "Hear what the unrighteous judge says. And will not God vindicate his elect, who cry to him day and night? Will he delay long over them? I tell you, he will vindicate them speedily. Nevertheless, when the Son of man comes, will he find faith on earth?"

The Parable of the Pharisee and the Tax Collector [18:9-14]

He also told this parable to some who trusted in themselves that they were righteous and despised others: "Two men went up into the temple to pray, one a Phar'isee and the other a tax collector. The Phar'isee stood and prayed thus with himself, 'God, I thank thee that I am not like other men, extortioners, unjust, adulterers, or even like this tax collector. I fast twice a week, I give tithes of all that I get.' But the tax collector, standing far off, would not even lift up his eyes to heaven, but beat his breast, saying, 'God, be merciful to me a sinner!' I tell you, this man went down to his house justified rather than the other; for every one who exalts himself will be humbled, but he who humbles himself will be exalted."

Jesus Blesses Little Children [18:15-17]

Now they were bringing even infants to him that he might touch them; and when the disciples saw it, they rebuked them. But Jesus called them to him, saying, "Let the children come to me, and do not hinder them; for to such belongs the kingdom of God. Truly, I say to you, whoever does not receive the kingdom of God like a child shall not enter it."

The Rich Young Ruler [18:18-30]

And a ruler asked him, "Good Teacher, what shall I do to inherit eternal life?" And Jesus said to him, "Why do you call me good? No one is good but God alone. You know the commandments: 'Do not commit adultery, Do not kill, Do not steal, Do not bear false witness, Honor your father and mother.' "[10] And he said, "All these I have observed from my youth." And when Jesus heard it, he said to him, "One thing you still lack. Sell all that you have and distribute to the poor, and you will have treasure in heaven; and come, follow me." But when he heard this he became sad, for he was very rich. Jesus looking at him said, "How hard it is for those who have riches to enter the kingdom of God! For it is easier for a

[b]Other ancient authorities add verse 36, "Two men will be in the field; one will be taken and the other left"
[c]Or vultures
[10]Exodus 20:12-16; Deuteronomy 5:16-20

camel to go through the eye of a needle than for a rich man to enter the kingdom of God." Those who heard it said, "Then who can be saved?" But he said, "What is impossible with men is possible with God." And Peter said, "Lo, we have left our homes and followed you." And he said to them, "Truly, I say to you, there is no man who has left house or wife or brothers or parents or children, for the sake of the kingdom of God, who will not receive manifold more in this time, and in the age to come eternal life."

Jesus Foretells His Death a Third Time [18:31-34]

And taking the twelve, he said to them, "Behold, we are going up to Jerusalem, and everything that is written of the Son of man by the prophets will be accomplished. For he will be delivered to the Gentiles, and will be mocked and shamefully treated and spit upon; they will scourge him and kill him, and on the third day he will rise." But they understood none of these things; this saying was hid from them, and they did not grasp what was said.

A Blind Beggar Healed near Jericho [18:35-43]

As he drew near to Jer'icho, a blind man was sitting by the roadside begging; and hearing a multitude going by, he inquired what this meant. They told him, "Jesus of Naz'areth is passing by." And he cried, "Jesus, Son of David, have mercy on me!" And those who were in front rebuked him, telling him to be silent; but he cried out all the more, "Son of David, have mercy on me!" And Jesus stopped, and commanded him to be brought to him; and when he came near, he asked him, "What do you want me to do for you?" He said, "Lord, let me receive my sight." And Jesus said to him, "Receive your sight; your faith has made you well." And immediately he received his sight and followed him, glorifying God; and all the people, when they saw it, gave praise to God.

Jesus and Zacchaeus [Luke 19:1-10]

HE entered Jer'icho and was passing through. And there was a man named Zacchae'us; he was a chief tax collector, and rich. And he sought to see who Jesus was, but could not, on account of the crowd, because he was small of stature. So he ran on ahead and climbed up into a sycamore tree to see him, for he was to pass that way. And when Jesus came to the place, he looked up and said to him, "Zacchae'us, make haste and come down; for I must stay at your house today." So he made haste and came down, and received him joyfully. And when they saw it they all murmured, "He has gone in to be the guest of a man who is a sinner." And Zacchae'us stood and said to the Lord, "Behold, Lord, the half of my goods I give to the poor; and if I have defrauded any one of anything, I restore it fourfold." And Jesus said to him, "Today salvation has come to this house, since he also is a son of Abraham. For the Son of man came to seek and to save the lost."

The Parable of the Pounds [19:11-27]

As they heard these things, he proceeded to tell a parable, because he was near to Jerusalem, and because they supposed that the kingdom of God was to appear immediately. He said therefore, "A nobleman went

UJA

88

into a far country to receive kingly power[d] and then return. Calling ten of his servants, he gave them ten pounds,[e] and said to them, 'Trade with these till I come.' But his citizens hated him and sent an embassy after him, saying, 'We do not want this man to reign over us.' When he returned, having received the kingly power,[d] he commanded these servants, to whom he had given the money, to be called to him, that he might know what they had gained by trading. The first came before him, saying, 'Lord, your pound has made ten pounds more.' And he said to him, 'Well done, good servant! Because you have been faithful in a very little, you shall have authority over ten cities.' And the second came, saying, 'Lord, your pound has made five pounds.' And he said to him, 'And you are to be over five cities.' Then another came, saying, 'Lord, here is your pound, which I kept laid away in a napkin; for I was afraid of you, because you are a severe man; you take up what you did not lay down, and reap what you did not sow.'

[d]Greek *a kingdom*
[e]The mina, rendered here by *pound*, was equal to about twenty dollars

He said to him, 'I will condemn you out of your own mouth, you wicked servant! You knew that I was a severe man, taking up what I did not lay down and reaping what I did not sow? Why then did you not put my money into the bank, and at my coming I should have collected it with interest?' And he said to those who stood by, 'Take the pound from him, and give it to him who has the ten pounds.' (And they said to him, 'Lord, he has ten pounds!') 'I tell you, that to every one who has will more be given; but from him who has not, even what he has will be taken away. But as for these enemies of mine, who did not want me to reign over them, bring them here and slay them before me.' "

The Triumphal Entry into Jerusalem
[19:28-44]

And when he had said this, he went on ahead, going up to Jerusalem. When he drew near to Beth'phage and Beth'any, at the mount that is called Ol'ivet, he sent two of the disciples, saying, "Go into the village opposite, where on entering you will find a

colt tied, on which no one has ever yet sat; untie it and bring it here. If any one asks you, 'Why are you untying it?' you shall say this, 'The Lord has need of it.' " So those who were sent went away and found it as he had told them. And as they were untying the colt, its owners said to them, "Why are you untying the colt?" And they said, "The Lord has need of it." And they brought it to Jesus, and throwing their garments on the colt they set Jesus upon it. And as he rode along, they spread their garments on the road. As he was now drawing near, at the descent of the Mount of Olives, the whole multitude of the disciples began to rejoice and praise God with a loud voice for all the mighty works that they had seen, saying, "Blessed is the King who comes in the name of the Lord! Peace in heaven and glory in the highest!"[11] And some of the Phar'isees in the multitude said to him, "Teacher, rebuke your disciples." He answered, "I tell you, if these were silent, the very stones would cry out."

And when he drew near and saw the city he wept over it, saying, "Would that even today you knew the things that make for peace! But now they are hid from your eyes. For the days shall come upon you, when your enemies will cast up a bank about you and surround you, and hem you in on every side, and dash you to the ground, you and your children within you, and they will not leave one stone upon another in you; because you did not know the time of your visitation."

The Cleansing of the Temple [19:45-48]

And he entered the temple and began to drive out those who sold, saying to them, "It is written, 'My house shall be a house of prayer'; but you have made it a den of robbers." [12]

And he was teaching daily in the temple. The chief priests and the scribes and the principal men of the people sought to destroy him; but they did not find anything they could do, for all the people hung upon his words.

Jesus' Authority Questioned [Luke 20:1-8]

ONE day, as he was teaching the people in the temple and preaching the gospel, the chief priests and the scribes with the elders came up and said to him, "Tell us by what authority you do these things, or who it is that gave you this authority." He answered them, "I also will ask you a question; now tell me, Was the baptism of John from heaven or from men?" And they discussed it with one another, saying, "If we say, 'From heaven,' he will say, 'Why did you not believe him?' But if we say, 'From men,' all the people will stone us; for they are convinced that John was a prophet." So they answered that they did not know whence it was. And Jesus said to them, "Neither will I tell you by what authority I do these things."

The Parable of the Vineyard and the Tenants [20:9-18]

And he began to tell the people this parable: "A man planted a vineyard, and let it out to tenants, and went into another country for a long while. When the time came, he sent a servant to the tenants, that they should give him some of the fruit of the

The outside southeast corner of the Temple area in Jerusalem. The huge drafted stones belong to the original wall built by Herod the Great just before the time of Christ. The stones at the top date from the Middle Ages. The Garden of Gethsemane is in the foreground, with the Mount of Olives visible in the distance

J. Lane Miller

[11]*Psalms* 118:26
[12]*Isaiah* 56:7; *Jeremiah* 7:11

vineyard; but the tenants beat him, and sent him away empty-handed. And he sent another servant; him also they beat and treated shamefully, and sent him away empty-handed. And he sent yet a third; this one they wounded and cast out. Then the owner of the vineyard said, 'What shall I do? I will send my beloved son; it may be they will respect him.' But when the tenants saw him, they said to themselves, 'This is the heir; let us kill him, that the inheritance may be ours.' And they cast him out of the vineyard and killed him. What then will the owner of the vineyard do to them? He will come and destroy those tenants, and give the vineyard to others." When they heard this, they said, "God forbid!" But he looked at them and said, "What then is this that is written:

'The very stone which the builders rejected

has become the head of the corner'?[13] Every one who falls on that stone will be broken to pieces; but when it falls on any one it will crush him."

Paying Taxes to Caesar [20:19–26]

The scribes and the chief priests tried to lay hands on him at that very hour, but they feared the people; for they perceived that he had told this parable against them. So they watched him, and sent spies, who pretended to be sincere, that they might take hold of what he said, so as to deliver him up

[13]Psalms 118:22

to the authority and jurisdiction of the governor. They asked him, "Teacher, we know that you speak and teach rightly, and show no partiality, but truly teach the way of God. Is it lawful for us to give tribute to Caesar, or not?" But he perceived their craftiness, and said to them, "Show me a coin.[f] Whose likeness and inscription has it?" They said, "Caesar's." He said to them, "Then render to Caesar the things that are Caesar's, and to God the things that are God's." And they were not able in the presence of the people to catch him by what he said; but marveling at his answer they were silent.

The Question about the Resurrection [20:27–40]

There came to him some Sad'ducees, those who say that there is no resurrection, and they asked him a question, saying, "Teacher, Moses wrote for us that if a man's brother dies, having a wife but no children, the man[g] must take the wife and raise up children for his brother. Now there were seven brothers; the first took a wife, and died without children; and the second and the third took her, and likewise all seven left no children and died. Afterward the woman also died. In the resurrection, therefore, whose wife will the woman be? For the seven had her as wife."

And Jesus said to them, "The sons of this

[f]Greek denarius
[g]Greek his brother

age marry and are given in marriage; but those who are accounted worthy to attain to that age and to the resurrection from the dead neither marry nor are given in marriage, for they cannot die any more, because they are equal to angels and are sons of God, being sons of the resurrection. But that the dead are raised, even Moses showed, in the passage about the bush, where he calls the Lord the God of Abraham and the God of Isaac and the God of Jacob. Now he is not God of the dead, but of the living; for all live to him." And some of the scribes answered, "Teacher, you have spoken well." For they no longer dared to ask him any question.

The Question about David's Son [20:41–44]

But he said to them, "How can they say that the Christ is David's son? For David himself says in the Book of Psalms,

'The Lord said to my Lord,
Sit at my right hand,
till I make thy enemies a stool for thy feet.'[14]

David thus calls him Lord; so how is he his son?"

Jesus Denounces the Scribes [20:45–47]

And in the hearing of all the people he said to his disciples, "Beware of the scribes, who like to go about in long robes, and love salutations in the market places and the best seats in the synagogues and the places of honor at feasts, who devour widows' houses and for a pretense make long prayers. They will receive the greater condemnation."

The Widow's Offering [Luke 21:1–4]

HE looked up and saw the rich putting their gifts into the treasury; and he saw a poor widow put in two copper coins. And he said, "Truly I tell you, this poor widow has put in more than all of them; for they all contributed out of their abundance, but she out of her poverty put in all the living that she had."

Signs and Persecutions [21:5–19]

And as some spoke of the temple, how it was adorned with noble stones and offerings, he said, "As for these things which you see, the days will come when there shall not be left here one stone upon another that will not be thrown down." And they asked him, "Teacher, when will this be, and what will be the sign when this is about to take place?" And he said, "Take heed that you are not led astray; for many will come in my name, saying, 'I am he!' and, 'The time is at hand!' Do not go after them. And when you hear of wars and tumults, do not be terrified; for this must first take place, but the end will not be at once."

Then he said to them, "Nation will rise against nation, and kingdom against kingdom; there will be great earthquakes, and in various places famines and pestilences; and there will be terrors and great signs from heaven. But before all this they will lay their hands on you and persecute you, delivering you up to the synagogues and prisons, and you will be brought before kings and governors for my name's sake. This will be a time for you to bear testimony. Settle it therefore in your minds, not to meditate beforehand how to answer; for I will give you a mouth and wisdom, which

[14]Psalms 110:1

SILVER ROMAN DENARII OF JESUS' TIME
as in Luke 7:41, 10:35 and 20:24

Obverse

Julius Caesar, before 44 B.C.

Augustus Caesar, 27 B.C.–14 A.D.

Tiberius Caesar, 14–37 A.D.

Reverse

Juno in two-horse chariot

Temple of Mars

Female figure (possibly Pax) holding branch

BRONZE LEPTA
"copper" as in Luke 12:59; "copper coins" in Luke 21:2

Obverse

Herod I, 37–4 B.C.

Pontius Pilate, Procurator under Tiberius Caesar 26–36 A.D.

Reverse

Double cornucopiae

Ritual Vessel called "simpulum" used in sacrifice

When there was peace in the Roman Empire, the doors of the Temple of Janus were shut, as in this coin of 66–67 A.D.

none of your adversaries will be able to withstand or contradict. You will be delivered up even by parents and brothers and kinsmen and friends, and some of you they will put to death; you will be hated by all for my name's sake. But not a hair of your head will perish. By your endurance you will gain your lives.

Jesus Foretells the Destruction of Jerusalem [21:20-24]

"But when you see Jerusalem surrounded by armies, then know that its desolation has come near. Then let those who are in Jude'a flee to the mountains, and let those who are inside the city depart, and let not those who are out in the country enter it; for these are days of vengeance, to fulfil all that is written. Alas for those who are with child and for those who give suck in those days! For great distress shall be upon the earth and wrath upon this people; they will fall by the edge of the sword, and be led captive among all nations; and Jerusalem will be trodden down by the Gentiles, until the times of the Gentiles are fulfilled.

Signs of the End [21:25-38]

"And there will be signs in sun and moon and stars, and upon the earth distress of nations in perplexity at the roaring of the sea and the waves, men fainting with fear and with foreboding of what is coming on the world; for the powers of the heavens will be shaken. And then they will see the Son of man coming in a cloud with power and great glory. Now when these things begin to take place, look up and raise your heads, because your redemption is drawing near."

And he told them a parable: "Look at the fig tree, and all the trees; as soon as they come out in leaf, you see for yourselves and know that the summer is already near. So also, when you see these things taking place, you know that the kingdom of God is near. Truly, I say to you, this generation will not pass away till all has taken place. Heaven and earth will pass away, but my words will not pass away.

"But take heed to yourselves lest your hearts be weighed down with dissipation and drunkenness and cares of this life, and that day come upon you suddenly like a snare; for it will come upon all who dwell upon the face of the whole earth. But watch at all times, praying that you may have strength to escape all these things that will take place, and to stand before the Son of man."

And every day he was teaching in the temple, but at night he went out and lodged on the mount called Ol'ivet. And early in the morning all the people came to him in the temple to hear him.

The Plot against Jesus [Luke 22:1-6]

NOW the feast of Unleavened Bread drew near, which is called the Passover. And the chief priests and the scribes were seeking how to put him to death; for they feared the people.

Then Satan entered into Judas called Iscar'iot, who was of the number of the twelve; he went away and conferred with the chief priests and captains how he might betray him to them. And they were glad, and engaged to give him money. So he agreed, and sought an opportunity to betray him to them in the absence of the multitude.

Bas-relief from Triumphal Arch of Titus, commemorating his capture of Jerusalem. Roman soldiers crowned with laurel carry the golden Seven-branched Lampstand, the Table of Showbread and the Sacred trumpets, taken from the Temple at Jerusalem.

The Last Supper [22:7-23]

Then came the day of Unleavened Bread, on which the passover lamb had to be sacrificed. So Jesus[h] sent Peter and John, saying, "Go and prepare the passover for us, that we may eat it." They said to him, "Where will you have us prepare it?" He said to them, "Behold, when you have entered the city, a man carrying a jar of water will meet you; follow him into the house which he enters, and tell the householder, 'The Teacher says to you, Where is the guest room, where I am to eat the passover with my disciples?' And he will show you a large upper room furnished; there make ready." And they went, and found it as he had told them; and they prepared the passover.

And when the hour came, he sat at table, and the apostles with him. And he said to them, "I have earnestly desired to eat this passover with you before I suffer; for I tell you I shall not eat it[i] until it is fulfilled in the kingdom of God." And he took a cup, and when he had given thanks he said, "Take this, and divide it among yourselves; for I tell you that from now on I shall not drink of the fruit of the vine until the kingdom of God comes." And he took bread, and when he had given thanks he broke it and gave it to them, saying, "This is my body.[j] But behold the hand of him who betrays me is with me on the table. For the Son of man goes as it has been determined; but woe to that man by whom he is betrayed!" And they began to question one another, which of them it was that would do this.

[h]Greek he

[i]Other ancient authorities read never eat it again
[j]Other ancient authorities add which is given for you. Do this in remembrance of me." And likewise the cup after supper, saying, "This cup which is poured out for you is the new covenant in my blood."

Before these large stones of Herod's time the Jews lament the destruction of Jerusalem, which Jesus predicted.

Old olive tree on Mount of Olives
J. Lane Miller

Philip Gendreau
Garden of Gethsemane and Mount of Olives

St. Stephen's Gate
Keystone View

Modern structure above ancient Praetorium
Matson Photo Service

The Dispute about Greatness [22:24–30]

A dispute also arose among them, which of them was to be regarded as the greatest. And he said to them, "The kings of the Gentiles exercise lordship over them; and those in authority over them are called benefactors. But not so with you; rather let the greatest among you become as the youngest, and the leader as one who serves. For which is the greater, one who sits at table, or one who serves? Is it not the one who sits at table? But I am among you as one who serves.

"You are those who have continued with me in my trials; as my Father appointed a kingdom for me, so do I appoint for you that you may eat and drink at my table in my kingdom, and sit on thrones judging the twelve tribes of Israel.

Peter's Denial Foretold [22:31–34]

"Simon, Simon, behold, Satan demanded to have you,[k] that he might sift you[k] like wheat, but I have prayed for you that your faith may not fail; and when you have turned again, strengthen your brethren." And he said to him, "Lord, I am ready to go with you to prison and to death." He said, "I tell you, Peter, the cock will not crow this day, until you three times deny that you know me."

Purse, Bag, and Sword [22:35–38]

And he said to them, "When I sent you out with no purse or bag or sandals, did you lack anything?" They said, "Nothing." He said to them, "But now, let him who has a purse take it, and likewise a bag. And let him who has no sword sell his mantle and buy one. For I tell you that this scripture must be fulfilled in me, 'And he was reckoned with transgressors'[15]; for what is written about me has its fulfilment." And they said, "Look, Lord, here are two swords." And he said to them, "It is enough."

[k]The Greek word for *you* here is plural; in verse 32 it is singular
[15]Isaiah 53:12

Jesus Prays in Gethsemane [22:39–46]

And he came out, and went, as was his custom, to the Mount of Olives; and the disciples followed him. And when he came to the place he said to them, "Pray that you may not enter into temptation." And he withdrew from them about a stone's throw, and knelt down and prayed, "Father, if thou art willing, remove this cup from me; nevertheless not my will, but thine, be done." And there appeared to him an angel from heaven, strengthening him. And being in an agony he prayed more earnestly; and his sweat became like great drops of blood falling down upon the ground.[l] And when he rose from prayer, he came to the disciples and found them sleeping for sorrow, and he said to them, "Why do you sleep? Rise and pray that you may not enter into temptation."

The Betrayal and Arrest of Jesus [22:47–53]

While he was still speaking, there came a crowd, and the man called Judas, one of the twelve, was leading them. He drew near to Jesus to kiss him; but Jesus said to him, "Judas, would you betray the Son of man with a kiss?" And when those who were about him saw what would follow, they said, "Lord, shall we strike with the sword?" And one of them struck the slave of the high priest and cut off his right ear. But Jesus said, "No more of this!" And he touched his ear and healed him. Then Jesus said to the chief priests and captains of the temple and elders, who had come out against him, "Have you come out as against a robber, with swords and clubs? When I was with you day after day in the temple, you did not lay hands on me. But this is your hour, and the power of darkness."

Peter Denies Jesus [22:54–62]

Then they seized him and led him away, bringing him into the high priest's house. Peter followed at a distance; and when they

[l]Other ancient authorities omit verses 43 and 44

Matson Photo Service

Large paving stones in the court of the Roman Praetorium, where Jesus appeared before Pontius Pilate. Roman soldiers are believed to have marked these stones for their games

Modern views on the Via Dolorosa

had kindled a fire in the middle of the courtyard and sat down together, Peter sat among them. Then a maid, seeing him as he sat in the light and gazing at him, said, "This man also was with him." But he denied it, saying, "Woman, I do not know him." And a little later some one else saw him and said, "You also are one of them." But Peter said, "Man, I am not." And after an interval of about an hour still another insisted, saying, "Certainly this man also was with him; for he is a Galile'an." But Peter said, "Man, I do not know what you are saying." And immediately, while he was still speaking, the cock crowed. And the Lord turned and looked at Peter. And Peter remembered the word of the Lord, how he had said to him, "Before the cock crows today, you will deny me three times." And he went out and wept bitterly.

Jesus Mocked and Beaten [22:63–65]

Now the men who were holding Jesus mocked him and beat him; they also blindfolded him and asked him, "Prophesy! Who is it that struck you?" And they spoke many other words against him, reviling him.

Jesus before the Council [22:66–71]

When day came, the assembly of the elders of the people gathered together, both chief priests and scribes; and they led him away to their council, and they said, "If you are the Christ, tell us." But he said to them, "If I tell you, you will not believe; and if I ask you, you will not answer. But from now on the Son of man shall be seated at the right hand of the power of God." And they all said, "Are you the Son of God, then?" And he said to them, "You say that I am." And they said, "What further testimony do we need? We have heard it ourselves from his own lips."

Jesus before Pilate [Luke 23:1–5]

THEN the whole company of them arose, and brought him before Pilate. And they began to accuse him, saying, "We found this man perverting our nation, and forbidding us to give tribute to Caesar, and saying that he himself is Christ a king." And Pilate asked him, "Are you the King of the Jews?" And he answered him, "You have said so." And Pilate said to the chief priests and the multitudes, "I find no crime in this man." But they were urgent, saying, "He stirs up the people, teaching throughout all Jude'a, from Gal'ilee even to this place."

Jesus before Herod [23:6–12]

When Pilate heard this, he asked whether the man was a Galile'an. And when he learned that he belonged to Herod's jurisdiction, he sent him over to Herod, who was himself in Jerusalem at that time. When Herod saw Jesus, he was very glad, for he had long desired to see him, because he had heard about him, and he was hoping to see some sign done by him. So he questioned him at some length; but he made no answer. The chief priests and the scribes stood by, vehemently accusing him. And Herod with his soldiers treated him with contempt and mocked him; then, arraying him in gorgeous apparel, he sent him back to Pilate. And Herod and Pilate became friends with each other that very day, for before this they had been at enmity with each other.

Jesus Sentenced to Die [23:13–25]

Pilate then called together the chief priests and the rulers and the people, and said to them, "You brought me this man as one who was perverting the people; and after examining him before you, behold, I did not find this man guilty of any of your charges against him; neither did Herod, for he sent him back to us. Behold, nothing deserving death has been done by him; I will therefore chastise him and release him."[m]

But they all cried out together, "Away with this man, and release to us Barab'bas" —a man who had been thrown into prison for an insurrection started in the city, and for murder. Pilate addressed them once

[m]Here, or after verse 19, other ancient authorities add verse 17, *Now he was obliged to release one man to them at the festival*

Matson Photo Service

Street scene in Jerusalem

Three Lions

Wide World

Underwood & Underwood

more, desiring to release Jesus; but they shouted out, "Crucify, crucify him!" A third time he said to them, "Why, what evil has he done? I have found in him no crime deserving death; I will therefore chastise him and release him." But they were urgent, demanding with loud cries that he should be crucified. And their voices prevailed. So Pilate gave sentence that their demand should be granted. He released the man who had been thrown into prison for insurrection and murder, whom they asked for; but Jesus he delivered up to their will.

The Crucifixion [23:26–38]

And as they led him away, they seized one Simon of Cyre'ne, who was coming in from the country, and laid on him the cross, to carry it behind Jesus. And there followed him a great multitude of the people, and of women who bewailed and lamented him. But Jesus turning to them said,

Ewing Galloway

"Daughters of Jerusalem, do not weep for me, but weep for yourselves and for your children. For behold, the days are coming when they will say, 'Blessed are the barren, and the wombs that never bore, and the breasts that never gave suck!' Then they will begin to say to the mountains, 'Fall on us'; and to the hills, 'Cover us.' For if they do this when the wood is green, what will happen when it is dry?"

Two others also, who were criminals, were led away to be put to death with him. And when they came to the place which is called The Skull, there they crucified him, and the criminals, one on the right and one on the left. And Jesus said, "Father, forgive them; for they know not what they do."[n] And they cast lots to divide his garments. And the people stood by, watching; but the rulers scoffed at him, saying, "He saved others; let him save himself, if he is the Christ of God, his Chosen One!" The soldiers also mocked him, coming up and offering him vinegar, and saying, "If you are the King of the Jews, save yourself!" There was also an inscription over him,[o] "This is the King of the Jews."

One of the criminals who were hanged railed at him, saying, "Are you not the Christ? Save yourself and us!" But the other rebuked him, saying, "Do you not fear God, since you are under the same sentence of condemnation? And we indeed justly; for we are receiving the due reward of our deeds; but this man has done nothing wrong." And he said, "Jesus, remember me when you come in your kingly power."[p] And he said to him, "Truly, I say to you, today you will be with me in Paradise."

It was now about the sixth hour, and there was darkness over the whole land[q] until the ninth hour, while the sun's light failed;[r] and the curtain of the temple was torn in two. Then Jesus, crying with a loud voice, said, "Father, into thy hands I commit my spirit!" And having said this he breathed his last. Now when the centurion saw what had taken place, he praised God, and said, "Certainly this man was innocent!" And all the multitudes who assembled to see the sight, when they saw what had taken place, returned home beating their breasts. And all his acquaintances and the women who had followed him from Gal'ilee stood at a distance and saw these things.

The Burial of Jesus [23:50–56]

Now there was a man named Joseph from the Jewish town of Arimathe'a. He was a member of the council, a good and righteous man, who had not consented to their purpose and deed, and he was looking for the kingdom of God. This man went to Pilate and asked for the body of Jesus. Then he took it down and wrapped it in a linen shroud, and laid him in a rock-hewn tomb, where no one had ever yet been laid. It was the day of Preparation, and the sabbath was beginning.[s] The women who had come with him from Gal'ilee followed, and saw the tomb, and how his body was laid; then they returned, and prepared spices and ointments.

On the sabbath they rested according to the commandment.

[n] Other ancient authorities omit the sentence *And Jesus . . . what they do*
[o] Other ancient authorities add *in letters of Greek and Latin and Hebrew*
[p] Greek *kingdom*
[q] Or *earth*
[r] Or *the sun was eclipsed*. Other ancient authorities read *the sun was darkened*
[s] Greek *was dawning*

The Resurrection [Luke 24:1–11]

BUT on the first day of the week, at early dawn, they went to the tomb, taking the spices which they had prepared. And they found the stone rolled away from the tomb, but when they went in they did not find the body.[t] While they were perplexed about this, behold, two men stood by them in dazzling apparel; and as they were frightened and bowed their faces to the ground, the men said to them, "Why do you seek the living among the dead?[u] Remember how he told you, while he was still in Gal'ilee, that the Son of man must be delivered into the hands of sinful men, and be crucified, and on the third day rise." And they remembered his words, and returning from the tomb they told all this to the eleven and to all the rest. Now it was

[t] Other ancient authorities add *of the Lord Jesus*
[u] Other ancient authorities add *He is not here, but has risen*

Keystone View

Mary Mag'dalene and Jo-an'na and Mary the mother of James and the other women with them who told this to the apostles; but these words seemed to them an idle tale, and they did not believe them.[v]

The Walk to Emmaus [24:13-35]

That very day two of them were going to a village named Emma'us, about seven miles[w] from Jerusalem, and talking with each other about all these things that had happened. While they were talking and discussing together, Jesus himself drew near and went with them. But their eyes were kept from recognizing him. And he said to them, "What is this conversation which you are holding with each other as you walk?" And they stood still, looking sad. Then one of them, named Cle'opas, answered him, "Are you the only visitor to Jerusalem who does not know the things that have happened there in these days?" And he said to them, "What things?" And they said to him, "Concerning Jesus of Naz'areth, who was a prophet mighty in deed and word before God and all the people, and how our chief priests and rulers delivered him up to be condemned to death, and crucified him. But we had hoped that he was the one to redeem Israel. Yes, and besides all this, it is now the third day since this happened. Moreover, some women of our company amazed us. They were at the tomb early in the morning and did not find his body; and they came back saying that they had even seen a vision of angels, who said that he was alive. Some of those who were with us went to the tomb, and found it just as the women had said; but him they did not see." And he said to them, "O foolish men, and slow of heart to believe all that the prophets have spoken! Was it not necessary that the Christ should suffer these things and enter into his glory?" And beginning with Moses and all the prophets, he interpreted to them in all the scriptures the things concerning himself.

So they drew near to the village to which they were going. He appeared to be going further, but they constrained him, saying, "Stay with us, for it is toward evening and the day is now far spent." So he went in to stay with them. When he was at table with them, he took the bread and blessed, and broke it, and gave it to them. And their eyes were opened and they recognized him; and he vanished out of their sight. They said to each other, "Did not our hearts burn within us while he talked to us on the road, while he opened to us the scriptures?" And they rose that same hour and returned to Jerusalem; and they found the eleven gathered together and those who were with them, who said, "The Lord has risen indeed, and has appeared to Simon!" Then they told what had happened on the road, and how he was known to them in the breaking of the bread.

Jesus Appears to His Disciples [24:36-43]

As they were saying this, Jesus himself stood among them.[x] But they were startled and frightened, and supposed that they saw a spirit. And he said to them, "Why are you troubled, and why do questionings rise in your hearts? See my hands and my feet, that it is I myself; handle me, and see; for a spirit has not flesh and bones as you see that I have."[y] And while they still disbelieved for joy, and wondered, he said to them, "Have you anything here to eat?" They gave him a piece of broiled fish, and he took it and ate before them.

The Great Commission [24:44-49]

Then he said to them, "These are my words which I spoke to you, while I was still with you, that everything written about me in the law of Moses and the prophets and the psalms must be fulfilled." Then he opened their minds to understand the scriptures, and said to them, "Thus it is written, that the Christ should suffer and on the third day rise from the dead, and that repentance and forgiveness of sins should be preached in his name to all nations,[z] beginning from Jerusalem. You are witnesses of these things. And behold, I send the promise of my Father upon you; but stay in the city, until you are clothed with power from on high."

The Ascension [24:50-53]

Then he led them out as far as Beth'any, and lifting up his hands he blessed them. While he blessed them, he parted from them.[a] And they[b] returned to Jerusalem with great joy, and were continually in the temple blessing God.

[v]Other ancient authorities add verse 12, *But Peter rose and ran to the tomb; stooping and looking in, he saw the linen cloths by themselves; and he went home wondering at what had happened*

[w]Greek *sixty stadia;* some ancient authorities read *a hundred and sixty stadia*

[x]Other ancient authorities add *and said to them, "Peace to you!"*

[y]Other ancient authorities add verse 40, *And when he had said this, he showed them his hands and his feet*

[z]Or *nations. Beginning from Jerusalem you are witnesses*

[a]Other ancient authorities add *and was carried up into heaven*

[b]Other ancient authorities add *worshipped him, and*

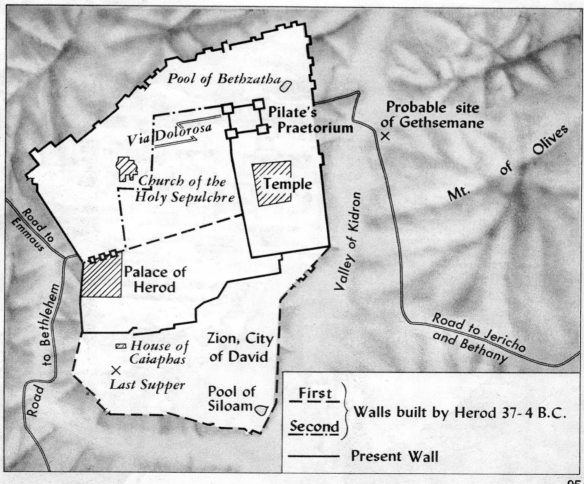

MAP OF JERUSALEM IN THE TIME OF CHRIST

The vast amount of rubble and later building make the identification of the places known to Jesus almost impossible. The sites printed in italics have not been definitely identified but have long been venerated by generations of Christians. The Church of the Holy Sepulchre has been honored since the 4th century as the site of the crucifixion. On the opposite page (upper left) modern pilgrims from many lands carry a cross along the Via Dolorosa. At the lower right is an Easter procession entering the restored Church of the Holy Sepulchre. The excavated rock tombs and the rolling stone may resemble in a general way the sepulchre of Joseph of Arimathea.

Pool of Bethzatha

Pilate's Praetorium

Probable site of Gethsemane

Via Dolorosa

Church of the Holy Sepulchre

Temple

Mt. of Olives

Road to Emmaus

Valley of Kidron

Palace of Herod

House of Caiaphas

Last Supper

Zion, City of David

Pool of Siloam

Road to Bethlehem

Road to Jericho and Bethany

First
Second } Walls built by Herod 37-4 B.C.

Present Wall

*Looking across the Temp...
...rusalem to the Mount ...
...yond the Dome of the Ro...
...Kidron Valley, lies th...
...Gethsemane. The high ...
summit of the Moun...*

He Gave His Only Son

LOOKING OVER THE KIDRON VALLEY TOWARD
GETHSEMANE AND THE MOUNT OF OLIVES

L. Kofod

THE GOSPEL ACCORDING TO JOHN

REVISED STANDARD VERSION

JUDEA AND SAMARIA

In the Gospel according to John much is told of the work of Jesus in Judea and Samaria. Together, Samaria and Judea occupy the central and southern highlands of Palestine, from the edge of the Plain of Esdraelon in the north to the dry slopes of the Negeb in the south, a distance of perhaps 90 miles. In the Old Testament, references to the hill-country of Judah and the hill-country of Ephraim are common and show that the chief impression made by these lands was their hilly character.

Judea is essentially a deeply cut tableland with an elevation of 2,593 feet at Jerusalem and of 3,370 feet farther south not far from Hebron. Beyond this the hills drop off into the arid reaches of the Negeb or Southland. On the west the plateau descends into the Shephelah or Lowlands, beyond which is the plain of the Mediterranean coastal region. On the east the Wilderness of Judea plunges steeply down into the profound depression in which are the Jordan River and the Dead Sea. At the most it is hardly more than 50 miles from south to north across Judea, and 30 miles from east to west, exclusive of the maritime plain.

Only on its more gentle slopes to the west, where Mediterranean clouds bring considerable rainfall, does Judea present the appearance of fertility. For the most part the highlands are overwhelmingly barren and arid. Indeed, George Adam Smith once remarked that the prevailing impression of Judea is of stone—piles of stones gathered from the fields, fields that are still stony, the boulders in the torrent beds, the gaunt ribs of the hills. A tawny land, arduous and forbidding—this, on the whole, is Judea.

In Old Testament times this region was occupied by the kingdom of Judah, with its capital at Jerusalem. Judah was ruled by kings of the Davidic line down to 587 B.C., when Jerusalem fell to the besieging armies of Nebuchadnezzar, king of Babylon. The Temple was destroyed and many of the inhabitants of Judah were carried away as captives to Babylon (2 Kings 25:1–21). In 539 B.C. Cyrus, king of Persia, issued a decree granting permission for the Jews to return to the land of Judah to rebuild the Temple at Jerusalem (Ezra 1:1–4).

After the conquest of the Persian Empire by Alexander the Great, Judea belonged first to Egypt and then to Syria. The revolt of the Jews led by the Maccabees against their Syrian overlords (in 166 B.C.) resulted in the establishment of a separate kingdom ruled by priests. Later, with the help of the Romans, Herod the Great reigned as king of Judea from 37 to 4 B.C. His kingdom included not only Judea but also Samaria, Idumea and Galilee, and the region east of the Jordan as well. After his death Judea, Samaria and Idumea passed into the hands of his son Archelaus. Archelaus was deposed and banished in A.D. 6. After that, procurators were sent out directly from Rome. Pontius Pilate, by whom Jesus was examined and sentenced to be crucified (John 18:28—19:16), was procurator of Judea, Samaria and Idumea from 26 to 36 A.D.

The residence of the procurator was ordinarily at Caesarea on the seacoast, a city built by Herod the Great to honor Augustus Caesar and preferred by the Romans to Jerusalem. On special occasions, however, as notably at Passover time, when turbulence might be expected among the crowds of pilgrims in the holy city, the procurator came to Jerusalem. Here was the Praetorium of Pilate, to which the Jews brought Jesus (John 18:28), and the Pavement (Lithostroton), where Pilate sentenced him to death (John 19:13).

SAMARIA

Samaria is more attractive in appearance than Judea. Viewed from a distance, the mountains of Samaria appear to form an almost continuous wall; and only at one point is there a clear sign of a break, at the valley of Shechem, between Mounts Ebal and Gerizim. The elevations of the twin peaks, which form a natural focus of the land, are 3,077 and 2,849 feet. It was at the feet of these two mountains that the Israelites stood as Joshua recited the blessings and curses of the law (Joshua 8:33–35).

The region of Samaria was later occupied by the northern kingdom of Israel. In 722–721 B.C. Samaria fell to the Assyrians, and the people of Israel were carried away into captivity by Sargon, king of Assyria, (2 Kings 17:6). Sargon and his successors repopulated the area by introducing colonists from Babylon, Hamath and other places (2 Kings

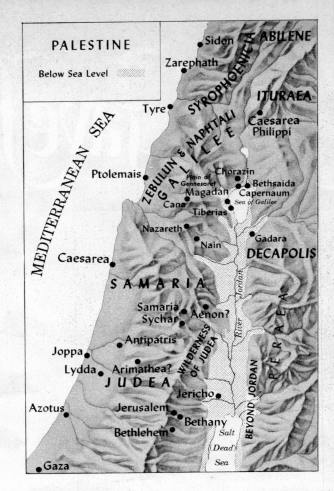

17:24; Ezra 4:2, 9, 10), who in the course of time intermarried with the Israelites who were left in the land. The Jews came to look upon the inhabitants of Samaria with suspicion as people not only of mixed race but also of mixed religion.

When the Jewish exiles returned to Jerusalem, the Samaritans asked permission to help in erecting the Temple, protesting that they had worshiped the God of Israel since the time of Esarhaddon (Ezra 4:2). When this offer was rejected, the Samaritans attempted to hinder the completion of the work (Ezra 4:4–6) and later also opposed the rebuilding of the walls of Jerusalem by Nehemiah (Nehemiah 4:1–23). Their leader at this time was Sanballat, whose son-in-law, Manasseh, was put out of the priesthood by Nehemiah because he had married a foreign woman (Nehemiah 13:28). According to Josephus, Sanballat built the rival Samaritan temple on Mount Gerizim and made his son-in-law its high priest.

From this time on the antipathy between the Jews and the Samaritans increased. According to 2 Maccabees 6:2, in the days of Antiochus Epiphanes (ca. 168 B.C.) the Samaritans disclaimed any relation to the Jews and gratified that tyrant by expressing a desire that their temple on Mount Gerizim be dedicated to Jupiter. About 128 B.C. the Jewish high priest John Hyrcanus took Shechem and Gerizim and destroyed the Samaritan temple. The people, however, continued to worship on the mountain where the sacred edifice had stood. Mount Gerizim is undoubtedly the mountain to which the Samaritan woman referred when she said, "Our fathers worshiped on this mountain" (John 4:20).

At the foot of the mountain, beside the main north-south road, Jacob's well (John 4:11) still exists. It is now about 75 feet in depth, and its water is superior to that of nearby springs and streams. The ancient town of Sychar, from which the woman of Samaria came to draw water (John 4:5–7), was a very short distance away. About two miles from Jacob's well there still exists a small community of Samaritans at Nablus.

(For additional geographical and historical material see other illustrated portions of the New Testament books of this series.)

The Jordan River

Jack Finegan

HE GAVE HIS ONLY SON

as reported in the Gospel according to JOHN

The Word

[John 1:1-5] In the beginning was the Word, and the Word was with God, and the Word was God. He was in the beginning with God; all things were made through him, and without him was not anything made that was made. In him was life,*a* and the life was the light of men. The light shines in the darkness, and the darkness has not overcome it.

John's Witness to the Light [1:6-8]

There was a man sent from God, whose name was John. He came for testimony, to bear witness to the light, that all might believe through him. He was not the light, but came to bear witness to the light.

The True Light [1:9–13]

The true light that enlightens every man was coming into the world. He was in the world, and the world was made through him, yet the world knew him not. He came to his own home, and his own people received him not. But to all who received him, who believed in his name, he gave power to become children of God; who were born,

aOr was not anything made. That which has been made was life in him

not of blood nor of the will of the flesh nor of the will of man, but of God.

The Word Made Flesh [1:14-18]

And the Word became flesh and dwelt among us, full of grace and truth; we have beheld his glory, glory as of the only Son from the Father. (John bore witness to him, and cried, "This was he of whom I said, 'He who comes after me ranks before me, for he was before me.'") And from his fulness have we all received, grace upon grace. For the law was given through Moses; grace and truth came through Jesus Christ. No one has ever seen God; the only Son,*b* who is in the bosom of the Father, he has made him known.

bOther ancient authorities read God

The Testimony of John the Baptist

[1:19–28]

And this is the testimony of John, when the Jews sent priests and Levites from Jerusalem to ask him, "Who are you?" He confessed, he did not deny, but confessed, "I am not the Christ." And they asked him, "What then? Are you Eli'jah?" He said, "I am not." "Are you the prophet?" And he answered, "No." They said to him then, "Who are you? Let us have an answer for those who sent us. What do you say about yourself?" He said, "I am the voice of one crying in the wilderness, 'Make straight the way of the Lord,' as the prophet Isai'ah said."[1]

Now they had been sent from the Phar'isees. They asked him, "Then why are you baptizing, if you are neither the Christ, nor Eli'jah, nor the prophet?" John answered them, "I baptize with water; but among you stands one whom you do not know, even he who comes after me, the thong of whose sandal I am not worthy to untie." This took place in Beth'any beyond the Jordan, where John was baptizing.

[1]*Isaiah 40:3*

99

"Behold, the Lamb of God" [1:29-34]

The next day he saw Jesus coming toward him, and said, "Behold, the Lamb of God, who takes away the sin of the world! This is he of whom I said, 'After me comes a man who ranks before me, for he was before me.' I myself did not know him; but for this I came baptizing with water, that he might be revealed to Israel." And John bore witness, "I saw the Spirit descend as a dove from heaven, and it remained on him. I myself did not know him; but he who sent me to baptize with water said to me, 'He on whom you see the Spirit descend and remain, this is he who baptizes with the Holy Spirit.' And I have seen and have borne witness that this is the Son of God."

The First Disciples [1:35-42]

The next day again John was standing with two of his disciples; and he looked at Jesus as he walked, and said, "Behold, the Lamb of God!" The two disciples heard him say this, and they followed Jesus. Jesus turned, and saw them following, and said to them, "What do you seek?" And they said to him, "Rabbi" (which means Teacher), "where are you staying?" He said to them, "Come and see." They came and saw where he was staying; and they stayed with him that day, for it was about the tenth hour. One of the two who heard John speak, and followed him, was Andrew, Simon Peter's brother. He first found his brother Simon, and said to him, "We have found the Messi'ah" (which means Christ). He brought him to Jesus. Jesus looked at him, and said, "So you are Simon the son of John? You shall be called Cephas" (which means Peter[c]).

[c]From the word for *rock* in Aramaic and Greek respectively

In the wilderness of Judea

Three Lions

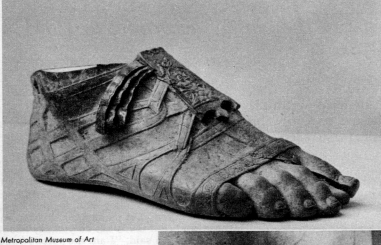

Metropolitan Museum of Art

Two types of sandals and thongs worn in New Testament times; the feet shown are from Graeco-Roman statues

A. Dönmez

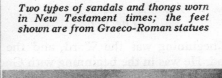

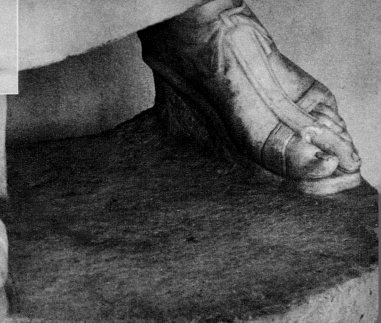

Fig tree, with first figs in early spring

Matson Photo Service

Down a path in the modern town of Nazareth

Matson Photo Service

Jack Finegan

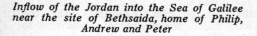

Inflow of the Jordan into the Sea of Galilee near the site of Bethsaida, home of Philip, Andrew and Peter

The Calling of Philip and Nathanael

[1:43–51]

The next day Jesus decided to go to Gal'-ilee. And he found Philip and said to him, "Follow me." Now Philip was from Beth-sa'ida, the city of Andrew and Peter. Philip found Nathan'a-el, and said to him, "We have found him of whom Moses in the law and also the prophets wrote, Jesus of Naz'-areth, the son of Joseph." Nathan'a-el said to him, "Can anything good come out of Naz'areth?" Philip said to him, "Come and see." Jesus saw Nathan'a-el coming to him, and said of him, "Behold, an Israelite indeed, in whom is no guile!" Nathan'a-el said to him, "How do you know me?" Jesus answered him, "Before Philip called you, when you were under the fig tree, I saw you." Nathan'a-el answered him, "Rabbi, you are the Son of God! You are the King of Israel!" Jesus answered him, "Because I said to you, I saw you under the fig tree, do you believe? You shall see greater things than these." And he said to him, "Truly, truly, I say to you, you will see heaven opened, and the angels of God ascending and descending upon the Son of man."

101

Kefr Kenna, traditional Cana of Galilee

A walled spring at the traditional Cana

A Wedding at Cana [John 2:1-12]

ON the third day there was a marriage at Cana in Gal'ilee, and the mother of Jesus was there; Jesus also was invited to the marriage, with his disciples. When the wine failed, the mother of Jesus said to him, "They have no wine." And Jesus said

A jar from the Dead Sea scroll cave, with an accompanying lid

The modern Greek church which commemorates the miracle of Christ at the marriage in Cana

By the Sea of Galilee

L. A. Fereday

to her, "O woman, what have you to do with me? My hour has not yet come." His mother said to the servants, "Do whatever he tells you." Now six stone jars were standing there, for the Jewish rites of purification, each holding twenty or thirty gallons. Jesus said to them, "Fill the jars with water." And they filled them up to the brim. He said to them, "Now draw some out, and take it to the steward of the feast." So they took it. When the steward of the feast tasted the water now become wine, and did not know where it came from (though the servants who had drawn the water knew), the steward of the feast called the bridegroom and said to him, "Every man serves the good wine first; and when men have drunk freely, then the poor wine; but you have kept the good wine until now." This, the first of his signs, Jesus did at Cana in Gal'ilee, and manifested his glory; and his disciples believed in him.

After this he went down to Caper'na-um, with his mother and his brothers and his disciples; and there they stayed for a few days.

103

The Temple of Jesus' time was destroyed by Titus in A.D. 70. The octagonal mosque in the center of the picture, known as the Dome of the Rock, was begun in A.D. 691 and covers the rock of the ancient Temple

Cleansing the Temple [2:13-25]

The Passover of the Jews was at hand, and Jesus went up to Jerusalem. In the temple he found those who were selling oxen and sheep and pigeons, and the money-changers at their business. And making a whip of cords, he drove them all, with the sheep and oxen, out of the temple; and he poured out the coins of the money-changers and overturned their tables. And he told those who sold the pigeons, "Take these things away; you shall not make my Father's house a house of trade." His disciples remembered that it was written, "Zeal for thy house will consume me."[2] The Jews then said to him, "What sign have you to show us for doing this?" Jesus answered them, "Destroy this temple, and in three days I will raise it up." The Jews then said, "It has taken forty-six years to build this temple, and will you raise it up in three days?" But he spoke of the temple of his body. When therefore he was raised from the dead, his disciples remembered that he had said this; and they believed the scripture and the word which Jesus had spoken.

Now when he was in Jerusalem at the Passover feast, many believed in his name when they saw the signs which he did; but Jesus did not trust himself to them, because he knew all men and needed no one to bear witness of man; for he himself knew what was in man.

[2]*Psalms 69:9*

Interview with Nicodemus [John 3:1-15]

NOW there was a man of the Phar'isees, named Nicode'mus, a ruler of the Jews. This man came to Jesus[d] by night and said to him, "Rabbi, we know that you are a teacher come from God; for no one can do these signs that you do, unless God is with him." Jesus answered him, "Truly, truly, I say to you, unless one is born anew,[e] he cannot see the kingdom of God." Nicode'mus said to him, "How can a man be born when he is old? Can he enter a second time into his mother's womb and be born?" Jesus answered, "Truly, truly, I say to you, unless one is born of water and the Spirit, he cannot enter the kingdom of God. That which is born of the flesh is flesh, and that which is born of the Spirit is spirit.[f] Do not marvel that I said to you, 'You must be born anew.'[e] The wind[f] blows where it wills, and you hear the sound of it, but you do not know whence it comes or whither it goes; so it is with every one who is born of the Spirit." Nicode'mus said to him, "How can this be?" Jesus answered him, "Are you a teacher of Israel, and yet you do not understand this? Truly, truly, I say to you, we speak of what we know, and bear wit-

[d]Greek *him*

[e]Or *from above*

[f]The same Greek word means both *wind* and *spirit*

ness to what we have seen; but you do not receive our testimony. If I have told you earthly things and you do not believe, how can you believe if I tell you heavenly things? No one has ascended into heaven but he who descended from heaven, the Son of man.[g] And as Moses lifted up the serpent in the wilderness, so must the Son of man be lifted up, that whoever believes in him may have eternal life."[h]

God so Loved the World [3:16-21]

For God so loved the world that he gave his only Son, that whoever believes in him should not perish but have eternal life. For God sent the Son into the world, not to condemn the world, but that the world might be saved through him. He who believes in him is not condemned; he who does not believe is condemned already, because he has not believed in the name of the only Son of God. And this is the judgment, that the light has come into the world, and men loved darkness rather than light, because their deeds were evil. For every one who does evil hates the light, and does not come to the light, lest his deeds should be exposed. But he who does what is true comes to the light, that it may be clearly seen that his deeds have been wrought in God.

[g]Other ancient authorities add *who is in heaven*

[h]Some interpreters hold that the quotation continues through verse 21

"He Must Increase, but I Must Decrease" [3:22-30]

After this Jesus and his disciples went into the land of Jude'a; there he remained with them and baptized. John also was baptizing at Ae'non near Salim, because there was much water there; and people came and were baptized. For John had not yet been put in prison.

Now a discussion arose between John's disciples and a Jew over purifying. And they came to John, and said to him, "Rabbi, he who was with you beyond the Jordan, to whom you bore witness, here he is, baptizing, and all are going to him." John answered, "No one can receive anything except what is given him from heaven. You yourselves bear me witness, that I said, I am not the Christ, but I have been sent before him. He who has the bride is the bridegroom; the friend of the bridegroom, who stands and hears him, rejoices greatly at the bridegroom's voice; therefore this joy of mine is now full. He must increase, but I must decrease."[i]

Eternal Life through the Son [3:31-36]

He who comes from above is above all; he who is of the earth belongs to the earth, and of the earth he speaks; he who comes from heaven is above all. He bears witness to what he has seen and heard, yet no one receives his testimony; he who receives his testimony sets his seal to this, that God is true. For he whom God has sent utters the words of God, for it is not by measure that he gives the Spirit; the Father loves the Son, and has given all things into his hand. He who believes in the Son has eternal life; he who does not obey the Son shall not see life, but the wrath of God rests upon him.

[i]Some interpreters hold that the quotation continues through verse 36

Going through a Jerusalem street

The Pool of the Sultan outside the walls of Jerusalem is the site of a cattle market

Excavated mound at Balata, ancient Shechem

Matson Photo Service

Jesus at Jacob's Well [John 4:1-6]

NOW when the Lord knew that the Phar'isees had heard that Jesus was making and baptizing more disciples than John (although Jesus himself did not baptize, but only his disciples), he left Jude'a and departed again to Gal'ilee. He had to pass through Samar'ia. So he came to a city of Samar'ia, called Sychar, near the field that Jacob gave to his son Joseph. Jacob's well was there, and so Jesus, wearied as he was with his journey, sat down beside the well. It was about the sixth hour.

Matson Photo Service

Site of traditional Jacob's Well

The Woman of Samaria [4:7-15]

There came a woman of Samar'ia to draw water. Jesus said to her, "Give me a drink." For his disciples had gone away into the city to buy food. The Samar'itan woman said to him, "How is it that you, a Jew, ask a drink of me, a woman of Samar'ia?" For Jews have no dealings with Samar'itans. Jesus answered her, "If you knew the gift of God, and who it is that is saying to you, 'Give me a drink,' you would have asked him, and he would have given you living

Modern Askar, often identified with Sychar

Matson Photo Service

water." The woman said to him, "Sir, you have nothing to draw with, and the well is deep; where do you get that living water? Are you greater than our father Jacob, who gave us the well, and drank from it himself, and his sons, and his cattle?" Jesus said to her, "Every one who drinks of this water will thirst again, but whoever drinks of the water that I shall give him will never thirst; the water that I shall give him will become in him a spring of water welling up to eternal life." The woman said to him, "Sir, give me this water, that I may not thirst, nor come here to draw."

"God Is Spirit" [4:16-26]

Jesus said to her, "Go, call your husband, and come here." The woman answered him, "I have no husband." Jesus said to her, "You are right in saying, 'I have no husband'; for you have had five husbands, and he whom you now have is not your husband; this you said truly." The woman said to him, "Sir, I perceive that you are a prophet. Our fathers worshiped on this mountain; and you say that in Jerusalem is the place where men ought to worship." Jesus said to her, "Woman, believe me, the hour is coming when neither on this mountain nor in Jerusalem will you worship the Father. You worship what you do not know; we worship what we know, for salvation is from the Jews. But the hour is coming, and now is, when the true worshipers will worship the Father in spirit and truth, for such the Father seeks to worship him. God is spirit, and those who worship him must worship in spirit and truth." The woman said to him, "I know that Messi'ah is coming (he who is called Christ); when he comes, he will show us all things." Jesus said to her, "I who speak to you am he."

"Can This Be the Christ?" [4:27-30]

Just then his disciples came. They marveled that he was talking with a woman, but none said, "What do you wish?" or, "Why are you talking with her?" So the woman left her water jar, and went away into the city, and said to the people, "Come, see a man who told me all that I ever did. Can this be the Christ?" They went out of the city and were coming to him.

106

Young wheat

"The fields are already white for harvest"

Fields White for Harvest [4:31-38]

Meanwhile the disciples besought him, saying, "Rabbi, eat." But he said to them, "I have food to eat of which you do not know." So the disciples said to one another, "Has any one brought him food?" Jesus said to them, "My food is to do the will of him who sent me, and to accomplish his work. Do you not say, 'There are yet four months, then comes the harvest'? I tell you, lift up your eyes, and see how the fields are already white for harvest. He who reaps receives wages, and gathers fruit for eternal life, so that sower and reaper may rejoice together. For here the saying holds true, 'One sows and another reaps.'[3] I sent you to reap that for which you did not labor; others have labored, and you have entered into their labor."

Many Samaritans Believe [4:39-42]

Many Samar'itans from that city believed in him because of the woman's testimony, "He told me all that I ever did." So when the Samar'itans came to him, they asked him to stay with them; and he stayed there two days. And many more believed because of his word. They said to the woman, "It is no longer because of your words that we believe, for we have heard for ourselves, and we know that this is indeed the Savior of the world."

Jesus Returns to Galilee [4:43-45]

After the two days he departed to Gal'ilee. For Jesus himself testified that a prophet has no honor in his own country. So when he came to Gal'ilee, the Galile'ans welcomed him, having seen all that he had done in Jerusalem at the feast, for they too had gone to the feast.

[3]Job 31:8; Micah 6:15

Samaritan observance of the Pass-over on Mount Gerizim in accord-ance with very ancient ceremonial

An Official's Son Healed [4:46-54]

So he came again to Cana in Gal'ilee, where he had made the water wine. And at Caper'na-um there was an official whose son was ill. When he heard that Jesus had come from Jude'a to Gal'ilee, he went and begged him to come down and heal his son, for he was at the point of death. Jesus therefore said to him, "Unless you see signs and wonders you will not believe." The official said to him, "Sir, come down before my child dies." Jesus said to him, "Go; your son will live." The man believed the word that Jesus spoke to him and went his way. As he was going down, his servants met him and told him that his son was living. So he asked them the hour when he began to mend, and they said to him, "Yesterday at the seventh hour the fever left him." The father knew that was the hour when Jesus had said to him, "Your son will live"; and he himself believed, and all his household. This was now the second sign that Jesus did when he had come from Jude'a to Gal'ilee.

The Samaritan Scroll of the Law, containing the Pentateuch and dating from the Middle Ages

Donald McLeish, London

It is so natural for shepherds to bring sheep to a certain city gate that in ancient Jerusalem one of the entrances was known as the Sheep Gate. Shown here is the Damascus Gate in the present north wall of Jerusalem. The ancient Sheep Gate may have been in the east wall near where St. Stephen's Gate now is

The Healing at the Pool [John 5:1-9a]

AFTER this there was a feast of the Jews, and Jesus went up to Jerusalem. Now there is in Jerusalem by the Sheep Gate a pool, in Hebrew called Beth-za'tha,[i] which has five porticoes. In these lay a multitude of invalids, blind, lame, paralyzed.[k] One man was there, who had been ill for thirty-eight years. When Jesus saw him and knew that he had been lying there a long time, he said to him, "Do you want to be healed?" The sick man answered him, "Sir, I have no man to put me into the pool when the water is troubled, and while I am going another steps down before me." Jesus said to him, "Rise, take up your pallet, and walk." And at once the man was healed, and he took up his pallet and walked.

[i]Other ancient authorities read *Bethesda*, others *Bethsaida*

[k]Other ancient authorities insert, wholly or in part, *waiting for the moving of the water; for an angel of the Lord went down at certain seasons into the pool, and troubled the water: whoever stepped in first after the troubling of the water was healed of whatever disease he had*

Breaking the Sabbath

[5:9b-18]

Now that day was the sabbath. So the Jews said to the man who was cured, "It is the sabbath, it is not lawful for you to carry your pallet." But he answered them, "The man who healed me said to me, 'Take up your pallet, and walk.' " They asked him, "Who is the man who said to you, 'Take up your pallet, and walk'?" Now the man who had been healed did not know who it was, for Jesus had withdrawn, as there was a crowd in the place. Afterward, Jesus found him in the temple, and said to him, "See, you are well! Sin no more, that nothing worse befall you." The man went away and told the Jews that it was Jesus who had healed him. And this was why the Jews persecuted Jesus, because he did this on the sabbath. But Jesus answered them, "My Father is working still, and I am working." This was why the Jews sought all the more to kill him, because he not only broke the sabbath but also called God his Father, making himself equal with God.

"The Son Gives Life" [5:19-24]

Jesus said to them, "Truly, truly, I say to you, the Son can do nothing of his own accord, but only what he sees the Father doing; for whatever he does, that the Son does likewise. For the Father loves the Son, and shows him all that he himself is doing; and greater works than these will he show him, that you may marvel. For as the Father raises the dead and gives them life, so also the Son gives life to whom he will. The Father judges no one, but has given all judgment to the Son, that all may honor the Son, even as they honor the Father. He who does not honor the Son does not honor the Father who sent him. Truly, truly, I say to you, he who hears my word and believes him who sent me, has eternal life; he does not come into judgment, but has passed from death to life.

Authority to Execute Judgment [5:25-29]

"Truly, truly, I say to you, the hour is coming, and now is, when the dead will hear the voice of the Son of God, and those

The Pool of Bethzatha or Bethesda, believed in early Christian times to be the site of the miracle

The Church of St. Anne, dating from the time of the Crusades and commemorating the miracle of the Pool of Bethzatha

who hear will live. For as the Father has life in himself, so he has granted the Son also to have life in himself, and has given him authority to execute judgment, because he is the Son of man. Do not marvel at this; for the hour is coming when all who are in the tombs will hear his voice and come forth, those who have done good, to the resurrection of life, and those who have done evil, to the resurrection of judgment.

Witnesses to Jesus [5:30–47]

"I can do nothing on my own authority; as I hear, I judge; and my judgment is just, because I seek not my own will but the will of him who sent me. If I bear witness to myself, my testimony is not true; there is

another who bears witness to me, and I know that the testimony which he bears to me is true. You sent to John, and he has borne witness to the truth. Not that the testimony which I receive is from man; but I say this that you may be saved. He was a burning and shining lamp, and you were willing to rejoice for a while in his light. But the testimony which I have is greater than that of John; for the works which the Father has granted me to accomplish, these very works which I am doing, bear me witness that the Father has sent me. And the Father who sent me has himself borne witness to me. His voice you have never heard, his form you have never seen; and you do not have his word abiding in you, for you do not believe him whom he has sent. You

search the scriptures, because you think that in them you have eternal life; and it is they that bear witness to me; yet you refuse to come to me that you may have life. I do not receive glory from men. But I know that you have not the love of God within you. I have come in my Father's name, and you do not receive me; if another comes in his own name, him you will receive. How can you believe, who receive glory from one another and do not seek the glory that comes from the only God? Do not think that I shall accuse you to the Father; it is Moses who accuses you, on whom you set your hope. If you believed Moses, you would believe me, for he wrote of me. But if you do not believe his writings, how will you believe my words?"

Combine Photos

L. Kofod

Village oven

Selling bread in the market

The Feeding of the Five Thousand

[John 6:1-15]

AFTER this Jesus went to the other side of the Sea of Gal'ilee, which is the Sea of Tiber'i-as. And a multitude followed him, because they saw the signs which he did on those who were diseased. Jesus went up into the hills, and there sat down with his disciples. Now the Passover, the feast of the Jews, was at hand. Lifting up his eyes, then, and seeing that a multitude was coming to him, Jesus said to Philip, "How are we to buy bread, so that these people may eat?" This he said to test him, for he himself knew what he would do. Philip answered him, "Two hundred denarii[1] would not buy enough bread for each of them to get a little." One of his disciples, Andrew, Simon Peter's brother, said to him, "There is a lad here who has five barley loaves and two fish; but what are they among so many?" Jesus said, "Make the people sit down." Now there was much grass in the place; so the men sat down, in number about five thousand. Jesus then took the loaves, and when he had given thanks, he distributed them to those who were seated; so also the fish, as much as they wanted. And when they had eaten their fill, he told his disciples, "Gather up the fragments left over, that nothing may be lost." So they gathered them up and filled twelve baskets with fragments from the five barley loaves, left by those who had eaten. When the people saw the sign which he had done, they said, "This is indeed the prophet who is to come into the world!"

Perceiving then that they were about to come and take him by force to make him king, Jesus withdrew again to the hills by himself.

Jesus Walks on the Sea [6:16-24]

When evening came, his disciples went down to the sea, got into a boat, and started across the sea to Caper'na-um. It was now dark, and Jesus had not yet come to them.

[1]The denarius was worth about twenty cents

The sea rose because a strong wind was blowing. When they had rowed about three or four miles,[m] they saw Jesus walking on the sea and drawing near to the boat. They were frightened, but he said to them, "It is I; do not be afraid." Then they were glad to take him into the boat, and immediately the boat was at the land to which they were going.

On the next day the people who remained on the other side of the sea saw that there had been only one boat there, and that Jesus had not entered the boat with his disciples, but that his disciples had gone away alone. However, boats from Tiber'i-as came near the place where they ate the bread after the Lord had given thanks. So when the people saw that Jesus was not there, nor his disciples, they themselves got into the boats and went to Caper'na-um, seeking Jesus.

The True Bread from Heaven [6:25-34]

When they found him on the other side of the sea, they said to him, "Rabbi, when did you come here?" Jesus answered them, "Truly, truly, I say to you, you seek me, not because you saw signs, but because you ate your fill of the loaves. Do not labor for the food which perishes, but for the food which endures to eternal life, which the Son of man will give to you; for on him has God the Father set his seal." Then they said to him, "What must we do, to be doing the works of God?" Jesus answered them, "This is the work of God, that you believe in him whom he has sent." So they said to him, "Then what sign do you do, that we may see, and believe you? What work do you perform? Our fathers ate the manna in the wilderness; as it is written, 'He gave them bread from heaven to eat.' "[4] Jesus then said to them, "Truly, truly, I say to you, it was not Moses who gave you the bread from heaven; my Father gives you the true bread from heaven. For the bread of God is that which comes down from heaven, and gives life to

[m]Greek *twenty-five or thirty stadia*

[4]*Exodus* 16:4, 15; *Numbers* 11:8; *Nehemiah* 9:15; *Psalms* 78:24; 105:40

the world." They said to him, "Lord, give us this bread always."

Jesus the Bread of Life [6:35-40]

Jesus said to them, "I am the bread of life; he who comes to me shall not hunger, and he who believes in me shall never thirst. But I said to you that you have seen me and yet do not believe. All that the Father gives me will come to me; and him who comes to me I will not cast out. For I have come down from heaven, not to do my own will, but the will of him who sent me; and this is the will of him who sent me, that I should lose nothing of all that he has given me, but raise it up at the last day. For this is the will of my Father, that every one who sees the Son and believes in him should have eternal life; and I will raise him up at the last day."

The Jews Murmur at Jesus [6:41-51]

The Jews then murmured at him, because he said, "I am the bread which came down from heaven." They said, "Is not this Jesus, the son of Joseph, whose father and mother we know? How does he now say, 'I have come down from heaven'?" Jesus answered them, "Do not murmur among yourselves. No one can come to me unless the Father who sent me draws him; and I will raise him up at the last day. It is written in the prophets, 'And they shall all be taught by God.'[5] Every one who has heard and learned from the Father comes to me. Not that any one has seen the Father except him who is from God; he has seen the Father. Truly, truly, I say to you, he who believes has eternal life. I am the bread of life. Your fathers ate the manna in the wilderness, and they died. This is the bread which comes down from heaven, that a man may eat of it and not die. I am the living bread which came down from heaven; if any one eats of this bread, he will live for ever; and the bread which I shall give for the life of the world is my flesh."

[5]*Isaiah* 54:13

Early morning on the Sea of Galilee

"My Flesh Is Food Indeed" [6:52–59]

The Jews then disputed among themselves, saying, "How can this man give us his flesh to eat?" So Jesus said to them, "Truly, truly, I say to you, unless you eat the flesh of the Son of man and drink his blood, you have no life in you; he who eats my flesh and drinks my blood has eternal life, and I will raise him up at the last day. For my flesh is food indeed, and my blood is drink indeed. He who eats my flesh and drinks my blood abides in me, and I in him. As the living Father sent me, and I live because of the Father, so he who eats me will live because of me. This is the bread which came down from heaven, not such as the fathers ate and died; he who eats this bread will live for ever." This he said in the synagogue, as he taught at Caper'na-um.

The Spirit Gives Life [6:60–65]

Many of his disciples, when they heard it, said, "This is a hard saying; who can listen to it?" But Jesus, knowing in himself that his disciples murmured at it, said to them, "Do you take offense at this? Then what if you were to see the Son of man ascending where he was before? It is the spirit that gives life, the flesh is of no avail; the words that I have spoken to you are spirit and life. But there are some of you that do not believe." For Jesus knew from the first who those were that did not believe, and who it was that should betray him. And he said, "This is why I told you that no one can come to me unless it is granted him by the Father."

The Words of Eternal Life [6:66–71]

After this many of his disciples drew back and no longer went about with him. Jesus said to the twelve, "Will you also go away?" Simon Peter answered him, "Lord, to whom shall we go? You have the words of eternal life; and we have believed, and have come to know, that you are the Holy One of God." Jesus answered them, "Did I not choose you, the twelve, and one of you is a devil?" He spoke of Judas the son of Simon Iscar'iot, for he, one of the twelve, was to betray him.

Tiberias on the Sea of Galilee, named by Herod Antipas in honor of Emperor Tiberius

111

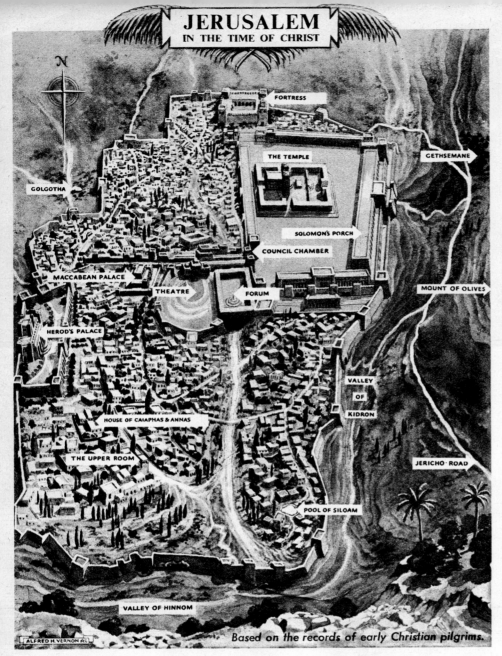

JERUSALEM
IN THE TIME OF CHRIST

FORTRESS

THE TEMPLE

GOLGOTHA

GETHSEMANE

SOLOMON'S PORCH

COUNCIL CHAMBER

MACCABEAN PALACE

THEATRE

FORUM

MOUNT OF OLIVES

HEROD'S PALACE

VALLEY OF KIDRON

HOUSE OF CAIAPHAS & ANNAS

THE UPPER ROOM

JERICHO·ROAD

POOL OF SILOAM

VALLEY OF HINNOM

ALFRED H. VERNON del.

Based on the records of early Christian pilgrims.

These Bokharan Jews are celebrating the Feast of Tabernacles in Jerusalem. Symbols of the feast are the lulab or palm branch, and the ethrog or citron

The Unbelief of Jesus' Brothers
[John 7:1–9]

AFTER this Jesus went about in Gal'ilee; he would not go about in Jude'a, because the Jews[n] sought to kill him. Now the Jews' feast of Tabernacles was at hand. So his brothers said to him, "Leave here and go to Jude'a, that your disciples may see the works you are doing. For no man works in secret if he seeks to be known openly. If you do these things, show yourself to the world." For even his brothers did not believe in him. Jesus said to them, "My time has not yet come, but your time is always here. The world cannot hate you, but it hates me because I testify of it that its works are evil. Go to the feast yourselves; I am not[o] going up to this feast, for my time has not yet fully come." So saying, he remained in Gal'ilee.

Jesus at the Feast of Tabernacles
[7:10–13]

But after his brothers had gone up to the feast, then he also went up, not publicly, but in private. The Jews were looking for him at the feast, and saying, "Where is he?" And there was much muttering about him among the people. While some said, "He is a good man," others said, "No, he is leading the people astray." Yet for fear of the Jews no one spoke openly of him.

Teaching in the Temple [7:14–24]

About the middle of the feast Jesus went up into the temple and taught. The Jews marveled at it, saying, "How is it that this man has learning,[p] when he has never studied?" So Jesus answered them, "My teaching is not mine, but his who sent me; if any man's will is to do his will, he shall know whether the teaching is from God or whether I am speaking on my own authority. He who speaks on his own authority seeks his own glory; but he who seeks the glory of him who sent him is true, and in him there is no falsehood. Did not Moses give you the law? Yet none of you keeps the law. Why do you seek to kill me?" The people answered, "You have a demon! Who is seeking to kill you?" Jesus answered them, "I did one deed, and you all marvel at it. Moses gave you circumcision (not that it is from Moses, but from the fathers), and you circumcise a man upon the sabbath. If on the sabbath a man receives circumcision, so that the law of Moses may not be broken, are you angry with me because on the sabbath I made a man's whole body well? Do not judge by appearances, but judge with right judgment."

Is This the Christ? [7:25–31]

Some of the people of Jerusalem therefore said, "Is not this the man whom they seek to kill? And here he is, speaking openly, and they say nothing to him! Can it be that the authorities really know that this is the Christ? Yet we know where this man comes from; and when the Christ appears, no one will know where he comes from." So Jesus proclaimed, as he taught in the temple, "You know me, and you know where I come

[n]Or *Judeans*

[o]Other ancient authorities add *yet*

[p]Or *this man knows his letters*

from? But I have not come of my own accord; he who sent me is true, and him you do not know. I know him, for I come from him, and he sent me." So they sought to arrest him; but no one laid hands on him, because his hour had not yet come. Yet many of the people believed him; they said, "When the Christ appears, will he do more signs than this man has done?"

Officers Sent To Arrest Jesus [7:32-36]

The Phar'isees heard the crowd thus muttering about him, and the chief priests and Phar'isees sent officers to arrest him. Jesus then said, "I shall be with you a little longer, and then I go to him who sent me; you will seek me and you will not find me; where I am you cannot come." The Jews said to one another, "Where does this man intend to go that we shall not find him? Does he intend to go to the Dispersion among the Greeks and teach the Greeks? What does he mean by saying, 'You will seek me and you will not find me,' and, 'Where I am you cannot come'?"

Rivers of Living Water [7:37-39]

On the last day of the feast, the great day, Jesus stood up and proclaimed, "If any one thirst, let him come to me and drink. He who believes in me, as*q* the scripture has said, 'Out of his heart shall flow rivers of

qOr let him come to me, and let him who believes in me drink. As

living water.' "[6] Now this he said about the Spirit, which those who believed in him were to receive; for as yet the Spirit had not been given, because Jesus was not yet glorified.

Division among the People [7:40-44]

When they heard these words, some of the people said, "This is really the prophet." Others said, "This is the Christ." But some said, "Is the Christ to come from Gal'ilee? Has not the scripture said that the Christ is descended from David, and comes from Beth'lehem, the village where David was?" So there was a division among the people over him. Some of them wanted to arrest him, but no one laid hands on him.

No Man Ever Spoke like This Man [7:45-52]

The officers then went back to the chief priests and Phar'isees, who said to them, "Why did you not bring him?" The officers answered, "No man ever spoke like this man!" The Phar'isees answered them, "Are you led astray, you also? Have any of the authorities or of the Phar'isees believed in him? But this crowd, who do not know the law, are accursed." Nicode'mus, who had gone to him before, and who was one of them, said to them, "Does our law judge a man without first giving him a hearing and learning what he does?" They replied, "Are

6Isaiah 44:3; 55:1; 58:11

you from Gal'ilee too? Search and you will see that no prophet is to rise from Gal'ilee."[r]

rOther ancient authorities add 7:53—8:11 either here or at the end of this gospel or after Luke 21:38, with variations of the text:

They went each to his own house, but Jesus went to the Mount of Olives. Early in the morning he came again to the temple; all the people came to him, and he sat down and taught them. The scribes and the Pharisees brought a woman who had been caught in adultery, and placing her in the midst they said to him, "Teacher, this woman has been caught in the act of adultery. Now in the law Moses commanded us to stone such. What do you say about her?" This they said to test him, that they might have some charge to bring against him. Jesus bent down and wrote with his finger on the ground. And as they continued to ask him, he stood up and said to them, "Let him who is without sin among you be the first to throw a stone at her." And once more he bent down and wrote with his finger on the ground. But when they heard it, they went away, one by one, beginning with the eldest, and Jesus was left alone with the woman standing before him. Jesus looked up and said to her, "Woman, where are they? Has no one condemned you?" She said, "No one, Lord." And Jesus said, "Neither do I condemn you; go, and do not sin again."

The traditional place of the giving of the Law is Jebel Musa, the Mountain of Moses, on the peninsula of Sinai. This photograph is taken from Jebel Musa looking northwest toward the Ras es-Safsaf, or Mountain of the Willow

The old Monastery of Saint Catherine lies in the valley at the foot of Mount Sinai

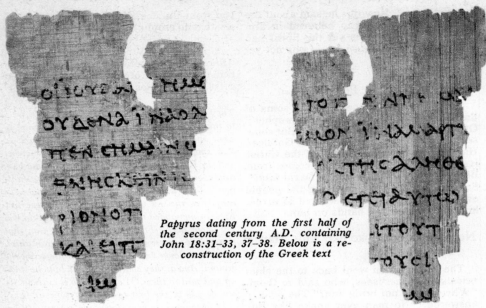

Papyrus dating from the first half of the second century A.D. containing John 18:31–33, 37–38. Below is a reconstruction of the Greek text

The John Rylands Library, Manchester

Recto.

οι ϊουδαιοι ημε ιν ουκ εξεστιν αποκτειναι   xviii. 31
ουδενα ϊνα ο λογος του ιησου πληρωθη ον ει   32
πεν σημαινω ν ποιω θανατω ημελλεν απο
θνησκειν ισ ηλθεν ουν παλιν εις το πραιτω   33
5 ριον ο π ιλατος και εφωνησεν τον ιησουν
και ειπ εν αυτω συ ει ο βασιλευς των ιου   34
δ αιω ν απεκριθη ιησους κτλ.

Verso.

εγω εις το υτο γ ε γεννημαι   37
και (εις τουτο) εληλυθα εις τον κο σμον ϊνα μαρτυ
10 ρησω τη αληθεια πας ο ων εκ της αληθε ι
ας ακουει μου της φωνης λεγει αυτω   38
ο πιλατος τι εστιν αληθεια κ αι τουτο
ειπων παλιν εξηλθεν προς τους ιου
δαιους και λεγει αυτοις εγω ουδ εμι αν

Jesus the Light of the World
[John 8:12–20]

AGAIN Jesus spoke to them, saying, "I am the light of the world; he who follows me will not walk in darkness, but will have the light of life." The Phar′isees then said to him, "You are bearing witness to yourself; your testimony is not true." Jesus answered, "Even if I do bear witness to myself, my testimony is true, for I know whence I have come and whither I am going, but you do not know whence I come or whither I am going. You judge according to the flesh, I judge no one. Yet even if I do judge, my judgment is true, for it is not I alone that judge, but I and he[a] who sent me. In your law it is written that the testimony of two men is true; I bear witness to myself, and the Father who sent me bears witness to me." They said to him therefore, "Where is your Father?" Jesus answered, "You know neither me nor my Father; if you knew me, you would know my Father also." These words he spoke in the treasury, as he taught in the temple; but no one arrested him, because his hour had not yet come.

"Where I Am Going, You Cannot Come" [8:21–30]

Again he said to them, "I go away, and you will seek me and die in your sin; where I am going, you cannot come." Then said the Jews, "Will he kill himself, since he says, 'Where I am going, you cannot come'?" He said to them, "You are from below, I am from above; you are of this world, I am not of this world. I told you that you would die in your sins, for you will die in your sins unless you believe that I am he." They said to him, "Who are you?" Jesus said to them, "Even what I have told you from the beginning.[b] I have much to say about you and

[a]Other ancient authorities read *the Father*

[b]Or *Why do I talk to you at all?*

much to judge; but he who sent me is true, and I declare to the world what I have heard from him." They did not understand that he spoke to them of the Father. So Jesus said, "When you have lifted up the Son of man, then you will know that I am he, and that I do nothing on my own authority but speak thus as the Father taught me. And he who sent me is with me; he has not left me alone, for I always do what is pleasing to him." As he spoke thus, many believed in him.

"The Truth Will Make You Free"
[8:31–38]

Jesus then said to the Jews who had believed in him, "If you continue in my word, you are truly my disciples, and you will know the truth, and the truth will make you free." They answered him, "We are descendants of Abraham, and have never been in bondage to any one. How is it that you say, 'You will be made free'?" Jesus answered them, "Truly, truly, I say to you, every one who commits sin is a slave to sin. The slave does not continue in the house for ever; the son continues for ever. So if the Son makes you free, you will be free indeed. I know that you are descendants of Abraham; yet you seek to kill me, because my word finds no place in you. I speak of what I have seen with my Father, and you do what you have heard from your father."

Children of the Devil [8:39–47]

They answered him, "Abraham is our father." Jesus said to them, "If you were Abraham's children, you would do what Abraham did, but now you seek to kill me, a man who has told you the truth which I heard from God; this is not what Abraham did. You do what your father did." They said to him, "We were not born of fornication; we have one Father, even God." Jesus said to them, "If God were your Father, you would love me, for I proceeded and came forth from God; I came not of my own accord, but he sent me. Why do you not understand what I say? It is because you cannot bear to hear my word. You are of your father the devil, and your will is to do your father's desires. He was a murderer from the beginning, and has nothing to do with the truth, because there is no truth in him. When he lies, he speaks according to his own nature, for he is a liar and the father of lies. But, because I tell the truth, you do not believe me. Which of you convicts me of sin? If I tell the truth, why do you not believe me? He who is of God hears the words of God; the reason why you do not hear them is that you are not of God."

"Before Abraham Was, I Am"
[8:48–59]

The Jews answered him, "Are we not right in saying that you are a Samar′itan and have a demon?" Jesus answered, "I have not a demon; but I honor my Father, and you dishonor me. Yet I do not seek my own glory; there is One who seeks it and he will be the judge. Truly, truly, I say to you, if any one keeps my word, he will never see death." The Jews said to him, "Now we know that you have a demon. Abraham died, as did the prophets; and you say, 'If any one keeps my word, he will never taste death.' Are you greater than our father

Abraham, who died? And the prophets died! Who do you claim to be?" Jesus answered, "If I glorify myself, my glory is nothing; it is my Father who glorifies me, of whom you say that he is your God. But you have not known him; I know him. If I said, I do not know him, I should be a liar like you; but I do know him and I keep his word. Your father Abraham rejoiced that he was to see my day; he saw it and was glad." The Jews then said to him, "You are not yet fifty years old, and have you seen Abraham?"ᵘ Jesus said to them, "Truly, truly, I say to you, before Abraham was, I am." So they took up stones to throw at him; but Jesus hid himself, and went out of the temple.

Jesus Heals the Man Born Blind

[John 9:1–12]

AS he passed by, he saw a man blind from his birth. And his disciples asked him, "Rabbi, who sinned, this man or his parents, that he was born blind?" Jesus answered, "It was not that this man sinned, or his parents, but that the works of God might be made manifest in him. We must work the works of him who sent me, while it is day; night comes, when no one can work. As long as I am in the world, I am the light of the world." As he said this, he spat on the ground and made clay of the spittle and anointed the man's eyes with the clay, saying to him, "Go, wash in the pool of Silo'am" (which means Sent). So he went and washed and came back seeing. The neighbors and those who had seen him before as a beggar, said, "Is not this the man who used to sit and beg?" Some said, "It is he"; others said, "No, but he is like him." He said, "I am the man." They said to him, "Then how were your eyes opened?" He answered, "The man called Jesus made clay and anointed my eyes and said to me, 'Go to Silo'am and wash'; so I went and washed and received my sight." They said to him, "Where is he?" He said, "I do not know."

The Pharisees Question the Healing

[9:13–23]

They brought to the Phar'isees the man who had formerly been blind. Now it was a sabbath day when Jesus made the clay and opened his eyes. The Phar'isees again asked him how he had received his sight. And he said to them, "He put clay on my eyes, and I washed, and I see." Some of the Phar'isees said, "This man is not from God, for he does not keep the sabbath." But others said, "How can a man who is a sinner do such signs?" There was a division among them. So they again said to the blind man, "What do you say about him, since he has opened your eyes?" He said, "He is a prophet."
The Jews did not believe that he had been blind and had received his sight, until they called the parents of the man who had received his sight, and asked them, "Is this your son, who you say was born blind? How then does he now see?" His parents answered, "We know that this is our son, and that he was born blind; but how he now sees we do not know, nor do we know who opened his eyes. Ask him; he is of age, he will speak for himself." His parents said this because they feared the Jews, for the

Jews had already agreed that if any one should confess him to be Christ, he was to be put out of the synagogue. Therefore his parents said, "He is of age, ask him."

"One Thing I Know" [9:24–34]

So for the second time they called the man who had been blind, and said to him, "Give God the praise; we know that this man is a sinner." He answered, "Whether he is a sinner, I do not know; one thing I know, that though I was blind, now I see." They said to him, "What did he do to you? How did he open your eyes?" He answered them, "I have told you already, and you would not listen. Why do you want to hear

it again? Do you too want to become his disciples?" And they reviled him, saying, "You are his disciple, but we are disciples of Moses. We know that God has spoken to Moses, but as for this man, we do not know where he comes from." The man answered, "Why, this is a marvel! You do not know where he comes from, and yet he opened my eyes. We know that God does not listen to sinners, but if any one is a worshiper of God and does his will, God listens to him. Never since the world began has it been heard that any one opened the eyes of a man born blind. If this man were not from God, he could do nothing." They answered him, "You were born in utter sin, and would you teach us?" And they cast him out.

Donald McLeish, London

These steps lead down to the modern Pool of Siloam, located in a part of the ancient pool

Palestine Exploration Fund

TRANSLATION

1st line "(Behold) the excavation! Now this had been the history of the excavation. While the workmen were still lifting up
2nd „ "the axe, each toward his neighbor, and while three cubits still remained to (cut through), (each heard) the voice of the other who called
3rd „ "to his neighbor since there was an excess in the rock on the right hand and on (the left). And on the day of the
4th „ "excavation the workmen struck, each to meet his neighbor, axe against axe, and there flowed
5th „ "the waters from the spring to the pool for a thousand two hundred cubits; and . . . .
6th „ "of a cubit was the height of the rock over the heads of the workmen."

From the Fountain of the Virgin a tunnel dating from the time of Hezekiah (ca. 700 B.C.) was hewn for about 1,777 feet through the rock to the Pool of Siloam. At the lower exit of this tunnel is found this carved inscription, one of the oldest in the Hebrew language

ᵘ"Other ancient authorities read *has Abraham seen you?*

Watering sheep near Bethlehem

Frank Hurley from Rapho-Guillumette

Gene Badger from Rapho-Guillumette

A good shepherd

L. A. Fereday

Two sheepfolds, each with a gap in the wall, or "door," guarded at night by the shepherds

Shepherds guarding their sheep at night

Matson Photo Service

Spiritual Blindness [9:35-41]

Jesus heard that they had cast him out, and having found him he said, "Do you believe in the Son of man?"[v] He answered, "And who is he, sir, that I may believe in him?" Jesus said to him, "You have seen him, and it is he who speaks to you." He said, "Lord, I believe"; and he worshiped him. Jesus said, "For judgment I came into this world, that those who do not see may see, and that those who see may become blind." Some of the Phár'isees near him heard this, and they said to him, "Are we also blind?" Jesus said to them, "If you were blind, you would have no guilt; but now that you say, 'We see,' your guilt remains.

The Parable of the Sheepfold
[John 10:1-6]

"TRULY, truly, I say to you, he who does not enter the sheepfold by the door but climbs in by another way, that man is a thief and a robber; but he who enters by the door is the shepherd of the sheep. To him the gatekeeper opens; the sheep hear his voice, and he calls his own sheep by name and leads them out. When he has brought out all his own, he goes before them, and the sheep follow him, for they know his voice. A stranger they will not follow, but they will flee from him, for they do not know the voice of strangers." This figure Jesus used with them, but they did not understand what he was saying to them.

Jesus the Good Shepherd [10:7-18]

So Jesus again said to them, "Truly, truly, I say to you, I am the door of the sheep. All who came before me are thieves and robbers; but the sheep did not heed them. I am the door; if any one enters by me, he will be saved, and will go in and out and find pasture. The thief comes only to steal and kill and destroy; I came that they

[v]Other ancient authorities read *the Son of God*

116

Evening over Jerusalem

may have life, and have it abundantly. I am the good shepherd. The good shepherd lays down his life for the sheep. He who is a hireling and not a shepherd, whose own the sheep are not, sees the wolf coming and leaves the sheep and flees; and the wolf snatches them and scatters them. He flees because he is a hireling and cares nothing for the sheep. I am the good shepherd; I know my own and my own know me, as the Father knows me and I know the Father; and I lay down my life for the sheep. And I have other sheep, that are not of this fold; I must bring them also, and they will heed my voice. So there shall be one flock, one shepherd. For this reason the Father loves me, because I lay down my life, that I may take it again. No one takes it from me, but I lay it down of my own accord. I have power to lay it down, and I have power to take it again; this charge I have received from my Father."

Division among the Jews [10:19-21]

There was again a division among the Jews because of these words. Many of them said, "He has a demon, and he is mad; why listen to him?" Others said, "These are not the sayings of one who has a demon. Can a demon open the eyes of the blind?"

"My Sheep Hear My Voice" [10:22-30]

It was the feast of the Dedication at Jerusalem; it was winter, and Jesus was walking in the temple, in the portico of Solomon. So the Jews gathered round him and said to him, "How long will you keep us in suspense? If you are the Christ, tell us plainly." Jesus answered them, "I told you, and you do not believe. The works that I do in my Father's name, they bear witness to me; but you do not believe, because you do not belong to my sheep. My sheep hear my voice, and I know them, and they follow me; and I give them eternal life, and they shall never perish, and no one shall snatch them out of my hand. My Father, who has

given them to me,*ʷ* is greater than all, and no one is able to snatch them out of the Father's hand. I and the Father are one."

The Jews Seek To Stone Jesus [10:31-39]

The Jews took up stones again to stone him. Jesus answered them, "I have shown you many good works from the Father; for which of these do you stone me?" The Jews answered him, "We stone you for no good work but for blasphemy; because you, being a man, make yourself God." Jesus answered them, "Is it not written in your law, 'I said, you are gods'?⁷ If he called them gods to whom the word of God came (and scripture cannot be broken), do you say of him whom

ʷOther ancient authorities read *What my Father has given to me*
⁷*Psalms* 82:6

the Father consecrated and sent into the world, 'You are blaspheming,' because I said, 'I am the Son of God'? If I am not doing the works of my Father, then do not believe me; but if I do them, even though you do not believe me, believe the works, that you may know and understand that the Father is in me and I am in the Father." Again they tried to arrest him, but he escaped from their hands.

Jesus Withdraws across the Jordan
[10:40-42]

He went away again across the Jordan to the place where John at first baptized, and there he remained. And many came to him; and they said, "John did no sign, but everything that John said about this man was true." And many believed in him there.

The Feast of the Dedication, or Hanukkah, was a festival of lights.
Here a Jewish girl in Jerusalem lights candles for this feast

Religious News Service

117

Bethany is in the center of this view from the top of the Russian Church tower on the summit of the Mount of Olives. The Dead Sea and the Mountains of Moab appear in the far distance

The Resurrection and the Life
[11:17–27]

Now when Jesus came, he found that Laz′a-rus[x] had already been in the tomb four days. Bethany was near Jerusalem, about two miles[y] off, and many of the Jews had come to Martha and Mary to console them concerning their brother. When Martha heard that Jesus was coming, she went and met him, while Mary sat in the house. Martha said to Jesus, "Lord, if you had been here, my brother would not have died. And even now I know that whatever you ask from God, God will give you." Jesus said to her, "Your brother will rise again." Martha said to him, "I know that he will rise again in the resurrection at the last day." Jesus said to her, "I am the resurrection and the life;[z] he who believes in me, though he die, yet shall he live, and whoever lives and believes in me shall never die. Do you believe this?" She said to him, "Yes, Lord; I believe that you are the Christ, the Son of God, he who is coming into the world."

Jesus Weeps [11:28–37]

When she had said this, she went and called her sister Mary, saying quietly, "The Teacher is here and is calling for you." And when she heard it, she rose quickly and went to him. Now Jesus had not yet come to the village, but was still in the place where Martha had met him. When the Jews who were with her in the house, consoling her, saw Mary rise quickly and go out, they followed her, supposing that she was going to the tomb to weep there. Then Mary, when she came where Jesus was and saw him, fell at his feet, saying to him, "Lord, if you had been here, my brother would not have died." When Jesus saw her weeping, and the Jews who came with her also weeping, he was deeply moved in spirit and troubled; and he said, "Where have you laid him?" They said to him, "Lord, come and see." Jesus wept. So the Jews said, "See how he loved him!" But some of them said, "Could not he who opened the eyes of the blind man have kept this man from dying?"

Lazarus Is Brought to Life
[11:38–44]

Then Jesus, deeply moved again, came to the tomb; it was a cave, and a stone lay upon it. Jesus said, "Take away the stone." Martha, the sister of the dead man, said to him, "Lord, by this time there will be an odor, for he has been dead four days." Jesus said to her, "Did I not tell you that if you would believe you would see the glory of God?" So they took away the stone. And Jesus lifted up his eyes and said, "Father, I thank thee that thou hast heard me. I knew that thou hearest me always, but I have said this on account of the people standing by, that they may believe that thou didst send me." When he had said this, he cried out with a loud voice, "Laz′arus, come out." The dead man came out, his hands and feet bound with bandages, and his face wrapped with a cloth. Jesus said to them, "Unbind him, and let him go."

Lazarus' Illness [John 11:1–4]

NOW a certain man was ill, Laz′arus of Beth′any, the village of Mary and her sister Martha. It was Mary who anointed the Lord with ointment and wiped his feet with her hair, whose brother Laz′arus was ill. So the sisters sent to him, saying, "Lord, he whom you love is ill." But when Jesus heard it he said, "This illness is not unto death; it is for the glory of God, so that the Son of God may be glorified by means of it."

The Death of Lazarus
[11:5–16]

Now Jesus loved Martha and her sister and Laz′arus. So when he heard that he was ill, he stayed two days longer in the place where he was. Then after this he said to the disciples, "Let us go into Jude′a again." The disciples said to him, "Rabbi, the Jews were but now seeking to stone you, and are you going there again?" Jesus answered, "Are there not twelve hours in the day? If any one walks in the day, he does not stumble, because he sees the light of this world. But if any one walks in the night, he stumbles, because the light is not in him." Thus he spoke, and then he said to them, "Our friend Laz′arus has fallen asleep, but I go to awake him out of sleep." The disciples said to him, "Lord, if he has fallen asleep, he will recover." Now Jesus had spoken of his death, but they thought that he meant taking rest in sleep. Then Jesus told them plainly, "Laz′arus is dead; and for your sake I am glad that I was not there, so that you may believe. But let us go to him." Thomas, called the Twin, said to his fellow disciples, "Let us also go, that we may die with him."

The road to Bethany past the Gate called Beautiful

[x]Greek *he*

[y]Greek *fifteen stadia*

[z]Other ancient authorities omit *and the life*

118

The Plot against Jesus

[11:45-54]

Many of the Jews therefore, who had come with Mary and had seen what he did, believed in him; but some of them went to the Phar'isees and told them what Jesus had done. So the chief priests and the Phar'isees gathered the council, and said, "What are we to do? For this man performs many signs. If we let him go on thus, every one will believe in him, and the Romans will come and destroy both our holy place[a] and our nation." But one of them, Cai'aphas, who was high priest that year, said to them, "You know nothing at all; you do not understand that it is expedient for you that one man should die for the people, and that the whole nation should not perish." He did not say this of his own accord, but being high priest that year he prophesied that Jesus should die for the nation, and not for the nation only, but to gather into one the children of God who are scattered abroad. So from that day on they took counsel how to put him to death.

Jesus therefore no longer went about openly among the Jews, but went from there to the country near the wilderness, to a town called E'phraim; and there he stayed with the disciples.

Orders for Jesus' Arrest

[11:55-57]

Now the Passover of the Jews was at hand, and many went up from the country to Jerusalem before the Passover, to purify themselves. They were looking for Jesus and saying to one another as they stood in the temple, "What do you think? That he will not come to the feast?" Now the chief priests and the Phar'isees had given orders that if any one knew where he was, he should let them know, so that they might arrest him.

The Anointing at Bethany [John 12:1-8]

SIX days before the Passover, Jesus came to Beth'any, where Laz'arus was, whom Jesus had raised from the dead. There they made him a supper; Martha served, and Laz'arus was one of those at table with him. Mary took a pound of costly ointment of pure nard and anointed the feet of Jesus and wiped his feet with her hair; and the house was filled with the fragrance of the ointment. But Judas Iscar'iot, one of his disciples (he who was to betray him), said, "Why was this ointment not sold for three hundred denarii[b] and given to the poor?" This he said, not that he cared for the poor but because he was a thief, and as he had the money box he used to take what was put into it. Jesus said, "Let her alone, let her keep it for the day of my burial. The poor you always have with you, but you do not always have me."

The Plot against Lazarus [12:9-11]

When the great crowd of the Jews learned that he was there, they came, not only on account of Jesus but also to see Laz'arus, whom he had raised from the dead. So the chief priests planned to put Laz'arus also to death, because on account of him many

[a]Greek our place

[b]The denarius was worth about twenty cents

of the Jews were going away and believing in Jesus.

Triumphal Entry into Jerusalem

[12:12-19]

The next day a great crowd who had come to the feast heard that Jesus was coming to Jerusalem. So they took branches of palm trees and went out to meet him, crying, "Hosanna! Blessed is he who comes in the name of the Lord, even the King of Israel!" And Jesus found a young ass and sat upon it; as it is written,

"Fear not, daughter of Zion;
behold, your king is coming,
sitting on an ass's colt!"[8]

His disciples did not understand this at first; but when Jesus was glorified, then they remembered that this had been written of him and had been done to him. The crowd that had been with him when he called Laz'arus out of the tomb and raised him from the dead bore witness. The reason why the crowd went to meet him was that they heard he had done this sign. The Phar-isees then said to one another, "You see that you can do nothing; look, the world has gone after him."

Greeks Seek Jesus

[12:20-26]

Now among those who went up to worship at the feast were some Greeks. So these came to Philip, who was from Beth-sa'ida in Gal'ilee, and said to him, "Sir, we wish to see Jesus." Philip went and told Andrew; Andrew went with Philip and they told Jesus. And Jesus answered them, "The hour has come for the Son of man to be glorified. Truly, truly, I say to you, unless a grain of wheat falls into the earth and dies, it remains alone; but if it dies, it bears much fruit. He who loves his life loses it, and he who hates his life in this world will keep it for eternal life. If any one serves me, he must follow me; and where I am, there shall my servant be also; if any one serves me, the Father will honor him.

The Son of Man Must Be Lifted Up

[12:27-36a]

"Now is my soul troubled. And what shall I say? 'Father, save me from this hour'? No, for this purpose I have come to this hour. Father, glorify thy name." Then a voice came from heaven, "I have glorified it, and I will glorify it again." The crowd standing by heard it and said that it had thundered. Others said, "An angel has spoken to him." Jesus answered, "This voice has come for your sake, not for mine. Now is the judgment of this world, now shall the ruler of this world be cast out; and I, when I am lifted up from the earth, will draw all men to myself." He said this to show by what death he was to die. The crowd answered him, "We have heard from the law that the Christ remains for ever. How can you say that the Son of man must be lifted up? Who is this Son of man?" Jesus said to them, "The light is with you for a little longer. Walk while you have the light, lest the darkness overtake you; he who walks in the darkness does not know where he goes. While you have the light, believe in the light, that you may become sons of light."

[8]Zechariah 9:9

American Schools of Oriental Research

Page from the ancient Hebrew Scrolls recently discovered in a cave near the Dead Sea, showing Isaiah 53:1

The Unbelief of the Jews [12:36b-43]

When Jesus had said this, he departed and hid himself from them. Though he had done so many signs before them, yet they did not believe in him; it was that the word spoken by the prophet Isai'ah might be fulfilled:

"Lord, who has believed our report, and to whom has the arm of the Lord been revealed?"[9]

Therefore they could not believe. For Isai'ah again said,

"He has blinded their eyes and hardened their heart,
lest they should see with their eyes and perceive with their heart,
and turn for me to heal them."[10]

Isai'ah said this because he saw his glory and spoke of him. Nevertheless many even of the authorities believed in him, but for fear of the Phar'isees they did not confess it, lest they should be put out of the synagogue: for they loved the praise of men more than the praise of God.

[9]Isaiah 53:1

[0]Isaiah 6:10

Palm trees in Palestine

Matson Photo Service

The Cenaculum, traditional site of the Last Supper

greater than his master; nor is he who is sent greater than he who sent him. If you know these things, blessed are you if you do them. I am not speaking of you all; I know whom I have chosen; it is that the scripture may be fulfilled, 'He who ate my bread has lifted his heel against me.'[11] I tell you this now, before it takes place, that when it does take place you may believe that I am he. Truly, truly, I say to you, he who receives any one whom I send receives me; and he who receives me receives him who sent me."

Jesus Foretells His Betrayal [13:21-30]

When Jesus had thus spoken, he was troubled in spirit, and testified, "Truly, truly, I say to you, one of you will betray me." The disciples looked at one another, uncertain of whom he spoke. One of his disciples, whom Jesus loved, was lying close to the breast of Jesus; so Simon Peter beckoned to him and said, "Tell us who it is of whom he speaks." So lying thus, close to the breast of Jesus, he said to him, "Lord, who is it?" Jesus answered, "It is he to whom I shall give this morsel when I have dipped it." So when he had dipped the morsel, he gave it to Judas, the son of Simon Iscar'iot. Then after the morsel, Satan entered into him. Jesus said to him, "What you are going to do, do quickly." Now no one at the table knew why he said this to him. Some thought that, because Judas had the money box, Jesus was telling him, "Buy what we need for the feast"; or, that he should give something to the poor. So, after receiving the morsel, he immediately went out; and it was night.

Love One Another [13:31-35]

When he had gone out, Jesus said, "Now is the Son of man glorified, and in him God is glorified; if God is glorified in him, God will also glorify him in himself, and glorify him at once. Little children, yet a little while I am with you. You will seek me; and as I said to the Jews so now I say to you, 'Where I am going you cannot come.' A new commandment I give to you, that you love one another; even as I have loved you, that you also love one another. By this all men will know that you are my disciples, if you have love for one another."

Peter's Denial Predicted [13:36-38]

Simon Peter said to him, "Lord, where are you going?" Jesus answered, "Where I am going you cannot follow me now; but you shall follow afterward." Peter said to him, "Lord, why cannot I follow you now? I will lay down my life for you." Jesus answered, "Will you lay down your life for me? Truly, truly, I say to you, the cock will not crow, till you have denied me three times.

The Way, the Truth and the Life

[John 14:1-7]

"LET not your hearts be troubled; believe[e] in God, believe also in me. In my Father's house are many rooms; if it were not so, would I have told you that I go to prepare a place for you? And when I go and prepare a place for you, I will come again and will take you to myself, that

The Authority of Christ's Word

[12:44-50]

And Jesus cried out and said, "He who believes in me, believes not in me but in him who sent me. And he who sees me sees him who sent me. I have come as light into the world, that whoever believes in me may not remain in darkness. If any one hears my sayings and does not keep them, I do not judge him; for I did not come to judge the world but to save the world. He who rejects me and does not receive my sayings has a judge; the word that I have spoken will be his judge on the last day. For I have not spoken on my own authority; the Father who sent me has himself given me commandment what to say and what to speak. And I know that his commandment is eternal life. What I say, therefore, I say as the Father has bidden me."

Washing the Disciples' Feet

[John 13:1-11]

NOW before the feast of the Passover, when Jesus knew that his hour had come to depart out of this world to the Father, having loved his own who were in the world, he loved them to the end. And during supper, when the devil had already put it into the heart of Judas Iscar'iot, Simon's son, to betray him, Jesus, knowing that the Father had given all things into his hands, and that he had come from God and was going to God, rose from supper, laid aside his garments, and girded himself with a towel. Then he poured water into a basin, and began to wash the disciples' feet, and to wipe them with the towel with which he was girded. He came to Simon Peter; and Peter said to him, "Lord, do you wash my feet?" Jesus answered him, "What I am doing you do not know now, but afterward you will understand." Peter said to him, "You shall never wash my feet." Jesus answered him, "If I do not wash you, you have no part in me." Simon Peter said to him, "Lord, not my feet only but also my hands and my head!" Jesus said to him, "He who has bathed does not need to wash, except for his feet,[c] but he is clean all over; and you are clean, but not all of you." For he knew who was to betray him; that was why he said, "You are not all clean."

The Example of Jesus [13:12-20]

When he had washed their feet, and taken his garments, and resumed his place, he said to them, "Do you know what I have done to you? You call me Teacher and Lord; and you are right, for so I am. If I then, your Lord and Teacher, have washed your feet, you also ought to wash one another's feet. For I have given you an example, that you also should do as I have done to you. Truly, truly, I say to you, a servant[d] is not

[c]Other ancient authorities omit *except for his feet*

[d]Or *slave*

[e]Or *you believe*

[11]Psalms 41:9

120

where I am you may be also. And you know the way where I am going."[j] Thomas said to him, "Lord, we do not know where you are going; how can we know the way?" Jesus said to him, "I am the way, and the truth, and the life; no one comes to the Father, but by me. If you had known me, you would have known my Father also; henceforth you know him and have seen him."

"Show Us the Father" [14:8–14]

Philip said to him, "Lord, show us the Father, and we shall be satisfied." Jesus said to him, "Have I been with you so long, and yet you do not know me, Philip? He who has seen me has seen the Father; how can you say, 'Show us the Father'? Do you not believe that I am in the Father and the Father in me? The words that I say to you I do not speak on my own authority; but the Father who dwells in me does his works. Believe me that I am in the Father and the Father in me; or else believe me for the sake of the works themselves.

"Truly, truly, I say to you, he who believes in me will also do the works that I do; and greater works than these will he do, because I go to the Father. Whatever you ask in my name, I will do it, that the Father may be glorified in the Son; if you ask[g] anything in my name, I will do it.

The Promise of the Counselor [14:15–17]

"If you love me, you will keep my commandments. And I will pray the Father, and he will give you another Counselor, to be with you for ever, even the Spirit of truth, whom the world cannot receive, because it neither sees him nor knows him; you know him, for he dwells with you, and will be in you.

The Inward Manifestation of Christ [14:18–24]

"I will not leave you desolate; I will come to you. Yet a little while, and the world will see me no more, but you will see me; because I live, you will live also. In that day you will know that I am in my Father, and you in me, and I in you. He who has my commandments and keeps them, he it is who loves me; and he who loves me will be loved by my Father, and I will love him and manifest myself to him." Judas (not Iscar'iot) said to him, "Lord, how is it that you will manifest yourself to us, and not to the world?" Jesus answered him, "If a man loves me, he will keep my word, and my Father will love him, and we will come to him and make our home with him. He who does not love me does not keep my words; and the word which you hear is not mine but the Father's who sent me.

The Gift of Peace [14:25–31]

"These things I have spoken to you, while I am still with you. But the Counselor, the Holy Spirit, whom the Father will send in my name, he will teach you all things, and bring to your remembrance all that I have said to you. Peace I leave with you; my peace I give to you; not as the world gives do I give to you. Let not your hearts be

troubled, neither let them be afraid. You heard me say to you, 'I go away, and I will come to you.' If you loved me, you would have rejoiced, because I go to the Father; for the Father is greater than I. And now I have told you before it takes place, so that when it does take place, you may believe. I will no longer talk much with you, for the ruler of this world is coming. He has no power over me; but I do as the Father has commanded me, so that the world may know that I love the Father. Rise, let us go hence.

Jesus the True Vine [John 15:1–11]

"I AM the true vine, and my Father is the vinedresser. Every branch of mine that bears no fruit, he takes away, and every branch that does bear fruit he prunes, that it may bear more fruit. You are already made clean by the word which I have spoken to you. Abide in me, and I in you. As the branch cannot bear fruit by itself, unless it abides in the vine, neither can you, unless you abide in me. I am the vine, you are the branches. He who abides in me, and I in him, he it is that bears much fruit, for apart from me you can do nothing. If a man does not abide in me, he is cast forth as a branch and withers; and the branches are gathered, thrown into the fire and burned. If you abide in me, and my words abide in you, ask whatever you will, and it shall be done for you. By this my Father is glorified, that you bear much fruit, and so prove to be my disciples. As the Father has loved me, so have I loved you; abide in my love. If you keep my commandments, you will abide in my love, just as I have kept my Father's commandments and abide in his love. These things I have spoken to you, that my joy may be in you, and that your joy may be full.

Greater Love Has No Man [15:12–17]

"This is my commandment, that you love one another as I have loved you. Greater love has no man than this, that a man lay down his life for his friends. You are my friends if you do what I command you. No longer do I call you servants,[h] for the servant[i] does not know what his master is doing; but I have called you friends, for all that I have heard from my Father I have made known to you. You did not choose me, but I chose you and appointed you that you should go and bear fruit and that your fruit should abide; so that whatever you ask the Father in my name, he may give it to you. This I command you, to love one another.

The World's Hatred

[15:18–16:4a]

"If the world hates you, know that it has hated me before it hated you. If you were of the world, the world would love its own; but because you are not of the world, but I chose you out of the world, therefore the world hates you. Remember the word that I said to you, 'A servant[i] is not greater than his master.' If they persecuted me, they will persecute you; if they kept my word, they will keep yours also. But all this they will do to you on my account, because they do not know him who sent me. If I had not come

Matson Photo Service

Pruning grapevines in Palestine

and spoken to them, they would not have sin; but now they have no excuse for their sin. He who hates me hates my Father also. If I had not done among them the works which no one else did, they would not have sin; but now they have seen and hated both me and my Father. It is to fulfil the word that is written in their law, 'They hated me without a cause.'[12] But when the Counselor comes, whom I shall send to you from the Father, even the Spirit of truth, who proceeds from the Father, he will bear witness to me; and you also are witnesses, because you have been with me from the beginning.

"I have said all this to you to keep you from falling away. They will put you out of the synagogues; indeed, the hour is coming when whoever kills you will think he is offering service to God. And they will do this because they have not known the Father, nor me. But I have said these things to you, that when their hour comes you may remember that I told you of them.

[j] Other ancient authorities read *where I am going you know, and the way you know*

[g] Other ancient authorities add *me*

[h] Or *slaves*

[i] Or *slave*

[12] Psalms 35:19; 69:4.

The Kidron Valley and the Garden of Gethsemane

The Work of the Counselor

[John 16:4b–11]

"I DID not say these things to you from the beginning, because I was with you. But now I am going to him who sent me; yet none of you asks me, 'Where are you going?' But because I have said these things to you, sorrow has filled your hearts. Nevertheless I tell you the truth: it is to your advantage that I go away, for if I do not go away, the Counselor will not come to you; but if I go, I will send him to you. And when he comes, he will convince the world of sin and of righteousness and of judgment: of sin, because they do not believe in me; of righteousness, because I go to the Father, and you will see me no more; of judgment, because the ruler of this world is judged.

The Spirit of Truth [16:12–15]

"I have yet many things to say to you, but you cannot bear them now. When the Spirit of truth comes, he will guide you into all the truth; for he will not speak on his own authority, but whatever he hears he will speak, and he will declare to you the things that are to come. He will glorify me, for he will take what is mine and declare it to you. All that the Father has is mine; therefore I said that he will take what is mine and declare it to you.

Sorrow Turned to Joy

[16:16–24]

"A little while, and you will see me no more; again a little while, and you will see me." Some of his disciples said to one another, "What is this that he says to us, 'A little while, and you will not see me, and again a little while, and you will see me'; and, 'because I go to the Father'?" They said, "What does he mean by 'a little while'? We do not know what he means." Jesus knew that they wanted to ask him; so he said to them, "Is this what you are asking yourselves, what I meant by saying, 'A little while, and you will not see me, and again a little while, and you will see me'? Truly, truly, I say to you, you will weep and lament, but the world will rejoice; you will be sorrowful, but your sorrow will turn into joy. When a woman is in travail she has sorrow, because her hour has come; but when she is delivered of the child, she no longer remembers the anguish, for joy that a child[i] is born into the world. So you have sorrow now, but I will see you again and your hearts will rejoice, and no one will take your joy from you. In that day you will ask nothing of me. Truly, truly, I say to you, if you ask anything of the Father, he will give it to you in my name. Hitherto you have asked nothing in my name; ask, and you will receive, that your joy may be full.

Going to the Father [16:25–28]

"I have said this to you in figures; the hour is coming when I shall no longer speak to you in figures but tell you plainly of the Father. In that day you will ask in my name; and I do not say to you that I shall pray the Father for you; for the Father himself loves

[i]Greek a human being

you, because you have loved me and have believed that I came from the Father. I came from the Father and have come into the world; again, I am leaving the world and going to the Father."

Jesus Has Overcome the World

[16:29–33]

His disciples said, "Ah, now you are speaking plainly, not in any figure! Now we know that you know all things, and need none to question you; by this we believe that you came from God." Jesus answered them, "Do you now believe? The hour is coming, indeed it has come, when you will be scattered, every man to his home, and will leave me alone; yet I am not alone, for the Father is with me. I have said this to you, that in me you may have peace. In the world you have tribulation; but be of good cheer, I have overcome the world."

The Prayer of Jesus [John 17:1–5]

WHEN Jesus had spoken these words, he lifted up his eyes to heaven and said, "Father, the hour has come; glorify thy Son that the Son may glorify thee, since thou hast given him power over all flesh, to give eternal life to all whom thou hast given him. And this is eternal life, that they know thee the only true God, and Jesus Christ whom thou hast sent. I glorified thee on earth, having accomplished the work which thou gavest me to do; and now, Father, glorify thou me in thy own presence with the glory which I had with thee before the world was made.

Jesus Prays for His Disciples [17:6–19]

"I have manifested thy name to the men whom thou gavest me out of the world; thine they were, and thou gavest them to me, and they have kept thy word. Now they know that everything that thou hast given me is from thee; for I have given them the words which thou gavest me, and they have received them and know in truth that I came from thee; and they have believed that thou didst send me. I am praying for them; I am not praying for the world but for those whom thou hast given me, for they are thine; all mine are thine, and thine are mine, and I am glorified in them. And now I am no more in the world, but they are in the world, and I am coming to thee. Holy Father, keep them in thy name, which thou hast given me, that they may be one, even as we are one. While I was with them, I kept them in thy name, which thou hast given me; I have guarded them, and none of them is lost but the son of perdition, that the scripture might be fulfilled. But now I am coming to thee; and these things I speak in the world, that they may have my joy fulfilled in themselves. I have given them thy word; and the world has hated them because they are not of the world, even as I am not of the world. I do not pray that thou shouldst take them out of the world, but that thou shouldst keep them from the evil one.[k] They are not of the world, even as I am not of the world. Sanctify them in the truth; thy word is truth. As thou didst send me into the world, so I have sent them into the world. And for their sake I consecrate myself, that they also may be consecrated in truth.

Jesus Prays for the Church [17:20–26]

"I do not pray for these only, but also for those who believe in me through their word, that they may all be one; even as thou, Father, art in me, and I in thee, that they also may be in us, so that the world may believe that thou hast sent me. The glory which thou hast given me I have given to them, that they may be one even as we are one, I in them and thou in me, that they may become perfectly one, so that the world may know that thou hast sent me and hast loved them even as thou hast loved me. Father, I desire that they also, whom thou hast given me, may be with me where I am, to behold my glory which thou hast given me in thy love for me before the foundation of the world. O righteous Father, the world has not known thee, but I have known thee; and these know that thou hast sent me. I made known to them thy name, and I will make it known, that the love with which thou hast loved me may be in them, and I in them."

The Arrest of Jesus [John 18:1–11]

WHEN Jesus had spoken these words, he went forth with his disciples across the Kidron valley, where there was a garden, which he and his disciples entered. Now Judas, who betrayed him, also knew the place; for Jesus often met there with his disciples. So Judas, procuring a band of soldiers and some officers from the chief priests and the Phar'isees, went there with lanterns and torches and weapons. Then Jesus, knowing all that was to befall

him, came forward and said to them, "Whom do you seek?" They answered him, "Jesus of Naz'areth." Jesus said to them, "I am he." Judas, who betrayed him, was standing with them. When he said to them, "I am he," they drew back and fell to the ground. Again he asked them, "Whom do you seek?" And they said, "Jesus of Naz'areth." Jesus answered, "I told you that I am he; so, if you seek me, let these men go." This was to fulfil the word which he had spoken, "Of those whom thou gavest me I lost not one." Then Simon Peter, having a sword, drew it and struck the high priest's slave and cut off his right ear. The slave's name was Malchus. Jesus said to Peter, "Put your sword into its sheath; shall I not drink the cup which the Father has given me?"

Jesus before Annas [18:12–14]

So the band of soldiers and their captain and the officers of the Jews seized Jesus and bound him. First they led him to Annas; for he was the father-in-law of Cai'aphas, who was high priest that year. It was Cai'aphas who had given counsel to the Jews that it was expedient that one man should die for the people.

Peter in the High Priest's Court

[18:15–18]

Simon Peter followed Jesus, and so did another disciple. As this disciple was known to the high priest, he entered the court of the high priest along with Jesus, while Peter stood outside at the door. So the other disciple, who was known to the high priest, went out and spoke to the maid who kept the door, and brought Peter in. The maid who kept the door said to Peter, "Are not you also one of this man's disciples?" He said, "I am not." Now the servants[l] and officers had made a charcoal fire, because it was cold, and they were standing and warming themselves; Peter also was with them, standing and warming himself.

The High Priest Questions Jesus

[18:19–24]

The high priest then questioned Jesus about his disciples and his teaching. Jesus answered him, "I have spoken openly to the world; I have always taught in synagogues and in the temple, where all Jews come together; I have said nothing secretly. Why do you ask me? Ask those who have heard me, what I said to them; they know what I said." When he had said this, one of the officers standing by struck Jesus with his hand, saying, "Is that how you answer the high priest?" Jesus answered him, "If I have spoken wrongly, bear witness to the wrong; but if I have spoken rightly, why do you strike me?" Annas then sent him bound to Cai'aphas the high priest.

Peter Denies Jesus [18:25–27]

Now Simon Peter was standing and warming himself. They said to him, "Are not you also one of his disciples?" He denied it and said, "I am not." One of the servants[l] of the high priest, a kinsman of the man whose ear Peter had cut off, asked, "Did I not see you in the garden with him?" Peter again denied it; and at once the cock crowed.

Matson Photo Service

This thorny tree, known as zizyphus spina Christi, is plentiful in Palestine. It was identified by the Crusaders with the thorn used for the crown that was put on the head of Jesus

Jesus before Pilate [18:28–32]

Then they led Jesus from the house of Cai'aphas to the praetor'ium. It was early. They themselves did not enter the praetor'ium, so that they might not be defiled, but might eat the passover. So Pilate went out to them and said, "What accusation do you bring against this man?" They answered him, "If this man were not an evildoer, we would not have handed him over." Pilate said to them, "Take him yourselves and judge him by your own law." The Jews said to him, "It is not lawful for us to put any man to death." This was to fulfil the word which Jesus had spoken to show by what death he was to die.

The King of the Jews [18:33–38a]

Pilate entered the praetor'ium again and called Jesus, and said to him, "Are you the King of the Jews?" Jesus answered, "Do you say this of your own accord, or did others say it to you about me?" Pilate answered, "Am I a Jew? Your own nation and the chief priests have handed you over to me; what have you done?" Jesus answered, "My kingship is not of this world; if my kingship were of this world, my servants would fight, that I might not be handed over to the Jews; but my kingship is not from the world." Pilate said to him, "So you are a king?" Jesus answered, "You say that I am a king. For this I was born, and for this I have come into the world, to bear witness to the truth. Every one who is of the truth hears my voice." Pilate said to him, "What is truth?"

Pilate's Verdict [18:38b–40]

After he had said this, he went out to the Jews again, and told them, "I find no crime in him. But you have a custom that I should release one man for you at the Passover; will you have me release for you the King of the Jews?" They cried out again, "Not this man, but Barab'bas!" Now Barab'bas was a robber.

[k]Or *from evil*

[l]Or *slaves*

Sisters of Zion, Jerusalem

The Lithostroton, or Pavement, showing the huge flagstones of the Roman Praetorium, where Jesus was judged by Pilate and mocked by the Roman soldiers. The Pavement is now located under a convent in the old city of Jerusalem, beneath the modern street level

Reproduction of markings found on the flagstones, believed to have been used by Roman soldiers for their games

Sisters of Zion, Jerusalem

"Here Is the Man!" [John 19:1–11]

THEN Pilate took Jesus and scourged him. And the soldiers plaited a crown of thorns, and put it on his head, and arrayed him in a purple robe; they came up to him, saying, "Hail, King of the Jews!" and struck him with their hands. Pilate went out again, and said to them, "Behold, I am bringing him out to you, that you may know that I find no crime in him." So Jesus came out, wearing the crown of thorns and the purple robe. Pilate said to them, "Here is the man!" When the chief priests and the officers saw him, they cried out, "Crucify him, crucify him!" Pilate said to them, "Take him yourselves and crucify him, for I find no crime in him." The Jews answered him, "We have a law, and by that law he ought to die, because he has made himself the Son of God." When Pilate heard these words, he was the more afraid; he entered the praetor'ium again and said to Jesus, "Where are you from?" But Jesus gave no answer. Pilate therefore said to him, "You will not speak to me? Do you not know that I have power to release you, and power to crucify you?" Jesus answered him, "You would have no power over me unless it had been given you from above; therefore he who delivered me to you has the greater sin."

Pilate Delivers Jesus To Be Crucified

[19:12–16]

Upon this Pilate sought to release him, but the Jews cried out, "If you release this man, you are not Caesar's friend; every one who makes himself a king sets himself against Caesar." When Pilate heard these words, he brought Jesus out and sat down on the judgment seat at a place called The Pavement, and in Hebrew, Gab'batha. Now it was the day of Preparation of the Passover; it was about the sixth hour. He said to the Jews, "Here is your King!" They cried out, "Away with him, away with him, crucify him!" Pilate said to them, "Shall I crucify your King?" The chief priests answered, "We have no king but Caesar." Then he handed him over to them to be crucified.

The Crucifixion [19:17–22]

So they took Jesus, and he went out, bearing his own cross, to the place called the place of a skull, which is called in Hebrew Gol'gotha. There they crucified him, and with him two others, one on either side, and Jesus between them. Pilate also wrote a title and put it on the cross; it read, "Jesus of Naz'areth, the King of the Jews." Many of the Jews read this title, for the place where Jesus was crucified was near the city; and it was written in Hebrew, in Latin, and in Greek. The chief priests of the Jews then said to Pilate, "Do not write, 'The King of the Jews,' but, 'This man said, I am King of the Jews.'" Pilate answered, "What I have written I have written."

Soldiers Cast Lots for Jesus' Garments

[19:23–24]

When the soldiers had crucified Jesus they took his garments and made four parts,

124

one for each soldier; also his tunic. But the tunic was without seam, woven from top to bottom; so they said to one another, "Let us not tear it, but cast lots for it to see whose it shall be." This was to fulfil the scripture,

"They parted my garments among them, and for my clothing they cast lots."[13]

Jesus' Care for His Mother [19:25-27]

So the soldiers did this. But standing by the cross of Jesus were his mother, and his mother's sister, Mary the wife of Clopas, and Mary Mag'dalene. When Jesus saw his mother, and the disciple whom he loved standing near, he said to his mother, "Woman, behold, your son!" Then he said to the disciple, "Behold, your mother!" And from that hour the disciple took her to his own home.

"It Is Finished" [19:28-30]

After this Jesus, knowing that all was now finished, said (to fulfil the scripture), "I thirst." A bowl full of vinegar stood there; so they put a sponge full of the vinegar on hyssop and held it to his mouth. When Jesus had received the vinegar, he said, "It is finished"; and he bowed his head and gave up his spirit.

Jesus' Side Pierced [19:31-37]

Since it was the day of Preparation, in order to prevent the bodies from remaining on the cross on the sabbath (for that sabbath was a high day), the Jews asked Pilate that their legs might be broken, and that they might be taken away. So the soldiers came and broke the legs of the first, and of the other who had been crucified with him; but when they came to Jesus and saw that he was already dead, they did not break his legs. But one of the soldiers pierced his side with a spear, and at once there came out blood and water. He who saw it has borne witness—his testimony is true, and he knows that he tells the truth—that you also may believe. For these things took place that the scripture might be fulfilled, "Not a bone of him shall be broken."[14] And again another scripture says, "They shall look on him whom they have pierced."[15]

The Burial of Jesus [19:38-42]

After this Joseph of Arimathe'a, who was a disciple of Jesus, but secretly, for fear of the Jews, asked Pilate that he might take away the body of Jesus, and Pilate gave him leave. So he came and took away his body. Nicode'mus also, who had at first come to him by night, came bringing a mixture of myrrh and aloes, about a hundred pounds' weight. They took the body of Jesus, and bound it in linen cloths with the spices, as is the burial custom of the Jews. Now in the place where he was crucified there was a garden, and in the garden a new tomb where no one had ever been laid. So because of the Jewish day of Preparation, as the tomb was close at hand, they laid Jesus there.

[13]*Psalms* 22:18

[14]*Exodus* 12:46; *Numbers* 9:12; *Psalms* 34:20

[15]*Zechariah* 12:10

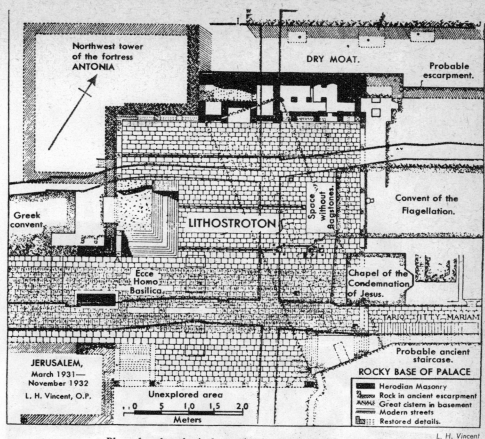

Plan of archaeological remains, around the Lithostroton

L. H. Vincent

Modern flowers and crown of thorns on the ancient Pavement where Jesus stood before Pilate

L. Kofod

Matson Photo Service

The Church of the Holy Sepulchre in Jerusalem, originally built by Emperor Constantine for his mother Helena. The present façade dates from the time of the Crusades

came and stood among them and said to them, "Peace be with you." When he had said this, he showed them his hands and his side. Then the disciples were glad when they saw the Lord. Jesus said to them again, "Peace be with you. As the Father has sent me, even so I send you." And when he had said this, he breathed on them, and said to them, "Receive the Holy Spirit. If you forgive the sins of any, they are forgiven; if you retain the sins of any, they are retained."

The Unbelief of Thomas [20:24-25]

Now Thomas, one of the twelve, called the Twin, was not with them when Jesus came. So the other disciples told him, "We have seen the Lord." But he said to them, "Unless I see in his hands the print of the nails, and place my finger in the mark of the nails, and place my hand in his side, I will not believe."

"My Lord and My God" [20:26-29]

Eight days later, his disciples were again in the house, and Thomas was with them. The doors were shut, but Jesus came and stood among them, and said, "Peace be with you." Then he said to Thomas, "Put your finger here, and see my hands; and put out your hand, and place it in my side; do not be faithless, but believing." Thomas answered him, "My Lord and my God!" Jesus said to him, "Have you believed because you have seen me? Blessed are those who have not seen and yet believe."

The Purpose of the Book [20:30-31]

Now Jesus did many other signs in the presence of the disciples, which are not written in this book; but these are written that you may believe that Jesus is the Christ, the Son of God, and that believing you may have life in his name.

Chapel of the Ascension on the Mount of Olives. The site of the Ascension was located on the Mount of Olives by the 4th century A.D.

Paul's Photos

The Empty Tomb [John 20:1-10]

NOW on the first day of the week Mary Mag'dalene came to the tomb early, while it was still dark, and saw that the stone had been taken away from the tomb. So she ran, and went to Simon Peter and the other disciple, the one whom Jesus loved, and said to them, "They have taken the Lord out of the tomb, and we do not know where they have laid him." Peter then came out with the other disciple, and they went toward the tomb. They both ran, but the other disciple outran Peter and reached the tomb first; and stooping to look in, he saw the linen cloths lying there, but he did not go in. Then Simon Peter came, following him, and went into the tomb; he saw the linen cloths lying, and the napkin, which had been on his head, not lying with the linen cloths but rolled up in a place by itself. Then the other disciple, who reached the tomb first, also went in, and he saw and believed; for as yet they did not know the scripture, that he must rise from the dead. Then the disciples went back to their homes.

Mary Magdalene Sees the Lord

[20:11-18]

But Mary stood weeping outside the tomb, and as she wept she stooped to look into the tomb; and she saw two angels in white, sitting where the body of Jesus had lain, one at the head and one at the feet. They said to her, "Woman, why are you weeping?" She said to them, "Because they have taken away my Lord, and I do not know where they have laid him." Saying this, she turned round and saw Jesus standing, but she did not know that it was Jesus. Jesus said to her, "Woman, why are you weeping? Whom do you seek?" Supposing him to be the gardener, she said to him, "Sir, if you have carried him away, tell me where you have laid him, and I will take him away." Jesus said to her, "Mary." She turned and said to him in Hebrew, "Rabbo'ni!" (which means Teacher). Jesus said to her, "Do not hold me, for I have not yet ascended to the Father; but go to my brethren and say to them, I am ascending to my Father and your Father, to my God and your God." Mary Mag'dalene went and said to the disciples, "I have seen the Lord"; and she told them that he had said these things to her.

Jesus Appears to His Disciples

[20:19-23]

On the evening of that day, the first day of the week, the doors being shut where the disciples were, for fear of the Jews, Jesus

Christ Appears by the Sea

[John 21:1-8]

AFTER this Jesus revealed himself again to the disciples by the Sea of Tiber'-i-as; and he revealed himself in this way. Simon Peter, Thomas called the Twin, Na-than'a-el of Cana in Gal'ilee, the sons of Zeb'edee, and two others of his disciples were together. Simon Peter said to them, "I am going fishing." They said to him, "We will go with you." They went out and got into the boat; but that night they caught nothing.

Just as day was breaking, Jesus stood on the beach; yet the disciples did not know that it was Jesus. Jesus said to them, "Children, have you any fish?" They answered him, "No." He said to them, "Cast the net on the right side of the boat, and you will find some." So they cast it, and now they were not able to haul it in, for the quantity of fish. That disciple whom Jesus loved said to Peter, "It is the Lord!" When Simon Peter heard that it was the Lord, he put on his clothes, for he was stripped for work, and sprang into the sea. But the other disciples came in the boat, dragging the net full of fish, for they were not far from the land, but about a hundred yards[m] off.

Breakfast on the Shore

[21:9-14]

When they got out on land, they saw a charcoal fire there, with fish lying on it, and bread. Jesus said to them, "Bring some of the fish that you have just caught." So Simon Peter went aboard and hauled the net ashore, full of large fish, a hundred and fifty-three of them; and although there were so many, the net was not torn. Jesus said to them, "Come and have breakfast." Now none of the disciples dared ask him, "Who are you?" They knew it was the Lord. Jesus came and took the bread and gave it to them, and so with the fish. This was now the third time that Jesus was revealed to the disciples after he was raised from the dead.

"Feed My Sheep"

[21:15-19]

When they had finished breakfast, Jesus said to Simon Peter, "Simon, son of John, do you love me more than these?" He said to him, "Yes, Lord; you know that I love you." He said to him, "Feed my lambs." A second time he said to him, "Simon, son of John, do you love me?" He said to him, "Yes, Lord; you know that I love you." He said to him, "Tend my sheep." He said to him the third time, "Simon, son of John, do you love me?" Peter was grieved because he said to him the third time, "Do you love me?" And he said to him, "Lord, you know everything; you know that I love you." Jesus said to him, "Feed my sheep. Truly, truly, I say to you, when you were young, you girded yourself and walked where you would; but when you are old, you will stretch out your hands, and another will gird you and carry you where you do not wish to go." (This he said to show by what death he was to glorify God.) And after this he said to him, "Follow me."

L. A. Fereday

"*Mensa Christi," or Table of Christ, by the Sea of Galilee, named by the Crusaders to commemorate the supposed site of Christ's appearance after the Resurrection*

The Beloved Disciple [21:20-25]

Peter turned and saw following them the disciple whom Jesus loved, who had lain close to his breast at the supper and had said, "Lord, who is it that is going to betray you?" When Peter saw him, he said to Jesus, "Lord, what about this man?" Jesus said to him, "If it is my will that he remain until I come, what is that to you? Follow me!" The saying spread abroad among the brethren that this disciple was not to die; yet Jesus did not say to him that he was not to die, but, "If it is my will that he remain until I come, what is that to you?"

This is the disciple who is bearing witness to these things, and who has written these things; and we know that his testimony is true.

But there are also many other things which Jesus did; were every one of them to be written, I suppose that the world itself could not contain the books that would be written.

Fishermen on the Sea of Galilee

Underwood and Underwood

"I AM THE GOOD SHEPHERD.
THE GOOD SHEPHERD LAYS DOWN HIS LIFE FOR THE SHEEP"

JOHN 10:11

A GOOD SHEPHERD

Matson

"FEED MY LAMBS" – "TEND MY SHEEP" – "FEED MY SHEEP" –
"FOLLOW ME" – "FOLLOW ME!"

Into All The World

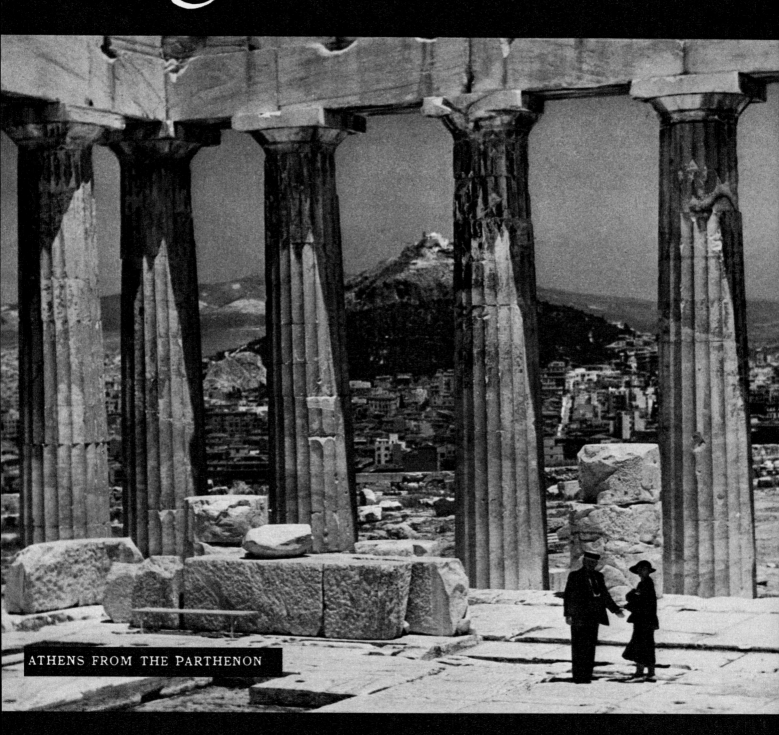

ATHENS FROM THE PARTHENON

THE ACTS OF THE APOSTLES

REVISED STANDARD VERSION

THE ROMAN EMPIRE

In New Testament times the Roman Empire controlled the Mediterranean Sea and its adjoining areas either directly or through allies. This great expansion of Roman power and influence was accomplished by force of arms, by treaties with friendly states or cities, by colonization and by grants of citizenship. The real power of the Emperor, however, was based upon his army. The Emperor Augustus, a well-trained and experienced soldier, placed his twenty-five legions in important strategic areas as a safeguard against revolt or invasion. Four legions were stationed in Syria.

Peace prevailed to an unusual extent in the Mediterranean area during the reign of the five Julian Emperors from 31 B.C. to A.D. 68. The doors of the Temple of Janus were closed for the first time in 29 B.C. to signify that there was peace throughout the Roman world. In Apostolic times these doors were closed much of the time. To publicize this Pax Romana some of Nero's coins bore the word "Peace" and showed the closed doors of the Temple of Janus; but although the forms of a republic were retained, the Senate and the Roman citizens were under the complete power of the Emperor, while the character of the Julian Emperors and of their households became more criminal and more corrupt all the time.

Roman rule and influence provided well-built roads, aqueducts, bridges, public buildings, temples, amphitheaters, harbors, docks, etc., together with a very considerable degree of law and order in the provinces. However, the beginning of Emperor worship—the cult of the Emperor—created new difficulties for those who insisted that Caesar's prerogative should not infringe upon God's.

Herod Agrippa I was able to thwart Caligula's demand that a statue of Caligula be installed in the Temple at Jerusalem, but the temples that were erected to Augustus at Caesarea, Pergamum, Pisidian Antioch and Apollonia created serious problems for Christians. It was in such an environment that the Gospel of God's good will to men was carried by the early disciples with great joy and zeal "into all the world."

ANTIOCH, on the Orontes River in Syria, where the disciples were first called Christians, was taken by the Romans from King Tigranes of Armenia about 66 B.C. A free—i.e., self-governing—city and the capital of the Province of Syria, it was the third largest city in the Roman Empire after Rome and Alexandria. Although beautified by Herod the Great, Augustus and Tiberius, its moral reputation was very bad. Today, a city of about 35,000, the splendors of its ancient past are gone.

ANTIOCH, in Pisidia, was made a free city by the Romans about 189 B.C. Augustus made it a Roman colony about 11 B.C. The city had two squares, the Square of Augustus and the Square of Tiberius. In the Square of Augustus was a great temple, used both for the worship of the chief local god *Men* and later also of the Roman Emperor. The phrase "the chief men of the city" in Acts 13:50 is verified by ancient inscriptions mentioning the rulers of Pisidian Antioch.

ATHENS was an ally of Rome against the Macedonians, but later deserted Rome and joined Mithridates of Pontus. As a result, Athens was stormed by the Romans under Sulla in 86 B.C. Though it sided later with Pompey and Brutus, the Romans permitted Athens to remain a free and sovereign city because of respect for its glorious past and its illustrious dead. Its famous buildings, statues, dramatists, philosophers and orators are still a precious heritage of all mankind.

CORINTH was defeated and completely destroyed by the Romans in 146 B.C., but was refounded by Julius Caesar 46 B.C. as a colony with Italian freedmen and dispossessed Greeks. Augustus made it the capital of the Province of Achaea and the seat of its proconsul. An inscription of the Emperor Claudius at Delphi (A.D. 51 or 52) refers to Lucius Junius Gallio, before whom Paul appeared, as "my friend and the proconsul of Achaea." Another inscription in a pavement of the theater is believed to refer to Erastus, the chamberlain of the city, whose greetings Paul included in the letter he wrote from Corinth to the Romans.

CYPRUS was captured from Ptolemy Auletes 58 B.C. and made a Roman province in 27 B.C. As a province of the Senate, its ruler was a proconsul, as stated in Acts. An inscription of about A.D. 55 found at Paphos refers to "the time of the proconsul Paulus." This is believed to be the proconsul Sergius Paulus mentioned in Acts 13:7.

DAMASCUS, mentioned in Genesis, is an ancient and important city in Syria on the main trade route from Mesopotamia to Palestine. Taken by Pompey in 64 B.C., it appears to have been controlled by the Nabateans when Paul commenced his ministry there. Situated in a fertile plain east of the Anti-Lebanon Mountains, whose snow-capped Mount Hermon is about 9,100 feet in height, it has always been a great center of trade.

EPHESUS. The last King of Pergamum, Attalus III Philometor, willed his kingdom, including Ephesus, to the Romans. Strabo says that Ephesus was "the largest emporium in Asia this side of the Taurus." Famous for its great Temple of Diana (Artemis), 340 x 160 feet, and for its theater and agora and public buildings, it was in size the fourth largest city of the Empire. But its claim to be the first city of Asia was contested by Smyrna and Pergamum. The use of the Greek word "Asiarchs" to describe the Ephesian officials in Acts 19:31 is confirmed by Strabo and by inscriptions and on coins. Later, its seaport silted up, its temple was sacked and burned by the Goths in A.D. 262. The ruins of the theater are shown on page 150.

JERUSALEM was captured by Pompey 63 B.C. Herod the Great became King of Judea by grant of the Roman Senate and reigned from 37 to 4 B.C. He built Caesarea in honor of Augustus Caesar and adorned and beautified the Temple at Jerusalem to please the Jews. On his death, his kingdom

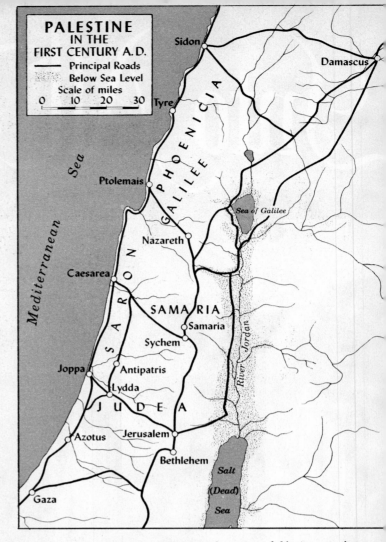

was divided between three living sons from two of his ten marriages. One of these, Herod Antipas, became tetrarch of Galilee and Peraea from 4 B.C. to A.D. 39. This was the Herod who took his brother's wife and was denounced by John the Baptist. The Nabatean King Aretas IV attacked and defeated him in battle for having divorced his first wife, who was Aretas' daughter. Herod Antipas built Tiberias on the Sea of Galilee to honor the Roman Emperor Tiberius. His nephew, later Herod Agrippa I, was employed by his uncle at Tiberias, but went to Rome and made friends with the youthful Caligula. Although put in jail by Tiberius for wishing Tiberius' death, he was made king over the tetrarchies of Philip and Lysanias in A.D. 37 when Caligula became Emperor. A few years later he was given the tetrarchy of Herod Antipas, who was banished to Lyons in Gaul. Herod Agrippa I began the building of the third north wall of Jerusalem, but this was ordered stopped by Claudius. His death in A.D. 44 is one of the most definitely established dates in the book of Acts. From A.D. 44 to the Jewish revolt in 66, Palestine was ruled by Roman procurators, among whom were Felix (about 52–60 A.D.) and Festus (60–62 A.D.).

PHILIPPI. After the Battle of Philippi, 42 B.C., Anthony and Octavian made Philippi a Roman colony, including in it its seaport Neapolis (the modern Kavalla) nine miles away. The Via Egnatia ran from Neapolis to Philippi through its ancient forum and across the Ganga River, about one mile west of the city. An air-view of the ruins of Philippi is shown on page 147.

THESSALONICA (modern Salonica), the largest city in Macedonia, was named after the sister of Alexander the Great. It was made a free city about 42 B.C. Ancient inscriptions confirm the use in Acts 17:6 of the Greek word "politarchs" as the rulers of Thessalonica, although the term is not found elsewhere in extant Greek literature.

TARSUS, in Cilicia, was the birthplace of Paul. It was the site of a famed school of philosophy which the historian Strabo said rivaled the schools of Athens and Alexandria. Its most famous philosopher, Athenodorus, was the teacher of the Emperor Augustus. Strongly Hellenized under the Seleucids, when it enjoyed autonomy and its own coinage, it was made the residence of the Roman governor of Cilicia by Pompey in 64 B.C. A free city from the time of Antony and Augustus, it was densely populated and prosperous. While in Paul's time Tarsus had a great harbor, Lake Rhegma on the Cydnus River, this was silted up during the decline and fall of the Roman Empire. Its Roman hippodrome, theater and other monuments for the most part lie beneath the level of the modern Turkish city.

The Matson Photo Service

The Mount of Olives, seen from the Kidron Valley. In the center is the traditional site of the Garden of Gethsemane. The modern road from Jerusalem starts at the lower left, runs to the Garden of Gethsemane and then goes around to the right on its way to Bethany and to Jericho

INTO ALL THE WORLD
as reported in the ACTS OF THE APOSTLES

The Promise of the Holy Spirit

[Acts 1:1–5] In the first book, O The-oph'ilus, I have dealt with all that Jesus began to do and teach, until the day when he was taken up, after he had given commandment through the Holy Spirit to the apostles whom he had chosen. To them he presented himself alive after his passion by many proofs, appearing to them during forty days, and speaking of the kingdom of God. And while staying[a] with them he charged them not to depart from Jerusalem, but to wait for the promise of the Father, which, he said, "you heard from me, for John baptized with water, but before many days you shall be baptized with the Holy Spirit."

The Ascension [1:6–11]

So when they had come together, they asked him, "Lord, will you at this time restore the kingdom to Israel?" He said to them, "It is not for you to know times or seasons which the Father has fixed by his own authority. But you shall receive power when the Holy Spirit has come upon you; and you shall be my witnesses in Jerusalem and in all Jude'a and Samar'ia and to the end of the earth." And when he had said this, as they were looking on, he was lifted up, and a cloud took him out of their sight. And while they were gazing into heaven as he went, behold, two men stood by them in white robes, and said, "Men of Gal'ilee, why do you stand looking into heaven? This Jesus, who was taken up from you into heaven, will

come in the same way as you saw him go into heaven."

Judas' Successor Chosen [1:12–26]

Then they returned to Jerusalem from the mount called Ol'ivet, which is near Jerusalem, a sabbath day's journey away; and when they had entered, they went up to the upper room, where they were staying, Peter and John and James and Andrew, Philip and Thomas, Barthol'omew and Matthew, James the son of Alphae'us and Simon the Zealot and Judas the son of James. All these with one accord devoted themselves to prayer, together with the women and Mary the mother of Jesus, and with his brothers.

In those days Peter stood up among the brethren (the company of persons was in all about a hundred and twenty), and said, "Brethren, the scripture had to be fulfilled,

which the Holy Spirit spoke beforehand by the mouth of David, concerning Judas who was guide to those who arrested Jesus. For he was numbered among us, and was allotted his share in this ministry. (Now this man bought a field with the reward of his wickedness; and falling headlong[b] he burst open in the middle and all his bowels gushed out. And it became known to all the inhabitants of Jerusalem, so that the field was called in their language Akel'dama, that is, Field of Blood.) For it is written in the Book of Psalms,

'Let his habitation become desolate, and let there be no one to live in it';[1]

and

'His office let another take.'[2]

So one of the men who have accompanied us during all the time that the Lord Jesus went in and out among us, beginning from the baptism of John until the day when he was taken up from us—one of these men must become with us a witness to his resurrection." And they put forward two, Joseph called Barsab'bas, who was surnamed Justus, and Matthi'as. And they prayed and said, "Lord, who knowest the hearts of all men, show which one of these two thou hast chosen to take the place in this ministry and apostleship from which Judas turned aside, to go to his own place." And they cast lots for them, and the lot fell on Matthi'as; and he was enrolled with the eleven apostles.

[a]Or *eating*

[b]Or *swelling up*

[1]*Psalms* 69:25   [2]*Psalms* 109:8

131

EGYPT

OSIRIS HORUS NEFERTEM

Brooklyn Museum
Egyptian hieroglyphics from Karnak

Metropolitan Museum of Art

1, 2

The Ten
Commandments
in Hebrew. 3
Nash papyrus 4
fragment of about
the first century B.C.
Exodus 20: 1-17
Deut. 5: 6-21 5

6, 7
8, 9, 10

JUDEA

V. Papatoannou
Zeus throwing a thunderbolt
GREECE
Thessalonica inscription mentioning "politarchs"
British Museum

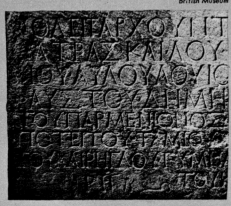

The Coming of the Holy Spirit

[Acts 2:1–13]

WHEN the day of Pen'tecost had come, they were all together in one place. And suddenly a sound came from heaven like the rush of a mighty wind, and it filled all the house where they were sitting. And there appeared to them tongues as of fire, distributed and resting on each one of them. And they were all filled with the Holy Spirit and began to speak in other tongues, as the Spirit gave them utterance.

Now there were dwelling in Jerusalem Jews, devout men from every nation under heaven. And at this sound the multitude came together, and they were bewildered, because each one heard them speaking in his own language. And they were amazed and wondered, saying, "Are not all these who are speaking Galile'ans? And how is it that we hear, each of us in his own native language? Par'thians and Medes and E'lamites and residents of Mesopota'mia, Jude'a and Cappado'cia, Pontus and Asia, Phryg'ia and Pamphyl'ia, Egypt and the parts of Libya belonging to Cyre'ne, and visitors from Rome, both Jews and proselytes, Cretans and Arabians, we hear them telling in our own tongues the mighty works of God." And all were amazed and perplexed, saying to one another, "What does this mean?" But others mocking said, "They are filled with new wine."

Peter's Address at Pentecost [2:14–42]

But Peter, standing with the eleven, lifted up his voice and addressed them, "Men of Jude'a and all who dwell in Jerusalem, let this be known to you, and give ear to my words. For these men are not drunk, as you suppose, since it is only the third hour of the day; but this is what was spoken by the prophet Joel:

'And in the last days it shall be, God declares,
that I will pour out my Spirit upon all flesh,
and your sons and your daughters shall prophesy,
and your young men shall see visions,
and your old men shall dream dreams;
yea, and on my menservants and my maidservants in those days
I will pour out my Spirit; and they shall prophesy.
And I will show wonders in the heaven above
and signs on the earth beneath,
blood, and fire, and vapor of smoke;
the sun shall be turned into darkness
and the moon into blood,
before the day of the Lord comes,
the great and manifest day.
And it shall be that whoever calls on the name of the Lord shall be saved.'[3]

"Men of Israel, hear these words: Jesus of Naz'areth, a man attested to you by God with mighty works and wonders and signs which God did through him in your midst, as you yourselves know—this Jesus, delivered up according to the definite plan and foreknowledge of God, you crucified and killed by the hands of lawless men. But God raised him up, having loosed the pangs of death, because it was not possible for him to be held by it. For David says concerning him,

'I saw the Lord always before me,
for he is at my right hand that I may not be shaken;

[3]Joel 2:28–32

Latin inscription at Rome recording religious events of A.D. 59

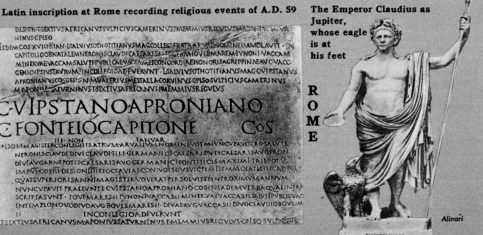

The Emperor Claudius as Jupiter, whose eagle is at his feet

ROME

Alinari

Dead Sea scroll of about first century B.C., open to Isaiah 40

John C. Trever

I AM the LORD your God, who brought you out of the land of Egypt, out of the house of bondage. You shall have no other gods before me. You shall not make for yourself a graven image, or any likeness of anything that is in heaven above, or that is in the earth beneath, or that is in the water under the earth; you shall not bow down to them or serve them; for I the LORD your God am a jealous God, visiting the iniquity of the fathers upon the children to the third and the fourth generation of those who hate me, but showing steadfast love to thousands of those who love me and keep my commandments . . .

Exodus 20:2–6

Ahura Mazda
Chief Parthian god

Fogg Museum of Art, Cambridge

Dietrich Reimer Verlag, Berlin

Parthian writing of about first century A.D.

---

therefore my heart was glad, and my tongue rejoiced;
moreover my flesh will dwell in hope.
For thou wilt not abandon my soul to Hades,
nor let thy Holy One see corruption.
Thou hast made known to me the ways of life;
thou wilt make me full of gladness with thy presence.'[4]

"Brethren, I may say to you confidently of the patriarch David that he both died and was buried, and his tomb is with us to this day. Being therefore a prophet, and knowing that God had sworn with an oath to him that he would set one of his descendants upon his throne, he foresaw and spoke of the resurrection of the Christ, that he was not abandoned to Hades, nor did his flesh see corruption. This Jesus God raised up, and of that we all are witnesses. Being therefore exalted at the right hand of God, and having received from the Father the promise of the Holy Spirit, he has poured out this which you see and hear. For David did not ascend into the heavens; but he himself says,

'The Lord said to my Lord, Sit at my right hand,
till I make thy enemies a stool for thy feet.'[5]

Let all the house of Israel therefore know assuredly that God has made him both Lord and Christ, this Jesus whom you crucified."

Now when they heard this they were cut to the heart, and said to Peter and the rest of the apostles, "Brethren, what shall we do?" And Peter said to them, "Repent, and

[4] *Psalms 16:8–11*
[5] *Psalms 110:1 (Matthew 22:44; Mark 12:36; Luke 20:42)*

be baptized every one of you in the name of Jesus Christ for the forgiveness of your sins; and you shall receive the gift of the Holy Spirit. For the promise is to you and to your children and to all that are far off, every one whom the Lord our God calls to him." And he testified with many other words and exhorted them, saying, "Save yourselves from this crooked generation." So those who received his word were baptized, and there were added that day about three thousand souls. And they devoted themselves to the apostles' teaching and fellowship, to the breaking of bread and the prayers.

Life among the Believers [2:43–47]

And fear came upon every soul; and many wonders and signs were done through the apostles. And all who believed were together and had all things in common; and they sold their possessions and goods and distributed them to all, as any had need. And day by day, attending the temple together and breaking bread in their homes, they partook of food with glad and generous hearts, praising God and having favor with all the people. And the Lord added to their number day by day those who were being saved.

A Lame Man Healed at the Gate of the Temple [Acts 3:1–10]

NOW Peter and John were going up to the temple at the hour of prayer, the ninth hour. And a man lame from birth was being carried, whom they laid daily at that gate of the temple which is called Beautiful to ask alms of those who entered the temple. Seeing Peter and John about to go into

Cybele, the mother goddess of Phrygia

David M. Robinson

P H R Y G I A

Phrygian tomb inscription

A VOICE cries: "In the wilderness prepare the way of the LORD, make straight in the desert a highway for our God. Every valley shall be lifted up, and every mountain and hill be made low; the uneven ground shall become level, and the rough places a plain. And the glory of the LORD shall be revealed, and all flesh shall see it together, for the mouth of the LORD has spoken." A voice says, "Cry!" And I said, "What shall I cry?" All flesh is grass . . . The grass withers, the flower fades; but the word of our God will stand for ever.

Isaiah 40:3–6, 8

Atargatis, chief goddess of Northern Arabia

American School of Oriental Research, Nelson Glueck

Nabatean inscription

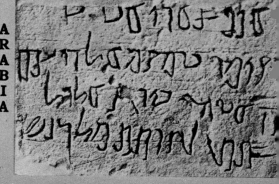

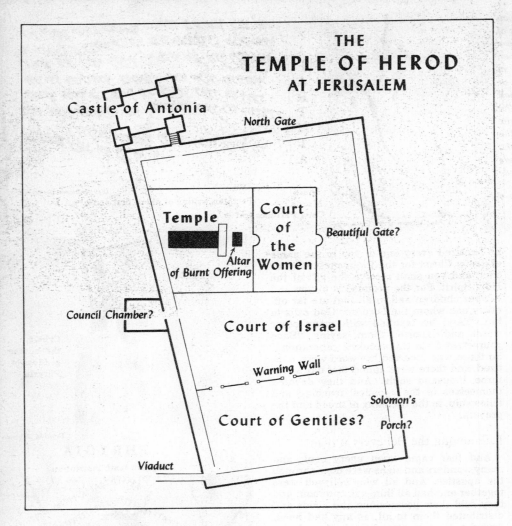

THE
TEMPLE OF HEROD
AT JERUSALEM

Castle of Antonia

North Gate

Temple

Court of the Women

Beautiful Gate?

Altar of Burnt Offering

Council Chamber?

Court of Israel

Warning Wall

Solomon's Porch?

Court of Gentiles?

Viaduct

having raised up his servant,[c] sent him to you first, to bless you in turning every one of you from your wickedness."

Peter and John before the Council

[Acts 4:1–22]

AND as they were speaking to the people, the priests and the captain of the temple and the Sad'ducees came upon them, annoyed because they were teaching the people and proclaiming in Jesus the resurrection from the dead. And they arrested them and put them in custody until the morrow, for it was already evening. But many of those who heard the word believed; and the number of the men came to about five thousand.

On the morrow their rulers and elders and scribes were gathered together in Jerusalem, with Annas the high priest and Cai'aphas and John and Alexander, and all who were of the high-priestly family. And when they had set them in the midst, they inquired, "By what power or by what name did you do this?" Then Peter, filled with the Holy Spirit, said to them, "Rulers of the people and elders, if we are being examined today concerning a good deed done to a cripple, by what means this man has been healed, be it known to you all, and to all the people of Israel, that by the name of Jesus Christ of Naz'areth, whom you crucified, whom God raised from the dead, by him this man is standing before you well. This is the stone which was rejected by you builders, but which has become the head of the corner.[8] And there is salvation in no one else, for there is no other name under heaven given among men by which we must be saved."

Now when they saw the boldness of Peter and John, and perceived that they were uneducated, common men, they wondered; and they recognized that they had been with Jesus. But seeing the man that had been healed standing beside them, they had nothing to say in opposition. But when they had commanded them to go aside out of the council, they conferred with one another, saying, "What shall we do with these men? For that a notable sign has been performed through them is manifest to all the inhabitants of Jerusalem, and we cannot deny it. But in order that it may spread no further among the people, let us warn them to speak no more to any one in this name." So they called them and charged them not to speak or teach at all in the name of Jesus. But Peter and John answered them, "Whether it is right in the sight of God to listen to you rather than to God, you must judge; for we cannot but speak of what we have seen and heard." And when they had further threatened them, they let them go, finding no way to punish them, because of the people; for all men praised God for what had happened. For the man on whom this sign of healing was performed was more than forty years old.

The Believers Pray for Boldness [4:23–31]

When they were released they went to their friends and reported what the chief priests and the elders had said to them. And when they heard it, they lifted their voices together to God and said, "Sovereign Lord, who didst make the heaven and the earth and the sea and everything in them,

the temple, he asked for alms. And Peter directed his gaze at him, with John, and said, "Look at us." And he fixed his attention upon them, expecting to receive something from them. But Peter said, "I have no silver and gold, but I give you what I have; in the name of Jesus Christ of Naz'areth, walk." And he took him by the right hand and raised him up; and immediately his feet and ankles were made strong. And leaping up he stood and walked and entered the temple with them, walking and leaping and praising God. And all the people saw him walking and praising God, and recognized him as the one who sat for alms at the Beautiful Gate of the temple; and they were filled with wonder and amazement at what had happened to him.

Peter's Address in Solomon's Portico

[3:11–26]

While he clung to Peter and John, all the people ran together to them in the portico called Solomon's, astounded. And when Peter saw it he addressed the people, "Men of Israel, why do you wonder at this, or why do you stare at us, as though by our own power or piety we had made him walk? The God of Abraham and of Isaac and of Jacob, the God of our fathers, glorified his servant[c] Jesus, whom you delivered up and denied in the presence of Pilate, when he had decided to release him. But you denied the Holy and Righteous One, and asked for a murderer to be granted to you, and killed

[c]Or child

the Author of life, whom God raised from the dead. To this we are witnesses. And his name, by faith in his name, has made this man strong whom you see and know; and the faith which is through Jesus[d] has given the man this perfect health in the presence of you all.

"And now, brethren, I know that you acted in ignorance, as did also your rulers. But what God foretold by the mouth of all the prophets, that his Christ should suffer, he thus fulfilled. Repent therefore, and turn again, that your sins may be blotted out, that times of refreshing may come from the presence of the Lord, and that he may send the Christ appointed for you, Jesus, whom heaven must receive until the time for establishing all that God spoke by the mouth of his holy prophets from of old. Moses said, 'The Lord God will raise up for you a prophet from your brethren as he raised me up. You shall listen to him in whatever he tells you.[6] And it shall be that every soul that does not listen to that prophet shall be destroyed from the people.' And all the prophets who have spoken, from Samuel and those who came afterwards, also proclaimed these days. You are the sons of the prophets and of the covenant which God gave to your fathers, saying to Abraham, 'And in your posterity shall all the families of the earth be blessed.'[7] God,

[d]Greek him

[6]Deuteronomy 18:15, 18

[7]Genesis 12:3; 22:18; 26:4; 28:14

[8]Psalms 118:22 (Matthew 21:42; Mark 12:10)

who by the mouth of our father David, thy servant,[c] didst say by the Holy Spirit,

'Why did the Gentiles rage,
and the peoples imagine vain things?
The kings of the earth set themselves in array,
and the rulers were gathered together,
against the Lord and against his Anointed'—[e][9]

for truly in this city there were gathered together against thy holy servant[c] Jesus, whom thou didst anoint, both Herod and Pontius Pilate, with the Gentiles and the peoples of Israel, to do whatever thy hand and thy plan had predestined to take place. And now, Lord, look upon their threats, and grant to thy servants[f] to speak thy word with all boldness, while thou stretchest out thy hand to heal, and signs and wonders are performed through the name of thy holy servant[c] Jesus." And when they had prayed, the place in which they were gathered together was shaken; and they were all filled with the Holy Spirit and spoke the word of God with boldness.

The Matson Photo Service

Air view of Jerusalem, showing the present Temple area. The octagonal building in the center is the "Dome of the Rock," first erected in A.D. 691. To the right, note the shadow in the Kidron Valley, and the road between Jerusalem and the Mount of Olives that leads to Bethany and Jericho

All Things in Common [4:32–37]

Now the company of those who believed were of one heart and soul, and no one said that any of the things which he possessed was his own, but they had everything in common. And with great power the apostles gave their testimony to the resurrection of the Lord Jesus, and great grace was upon them all. There was not a needy person among them, for as many as were possessors of lands or houses sold them, and brought the proceeds of what was sold and laid it at the apostles' feet; and distribution was made to each as any had need. Thus Joseph who was surnamed by the apostles Bar'nabas (which means, Son of encouragement), a Levite, a native of Cyprus, sold a field which belonged to him, and brought the money and laid it at the apostles' feet.

Ananias and Sapphira [Acts 5:1–11]

BUT a man named Anani'as with his wife Sapphi'ra sold a piece of property, and with his wife's knowledge he kept back some of the proceeds, and brought only a part and laid it at the apostles' feet. But Peter said, "Anani'as, why has Satan filled your heart to lie to the Holy Spirit and to keep back part of the proceeds of the land? While it remained unsold, did it not remain your own? And after it was sold, was it not at your disposal? How is it that you have contrived this deed in your heart? You have not lied to men but to God." When Anani'as heard these words, he fell down and died. And great fear came upon all who heard of it. The young men rose and wrapped him up and carried him out and buried him.

After an interval of about three hours his wife came in, not knowing what had happened. And Peter said to her, "Tell me whether you sold the land for so much."

And she said, "Yes, for so much." But Peter said to her, "How is it that you have agreed together to tempt the Spirit of the Lord? Hark, the feet of those that have buried your husband are at the door, and they will carry you out." Immediately she fell down at his feet and died. When the young men came in they found her dead, and they carried her out and buried her beside her husband. And great fear came upon the whole church, and upon all who heard of these things.

Many Signs and Wonders Performed [5:12–16]

Now many signs and wonders were done among the people by the hands of the apostles. And they were all together in Solomon's Portico. None of the rest dared join them, but the people held them in high honor. And more than ever believers were added to the Lord, multitudes both of men and women, so that they even carried out the sick into the streets, and laid them on beds and pallets, that as Peter came by at least his shadow might fall on some of them. The people also gathered from the towns around Jerusalem, bringing the sick and those afflicted with unclean spirits, and they were all healed.

The Apostles Persecuted [5:17–42]

But the high priest rose up and all who were with him, that is, the party of the

These huge drafted stones were part of the ancient wall of Jerusalem erected by Herod the Great

Burton Holmes, Ewing Galloway

[c] Or *child*

[e] Or *Christ*

[f] Or *slaves*

[9] *Psalms* 2:1–2

Jerusalem: This Greek inscription, which is believed to have been part of the synagogue of the Libertines (Acts 6:9), says in part:

"Theodotos, son of Vettenos . . . built the synagogue for the reading of the law and for the teaching of the commandments . . ."

Sad'ducees, and filled with jealousy they arrested the apostles and put them in the common prison. But at night an angel of the Lord opened the prison doors and brought them out and said, "Go and stand in the temple and speak to the people all the words of this Life." And when they heard this, they entered the temple at daybreak and taught.

Now the high priest came and those who were with him and called together the council and all the senate of Israel, and sent to the prison to have them brought. But when the officers came, they did not find them in the prison, and they returned and reported, "We found the prison securely locked and the sentries standing at the doors, but when we opened it we found no one inside." Now when the captain of the temple and the chief priests heard these words, they were much perplexed about them, wondering what this would come to. And some one came and told them, "The men whom you put in prison are standing in the temple and teaching the people." Then the captain with the officers went and brought them, but without violence, for they were afraid of being stoned by the people.

And when they had brought them, they set them before the council. And the high priest questioned them, saying, "We strictly charged you not to teach in this name, yet here you have filled Jerusalem with your teaching and you intend to bring this man's blood upon us." But Peter and the apostles answered, "We must obey God rather than men. The God of our fathers raised Jesus whom you killed by hanging him on a tree. God exalted him at his right hand as Leader and Savior, to give repentance to Israel and forgiveness of sins. And we are witnesses to these things, and so is the Holy Spirit whom God has given to those who obey him."

When they heard this they were enraged and wanted to kill them. But a Phar'isee in the council named Gama'li-el, a teacher of the law, held in honor by all the people, stood up and ordered the men to be put outside for a while. And he said to them, "Men of Israel, take care what you do with these men. For before these days Theu'das arose, giving himself out to be somebody, and a number of men, about four hundred, joined him; but he was slain and all who followed him were dispersed and came to nothing. After him Judas the Galile'an arose in the days of the census and drew away some of the people after him; he also perished, and all who followed him were scattered. So in the present case I tell you, keep away from these men and let them alone; for if this plan or this undertaking is of men, it will fail; but if it is of God, you will not be able to overthrow them. You might even be found opposing God!"

So they took his advice, and when they had called in the apostles, they beat them and charged them not to speak in the name of Jesus, and let them go. Then they left the presence of the council, rejoicing that they were counted worthy to suffer dishonor for the name. And every day in the temple and at home they did not cease teaching and preaching Jesus as the Christ.

The Appointment of the Seven [Acts 6:1–7]

NOW in these days when the disciples were increasing in number, the Hel'lenists murmured against the Hebrews because their widows were neglected in the daily distribution. And the twelve summoned the body of the disciples and said, "It is not right that we should give up preaching the word of God to serve tables. Therefore, brethren, pick out from among you seven men of good repute, full of the Spirit and of wisdom, whom we may appoint to this duty. But we will devote ourselves to prayer and to the ministry of the word." And what they said pleased the whole multitude, and they chose Stephen, a man full of faith and of the Holy Spirit, and Philip, and Proch'orus, and Nica'nor, and Timon, and Par'menas, and Nicola'us, a proselyte of An'tioch. These they set before the apostles, and they prayed and laid their hands upon them.

And the word of God increased; and the number of the disciples multiplied greatly in Jerusalem, and a great many of the priests were obedient to the faith.

The Arrest of Stephen [6:8–15]

And Stephen, full of grace and power, did great wonders and signs among the people. Then some of those who belonged to the synagogue of the Freedmen (as it was

This outcropping of rock, 58 feet long and 51 feet wide, is believed to have been part of Solomon's Temple and the second Temple of Ezra and Nehemiah, perhaps the altar of sacrifice. Since A.D. 691 it has been covered by "The Dome of the Rock," erected by Abd el Malik, with subsequent additions

called), and of the Cyre′nians, and of the Alexandrians, and of those from Cili′cia and Asia, arose and disputed with Stephen. But they could not withstand the wisdom and the Spirit with which he spoke. Then they secretly instigated men, who said, "We have heard him speak blasphemous words against Moses and God." And they stirred up the people and the elders and the scribes, and they came upon him and seized him and brought him before the council, and set up false witnesses who said, "This man never ceases to speak words against this holy place and the law; for we have heard him say that this Jesus of Naz′areth will destroy this place, and will change the customs which Moses delivered to us." And gazing at him, all who sat in the council saw that his face was like the face of an angel.

Stephen's Defense [Acts 7:1–8]

AND the high priest said, "Is this so?" And Stephen said:

"Brethren and fathers, hear me. The God of glory appeared to our father Abraham, when he was in Mesopota′mia, before he lived in Haran,[10] and said to him, 'Depart from your land and from your kindred and go into the land which I will show you.' Then he departed from the land of the Chalde′ans, and lived in Haran. And after his father died, God removed him from there into this land in which you are now living; yet he gave him no inheritance in it, not even a foot's length, but promised to give it to him in possession and to his posterity after him, though he had no child. And God spoke to this effect, that his posterity would be aliens in a land belonging to others, who would enslave them and ill-treat them four hundred years. 'But I will judge the nation which they serve,' said God, 'and after that they shall come out and worship me in this place.' And he gave him the covenant of circumcision. And so Abraham became the father of Isaac, and circumcised him on the eighth day; and Isaac became the father of Jacob, and Jacob of the twelve patriarchs.

The Era of the Patriarchs [7:9–16]

"And the patriarchs, jealous of Joseph, sold him into Egypt; but God was with him, and rescued him out of all his afflictions, and gave him favor and wisdom before Pharaoh, king of Egypt, who made him governor over Egypt and over all his household. Now there came a famine throughout all Egypt and Canaan, and great affliction, and our fathers could find no food. But when Jacob heard that there was grain in Egypt, he sent forth our fathers the first time. And at the second visit Joseph made himself known to his brothers, and Joseph's family became known to Pharaoh. And Joseph sent and called to him Jacob his father and all his kindred, seventy-five souls; and Jacob went down into Egypt. And he died, himself and our fathers, and they were carried back to Shechem and laid in the tomb that Abraham had bought for a sum of silver from the sons of Hamor in Shechem.

[10]In this speech Stephen refers to many events in the history of the Jews which are recorded in the Old Testament books of Genesis, Exodus, Deuteronomy and others

American Foundation for the Study of Man
Mount Sinai with an ancient monastery occupied for the past 1500 years by Greek-speaking Christians. Here was preserved the famous Bible manuscript called "Codex Sinaiticus"

The Exile of Moses [7:17–29]

"But as the time of the promise drew near, which God had granted to Abraham, the people grew and multiplied in Egypt till there arose over Egypt another king who had not known Joseph. He dealt craftily with our race and forced our fathers to expose their infants, that they might not be kept alive. At this time Moses was born, and was beautiful before God. And he was brought up for three months in his father's house; and when he was exposed, Pharaoh's daughter adopted him and brought him up as her own son. And Moses was instructed in all the wisdom of the Egyptians, and he was mighty in his words and deeds.

"When he was forty years old, it came into his heart to visit his brethren, the sons of Israel. And seeing one of them being wronged, he defended the oppressed man and avenged him by striking the Egyptian. He supposed that his brethren understood that God was giving them deliverance by his hand, but they did not understand. And on the following day he appeared to them as they were quarreling and would have reconciled them, saying, 'Men, you are brethren, why do you wrong each other?' But the man who was wronging his neighbor thrust him aside, saying, 'Who made you a ruler and a judge over us? Do you want to kill me as you killed the Egyptian yesterday?' At this retort Moses fled, and became an exile in the land of Mid′ian, where he

became the father of two sons.

God's Call to Moses [7:30–34]

"Now when forty years had passed, an angel appeared to him in the wilderness of Mount Si′nai, in a flame of fire in a bush. When Moses saw it he wondered at the sight; and as he drew near to look, the voice of the Lord came, 'I am the God of your fathers, the God of Abraham and of Isaac and of Jacob.' And Moses trembled and did not dare to look. And the Lord said to him, 'Take off the shoes from your feet, for the place where you are standing is holy ground. I have surely seen the ill-treatment of my people that are in Egypt and heard their groaning, and I have come down to deliver them. And now come, I will send you to Egypt.'

The Israelites in the Wilderness [7:35–43]

"This Moses whom they refused, saying, 'Who made you a ruler and a judge?' God sent us both ruler and deliverer by the hand of the angel that appeared to him in the bush. He led them out, having performed wonders and signs in Egypt and at the Red Sea, and in the wilderness for forty years. This is the Moses who said to the Israelites, 'God will raise up for you a prophet from your brethren as he raised me up.' This is he who was in the congrega-

137

St. Stephen's Gate: This medieval gate commemorates the first Christian martyr, who was cast outside of the walls of Jerusalem and stoned

tion in the wilderness with the angel who spoke to him at Mount Si'nai, and with our fathers; and he received living oracles to give to us. Our fathers refused to obey him, but thrust him aside, and in their hearts they turned to Egypt, saying to Aaron, 'Make for us gods to go before us; as for this Moses who led us out from the land of Egypt, we do not know what has become of him.' And they made a calf in those days, and offered a sacrifice to the idol and rejoiced in the works of their hands. But God turned and gave them over to worship the host of heaven, as it is written in the book of the prophets:

'Did you offer to me slain beasts and
    sacrifices,
forty years in the wilderness, O house of
    Israel?
And you took up the tent of Moloch,
and the star of the god Rephan,
the figures which you made to worship;
and I will remove you beyond Babylon.'[11]

Where God Dwells [7:44-53]

"Our fathers had the tent of witness in the wilderness, even as he who spoke to Moses directed him to make it, according to the pattern that he had seen. Our fathers in turn brought it in with Joshua when they dispossessed the nations which God thrust out before our fathers. So it was until the days of David, who found favor in the sight of God and asked leave to find a habitation for the God of Jacob. But it was Solomon who built a house for him. Yet the Most High does not dwell in houses made with hands; as the prophet says,

'Heaven is my throne,
and earth my footstool.
What house will you build for me, says
    the Lord,
or what is the place of my rest?

[11]Amos 5:25-27

Did not my hand make all these
    things?'[12]

"You stiff-necked people, uncircumcised in heart and ears, you always resist the Holy Spirit. As your fathers did, so do you. Which of the prophets did not your fathers persecute? And they killed those who announced beforehand the coming of the Righteous One, whom you have now betrayed and murdered, you who received the law as delivered by angels and did not keep it."

The Stoning of Stephen [7:54—8:1a]

Now when they heard these things they were enraged, and they ground their teeth against him. But he, full of the Holy Spirit, gazed into heaven and saw the glory of God, and Jesus standing at the right hand of God; and he said, "Behold, I see the heavens opened, and the Son of man standing at the right hand of God." But they cried out with a loud voice and stopped their ears and rushed together upon him. Then they cast him out of the city and stoned him; and the witnesses laid down their garments at the feet of a young man named Saul. And as they were stoning Stephen, he prayed, "Lord Jesus, receive my spirit." And he knelt down and cried with a loud voice, "Lord, do not hold this sin against them." And when he had said this, he fell asleep. And Saul was consenting to his death.

Saul Persecutes the Church [Acts 8:1b-3]

AND on that day a great persecution arose against the church in Jerusalem; and they were all scattered throughout the

[12]Isaiah 66:1-2

region of Jude'a and Samar'ia, except the apostles. Devout men buried Stephen, and made great lamentation over him. But Saul laid waste the church, and entering house after house, he dragged off men and women and committed them to prison.

The Gospel Preached in Samaria [8:4-8]

Now those who were scattered went about preaching the word. Philip went down to a city of Samar'ia, and proclaimed to them the Christ. And the multitudes with one accord gave heed to what was said by Philip, when they heard him and saw the signs which he did. For unclean spirits came out of many who were possessed, crying with a loud voice; and many who were paralyzed or lame were healed. So there was much joy in that city.

The Conversion of Simon the Magician
[8:9-25]

But there was a man named Simon who had previously practiced magic in the city and amazed the nation of Samar'ia, saying that he himself was somebody great. They all gave heed to him, from the least to the greatest, saying, "This man is that power of God which is called Great." And they gave heed to him, because for a long time he had amazed them with his magic. But when they believed Philip as he preached good news about the kingdom of God and the name of Jesus Christ, they were baptized, both men and women. Even Simon himself believed, and after being baptized he continued with Philip. And seeing signs and great miracles performed, he was amazed.

Now when the apostles at Jerusalem heard that Samar'ia had received the word of God, they sent to them Peter and John, who came down and prayed for them that they might receive the Holy Spirit; for it had not yet fallen on any of them, but they had only been baptized in the name of the Lord Jesus. Then they laid their hands on them and they received the Holy Spirit. Now when Simon saw that the Spirit was given through the laying on of the apostles' hands, he offered them money, saying, "Give me also this power, that any one on whom I lay my hands may receive the Holy Spirit." But Peter said to him, "Your silver perish with you, because you thought you could obtain the gift of God with money! You have neither part nor lot in this matter, for your heart is not right before God. Repent therefore of this wickedness of yours, and pray to the Lord that, if possible, the intent of your heart may be forgiven you. For I see that you are in the gall of bitterness and in the bond of iniquity." And Simon answered, "Pray for me to the Lord, that nothing of what you have said may come upon me."

Now when they had testified and spoken the word of the Lord, they returned to Jerusalem, preaching the gospel to many villages of the Samar'itans.

Philip and the Ethiopian Eunuch
[8:26-40]

But an angel of the Lord said to Philip, "Rise and go toward the south[g] to the road that goes down from Jerusalem to Gaza."

[g]Or at noon

This is a desert road. And he rose and went. And behold, an Ethiopian, a eunuch, a minister of Canda'ce the queen of the Ethiopians, in charge of all her treasure, had come to Jerusalem to worship and was returning; seated in his chariot, he was reading the prophet Isai'ah. And the Spirit said to Philip, "Go up and join this chariot." So Philip ran to him, and heard him reading Isai'ah the prophet, and asked, "Do you understand what you are reading?" And he said, "How can I, unless some one guides me?" And he invited Philip to come up and sit with him. Now the passage of the scripture which he was reading was this:

"As a sheep led to the slaughter
or a lamb before its shearer is dumb,
so he opens not his mouth.
In his humiliation justice was denied him.
Who can describe his generation?
For his life is taken up from the
earth."[13]

And the eunuch said to Philip, "About whom, pray, does the prophet say this, about himself or about some one else?" Then Philip opened his mouth, and beginning with this scripture he told him the good news of Jesus. And as they went along the road they came to some water, and the eunuch said, "See, here is water! What is to prevent my being baptized?"[h] And he commanded the chariot to stop, and they both went down into the water, Philip and the eunuch, and he baptized him. And when they came up out of the water, the Spirit of the Lord caught up Philip; and the eunuch saw him no more, and went on his way rejoicing. But Philip was found at Azo'tus, and passing on he preached the gospel to all the towns till he came to Caesare'a.

The Conversion of Saul [Acts 9:1–19a]

BUT Saul, still breathing threats and murder against the disciples of the Lord, went to the high priest and asked him for letters to the synagogues at Damascus, so that if he found any belonging to the Way, men or women, he might bring them bound to Jerusalem. Now as he journeyed he approached Damascus, and suddenly a light from heaven flashed about him. And he fell to the ground and heard a voice saying to him, "Saul, Saul, why do you persecute me?" And he said, "Who are you, Lord?" And he said, "I am Jesus, whom you are persecuting; but rise and enter the city, and you will be told what you are to do." The men who were traveling with him stood speechless, hearing the voice but seeing no one. Saul arose from the ground; and when his eyes were opened, he could see nothing; so they led him by the hand and brought him into Damascus. And for three days he was without sight, and neither ate nor drank.

Now there was a disciple at Damascus named Anani'as. The Lord said to him in a vision, "Anani'as." And he said, "Here I am, Lord." And the Lord said to him, "Rise and go to the street called Straight, and inquire in the house of Judas for a man of

[h] Other ancient authorities add all or most of verse 37, *And Philip said, "If you believe with all your heart, you may." And he replied, "I believe that Jesus Christ is the Son of God."*

[13] *Isaiah 53:7–8*

Museum of Fine Arts, Boston

These pyramids at Meroë (about 133 miles north of Khartoum on the Nile) are the tombs of the Candaces (or Queens) and Kings of Ethiopia, ca. 300 B.C. to A.D. 350

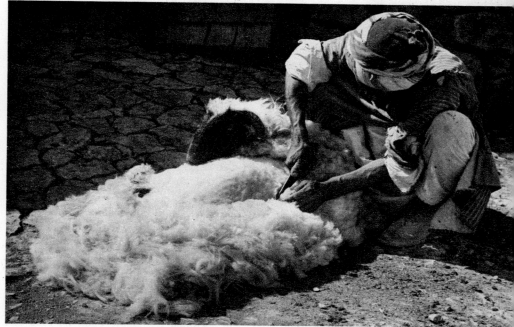

The Matson Photo Service

"Like a sheep that before its shearers is dumb, so he opened not his mouth." Isa. 53:7

Bas-relief of Candace (or Queen) Amanitēre on the walls of the Lion Temple at Naga, Nubia. Amanitēre, who died about A.D. 15, is in the center, with prince on the left and lion god on the extreme right

Oriental Institute, University of Chicago

immediately he proclaimed Jesus, saying, "He is the Son of God." And all who heard him were amazed, and said, "Is not this the man who made havoc in Jerusalem of those who called on this name? And he has come here for this purpose, to bring them bound before the chief priests." But Saul increased all the more in strength, and confounded the Jews who lived in Damascus by proving that Jesus was the Christ.

Saul Escapes from the Jews [9:23–25]

When many days had passed, the Jews plotted to kill him, but their plot became known to Saul. They were watching the gates day and night, to kill him; but his disciples took him by night and let him down over the wall, lowering him in a basket.

Saul at Jerusalem [9:26–31]

And when he had come to Jerusalem he attempted to join the disciples; and they were all afraid of him, for they did not believe that he was a disciple. But Bar'-nabas took him, and brought him to the apostles, and declared to them how on the road he had seen the Lord, who spoke to him, and how at Damascus he had preached boldly in the name of Jesus. So he went in and out among them at Jerusalem, preaching boldly in the name of the Lord. And he spoke and disputed against the Hellenists; but they were seeking to kill him. And when the brethren knew it, they brought him down to Caesare'a, and sent him off to Tarsus.

So the church throughout all Jude'a and Gal'ilee and Samar'ia had peace and was built up; and walking in the fear of the Lord and in the comfort of the Holy Spirit it was multiplied.

Peter Heals Aeneas [9:32–35]

Now as Peter went here and there among them all, he came down also to the saints that lived at Lydda. There he found a man named Aene'as, who had been bedridden for eight years and was paralyzed. And Peter said to him, "Aene'as, Jesus Christ heals you; rise and make your bed." And immediately he rose. And all the residents of Lydda and Sharon saw him, and they turned to the Lord.

Dorcas Restored to Life [9:36–43]

Now there was at Joppa a disciple named Tab'itha, which means Dorcas or Gazelle. She was full of good works and acts of charity. In those days she fell sick and died; and when they had washed her, they laid her in an upper room. Since Lydda was near Joppa, the disciples, hearing that Peter was there, sent two men to him entreating him, "Please come to us without delay." So Peter rose and went with them. And when he had come, they took him to the upper room. All the widows stood beside him weeping, and showing coats and garments which Dorcas made while she was with them. But Peter put them all outside and knelt down and prayed; then turning to the body he said, "Tab'itha, rise." And she opened her eyes, and when she saw Peter she sat up. And he gave her his hand and lifted her up. Then calling the saints and widows he presented her alive. And it became known throughout all Joppa, and many believed in the Lord. And he stayed in Joppa for many days with one Simon, a tanner.

Ewing Galloway

Damascus: The Street called Straight, one of the oldest known streets in the world

Tarsus named Saul; for behold, he is praying, and he has seen a man named Anani'as come in and lay his hands on him so that he might regain his sight." But Anani'as answered, "Lord, I have heard from many about this man, how much evil he has done to thy saints at Jerusalem; and here he has authority from the chief priests to bind all who call upon thy name." But the Lord said to him, "Go, for he is a chosen instrument of mine to carry my name before the Gentiles and kings and the sons of Israel; for I will show him how much he must suffer for the sake of my name." So Anani'as

departed and entered the house. And laying his hands on him he said, "Brother Saul, the Lord Jesus who appeared to you on the road by which you came, has sent me that you may regain your sight and be filled with the Holy Spirit." And immediately something like scales fell from his eyes and he regained his sight. Then he rose and was baptized, and took food and was strengthened.

Saul Preaches at Damascus [9:19b–22]

For several days he was with the disciples at Damascus. And in the synagogues

Part of the Damascus wall as it is today

J. Lane Miller

Cornelius' Vision [Acts 10:1-8]

AT Caesare'a there was a man named Cornelius, a centurion of what was known as the Italian Cohort, a devout man who feared God with all his household, gave alms liberally to the people, and prayed constantly to God. About the ninth hour of the day he saw clearly in a vision an angel of God coming in and saying to him, "Cornelius." And he stared at him in terror, and said, "What is it, Lord?" And he said to him, "Your prayers and your alms have ascended as a memorial before God. And now send men to Joppa, and bring one Simon who is called Peter; he is lodging with Simon, a tanner, whose house is by the seaside." When the angel who spoke to him had departed, he called two of his servants and a devout soldier from among those that waited on him, and having related everything to them, he sent them to Joppa.

Peter's Vision [10:9-16]

The next day, as they were on their journey and coming near the city, Peter went up on the housetop to pray, about the sixth hour. And he became hungry and desired something to eat; but while they were preparing it, he fell into a trance and saw the heaven opened, and something descending, like a great sheet, let down by four corners upon the earth. In it were all kinds of animals and reptiles and birds of the air. And there came a voice to him, "Rise, Peter; kill and eat." But Peter said, "No, Lord; for I have never eaten anything that is common or unclean." And the voice came to him again a second time, "What God has cleansed, you must not call common." This happened three times, and the thing was taken up at once to heaven.

Cornelius Sends for Peter [10:17-33]

Now while Peter was inwardly perplexed as to what the vision which he had seen might mean, behold, the men that were sent by Cornelius, having made inquiry for Simon's house, stood before the gate and called out to ask whether Simon who was called Peter was lodging there. And while Peter was pondering the vision, the Spirit said to him, "Behold, three men are looking for you. Rise and go down, and accompany them without hesitation; for I have sent them." And Peter went down to the men and said, "I am the one you are looking for; what is the reason for your coming?" And they said, "Cornelius, a centurion, an upright and God-fearing man, who is well spoken of by the whole Jewish nation, was directed by a holy angel to send for you to come to his house, and to hear what you have to say." So he called them in to be his guests.

The next day he rose and went off with them, and some of the brethren from Joppa accompanied him. And on the following day they entered Caesare'a. Cornelius was expecting them and had called together his kinsmen and close friends. When Peter entered, Cornelius met him and fell down at his feet and worshiped him. But Peter lifted him up, saying, "Stand up; I too am a man." And as he talked with him, he went in and found many persons gathered; and he said to them, "You yourselves know how unlawful it is for a Jew to associate with or

Tarsus: The Roman gateway in the west wall, leading to the seaport and to Iconium. To the left is the modern road which follows the ancient route

to visit any one of another nation; but God has shown me that I should not call any man common or unclean. So when I was sent for, I came without objection. I ask then why you sent for me."

And Cornelius said, "Four days ago, about this hour, I was keeping the ninth hour of prayer in my house; and behold, a man stood before me in bright apparel, saying, 'Cornelius, your prayer has been heard and your alms have been remembered before God. Send therefore to Joppa and ask for Simon who is called Peter; he is lodging in the house of Simon, a tanner, by the seaside.' So I sent to you at once, and you have been kind enough to come. Now therefore we are all here present in the sight of God, to hear all that you have been commanded by the Lord."

Peter Speaks in Cornelius' House

[10:34-43]

And Peter opened his mouth and said: "Truly I perceive that God shows no partiality, but in every nation any one who fears him and does what is right is acceptable to him. You know the word which he sent to Israel, preaching good news of peace by Jesus Christ (he is Lord of all), the word which was proclaimed throughout all Jude'a, beginning from Gal'ilee after the baptism which John preached: how God anointed Jesus of Naz'areth with the Holy Spirit and with power; how he went about doing good and healing all that were oppressed by the devil, for God was with him. And we are witnesses to all that he did both in the country of the Jews and in Jerusalem. They put him to death by hanging him on a tree; but God raised him on the third day and made him manifest; not to all the people but to us who were chosen by God as witnesses, who ate and drank with him after he rose from the dead. And he commanded us to preach to the people, and to testify that he is the one ordained by God to be judge of the living and the dead. To him all the prophets bear witness that every one who believes in him receives forgiveness of sins through his name."

The Gentiles Receive the Holy Spirit

[10:44-48]

While Peter was still saying this, the Holy Spirit fell on all who heard the word. And the believers from among the circumcised who came with Peter were amazed, because the gift of the Holy Spirit had been poured out even on the Gentiles. For they heard them speaking in tongues and

Marshlands south of Tarsus, where formerly the great inland harbor, Lake Rhegma, teemed with ships. Silt deposited by the Cydnus River has filled up the lake

Antioch on the Orontes River, at the foot of Mount Silpius, was the third largest city in the Roman Empire. Here the disciples were first called Christians

Wide World

three men arrived at the house in which we were, sent to me from Caesare'a. And the Spirit told me to go with them, making no distinction. These six brethren also accompanied me, and we entered the man's house. And he told us how he had seen the angel standing in his house and saying, 'Send to Joppa and bring Simon called Peter; he will declare to you a message by which you will be saved, you and all your household.' As I began to speak, the Holy Spirit fell on them just as on us at the beginning. And I remembered the word of the Lord, how he said, 'John baptized with water, but you shall be baptized with the Holy Spirit.' If then God gave the same gift to them as he gave to us when we believed in the Lord Jesus Christ, who was I that I could withstand God?" When they heard this they were silenced. And they glorified God, saying, "Then to the Gentiles also God has granted repentance unto life."

The Church at Antioch [11:19–30]

Now those who were scattered because of the persecution that arose over Stephen traveled as far as Phoeni'cia and Cyprus and An'tioch, speaking the word to none except Jews. But there were some of them, men of Cyprus and Cyre'ne, who on coming to An'tioch spoke to the Greeks' also, preaching the Lord Jesus. And the hand of the Lord was with them, and a great number that believed turned to the Lord. News of this came to the ears of the church in Jerusalem, and they sent Bar'nabas to An'tioch. When he came and saw the grace of God, he was glad; and he exhorted them all to remain faithful to the Lord with steadfast purpose; for he was a good man, full of the Holy Spirit and of faith. And a large company was added to the Lord. So Bar'nabas went to Tarsus to look for Saul; and when he had found him, he brought him to Antioch. For a whole year they met with[j] the church, and taught a large company of people; and in An'tioch the disciples were for the first time called Christians.

Now in these days prophets came down from Jerusalem to An'tioch. And one of them named Ag'abus stood up and foretold by the Spirit that there would be a great famine over all the world; and this took place in the days of Claudius. And the disciples determined, every one according to his ability, to send relief to the brethren who lived in Jude'a; and they did so, sending it to the elders by the hand of Bar'nabas and Saul.

Peter's Report to the Church at Jerusalem [Acts 11:1–18]

NOW the apostles and the brethren who were in Jude'a heard that the Gentiles also had received the word of God. So when Peter went up to Jerusalem, the circumcision party criticized him, saying,

extolling God. Then Peter declared, "Can any one forbid water for baptizing these people who have received the Holy Spirit just as we have?" And he commanded them to be baptized in the name of Jesus Christ. Then they asked him to remain for some days.

"Why did you go to uncircumcised men and eat with them?" But Peter began and explained to them in order: "I was in the city of Joppa praying; and in a trance I saw a vision, something descending, like a great sheet, let down from heaven by four corners; and it came down to me. Looking at it closely I observed animals and beasts of prey and reptiles and birds of the air. And I heard a voice saying to me, 'Rise, Peter; kill and eat.' But I said, 'No, Lord; for nothing common or unclean has ever entered my mouth.' But the voice answered a second time from heaven, 'What God has cleansed you must not call common.' This happened three times, and all was drawn up again into heaven. At that very moment

James Killed and Peter Imprisoned

[Acts 12:1–5]

ABOUT that time Herod the king laid violent hands upon some who belonged to the church. He killed James the brother of John with the sword; and when he saw that it pleased the Jews, he proceeded to arrest Peter also. This was during the days of Unleavened Bread. And when he had seized him, he put him in prison, and delivered him to four squads of soldiers to guard him, intending after the Passover to bring him out to the people.

'Other ancient authorities read *Hellenists*
[j]Or *were guests of*

Paphos on the Island of Cyprus. Ancient Roman pillars still stand near the church named after Paul

T. Goell

So Peter was kept in prison; but earnest prayer for him was made to God by the church.

Peter Delivered from Prison [12:6-19]

The very night when Herod was about to bring him out, Peter was sleeping between two soldiers, bound with two chains, and sentries before the door were guarding the prison; and behold, an angel of the Lord appeared, and a light shone in the cell; and he struck Peter on the side and woke him, saying, "Get up quickly." And the chains fell off his hands. And the angel said to him, "Dress yourself and put on your sandals." And he did so. And he said to him, "Wrap your mantle around you and follow me." And he went out and followed him; he did not know that what was done by the angel was real, but thought he was seeing a vision. When they had passed the first and the second guard, they came to the iron gate leading into the city. It opened to them of its own accord, and they went out and passed on through one street; and immediately the angel left him. And Peter came to himself, and said, "Now I am sure that the Lord has sent his angel and rescued me from the hand of Herod and from all that the Jewish people were expecting."

When he realized this, he went to the house of Mary, the mother of John whose other name was Mark, where many were gathered together and were praying. And when he knocked at the door of the gateway, a maid named Rhoda came to answer. Recognizing Peter's voice, in her joy she did not open the gate but ran in and told that Peter was standing at the gate. They said to her, "You are mad." But she insisted that it was so. They said, "It is his angel!" But Peter continued knocking; and when they opened, they saw him and were amazed. But motioning to them with his hand to be silent, he described to them how the Lord had brought him out of the prison. And he said, "Tell this to James and to the brethren." Then he departed and went to another place.

Now when day came, there was no small stir among the soldiers over what had become of Peter. And when Herod had sought for him and could not find him, he examined the sentries and ordered that they should be put to death. Then he went down from Jude'a to Caesare'a, and remained there.

The Death of Herod [12:20-23]

Now Herod was angry with the people of Tyre and Sidon; and they came to him in a body, and having persuaded Blastus, the king's chamberlain, they asked for peace, because their country depended on the king's country for food. On an appointed day Herod put on his royal robes, took his seat upon the throne, and made an oration to them. And the people shouted, "The voice of a god, and not of man!" Immediately an angel of the Lord smote him, because he did not give God the glory; and he was eaten by worms and died.

Barnabas and Saul [12:24-13:3]

But the word of God grew and multiplied. And Bar'nabas and Saul returned from[k]

[k]Other ancient authorities read *to*

Gemma Augustea: The upper half of this cameo shows the Emperor Augustus in the role of Jupiter, whose eagle is at his feet; seated next to him is the goddess Roma. Tiberius, dismounting from a triumphal chariot, and Germanicus to his left, are returning from a victory over northern enemies, ca. A.D. 12. Both Augustus and Tiberius hold scepters. The lower half shows captives in distress, with Roman soldiers erecting a trophy of victory

Kunsthistorisches Museum, Vienna

Jerusalem when they had fulfilled their mission, bringing with them John whose other name was Mark.

Now in the church at An'tioch there were prophets and teachers, Bar'nabas, Sym'eon who was called Niger, Lucius of Cyre'ne, Mana'-en a member of the court of Herod the tetrarch, and Saul. While they were worshiping the Lord and fasting, the Holy Spirit said, "Set apart for me Bar'nabas and Saul for the work to which I have called them." Then after fasting and praying they laid their hands on them and sent them off.

The Apostles Preach in Cyprus

[Acts 13:4-12]

SO, being sent out by the Holy Spirit, they went down to Seleu'cia; and from there they sailed to Cyprus. When they arrived at Sal'amis, they proclaimed the word of God in the synagogues of the Jews. And they had John to assist them. When they had gone through the whole island as far as Paphos, they came upon a certain magician, a Jewish false prophet, named Bar-Jesus. He was with the proconsul, Ser'gius Paulus, a man of intelligence, who summoned Bar'nabas and Saul and sought to hear the word of God. But El'ymas the magician (for that is the meaning of his name) withstood them, seeking to turn away the proconsul from the faith. But Saul, who is also called Paul, filled with the Holy Spirit, looked intently at him and said, "You son of the devil, you enemy of all righteousness, full of all deceit and villainy, will you not stop making crooked the straight paths of the Lord? And now, behold, the hand of the Lord is upon you, and you shall be blind and unable to see the sun for a time." Immediately mist and darkness fell upon him and he went about seeking people to lead him by the hand. Then the proconsul believed, when he saw what had occurred, for he was astonished at the teaching of the Lord.

Paul and Barnabas at Antioch of Pisidia

[13:13-43]

Now Paul and his company set sail from Paphos, and came to Perga in Pamphyl'ia. And John left them and returned to Jerusalem; but they passed on from Perga and came to An'tioch of Pisid'ia. And on the sabbath day they went into the synagogue and sat down. After the reading of the law

Excavated section of the third wall north of Jerusalem, started by Herod Agrippa I but stopped by the Romans

E. L. Sukenik

David M. Robinson

Pisidian Antioch: These steps mounting from the Square of Tiberius to the Square and Temple of Augustus were seen by Paul

and the prophets, the rulers of the synagogue sent to them, saying, "Brethren, if you have any word of exhortation for the people, say it." So Paul stood up, and motioning with his hand said:

"Men of Israel, and you that fear God, listen. The God of this people Israel chose our fathers and made the people great during their stay in the land of Egypt, and with uplifted arm he led them out of it. And for about forty years he bore with[m] them in the wilderness. And when he had destroyed seven nations in the land of Canaan, he gave them their land as an inheritance, for about four hundred and fifty years. And after that he gave them judges until Samuel the prophet. Then they asked for a king;

[m]Other ancient authorities read *cared for* (Deut. 1:31)

and God gave them Saul the son of Kish, a man of the tribe of Benjamin, for forty years. And when he had removed him, he raised up David to be their king; of whom he testified and said, 'I have found in David the son of Jesse a man after my heart,[14] who will do all my will.' Of this man's posterity God has brought to Israel a Savior, Jesus, as he promised. Before his coming John had preached a baptism of repentance to all the people of Israel. And as John was finishing his course, he said, 'What do you suppose that I am? I am not he. No, but after me one is coming, the sandals of whose feet I am not worthy to untie.'

"Brethren, sons of the family of Abraham, and those among you that fear God, to

[14]I Samuel 13:14; Psalms 89:20

The Mound at Derbe

Underwood & Underwood

us has been sent the message of this salvation. For those who live in Jerusalem and their rulers, because they did not recognize him nor understand the utterances of the prophets which are read every sabbath, fulfilled these by condemning him. Though they could charge him with nothing deserving death, yet they asked Pilate to have him killed. And when they had fulfilled all that was written of him, they took him down from the tree, and laid him in a tomb. But God raised him from the dead; and for many days he appeared to those who came up with him from Gal'ilee to Jerusalem, who are now his witnesses to the people. And we bring you the good news that what God promised to the fathers, this he has fulfilled to us their children by raising Jesus; as also it is written in the second psalm,

'Thou art my Son,
today I have begotten thee.'[15]

And as for the fact that he raised him from the dead, no more to return to corruption, he spoke in this way,

'I will give you the holy and sure blessings of David.'[16]

Therefore he says also in another psalm,

'Thou wilt not let thy Holy One see corruption.'[17]

For David, after he had served the counsel of God in his own generation, fell asleep, and was laid with his fathers, and saw corruption; but he whom God raised up saw no corruption. Let it be known to you therefore, brethren, that through this man forgiveness of sins is proclaimed to you, and by him every one that believes is freed from everything from which you could not be freed by the law of Moses. Beware, therefore, lest there come upon you what is said in the prophets:

'Behold, you scoffers, and wonder, and perish;
for I do a deed in your days,
a deed you will never believe, if one declares it to you.' "[18]

As they went out, the people begged that these things might be told them the next sabbath. And when the meeting of the synagogue broke up, many Jews and devout converts to Judaism followed Paul and Bar'nabas, who spoke to them and urged them to continue in the grace of God.

The Result of Hearing the Word of God

[13:44-52]

The next sabbath almost the whole city gathered together to hear the word of God. But when the Jews saw the multitudes, they were filled with jealousy, and contradicted what was spoken by Paul, and reviled him. And Paul and Bar'nabas spoke out boldly, saying, "It was necessary that the word of God should be spoken first to you. Since you thrust it from you, and judge yourselves unworthy of eternal life, behold, we turn to the Gentiles. For so the Lord has commanded us, saying,

'I have set you to be a light for the Gentiles,

[15]Psalms 2:7

[16]Isaiah 55:3

[17]Psalms 16:10

[18]Habakkuk 1:5

144

that you may bring salvation to the utter-most parts of the earth.' "[19]

And when the Gentiles heard this, they were glad and glorified the word of God; and as many as were ordained to eternal life believed. And the word of the Lord spread throughout all the region. But the Jews incited the devout women of high standing and the leading men of the city, and stirred up persecution against Paul and Bar'nabas, and drove them out of their district. But they shook off the dust from their feet against them, and went to Ico'-nium. And the disciples were filled with joy and with the Holy Spirit.

Paul and Barnabas at Iconium [Acts 14:1–7]

NOW at Ico'nium they entered together into the Jewish synagogue, and so spoke that a great company believed, both of Jews and of Greeks. But the unbelieving Jews stirred up the Gentiles and poisoned their minds against the brethren. So they remained for a long time, speaking boldly for the Lord, who bore witness to the word of his grace, granting signs and wonders to be done by their hands. But the people of the city were divided; some sided with the Jews, and some with the apostles. When an attempt was made by both Gentiles and Jews, with their rulers, to molest them and to stone them, they learned of it and fled to Lystra and Derbe, cities of Lycao'nia, and to the surrounding country; and there they preached the gospel.

Paul Stoned at Lystra [14:8–23]

Now at Lystra there was a man sitting, who could not use his feet; he was a cripple from birth, who had never walked. He listened to Paul speaking; and Paul, looking intently at him and seeing that he had faith to be made well, said in a loud voice, "Stand upright on your feet." And he sprang up and walked. And when the crowds saw what Paul had done, they lifted up their voices, saying in Lycao'nian, "The gods have come down to us in the likeness of men!" Bar'nabas they called Zeus, and Paul, because he was the chief speaker, they called Hermes. And the priest of Zeus, whose temple was in front of the city, brought oxen and garlands to the gates and wanted to offer sacrifice with the people. But when the apostles Bar'-nabas and Paul heard of it, they tore their garments and rushed out among the multitude, crying, "Men, why are you doing this? We also are men, of like nature with you, and bring you good news, that you should turn from these vain things to a living God who made the heaven and the earth and the sea and all that is in them. In past generations he allowed all the nations to walk in their own ways; yet he did not leave himself without witness, for he did good and gave you from heaven rains and fruitful seasons, satisfying your hearts with food and gladness." With these words they scarcely restrained the people from offering sacrifice to them.

But Jews came there from An'tioch and Ico'nium; and having persuaded the people, they stoned Paul and dragged him out of the city, supposing that he was dead. But when the disciples gathered about him, he rose up and entered the city; and on the

[19] Isaiah 49:6

Underwood & Underwood

Site of Lystra, looking south toward the Taurus Mountains

next day he went on with Bar'nabas to Derbe. When they had preached the gospel to that city and had made many disciples, they returned to Lystra and to Ico'nium and to An'tioch, strengthening the souls of the disciples, exhorting them to continue in the faith, and saying that through many tribulations we must enter the kingdom of God. And when they had appointed elders for them in every church, with prayer and fasting, they committed them to the Lord in whom they believed.

The Return to Antioch of Pisidia
[14:24–28]

Then they passed through Pisid'ia, and came to Pamphyl'ia. And when they had spoken the word in Perga, they went down to Attali'a; and from there they sailed to An'tioch, where they had been commended to the grace of God for the work which they had fulfilled. And when they arrived, they gathered the church together and declared all that God had done with them, and how he had opened a door of faith to the Gentiles. And they remained no little time with the disciples.

The Council at Jerusalem
[Acts 15:1–21]

BUT some men came down from Jude'a and were teaching the brethren, "Unless you are circumcised according to the

Antioch (from Mount Silpius): The Orontes River and the road leading to the Mediterranean, twenty miles away, are visible across the top of the picture

The Matson Photo Service

Old Roman Road to Tarsus from the Cilician Gates

The Cilician Gates, going south toward Tarsus

Air view of Neapolis (modern Cavalla)

custom of Moses, you cannot be saved." And when Paul and Bar'nabas had no small dissension and debate with them, Paul and Bar'nabas and some of the others were appointed to go up to Jerusalem to the apostles and the elders about this question. So, being sent on their way by the church, they passed through both Phoeni'cia and Samar'ia, reporting the conversation of the Gentiles, and they gave great joy to all the brethren. When they came to Jerusalem, they were welcomed by the church and the apostles and the elders, and they declared all that God had done with them. But some believers who belonged to the party of the Phar'isees rose up, and said, "It is necessary to circumcise them, and to charge them to keep the law of Moses."

The apostles and the elders were gathered together to consider this matter. And after there had been much debate, Peter rose and said to them, "Brethren, you know that in the early days God made choice among you, that by my mouth the Gentiles should hear the word of the gospel and believe. And God who knows the heart bore witness to them, giving them the Holy Spirit just as he did to us; and he made no distinction between us and them, but cleansed their hearts by faith. Now therefore why do you make trial of God by putting a yoke upon the neck of the disciples which neither our fathers nor we have been able to bear? But we believe that we shall be saved through the grace of the Lord Jesus, just as they will."

And all the assembly kept silence; and they listened to Bar'nabas and Paul as they related what signs and wonders God had done through them among the Gentiles. After they finished speaking, James replied, "Brethren, listen to me. Sym'eon has related how God first visited the Gentiles, to take out of them a people for his name. And with this the words of the prophets agree, as it is written,

'After this I will return,
and I will rebuild the dwelling of David,
which has fallen;
I will rebuild its ruins,
and I will set it up,
that the rest of men may seek the Lord,
and all the Gentiles who are called by
my name,
says the Lord, who has made these things
known from of old.'[20]

Therefore my judgment is that we should not trouble those of the Gentiles who turn to God, but should write to them to abstain from the polutions of idols and from unchastity and from what is strangled[n] and from blood. For from early generations Moses has had in every city those who preach him, for he is read every sabbath in the synagogues."

The Reply of the Council [15:22-35]

Then it seemed good to the apostles and the elders, with the whole church, to choose men from among them and send them to An'tioch with Paul and Bar'nabas. They sent Judas called Barsab'bas, and Silas, leading men among the brethren, with the following letter: "The brethren, both the apostles and the elders, to the brethren who are of the Gentiles in An'tioch and Syria and Cili'cia, greeting. Since we have heard that some persons from us have troubled you with words, unsettling your minds, although we gave them no instructions, it has seemed good to us in assembly to choose men and send them to you with our beloved Bar'nabas and Paul, men who have risked their lives for the sake of our Lord Jesus Christ. We have therefore sent Judas and Silas, who themselves will tell you the same things by word of mouth. For it has seemed good to the Holy Spirit and to us to lay upon you no greater burden than these necessary things: that you abstain from what has been sacrificed to idols and from blood and from what is strangled[n] and from unchastity. If you keep yourselves from these, you will do well. Farewell."

So when they were sent off, they went down to An'tioch; and having gathered the congregation together, they delivered the letter. And when they read it, they rejoiced at the exhortation. And Judas and Silas, who were themselves prophets, exhorted the brethren with many words and strengthened them. And after they had spent some time, they were sent off in peace by the brethren to those who had sent them.[o] But Paul and Bar'nabas remained in An'tioch, teaching and preaching the word of the Lord, with many others also.

Paul Separates from Barnabas [15:36-41]

And after some days Paul said to Bar'nabas, "Come, let us return and visit the brethren in every city where we proclaimed the word of the Lord, and see how they are." And Bar'nabas wanted to take with them John called Mark. But Paul thought best not to take with them one who had withdrawn from them in Pamphyl'ia, and had not gone with them to the work. And there arose a sharp contention, so that they separated from each other; Bar'nabas took Mark with him and sailed away to Cyprus, but Paul chose Silas and departed, being commended by the brethren to the grace of the Lord. And he went through Syria and Cili'cia, strengthening the churches.

Timothy Accompanies Paul and Silas

[Acts 16:1-5]

AND he came also to Derbe and to Lystra. A disciple was there, named Timothy, the son of a Jewish woman who was a believer; but his father was a Greek. He was well spoken of by the brethren at Lystra and Ico'nium. Paul wanted Timothy to accompany him; and he took him and circumcised him because of the Jews that were in those places, for they all knew that his father was a Greek. As they went on their way through the cities, they delivered to them for observance the decisions which had been reached by the apostles and elders who were at Jerusalem. So the churches were strengthened in the faith, and they increased in numbers daily.

Paul's Vision of the Man of Macedonia

[16:6-10]

And they went through the region of Phry'gia and Gala'tia, having been for-

---

[n]Other early authorities omit *and from what is strangled*

[20]*Amos* 9:11-12

[o]Other ancient authorities insert verse 34, *But it seemed good to Silas to remain there*

bidden by the Holy Spirit to speak the word in Asia. And when they had come opposite My′sia, they attempted to go into Bithyn′ia, but the Spirit of Jesus did not allow them; so, passing by My′sia, they went down to Troas. And a vision appeared to Paul in the night: a man of Macedo′nia was standing beseeching him and saying, "Come over to Macedo nia and help us." And when he had seen the vision, immediately we sought to go on into Macedo′nia, concluding that God had called us to preach the gospel to them.

The Conversion of Lydia [16:11–15]

Setting sail therefore from Troas, we made a direct voyage to Sam′othrace, and the following day to Ne-ap′olis, and from there to Phil′ippi, which is the leading city of the district*ˣ* of Macedo′nia, and a Roman colony. We remained in this city some days; and on the sabbath day we went outside the gate to the riverside, where we supposed there was a place of prayer; and we sat down and spoke to the women who had come together. One who heard us was a woman named Lydia, from the city of Thyati′ra, a seller of purple goods, who was a worshiper of God. The Lord opened her heart to give heed to what was said by Paul. And when she was baptized, with her household, she besought us, saying, "If you have judged me to be faithful to the Lord, come to my house and stay." And she prevailed upon us.

The Imprisonment at Philippi [16:16–40]

As we were going to the place of prayer, we were met by a slave girl who had a spirit of divination and brought her owners much gain by soothsaying. She followed Paul and us, crying, "These men are servants of the Most High God, who proclaim to you the way of salvation." And this she did for many days. But Paul was annoyed, and turned and said to the spirit, "I charge you in the name of Jesus Christ to come out of her." And it came out that very hour.

But when her owners saw that their hope of gain was gone, they seized Paul and Silas and dragged them into the market place before the rulers; and when they had brought them to the magistrates they said, "These men are Jews and they are disturbing our city. They advocate customs which it is not lawful for us Romans to accept or practice." The crowd joined in attacking them; and the magistrates tore the garments off them and gave orders to beat them with rods. And when they had inflicted many blows upon them, they threw them into prison, charging the jailer to keep them safely. Having received this charge, he put them into the inner prison and fastened their feet in the stocks.

But about midnight Paul and Silas were praying and singing hymns to God, and the prisoners were listening to them, and suddenly there was a great earthquake, so that the foundations of the prison were shaken; and immediately all the doors were opened and every one's fetters were unfastened. When the jailer woke and saw that the prison doors were open, he drew his sword and was about to kill himself, supposing that the prisoners had escaped. But Paul cried with a loud voice, "Do not harm yourself, for we are all here." And he called for

*ˣ*The Greek text is uncertain

Greek Government

Air view of Philippi. The ruins of two Christian churches are visible in the center foreground. Between these ruins and the road are the remains of the Roman forum

lights and rushed in, and trembling with fear he fell down before Paul and Silas, and brought them out and said, "Men, what must I do to be saved?" And they said, "Believe in the Lord Jesus, and you will be saved, you and your household." And they spoke the word of the Lord to him and to all that were in his house. And he took them the same hour of the night, and washed their wounds, and he was baptized at once, with all his family. Then he brought them up into his house, and set food before them; and he rejoiced with all his household that he had believed in God.

But when it was day, the magistrates sent the police, saying, "Let those men go." And the jailer reported the words to Paul, saying, "The magistrates have sent to let you go; now therefore come out and go in peace." But Paul said to them, "They have beaten us publicly, uncondemned, men who are Roman citizens, and have thrown us into prison; and do they now cast us out secretly? No! let them come themselves and take us out." The police reported these words to the magistrates, and they were afraid when they heard that they were Roman citizens; so they came and apologized to them. And they took them out and asked them to leave the city. So they went out of the prison, and visited Lydia; and when they had seen the brethren, they exhorted them and departed.

The Uproar in Thessalonica [Acts 17:1–9]

NOW when they had passed through Amphip′olis and Apollo′nia, they came to Thessaloni′ca, where there was a synagogue of the Jews. And Paul went in, as was his custom, and for three weeks*ᵖ* he argued with them from the scriptures, explaining and proving that it was necessary for the Christ to suffer and to rise from the dead, and saying, "This Jesus, whom I proclaim to you, is the Christ." And some of them were persuaded, and joined Paul and Silas; as did a great many of the devout Greeks and not a few of the leading women. But the Jews were jealous, and taking some wicked fellows of the rabble, they gathered a crowd, set the city in an uproar, and attacked the house of Jason, seeking to bring them out to the people. And when they could not find them, they dragged Jason and some of the brethren before the city authorities, crying, "These men who have turned the world upside down have come here also, and Jason has received them; and they are all acting against the decrees of Caesar, saying that there is another king, Jesus." And the people and the city authorities were disturbed when they heard this. And when they had taken security from Jason and the rest, they let them go.

*ᵖ*Or *sabbaths*

Air view of Thessalonica (modern Salonica)

Greek Government

Agora Excavations, Athens

Athens: The Acropolis and the Areopagus, seen from the northwest

The Apostles at Beroea [17:10–15]

The brethren immediately sent Paul and Silas away by night to Beroe'a; and when they arrived they went into the Jewish synagogue. Now these Jews were more noble than those in Thessaloni'ca, for they received the word with all eagerness, examining the scriptures daily to see if these things were so. Many of them therefore believed, with not a few Greek women of high standing as well as men. But when the Jews of Thessaloni'ca learned that the word of God was proclaimed by Paul at Beroe'a also, they came there too, stirring up and inciting the crowds. Then the brethren immediately sent Paul off on his way to the sea, but Silas and Timothy remained there. Those who conducted Paul brought him as far as Athens; and receiving a command for Silas and Timothy to come to him as soon as possible, they departed.

Paul at Athens [17:16–34]

Now while Paul was waiting for them at Athens, his spirit was provoked within him as he saw that the city was full of idols. So he argued in the synagogue with the Jews and the devout persons, and in the market place every day with those who chanced to be there. Some also of the Epicure'an and Stoic philosophers met him. And some said, "What would this babbler say?" Others said, "He seems to be a preacher of foreign divinities"—because he preached Jesus and the resurrection. And they took hold of him and brought him to the Are-op'agus, saying, "May we know what this new teaching is which you present? For you bring some strange things to our ears; we wish to know therefore what these things mean." Now all the Athenians and the foreigners who lived there spent their time in nothing except telling or hearing something new.

The Areopagus: A bronze plaque of Paul's speech is seen on the lower right. The rock-cut steps lead to the top of the rock

American School of Classical Studies, Athens

So Paul, standing in the middle of the Are-op'agus, said: "Men of Athens, I perceive that in every way you are very religious. For as I passed along, and observed the objects of your worship, I found also an altar with this inscription, 'To an unknown god.' What therefore you worship as unknown, this I proclaim to you. The God who made the world and everything in it, being Lord of heaven and earth, does not live in shrines made by man, nor is he served by human hands, as though he needed anything, since he himself gives to all men life and breath and everything. And he made from one every nation of men to live on all the face of the earth, having determined allotted periods and the boundaries of their habitation, that they should seek God, in the hope that they might feel after him and find him. Yet he is not far from each one of us, for

'In him we live and move and have our being';*

as even some of your poets have said,

'For we are indeed his offspring.'**

Being then God's offspring, we ought not to think that the Deity is like gold, or silver, or stone, a representation by the art and imagination of man. The times of ignorance God overlooked, but now he commands all men everywhere to repent, because he has fixed a day on which he will judge the world in righteousness by a man whom he has appointed, and of this he has given assurance to all men by raising him from the dead."

Now when they heard of the resurrection of the dead, some mocked; but others said, "We will hear you again about this." So Paul went out from among them. But some men joined him and believed, among them Dionys'ius the Are-op'agite and a woman named Dam'aris and others with them.

Paul at Corinth [Acts 18:1–17]

AFTER this he left Athens and went to Corinth. And he found a Jew named Aquil'a, a native of Pontus, lately come from Italy with his wife Priscilla, because Claudius had commanded all the Jews to leave Rome. And he went to see them; and because he was of the same trade he stayed with them, and they worked, for by trade they were tentmakers. And he argued in the synagogue every sabbath, and persuaded Jews and Greeks.

When Silas and Timothy arrived from Macedo'nia, Paul was occupied with preaching, testifying to the Jews that the Christ was Jesus. And when they opposed and reviled him, he shook out his garments and said to them, "Your blood be upon your heads! I am innocent. From now on I will go to the Gentiles." And he left there and went to the house of a man named Titius[q] Justus, a worshiper of God; his house was next door to the synagogue. Crispus, the ruler of the synagogue, believed in the Lord, together with all his household; and many of the Corinthians hearing Paul believed and were baptized. And the Lord said to Paul one night in a vision, "Do not be afraid, but speak and do not be silent; for I am with you, and no man shall attack you to harm you; for I have many people in this city." And he stayed

*Epimenides

**Aratus, *Phænomena*, 5

[q]Other early authorities read *Titus*

a year and six months, teaching the word of God among them.

But when Gal'lio was proconsul of Achai'a, the Jews made a united attack upon Paul and brought him before the tribunal, saying, "This man is persuading men to worship God contrary to the law." But when Paul was about to open his mouth, Gal'lio said to the Jews, "If it were a matter of wrongdoing or vicious crime, I should have reason to bear with you, O Jews; but since it is a matter of questions about words and names and your own law, see to it yourselves; I refuse to be a judge of these things." And he drove them from the tribunal. And they all seized Sos'thenes, the ruler of the synagogue, and beat him in front of the tribunal. But Gal'lio paid no attention to this.

Paul Returns to Antioch [18:18–23]

After this Paul stayed many days longer, and then took leave of the brethren and sailed for Syria, and with him Priscilla and Aquil'a. At Cenchre'ae he cut his hair, for he had a vow. And they came to Eph'esus, and he left them there; but he himself went into the synagogue and argued with the Jews. When they asked him to stay for a longer period, he declined; but on taking leave of them he said, "I will return to you if God wills," and he set sail from Eph'esus.

When he had landed at Caesare'a, he went up and greeted the church, and then went down to An'tioch. After spending some time there he departed and went from place to place through the region of Gala'tia and Phryg'ia, strengthening all the disciples.

Apollos Preaches [18:24–28]

Now a Jew named Apol'los, a native of Alexandria, came to Eph'esus. He was an eloquent man, well versed in the scriptures. He had been instructed in the way of the Lord; and being fervent in spirit, he spoke and taught accurately the things concerning Jesus, though he knew only the baptism of John. He began to speak boldly in the synagogue; but when Priscilla and Aquil'a heard him, they took him and expounded to him the way of God more accurately. And when he wished to cross to Achai'a, the brethren encouraged him, and wrote to the disciples to receive him. When he arrived, he greatly helped those who through grace had believed, for he powerfully confuted the Jews in public, showing by the scriptures that the Christ was Jesus.

Paul at Ephesus [Acts 19:1–10]

WHILE Apol'los was at Corinth, Paul passed through the upper country and came to Eph'esus. There he found some disciples. And he said to them, "Did you receive the Holy Spirit when you believed?" And they said, "No, we have never even heard that there is a Holy Spirit." And he said, "Into what then were you baptized?" They said, "Into John's baptism." And Paul said, "John baptized with the baptism of repentance, telling the people to believe in the one who was to come after him, that is, Jesus." On hearing this, they were baptized in the name of the Lord Jesus. And when Paul had laid his hands upon them, the Holy Spirit came on them; and they spoke with tongues and prophesied. There were about twelve of them in all.

149

The "Judgment seat" or Bema, where Paul appeared before Gallio, is in the center foreground. The Acrocorinth is in the background

And he entered the synagogue and for three months spoke boldly, arguing and pleading about the kingdom of God; but when some were stubborn and disbelieved, speaking evil of the Way before the congregation, he withdrew from them, taking the disciples with him, and argued daily in the hall of Tyran'nus.^r This continued for two years, so that all the residents of Asia heard the word of the Lord, both Jews and Greeks.

The Sons of Sceva [19:11–20]

And God did extraordinary miracles by the hands of Paul, so that handkerchiefs or aprons were carried away from his body to the sick, and diseases left them and the evil spirits came out of them. Then some of the itinerant Jewish exorcists undertook to pronounce the name of the Lord Jesus over those who had evil spirits, saying, "I adjure you by the Jesus whom Paul preaches." Seven sons of a Jewish high priest named Sceva were doing this. But the evil spirit answered them, "Jesus I know, and Paul I

^r Other ancient authorities add *from the fifth hour to the tenth*

know; but who are you?" And the man in whom the evil spirit was leaped on them, mastered all of them, and overpowered them, so that they fled out of that house naked and wounded. And this became known to all residents of Eph'esus, both Jews and Greeks; and fear fell upon them all; and the name of the Lord Jesus was extolled. Many also of those who were now believers came, confessing and divulging their practices. And a number of those who practiced magic arts brought their books together and burned them in the sight of all; and they counted the value of them and found it came to fifty thousand pieces of silver. So the word of the Lord grew and prevailed mightily.

The Riot at Ephesus [19:21–41]

Now after these events Paul resolved in the Spirit to pass through Macedo'nia and Achai'a and go to Jerusalem, saying, "After I have been there, I must also see Rome." And having sent into Macedo'nia two of his helpers, Timothy and Eras'tus, he himself stayed in Asia for a while.

Corinth: The Temple of Apollo

William A. McDonald

The theater at Ephesus

About that time there arose no little stir concerning the Way. For a man named Deme'trius, a silversmith, who made silver shrines of Ar'temis, brought no little business to the craftsmen. These he gathered together, with the workmen of like occupation, and said, "Men, you know that from this business we have our wealth. And you see and hear that not only at Eph'esus but almost throughout all Asia this Paul has persuaded and turned away a considerable company of people, saying that gods made with hands are not gods. And there is danger not only that this trade of ours may come into disrepute but also that the temple of the great goddess Ar'temis may count for nothing, and that she may even be deposed from her magnificence, she whom all Asia and the world worship."

When they heard this they were enraged, and cried out, "Great is Ar'temis of the Ephe'sians!" So the city was filled with the confusion; and they rushed together into the theater, dragging with them Ga'ius and Aristar'chus, Macedo'nians who were Paul's companions in travel. Paul wished to go in among the crowd, but the disciples would not let him; some of the A'si-archs also, who were friends of his, sent to him and begged him not to venture into the theater. Now some cried one thing, some another; for the assembly was in confusion, and most of them did not know why they had come

together. Some of the crowd prompted Alexander, whom the Jews had put forward. And Alexander motioned with his hand, wishing to make a defense to the people. But when they recognized that he was a Jew, for about two hours they all with one voice cried out, "Great is Ar'temis of the Ephe'sians!" And when the town clerk had quieted the crowd, he said, "Men of Eph'esus, what man is there who does not know that the city of the Ephe'sians is temple keeper of the great Ar'temis, and of the sacred stone that fell from the sky?[s] Seeing then that these things cannot be contradicted, you ought to be quiet and do nothing rash. For you have brought these men here who are neither sacreligious nor blasphemers of our goddess. If therefore Deme'trius and the craftsmen with him have a complaint against any one, the courts are open, and there are proconsuls; let them bring charges against one another. But if you seek anything further,[t] it shall be settled in the regular assembly. For we are in danger of being charged with rioting today, there being no cause that we can give to justify this commotion." And when he had said this, he dismissed the assembly.

[s]The meaning of the Greek is uncertain

[t]Other ancient authorities read *about other matters*

Ephesus: The street that leads from the theater to the harbor, which is now silted up

William A. McDonald

Paul's Journey to Macedonia and Greece [Acts 20:1–6]

AFTER the uproar ceased, Paul sent for the disciples and having exhorted them took leave of them and departed for Macedo'nia. When he had gone through these parts and had given them much encouragement, he came to Greece. There he spent three months, and when a plot was made against him by the Jews as he was about to set sail for Syria, he determined to return through Macedo'nia. So'pater of Beroe'a, the son of Pyrrhus, accompanied him; and of the Thessalo'nians, Aristar'chus and Secun'dus; and Gaius of Derbe, and Timothy; and the Asians, Tych'icus and Troph'imus. These went on and were waiting for us at Troas, but we sailed away from Phil'ippi after the days of Unleavened Bread, and in five days we came to them at Troas, where we stayed for seven days.

Paul's Farewell Visit at Troas [20:7–12]

On the first day of the week, when we were gathered together to break bread, Paul talked with them, intending to depart on the morrow; and he prolonged his speech until midnight. There were many lights in the upper chamber where we were gathered. And a young man named Eu'tychus was sitting in the window. He sank into a deep sleep as Paul talked still longer; and being overcome by sleep, he fell down from the third story and was taken up dead. But Paul went down and bent over him, and, embracing him said, "Do not be alarmed, for his life is in him." And when Paul had gone up and had broken bread and eaten, he conversed with them a long while, until daybreak, and so departed. And they took the lad away alive, and were not a little comforted.

The Voyage from Troas to Miletus [20:13–16]

But going ahead to the ship, we set sail for Assos, intending to take Paul aboard there; for so he had arranged, intending himself to go by land. And when he met us at Assos, we took him on board and came to Mityle'ne. And sailing from there we came the following day opposite Chios; the next day we touched at Samos; and[u] the day after that we came to Mile'tus. For Paul had decided to sail past Eph'esus, so that he might not have to spend time in Asia; for he was hastening to be at Jerusalem, if possible, on the day of Pen'tecost.

Paul Speaks to the Ephesian Elders [20:17–38]

And from Mile'tus he sent to Eph'esus and called to him the elders of the church. And when they came to him, he said to them:

"You yourselves know how I lived among you all the time from the first day that I set foot in Asia, serving the Lord with all humility and with tears and with trials which befell me through the plots of the Jews; how I did not shrink from declaring to you anything that was profitable, and teaching you in public and from house to house, testifying both to Jews and to Greeks of repentance

[u]Other ancient authorities add *after remaining at Trogyllium*

to God and of faith in our Lord Jesus Christ. And now, behold, I am going to Jerusalem, bound in the Spirit, not knowing what shall befall me there; except that the Holy Spirit testifies to me in every city that imprisonment and afflictions await me. But I do not account my life of any value nor as precious to myself, if only I may accomplish my course and the ministry which I received from the Lord Jesus, to testify to the gospel of the grace of God. And now, behold, I know that all you among whom I have gone about preaching the kingdom will see my face no more. Therefore I testify to you this day that I am innocent of the blood of all of you, for I did not shrink from declaring to you the whole counsel of God. Take heed to yourselves and to all the flock, in which the Holy Spirit has made you guardians, to feed the church of the Lord[v] which he obtained with his own blood.[w] I know that after my departure fierce wolves will come in among you, not sparing the flock; and from among your own selves will arise men speaking perverse things, to draw away the disciples after them. Therefore be alert, remembering that for three years I did not cease night or day to admonish every one with tears. And now I commend you to God and to the word of his grace, which is able to build you up and to give you the inheritance among all those who are sanctified. I coveted no one's silver or gold or apparel. You yourselves know that these hands ministered to my necessities, and to those who were with me. In all things I have shown you that by so toiling one must help the weak, remembering the words of the Lord Jesus, how he said, 'It is more blessed to give than to receive.' "

And when he had spoken thus, he knelt down and prayed with them all. And they all wept and embraced Paul and kissed him, sorrowing most of all because of the word he had spoken, that they should see his face no more. And they brought him to the ship.

Paul's Journey to Jerusalem [Acts 21:1–16]

AND when we had parted from them and set sail, we came by a straight course to Cos, and the next day to Rhodes, and from there to Pat'ara.[x] And having found a ship crossing to Phoeni'cia, we went aboard, and set sail. When we had come in sight of Cyprus, leaving it on the left we sailed to Syria, and landed at Tyre; for there the ship was to unload its cargo. And having sought out the disciples, we stayed there for seven days. Through the Spirit they told Paul not to go on to Jerusalem. And when our days there were ended, we departed and went on our journey; and they all, with wives and children, brought us on our way till we were outside the city; and kneeling down on the beach we prayed and bade one another farewell. Then we went on board the ship, and they returned home.

When we had finished the voyage from Tyre, we arrived at Ptolema'is; and we greeted the brethren and stayed with them for one day. On the morrow we departed and came to Caesare'a; and we entered the house of Philip the evangelist, who was one of the seven, and stayed with him. And he had four unmarried daughters, who prophe-

The harbor of Lindos on the Island of Rhodes

J. Lane Miller

sied. While we were staying for some days, a prophet named Ag'abus came down from Jude'a. And coming to us he took Paul's girdle and bound his own feet and hands, and said, "Thus says the Holy Spirit, 'So shall the Jews at Jerusalem bind the man who owns this girdle and deliver him into the hands of the Gentiles.' " When we heard this, we and the people there begged him not to go up to Jerusalem. Then Paul answered, "What are you doing, weeping and breaking my heart? For I am ready not only to be imprisoned but even to die at Jerusalem for the name of the Lord Jesus." And when he would not be persuaded, we ceased and said, "The will of the Lord be done."

After these days we made ready and went up to Jerusalem. And some of the disciples from Caesare'a went with us, bringing us to the house of Mnason of Cyprus, an early disciple, with whom we should lodge.

Paul Visits James [21:17–26]

When we had come to Jerusalem, the brethren received us gladly. On the following day Paul went in with us to James; and all the elders were present. After greeting them, he related one by one the things that God had done among the Gentiles through his ministry. And when they heard it, they glorified God. And they said to him, "You see, brother, how many thousands there are among the Jews of those who have believed; they are all zealous for the law, and they have been told about you that you teach all the Jews who are among the Gentiles to forsake Moses, telling them not to circumcise their children or observe the customs. What then is to be done? They will certainly hear that you have come. Do therefore what we tell you. We have four men who are under a vow; take these men and purify yourself along with them and pay their expenses, so that they may shave their heads. Thus all will know that there is nothing in what they have been told about you but that you yourself live in observance of the law. But as for the Gentiles who have believed, we have sent a letter with our judgment that they should abstain from what has been sacrificed to idols and from blood and from what is strangled[y] and from unchastity." Then Paul took the men, and the next day he purified himself with them and went into the temple, to give notice when the days of purification would be fulfilled and the offering presented for every one of them.

[y]Other early authorities omit *and from what is strangled*

Tyre: "And we kneeled down on the shore, and prayed"

J. Lane Miller

[v]Other ancient authorities read *of God*

[w]Or *with the blood of his Own*

[x]Other ancient authorities add *and Myra*

Warning notice from Herod's Temple in Jerusalem: "No stranger is to enter within the balustrade round the Temple and enclosure. Whoever is caught will be responsible to himself for his death, which will ensue"

Paul Tells of His Conversion [Acts 22:6-16]

"AS I made my journey and drew near to Damascus, about noon a great light from heaven suddenly shone about me. And I fell to the ground and heard a voice saying to me, 'Saul, Saul, why do you persecute me?' And I answered, 'Who are you, Lord?' And he said to me, 'I am Jesus of Naz'areth whom you are persecuting.' Now those who were with me saw the light but did not hear the voice of the one who was speaking to me. And I said, 'What shall I do, Lord?' And the Lord said to me, 'Rise, and go into Damascus, and there you will be told all that is appointed for you to do.' And when I could not see because of the brightness of that light, I was led by the hand by those who were with me, and came into Damascus.

"And one Anani'as, a devout man according to the law, well spoken of by all the Jews who lived there, came to me, and standing by me said to me, 'Brother Saul, receive your sight.' And in that very hour I received my sight and saw him. And he said, 'The God of our fathers appointed you to know his will, to see the Just One and to hear a voice from his mouth; for you will be a witness for him to all men of what you have seen and heard. And now why do you wait? Rise and be baptized, and wash away your sins, calling on his name.'

Paul's Arrest [21:27-36]

When the seven days were almost completed, the Jews from Asia, who had seen him in the temple, stirred up all the crowd, and laid hands on him, crying out, "Men of Israel, help! This is the man who is teaching men everywhere against the people and the law and this place; moreover he also brought Greeks into the temple, and he has defiled this holy place." For they had previously seen Troph'imus the Ephe'sian with him in the city, and they supposed that Paul had brought him into the temple. Then all the city was aroused, and the people ran together; they seized Paul and dragged him out of the temple, and at once the gates were shut. And as they were trying to kill him, word came to the tribune of the cohort that all Jerusalem was in confusion. He at once took soldiers and centurions, and ran down to them; and when they saw the tribune and the soldiers, they stopped beating Paul. Then the tribune came up and arrested him, and ordered him to be bound with two chains. He inquired who he was and what he had done. Some in the crowd shouted one thing, some another; and as he could not learn the facts because of the uproar, he ordered him to be brought into the barracks. And when he came to the steps, he was actually carried by the soldiers because of the violence of the crowd; for the mob of people followed, crying, "Away with him!"

Paul's Defense [21:37-22:5]

As Paul was about to be brought into the barracks, he said to the tribune, "May I say something to you?" And he said, "Do you know Greek? Are you not the Egyptian, then, who recently stirred up a revolt and led the four thousand men of the Assassins out into the wilderness?" Paul replied, "I am a Jew, from Tarsus in Cili'cia, a citizen of no mean city; I beg you, let me speak to the people." And when he had given him leave, Paul, standing on the steps, motioned with his hand to the people; and when there was a great hush, he spoke to them in the Hebrew language, saying:

"Brethren and fathers, hear the defense which I now make before you."

And when they heard that he addressed them in the Hebrew language, they were the more quiet. And he said:

"I am a Jew, born at Tarsus in Cili'cia, but brought up in this city at the feet of Gama'li-el, educated according to the strict manner of the law of our fathers, being zealous for God as you all are this day. I persecuted this Way to the death, binding and delivering to prison both men and women, as the high priest and the whole council of elders bear me witness. From them I received letters to the brethren, and I journeyed to Damascus to take those also who were there and bring them in bonds to Jerusalem to be punished.

Paul's Call to the Gentiles [22:17-21]

"When I had returned to Jerusalem and was praying in the temple, I fell into a trance and saw him saying to me, 'Make haste and get quickly out of Jerusalem, because they will not accept your testimony about me.' And I said, 'Lord, they themselves know that in every synagogue I imprisoned and beat those who believed in thee. And when the blood of Stephen thy witness was shed, I also was standing by and approving, and keeping the garments of those who killed him.' And he said to me, 'Depart; for I will send you far away to the Gentiles.' "

Paul in the Tribune's Custody [22:22-29]

Up to this word they listened to him; then they lifted up their voices and said, "Away with such a fellow from the earth! For he ought not to live." And as they cried out and waved their garments and threw dust into the air, the tribune commanded him to be brought into the barracks, and ordered him to be examined by scourging, to find out why they shouted thus against him. But when they had tied him up with the thongs, Paul said to the centurion who was standing by, "Is it lawful for you to scourge a man who is a Roman citizen, and uncondemned?" When the centurion heard that, he went to the tribune and said to him, "What are you about to do? For this man is a Roman citizen." So the tribune came and said to him, "Tell me, are you a Roman citizen?" And he said, "Yes." The tribune answered, "I bought this citizenship for a large sum." Paul said, "But I was born a citizen." So those who were about to examine him withdrew from him instantly; and the tribune also was afraid, for he realized that Paul was a Roman citizen and that he had bound him.

Paul before the Council [22:30-23:11]

But on the morrow, desiring to know the real reason why the Jews accused him, he

The lead in this inscription at Corinth is gone, but the generous act of Erastus, who "laid this pavement at his own expense in return for being elected aedile," still endures. Many identify him with the Erastus of Acts 19:22, Romans 16:23, and 2 Timothy 4:20

unbound him, and commanded the chief priests and all the council to meet, and he brought Paul down and set him before them.

And Paul, looking intently at the council, said, "Brethren, I have lived before God in all good conscience up to this day." And the high priest Anani'as commanded those who stood by him to strike him on the mouth. Then Paul said to him, "God shall strike you, you whitewashed wall! Are you sitting to judge me according to the law, and yet contrary to the law you order me to be struck?" Those who stood by said, "Would you revile God's high priest?" And Paul said, "I did not know, brethren, that he was the high priest; for it is written, 'You shall not speak evil of a ruler of your people.' "[21]

But when Paul perceived that one part were Sad'ducees and the other Phar'isees, he cried out in the council, "Brethren, I am a Phar'isee, a son of Phar'isees; with respect to the hope and the resurrection of the dead I am on trial." And when he had said this, a dissension arose between the Phar'isees and the Sad'ducees; and the assembly was divided. For the Sad'ducees say that there is no resurrection, nor angel, nor spirit; but the Phar'isees acknowledge them all. Then a great clamor arose; and some of the scribes of the Phar'isees' party stood up and contended, "We find nothing wrong in this man. What if a spirit or an angel spoke to him?" And when the dissension became violent, the tribune, afraid that Paul would be torn in pieces by them, commanded the soldiers to go down and take him by force from among them and bring him into the barracks.

The following night the Lord stood by him and said, "Take courage, for as you have testified about me at Jerusalem, so you must bear witness also at Rome."

The Plot against Paul's Life [Acts 23:12–22]

WHEN it was day, the Jews made a plot and bound themselves by an oath neither to eat nor drink till they had killed Paul. There were more than forty who made this conspiracy. And they went to the chief priests and elders, and said, "We have strictly bound ourselves by an oath to taste no food till we have killed Paul. You therefore, along with the council, give notice now to the tribune to bring him down to you, as though you were going to determine his case more exactly. And we are ready to kill him before he comes near."

Now the son of Paul's sister heard of their ambush; so he went and entered the barracks and told Paul. And Paul called one of the centurions and said, "Bring this young man to the tribune; for he has something to tell him." So he took him and brought him to the tribune and said, "Paul the prisoner called me and asked me to bring this young man to you, as he has something to say to you." The tribune took him by the hand, and going aside asked him privately, "What is it that you have to tell me?" And he said, "The Jews have agreed to ask you to bring Paul down to the council tomorrow, as though they were going to inquire somewhat more closely about him. But do not yield to them; for more than forty of their men lie in ambush for him, having bound themselves by an oath neither to eat nor drink till they have killed him; and now they are ready, waiting for the promise from you." So the tribune dis-

[21] Exodus 22:28

Sisters of Zion, Jerusalem

Castle of Antonia, Jerusalem. These huge Herodian flagstones, three feet square and over one foot thick, support the modern pillars and vaults above them. They are believed to have been part of the pavement of the courtyard in the Castle of Antonia, where Paul was confined. They still show the diagrams and markings of the Roman soldiers' games

missed the young man, charging him, "Tell no one that you have informed me of this."

Paul Sent to Felix the Governor

[23:23–35]

Then he called two of the centurions and said, "At the third hour of the night get ready two hundred soldiers with seventy horsemen and two hundred spearmen to go as far as Caesare'a. Also provide mounts for Paul to ride, and bring him safely to Felix the governor." And he wrote a letter to this effect:

"Claudius Lys'ias to his Excellency the governor Felix, greeting. This man was seized by the Jews, and was about to be killed by them, when I came upon them with the soldiers and rescued him, having learned that he was a Roman citizen. And desiring to know the charge on which they accused him, I brought him down to their council. I found that he was accused about questions of their law, but charged with nothing deserving death or imprisonment. And when it was disclosed to me that there would be a plot against the man, I sent him to you at once, ordering his accusers also to state before you what they have against him."

So the soldiers, according to their instructions, took Paul and brought him by night to Antip'atris. And on the morrow they returned to the barracks, leaving the horsemen to go on with him. When they came to Caesare'a and delivered the letter to the governor, they presented Paul also before him. On reading the letter, he asked to what province he belonged. When he learned that he was from Cili'cia he said, "I will hear you when your accusers arrive." And he commanded him to be guarded in Herod's praetor'ium.

The Case against Paul [Acts 24:1–9]

AND after five days the high priest Anani'as came down with some elders and a spokesman, one Tertul'lus. They laid before the governor their case against Paul; and when he was called, Tertul'lus began to accuse him, saying:

"Since through you we enjoy much peace, and since by your provision, most excellent Felix, reforms are introduced on behalf of this nation, in every way and everywhere we accept this with all gratitude. But, to detain you no further, I beg you in your kind-

Part of the ancient cistern that supplied water to the Castle of Antonia. Titus battering rams are believed to have knocked down these large fragments of the superstructure of the Castle in A.D. 70, when Jerusalem was destroyed

Sisters of Zion, Jerusalem

ness to hear us briefly. For we have found this man a pestilent fellow, an agitator among all the Jews throughout the world, and a ringleader of the sect of the Naz′arenes. He even tried to profane the temple, but we seized him.[2] By examining him yourself you will be able to learn from him about everything of which we accuse him."

The Jews also joined in the charge, affirming that all this was so.

Paul's Defense before Felix [24:10–21]

And when the governor had motioned to him to speak, Paul replied:

"Realizing that for many years you have been judge over this nation, I cheerfully make my defense. As you may ascertain, it is not more than twelve days since I went up to worship at Jerusalem; and they did not find me disputing with any one or stirring up a crowd, either in the temple or in the synagogues, or in the city. Neither can they prove to you what they now bring up against me. But this I admit to you, that according to the Way, which they call a sect, I worship the God of our fathers, believing everything laid down by the law or written in the prophets, having a hope in God which these themselves accept, that there will be a resurrection of both the just and the unjust. So I always take pains to have a clear conscience toward God and toward men. Now after some years I came to bring to my nation alms and offerings. As I was doing this, they found me purified in the temple, without any crowd or tumult. But some Jews from Asia—they ought to be here before you and to make an accusation,

[2] Other ancient authorities add *and we would have judged him according to our law. But the chief captain Lysias came and with great violence took him out of our hands, commanding his accusers to come before you.*

if they have anything against me. Or else let these men themselves say what wrongdoing they found when I stood before the council, except this one thing which I cried out while standing among them, 'With respect to the resurrection of the dead I am on trial before you this day.'"

Paul Held in Custody [24:22–27]

But Felix, having a rather accurate knowledge of the Way, put them off, saying, "When Lys′ias the tribune comes down, I will decide your case." Then he gave orders to the centurion that he should be kept in custody but should have some liberty, and that none of his friends should be prevented from attending to his needs.

After some days Felix came with his wife Drusil′la, who was a Jewess; and he sent for Paul and heard him speak upon faith in Christ Jesus. And as he argued about justice and self-control and future judgment, Felix was alarmed and said, "Go away for the present; when I have an opportunity I will summon you." At the same time he hoped that money would be given him by Paul. So he sent for him often and conversed with him. But when two years had elapsed, Felix was succeeded by Porcius Festus; and desiring to do the Jews a favor, Felix left Paul in prison.

Paul Appeals to Caesar [Acts 25:1–12]

NOW when Festus had come into his province, after three days he went up to Jerusalem from Caesare′a. And the chief priests and the principal men of the Jews informed him against Paul; and they urged him, asking as a favor to have the man sent to Jerusalem, planning an ambush to kill him on the way. Festus replied that Paul was being kept at Caesare′a, and that he

himself intended to go there shortly. "So," said he, "let the men of authority among you go down with me, and if there is anything wrong about the man, let them accuse him."

When he had stayed among them not more than eight or ten days, he went down to Caesare′a; and the next day he took his seat on the tribunal and ordered Paul to be brought. And when he had come, the Jews who had gone down from Jerusalem stood about him, bringing against him many serious charges which they could not prove. Paul said in his defense, "Neither against the law of the Jews, nor against the temple, nor against Caesar have I offended at all." But Festus, wishing to do the Jews a favor, said to Paul, "Do you wish to go up to Jerusalem, and there be tried on these charges before me?" But Paul said, "I am standing before Caesar's tribunal, where I ought to be tried; to the Jews I have done no wrong, as you know very well. If then I am a wrongdoer, and have committed anything for which I deserve to die, I do not seek to escape death; but if there is nothing in their charges against me, no one can give me up to them. I appeal to Caesar." Then Festus, when he had conferred with his council, answered, "You have appealed to Caesar; to Caesar you shall go."

Paul Brought before Agrippa and Bernice [25:13–27]

Now when some days had passed, Agrip′pa the king and Bernice arrived at Caesare′a to welcome Festus. And as they stayed there many days, Festus laid Paul's case before the king, saying, "There is a man left prisoner by Felix; and when I was at Jerusalem, the chief priests and the elders of the Jews gave information about him, asking for sentence against him. I answered them that it was not the custom of the

Romans to give up any one before the accused met the accusers face to face, and had opportunity to make his defense concerning the charge laid against him. When therefore they came together here, I made no delay, but on the next day took my seat on the tribunal and ordered the man to be brought in. When the accusers stood up, they brought no charge in his case of such evils as I supposed; but they had certain points of dispute with him about their own superstition and about one Jesus, who was dead, but whom Paul asserted to be alive. Being at a loss how to investigate these questions, I asked whether he wished to go to Jerusalem and be tried there regarding them. But when Paul had appealed to be kept in custody for the decision of the emperor, I commanded him to be held until I could send him to Caesar." And Agrip'pa said to Festus, "I should like to hear the man myself." "Tomorrow," said he, "you shall hear him."

So on the morrow Agrip'pa and Bernice came with great pomp, and they entered the audience hall with the military tribunes and the prominent men of the city. Then by command of Festus Paul was brought in. And Festus said, "King Agrip'pa and all who are present with us, you see this man about whom the whole Jewish people petitioned me, both at Jerusalem and here, shouting that he ought not to live any longer. But I found that he had done nothing deserving death; and as he himself appealed to the emperor, I decided to send him. But I have nothing definite to write to my lord about him. Therefore I have brought him before you, and, especially before you, King Agrip'pa, that, after we have examined him, I may have something to write. For it seems to me unreasonable, in sending a prisoner, not to indicate the charges against him."

Paul Defends Himself before Agrippa

[Acts 26:1–11]

AGRIP'PA said to Paul, "You have permission to speak for yourself." Then Paul stretched out his hand and made his defense:

"I think myself fortunate that it is before you, King Agrip'pa, I am to make my defense today against all the accusations of the Jews, because you are especially familiar with all customs and controversies of the Jews; therefore I beg you to listen to me patiently.

"My manner of life from my youth, spent from the beginning among my own nation and at Jerusalem, is known by all the Jews. They have known for a long time, if they are willing to testify, that according to the strictest party of our religion I have lived as a Phar'isee. And now I stand here on trial for hope in the promise made by God to our fathers, to which our twelve tribes hope to attain, as they earnestly worship night and day. And for this hope I am accused by Jews, O king! Why is it thought incredible by any of you that God raises the dead?

"I myself was convinced that I ought to do many things in opposing the name of Jesus of Naz'areth. And I did so in Jerusalem; I not only shut up many of the saints in prison, by authority from the chief priests, but when they were put to death I cast my vote against them. And I punished them often in all the synagogues and tried to make them blaspheme; and in raging fury against them, I persecuted them even to foreign cities.

J. L. Kelso

Jericho: Excavation of the great stairway at the eastern end of the grand façade of the civic center at Archelaus' palace at Jericho. Herod Agrippa I is believed to have occupied this palace in the winter-time with his children, Herod Agrippa II and Bernice

Paul Tells of His Conversion [26:12–18]

"Thus I journeyed to Damascus with the authority and commission of the chief priests. At midday, O king, I saw on the way a light from heaven, brighter than the sun, shining round me and those who journeyed with me. And when we had all fallen to the ground, I heard a voice saying to me in the Hebrew language, 'Saul, Saul, why do you persecute me? It hurts you to kick against the goads.' And I said, 'Who are you, Lord?' And the Lord said, 'I am Jesus whom you are persecuting. But rise and stand upon your feet; for I have appeared to you for this purpose, to appoint you to serve and bear witness to the things in which you have seen me and to those in which I will appear to you, delivering you from the people and from the Gentiles—to whom I send you to open their eyes, that they may turn from darkness to light and from the power of Satan to God, that they may receive forgiveness of sins and a place among those who are sanctified by faith in me.'

Paul's Testimony to Jews and Gentiles [26:19–23]

"Wherefore, O King Agrip'pa, I was not disobedient to the heavenly vision, but declared first to those at Damascus, then at Jerusalem and throughout all the country of Jude'a, and also to the Gentiles, that they should repent and turn to God and perform deeds worthy of their repentance. For this reason the Jews seized me in the temple and tried to kill me. To this day I have had the help that comes from God, and so I stand here testifying both to small and great, saying nothing but what the prophets and Moses said would come to pass: that the Christ must suffer, and that, by being the first to rise from the dead, he would proclaim light both to the people and to the Gentiles."

Paul Appeals to Agrippa to Believe

[26:24–32]

And as he thus made his defense, Festus said with a loud voice, "Paul, you are mad; your great learning is turning you mad." But Paul said, "I am not mad, most excellent Festus, but I am speaking the sober truth. For the king knows about these things, and to him I speak freely; for I am persuaded that none of these things has escaped his notice, for this was not done in a corner. King Agrip'pa, do you believe the prophets? I know that you believe." And Agrip'pa said to Paul, "In a short time you think to make me a Christian!" And Paul said, "Whether short or long, I would to God that not only you but also all who hear me this day might become such as I am—except for these chains."

Then the king rose, and the governor and Bernice and those who were sitting with them; and when they had withdrawn, they said to one another, "This man is doing nothing to deserve death or imprisonment." And Agrip'pa said to Festus, "This man could have been set free if he had not appealed to Caesar."

Paul Sails for Rome [Acts 27:1–12]

AND when it was decided that we should sail for Italy, they delivered Paul and some other prisoners to a centurion of the Augus'tan Cohort, named Julius. And embarking in a ship of Adramyt'tium, which

CAESAREA

SIDON

SEA NORTH OF CYPRUS

Gordon Grant

In the autumn, the prevailing wind in the eastern Mediterranean is a little north of west. The grain ships, therefore, sailed almost due north from Alexandria to Myra, as they could not sail closer than about seven points to the wind. From there they worked their way along the coast of Asia Minor as far north as possible before sailing south of Greece and heading for the straits of Messina.

1½ times Actual Size

This debased silver Tetradrachm of Nero struck at Alexandria shows a sailing vessel.

was about to sail to the ports along the coast of Asia, we put to sea, accompanied by Aristar'chus, a Macedo'nian from Thessaloni'ca. The next day we put in at Sidon; and Julius treated Paul kindly, and gave him leave to go to his friends and be cared for. And putting to sea from there we sailed under the lee of Cyprus, because the winds were against us. And when we had sailed across the sea which is off Cili'cia and Pamphyl'ia, we came to Myra in Lyc'ia. There the centurion found a ship of Alexandria sailing for Italy, and put us on board. We sailed slowly for a number of days, and arrived with difficulty off Cni'dus, and as the wind did not allow us to go on, we sailed under the lee of Crete off Salmo'-ne. Coasting along it with difficulty, we came to a place called Fair Havens, near which was the city of Lase'a.

As much time had been lost, and the voyage was already dangerous because the fast had already gone by, Paul advised them, saying, "Sirs, I perceive that the voyage will be with injury and much loss, not only of the cargo and the ship, but also of our lives." But the centurion paid more attention to the captain and to the owner of the ship than to what Paul said. And because the harbor was not suitable to winter in, the majority advised to put to sea from there, on the chance that somehow they could reach Phoenix, a harbor of Crete, looking northeast and southeast,[a] and winter there.

The Storm at Sea [27:13–38]

And when the south wind blew gently, supposing that they had obtained their purpose, they weighed anchor and sailed along Crete, close inshore. But soon a tempestuous wind, called the northeaster, struck down from the land; and when the

[a] Or southwest and northwest

ship was caught and could not face the wind, we gave way to it and were driven. And running under the lee of a small island called Cauda,[b] we managed with difficulty to secure the boat; after hoisting it up, they took measures[c] to undergird the ship; then, fearing that they should run on the Syr'tis, they lowered the gear, and so were driven. As we were violently storm-tossed, they began next day to throw the cargo overboard; and the third day they cast out with their own hands the tackle of the ship. And when neither sun nor stars appeared for many a day, and no small tempest lay on us, all hope of our being saved was at last abandoned.

As they had been long without food, Paul then came forward among them and said, "Men, you should have listened to me, and should not have set sail from Crete and incurred this injury and loss. I now bid you take heart; for there will be no loss of life among you, but only of the ship. For this very night there stood by me an angel of the God to whom I belong and whom I worship, and he said, 'Do not be afraid, Paul; you must stand before Caesar; and lo, God has granted you all those who sail with you.' So take heart, men, for I have faith in God that it will be exactly as I have been told. But we shall have to run on some island."

When the fourteenth night had come, as we were drifting across the sea of A'dria, about midnight the sailors suspected that they were nearing land. So they sounded and found twenty fathoms; a little farther on they sounded again and found fifteen fathoms. And fearing that we might run on the rocks, they let out four anchors from the stern, and prayed for day to come. And as the sailors were seeking to escape from

[b] Other ancient authorities read Clauda
[c] Greek helps

MALTA: ST. PAUL'S BAY

STATUE OF ST. PAUL ON SELMUN ISLAND

AIR VIEW OF SYRACUSE

MYRA: ROCK TOMB

MUROS AND FAIR HAVENS

Greek Government

Greek Government

CAUDA (MODERN GAUDHO)

the ship, and had lowered the boat into the sea, under pretense of laying out anchors from the bow, Paul said to the centurion and the soldiers, "Unless these men stay in the ship, you cannot be saved." Then the soldiers cut away the ropes of the boat, and let it go.

As day was about to dawn, Paul urged them all to take some food, saying, "Today is the fourteenth day that you have continued in suspense and without food, having taken nothing. Therefore I urge you to take some food; it will give you strength, since not a hair is to perish from the head of any of you." And when he had said this, he took bread, and giving thanks to God in the presence of all he broke it and began to eat. Then they were all encouraged and ate some food themselves. (We were in all two hundred and seventy-six[d] persons in the ship.) And when they had eaten enough, they lightened the ship, throwing out the wheat into the sea.

The Shipwreck [Acts 27:39–44]

Now when it was day, they did not recognize the land, but they noticed a bay with a beach, on which they planned if possible to bring the ship ashore. So they cast off the anchors and left them in the sea, at the same time loosening the ropes that tied the rudders; then hoisting the foresail to the wind they made for the beach. But striking a shoal[e] they ran the vessel aground; the bow stuck and remained immovable, and the stern was broken up by the surf. The soldiers' plan was to kill the prisoners, lest any should swim away and escape; but the centurion, wishing to save Paul, kept them from carrying out their purpose. He

[d]Other ancient authorities read *seventy-six* or *about seventy-six*

[e]Greek *place of two seas*

ordered those who could swim to throw themselves overboard first and make for the land, and the rest on planks or on pieces of the ship. And so it was that all escaped to land.

Paul on the Island of Malta

[Acts 28:1–10]

AFTER we had escaped, we then learned that the island was called Malta. And the natives showed us unusual kindness, for they kindled a fire and welcomed us all, because it had begun to rain and was cold. Paul had gathered a bundle of sticks and put them on the fire, when a viper came out because of the heat and fastened on his hand. When the natives saw the creature hanging from his hand, they said to one another, "No doubt this man is a murderer. Though he has escaped from the sea, justice has not allowed him to live." Hè, however, shook off the creature into the fire and suffered no harm. They waited, expecting him to swell up or suddenly fall down dead; but when they had waited a long time and saw no misfortune come to him, they changed their minds and said that he was a god.

Now in the neighborhood of that place were lands belonging to the chief man of the island, named Pub′lius, who received us and entertained us hospitably for three days. It happened that the father of Pub′lius lay sick with fever and dysentery; and Paul visited him and prayed, and putting his hands on him healed him. And when this had taken place, the rest of the people on the island who had diseases also came and were cured. They presented many gifts to us;[f] and when we sailed, they put on board whatever we needed.

[f]Or *honored us with many honors*

Jules Sotias

As the population of Rome increased and agriculture in Italy decayed, the need for grain from Egypt became more acute. Without grain ships from Alexandria it would not have been possible to feed the growing population of Rome, of whom 200,000 received free rations of grain under Augustus. Ostia, at the mouth of the Tiber River, was the harbor nearest Rome, but constant dredging was needed to keep it open for navigation.

Actual Size

This bronze Sestertius of Nero struck at Rome shows the harbor of Ostia filled with ships.

American Numismatic Society

STRAIT OF MESSINA NEAR RHEGIUM

J. Lane Miller

PUTEOLI, ITALY

J. Lane Miller

THE APPIAN WAY — Ernest Nash

them for seven days. And so we came to Rome. And the brethren there, when they heard of us, came as far as the Forum of Ap'pius and Three Taverns to meet us. On seeing them Paul thanked God and took courage. And when we came into Rome, Paul was allowed to stay by himself, with the soldier that guarded him.

Paul Preaches in Rome

[28:17–31]

After three days he called together the local leaders of the Jews; and when they had gathered, he said to them, "Brethren, though I had done nothing against the people or the customs of our fathers, yet I was delivered prisoner from Jerusalem into the hands of the Romans. When they had examined me, they wished to set me at liberty, because there was no reason for the death penalty in my case. But when the Jews objected, I was compelled to appeal to Caesar—though I had no charge to bring against my nation. For this reason therefore I have asked to see you and speak with you, since it is because of the hope of Israel that I am bound with this chain." And they said to him, "We have received no letters from Jude'a about you, and none of the brethren coming here has reported or spoken any evil about you. But we desire to hear from you what your views are; for with regard to this sect we know that everywhere it is spoken against."

When they had appointed a day for him, they came to him at his lodgings in great numbers. And he expounded the matter to them from morning to evening, testifying to the kingdom of God and trying to convince them about Jesus both from the law of Moses and from the prophets. And some were convinced by what he said, while others disbelieved. So, as they disagreed among themselves, they departed, after Paul had made one statement: "The Holy Spirit was right in saying to your fathers through Isai'ah the prophet:

'Go to this people, and say,
You shall indeed hear but never understand,
and you shall indeed see but never perceive.
For this people's heart has grown dull,
and their ears are heavy of hearing,
and their eyes they have closed;
lest they should perceive with their eyes,
and hear with their ears,
and understand with their heart,
and turn for me to heal them.'[22]
Let it be known to you then that this

[22]Isa. 6:9–10 (Matthew 13:14; John 12:40)

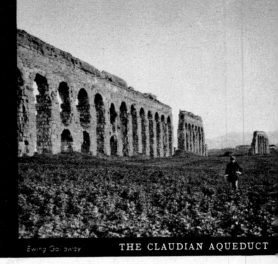

THE CLAUDIAN AQUEDUCT — Ewing Galloway

salvation of God has been sent to the Gentiles; they will listen."[g]

And he lived there two whole years at his own expense,[h] and welcomed all who came to him, preaching the kingdom of God and teaching about the Lord Jesus Christ quite openly and unhindered.

[g]Other ancient authorities add verse 29, And when he had said these words, the Jews departed, holding much dispute among themselves
[h]Or in his own hired dwelling

Paul Arrives at Rome [28:11–16]

After three months we set sail in a ship which had wintered in the island, a ship of Alexandria, with the Twin Brothers as figurehead. Putting in at Syracuse, we stayed there for three days. And from there we made a circuit and arrived at Rhe'gium; and after one day a south wind sprang up, and on the second day we came to Puteo'li. There we found brethren, and were invited to stay with

ROME: THE PORTA CAPENA — John H. Kent

THE ROMAN FORUM — Philip Gendreau

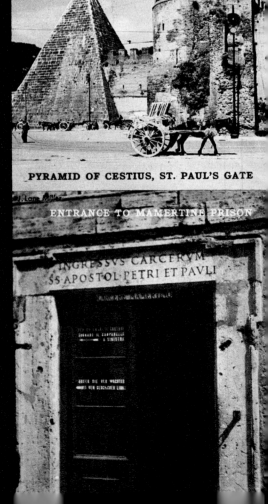

PYRAMID OF CESTIUS, ST. PAUL'S GATE — Ernest Nash

ENTRANCE TO MAMERTINE PRISON

INGRESSVS CARCERVM
SS APOSTOL PETRI ET PAVLI

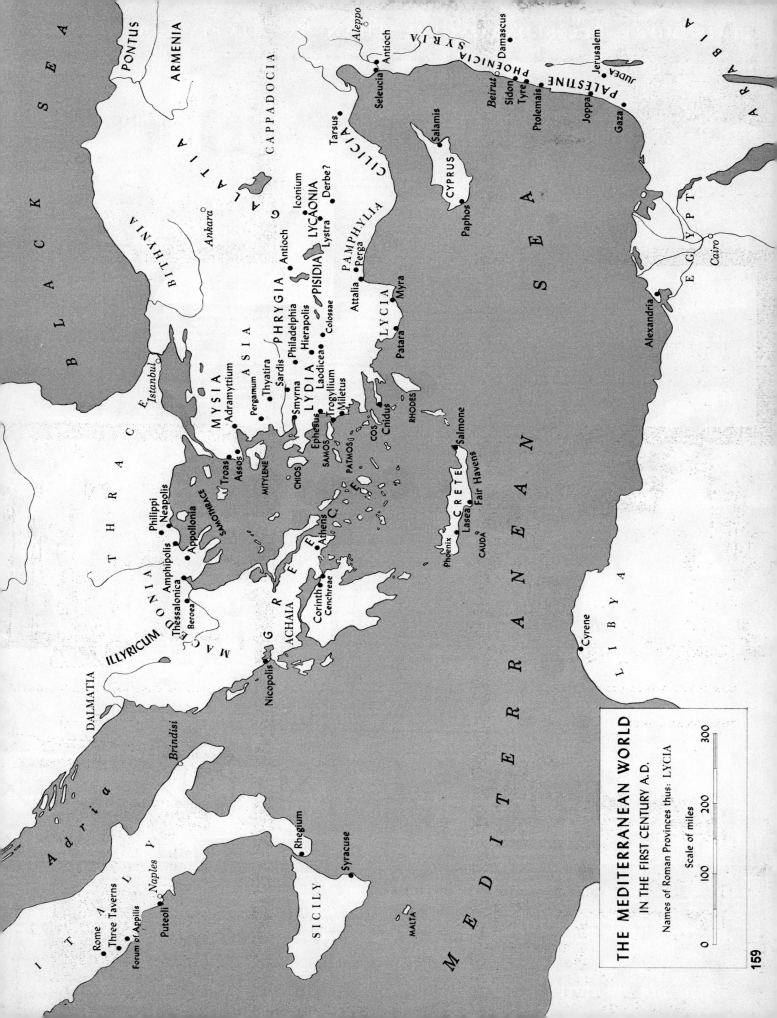

BLACK SEA

PONTUS

ARMENIA

Aleppo

Antioch

SYRIA

Damascus

Seleucia

PHOENICIA

Beirut
Sidon
Tyre
Ptolemais

PALESTINE

Jerusalem
Judea

Joppa

Gaza

ARABIA

CAPPADOCIA

G A L A T I A

Ankara

Tarsus

CILICIA

Iconium

LYCAONIA

Derbe?

Lystra

Antioch

PISIDIA

PHRYGIA

Salamis

CYPRUS

Paphos

BITHYNIA

PAMPHYLIA

Perga
Attalia

LYCIA

Myra

Patara

EGYPT

Cairo

Istanbul

MYSIA

ASIA

Adramyttium

Pergamum

Thyatira

Sardis

Smyrna

LYDIA

Philadelphia

Hierapolis

Colossae

Laodicea

Ephesus

Trogyllium

Miletus

SAMOS

CHIOS

MITYLENE

Assos

Troas

PATMOS

COS

Cnidus

RHODES

Alexandria

M E D I T E R R A N E A N   S E A

T H R A C E

Philippi

Neapolis

Amphipolis

Apollonia

SAMOTHRACE

Thessalonica

Beroea

ILLYRICUM

MACEDONIA

Nicopolis

G R E E C E

Athens

ACHAIA

Corinth

Cenchreae

CRETE

Salmone

Fair Havens

Lasea

Phoenix

CAUDA

CYRENE

Cyrene

LIBYA

DALMATIA

Brindisi

Adria

Naples

Rome
Three Taverns

I T A L Y

Forum of Appius

Puteoli

Rhegium

Syracuse

SICILY

MALTA

THE MEDITERRANEAN WORLD
IN THE FIRST CENTURY A.D.

Names of Roman Provinces thus: LYCIA

Scale of miles

0   100   200   300

159

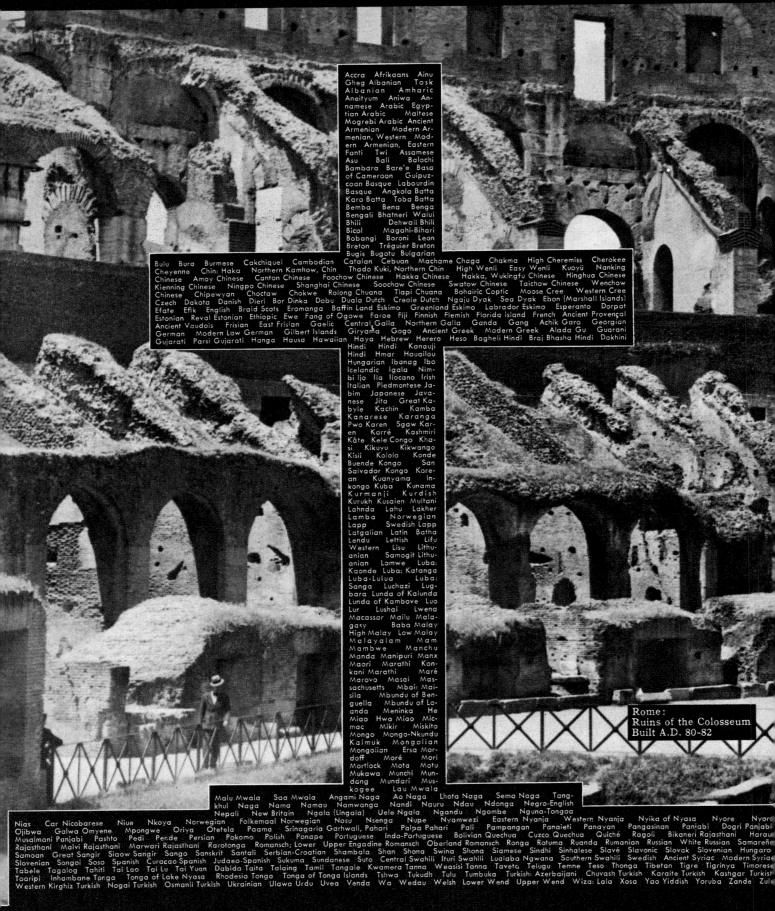

Accra Afrikaans Ainu Gheg Albanian Tosk Albanian Amharic Aneityum Aniwa Annamese Arabic Egyptian Arabic Maltese Mogrebi Arabic Ancient Armenian Modern Armenian, Western Modern Armenian, Eastern Fanti Twi Assamese Asu Bali Balochi Bambara Bare'e Basa of Cameroon Guipuzcoan Basque Labourdin Basque Angkola Batta Karo Batta Toba Batta Bemba Bena Benga Bengali Bhatneri Waiui Bhili Dehwali Bhili Bicol Magahi-Bihari Bobangi Boroni Leon Breton Tréguier Breton Bugis Bugotu Bulgarian

Bulu Bura Burmese Cakchiquel Cambodian Catalan Cebuan Machame Chaga Chakma High Cheremiss Cherokee Cheyenne Chin: Haka Northern Kamhow, Chin Thado Kuki, Northern Chin High Wenli Easy Wenli Kuoyü Nanking Chinese Amoy Chinese Canton Chinese Foochow Chinese Hakka Chinese Hakka, Wukingfu Chinese Hinghua Chinese Kienning Chinese Ningpo Chinese Shanghai Chinese Soochow Chinese Swatow Chinese Taichow Chinese Wenchow Chinese Chipewyan Choctaw Chokwe Rolong Chuana Tlapi Chuana Bohairic Coptic Moose Cree Western Cree Czech Dakota Danish Dieri Bor Dinka Dobu Duala Dutch Creole Dutch Ngaju Dyak Sea Dyak Ebon (Marshall Islands) Efate Efik English Braid Scots Eromanga Baffin Land Eskimo Greenland Eskimo Labrador Eskimo Esperanto Dorpat Estonian Reval Estonian Ethiopic Ewe Fang of Ogowe Faroe Fiji Finnish Flemish Florida Island French Ancient Provençal Ancient Vaudois Frisian East Frisian Gaelic Central Galla Northern Galla Ganda Gang Achik Garo Georgian German Modern Low German Gilbert Islands Giryama Gogo Ancient Greek Modern Greek Alada Gu Guarani Gujarati Parsi Gujarati Hanga Hausa Hawaiian Haya Hebrew Herero Heso Bagheli Hindi Braj Bhasha Hindi Dakhini

Hindi Hindi Kanauji Hindi Hmar Houailou Hungarian Ibanag Ibo Icelandic Igala Nimbi Ijo Ila Ilocano Irish Italian Piedmontese Jabim Japanese Javanese Jita Great Kabyle Kachin Kamba Kanarese Karanga Pwo Karen Sgaw Karen Karré Kashmiri Kâte Kele Congo Khasi Kikuyu Kikwango Kisii Kololo Konde Buende Kongo San Saivador Kongo Korean Kuanyama Inkongo Kuba Kunama Kurmanji Kurdish Kurukh Kusaien Multani Lahnda Lahu Lakher Lamba Norwegian Lapp Swedish Lapp Latgalian Latin Batha Lendu Lettish Lifu Western Lisu Lithuanian Samogit Lithuanian Lomwe Luba: Kaonde Luba: Katanga Luba-Lulua Luba: Sanga Luchazi Lugbara Lunda of Kalunda Lunda of Kambove Luo Lur Lushai Lwena Macassar Mailu Malagasy Baba Malay High Malay Low Malay Malayalam Mam Mambwe Manchu Manda Manipuri Manx Maori Marathi Konkani Marathi Maré Marovo Masai Massachusetts Mbai: Maisila Mbundu of Benguella Mbundu of Loanda Meninka He Miao Hwa Miao Micmac Mikir Miskito Mongo Mongo-Nkundu Kalmuk Mongolian Mongolian Ersa Mordoff Moré Mori Mortlock Mota Motu Mukawa Munchi Mundang Mundari Muskogee Lau Mwala

Malu Mwala Saa Mwala Angami Naga Ao Naga Lhota Naga Sema Naga Tangkhul Naga Nama Namau Namwanga Nandi Nauru Ndau Ndonga Negro-English Nepali New Britain Ngala (Lingala) Uele Ngala Ngandu Ngombe Nguna-Tongoa

Nias Car Nicobarese Niue Nkoya Norwegian Folkemaal Norwegian Nosu Nsenga Nupe Nyamwezi Eastern Nyanja Western Nyanja Nyika of Nyasa Nyore Nyore Ojibwa Galwa Omyene Mpongwe Oriya Otetela Paama Srinagaria Garhwali, Pahari Palpa Pahari Pali Pampangan Panaieti Panayan Pangasinan Panjabi Dogri Panjabi Musalmani Panjabi Pashto Pedi Perde Persian Pokomo Polish Ponape Portuguese Indo-Portuguese Bolivian Quechua Cuzco Quechua Quiché Ragoli Bikaneri Rajasthani Harau Rajasthani Malvi Rajasthani Marwari Rajasthani Rarotonga Romansch; Lower Upper Engadine Romansch Oberland Romansch Ronga Rotuma Ruanda Rumanian Russian White Russian Samareño Samoan Great Sangir Siaow Sangir Sango Sanskrit Santali Serbian-Croatian Shambala Shan Shona Swina Shona Siamese Sindhi Sinhalese Slavé Slavonic Slovak Slovenian Hungaro Slovenian Songoi Sosa Spanish Curacao Spanish Judaeo-Spanish Sukuma Sundanese Suto Central Swahili Ituri Swahili Lualaba Ngwana Southern Swahili Swedish Ancient Syriac Modern Syriac Tabele Tagalog Tahiti Tai Lao Tai Lu Tai Yuan Dabida Taita Talaing Tamil Tangale Kwamera Tanna Weasisi Tanna Taveta Telugu Temne Teso Thonga Tibetan Tigre Tigrinya Timorese Toaripi Inhambane Tonga Tonga of Lake Nyasa Rhodesia Tonga Tonga of Tonga Islands Tshwa Tukudh Tulu Tumbuka Turkish: Azerbaijani Chuvash Turkish Karaite Turkish Kashgar Turkish Western Kirghiz Turkish Nogai Turkish Osmanli Turkish Ukrainian Ulawa Urdu Uvea Venda Wa Wedau Welsh Lower Wend Upper Wend Wiza: Lala Xosa Yao Yiddish Yoruba Zande Zulu

More Than Conquerors

ROME. THE RUINS OF THE ROMAN
FORUM AND THE TRIUMPHAL ARCH OF
TITUS AS SEEN THROUGH THE ARCH OF
SEPTIMIUS SEVERUS, ERECTED A.D. 203

Letters of Paul to the Romans and to the Corint

ROME

ROME was the capital of the Mediterranean world in early Christian times. According to traditional chronology the city was founded in 753 B.C. A primitive monarchy endured until about 500 B.C., and then a republic was maintained until about 30 B.C. It was not until after the death of Alexander the Great (323 B.C.) and the disintegration of his far-flung empire that the opportunity was ripe for Rome to rise to world mastery. Carthage, its North African rival, was destroyed in 146 B.C., and by 64 B.C. the famous general Pompey had occupied Asia Minor and Syria. A year later he conquered Palestine and, much to the horror of the Jews, he entered the Holy of Holies in the Temple at Jerusalem. However, in 49 B.C. Julius Caesar came back to Rome from his conquest of Gaul and soon vanquished the forces of Pompey. The triumph of Caesar was short-lived, for conspirators took his life in 44 B.C.; but he had designated Octavian, his grand-nephew, as heir to his empire. Octavian in turn faced the rivalry of Mark Antony, but in 31 B.C. defeated him and his ally, Cleopatra of Egypt, in the naval battle of Actium. Receiving the title Augustus (Luke 2:1) in 27 B.C., Octavian reigned over an empire largely at peace until his death in A.D. 14. His successor was Tiberius (Luke 3:1), who was on the throne until A.D. 37, and thus the entire lifetime of Jesus fell within the reigns of the two emperors Augustus and Tiberius. Paul's missionary activities and letters date from the reigns of Claudius (Acts 11:28; 18:2), A.D. 41–54, and Nero (Acts 25:11), A.D. 54–68.

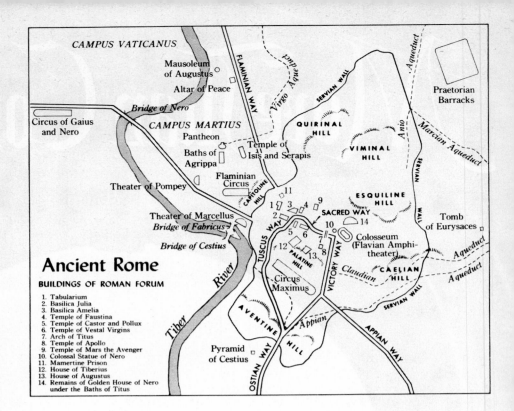

Ancient Rome

BUILDINGS OF ROMAN FORUM

1. Tabularium
2. Basilica Julia
3. Basilica Amelia
4. Temple of Faustina
5. Temple of Castor and Pollux
6. Temple of Vestal Virgins
7. Arch of Titus
8. Temple of Apollo
9. Temple of Mars the Avenger
10. Colossal Statue of Nero
11. Mamertine Prison
12. House of Tiberius
13. House of Augustus
14. Remains of Golden House of Nero under the Baths of Titus

The location of Rome, approximately in the center of the Mediterranean world, was favorable to its supremacy. Not only war but also commerce found the city strategically placed, and through its seaport of Ostia, seventeen miles away, it enjoyed connections by sea with all the main regions of the empire. Great highways radiated in all directions, so that it was said, "All roads lead to Rome." The Ostian Way, as its name indicates, came from Ostia. The Appian Way led to Rome from the very bottom tip of Italy, while the Flaminian Way came from the north.

The immediate site of the city was upon seven famous hills beside the Tiber River—the Aventine, the Caelian, the Palatine, the Capitoline, the Esquiline, the Viminal and the Quirinal. Around the central area, in republican days the Servian Wall was built.

The very center of the city was the Forum. On one side was the Palatine Hill, with the residences of the emperors; on the other was the Capitoline, with a mighty temple to Jupiter. In and near the Forum were palaces, temples, office buildings, law courts, triumphal arches, shops and stores. In the Forum was the golden mile-post on which were shown the distances to the corners of the empire, including London on the west and Jerusalem on the east. When at a later period the Triumphal Arch of Titus and the Basilica of Constantine were added, the Forum extended almost to the Colosseum. Although most of the ancient city is now in ruins, the fallen stones and fragments of standing columns and walls still give an almost indescribable impression of the grandeur that was Rome.

For the pleasure of the people there were many public gardens and parks in Rome. Large theaters provided for the presentation of plays. Public baths were characteristic, and already in 33 B.C. were said to number no fewer than one hundred and seventy. In these beautifully fitted-out establishments there was opportunity for exercise, reading and the hearing of lectures, as well as bathing. Amphitheaters and circuses were available for amusements, chief of which was chariot racing. Gradually, however, the people developed a taste for bloodier sports, and in the reign of Nero the arena of the Circus of Caligula was stained with the blood of Christians. The great Colosseum was not begun until the time of Vespasian and not completed until A.D. 80 under Titus.

The living conditions of the common people, however, were not as favorable as the external magnificence of the public buildings might suggest. Turning aside from the great avenues, one could quickly lose oneself in the crooked, constricted streets which formed a veritable labyrinth throughout much of the city. By law these lanes could not be less than nine and one-half feet wide, but balconies often projected so far from the houses on either side that neighbors could touch hands across the street. In the daytime the streets were crowded and noisy, and at night many were unlighted and became the haunt of ruffians. Wheeled vehicles were kept off during the day but rumbled past throughout the night. Slop was thrown out of upper windows, and filth accumulated on the pavements. During the rains water poured down the streets and large stepping-stones were needed for crossing intersections. The tenements in which the majority of the population lived covered large areas of the city. Usually built of concrete and wood, erected as cheaply as possible, crowded tightly together and pushed up to the legal limit of seventy feet in height, these buildings were often allowed to come into such disrepair that they were in danger of collapse. Juvenal wrote about Rome, "We inhabit a city propped up for the most part by slats: for that is how the landlord patches up the cracks in the old wall, bidding the inmates sleep at ease under a roof ready to tumble about their ears." Through these narrow streets and among these crowded tenements the great fire of A.D. 64 raged with irresistible violence.

CORINTH

Once a rival of Rome and destroyed by the Romans in 146 B.C., the same year in which Carthage fell, the city of Corinth became in New Testament times a teeming metropolis of commerce. Its site was both strategic and striking. Located on the Isthmus of Corinth, it commanded the ports of Lechaeum (about one mile to the west) and Cenchreae (about eight miles to the east). Across the narrow neck of land, not cut by a canal until modern times, smaller ships were moved on a sort of tramway, while the cargoes of larger ones were readily transshipped. By either expedient a potentially stormy and certainly lengthy circumnavigation of the southern capes of Greece was avoided.

As revealed by modern excavations, the heart of the city of New Testament times was the agora or market place. This was a rectangular area, 600 feet long and 300 feet wide, paved with marble. To the south was the stoa or covered walk where people promenaded and talked religion, philosophy and business. Its 500-foot length made it the largest in all Greece. Paul no doubt found occasion to teach here. To the north of the agora were all kinds of shops and public buildings, and near the center was the large outdoor speakers' stand or bema, in front of which Paul must have stood before Gallio (Acts 18:12–17). Outside the agora were a large theater and a smaller odeum or music hall. On a low hill not far away was the beautiful temple of Apollo, seven of whose pillars are still standing. Another temple was that of Asklepios, where there were arrangements for baths and meals for the patients who came to seek help from the god of healing. On the summit of Acrocorinth, the 1,800-foot rock fortress behind the city, was the temple of Aphrodite, the Greek goddess of love, which only served to increase the evil propensities of this cosmopolitan city. They are described in Paul's letters to Corinth; and he may have had Corinth in mind when in Romans 1:18–32 he described the depths of human degradation.

Ernest Nash

In the Roman Forum were the Temple of Vesta and the House of the Vestal Virgins. The Vestal Virgins guarded the sacred fire and the palladium or image of Pallas Athena (Minerva), said to have been brought by Aeneas from Troy

Ernest Nash

Basilica Julia (public building) on the Roman Forum and the Sacred Way, begun by Julius Caesar 54 B.C., dedicated by Augustus A.D. 12 to the memory of his adopted sons, Gaius and Lucius Caesar

THE LETTER OF PAUL TO THE ROMANS

Greetings

American Numismatic Society

[Romans 1:1-7] Paul, a servant[a] of Jesus Christ, called to be an apostle, set apart for the gospel of God which he promised beforehand through his prophets in the holy scriptures, the gospel concerning his Son, who was descended from David according to the flesh and designated Son of God in power according to the Spirit of holiness by his resurrection from the dead, Jesus Christ our Lord, through whom we have received grace and apostleship to bring about the obedience of faith for the sake of his name among all the nations, including yourselves who are called to belong to Jesus Christ;

To all God's beloved in Rome, who are called to be saints:

Grace to you and peace from God our Father and the Lord Jesus Christ.

Paul's Desire To Visit Rome [1:8-15]

First, I thank my God through Jesus Christ for all of you, because your faith is proclaimed in all the world. For God is my witness, whom I serve with my spirit in the gospel of his Son, that without ceasing I mention you always in my prayers, asking that somehow by God's will I may now at last succeed in coming to you. For I long to see you, that I may impart to you some

[a]Or slave

spiritual gift to strengthen you, that is, that we may be mutually encouraged by each other's faith, both yours and mine. I want you to know, brethren, that I have often intended to come to you (but thus far have been prevented), in order that I may reap some harvest among you as well as among the rest of the Gentiles. I am under obligation both to Greeks and to barbarians, both to the wise and to the foolish: so I am eager to preach the gospel to you also who are in Rome.

(1) *This coin of Julius Caesar, ca. 48 B.C., shows Aeneas carrying his father Anchises from burning Troy. Julius Caesar claimed that he was descended from Venus through Aeneas. Note the palladium or image of Pallas Athena (Minerva) carried by Anchises*

(2) *This coin, issued by Brutus, with his head on the obverse, shows on the reverse a liberty cap between two daggers in justification of the stabbing of Julius Caesar on the Ides of March, 44 B.C.*

(3) *This coin of Octavian, who was later known as Augustus Caesar, 27 B.C.–A.D. 14, bears the legend CAESAR.DIVI.F, "Caesar, son of the deified (Julius)." It shows Octavian with globe beneath his foot, the aplustre of Neptune in his right hand, and the long scepter of Jupiter in his left hand*

(4) *After the murder of Caligula, the Praetorian Guard proclaimed his uncle Claudius his successor. This coin shows Claudius clasping hands with a Praetorian soldier*

Mausoleum of Augustus, erected 28 B.C., which contained in urns his ashes and those of Germanicus, Livia, Tiberius, Caligula and many other members of his dynasty

Gabinetto Fotografico Nazionale, Rome

↓

The Way of Victory between the palaces of the early emperors on the Palatine Hill. Augustus boasted that he found Rome a city of brick and left it a city of marble. Later generations have removed most of the marble, leaving the brick

↓

Gallerie Musei Vaticani, Rome

Kunsthistorisches Museum, Vienna

Silver plate found at Aquileia which represents an early Roman emperor as Triptolemus, god of agriculture, offering gifts to Demeter enthroned on the right. The Seasons feed the snakes of the winged imperial chariot. Psyche and love-gods bring additional gifts. Below is Tellus with her cow to symbolize the fertility of the earth

The Cornucopia Cameo, showing Claudius and Agrippina the Younger at the left, and Germanicus and Agrippina the Elder on the right. Nero's claim to the empire came through the four persons on this cameo. Agrippina the Younger was the sister of the Roman Emperor Caligula and the mother of Nero. She was born in Germany and is reported to have poisoned her second husband in order to marry Claudius, her uncle. Claudius, A.D. 41–54, was grandson of Livia, wife of Augustus, and so not of the Julian family. Agrippina married her son Nero to Claudius' daughter Octavia when he was barely fifteen, and then persuaded Claudius to adopt Nero as his heir in place of his own son Britannicus. Agrippina the Younger then poisoned Claudius to make Nero emperor in A.D. 54. Nero in turn is accused of her death in A.D. 59 and also of poisoning Britannicus at a banquet in A.D. 55

The Power of the Gospel [1:16–17]

For I am not ashamed of the gospel: it is the power of God for salvation to every one who has faith, to the Jew first and also to the Greek. For in it the righteousness of God is revealed through faith for faith; as it is written, "He who through faith is righteous shall live.[b1]"

The Guilt of Mankind [1:18–23]

For the wrath of God is revealed from heaven against all ungodliness and wickedness of men who by their wickedness suppress the truth. For what can be known about God is plain to them, because God has shown it to them. Ever since the creation of the world his invisible nature, namely, his eternal power and deity, has been clearly perceived in the things that have been made.[2] So they are without excuse; for although they knew God they did not honor him as God or give thanks to him, but they became futile in their thinking and their senseless minds were darkened. Claiming to be wise, they became fools, and exchanged the glory of the immortal God for images resembling mortal man or birds or animals or reptiles.

The Downward Course of Man [1:24–32]

Therefore God gave them up in the lusts of their hearts to impurity, to the dishonoring of their bodies among themselves, because they exchanged the truth about God

[b]Or *The righteous shall live by faith*
[1]*Habakkuk 2:4*

for a lie and worshiped and served the creature rather than the Creator, who is blessed for ever! Amen.

For this reason God gave them up to dishonorable passions. Their women exchanged natural relations for unnatural, and the men likewise gave up natural relations with women and were consumed with passion for one another, men committing shameless acts with men and receiving in their own persons the due penalty for their error.

And since they did not see fit to acknowledge God, God gave them up to a base mind and to improper conduct. They were filled with all manner of wickedness, evil, covetousness, malice. Full of envy, murder, strife, deceit, malignity, they are gossips, slanderers, haters of God, insolent, haughty, boastful, inventors of evil, disobedient to parents, foolish, faithless, heartless, ruthless. Though they know God's decree that those who do such things deserve to die, they not only do them but approve those who practice them.

God's Righteous Judgment [Romans 2:1–11]

THEREFORE you have no excuse, O man, whoever you are, when you judge another; for in passing judgment upon him you condemn yourself, because you, the judge, are doing the very same things. We know that the judgment of God rightly falls upon those who do such things. Do you suppose, O man, that when you judge those who do such things and yet do them yourself, you will escape the judgment of God?

Or do you presume upon the riches of his kindness and forbearance and patience? Do you not know that God's kindness is meant to lead you to repentance? But by your hard and impenitent heart you are storing up wrath for yourself on the day of wrath when God's righteous judgment will be revealed. For he will render to every man according to his works: to those who by patience in well-doing seek for glory and honor and immortality, he will give eternal life; but for those who are factious and do not obey the truth, but obey wickedness, there will be wrath and fury. There will be tribulation and distress for every human being who does evil, the Jew first and also the Greek, but glory and honor and peace for every one who does good, the Jew first and also the Greek. For God shows no partiality.

"A Law to Themselves" [2:12–16]

All who have sinned without the law will also perish without the law, and all who have sinned under the law will be judged by the law. For it is not the hearers of the law who are righteous before God, but the doers of the law who will be justified. When Gentiles who have not the law do by nature what the law requires, they are a law to themselves, even though they do not have the law. They show that what the law requires is written on their hearts, while their conscience also bears witness and their conflicting thoughts accuse or perhaps excuse them on that day when, according to my gospel, God judges the secrets of men by Christ Jesus.

The Jews and the Law [2:17–24]

But if you call yourself a Jew and rely upon the law and boast of your relation to God and know his will and approve what is excellent, because you are instructed in the law, and if you are sure that you are a guide to the blind, a light to those who are in darkness, a corrector of the foolish, a teacher of children, having in the law the embodiment of knowledge and truth—you then who teach others, will you not teach yourself? While you preach against stealing, do you steal? You who say that one must not commit adultery, do you commit adultery? You who abhor idols, do you rob temples? You who boast in the law, do you dishonor God by breaking the law? For, as it is written, "The name of God is blasphemed among the Gentiles because of you."[2]

True Circumcision [2:25–29]

Circumcision indeed is of value if you obey the law; but if you break the law, your circumcision becomes uncircumcision. So, if a man who is uncircumcised keeps the precepts of the law, will not his uncircumcision be regarded as circumcision? Then those who are physically uncircumcised but keep the law will condemn you who have the written code and circumcision but break the law. For he is not a real Jew who is one outwardly, nor is true circumcision something external and physical. He is a Jew who is one inwardly, and real circumcision is a matter of the heart, spiritual and not literal. His praise is not from men but from God.

The Advantage of the Jews

[Romans 3:1–8]

THEN what advantage has the Jew? Or what is the value of circumcision? Much in every way. To begin with, the Jews are entrusted with the oracles of God. What if some were unfaithful? Does their faithlessness nullify the faithfulness of God? By no means! Let God be true though every man be false, as it is written,

"That thou mayest be justified in thy words,
and prevail when thou art judged."[3]

But if our wickedness serves to show the justice of God, what shall we say? That God is unjust to inflict wrath on us? (I speak in a human way.) By no means! For then how could God judge the world? But if through my falsehood God's truthfulness abounds to his glory, why am I still being condemned as a sinner? And why not do evil that good may come?—as some people slanderously charge us with saying. Their condemnation is just.

None Is Righteous [3:9–20]

What then? Are we Jews any better off?[c] No, not at all; for I[d] have already charged that all men, both Jews and Greeks, are under the power of sin, as it is written:

"None is righteous, no, not one;
no one understands, no one seeks for God.
All have turned aside, together they have gone wrong;

[c]Or at any disadvantage?
[d]Greek we
[2]Isaiah 52:5
[3]Psalms 51:4

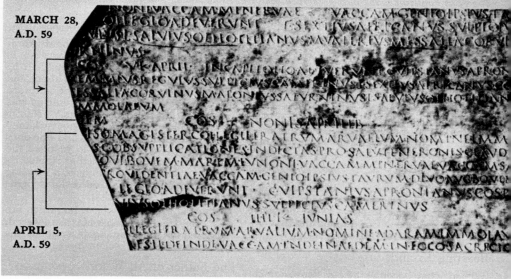

College of Arval Brethren inscriptions. On November 6, A.D. 58, the College of the Arval Brethren celebrated the birthday of Agrippina, mother of the Emperor Nero, by sacrificing on the Capitol: "to Jupiter, a bull; to Juno, a cow; to Minerva, a cow; to Public Welfare, a cow; to Concord, a cow." Agrippina was murdered between March 19 and 23, A.D. 59. The College of the Arval Brethren met on March 28, but no mention is made of the reason for the meeting. On April 5 this same College celebrated her assassination as an act by which her son, the Emperor Nero, was saved, and in fulfillment of a decree by the Senate gave public and official thanksgiving by sacrificing "to Jupiter, a bull; to Juno, a cow; to Minerva, a cow; to Public Welfare, a cow; to Providence, a cow; to the Genius of the Emperor, a steer; to the deified Augustus, a bull"

NOV. 6, A.D. 58

MARCH 28, A.D. 59

APRIL 5, A.D. 59

Herbert Bloch

Ernest Nash

no one does good, not even one."[4]
"Their throat is an open grave,
they use their tongues to deceive."[5]
"The venom of asps is under their lips."[6]
"Their mouth is full of curses and bitterness."[7]
"Their feet are swift to shed blood,
in their paths are ruin and misery,
and the way of peace they do not know."[8]
"There is no fear of God before their eyes."[9]

Now we know that whatever the law says it speaks to those who are under the law, so that every mouth may be stopped, and the whole world may be held accountable to God. For no human being will be justified in his sight by works of the law, since through the law comes knowledge of sin.

[4]Psalms 14:1–3; 53:1–3
[5]Psalms 5:9
[6]Psalms 140:3
[7]Psalms 10:7
[8]Isaiah 59:7–8
[9]Psalms 36–1

Part of the Servian Wall, built, according to tradition, by the sixth king of Rome, Servius Tullius, but in reality dating from the fourth century B.C.

Ernest Nash

On this coin of Tiberius the ideal of justice is proclaimed. On other coins peace and public welfare are broadcast as objectives of imperial propaganda. Although the Romans established law courts and had judges, these alone could not effectively curb lawlessness and crime

British Museum

The Pons Fabricius is the best-preserved bridge in Rome, being practically the original structure built in 62 B.C.

Righteousness through Faith

[3:21–26]

But now the righteousness of God has been manifested apart from law, although the law and the prophets bear witness to it, the righteousness of God through faith in Jesus Christ for all who believe. For there is no distinction; since all have sinned and fall short of the glory of God, they are justified by his grace as a gift, through the redemption which is in Christ Jesus, whom God put forward as an expiation by his blood, to be received by faith. This was to show God's righteousness, because in his divine forbearance he had passed over former sins; it was to prove at the present time that he himself is righteous and that he justifies him who has faith in Jesus.

Boasting Excluded [3:27–31]

Then what becomes of our boasting? It is excluded. On what principle? On the principle of works? No, but on the principle of faith. For we hold that a man is justified by faith apart from works of law. Or is God the God of Jews only? Is he not the God of Gentiles also? Yes, of Gentiles also, since God is one; and he will justify the circumcised on the ground of their faith and the uncircumcised through their faith. Do we then overthrow the law by this faith? By no means! On the contrary, we uphold the law.

The Example of Abraham [Romans 4:1–8]

WHAT then shall we say about[e] Abraham, our forefather according to the flesh? For if Abraham was justified by works, he has something to boast about, but not before God. For what does the scripture say? "Abraham believed God, and it was reckoned to him as righteousness."[10] Now to one who works, his wages are not reckoned as a gift but as his due. And to one who does not work but trusts him who justifies the ungodly, his faith is reckoned as righteousness. So also David pronounces a blessing upon the man to whom God reckons righteousness apart from works:

"Blessed are those whose iniquities are forgiven, and whose sins are covered; blessed is the man against whom the Lord will not reckon his sin."[11]

The Father of All Who Believe [4:9–12]

Is this blessing pronounced only upon the circumcised, or also upon the uncircumcised? We say that faith was reckoned to Abraham as righteousness. How then was it reckoned to him? Was it before or after he had been circumcised? It was not after, but before he was circumcised. He received circumcision as a sign or seal of the right-

[e]Other ancient authorities read was gained by
[10]Genesis 15:6
[11]Psalms 32:1–2

Keystone View Co.

eousness which he had by faith while he was still uncircumcised. The purpose was to make him the father of all who believe without being circumcised and who thus have righteousness reckoned to them, and likewise the father of the circumcised who are not merely circumcised but also follow the example of the faith which our father Abraham had before he was circumcised.

The Promise Not through Law [4:13–15]

The promise to Abraham and his descendants, that they should inherit the world, did not come through the law but through the righteousness of faith. If it is the adherents of the law who are to be the heirs, faith is null and the promise is void. For the law brings wrath, but where there is no law there is no transgression.

The Promise Depends on Faith [4:16–25]

That is why it depends on faith, in order that the promise may rest on grace and be guaranteed to all his descendants—not only to the adherents of the law but also to those who share the faith of Abraham, for he is the father of us all, as it is written, "I have made you the father of many nations"[12]—in the presence of the God in whom he believed, who gives life to the dead and calls into existence the things that do not exist. In hope he believed against hope, that he should become the father of many nations; as he had been told, "So shall your descendants be."[13] He did not weaken in faith when he considered his own body, which was as good as dead because he was about a hundred years old, or when he considered the barrenness of Sarah's womb. No distrust made him waver concerning the promise of God, but he grew strong in his faith as he gave glory to God, fully convinced that God was able to do what he had promised. That is why his faith was "reckoned to him as righteousness." But the words, "it was reckoned to him," were written not for his sake alone, but for ours

[12]Genesis 17:5
[13]Genesis 15:5

Ruins of the ziggurat or temple tower of ancient Ur. According to the Book of Genesis Ur was the original home of Abraham

also. It will be reckoned to us who believe in him that raised from the dead Jesus our Lord, who was put to death for our trespasses and raised for our justification.

Peace with God through Christ

[Romans 5:1-5]

THEREFORE, since we are justified by faith, we[f] have peace with God through our Lord Jesus Christ. Through him we have obtained access[g] to this grace in which we stand, and we[h] rejoice in our hope of sharing the glory of God. More than that, we[h] rejoice in our sufferings, knowing that suffering produces endurance, and endurance produces character, and character produces hope, and hope does not disappoint us, because God's love has been poured into our hearts through the Holy Spirit which has been given to us.

Christ Died for the Ungodly [5:6-11]

While we were yet helpless, at the right time Christ died for the ungodly. Why, one will hardly die for a righteous man—though perhaps for a good man one will dare even to die. But God shows his love for us in that while we were yet sinners Christ died for us. Since, therefore, we are now justified by his blood, much more shall we be saved by him from the wrath of God. For if while we were enemies we were reconciled to God by the death of his Son, much more, now that we are reconciled, shall we be saved by his life. Not only so, but we also rejoice in God through our Lord Jesus Christ, through whom we have now received our reconciliation.

The Reign of Sin and Death [5:12-14]

Therefore as sin came into the world through one man and death through sin, and so death spread to all men because all men sinned—sin indeed was in the world before the law was given, but sin is not counted where there is no law. Yet death reigned from Adam to Moses, even over those whose sins were not like the transgression of Adam, who was a type of the one who was to come.

The Gift of Righteousness [5:15-17]

But the free gift is not like the trespass. For if many died through one man's trespass, much more have the grace of God and the free gift in the grace of that one man Jesus Christ abounded for many. And the free gift is not like the effect of that one man's sin. For the judgment following one trespass brought condemnation, but the free gift following many trespasses brings justification. If, because of one man's trespass, death reigned through that one man, much more will those who receive the abundance of grace and the free gift of righteousness reign in life through the one man Jesus Christ.

Abounding Grace [5:18-21]

Then as one man's trespass led to condemnation for all men, so one man's act of righteousness leads to acquittal and life for all men. For as by one man's dis-

[f]Other ancient authorities read *let us*
[g]Other ancient authorities add *by faith*
[h]Or *let us*

Matson Photo Service

Ras Safsaf, one of the Sinai peaks at the foot of which the Israelites are said to have encamped while Moses was receiving the law

obedience many were made sinners, so by one man's obedience many will be made righteous. Law came in, to increase the trespass; but where sin increased, grace abounded all the more, so that, as sin reigned in death, grace also might reign through righteousness to eternal life through Jesus Christ our Lord.

Dead to Sin [Romans 6:1-4]

WHAT shall we say then? Are we to continue in sin that grace may abound? By no means! How can we who died to sin still live in it? Do you not know that all of us who have been baptized into Christ Jesus were baptized into his death? We were buried therefore with him by baptism into death, so that as Christ was raised from the dead by the glory of the Father, we too might walk in newness of life.

Alive to God in Christ [6:5-11]

For if we have been united with him in a death like his, we shall certainly be united with him in a resurrection like his. We know that our old self was crucified with him so that the sinful body might be destroyed, and we might no longer be enslaved to sin. For he who has died is freed from sin. But if we have died with Christ, we believe that we shall also live with him. For we know that Christ being raised from the dead will never die again; death no longer has dominion over him. The death he died he died to sin, once for all, but the life he lives he lives to God. So you also must consider yourselves dead to sin and alive to God in Christ Jesus.

Perhaps a fourth of the population of Rome were slaves. Many of these slaves were men of high intellect and culture. These busts from the Second Columbarium of the Vigna Codini on the Appian Way represent slaves who provided for their own burial.
Top: Salvius, slave of the Emperor (Tiberius), in charge of his silver plate.
Bottom: Sinnio, bodyguard of the Emperor (Tiberius), previously in the household of Drusus (Tiberius' brother)

Felbermeyer

167

Louvre

Hammurabi, King of Babylonia in the patriarchal age, receiving his law code from the sun god. This code is inscribed on the lower part of the cylinder

Yield Yourselves to God [6:12-14]

Let not sin therefore reign in your mortal bodies, to make you obey their passions. Do not yield your members to sin as instruments of wickedness, but yield yourselves to God as men who have been brought from death to life, and your members to God as instruments of righteousness. For sin will have no dominion over you, since you are not under law but under grace.

Slaves of Righteousness [6:15-19]

What then? Are we to sin because we are not under law but under grace? By no means! Do you not know that if you yield yourselves to any one as obedient slaves, you are slaves of the one whom you obey, either of sin, which leads to death, or of obedience, which leads to righteousness? But thanks be to God, that you who were once slaves of sin have become obedient from the heart to the standard of teaching to which you were committed, and, having been set free from sin, have become slaves of righteousness. I am speaking in human terms, because of your natural limitations. For just as you once yielded your members to impurity and to greater and greater iniquity, so now yield your members to righteousness for sanctification.

The Wages of Sin [6:20-23]

When you were slaves of sin, you were free in regard to righteousness. But then what return did you get from the things of which you are now ashamed? The end of those things is death. But now that you have been set free from sin and have become slaves of God, the return you get is sanctification and its end, eternal life. For the wages of sin is death, but the free gift of God is eternal life in Christ Jesus our Lord.

Discharged from the Law [Romans 7:1-6]

DO you not know, brethren—for I am speaking to those who know the law—that the law is binding on a person only during his life? Thus a married woman is bound by law to her husband as long as he lives; but if her husband dies she is discharged from the law concerning the husband. Accordingly, she will be called an adulteress if she lives with another man while her husband is alive. But if her husband dies she is free from that law, and if she marries another man she is not an adulteress.

The Purpose of the Law [7:7-12]

Likewise, my brethren, you have died to the law through the body of Christ, so that you may belong to another, to him who has been raised from the dead in order that we may bear fruit for God. While we were living in the flesh, our sinful passions, aroused by the law, were at work in our members to bear fruit for death. But now we are discharged from the law, dead to that which held us captive, so that we serve not under the old written code but in the new life of the Spirit.

What then shall we say? That the law is sin? By no means! Yet, if it had not been for the law, I should not have known sin. I should not have known what it is to covet if the law had not said, "You shall not covet."[14] But sin, finding opportunity in the commandment, wrought in me all kinds of covetousness. Apart from the law sin lies dead. I was once alive apart from the law, but when the commandment came, sin revived and I died; the very commandment which promised life proved to be death to me. For sin, finding opportunity in the commandment, deceived me and by it killed me. So the law is holy, and the commandment is holy and just and good.

Indwelling Sin [7:13-20]

Did that which is good, then, bring death to me? By no means! It was sin, working death in me through what is good, in order that sin might be shown to be sin, and through the commandment might become sinful beyond measure. We know that the law is spiritual; but I am carnal, sold under sin. I do not understand my own actions. For I do not do what I want, but I do the very thing I hate. Now if I do what I do not want, I agree that the law is good. So then it is no longer I that do it, but sin which dwells within me. For I know that nothing good dwells within me, that is, in my flesh. I can will what is right, but I cannot do it. For I do not do the good I want, but the evil I do not want is what I do. Now if I do what I do not want, it is no longer I that do it, but sin which dwells within me.

The War Within [7:21-25]

So I find it to be a law that when I want to do right, evil lies close at hand. For I delight in the law of God, in my inmost self,

[14]*Exodus* 20:17; *Deuteronomy* 5:21

but I see in my members another law at war with the law of my mind and making me captive to the law of sin which dwells in my members. Wretched man that I am! Who will deliver me from this body of death? Thanks be to God through Jesus Christ our Lord! So then, I of myself serve the law of God with my mind, but with my flesh I serve the law of sin.

No Condemnation for Those in Christ

[Romans 8:1-8]

THERE is therefore now no condemnation for those who are in Christ Jesus. For the law of the Spirit of life in Christ Jesus has set me free from the law of sin and death. For God has done what the law, weakened by the flesh, could not do: sending his own Son in the likeness of sinful flesh and for sin,[i] he condemned sin in the flesh, in order that the just requirement of the law might be fulfilled in us, who walk not according to the flesh but according to the Spirit. For those who live according to the flesh set their minds on the things of the flesh, but those who live according to the Spirit set their minds on the things of the Spirit. To set the mind on the flesh is death, but to set the mind on the Spirit is life and peace. For the mind that is set on the flesh is hostile to God; it does not submit to God's law, indeed it cannot; and those who are in the flesh cannot please God.

The Indwelling Spirit [8:9-11]

But you are not in the flesh, you are in the Spirit, if the Spirit of God really dwells in you. Any one who does not have the Spirit of Christ does not belong to him. But if Christ is in you, although your bodies are dead because of sin, your spirits are alive because of righteousness. If the Spirit of him who raised Jesus from the dead dwells in you, he who raised Christ Jesus from the dead will give life to your mortal bodies also through his Spirit which dwells in you.

Fellow Heirs with Christ [8:12-17]

So then, brethren, we are debtors, not to the flesh, to live according to the flesh—for if you live according to the flesh you will die, but if by the Spirit you put to death the deeds of the body you will live. For all who are led by the Spirit of God are sons of God. For you did not receive the spirit of slavery to fall back into fear, but you have received the spirit of sonship. When we cry, "Abba! Father!" it is the Spirit himself bearing witness with our spirit that we are children of God, and if children, then heirs, heirs of God and fellow heirs with Christ, provided we suffer with him in order that we may also be glorified with him.

Longing for the Coming Glory [8:18-25]

I consider that the sufferings of this present time are not worth comparing with the glory that is to be revealed to us. For the creation waits with eager longing for the revealing of the sons of God; for the creation was subjected to futility, not of its own will but by the will of him who subjected it in hope; because the creation itself will be set free from its bondage to decay and obtain the glorious liberty of the children of God. We know that the whole creation has been groaning in travail together until now;

[i]*Or and as a sin offering*

and not only the creation, but we ourselves, who have the first fruits of the Spirit, groan inwardly as we wait for adoption as sons, the redemption of our bodies. For in this hope we were saved. Now hope that is seen is not hope. For who hopes for what he sees? But if we hope for what we do not see, we wait for it with patience.

The Intercession of the Spirit [8:26–27]

Likewise the Spirit helps us in our weakness; for we do not know how to pray as we ought, but the Spirit himself intercedes for us with sighs too deep for words. And he who searches the hearts of men knows what is the mind of the Spirit, because^j the Spirit intercedes for the saints according to the will of God.

Called According to His Purpose
[8:28–30]

We know that in everything God works for good^k with those who love him,^{l} who are called according to his purpose. For those whom he foreknew he also predestined to be conformed to the image of his Son, in order that he might be the first-born among many brethren. And those whom he predestined he also called; and those whom he called he also justified; and those whom he justified he also glorified.

More than Conquerors [8:31–39]

What then shall we say to this? If God is for us, who is against us? He who did not spare his own Son but gave him up for us all, will he not also give us all things with him? Who shall bring any charge against God's elect? It is God who justifies; who is to condemn? Is it Christ Jesus, who died, yes, who was raised from the dead, who is at the right hand of God, who indeed intercedes for us?^{m} Who shall separate us from the love of Christ? Shall tribulation, or distress, or persecution, or famine, or nakedness, or peril, or sword? As it is written,

"For thy sake we are being killed all the day long;
we are regarded as sheep to be slaughtered."[15]

No, in all these things we are more than conquerors through him who loved us. For I am sure that neither death, nor life, nor angels, nor principalities, nor things present, nor things to come, nor powers, nor height, nor depth, nor anything else in all creation, will be able to separate us from the love of God in Christ Jesus our Lord.

Paul's Concern for Israel [Romans 9:1–5]

I AM speaking the truth in Christ, I am not lying; my conscience bears me witness in the Holy Spirit, that I have great sorrow and unceasing anguish in my heart. For I could wish that I myself were accursed and cut off from Christ for the sake of my brethren, my kinsmen by race. They are Israelites, and to them belong the sonship, the glory, the covenants, the giving of the law, the worship, and the promises; to them

A woman making pottery by hand in Palestine

belong the patriarchs, and of their race, according to the flesh, is the Christ. God who is over all be blessed for ever.^{n} Amen.

Children of the Promise [9:6–13]

But it is not as though the word of God had failed. For not all who are descended from Israel belong to Israel, and not all are children of Abraham because they are his descendants; but, "Through Isaac shall your descendants be named."[16] This means that it is not the children of the flesh who are the children of God, but the children of the promise are reckoned as descendants. For this is what the promise said, "About this time I will return and Sarah shall have a son."[17] And not only so, but also when Rebec'ca had conceived children by one man, our forefather Isaac, though they were not yet born and had done nothing either good or bad, in order that God's purpose of election might continue, not because of works but because of his call, she was told, "The elder will serve the younger."[18] As it is written, "Jacob I loved, but Esau I hated."[19]

God's Mercy [9:14–18]

What shall we say then? Is there injustice on God's part? By no means! For he says to Moses, "I will have mercy on whom I have mercy, and I will have compassion on whom I have compassion."[20] So it depends not upon man's will or exertion, but upon God's mercy. For the scripture says to Pharaoh, "I have raised you up for the very purpose of showing my power in you, so that my name may be proclaimed in all the earth."[21] So then he has mercy upon

whomever he wills, and he hardens the heart of whomever he wills.

The Potter and the Clay [9:19–26]

You will say to me then, "Why does he still find fault? For who can resist his will?" But who are you, a man, to answer back to God? Will what is molded say to its molder, "Why have you made me thus?" Has the potter no right over the clay, to make out of the same lump one vessel for beauty and another for menial use? What if God, desiring to show his wrath and to make known his power, has endured with much patience the vessels of wrath made for destruction, in order to make known the riches of his glory for the vessels of mercy, which he has prepared beforehand for glory, even us whom he has called, not from the Jews only but also from the Gentiles? As indeed he says in Hose'a,

"Those who were not my people
I will call 'my people,'
and her who was not beloved
I will call 'my beloved.' "[22]
"And in the very place where it was said
to them, 'You are not my people,'
they will be called 'sons of the living
God.' "[23]

The Saved Remnant [9:27–29]

And Isai'ah cries out concerning Israel: "Though the number of the sons of Israel be as the sand of the sea, only a remnant of them will be saved; for the Lord will execute his sentence upon the earth with rigor and dispatch."[24] And as Isai'ah predicted,

"If the Lord of hosts had not left us
children,
we would have fared like Sodom and
been made like Gomor'rah."[25]

^{j}Or *that*
^{k}Other ancient authorities read *in everything he works for good*, or *everything works for good*
^{l}Greek *God*
^{m}Or *It is Christ Jesus . . . for us*
[15]*Psalms* 44:22

^{n}Or *Christ, who is God over all, blessed for ever*
[16]*Genesis* 21:12
[17]*Genesis* 18:10
[18]*Genesis* 25:23
[19]*Malachi* 1:2,3
[20]*Exodus* 33:19
[21]*Exodus* 9:16
[22]*Hosea* 2:23
[23]*Hosea* 1:10
[24]*Isaiah* 10:22–23
[25]*Isaiah* 1:9

American Society of Civil Engineers

Paul's travels were aided by the excellent Roman roads. This street in Pompeii was probably a one-way thoroughfare to facilitate quick travel through the city. The stepping-stones across the street were useful to pedestrians to keep their feet dry but were stumbling blocks to traffic

The Stumbling Stone [9:30-33]

What shall we say, then? That Gentiles who did not pursue righteousness have attained it, that is, righteousness through faith; but that Israel who pursued the righteousness which is based on law did not succeed in fulfilling that law. Why? Because they did not pursue it through faith, but as if it were based on works. They have stumbled over the stumbling stone, as it is written,

"Behold, I am laying in Zion a stone
that will make men stumble,
a rock that will make them fall;
and he who believes in him will not be
put to shame."[26]

God's Righteousness [Romans 10:1-4]

BRETHREN, my heart's desire and prayer to God for them is that they may be saved. I bear them witness that they have a zeal for God, but it is not enlightened. For, being ignorant of the righteousness that comes from God, and seeking to establish their own, they did not submit to God's righteousness. For Christ is the end of the law, that every one who has faith may be justified.

[26]*Isaiah* 28:16

The Dead Sea. Traditional site near the place where Sodom is believed to be buried

Salvation through Faith [10:5-13]

Moses writes that the man who practices the righteousness which is based on the law shall live by it. But the righteousness based on faith says, Do not say in your heart, "Who will ascend into heaven?" (that is, to bring Christ down) or "Who will descend into the abyss?" (that is, to bring Christ up from the dead). But what does it say? The word is near you, on your lips and in your heart[27] (that is, the word of faith which we preach); because, if you confess with your lips that Jesus is Lord and believe in your heart that God raised him from the dead, you will be saved. For man believes with his heart and so is justified, and he confesses with his lips and so is saved. The scripture says, "No one who believes in him will be put to shame."[28] For there is no distinction between Jew and Greek; the same Lord is Lord of all and bestows his riches upon all who call upon him. For, "every one who calls upon the name of the Lord will be saved."[29]

Hearing and Believing [10:14-21]

But how are men to call upon him in whom they have not believed? And how are they to believe in him of whom they have never heard? And how are they to hear without a preacher? And how can

[27]*Deuteronomy* 30:14   [29]*Joel* 2:32
[28]*Isaiah* 28:16

men preach unless they are sent? As it is written, "How beautiful are the feet of those who preach good news!"[30] But they have not all heeded the gospel; for Isai'ah says, "Lord, who has believed what he has heard from us?"[31] So faith comes from what is heard, and what is heard comes by the preaching of Christ.

But I ask, have they not heard? Indeed they have; for

"Their voice has gone out to all the earth,
and their words to the ends of the world."[32]
Again I ask, did Israel not understand? First Moses says,

"I will make you jealous of those who are
not a nation;
with a foolish nation I will make you
angry."[33]
Then Isai'ah is so bold as to say,

"I have been found by those who did not
seek me;
I have shown myself to those who did
not ask for me."[34]
But of Israel he says, "All day long I have held out my hands to a disobedient and contrary people."[35]

The Remnant Chosen by Grace

[Romans 11:1-6]

I ASK, then, has God rejected his people? By no means! I myself am an Israelite, a descendant of Abraham, a member of the tribe of Benjamin. God has not rejected his people whom he foreknew. Do you not know what the scripture says of Eli'jah, how he pleads with God against Israel? "Lord, they have killed thy prophets, they have demolished thy altars, and I alone am left, and they seek my life."[36] But what is God's reply to him? "I have kept for myself seven thousand men who have not bowed the knee to Ba'al."[37] So too at the present time there is a remnant, chosen by grace. But if it is by grace, it is no longer on the basis of works; otherwise grace would no longer be grace.

A Spirit of Stupor [11:7-10]

What then? Israel failed to obtain what it sought. The elect obtained it, but the rest

[30]*Isaiah* 52:7   [34]*Isaiah* 65:1
[31]*Isaiah* 53:1   [35]*Isaiah* 65:2
[32]*Psalms* 19:4   [36]*I Kings* 19:10
[33]*Deuteronomy* 32:21   [37]*I Kings* 19:18

The traditional place of sacrifice on Mount Carmel, where Elijah challenged the prophets of Baal

Matson Photo Service

*Rome, two bas-reliefs showing the baking of bread, from the tomb of Eurysaces the baker, built
at the fork of two roads outside the Porta Maggiore. First century B.C. Rome was famous for its
"bread and circuses"*

were hardened, as it is written,

"God gave them a spirit of stupor,
eyes that should not see and ears that
should not hear,
down to this very day."[38]
And David says,
"Let their feast become a snare and a trap,
a pitfall and a retribution for them;
let their eyes be darkened so that they
cannot see,
and bend their backs for ever."[39]

Salvation to the Gentiles [11:11–16]

So I ask, have they stumbled so as to
fall? By no means! But through their trespass salvation has come to the Gentiles,
so as to make Israel jealous. Now if their
trespass means riches for the world, and
if their failure means riches for the Gentiles, how much more will their full in-
clusion mean!

Now I am speaking to you Gentiles. Inasmuch then as I am an apostle to the
Gentiles, I magnify my ministry in order to
make my fellow Jews jealous, and thus
save some of them. For if their rejection
means the reconciliation of the world, what
will their acceptance mean but life from the
dead? If the dough offered as first fruits is
holy, so is the whole lump; and if the root is
holy, so are the branches.

Branches of the Olive Tree [11:17–24]

But if some of the branches were broken
off, and you, a wild olive shoot, were grafted
in their place to share the richness[o] of the
olive tree, do not boast over the branches.
If you do boast, remember it is not you
that support the root, but the root that
supports you. You will say, "Branches were
broken off so that I might be grafted in."
That is true. They were broken off because
of their unbelief, but you stand fast only
through faith. So do not become proud,
but stand in awe. For if God did not spare
the natural branches, neither will he spare
you. Note then the kindness and the severity of God: severity toward those who have
fallen, but God's kindness to you, provided
you continue in his kindness; otherwise
you too will be cut off. And even the others,

[o]Other ancient authorities read *rich root*
[38]*Isaiah* 29:10; *Deuteronomy* 29:4
[39]*Psalms* 69:22–23

if they do not persist in their unbelief, will
be grafted in, for God has the power to graft
them in again. For if you have been cut
from what is by nature a wild olive tree, and
grafted, contrary to nature, into a cultivated olive tree, how much more will these
natural branches be grafted back into their
own olive tree.

The Restoration of Israel [11:25–32]

Lest you be wise in your own conceits, I
want you to understand this mystery,
brethren: a hardening has come upon part
of Israel, until the full number of the Gentiles come in, and so all Israel will be saved;
as it is written,

"The Deliverer will come from Zion,
he will banish ungodliness from Jacob";[40]
"and this will be my convenant with them
when I take away their sins."[41]
As regards the gospel they are enemies of
God, for your sake; but as regards election
they are beloved for the sake of their fore-

[40]*Isaiah* 59:20
[41]*Jeremiah* 31:33–34; *Isaiah* 27:9

fathers. For the gifts and the call of God
are irrevocable. Just as you were once disobedient to God but now have received
mercy because of their disobedience, so
they have now been disobedient in order
that by the mercy shown to you they also
may[p] receive mercy. For God has consigned
all men to disobedience, that he may have
mercy upon all.

The Depth of the Riches of God
[11:33–36]

O the depth of the riches and wisdom
and knowledge of God! How unsearchable
are his judgments and how inscrutable his
ways!

"For who has known the mind of the Lord,
or who has been his counselor?"[42]
"Or who has given a gift to him
that he might be repaid?"[43]
For from him and through him and to him
are all things. To him be glory for ever.
Amen.

[p]Other ancient authorities add *now*
[42]*Isaiah* 40:13   [43]*Job* 35:7; 41:11

*An ancient olive tree
in Palestine, probably
as old as the Christian
era. "If God did not
spare the natural
branches, neither will
he spare you"*

Procession of lictors and magistrates, from the Altar of Peace of Augustus. The fasces carried in the left hand and over the left shoulder represent the judicial authority of the Roman magistrates

A Living Sacrifice [Romans 12:1–2]

I APPEAL to you therefore, brethren, by the mercies of God, to present your bodies as a living sacrifice, holy and acceptable to God, which is your spiritual worship. Do not be conformed to this world[a] but be transformed by the renewal of your mind, that you may prove what is the will of God, what is good and acceptable and perfect.[r]

Members of the Body of Christ [12:3–8]

For by the grace given to me I bid every one among you not to think of himself more highly than he ought to think, but to think with sober judgment, each according to the measure of faith which God has assigned him. For as in one body we have many members, and all the members do not have the same function, so we, though many, are one body in Christ, and individually members one of another. Having gifts that differ according to the grace given to us, let us use them: if prophecy, in proportion to our faith; if service, in our serving; he who teaches, in his teaching; he who exhorts, in his exhortation; he who contributes, in liberality; he who gives aid, with zeal; he who does acts of mercy, with cheerfulness.

Aglow with the Spirit [12:9–13]

Let love be genuine; hate what is evil, hold fast to what is good; love one another with brotherly affection; outdo one another in showing honor. Never flag in zeal, be aglow with the Spirit, serve the Lord. Rejoice in your hope, be patient in tribulation, be constant in prayer. Contribute to the needs of the saints, practice hospitality.

[a]Greek *age*   [r]Or *what is the good and acceptable and perfect will of God*

Altar dedicated to an "Unknown God," found at the northwest corner of the Palatine Hill, near the Scalae Caci. The inscription begins, SEI DEO SEI DEIVAE SAC, "Sacred, whether it be to a god or to a goddess." (Late republican replacement of an earlier monument)

Felbermeyer

Overcome Evil with Good [12:14–21]

Bless those who persecute you; bless and do not curse them. Rejoice with those who rejoice, weep with those who weep. Live in harmony with one another; do not be haughty, but associate with the lowly;[s] never be conceited. Repay no one evil for evil, but take thought for what is noble in the sight of all. If possible, so far as it depends upon you, live peaceably with all. Beloved, never avenge yourselves, but leave it[t] to the wrath of God; for it is written, "Vengeance is mine, I will repay, says the Lord."[44] No, "if your enemy is hungry, feed him; if he is thirsty, give him drink; for by so doing you will heap burning coals upon his head."[45] Do not be overcome by evil, but overcome evil with good.

Subject to Authorities [Romans 13:1–7]

LET every person be subject to the governing authorities. For there is no authority except from God, and those that exist have been instituted by God. Therefore he who resists the authorities resists what God has appointed, and those who resist will incur judgment. For rulers are not a terror to good conduct, but to bad. Would you have no fear of him who is in authority? Then do what is good, and you will receive his approval, for he is God's servant for your good. But if you do wrong, be afraid, for he does not bear the sword in vain; he is the servant of God to execute his wrath on the wrongdoer. Therefore one must be subject, not only to avoid God's wrath but also for the sake of conscience. For the same reason you also pay taxes, for the authorities are ministers of God, attending to this very thing. Pay all of them their dues, taxes to whom taxes are due, revenue to whom revenue is due, respect to whom respect is due, honor to whom honor is due.

Love Fulfills the Law [13:8–10]

Owe no one anything, except to love one another; for he who loves his neighbor has fulfilled the law. The commandments, "You shall not commit adultery, You shall not kill, You shall not steal, You shall not covet"[46] and any other commandment, are summed up in this sentence, "You shall

[s]Or *give yourselves to humble tasks*
[t]Greek *give place*
[44]*Deuteronomy* 32:35
[45]*Proverbs* 25:21–22
[46]*Exodus* 20:13–17; *Deuteronomy* 5:17–21

love your neighbor as yourself."[47] Love does no wrong to a neighbor; therefore love is the fulfilling of the law.

"The Day Is at Hand" [13:11–14]

Besides this you know what hour it is, how it is full time now for you to wake from sleep. For salvation is nearer to us now than when we first believed; the night is far gone, the day is at hand. Let us then cast off the works of darkness and put on the armor of light; let us conduct ourselves becomingly as in the day, not in reveling and drunkenness, not in debauchery and licentiousness, not in quarreling and jealousy. But put on the Lord Jesus Christ, and make no provision for the flesh, to gratify its desires.

Those Weak in Faith [Romans 14:1–4]

AS for the man who is weak in faith, welcome him, but not for disputes over opinions. One believes he may eat anything, while the weak man eats only vegetables. Let not him who eats despise him who abstains, and let not him who abstains pass judgment on him who eats; for God has welcomed him. Who are you to pass judgment on the servant of another? It is before his own master that he stands or falls. And he will be upheld, for the Master is able to make him stand.

Living to the Lord [14:5–9]

One man esteems one day as better than another, while another man esteems all days alike. Let every one be fully convinced in his own mind. He who observes the day, observes it in honor of the Lord. He also who eats, eats in honor of the Lord, since he gives thanks to God; while he who abstains, abstains in honor of the Lord and gives thanks to God. None of us lives to himself, and none of us dies to himself. If we live, we live to the Lord, and if we die, we die to the Lord; so then, whether we live or whether we die, we are the Lord's. For to this end Christ died and lived again, that he might be Lord both of the dead and of the living.

The Judgment Seat of God [14:10–12]

Why do you pass judgment on your brother? Or you, why do you despise your brother? For we shall all stand before the judgment seat of God; for it is written,

"As I live, says the Lord, every knee shall
    bow to me,
and every tongue shall give praise[u] to
    God."[48]

So each of us shall give account of himself to God.

Pursue What Makes for Peace [14:13–23]

Then let us no more pass judgment on one another, but rather decide never to put a stumbling block or hindrance in the way of a brother. I know and am persuaded in the Lord Jesus that nothing is unclean in itself; but it is unclean for any one who thinks it unclean. If your brother is being injured by what you eat, you are no longer walking in love. Do not let what you eat cause the ruin of one for whom Christ died. So do not let what is good to you be spoken

[u]Or *confess*   [48]*Isaiah* 45:23
[47]*Leviticus* 19:18

A bull, a ram and a pig being led to an altar of sacrifice. Bas-relief from the Altar of Domitius Ahenobarbus (35–30 B.C.) Louvre

of as evil. For the kingdom of God does not mean food and drink but righteousness and peace and joy in the Holy Spirit; he who thus serves Christ is acceptable to God and approved by men. Let us then pursue what makes for peace and for mutual upbuilding. Do not, for the sake of food, destroy the work of God. Everything is indeed clean, but it is wrong for any one to make others fall by what he eats; it is right not to eat meat or drink wine or do anything that makes your brother stumble.[v] The faith that you have, keep between yourself and God; happy is he who has no reason to judge himself for what he approves. But he who has doubts is condemned, if he eats, because he does not act from faith; for whatever does not proceed from faith is sin.[w]

The Strong and the Weak [Romans 15:1–6]

WE who are strong ought to bear with the failings of the weak, and not to please ourselves; let each of us please his neighbor for his good, to edify him. For Christ did not please himself; but, as it is written, "The reproaches of those who reproached thee fell on me."[49] For whatever was written in former days was written for our instruction, that by steadfastness and by the encouragement of the scriptures we might have hope. May the God of steadfastness and encouragement grant you to live in such harmony with one another, in accord with Christ Jesus, that together you may with one voice glorify the God and Father of our Lord Jesus Christ.

"In Him Shall the Gentiles Hope"

[15:7–13]

Welcome one another, therefore, as Christ has welcomed you, for the glory of God. For I tell you that Christ became a servant to the circumcised to show God's truthfulness, in order to confirm the promises given to the patriarchs, and in order that the Gentiles might glorify God for his mercy. As it is written,

"Therefore I will praise thee among the Gentiles,
and sing to thy name";[50]
and again it is said,
"Rejoice, O Gentiles, with his people";[51]
and again,
"Praise the Lord, all Gentiles,
and let all the peoples praise him";[52]

[v]Other ancient authorities add *or be upset or be weakened*
[w]Other authorities, some ancient, insert here Ch 16:25–27
[49]*Psalms* 69:9   [51]*Deuteronomy* 32:43
[50]*Psalms* 18:49; 2 *Samuel* 22:50 [52]*Psalms* 117:1

and further Isai'ah says,
"The root of Jesse shall come,
he who rises to rule the Gentiles;
in him shall the Gentiles hope."[53]
May the God of hope fill you with all joy and peace in believing, so that by the power of the Holy Spirit you may abound in hope.

A Minister to the Gentiles [15:14–21]

I myself am satisfied about you, my brethren, that you yourselves are full of goodness, filled with all knowledge, and able to instruct one another. But on some points I have written to you very boldly by way of reminder, because of the grace given me by God to be a minister of Christ Jesus to the Gentiles in the priestly service of the gospel of God, so that the offering of the Gentiles may be acceptable, sanctified by the Holy Spirit. In Christ Jesus, then, I have reason to be proud of my work for God. For I will not venture to speak of anything except what Christ has wrought through me to win obedience from the Gentiles, by word and deed, by the power of signs and wonders, by the power of the Holy Spirit, so that from Jerusalem and as far round as Illyr'icum I have fully preached the gospel of Christ, thus making it my ambition to preach the gospel, not where Christ has already been named, lest I build on another man's foundation, but as it is written,

"They shall see who have never been told of him,
and they shall understand who have never heard of him."[54]

Paul Plans to Visit Rome [15:22–33]

This is the reason why I have so often been hindered from coming to you. But

[53]*Isaiah* 11:10   [54]*Isaiah* 52:15

now, since I no longer have any room for work in these regions, and since I have longed for many years to come to you, I hope to see you in passing as I go to Spain, and to be sped on my journey there by you, once I have enjoyed your company for a little. At present, however, I am going to Jerusalem with aid for the saints. For Macedo'nia and Acha'ia have been pleased to make some contribution for the poor among the saints at Jerusalem; they were pleased to do it, and indeed they are in debt to them, for if the Gentiles have come to share in their spiritual blessings, they ought also to be of service to them in material blessings. When therefore I have completed this, and have delivered to them. what has been raised,[x] I shall go on by way of you to Spain; and I know that when I come to you I shall come in the fulness of the blessing[y] of Christ.

I appeal to you, brethren, by our Lord Jesus Christ and by the love of the Spirit, to strive together with me in your prayers to God on my behalf, that I may be delivered from the unbelievers in Jude'a, and that my service for Jerusalem may be acceptable to the saints, so that by God's will I may come to you with joy and be refreshed in your company. The God of peace be with you all. Amen.

Commendation of Phoebe [Romans 16:1–2]

I COMMEND to you our sister Phoebe, a deaconess of the church at Cenchre'ae, that you may receive her in the Lord as befits the saints, and help her in whatever she may require from you, for she has been a helper of many and of myself as well.

[x]Greek *sealed to them this fruit*
[y]Other ancient authorities insert *of the gospel*

This great aqueduct, completed by the Emperor Claudius about A.D. 50, is over forty miles long. About three fourths are underground, but the last ten miles are supported on tall, massive arches. It brought water not only to the city but also to the emperor's palace on the Palatine Hill. The water-supply department of the city of Rome employed in the first century A.D. 240 "public" slaves who were responsible to the emperor and 460 "slaves of Caesar." The Romans built such well-constructed aqueducts that four are still in use. In the foreground is The Appian Way

Gallerie Musei Vaticani, Rome

Part of the ruins of the Circus Maximus, the first and largest circus in Rome, which seated over 150,000 people. In 31 B.C. and in A.D. 36 it was partly destroyed by fire. The great fire of June, A.D. 64 broke out in the wooden storerooms on the Palatine side of the circus. This great fire gave Nero an opportunity to claim over 100 acres of land for the site of his Golden House and gardens. Nero rebuilt the Circus Maximus and it was in use again in A.D. 68, when he returned from Greece. The remains date largely from Trajan (A.D. 98–117)

Metropolitan Museum of Art

Roman racing chariot with four horses turning the post. Racing colors were blue, green, red and white. Nero's color was green. He contended in chariot races as well as in dancing, musical and theatrical contests. First century A.D.

British Museum

The Theater of Marcellus, planned by Julius Caesar and finished in 13–11 B.C. by Augustus, who named it after his deceased son-in-law Marcellus. It seated about 12,000 spectators. The construction of the walls and seats is like that used later in the Colosseum. Less than one third of the exterior is now standing

Gabinetto Fotografico Nazionale, Rome

This bas-relief from the Theater of Marcellus shows a contest between Roman gladiators and wild beasts. The Romans delighted in such gory spectacles

Felbermeyer

Personal Greetings [16:3-16]

Greet Prisca and Aqui'la, my fellow workers in Christ Jesus, who risked their necks for my life, to whom not only I but also all the churches of the Gentiles give thanks; greet also the church in their house. Greet my beloved Epae'netus, who was the first convert in Asia for Christ. Greet Mary, who has worked hard among you. Greet Andron'icus and Ju'nias, my kinsmen and my fellow prisoners; they are men of note among the apostles, and they were in Christ before me. Greet Amplia'tus, my beloved in the Lord. Greet Urba'nus, our fellow worker in Christ, and my beloved Stachys. Greet Apel'les, who is approved in Christ. Greet those who belong to the family of Aristob'ulus. Greet my kinsman Hero'dion. Greet those in the Lord who belong to the family of Narcis'sus. Greet those workers in the Lord, Tryphae'na and Trypho'sa. Greet the beloved Persis, who has worked hard in the Lord. Greet Rufus, eminent in the Lord, also his mother and mine. Greet Asyn'critus, Phlegon, Hermes, Patro'bas, Hermas, and the brethren who are with them. Greet Philol'ogus, Julia, Nereus and his sister, and Olym'pas, and all the saints who are with them. Greet one another with a holy kiss. All the churches of Christ greet you.

Warning against Deceivers [16:17-20]

I appeal to you, brethren, to take note of those who create dissensions and difficulties, in opposition to the doctrine which you have been taught; avoid them. For such persons do not serve our Lord Christ, but their own appetites,[z] and by fair and flattering words they deceive the hearts of the simple-minded. For while your obedience is known to all, so that I rejoice over you, I would have you wise as to what is good and guileless as to what is evil; then the God of peace will soon crush Satan under your feet. The grace of our Lord Jesus Christ be with you.[a]

Greetings from Paul's Associates

[16:21-24]

Timothy, my fellow worker, greets you; so do Lucius and Jason and Sosip'ater, my kinsmen.

I Tertius, the writer of this letter, greet you in the Lord.

Gaius, who is host to me and to the whole church, greets you. Eras'tus, the city treasurer, and our brother Quartus, greet you.[b]

Concluding Doxology [16:25-27]

Now to him who is able to strengthen you according to my gospel and the preaching of Jesus Christ, according to the revelation of the mystery which was kept secret for long ages but is now disclosed and through the prophetic writings is made known to all nations, according to the command of the eternal God, to bring about the obedience of the faith—to the only wise God be glory for evermore through Jesus Christ! Amen.

[z] Greek *their own belly*
[a] Other ancient authorities omit this sentence
[b] Other ancient authorities insert verse 24, *The grace of our Lord Jesus Christ be with you all. Amen.*

General view of the ancient Agora at Corinth, seen from the east. The Bema, where Paul appeared before Gallio A.D. 51–53, is at the middle left. The Lechaeum Road comes in from the right foreground and the road to Cenchreae leaves on the left near the Bema. The Temple of Apollo is on the extreme right

THE FIRST LETTER OF PAUL TO THE CORINTHIANS

Greetings

[1 Corinthians 1:1–3] Paul, called by the will of God to be an apostle of Christ Jesus, and our brother Sos'thenes,

To the church of God which is at Corinth, to those sanctified in Christ Jesus, called to be saints together with all those who in every place call on the name of our Lord Jesus Christ, both their Lord and ours:

Grace to you and peace from God our Father and the Lord Jesus Christ.

Thanksgiving [1:4–9]

I give thanks to God[a] always for you because of the grace of God which was given you in Christ Jesus, that in every way you were enriched in him with all speech and all knowledge—even as the testimony to Christ was confirmed among you—so that you are not lacking in any spiritual gift, as you wait for the revealing of our Lord Jesus Christ; who will sustain you to the end, guiltless in the day of our Lord Jesus Christ. God is faithful, by whom you were called into the fellowship of his Son, Jesus Christ our Lord.

Divisions in the Church [1:10–17]

I appeal to you, brethren, by the name of our Lord Jesus Christ, that all of you agree and that there be no dissensions among you, but that you be united in the same mind and the same judgment. For it has been reported to me by Chloe's people that there is quarreling among you, my brethren. What I mean is that each one of you says, "I belong to Paul," or "I belong to Apol'los," or "I belong to Cephas," or "I belong to Christ." Is Christ divided? Was Paul crucified for you? Or were you baptized in the name of Paul? I am thankful[b]

that I baptized none of you except Crispus and Gaius; lest any one should say that you were baptized in my name. (I did baptize also the household of Steph'anas. Beyond that, I do not know whether I baptized any one else.) For Christ did not send me to baptize but to preach the gospel, and not with eloquent wisdom, lest the cross of Christ be emptied of its power.

Christ the Power and Wisdom of God
[1:18–25]

For the word of the cross is folly to those who are perishing, but to us who are being saved it is the power of God. For it is written,

"I will destroy the wisdom of the wise,
and the cleverness of the clever I will thwart."[1]

Where is the wise man? Where is the scribe? Where is the debater of this age? Has not God made foolish the wisdom of the world? For since, in the wisdom of God, the world did not know God through wisdom, it pleased God through the folly of what we preach to save those who believe. For Jews demand signs and Greeks seek wisdom, but we preach Christ crucified, a stumbling block to Jews and folly to Gentiles, but to those who are called, both Jews and Greeks, Christ the power of God and the wisdom of God. For the foolishness of God is wiser than men, and the weakness of God is stronger than men.

[a]Other ancient authorities read *my God*

[b]Other ancient authorities read *I thank God*

[1]*Isaiah* 29:14

175

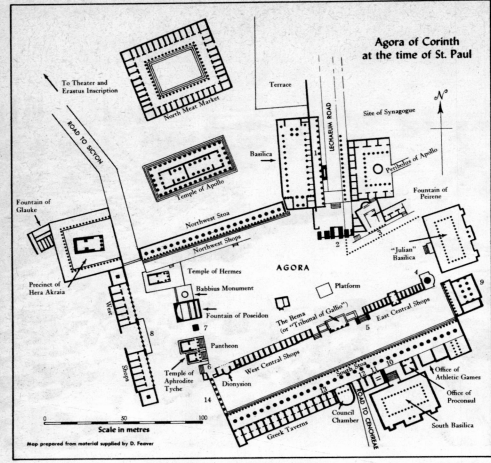

Agora of Corinth
at the time of St. Paul

To Theater and Erastus Inscription

ROAD TO SICYON

North Meat Market

Terrace

LECHAEUM ROAD

Site of Synagogue

Basilica

Peribolus of Apollo

Temple of Apollo

Fountain of Peirene

Fountain of Glauke

Northwest Stoa

Northwest Shops

"Julian" Basilica

Precinct of Hera Akraia

Temple of Hermes

AGORA

Babbius Monument

Platform

West

Fountain of Poseidon

The Bema (or "Tribunal of Gallio")

East Central Shops

Shops

Pantheon

West Central Shops

South Stoa

Office of Athletic Games

Temple of Aphrodite Tyche

Dionysion

Office of Proconsul

Council Chamber

ROAD TO CENCHREAE

Greek Taverns

South Basilica

0   50   100
Scale in metres

Map prepared from material supplied by D. Feaver

LEGEND OF NUMBERED ITEMS: 1. Shops under Basilica on Lechaeum Road 2. Propylaea 3. Colonnade above Peirene 4. Circular Monument 5. Monumental Archway 6. Reservoir 7. Monument 8. Monumental Stairway 9. Archives Building 10. Entrance court to Southern Basilica 11. Ornamental Fountain 12. Cult Rooms connected with fountain 13. Shop with cult statue of Serapis 14. Aqueduct with archaic columns

What God Has Chosen [1:26–31]

For consider your call, brethren; not many of you were wise according to worldly standards, not many were powerful, not many were of noble birth; but God chose what is foolish in the world to shame the wise, God chose what is weak in the world to shame the strong, God chose what is low and despised in the world, even things that are not, to bring to nothing things that are, so that no human being might boast in the presence of God. He is the source of your life in Christ Jesus, whom God made our wisdom, our righteousness and sanctification and redemption; therefore, as it is written, "Let him who boasts, boast of the Lord."[2]

Proclaiming Christ Crucified

[1 Corinthians 2:1–5]

WHEN I came to you, brethren, I did not come proclaiming to you the testimony[c] of God in lofty words or wisdom. For I decided to know nothing among you except Jesus Christ and him crucified. And I was with you in weakness and in much fear and trembling; and my speech and my message were not in plausible words of wisdom, but in demonstration of the Spirit and power, that your faith might not rest in the wisdom of men but in the power of God.

[c]Other ancient authorities read *mystery* (or *secret*)

[2]*Jeremiah 9:24*

The Spirit of God [2:6–13]

Yet among the mature we do impart wisdom, although it is not a wisdom of this age or of the rulers of this age, who are doomed to pass away. But we impart a secret and hidden wisdom of God, which God decreed before the ages for our glorification. None of the rulers of this age understood this; for if they had, they would not have crucified the Lord of glory. But, as it is written,

"What no eye has seen, nor ear heard,
    nor the heart of man conceived,
what God has prepared for those who
    love him,"[3]

God has revealed to us through the Spirit. For the Spirit searches everything, even the depths of God. For what person knows a man's thoughts except the spirit of the man which is in him? So also no one comprehends the thoughts of God except the Spirit of God. Now we have received not the spirit of the world, but the Spirit which is from God, that we might understand the gifts bestowed on us by God. And we impart this in words not taught by human wisdom but taught by the Spirit, interpreting spiritual truths to those who possess the Spirit.[d]

[3]*Isaiah 64:4*

[d]Or *interpreting spiritual truths in spiritual language;* or *comparing spiritual things with spiritual*

God's Gifts Spiritually Discerned
[2:14–16]

The unspiritual[e] man does not receive the gifts of the Spirit of God, for they are folly to him, and he is not able to understand them because they are spiritually discerned. The spiritual man judges all things, but is himself to be judged by no one. "For who has known the mind of the Lord so as to instruct him?"[4] But we have the mind of Christ.

Men of the Flesh [1 Corinthians 3:1–4]

BUT, I, brethren, could not address you as spiritual men, but as men of the flesh, as babes in Christ. I fed you with milk, not solid food; for you were not ready for it; and even yet you are not ready, for you are still of the flesh. For while there is jealousy and strife among you, are you not of the flesh, and behaving like ordinary men? For when one says, "I belong to Paul," and another, "I belong to Apol'los," are you not merely men?

Fellow Workmen for God [3:5–9]

What then is Apol'los? What is Paul? Servants through whom you believed, as the Lord assigned to each. I planted, Apol'los watered, but God gave the growth. So neither he who plants nor he who waters is anything, but only God who gives the growth. He who plants and he who waters are equal, and each shall receive his wages according to his labor. For we are fellow workers for God;[f] you are God's field, God's building.

Jesus Christ the Only Foundation
[3:10–15]

According to the commission of God given to me, like a skilled master builder I laid a foundation, and another man is building upon it. Let each man take care how he builds upon it. For no other foundation can any one lay than that which is laid, which is Jesus Christ. Now if any one builds on the foundation with gold, silver, precious stones, wood, hay, stubble—each man's work will become manifest; for the Day will disclose it, because it will be revealed with fire, and the fire will test what sort of work each one has done. If the work which any man has built on the foundation survives, he will receive a reward. If any man's work is burned up, he will suffer loss, though he himself will be saved, but only as through fire.

"You Are God's Temple" [3:16–17]

Do you not know that you are God's temple and that God's Spirit dwells in you? If any one destroys God's temple, God will destroy him. For God's temple is holy, and that temple you are.

The Wisdom of This World [3:18–23]

Let no one deceive himself. If any one among you thinks that he is wise in this age, let him become a fool that he may become wise. For the wisdom of this world is folly with God. For it is written, "He catches

[e]Or *natural*
[f]Greek *God's fellow workers*
[4]*Isaiah 40:13*

the wise in their craftiness,"5 and again, "The Lord knows that the thoughts of the wise are futile."6 So let no one boast of men. For all things are yours, whether Paul or Apol'los or Cephas or the world or life or death or the present or the future, all are yours; and you are Christ's; and Christ is God's.

Stewards of the Mysteries of God

[1 Corinthians 4:1–7]

THIS is how one should regard us, as servants of Christ and stewards of the mysteries of God. Moreover it is required of stewards that they be found trustworthy. But with me it is a very small thing that I should be judged by you or by any human court. I do not even judge myself. I am not aware of anything against myself, but I am not thereby acquitted. It is the Lord who judges me. Therefore do not pronounce judgment before the time, before the Lord comes, who will bring to light the things now hidden in darkness and will disclose the purposes of the heart. Then every man will receive his commendation from God.

I have applied all this to myself and Apol'los for your benefit, brethren, that you may learn by us to live according to scripture, that none of you may be puffed up in favor of one against another. For who sees anything different in you? What have you that you did not receive? If then you received it, why do you boast as if it were not a gift?

Fools for Christ's Sake [4:8–13]

Already you are filled! Already you have become rich! Without us you have become kings! And would that you did reign, so that we might share the rule with you! For I think that God has exhibited us apostles as last of all, like men sentenced to death; because we have become a spectacle to the world, to angels and to men. We are fools for Christ's sake, but you are wise in Christ. We are weak, but you are strong. You are held in honor, but we in disrepute. To the present hour we hunger and thirst, we are ill-clad and buffeted and homeless, and we labor, working with our own hands. When reviled, we bless; when persecuted, we endure; when slandered, we try to conciliate; we have become, and are now, as the refuse of the world, the offscouring of all things.

"Be Imitators of Me" [4:14–21]

I do not write this to make you ashamed, but to admonish you as my beloved children. For though you have countless guides in Christ, you do not have many fathers. For I became your father in Christ Jesus through the gospel. I urge you, then, be imitators of me. Therefore I sent9 to you Timothy, my beloved and faithful child in the Lord, to remind you of my ways in Christ, as I teach them everywhere in every church. Some are arrogant, as though I were not coming to you. But I will come to you soon, if the Lord wills, and I will find out not the talk of these arrogant people but their power. For the kingdom of God does not consist in talk but in power. What do you wish? Shall I come to you with a rod, or with love in a spirit of gentleness?

9Or am sending
5Job 5:13
6Psalms 94:11

Fragments containing the famous Delphic inscription which mentions the Emperor Claudius and Gallio, proconsul of Achaia, before whose bema, or judgment seat, Paul appeared (Acts 18:12–17). This inscription makes it possible to date Paul's arrival in Corinth at about A.D. 51–53. Gallio was the brother of Seneca, who was the tutor of Nero

A Case of Immorality [1 Corinthians 5:1–2]

IT is actually reported that there is immorality among you, and of a kind that is not found even among pagans; for a man is living with his father's wife. And you are arrogant! Ought you not rather to mourn? Let him who has done this be removed from among you.

Judgment on the Immoral Man [5:3–5]

For though absent in body I am present in spirit, and as if present, I have already pronounced judgment in the name of the Lord Jesus on the man who has done such a thing. When you are assembled, and my spirit is present, with the power of our Lord Jesus, you are to deliver this man to Satan for the destruction of the flesh, that his spirit may be saved in the day of the Lord Jesus.h

Christ Our Paschal Lamb [5:6–8]

Your boasting is not good. Do you not know that a little leaven leavens the whole lump? Cleanse out the old leaven that you may be a new lump, as you really are unleavened. For Christ, our paschal lamb, has been sacrificed. Let us, therefore, celebrate the festival, not with the old leaven, the leaven of malice and evil, but with the unleavened bread of sincerity and truth.

hOther ancient authorities omit Jesus.

Associating with Immoral Men [5:9–13]

I wrote to you in my letter not to associate with immoral men; not at all meaning the immoral of this world, or the greedy and robbers, or idolaters, since then you would need to go out of the world. But rather I wrotei to you not to associate with any one who bears the name of brother if he is guilty of immorality or greed, or is an idolater, reviler, drunkard, or robber—not even to eat with such a one. For what have I to do with judging outsiders? Is it not those inside the church whom you are to judge? God judges those outside. "Drive out the wicked person from among you."7

Lawsuits among Christians

[1 Corinthians 6:1–8]

WHEN one of you has a grievance against a brother, does he dare go to law before the unrighteous instead of the saints? Do you not know that the saints will judge the world? And if the world is to be judged by you, are you incompetent to try trivial cases? Do you not know that we are to judge angels? How much more, matters pertaining to this life! If then you have such cases, why do you lay them before those who are least esteemed by the church? I say this to your shame. Can it be that there is no man among you wise enough to decide between members of the brotherhood, but brother goes to law against brother, and that before unbelievers?

iOr now I write.   7Deuteronomy 17:7.

Obverse, head of Aphrodite; reverse, Doric capital surmounted by a lioness standing over a prostrate ram (Tomb of Lais). Time of Augustus

Obverse, head of Helios (the sun god) with radiate crown; reverse, statue of Neptune on a mole in the harbor of Cenchreae

Obverse, head of Tiberius; reverse, hexastyle temple inscribed GEN IVLI in honor of the Julian emperors

Obverse, head of Claudius; reverse, Temple of Aphrodite on Acrocorinth, where there were once reported to be a thousand prostitutes

Obverse, head of Drusus Caesar (?); reverse, seated cult-statue of a woman with left arm upraised, symbolizing the Julian line of Roman Emperors

Obverse, head of Antoninus Pius; reverse, statue of Aphrodite looking at her reflection in a shield—a copy of a cult-statue in the Temple of Aphrodite on Acrocorinth. It is believed that this statue dates from the time of Julius Caesar

American Numismatic Society

To have lawsuits at all with one another is defeat for you. Why not rather suffer wrong? Why not rather be defrauded? But you yourselves wrong and defraud, and that even your own brethren.

"The Unrighteous Will Not Inherit the Kingdom" [6:9-11]

Do you not know that the unrighteous will not inherit the kingdom of God? Do not be deceived; neither the immoral, nor idolaters, nor adulterers, nor homosexuals,[j] nor thieves, nor the greedy, nor drunkards, nor revilers, nor robbers will inherit the kingdom of God. And such were some of you. But you were washed, you were sanctified, you were justified in the name of the Lord Jesus Christ and in the Spirit of our God.

"Glorify God in Your Body" [6:12-20]

"All things are lawful for me," but not all things are helpful. "All things are lawful for

[j] Two Greek words are rendered by this expression

me," but I will not be enslaved by anything. "Food is meant for the stomach and the stomach for food"—and God will destroy both one and the other. The body is not meant for immorality, but for the Lord, and the Lord for the body. And God raised the Lord and will also raise us up by his power. Do you not know that your bodies are members of Christ? Shall I therefore take the members of Christ and make them members of a prostitute? Never! Do you not know that he who joins himself to a prostitute becomes one body with her? For, as it is written, "The two shall become one."[k][8] But he who is united to the Lord becomes one spirit with him. Shun immorality. Every other sin which a man commits is outside the body; but the immoral man sins against his own body. Do you not know that your body is a temple of the Holy Spirit within you, which you have from God? You are not your own; you were bought with a price. So glorify God in your body.

[k] Greek one flesh   [8] Genesis 2:24

Gambling counters and dice found in Corinth. Corinth was known throughout the world for its many taverns, brothels and gambling places

American School of Classical Studies, Athens

Concerning Marriage [1 Corinthians 7:1-9]

NOW concerning the matters about which you wrote. It is well for a man not to touch a woman. But because of the temptation to immorality, each man should have his own wife and each woman her own husband. The husband should give to his wife her conjugal rights, and likewise the wife to her husband. For the wife does not rule over her own body, but the husband does; likewise the husband does not rule over his own body, but the wife does. Do not refuse one another except perhaps by agreement for a season, that you may devote yourselves to prayer; but then come together again, lest Satan tempt you through lack of self-control. I say this by way of concession, not of command. I wish that all were as I myself am. But each has his own special gift from God, one of one kind and one of another.

To the unmarried and the widows I say that it is well for them to remain single as I do. But if they cannot exercise self-control, they should marry. For it is better to marry than to be aflame with passion.

Concerning Divorce [7:10-16]

To the married I give charge, not I but the Lord, that the wife should not separate from her husband (but if she does, let her remain single or else be reconciled to her husband)—and that the husband should not divorce his wife.

To the rest I say, not the Lord, that if any brother has a wife who is an unbeliever, and she consents to live with him, he should not divorce her. If any woman has a husband who is an unbeliever, and he consents to live with her, she should not divorce him. For the unbelieving husband is consecrated through his wife, and the unbelieving wife is consecrated through her husband. Otherwise, your children would be unclean, but as it is they are holy. But if the unbelieving partner desires to separate, let it be so; in such a case the brother or sister is not bound. For God has called us[l] to peace. Wife, how do you know whether you will save your husband? Husband, how do you know whether you will save your wife?

The Life Assigned by the Lord [7:17-24]

Only, let every one lead the life which the Lord has assigned to him, and in which God has called him. This is my rule in all the churches. Was any one at the time of his call already circumcised? Let him not seek to remove the marks of circumcision. Was any one at the time of his call uncircumcised? Let him not seek circumcision. For neither circumcision counts for anything nor uncircumcision, but keeping the commandments of God. Every one should remain in the state in which he was called. Were you a slave when called? Never mind. But if you can gain your freedom, avail yourself of the opportunity.[x] For he who was called in the Lord as a slave is a freedman of the Lord. Likewise he who was free when called is a slave of Christ. You were bought with a price; do not become slaves of men. So, brethren, in whatever state each was called, there let him remain with God.

[l] Other ancient authorities read you
[x] Or make use of your present condition instead

Concerning the Unmarried [7:25-31]

Now concerning the unmarried, I have no command of the Lord, but I give my opinion as one who by the Lord's mercy is trustworthy. I think that in view of the impending[m] distress it is well for a person to remain as he is. Are you bound to a wife? Do not seek to be free. Are you free from a wife? Do not seek marriage. But if you marry, you do not sin, and if a girl marries she does not sin. Yet those who marry will have worldly troubles, and I would spare you that. I mean, brethren, the appointed time has grown very short; from now on, let those who have wives live as though they had none, and those who mourn as though they were not mourning, and those who rejoice as though they were not rejoicing, and those who buy as though they had no goods, and those who deal with the world as though they had no dealings with it. For the form of this world is passing away.

Anxious about Worldly Affairs [7:32-35]

I want you to be free from anxieties. The unmarried man is anxious about the affairs of the Lord, how to please the Lord; but the married man is anxious about worldly affairs, how to please his wife, and his interests are divided. And the unmarried woman or girl is anxious about the affairs of the Lord, how to be holy in body and spirit; but the married woman is anxious about worldly affairs, how to please her husband. I say this for your own benefit, not to lay any restraint upon you, but to promote good order and to secure your undivided devotion to the Lord.

Keeping One's Betrothed [7:36-38]

If any one thinks that he is not behaving properly toward his betrothed, if his passions are strong, and it has to be, let him do as he wishes: let them marry—it is no sin. But whoever is firmly established in his heart, being under no necessity but having his desire under control, and has determined this in his heart, to keep her as his betrothed, he will do well. So that he who marries his betrothed does well; and he who refrains from marriage will do better.

[m]Or present

Felbermeyer

Shepherd offering kid before idol of Dionysus, god of wine. On the table is a basket of cheese, and hanging from a branch is a shepherd's flute as an offering to the god. The other vessel is a censer of incense used during sacrifice. From the name Corinth is derived the word "currant," originally meaning a small sweet grape

Concerning Remarriage [7:39-40]

A wife is bound to her husband as long as he lives. If the husband dies, she is free to be married to whom she wishes, only in the Lord. But in my judgment she is happier if she remains as she is. And I think that I have the Spirit of God.

Food Offered to Idols [1 Corinthians 8:1-6]

NOW concerning food offered to idols: we know that "all of us possess knowledge." "Knowledge" puffs up, but love builds up. If any one imagines that he knows something, he does not yet know as he ought to know. But if one loves God, one is known by him.

Hence, as to the eating of food offered to idols, we know that "an idol has no real existence," and that "there is no God but one."[9] For although there may be so-called gods in heaven or on earth—as indeed there are many "gods" and many "lords"—yet for us there is one God, the Father,

[9]Deuteronomy 6:4

from whom are all things and for whom we exist, and one Lord, Jesus Christ, through whom are all things and through whom we exist.

Knowledge and Love [8:7-13]

However, not all possess this knowledge. But some, through being hitherto accustomed to idols, eat food as really offered to an idol; and their conscience, being weak, is defiled. Food will not commend us to God. We are no worse off if we do not eat, and no better off if we do. Only take care lest this liberty of yours somehow become a stumbling block to the weak. For if any one sees you, a man of knowledge, at table in an idol's temple, might he not be encouraged, if his conscience is weak, to eat food offered to idols? And so by your knowledge this weak man is destroyed, the brother for whom Christ died. Thus, sinning against your brethren and wounding their conscience when it is weak, you sin against Christ. Therefore, if food is a cause of my brother's falling, I will never eat meat, lest I cause my brother to fall.

Scene of sacrifice of a pig, a sheep and a bull (the so-called Suovetaurilia). Second half of first century A.D.

Louvre

179

Roman soldiers being paid. From the Altar of Domitius Ahenobarbus (35–30 B.C.)

The Rights of an Apostle

[1 Corinthians 9:1–7]

AM I not free? Am I not an apostle? Have I not seen Jesus our Lord? Are not you my workmanship in the Lord? If to others I am not an apostle, at least I am to you; for you are the seal of my apostleship in the Lord.

This is my defense to those who would examine me. Do we not have the right to our food and drink? Do we not have the right to be accompanied by a wife,[n] as the other apostles and the brothers of the Lord and Cephas? Or is it only Bar′nabas and I who have no right to refrain from working for a living? Who serves as a soldier at his own expense? Who plants a vineyard without eating any of its fruit? Who tends a flock without getting some of the milk?

Reaping Material Benefits [9:8–14]

Do I say this on human authority? Does not the law say the same? For it is written in the law of Moses, "You shall not muzzle

[n]Greek *a sister as wife.*

an ox when it is treading out the grain."[10] Is it for oxen that God is concerned? Does he not speak entirely for our sake? It was written for our sake, because the plowman should plow in hope and the thresher thresh in hope of a share in the crop. If we have sown spiritual good among you, is it too much if we reap your material benefits? If others share this rightful claim upon you, do not we still more?

Nevertheless, we have not made use of this right, but we endure anything rather than put an obstacle in the way of the gospel of Christ. Do you not know that those who are employed in the temple service get their food from the temple, and those who serve at the altar share in the sacrificial offerings? In the same way, the Lord commanded that those who proclaim the gospel should get their living by the gospel.

Surrender of Rights [9:15–18]

But I have made no use of any of these rights, nor am I writing this to secure any

[10]Deuteronomy 25:4

such provision. For I would rather die than have any one deprive me of my ground for boasting. For if I preach the gospel, that gives me no ground for boasting. For necessity is laid upon me. Woe to me if I do not preach the gospel! For if I do this of my own will, I have a reward; but if not of my own will, I am entrusted with a commission. What then is my reward? Just this: that in my preaching I may make the gospel free of charge, not making full use of my right in the gospel.

All Things to All Men [9:19–23]

For though I am free from all men, I have made myself a slave to all, that I might win the more. To the Jews I became as a Jew, in order to win Jews; to those under the law I became as one under the law—though not being myself under the law—that I might win those under the law. To those outside the law I became as one outside the law—not being without law toward God but under the law of Christ—that I might win those outside the law. To the weak I

Two bronze tablets of a military diploma granting citizenship to honorably discharged soldiers and their wives. Roman, second century

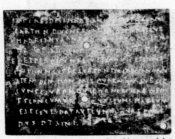

"You shall not muzzle an ox when it is treading out the grain" (1 Cor. 9:9). In modern Palestine oxen are often muzzled, as shown in this threshing scene

180

Metropolitan Museum of Art

Cup bearing the Greek inscription, "Win the victory"

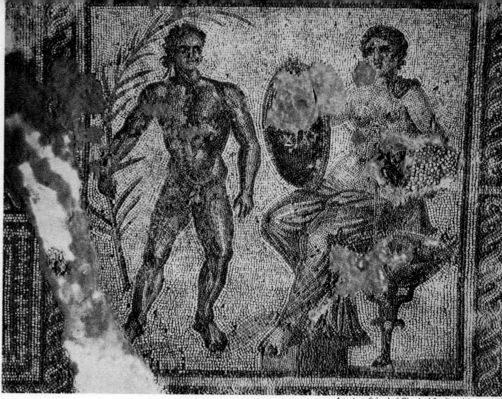

American School of Classical Studies, Athens

"Do you not know that in a race all the runners compete, but only one receives the prize?" (1 Cor. 9:24.) Roman mosaic showing athlete being crowned with celery and standing with palm branch in hand before the goddess of good fortune. From an office in South Stoa at Corinth, believed to be that of the administrator of the Isthmian Games

became weak, that I might win the weak. I have become all things to all men, that I might by all means save some. I do it all for the sake of the gospel, that I may share in its blessings.

Run to Obtain the Prize [9:24–27]

Do you not know that in a race all the runners compete, but only one receives the prize? So run that you may obtain it. Every athlete exercises self-control in all things. They do it to receive a perishable wreath, but we an imperishable. Well, I do not run aimlessly, I do not box as one beating the air; but I pommel my body and subdue it, lest after preaching to others I myself should be disqualified.

Christ the Rock   [I Corinthians 10:1–5]

I WANT you to know, brethren, that our fathers were all under the cloud, and all passed through the sea, and all were baptized into Moses in the cloud and in the sea, and all ate the same supernatural[o] food and all drank the same supernatural[o] drink. For they drank from the supernatural[o] Rock which followed them, and the Rock was Christ. Nevertheless with most of them God was not pleased; for they were overthrown in the wilderness.

God and Temptation [10:6–13]

Now these things are warnings for us, not to desire evil as they did. Do not be idolaters as some of them were; as it is written, "The people sat down to eat and drink and rose up to dance."[11] We must not indulge in immorality as some of them did, and twenty-three thousand fell in a single day. We must not put the Lord[p] to the test, as some of them did and were destroyed by serpents; nor grumble, as some of them did and were destroyed by the Destroyer. Now these things happened to them as a warning, but they were written down for our instruction, upon whom the end of the ages

has come. Therefore let any one who thinks that he stands take heed lest he fall. No temptation has overtaken you that is not common to man. God is faithful, and he will not let you be tempted beyond your strength, but with the temptation will also provide the way of escape, that you may be able to endure it.

A Warning Against Idolatry [10:14–22]

Therefore, my beloved, shun the worship of idols. I speak as to sensible men; judge for yourselves what I say. The cup of blessing which we bless, is it not a participation[q]

[q]Or *communion*

in the blood of Christ? The bread which we break, is it not a participation[q] in the body of Christ? Because there is one bread, we who are many are one body, for we all partake of the one bread. Consider the practice of Israel; are not those who eat the sacrifices partners in the altar? What do I imply then? That food offered to idols is anything, or that an idol is anything? No, I imply that what pagans sacrifice they offer to demons and not to God. I do not want you to be partners with demons. You cannot drink the cup of the Lord and the cup of demons. You cannot partake of the table of the Lord and the table of demons. Shall we provoke the Lord to jealousy? Are we stronger than he?

"I do not box as one beating the air" (1 Cor. 9:26). Ancient boxing match. Note thongs of oxhide wrapped around hands. Black-figured Panathenaic amphora, sixth century B.C.

Metropolitan Museum of Art

[o]Greek *spiritual*
[p]Other ancient authorities read *Christ*
[11]Exodus 32:6

American School of Classical Studies, Athens

Ruins of the shops on the northwest side of the market place in ancient Corinth. This market place was over 500 feet long and was decorated with a colonnade of 71 Doric columns and an inner row of 34. It had 33 shops, each of which had a storeroom and a supply of cool water

American School of Classical Studies, Athens

Inscription from Corinth. The second word from the bottom in the lower left-hand corner means "meat market" and is the same word in Latin which Paul employs in Greek in 1 Cor. 10:25

Shops in the market place at Corinth had cisterns connected, like this one, with subterranean channels in which ran cooling waters from the fountain of Peirene

American School
of Classical Studies, Athens

Liberty and Another's Conscience

[10:23–30]

"All things are lawful," but not all things are helpful. "All things are lawful," but not all things build up. Let no one seek his own good, but the good of his neighbor. Eat whatever is sold in the meat market without raising any question on the ground of conscience. For "the earth is the Lord's, and everything in it."[12] If one of the unbelievers invites you to dinner and you are disposed to go, eat whatever is set before you without raising any question on the ground of conscience. (But if some one says to you, "This has been offered in sacrifice," then out of consideration for the man who informed you, and for conscience' sake—I mean his conscience, not yours—do not eat it.) For why should my liberty be determined by another man's scruples? If I partake with thankfulness, why am I denounced because of that for which I give thanks?

[12]*Psalms* 24:1; 50:12

Do All to the Glory of God [10:31—11:1]

So, whether you eat or drink, or whatever you do, do all to the glory of God. Give no offense to Jews or to Greeks or to the church of God, just as I try to please all men in everything I do, not seeking my own advantage, but of many, that they may be saved. Be imitators of me, as I am of Christ.

The Covering of Women's Heads

[1 Corinthians 11:2–16]

I COMMEND you because you remember me in everything and maintain the traditions even as I have delivered them to you. But I want you to understand that the head of every man is Christ, the head of a woman is her husband, and the head of Christ is God. Any man who prays or prophesies with his head covered dishonors his head, but any woman who prays or prophesies with her head unveiled dishonors her head—it is the same as if her head were shaven. For if

Metropolitan Museum of Art

Alinari

Greco-Roman women's hairdress

Greco-Roman women's hairdress

This Greco-Roman woman wears a veil, which was not necessarily used to cover the face

a woman will not veil herself, then she should cut off her hair; but if it is disgraceful for a woman to be shorn or shaven, let her wear a veil. For a man ought not to cover his head, since he is the image and glory of God; but woman is the glory of man. (For man was not made from woman, but woman from man. Neither was man created for woman, but woman for man.) That is why a woman ought to have a veil[r] on her head, because of the angels. (Nevertheless, in the Lord woman is not independent of man nor man of woman; for as woman was made from man, so man is now born of woman. And all things are from God.) Judge for yourselves; is it proper for a woman to pray to God with her head uncovered? Does not nature itself teach you that for a man to wear long hair is degrading to him, but if a woman has long hair, it is her pride? For her hair is given to her for a covering. If any one is disposed to be contentious, we recognize no other practice, nor do the churches of God.

Abuses at the Lord's Supper [11:17–22]

But in the following instructions I do not commend you, because when you come together it is not for the better but for the worse. For, in the first place, when you assemble as a church, I hear that there are divisions among you; and I partly believe it, for there must be factions among you in order that those who are genuine among you may be recognized. When you meet together, it is not the Lord's supper that you eat. For in eating, each one goes ahead with his own meal, and one is hungry and another is drunk. What! Do you not have houses to eat and drink in? Or do you despise the church of God and humiliate those who have nothing? What shall I say to you? Shall I commend you in this? No, I will not.

The Lord's Supper [11:23–26]

For I received from the Lord what I also delivered to you, that the Lord Jesus on the night when he was betrayed took bread, and when he had given thanks, he broke it, and said, "This is my body which is for[s] you. Do this in remembrance of me." In the same way also the cup, after supper, saying, "This cup is the new covenant in my blood. Do this, as often as you drink it, in remembrance of me." For as often as you eat this bread and drink the cup, you proclaim the Lord's death until he comes.

Discerning the Lord's Body [11:27–34]

Whoever, therefore, eats the bread or drinks the cup of the Lord in an unworthy manner will be guilty of profaning the body and blood of the Lord. Let a man examine himself, and so eat of the bread and drink of the cup. For any one who eats and drinks without discerning the body eats and drinks judgment upon himself. That is why many of you are weak and ill, and some have died.[t] But if we judged ourselves truly, we should not be judged. But when we are judged by the Lord, we are chastened[u] so

[r] Greek *authority* (the veil being a symbol of this)
[s] Other ancient authorities read *broken for*
[t] Greek *have fallen asleep* (as in 15: 6, 20)
[u] Or *when we are judged we are being chastened by the Lord*

Felbermeyer

"*Led astray to dumb idols*" (1 Cor. 12:2). *At the left of the table a young woman is holding a knife and a kid, ready for sacrifice to Dionysus, the small bearded, crowned figure in the center, holding a cup in his right hand and a staff with a pine cone in his left. On the altar a fire is burning. The woman on the right offers a basket of food. Terra-cotta vase, fourth century B.C.*

that we may not be condemned along with the world.

So then, my brethren, when you come together to eat, wait for one another—if any one is hungry, let him eat at home—lest you come together to be condemned. About the other things I will give directions when I come.

Various Gifts, One Spirit

[I Corinthians 12:1–11]

NOW concerning spiritual gifts, brethren, I do not want you to be uninformed. You know that when you were heathen, you were led astray to dumb idols, however you may have been moved. Therefore I want you to understand that no one speaking by the Spirit of God ever says "Jesus be cursed!" and no one can say "Jesus is Lord" except by the Holy Spirit.

Now there are varieties of gifts, but the same Spirit; and there are varieties of service, but the same Lord; and there are varieties of working, but it is the same God who inspires them all in every one. To each is given the manifestation of the Spirit for the common good. To one is given through the Spirit the utterance of wisdom, and to another the utterance of knowledge according to the same Spirit, to another faith by the same Spirit, to another gifts of healing by the one Spirit, to another the working of miracles, to another prophecy, to another the ability to distinguish between spirits, to another various kinds of tongues, to another the interpretation of tongues. All these are inspired by one and the same Spirit, who apportions to each one individually as he wills.

Many Members, One Body [12:12–26]

For just as the body is one and has many members, and all the members of the body, though many, are one body, so it is with Christ. For by one Spirit we were all baptized into one body—Jews or Greeks, slaves or free—and all were made to drink of one Spirit.

For the body does not consist of one member but of many. If the foot should say, "Because I am not a hand, I do not belong to the body," that would not make it any less a part of the body. And if the ear should say, "Because I am not an eye, I do not belong to the body," that would not make it any less a part of the body. If the whole body were an eye, where would be the hearing? If the whole body were an ear, where would be the sense of smell? But as it is, God arranged the organs in the body, each one of them, as he chose. If all were a single organ, where would the body be? As it is, there are many parts, yet one body. The eye cannot say to the hand, "I have no need of you," nor again the head to the feet, "I have no need of you." On the contrary, the parts of the body which seem to be weaker are indispensable, and those parts of the body which we think less honorable we invest with the greater honor, and our unpresentable parts are treated with greater modesty, which our more presentable parts do not require. But God has so adjusted the body, giving the greater honor to the inferior part, that there may be no discord in the body, but that the members may have the same care for one another. If one member suffers, all suffer together; if one member is honored, all rejoice together.

You Are the Body of Christ [12:27–31]

Now you are the body of Christ and individually members of it. And God has appointed in the church first apostles, second prophets, third teachers, then workers of miracles, then healers, helpers, administrators, speakers in various kinds of tongues. Are all apostles? Are all prophets? Are all teachers? Do all work miracles? Do all possess gifts of healing? Do all speak with tongues? Do all interpret? But earnestly desire the higher gifts.

And I will show you a still more excellent way.

Prophecy Superior to Tongues
[1 Corinthians 14:1-5]

MAKE love your aim, and earnestly desire the spiritual gifts, especially that you may prophesy. For one who speaks in a tongue speaks not to men but to God; for no one understands him, but he utters mysteries in the Spirit. On the other hand, he who prophesies speaks to men for their upbuilding and encouragement and consolation. He who speaks in a tongue edifies himself, but he who prophesies edifies the church. Now I want you all to speak in tongues, but even more to prophesy. He who prophesies is greater than he who speaks in tongues, unless some one interprets, so that the church may be edified.

Speaking into the Air [14:6-12]

Now, brethren, if I come to you speaking in tongues, how shall I benefit you unless I bring you some revelation or knowledge or prophecy or teaching? If even lifeless instruments, such as the flute or the harp, do not give distinct notes, how will any one know what is played? And if the bugle gives an indistinct sound, who will get ready for battle? So with yourselves; if you in a tongue utter speech that is not intelligible, how will any one know what is said? For you will be speaking into the air. There are doubtless many different languages in the world, and none is without meaning; but if I do not know the meaning of the language, I shall be a foreigner to the speaker and the speaker a foreigner to me. So with yourselves; since you are eager for manifestations of the Spirit, strive to excel in building up the church.

The Power to Interpret [14:13-19]

Therefore, he who speaks in a tongue should pray for the power to interpret. For if I pray in a tongue, my spirit prays but my mind is unfruitful. What am I to do? I will pray with the spirit and I will pray with the mind also; I will sing with the spirit and I will sing with the mind also. Otherwise, if you bless[w] with the spirit, how can any one in the position of an outsider[x] say the "Amen" to your thanksgiving when he does not know what you are saying? For you may give thanks well enough, but the other man is not edified. I thank God that I speak in tongues more than you all; nevertheless, in church I would rather speak five words with my mind, in order to instruct others, than ten thousand words in a tongue.

The Purpose of Tongues [14:20-25]

Brethren, do not be children in your thinking; be babes in evil, but in thinking be mature. In the law it is written, "By men of strange tongues and by the lips of foreigners will I speak to this people, and even then they will not listen to me, says the Lord."[13] Thus, tongues are a sign not for believers but for unbelievers, while prophecy is not for unbelievers but for believers. If, therefore, the whole church assembles and all speak in tongues, and outsiders or unbelievers enter, will they not say that you are mad? But if all prophesy, and an unbeliever or outsider enters, he is convicted by all, he is called to account by all, the secrets of his

[w]That is *give thanks to God*
[x]Or *him that is without gifts*
[13]Isaiah 28:11-12

Metropolitan Museum of Art

Fresco from Boscoreale near Pompeii, showing a woman playing a cithara (a kind of lyre)

The Pre-eminence of Love
[1 Corinthians 13:1-3]

IF I speak in the tongues of men and of angels, but have not love, I am a noisy gong or a clanging cymbal. And if I have prophetic powers, and understand all mysteries and all knowledge, and if I have all faith, so as to remove mountains, but have not love, I am nothing. If I give away all I have, and if I deliver my body to be burned,[v] but have not love, I gain nothing.

The Characteristics of Love [13:4-7]

Love is patient and kind; love is not jealous or boastful; it is not arrogant or rude. Love does not insist on its own way; it is not irritable or resentful; it does not rejoice at wrong, but rejoices in the right. Love bears all things, believes all things, hopes all things, endures all things.

Love Never Ends [13:8-13]

Love never ends; as for prophecies, they will pass away; as for tongues, they will cease; as for knowledge, it will pass away. For our knowledge is imperfect and our prophecy is imperfect; but when the perfect comes, the imperfect will pass away. When I was a child, I spoke like a child, I thought like a child, I reasoned like a child; when I became a man, I gave up childish ways. For now we see in a mirror dimly, but then face to face. Now I know in part; then I shall understand fully, even as I have been fully understood. So faith, hope, love abide, these three; but the greatest of these is love.

[v]Other ancient authorities read *body that I may glory*

Metropolitan Museum of Art

An Etruscan mirror.
Third or fourth century B.C.

heart are disclosed; and so, falling on his face, he will worship God and declare that God is really among you.

Order in Worship [14:26–33a]

What then, brethren? When you come together, each one has a hymn, a lesson, a revelation, a tongue, or an interpretation. Let all things be done for edification. If any speak in a tongue, let there be only two or at most three, and each in turn; and let one interpret. But if there is no one to interpret, let each of them keep silence in church and speak to himself and to God. Let two or three prophets speak, and let the others weigh what is said. If a revelation is made to another sitting by, let the first be silent. For you can all prophesy one by one, so that all may learn and all be encouraged; and the spirits of prophets are subject to prophets. For God is not a God of confusion but of peace.

Women Subordinate

[14:33b–36]

As in all the churches of the saints, the women should keep silence in the churches. For they are not permitted to speak, but should be subordinate, as even the law says. If there is anything they desire to know, let them ask their husbands at home. For it is shameful for a woman to speak in church. What! Did the word of God originate with you, or are you the only ones it has reached?

Acknowledge the Lord's Commands

[14:37–40]

If any one thinks that he is a prophet, or spiritual, he should acknowledge that what I am writing to you is a command of the Lord. If any one does not recognize this, he is not recognized. So, my brethren, earnestly desire to prophesy, and do not forbid speaking in tongues; but all things should be done decently and in order.

The Resurrection of Christ

[I Corinthians 15:1–11]

NOW I would remind you, brethren, in what terms I preached to you the gospel, which you received, in which you stand, by which you are saved, if you hold it fast—unless you believed in vain.

For I delivered to you as of first importance what I also received, that Christ died for our sins in accordance with the scriptures, that he was buried, that he was raised on the third day in accordance with the scriptures, and that he appeared to Cephas, then to the twelve. Then he appeared to more than five hundred brethren at one time, most of whom are still alive, though some have fallen asleep. Then he appeared to James, then to all the apostles. Last of all, as to one untimely born, he appeared also to me. For I am the least of the apostles, unfit to be called an apostle, because I persecuted the church of God. But by the grace of God I am what I am, and his grace toward me was not in vain. On the contrary, I worked harder than any of them, though it was not I, but the grace of God which is with me. Whether then it was I or they, so we preach and so you believed.

The Resurrection of the Dead [15:12–19]

Now if Christ is preached as raised from the dead, how can some of you say that

185

Deutsches Archaeologisches Institut, Rome

Sale of a piece of cloth. In Corinth, Paul met Aquila and Priscilla, who, like him, were tentmakers. Heavy cloth made of the hair of black Cilician goats was preferred for making tents

there is no resurrection of the dead? But if there is no resurrection of the dead, then Christ has not been raised; if Christ has not been raised, then our preaching is in vain and your faith is in vain. We are even found to be misrepresenting God, because we testified of God that he raised Christ, whom he did not raise if it is true that the dead are not raised. For if the dead are not raised, then Christ has not been raised. If Christ has not been raised, your faith is futile and you are still in your sins. Then those also who have fallen asleep in Christ have perished. If for this life only we have hoped in Christ, we are of all men most to be pitied.

Christ the First Fruits [15:20–28]

But in fact Christ has been raised from the dead, the first fruits of those who have fallen asleep. For as by a man came death, by a man has come also the resurrection of the dead. For as in Adam all die, so also in Christ shall all be made alive. But each in his own order: Christ the first fruits, then at his coming those who belong to Christ. Then comes the end, when he delivers the kingdom to God the Father after destroying every rule and every authority and power. For he must reign until he has put all his enemies under his feet. The last enemy to be destroyed is death. "For God² has put all things in subjection under his feet."[14] But when it says, "All things are put in subjection under him," it is plain that he is excepted who put all things under him. When all things are subjected to him, then the Son himself will also be subjected to him who put all things under him, that God may be everything to every one.

²Greek *he*
[14]*Psalms 8:6*

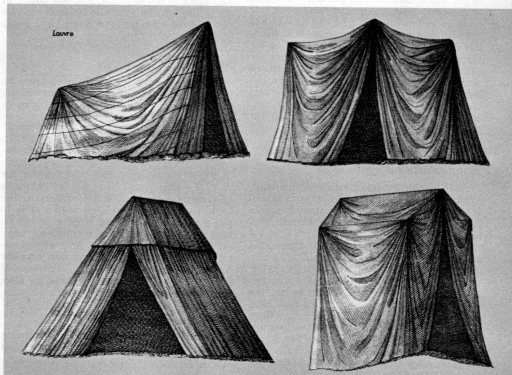

Louvre

As a tentmaker, Paul knew many varieties of tents. These four kinds were used by the soldiers on Trajan's column (A.D. 113)

New York Times

Part of colonnade and row of 33 taverns, with 40-foot-deep wells connected at the bottom with a channel of fresh running water in which milk, meat and wine could be kept cool. Wine jars, mixing bowls, drinking cups, dice and flutes have been recovered from the wells of the taverns into which the Romans hurled them 146 B.C., when they sacked the city

J. Lane Miller

Corinth: The Lechaeum Road

Baptism on Behalf of the Dead [15:29–34]

Otherwise, what do people mean by being baptized on behalf of the dead? If the dead are not raised at all, why are people baptized on their behalf? Why am I in peril every hour? I protest, brethren, by my pride in you which I have in Christ Jesus our Lord, I die every day! What do I gain if, humanly speaking, I fought with beasts at Eph'esus? If the dead are not raised, "Let us eat and drink, for tomorrow we die."[15] Do not be deceived: "Bad company ruins good morals." Come to your right mind, and sin no more. For some have no knowledge of God. I say this to your shame.

How the Dead Are Raised [15:35–41]

But some one will ask, "How are the dead raised? With what kind of body do they come?" You foolish man! What you sow does not come to life unless it dies. And what you sow is not the body which is to be, but a bare kernel, perhaps of wheat or of some other grain. But God gives it a body as he has chosen, and to each kind of seed its own body. For not all flesh is alike, but there is one kind for men, another for animals, another for birds, and another for fish. There are celestial bodies and there are terrestrial bodies; but the glory of the celestial is one, and the glory of the terrestrial is another. There is one glory of the sun, and another glory of the moon, and another glory of the stars; for star differs from star in glory.

The Spiritual Body [15:42–50]

So is it with the resurrection of the dead. What is sown is perishable, what is raised is imperishable. It is sown in dishonor, it is raised in glory. It is sown in weakness, it is raised in power. It is sown a physical body, it is raised a spiritual body. If there is a physical body, there is also a spiritual body. Thus it is written, "The first man Adam became a living being";[16] the last Adam became a life-giving spirit. But it is not the spiritual which is first but the physical, and then the spiritual. The first man was from the earth, a man of dust; the second man is from heaven. As was the man of dust, so are those who are of the dust; and as is the man of heaven, so are those who are of heaven.

Just as we have borne the image of the man of dust, we shall[a] also bear the image of the man of heaven. I tell you this, brethren: flesh and blood cannot inherit the kingdom of God, nor does the perishable inherit the imperishable.

Victory over Death [15:51–57]

Lo! I tell you a mystery. We shall not all sleep, but we shall all be changed, in a moment, in the twinkling of an eye, at the last trumpet. For the trumpet will sound, and the dead will be raised imperishable, and we shall be changed. For this perishable nature must put on the imperishable, and this mortal nature must put on immortality. When the perishable puts on the imperishable, and the mortal puts on immortality, then shall come to pass the saying that is written:

"Death is swallowed up in victory."[17]
"O death, where is thy victory?
O death, where is thy sting?"[18]

The sting of death is sin, and the power of sin is the law. But thanks be to God, who gives us the victory through our Lord Jesus Christ.

Be Steadfast [15:58]

Therefore, my beloved brethren, be steadfast, immovable, always abounding in the work of the Lord, knowing that in the Lord your labor is not in vain.

The Contribution for the Saints

[1 Corinthians 16:1–4]

NOW concerning the contribution for the saints: as I directed the churches of Galatia, so you also are to do. On the first day of every week, each of you is to put something aside and store it up, as he may prosper, so that contributions need not be made when I come. And when I arrive, I will send those whom you accredit by letter to carry your gift to Jerusalem. If it seems advisable that I should go also, they will accompany me.

Plans for Travel [16:5–9]

I will visit you after passing through Macedo'nia, for I intend to pass through Macedo'nia, and perhaps I will stay with you or even spend the winter, so that you may speed me on my journey, wherever I go. For I do not want to see you now just in passing; I hope to spend some time with you, if the Lord permits. But I will stay in Eph'esus until Pen'tecost, for a wide door for effective work has opened to me, and there are many adversaries.

The Coming of Timothy and Apollos

[16:10–12]

When Timothy comes, see that you put him at ease among you, for he is doing the work of the Lord, as I am. So let no one despise him. Speed him on his way in peace, that he may return to me; for I am expecting him with the brethren.

As for our brother Apol'los, I strongly urged him to visit you with the other brethren, but it was not at all his will[b] to come now. He will come when he has opportunity.

Exhortations and Greetings [16:13–20]

Be watchful, stand firm in your faith, be courageous, be strong. Let all that you do be done in love.

Now, brethren, you know that the household of Steph'anas were the first converts in Achai'a, and they have devoted themselves to the service of the saints; I urge you to be subject to such men and to every fellow worker and laborer. I rejoice at the coming of Steph'anas and Fortuna'tus and Acha'icus, because they have made up for your absence; for they refreshed my spirit as well as yours. Give recognition to such men.

The churches of Asia send greetings. Aqui'la and Prisca, together with the church in their house, send you hearty greetings in the Lord. All the brethren send greetings. Greet one another with a holy kiss.

Benediction [16:21–24]

I, Paul, write this greeting with my own hand. If any one has no love for the Lord, let him be accursed. Our Lord, come![c] The grace of the Lord Jesus be with you. My love be with you all in Christ Jesus. Amen.

[15]Isaiah 22:13   [16]Genesis 2:7
[a]Other ancient authorities read *let us*
[17]Isaiah 25:8
[18]Hosea 13:14
[b]Or *God's will for him*
[c]Greek *Maranatha*

Ewing Galloway

The Corinth Canal was opened in 1893. Julius Caesar desired to dig it. Nero, with a golden shovel, actually started the digging at the western end. Roman soldiers and 6,000 Jews captured by Vespasian continued the work, but upon Nero's death on June 8, A.D. 68 the digging stopped before the canal was one-fifth completed

THE SECOND LETTER OF PAUL TO THE CORINTHIANS

Greetings

[2 Corinthians 1:1–2] Paul, an apostle of Christ Jesus by the will of God, and Timothy our brother,

To the church of God which is at Corinth, with all the saints who are in the whole of Achai'a:

Grace to you and peace from God our Father and the Lord Jesus Christ.

The God of All Comfort [1:3–7]

Blessed be the God and Father of our Lord Jesus Christ, the Father of mercies and God of all comfort, who comforts us in all our affliction, so that we may be able to comfort those who are in any affliction, with the comfort with which we ourselves are comforted by God. For as we share abundantly in Christ's sufferings, so through Christ we share abundantly in comfort too.[a] If we are afflicted, it is for your comfort and salvation; and if we are comforted, it is for your comfort, which you experience when you patiently endure the same sufferings that we suffer. Our hope for you is unshaken; for we know that as you share in our sufferings, you will also share in our comfort.

Paul's Affliction in Asia [1:8–11]

For we do not want you to be ignorant, brethren, of the affliction we experienced in Asia; for we were so utterly, unbearably crushed that we despaired of life itself. Why, we felt that we had received the sentence of death; but that was to make us rely not on ourselves but on God who raises the dead; he delivered us from so deadly a peril, and he will deliver us; on him we have set our hope that he will deliver us again. You also must help us by prayer, so that many will give thanks on our behalf for the blessing granted us in answer to many prayers.

Paul's Sincerity [1:12–14]

For our boast is this, the testimony of our conscience that we have behaved in the world, and still more toward you, with holiness and godly sincerity, not by earthly wisdom but by the grace of God. For we write you nothing but what you can read and understand; I hope you will understand fully, as you have understood in part, that you can be proud of us as we can be of you, on the day of the Lord Jesus.

Paul's Plans to Visit Corinth [1:15–22]

Because I was sure of this, I wanted to come to you first, so that you might have a double pleasure;[b] I wanted to visit you on my way to Macedo'nia, and to come back to you from Macedo'nia and have you send me on my way to Jude'a. Was I vacillating when I wanted to do this? Do I make my plans like a worldly man, ready to say Yes and No at once? As surely as God is faithful, our word to you has not been Yes and No. For the Son of God, Jesus Christ, whom we preached among you, Silva'nus and Timothy and I, was not Yes and No; but in him it is always Yes. For all the promises of God find their Yes in him. That is why we utter the Amen through him, to the glory of God. But it is God who establishes us with you in Christ, and has commissioned us; he has put his seal upon us and given us his Spirit in our hearts as a guarantee.

Why Paul Remained Away [1:23–2:11]

But I call God to witness against me—it was to spare you that I refrained from coming to Corinth. Not that we lord it over your faith; we work with you for your joy, for you stand firm in your faith. For I made up my mind not to make you another painful visit. For if I cause you pain, who is there to make me glad but the one whom I have pained? And I wrote as I did, so that when I came I might not be pained by those who should have made me rejoice, for I felt sure of all of you, that my joy would be the joy of you all. For I wrote you out of much affliction and anguish of heart and with many tears, not to cause you pain but to let you know the abundant love that I have for you.

But if any one has caused pain, he has caused it not to me, but in some measure—not to put it too severely—to you all. For such a one this punishment by the majority is enough; so you should rather turn to forgive and comfort him, or he may be overwhelmed by excessive sorrow. So I beg you to reaffirm your love for him. For this is why I wrote, that I might test you and know whether you are obedient in everything. Any one whom you forgive, I also forgive. What I have forgiven, if I have forgiven anything, has been for your sake in the presence of Christ, to keep Satan from gaining the advantage over us; for we are not ignorant of his designs.

Paul's Anxiety at Troas
[2 Corinthians 2:12–13]

WHEN I came to Troas to preach the gospel of Christ, a door was opened for me in the Lord; but my mind could not rest because I did not find my brother Titus there. So I took leave of them and went on to Macedo'nia.

Triumphant in Christ [2:14–17]

But thanks be to God, who in Christ always leads us in triumph, and through us spreads the fragrance of the knowledge of him everywhere. For we are the aroma of Christ to God among those who are being saved and among those who are perishing, to one a fragrance from death to death, to the other a fragrance from life to life. Who is sufficient for these things? For we are not, like so many, peddlers of God's word; but as men of sincerity, as commissioned by God, in the sight of God we speak in Christ.

Letters of Recommendation
[2 Corinthians 3:1–3]

ARE we beginning to commend ourselves again? Or do we need, as some do, letters of recommendation to you, or from you? You yourselves are our letter of recommendation, written on your[c] hearts, to be known and read by all men; and you show that you are a letter from Christ delivered by us, written not with ink but with the Spirit of the living God, not on tablets of stone but on tablets of human hearts.

Ministers of a New Covenant [3:4–6]

Such is the confidence that we have through Christ toward God. Not that we are sufficient of ourselves to claim anything as coming from us; our sufficiency is from God, who has qualified us to be ministers of a new covenant, not in a written code but in the Spirit; for the written code kills, but the Spirit gives life.

[a]Or *For as the sufferings of Christ abound for us, so also our comfort abounds through Christ*

[b]Other ancient authorities read *favor*

[c]Other ancient authorities read *our*

Philip Gendreau

"If the earthly tent we live in is destroyed, we have a building from God" (2 Cor. 5:1). A modern Bedouin tent pitched beside an oasis in North Africa. Paul worked hard as a tentmaker in order to make the Gospel "free of charge" (1 Cor. 9:18)

Superiority of the New Dispensation

[3:7–11]

Now if the dispensation of death, carved in letters on stone, came with such splendor that the Israelites could not look at Moses' face because of its brightness, fading as this was, will not the dispensation of the Spirit be attended with greater splendor? For if there was splendor in the dispensation of condemnation, the dispensation of righteousness must far exceed it in splendor. Indeed, in this case, what once had splendor has come to have no splendor at all, because of the splendor that surpasses it. For if what faded away came with splendor, what is permanent must have much more splendor.

Beholding the Glory of the Lord

[3:12–18]

Since we have such a hope, we are very bold, not like Moses, who put a veil over his face so that the Israelites might not see the end of the fading splendor. But their minds were hardened; for to this day, when they read the old covenant, that same veil remains unlifted, because only through Christ is it taken away. Yes, to this day whenever Moses is read a veil lies over their minds; but when a man turns to the Lord the veil is removed. Now the Lord is the Spirit, and where the Spirit of the Lord is, there is freedom. And we all, with unveiled face, beholding[d] the glory of the Lord, are being changed into his likeness from one degree of glory to another; for this comes from the Lord who is the Spirit.

The Light of the Gospel [2 Corinthians 4:1–6]

THEREFORE, having this ministry by the mercy of God,[e] we do not lose heart. We have renounced disgraceful, underhanded ways; we refuse to practice cunning or to tamper with God's word, but by the open statement of the truth we would commend ourselves to every man's conscience in the sight of God. And even if our gospel is veiled, it is veiled only to those who are perishing. In their case the god of this world has blinded the minds of the unbelievers, to keep them from seeing the light of the gospel of the glory of Christ, who is the likeness of God. For what we preach is not ourselves, but Jesus Christ as Lord, with ourselves as your servants[f] for Jesus' sake. For it is the God who said, "Let light shine out of darkness,"[1] who has

shone in our hearts to give the light of the knowledge of the glory of God in the face of Christ.

Treasure in Earthen Vessels [4:7–12]

But we have this treasure in earthen vessels, to show that the transcendent power belongs to God and not to us. We are afflicted in every way, but not crushed; perplexed, but not driven to despair; persecuted, but not forsaken; struck down, but not destroyed; always carrying in the body the death of Jesus, so that the life of Jesus may also be manifested in our bodies. For while we live we are always being given up to death for Jesus' sake, so that the life of Jesus may be manifested in our mortal flesh. So death is at work in us, but life in you.

The Spirit of Faith [4:13–15]

Since we have the same spirit of faith as he had who wrote, "I believed, and so I spoke,"[2] we too believe, and so we speak, knowing that he who raised the Lord Jesus will raise us also with Jesus and bring us with you into his presence. For it is all for your sake, so that as grace extends to more and more people it may increase thanksgiving, to the glory of God.

An Eternal Weight of Glory [4:16–18]

So we do not lose heart. Though our outer nature is wasting away, our inner nature is being renewed every day. For this slight momentary affliction is preparing for us an eternal weight of glory beyond all comparison, because we look not to the things that are seen but to the things that are unseen; for the things that are seen are transient, but the things that are unseen are eternal.

A House Not Made with Hands

[2 Corinthians 5:1–5]

FOR we know that if the earthly tent we live in is destroyed, we have a building from God, a house not made with hands, eternal in the heavens. Here indeed we groan, and long to put on our heavenly dwelling, so that by putting it on we may not be found naked. For while we are still in this tent, we sigh with anxiety; not that we would be unclothed, but that we would be further clothed, so that what is mortal may be swallowed up by life. He who has prepared us for this very thing is God, who has given us the Spirit as a guarantee.

At Home with the Lord [5:6–10]

So we are always of good courage; we know that while we are at home in the body we are away from the Lord, for we walk by faith, not by sight. We are of good courage, and we would rather be away from the body and at home with the Lord. So whether we are at home or away, we make it our aim to please him. For we must all appear before the judgment seat of Christ, so that each one may receive good or evil, according to what he has done in the body.

The Love of Christ Controls Us

[5:11–15]

Therefore, knowing the fear of the Lord, we persuade men; but what we are is known to God, and I hope it is known also to your conscience. We are not commending ourselves to you again but giving you cause to be proud of us, so that you may be able to answer those who pride themselves on a man's position and not on his heart. For if we are beside ourselves, it is for God; if we are in our right mind, it is for you. For the love of Christ controls us, because we are convinced that one has died for all; therefore all have died. And he died for all, that those who live might live no longer for themselves but for him who for their sake died and was raised.

The Ministry of Reconciliation [5:16–21]

From now on, therefore, we regard no one from a human point of view; even though we once regarded Christ from a human point of view, we regard him thus no longer. Therefore, if any one is in Christ, he is a new creation;[g] the old has passed away, behold, the new has come. All this is from God, who through Christ reconciled us to himself and gave us the ministry of reconciliation; that is, God was in Christ reconciling[h] the world to himself, not counting their trespasses against them, and entrusting to us the message of reconciliation. So we are ambassadors for Christ, God making his appeal through us. We beseech you on behalf of Christ, be reconciled to God. For our sake he made him to be sin who knew no sin, so that in him we might become the righteousness of God.

Paul's Credentials [2 CORINTHIANS 6:1–13]

WORKING together with him, then, we entreat you not to accept the grace of God in vain. For he says,

"At the acceptable time I have listened to you,
and helped you on the day of salvation."[3]

Behold, now is the acceptable time; behold, now is the day of salvation. We put no obstacle in any one's way, so that no fault may be found with our ministry, but as servants of God we commend ourselves in every way: through great endurance, in afflictions, hardships, calamities, beatings, imprisonments, tumults, labors, watching, hunger; by purity, knowledge, forbearance, kindness, the Holy Spirit, genuine love, truthful speech, and the power of God; with the weapons of righteousness for the right hand and for the left; in honor and dishonor, in ill repute and good repute. We are treated as impostors, and yet are true; as

---

[d]Or *reflecting*   [e]Greek *as we have received mercy*
[f]Or *slaves*   [1]*Genesis* 1:3

[2]*Psalms* 116:10

[g]Or *creature*   [h]Or *in Christ God was reconciling*
[3]*Isaiah* 49:8

unknown, and yet well known; as dying, and behold we live; as punished, and yet not killed; as sorrowful, yet always rejoicing; as poor, yet making many rich; as having nothing, and yet possessing everything.

Our mouth is open to you, Corinthians; our heart is wide. You are not restricted by us, but you are restricted in your own affections. In return—I speak as to children —widen your hearts also.

Separation from Evil [6:14—7:1]

Do not be mismated with unbelievers. For what partnership have righteousness and iniquity? Or what fellowship has light with darkness? What accord has Christ with Be'lial?[i] Or what has a believer in common with an unbeliever? What agreement has the temple of God with idols? For we are the temple of the living God; as God said,

"I will live in 'them and move among them,
and I will be their God,
and they shall be my people.[4]
Therefore come out from them,
and be separate from them, says the Lord,
and touch nothing unclean;
then I will welcome you,[5]
and I will be a father to you,
and you shall be my sons and daughters,
says the Lord Almighty."[6]

Since we have these promises, beloved, let us cleanse ourselves from every defilement of body and spirit, and make holiness perfect in the fear of God.

Paul's Joy in Affliction [2 Corinthians 7:2-4]

OPEN your hearts to us; we have wronged no one, we have corrupted no one, we have taken advantage of no one. I do not say this to condemn you, for I said before that you are in our hearts, to die together and to live together. I have great confidence in you; I have great pride in you; I am filled with comfort. With all our affliction, I am overjoyed.

Rejoicing in the Church's Repentance
[7:5-13a]

For even when we came into Macedo'nia, our bodies had no rest but we were afflicted at every turn—fighting without and fear within. But God, who comforts the downcast, comforted us by the coming of Titus, and not only by his coming but also by the comfort with which he was comforted in you, as he told us of your longing, your mourning, your zeal for me, so that I rejoiced still more. For even if I made you sorry with my letter, I do not regret it (though I did regret it), for I see that that letter grieved you, though only for a while. As it is, I rejoice, not because you were grieved, but because you were grieved into repenting; for you felt a godly grief, so that you suffered no loss through us. For godly grief produces a repentance that leads to salvation and brings no regret, but worldly grief produces death. For see what earnestness this godly grief has produced in you, what eagerness to clear yourselves, what indignation, what alarm, what longing, what zeal, what punishment! At every point you have proved yourselves guiltless in the mat-

Combine Photos

"Do not be mismated with unbelievers" (2 Cor. 6:14). Horse and donkey hitched together to thresh grain

ter. So although I wrote to you, it was not on account of the one who did the wrong, nor on account of the one who suffered the wrong, but in order that your zeal for us might be revealed to you in the sight of God. Therefore we are comforted.

The Joy of Titus [7:13b-16]

And besides our own comfort we rejoiced still more at the joy of Titus, because his mind has been set at rest by you all. For if I have expressed to him some pride in you, I was not put to shame; but just as everything we said to you was true, so our boasting before Titus has proved true. And his heart goes out all the more to you, as he remembers the obedience of you all, and the fear and trembling with which you received him. I rejoice, because I have perfect confidence in you.

The Example of Macedonia
[2 Corinthians 8:1-7]

WE want you to know, brethren, about the grace of God which has been shown in the churches of Macedo'nia, for in a severe test of affliction, their abundance of joy and their extreme poverty have overflowed in a wealth of liberality on their part. For they gave according to their means, as I can testify, and beyond their means, of their own free will, begging us earnestly for the favor of taking part in the relief of the saints—and this, not as we expected, but first they gave themselves to the Lord and to us by the will of God. Accordingly we have urged Titus that as he had already made a beginning, he should also complete among you this gracious work. Now as you excel in everything—in faith, in utterance, in knowledge, in all earnestness, and in your love for us—see that you excel in this gracious work also.

Equality through Sharing [8:8-15]

I say this not as a command, but to prove by the earnestness of others that your love also is genuine. For you know the grace of our Lord Jesus Christ, that though he was rich, yet for your sake he became poor, so that by his poverty you might become rich. And in this matter I give my advice: it is best for you now to complete what a year ago you began not only to do but to desire, so that your readiness in desiring it may be matched by your completing it out of what you have. For if the readiness is there, it is acceptable according to what a man has,

not according to what he has not. I do not mean that others should be eased and you burdened, but that as a matter of equality your abundance at the present time should supply their want, so that their abundance may supply your want, that there may be equality. As it is written, "He who gathered much had nothing over, and he who gathered little had no lack."[7]

Paul Sends Messengers to Corinth
[8:16-24]

But thanks be to God who puts the same earnest care for you into the heart of Titus. For he not only accepted our appeal, but being himself very earnest he is going to you of his own accord. With him we are sending the brother who is famous among all the churches for his preaching of the gospel; and not only that, but he has been appointed by the churches to travel with us in this gracious work which we are carrying on, for the glory of the Lord and to show our good will. We intend that no one should blame us about this liberal gift which we are administering, for we aim at what is honorable not only in the Lord's sight but also in the sight of men. And with them we are sending our brother whom we have often tested and found earnest in many matters, but who is now more earnest than ever because of his great confidence in you. As for Titus, he is my partner and fellow worker in your service; and as for our brethren, they are messengers[j] of the churches, the glory of Christ. So give proof, before the churches, of your love and of our boasting about you to these men.

The Offering for the Saints
[2 Corinthians 9:1-5]

NOW it is superfluous for me to write to you about the offering for the saints, for I know your readiness, of which I boast about you to the people of Macedo'nia, saying that Achai'a has been ready since last year; and your zeal has stirred up most of them. But I am sending the brethren so that our boasting about you may not prove vain in this case, so that you may be ready, as I said you would be; lest if some Macedo'nians come with me and find that you are not ready, we be humiliated—to say nothing of you—for being so confident. So I thought it necessary to urge the brethren to go on to you before me, and arrange in

[i] Greek Beliar
[4] Exodus 25:8, 29:45; Leviticus 26:12; Jeremiah 31:1
[5] Isaiah 52:11; Ezekiel 37:27
[6] 2 Samuel 7:8, 14; Hosea 1:10; Isaiah 43:6

[j] Greek apostles   [7] Exodus 16:18

R. S. Robinson

Plowing

Threshing

Pitching wheat straw   R. S. Robinson

advance for this gift you have promised, so that it may be ready not as an exaction but as a willing gift.

God Loves a Cheerful Giver [9:6–15]

The point is this: he who sows sparingly will also reap sparingly, and he who sows bountifully will also reap bountifully. Each one must do as he has made up his mind, not reluctantly or under compulsion, for God loves a cheerful giver. And God is able to provide you with every blessing in abundance, so that you may always have enough of everything and may provide in abundance for every good work. As it is written,

"He scatters abroad, he gives to the poor;
his righteousness[k] endures for ever."[8]

He who supplies seed to the sower and bread for food will supply and multiply your resources[l] and increase the harvest of your righteousness.[k] You will be enriched in every way for great generosity, which through us will produce thanksgiving to God; for the rendering of this service not only supplies the wants of the saints but also overflows in many thanksgivings to God. Under the test of this service, you[m] will glorify God by your obedience in acknowledging the gospel of Christ, and by the generosity of your contribution for them and for all others; while they long for you and pray for you, because of the surpassing grace of God in you. Thanks be to God for his inexpressible gift!

The Weapons of Our Warfare

[2 Corinthians 10:1–6]

I, PAUL, myself entreat you, by the meekness and gentleness of Christ—I who am humble when face to face with you, but bold to you when I am away!—I beg of you that when I am present I may not have to show boldness with such confidence as I count on showing against some who suspect us of acting in worldly fashion. For though we live in the world we are not carrying on a worldly war, for the weapons of our warfare are not worldly but have divine power to destroy strongholds. We destroy arguments and every proud obstacle to the knowledge of God, and take every thought captive to obey Christ, being ready to punish every disobedience, when your obedience is complete.

Paul's Boasting [10:7–12]

Look at what is before your eyes. If any one is confident that he is Christ's, let him remind himself that as he is Christ's, so are we. For even if I boast a little too much of our authority, which the Lord gave for building you up and not for destroying you, I shall not be put to shame. I would not seem to be frightening you with letters. For they say, "His letters are weighty and strong, but his bodily presence is weak, and his speech of no account." Let such people understand that what we say by letter when absent, we do when present. Not that we venture to class or compare ourselves with some of those who commend themselves. But when they measure themselves by one another, and compare themselves with one another, they are without understanding.

[k]Or *benevolence*   [m]Or *they*
[l]Greek *sowing*   [8]*Psalms* 112:9

190

Boasting in the Lord [10:13–18]

But we will not boast beyond limit, but will keep to the limits God has apportioned us, to reach even to you. For we are not overextending ourselves, as though we did not reach you; we were the first to come all the way to you with the gospel of Christ. We do not boast beyond limit, in other men's labors; but our hope is that as your faith increases, our field among you may be greatly enlarged, so that we may preach the gospel in lands beyond you, without boasting of work already done in another's field. "Let him who boasts, boast of the Lord."[9] For it is not the man who commends himself that is accepted, but the man whom the Lord commends.

A Divine Jealousy [2 Corinthians 11:1–6]

I WISH you would bear with me in a little foolishness. Do bear with me! I feel a divine jealousy for you, for I betrothed you to Christ to present you as a pure bride to her one husband. But I am afraid that as the serpent deceived Eve by his cunning, your thoughts will be led astray from a sincere and pure devotion to Christ. For if some one comes and preaches another Jesus than the one we preached, or if you receive a different spirit from the one you received, or if you accept a different gospel from the one you accepted, you submit to it readily enough. I think that I am not in the least inferior to these superlative apostles. Even if I am unskilled in speaking, I am not in knowledge; in every way we have made this plain to you in all things.

Paul's Self-Support [11:7–11]

Did I commit a sin in abasing myself so that you might be exalted, because I preached God's gospel without cost to you? I robbed other churches by accepting support from them in order to serve you. And when I was with you and was in want, I did not burden any one, for my needs were supplied by the brethren who came from Mace-do'nia. So I refrained and will refrain from burdening you in any way. As the truth of Christ is in me, this boast of mine shall not be silenced in the regions of Achai'a. And why? Because I do not love you? God knows I do!

False Apostles [11:12–15]

And what I do I will continue to do, in order to undermine the claim of those who would like to claim that in their boasted mission they work on the same terms as we do. For such men are false apostles, deceitful workmen, disguising themselves as apostles of Christ. And no wonder, for even Satan disguises himself as an angel of light. So it is not strange if his servants also disguise themselves as servants of righteousness. Their end will correspond to their deeds.

Paul's Sufferings as an Apostle [11:16–29]

I repeat, let no one think me foolish; but even if you do, accept me as a fool, so that I too may boast a little. (What I am saying I say not with the Lord's authority but as a fool, in this boastful confidence; since many boast of worldly things, I too will boast.) For you gladly bear with fools, being wise

[9]*Jeremiah* 9:24

yourselves! For you bear it if a man makes slaves of you, or preys upon you, or takes advantage of you, or puts on airs, or strikes you in the face. To my shame, I must say, we were too weak for that!

But whatever any one dares to boast of—I am speaking as a fool—I also dare to boast of that. Are they Hebrews? So am I. Are they Israelites? So am I. Are they descendants of Abraham? So am I. Are they servants of Christ? I am a better one—I am talking like a madman—with far greater labors, far more imprisonments, with countless beatings, and often near death. Five times I have received at the hands of the Jews the forty lashes less one. Three times I have been beaten with rods; once I was stoned. Three times I have been shipwrecked; a night and a day I have been adrift at sea; on frequent journeys, in danger from rivers, danger from robbers, danger from my own people, danger from Gentiles, danger in the city, danger in the wilderness, danger at sea, danger from false brethren; in toil and hardship, through many a sleepless night, in hunger and thirst, often without food, in cold and exposure. And, apart from other things, there is the daily pressure upon me of my anxiety for all the churches. Who is weak, and I am not weak? Who is made to fall, and I am not indignant?

Paul's Escape at Damascus [11:30-33]

If I must boast, I will boast of the things that show my weakness. The God and Father of the Lord Jesus, he who is blessed for ever, knows that I do not lie. At Damascus, the governor under King Ar'etas guarded the city of Damascus in order to seize me, but I was let down in a basket through a window in the wall, and escaped his hands.

A Thorn in the Flesh [2 Corinthians 12:1-10]

I MUST boast; there is nothing to be gained by it, but I will go on to visions and revelations of the Lord. I know a man in Christ who fourteen years ago was caught up to the third heaven—whether in the body or out of the body I do not know, God knows. And I know that this man was caught up into Paradise—whether in the body or out of the body I do not know, God knows—and he heard things that cannot be told, which man may not utter. On behalf of this man I will boast, but on my own behalf I will not boast, except of my weaknesses. Though if I wish to boast, I shall not be a fool, for I shall be speaking the truth. But I refrain from it, so that no one may think more of me than he sees in me or hears from me. And to keep me from being too elated by the abundance of revelations, a thorn was given me in the flesh, a messenger of Satan, to harass me, to keep me from being too elated. Three times I besought the Lord about this, that it should leave me; but he said to me, "My grace is sufficient for you, for my power is made perfect in weakness." I will all the more gladly boast of my weaknesses, that the power of Christ may rest upon me. For the sake of Christ, then, I am content with weaknesses, insults, hardships, persecutions, and calamities; for when I am weak, then I am strong.

The Signs of an Apostle [12:11-13]

I have been a fool! You forced me to it, for I ought to have been commended by you. For I am not at all inferior to these

superlative apostles, even though I am nothing. The signs of a true apostle were performed among you in all patience, with signs and wonders and mighty works. For in what were you less favored than the rest of the churches, except that I myself did not burden you? Forgive me this wrong!

Paul's Approaching Visit [12:14-18]

Here for the third time I am ready to come to you. And I will not be a burden, for I seek not what is yours but you; for children ought not to lay up for their parents, but parents for their children. I will most gladly spend and be spent for your souls. If I love you the more, am I to be loved the less? But granting that I myself did not burden you, I was crafty, you say, and got the better of you by guile. Did I take advantage of you through any of those whom I sent to you? I urged Titus to go, and sent the brother with him. Did Titus take advantage of you? Did we not act in the same spirit? Did we not take the same steps?

Paul's Concern for a Pure Church [12:19-21]

Have you been thinking all along that we have been defending ourselves before you? It is in the sight of God that we have been speaking in Christ, and all for your upbuilding, beloved. For I fear that perhaps I may come and find you not what I wish, and that you may find me not what you wish; that perhaps there may be quarreling, jealousy, anger, selfishness, slander, gossip, conceit, and disorder. I fear that when I come again my God may humble me before you, and I may have to mourn over many of those who sinned before and have not repented of the impurity, immorality, and licentiousness which they have practiced.

Warning to Sinners [2 Corinthians 13:1-4]

THIS is the third time I am coming to you. Any charge must be sustained by the evidence of two or three witnesses. I warned those who sinned before and all the others, and I warn them now while absent, as I did when present on my second visit, that if I come again I will not spare them—since you desire proof that Christ is speaking in me. He is not weak in dealing with you, but is powerful in you. For he was crucified in weakness, but lives by the power of God. For we are weak in him, but in dealing with you we shall live with him by the power of God.

Examine Yourselves [13:5-10]

Examine yourselves, to see whether you are holding to your faith. Test yourselves. Do you not realize that Jesus Christ is in you?—unless indeed you fail to meet the test! I hope you will find out that we have not failed. But we pray God that you may not do wrong—not that we may appear to have met the test, but that you may do what is right, though we may seem to have failed. For we cannot do anything against the truth, but only for the truth. For we are glad when we are weak and you are strong. What we pray for is your improvement. I write this while I am away from you, in order that when I come I may not have to be severe in my use of the authority which the Lord has given me for building up and not for tearing down.

A Final Appeal [13:11-13]

Finally, brethren, farewell. Mend your ways, heed my appeal, agree with one another, live in peace, and the God of love and peace will be with you. Greet one another with a holy kiss. All the saints greet you.

Benediction [13:14]

The grace of the Lord Jesus Christ and the love of God and the fellowship of[n] the Holy Spirit be with you all.

[n]Or and participation in

Malta. St. Paul's Bay, traditional site of Paul's landing after his later shipwreck on the way to Rome

DO YOU NOT KNOW THAT YOU ARE GOD'S TEMPLE
AND THAT GOD'S SPIRIT DWELLS IN YOU?

1 COR. 3:16

TEMPLE OF APOLLO, CORINTH. OF THE 38 COLUMNS
SEEN BY PAUL, ONLY 7 ARE NOW STANDING

J. Lane Miller

IF ANY ONE DESTROYS GOD'S TEMPLE, GOD WILL DESTROY HIM.
FOR GOD'S TEMPLE IS HOLY, AND THAT TEMPLE YOU ARE

A Cloud of Witnesses

THE STADIUM AT DELPHI, GREECE

de Mire

THE LETTERS OF PAUL TO THE GALATIANS, EPHESIANS, PHILIPPIANS, COLOSSIANS, THESSALONIANS, AND TO TIMOTHY, TITUS AND PHILEMON, AND THE LETTER TO THE HEBREWS   REVISED STANDARD VERSION

GALATIA

GALATIA was the name of a region in Asia Minor. The name was derived from the Gauls, who came in and formed a small state in the third century B.C. In the first century B.C. Asia Minor was conquered and reorganized by the Roman general Pompey. The eventual result was the establishment of Galatia as a province of the Roman empire. But as an imperial province Galatia was no longer limited to the district occupied originally by the invading Gauls. Other territories were added, and altogether Galatia, as a Roman province, included a considerable portion of Central Asia Minor. The original area, to which the name Galatia belongs ethnographically, was located around Ancyra in the north. The larger province, to which the name Galatia applied properly in Roman times, included the towns of Antioch, Iconium, Lystra, and Derbe in the south. Since the Book of Acts does not narrate a trip by Paul to the vicinity of Ancyra, but does tell (Acts 13:14—14:23; 16:1–5) about his repeated visits to the other cities, it is supposed by some scholars that it was the Christians in the latter places to whom he addressed the letter called "Galatians."

ANTIOCH OF PISIDIA, so called to distinguish it from Antioch on the Orontes River in Syria, was founded by Seleucus I about 300 B.C. Under Augustus it was given the honor of being a Roman colony. The city enjoyed a beautiful site on the Anthius River at the foot of a mountain. There were two large squares, named for Augustus and Tiberius respectively, and a great temple, a gateway and other architectural monuments, built in impressive Roman style. It was in this city that Paul preached the sermon recorded in Acts 13:16–41.

ICONIUM is situated on a large plain, bounded by hills, to two of which are attached the names of the early Christian martyrs Philip and Thecla. The deity most worshiped at Iconium seems to have been the Phrygian mother-goddess Cybele. By the second century of the Christian era the city had the status of a Roman colony, and thereby the rights of its citizens were improved. Today, Iconium still exists as a relatively large city and has even preserved its name almost intact, being known as Konia.

LYSTRA, the ancient site of which is now only a mound, was identified by the discovery of a stone altar bearing an inscription in Latin which contained the name of the city. As shown by this inscription, this city, too, was a colony of Rome. Both Greeks and native Lycaonians seem to have mingled in its population. It was here that Paul and Barnabas were taken as gods (Acts 14:8–18) and Paul was stoned (Acts 14:19–20). It was also the home of Timothy (Acts 16:1–3).

DERBE was on the southeastern edge of the Lycaonian plain and was reached by the same Roman road which led through the towns already mentioned. It is possible that a large mound, called Gudelisin, is the site of this city. Derbe seems to have had many of the marks of a frontier city and to have exhibited the lowest culture of any of this group of Galatian cities. Even ancient coins are rarely found there.

COLOSSAE (COLOSSE) AND ENVIRONS

COLOSSAE was located toward the upper end of the Lycus valley, where it narrows to a width of two miles and is walled by high precipices. Situated on the important trade route between Ephesus and the Euphrates valley, it teemed with many types of philosophic and religious thought. Paul was forbidden by the Holy Spirit (Acts 16:6) to preach in the province of Asia, where Colossae was located. Though Epaphras, who had founded the church there (Col. 1:7), was probably Paul's convert, Paul was writing to strangers in his Colossian letter (Col. 2:1). The ruins of the ancient city are now mostly covered by earth.

LAODICEA (Col. 4:13–16) was a dozen miles to the west of Colossae. It was one of the seven cities of the Province of Asia whose churches were addressed in Rev. 2:1—3:22, treated more extensively in the introduction to the illustrated Book of James to Revelation.

HIERAPOLIS (Col. 4:13), not far from Laodicea, stood on a spectacular terrace 500 feet above the bottom of the Lycus valley. Hot

springs pour out from the terrace, and at the edge of the cliff are the ruins of extensive baths. The city is mentioned in an inscription soon after 190 B.C., and coins of the city are known from the time of Augustus to that of Nero. In A.D. 60, however, an earthquake did great damage there, and it seems to have been early in the second century before it was again a flourishing place. Hierapolis had a long main street, with covered sidewalks on either side, and was adorned with a gymnasium, temples and theaters. The Roman theater, overlooking the city and the valley below, was especially large and impressive. Such famous personages as Philip the Evangelist, Papias and the pagan philosopher Epictetus lived at Hierapolis.

OTHER PLACES

Among places mentioned in 1 and 2 Timothy and Titus are Miletus (Acts 20:15, 17 or Miletum, 2 Timothy 4:20) and Crete (Titus 1:5). Miletus was one of a dozen ancient Greek colonies on the coast of Asia Minor which had united to form the famous Ionian League. Situated near the mouth of the Maeander River, Miletus controlled the trade of that river valley and became a flourishing commercial center. After capture and destruction at the hands first of Darius the Persian and then of Alexander the Great, it fell from its prosperous position and lost its trade to Ephesus. Even its fine harbors were silted up, and the very site is now several miles from the sea. Its extensive ruins include a fine theater. The famous philosophers Thales, Anaximander and Anaximenes lived there.

CRETE is one of the largest islands of the Mediterranean, one hundred sixty miles long and seven to thirty-five miles wide. It is largely mountainous, yet there are many fertile valleys, and, particularly on the north side, good harbors. There were many ancient cities there, and archaeology has revealed the existence of a flourishing civilization, the Minoan, dating back to about 3,000 B.C. It continued down to about 1,400 B.C., when the Mycenaean peoples from the Greek mainland overran the island. The proverb quoted in the letter to Titus (1:12), giving an uncomplimentary description of the character of the Cretans, was written by Epimenides, a poet who lived at Knossos in Crete in the sixth century B.C.

TROAS was a chief city and port of the Roman Province of Asia. Its modern name is Eskistanbul. Troas lies southwest of the ancient Ilium or Troy of Homer's Iliad. It was here that Paul had a vision of a man beckoning him to come over into Macedonia (Acts 16:8–11). Paul spent a week here preaching and teaching (Acts 20:6–12). Excavations show the existence of a Roman theater, temple, baths and aqueducts.

Ephesus, Philippi and Thessalonica are described in the introduction to the illustrated Book of Acts.

PICTORIAL GALATIANS, EPHESIANS, PHILIPPIANS, COLOSSIANS, 1 AND 2 THESSALONIANS, 1 AND 2 TIMOTHY, TITUS, PHILEMON AND HEBREWS (RS550P), COPYRIGHT 1963, AMERICAN BIBLE SOCIETY, NEW YORK, N. Y.
REVISED STANDARD VERSION, COPYRIGHT 1946 BY THE DIVISION OF CHRISTIAN EDUCATION, NATIONAL COUNCIL OF CHURCHES, U. S. A.

Tarsus in Cilicia. Ancient Roman brick wall with tunnel cut through to make modern street. Paul was born and brought up here

Sabit Merey

THE LETTER OF PAUL
TO THE
GALATIANS

Greetings

[Galatians 1:1–5] Paul an apostle—not from men nor through man, but through Jesus Christ and God the Father, who raised him from the dead—and all the brethren who are with me,

To the churches of Gala'tia:

Grace to you and peace from God the Father and our Lord Jesus Christ, who gave himself for our sins to deliver us from the present evil age, according to the will of our God and Father; to whom be the glory for ever and ever. Amen.

T. Goell

Cilician goats. In Paul's time the hair of such goats was used to make tent cloth at Tarsus

Weaver and loom in eastern Asia Minor
Goell & Doerner

There Is No Other Gospel [1:6–10]

I am astonished that you are so quickly deserting him who called you in the grace of Christ and turning to a different gospel—not that there is another gospel, but there are some who trouble you and want to pervert the gospel of Christ. But even if we, or an angel from heaven, should preach to you a gospel contrary to that which we preached to you, let him be accursed. As we have said before, so now I say again, If any one is preaching to you a gospel contrary to that which you received, let him be accursed.

Am I now seeking the favor of men, or of God? Or am I trying to please men? If I were still pleasing men, I should not be a servant[a] of Christ.

Paul's Becoming an Apostle [1:11–24]

For I would have you know, brethren, that the gospel which was preached by me is not man's[b] gospel. For I did not receive it from man, nor was I taught it, but it came through a revelation of Jesus Christ. For you have heard of my former life in Juda-ism, how I persecuted the church of God violently and tried to destroy it; and I advanced in Judaism beyond many of my own age among my people, so extremely zealous was I for the traditions of my fathers. But when he who had set me apart before I was born, and had called me through his grace, was pleased to reveal his Son to[c] me, in order that I might preach him among the Gentiles, I did not confer with flesh and blood, nor did I go up to Jerusalem to those who were apostles before me, but I went away into Arabia; and again I returned to Damascus.

Then after three years I went up to Jerusalem to visit Cephas, and remained with him fifteen days. But I saw none of the other apostles except James the Lord's brother. (In what I am writing to you, before God, I do not lie!) Then I went into the regions of Syria and Cili'cia. And I was still not known by sight to the churches of Christ in Jude'a; they only heard it said, "He who once persecuted us is now preaching the faith he once tried to destroy." And they glorified God because of me.

[a]Or *slave*
[b]Greek *according to man*

[c]Greek *in*

195

The sanctuary of the Moon God MEN, Pisidian Antioch

Goell & Doerner

The plain of Iconium. A shepherd with sheep and goats

Goell & Doerner

The mound of Derbe. Animals are drinking from a spring at its base

Goell & Doerner

Paul Accepted by the Other Apostles

[Galatians 2:1–10]

THEN after fourteen years I went up again to Jerusalem with Bar′nabas, taking Titus along with me. I went up by revelation; and I laid before them (but privately before those who were of repute) the gospel which I preach among the Gentiles, lest somehow I should be running or had run in vain. But even Titus, who was with me, was not compelled to be circumcised, though he was a Greek. But because of false brethren secretly brought in, who slipped in to spy out our freedom which we have in Christ Jesus, that they might bring us into bondage—to them we did not yield submission even for a moment, that the truth of the gospel might be preserved for you. And from those who were reputed to be something (what they were makes no difference to me; God shows no partiality) —those, I say, who were of repute added nothing to me; but on the contrary, when they saw that I had been entrusted with the gospel to the uncircumcised, just as Peter had been entrusted with the gospel to the circumcised (for he who worked through Peter for the mission to the circumcised worked through me also for the Gentiles), and when they perceived the grace that was given to me, James and Cephas and John, who were reputed to be pillars, gave to me and Bar′nabas the right hand of fellowship, that we should go to the Gentiles and they to the circumcised; only they would have us remember the poor, which very thing I was eager to do.

Paul Rebukes Peter at Antioch [2:11–21]

But when Cephas came to An′tioch I opposed him to his face, because he stood condemned. For before certain men came from James, he ate with the Gentiles; but when they came he drew back and separated himself, fearing the circumcision party. And with him the rest of the Jews acted insincerely, so that even Bar′nabas was carried away by their insincerity. But when I saw that they were not straightforward about the truth of the gospel, I said to Cephas before them all, "If you, though a Jew, live like a Gentile and not like a Jew, how can you compel the Gentiles to live like Jews?" We ourselves, who are Jews by birth and not Gentile sinners, yet who know that a man is not justified[d] by works of the law but through faith in Jesus Christ, even we have believed in Christ Jesus, in order to be justified by faith in Christ, and not by the works of the law, because by works of the law shall no one be justified.

[d] Or *reckoned righteous;* and so elsewhere

Goell & Doerner

The ancient site and mound of Lystra, with stream below

This stone found at Lystra is inscribed by the City Council to the deified Augustus. Probably it served as base for his statue

But if, in our endeavor to be justified in Christ, we ourselves were found to be sinners, is Christ then an agent of sin? Certainly not! But if I build up again those things which I tore down, then I prove myself a transgressor. For I through the law died to the law, that I might live to God. I have been crucified with Christ; it is no longer I who live, but Christ who lives in me; and the life I now live in the flesh I live by faith in the Son of God, who loved me and gave himself for me. I do not nullify the grace of God; for if justification[e] were through the law, then Christ died to no purpose.

Law or Faith [Galatians 3:1–14]

O FOOLISH Gala'tians! Who has bewitched you, before whose eyes Jesus Christ was publicly portrayed as crucified? Let me ask you only this: Did you receive the Spirit by works of the law, or by hearing with faith? Are you so foolish? Having begun with the Spirit, are you now ending with the flesh? Did you experience so many things in vain?—if it really is in vain. Does he who supplies the Spirit to you and works miracles among you do so by works of the law, or by hearing with faith?

Thus Abraham "believed God, and it was reckoned to him as righteousness."[1] So you see that it is men of faith who are the sons of Abraham. And the scripture, foreseeing that God would justify the Gentiles by faith, preached the gospel beforehand to Abraham, saying, "In you shall all the nations be blessed."[2] So then, those who are men of faith are blessed with Abraham who had faith.

For all who rely on works of the law are under a curse; for it is written, "Cursed be every one who does not abide by all things written in the book of the law, and do them."[3] Now it is evident that no man is justified before God by the law; for "He who through faith is righteous shall live";[f][4] but the law does not rest on faith, for "He who does them shall live by them."[5] Christ redeemed us from the curse of the law, having become a curse for us—for it is written, "Cursed be every one who hangs on a tree"[6]—that in Christ Jesus the blessing of Abraham might come upon the Gentiles, that we might receive the promise of the Spirit through faith.

The Law and the Promise [3:15–20]

To give a human example, brethren: no one annuls even a man's will,[g] or adds to it, once it has been ratified. Now the promises were made to Abraham and to his offspring. It does not say, "And to offsprings," referring to many; but, referring to one, "And to your offspring,"[7] which is Christ. This is what I mean: the law, which came four hundred and thirty years afterward, does not annul a covenant previously ratified by God, so as to make the promise void. For if the inheritance is by the law, it is no longer by promise; but God gave it to Abraham by a promise.

Why then the law? It was added because of transgressions, till the offspring should come to whom the promise had

University of Michigan, Kelsey Museum of Archaeology

Pisidia. Ruins of aqueduct serving ancient Antioch

been made; and it was ordained by angels through an intermediary. Now an intermediary implies more than one; but God is one.

The Purpose of the Law [3:21—4:7]

Is the law then against the promises of God? Certainly not; for if a law had been given which could make alive, then righteousness would indeed be by the law. But the scripture consigned all things to sin, that what was promised to faith in Jesus Christ might be given to those who believe.

Now before faith came, we were confined under the law, kept under restraint until faith should be revealed. So that the law was our custodian until Christ came, that we might be justified by faith. But now that faith has come, we are no longer under a custodian; for in Christ Jesus you are all sons of God, through faith. For as many of you as were baptized into Christ have put on Christ. There is neither Jew nor Greek, there is neither slave nor free, there is neither male nor female; for you are all one in Christ Jesus. And if you are Christ's, then you are Abraham's offspring, heirs according to promise.

I mean that the heir, as long as he is a child, is no better than a slave, though he is the owner of all the estate; but he is under guardians and trustees until the date set by the father. So with us; when we were children, we were slaves to the elemental spirits of the universe. But when the time had fully come, God sent forth his Son, born of woman, born under the law, to redeem those who were under the law, so that we might receive adoption as sons. And because you are sons, God has sent the Spirit of his Son into our hearts, crying, "Abba! Father!" So through God you are no longer a slave but a son, and if a son then an heir.

Paul's Concern for the Believers

[Galatians 4:8–20]

FORMERLY, when you did not know God, you were in bondage to beings that by nature are no gods; but now that you have come to know God, or rather to be known by God, how can you turn back again to the weak and beggarly elemental spirits, whose slaves you want to be once more? You observe days, and months, and seasons, and years! I am afraid I have labored over you in vain.

Antioch on the Orontes, where the disciples were first called Christians and where Peter and Paul met (Gal. 2:11)

Richard Stillwell

[e]Or *righteousness*
[f]Or *the righteous shall live by faith*
[g]Or *covenant* (as in verse 17)
[1]*Genesis* 15:6   [5]*Leviticus* 18:5
[2]*Genesis* 12:3; 18:18   [6]*Deuteronomy* 21:23
[3]*Deuteronomy* 27:26   [7]*Genesis* 12:7
[4]*Habakkuk* 2:4

Among the mountains of Sinai in Arabia, traditional site of Israelite encampment

Matson Photo Service

Sale of a slave standing on podium between a
slave dealer in Roman toga on the right and
his auctioneer in Greek garb on the left.
From funeral stele in the Museo Campano in
Capua, Italy. First century B.C.

Gallic (Galatian) chieftain slaying wife and self
to escape capture and bondage

Anderson

F. K. Doerner

*Ancyra (capital of the Roman province of Galatia). Part of the inscription in the temple of the
deified Augustus, which describes achievements of his reign and is of great historical importance.
It begins by stating that it is a copy of an inscription on bronze pillars at Rome*

Brethren, I beseech you, become as I am, for I also have become as you are. You did me no wrong; you know it was because of a bodily ailment that I preached the gospel to you at first; and though my condition was a trial to you, you did not scorn or despise me, but received me as an angel of God, as Christ Jesus. What has become of the satisfaction you felt? For I bear you witness that, if possible, you would have plucked out your eyes and given them to me. Have I then become your enemy by telling you the truth?[h] They make much of you, but for no good purpose; they want to shut you out, that you may make much of them. For a good purpose it is always good to be made much of, and not only when I am present with you. My little children, with whom I am again in travail until Christ be formed in you! I could wish to be present with you now and to change my tone, for I am perplexed about you.

The Allegory of Hagar and Sarah

[4:21-31]

Tell me, you who desire to be under law, do you not hear the law? For it is written that Abraham had two sons, one by a slave and one by a free woman. But the son of the slave was born according to the flesh, the son of the free woman through promise. Now this is an allegory: these women are two covenants. One is from Mount Si'nai, bearing children for slavery; she is Hagar. Now Hagar is Mount Si'nai in Arabia;[i] she corresponds to the present Jerusalem, for she is in slavery with her children. But the Jerusalem above is free, and she is our mother. For it is written,

"Rejoice, O barren one that dost not bear;
break forth and shout, thou who art not in travail;

[h] Or by dealing truly with you
[i] Other ancient authorities read *For Sinai is a mountain in Arabia*

for the desolate hath more children than she who hath a husband."[8]
Now we,[j] brethren, like Isaac, are children of promise. But as at that time he who was born according to the flesh persecuted him who was born according to the Spirit, so it is now. But what does the scripture say? "Cast out the slave and her son; for the son of the slave shall not inherit with the son of the free woman."[9] So, brethren, we are not children of the slave but of the free woman.

Stand Fast in Liberty [Galatians 5:1-15]

FOR freedom Christ has set us free; stand fast therefore, and do not submit again to a yoke of slavery.

Now I, Paul, say to you that if you receive circumcision, Christ will be of no advantage to you. I testify again to every man who receives circumcision that he is bound to keep the whole law. You are severed from Christ, you who would be justified by the law; you have fallen away from grace. For through the Spirit, by faith, we wait for the hope of righteousness. For in Christ Jesus neither circumcision nor uncircumcision is of any avail, but faith working through love. You were running well; who hindered you from obeying the truth? This persuasion is not from him who called you. A little leaven leavens the whole lump. I have confidence in the Lord that you will take no other view than mine; and he who is troubling you will bear his judgment, whoever he is. But if I, brethren, still preach circumcision, why am I still persecuted? In that case the stumbling block of the cross has been removed. I wish those who unsettle you would mutilate themselves!

For you were called to freedom, brethren; only do not use your freedom as an opportunity for the flesh, but through love be ser-

[j] Other ancient authorities read *you*
[8] Isaiah 54:1   [9] Genesis 21:10

Reconstruction of Temple of Augustus at Ancyra (Ankara)

Deutsches Archäologisches Institut, Berlin

Turkish Information Office

Ruins of the Temple of Augustus at Ancyra (Ankara). The inscription is on the lower part of the outside wall on the right

(1) God of Antioch, MEN, with Phrygian cap. Long scepter in right hand and statue of cock at right foot; bull's head under left foot

(2) Zeus of Iconium, with scepter and thunderbolt. Coin of first century B.C.

(3) Founder of Colonia Lystra tracing limits of city with a plow drawn by a white bull and a cow

(4) Heracles of Derbe with a club. Coin of Antoninus Pius, A.D. 138–161.

(5) Cybele seated, with lions at her feet, wearing crown of towers and holding a tympanum. Coin of Gordian III, A.D. 224–244.

(6) Perseus destroying the opponents of Hellenism by holding up the head of Medusa. Coin of Hadrian, A.D. 117–138.

(7) City goddess of Lystra, sitting on rocks, with crescent on her head and grain-ears in her hand. A river is at her feet

(8) Victory writing on a shield, probably from a statue at Derbe. Coin of Empress Lucilla

W. M. Ramsay

vants of one another. For the whole law is fulfilled in one word, "You shall love your neighbor as yourself."[10] But if you bite and devour one another take heed that you are not consumed by one another.

The Fruit of the Spirit and the Works of the Flesh [5:16–26]

But I say, walk by the Spirit, and do not gratify the desires of the flesh. For the desires of the flesh are against the Spirit, and the desires of the Spirit are against the flesh; for these are opposed to each other, to prevent you from doing what you would. But if you are led by the Spirit you are not under the law. Now the works of the flesh are plain: immorality, impurity, licentiousness, idolatry, sorcery, enmity, strife, jealousy, anger, selfishness, dissension, party spirit, envy,[k] drunkenness, carousing, and the like. I warn you, as I warned you before, that those who do such things shall not inherit the kingdom of God. But the fruit of the Spirit is love, joy, peace, patience, kindness, goodness, faithfulness, gentleness, self-control; against such there is no law. And those who belong to Christ Jesus have crucified the flesh with its passions and desires.

If we live by the Spirit, let us also walk by the Spirit. Let us have no self-conceit, no provoking of one another, no envy of one another.

Bear One Another's Burdens

[Galatians 6:1–10]

BRETHREN, if a man is overtaken in any trespass, you who are spiritual should restore him in a spirit of gentleness. Look to yourself, lest you too be tempted. Bear one another's burdens, and so fulfil the law of Christ. For if any one thinks he is something, when he is nothing, he deceives himself. But let each one test his own work, and then his reason to boast will be in himself alone and not in his neighbor. For each man will have to bear his own load.

Let him who is taught the word share all good things with him who teaches.

Do not be deceived; God is not mocked, for whatever a man sows, that he will also reap. For he who sows to his own flesh will from the flesh reap corruption; but he who sows to the Spirit will from the Spirit reap eternal life. And let us not grow weary in well-doing, for in due season we shall reap,

if we do not lose heart. So then, as we have opportunity, let us do good to all men, and especially to those who are of the household of faith.

Final Warning and Greeting [6:11–18]

See with what large letters I am writing to you with my own hand. It is those who want to make a good showing in the flesh that would compel you to be circumcised, and only in order that they may not be persecuted for the cross of Christ. For even those who receive circumcision do not themselves keep the law, but they desire to have you circumcised that they may glory in your flesh. But far be it from me to glory except in the cross of our Lord Jesus Christ, by which[l] the world has been crucified to me, and I to the world. For neither circumcision counts for anything, nor uncircumcision, but a new creation. Peace and mercy be upon all who walk by this rule, upon the Israel of God.

Henceforth let no man trouble me; for I bear on my body the marks of Jesus.

The grace of our Lord Jesus Christ be with your spirit, brethren. Amen.

[l]Or *through whom*

British Museum

American Numismatic Society

(1) Obverse, head of Diana. (2) Reverse, cult image of Diana. Gold stater of Ephesus. First century B.C.

(3) Diana and stag on coin of Hadrian, A.D. 117–138. (4) Sacred cart of Diana on coin of Antoninus Pius, A.D. 138–161

THE LETTER OF PAUL TO THE
EPHESIANS

Greetings

[Ephesians 1:1–2] Paul, an apostle of Christ Jesus by the will of God,
    To the saints who are also faithful[a] in Christ Jesus:
    Grace to you and peace from God our Father and the Lord Jesus Christ.

Spiritual Blessings in Christ [1:3–14]

Blessed be the God and Father of our Lord Jesus Christ, who has blessed us in Christ with every spiritual blessing in the

heavenly places, even as he chose us in him before the foundation of the world, that we should be holy and blameless before

[a] Other ancient authorities read *who are at Ephesus and faithful*

[k]Other ancient authorities add *murder*
[10]Leviticus 19:18

Ephesus. Reconstruction of Temple of Diana

him. He destined us in love[b] to be his sons through Jesus Christ, according to the purpose of his will, to the praise of his glorious grace which he freely bestowed on us in the Beloved. In him we have redemption through his blood, the forgiveness of our trespasses, according to the riches of his grace which he lavished upon us. For he has made known to us in all wisdom and insight the mystery of his will, according to his purpose which he set forth in Christ as a plan for the fulness of time, to unite all things in him, things in heaven and things on earth.

In him, according to the purpose of him who accomplishes all things according to the counsel of his will, we who first hoped in Christ have been destined and appointed to live for the praise of his glory.

[b]Or *before him in love, having destined us*

In him you also, who have heard the word of truth, the gospel of your salvation, and have believed in him, were sealed with the promised Holy Spirit, which is the guarantee of our inheritance until we acquire possession of it, to the praise of his glory.

Prayer for Wisdom and Knowledge

[1:15–23]

For this reason, because I have heard of your faith in the Lord Jesus and your love[c] toward all the saints, I do not cease to give thanks for you, remembering you in my prayers, that the God of our Lord Jesus Christ, the Father of glory, may give you a spirit of wisdom and of revelation in the knowledge of him, having the eyes of your

[c]Other ancient authorities omit *your love*

hearts enlightened, that you may know what is the hope to which he has called you, what are the riches of his glorious inheritance in the saints, and what is the immeasurable greatness of his power in us who believe, according to the working of his great might which he accomplished in Christ when he raised him from the dead and made him sit at his right hand in the heavenly places, far above all rule and authority and power and dominion, and above every name that is named, not only in this age but also in that which is to come; and he has put all things under his feet and has made him the head over all things for the church, which is his body, the fulness of him who fills all in all.

From Death to Life [Ephesians 2:1–10]

AND you he made alive, when you were dead through the trespasses and sins in which you once walked, following the course of this world, following the prince of the power of the air; the spirit that is now at work in the sons of disobedience. Among these we all once lived in the passions of our flesh, following the desires of body and mind, and so we were by nature children of wrath, like the rest of mankind. But God, who is rich in mercy, out of the great love with which he loved us, even when we were dead through our trespasses, made us alive together with Christ (by grace you have been saved), and raised us up with him, and made us sit with him in the heavenly places in Christ Jesus, that in the coming ages he might show the immeasurable riches of his grace in kindness toward us in Christ Jesus. For by grace you have been saved through faith; and this is not your own doing, it is the gift of God—not because of works, lest any man should boast. For we are his workmanship, created in Christ Jesus for good works, which God prepared beforehand, that we should walk in them.

Made One in Christ [2:11–22]

Therefore remember that at one time you Gentiles in the flesh, called the uncircumcision by what is called the circumcision, which is made in the flesh by hands—remember that you were at that time separated from Christ, alienated from the commonwealth of Israel, and strangers to the covenants of promise, having no hope and without God in the world. But now in Christ Jesus you who once were far off have been brought near in the blood of Christ. For he is our peace, who has made us both one, and has broken down the dividing wall of hostility, by abolishing in his flesh the law of commandments and ordinances, that he might create in himself one new man in place of the two, so making peace, and might reconcile us both to God in one body through the cross, thereby bringing the hostility to an end. And he came and preached peace to you who were far off and peace to those who were near; for through him we both have access in one Spirit to the Father. So then you are no longer strangers and sojourners, but you are fellow citizens with the saints and members of the household of God, built upon the foundation of the apostles and prophets, Christ Jesus himself being the cornerstone, in whom the whole structure is joined together and grows into a holy temple in the Lord; in whom you also are built into it for a dwelling place of God in the Spirit.

Ephesus. Ruins of the Temple of Diana in foreground

Paul's Ministry to the Gentiles

[Ephesians 3:1–13]

FOR this reason I, Paul, a prisoner for Christ Jesus on behalf of you Gentiles—assuming that you have heard of the stewardship of God's grace that was given to me for you, how the mystery was made known to me by revelation, as I have written briefly. When you read this you can perceive my insight into the mystery of Christ, which was not made known to the sons of men in other generations as it has now been revealed to his holy apostles and prophets by the Spirit; that is, how the Gentiles are fellow heirs, members of the same body, and partakers of the promise in Christ Jesus through the gospel.

Of this gospel I was made a minister according to the gift of God's grace which was given me by the working of his power. To me, though I am the very least of all the saints, this grace was given, to preach to the Gentiles the unsearchable riches of Christ, and to make all men see what is the plan of the mystery hidden for ages in[d] God who created all things; that through the church the manifold wisdom of God might now be made known to the principalities and powers in the heavenly places. This was according to the eternal purpose which he has realized in Christ Jesus our Lord, in whom we have boldness and confidence of access through our faith in him. So I ask you not to[e] lose heart over what I am suffering for you, which is your glory.

To Know The Love of Christ [3:14–21]

For this reason I bow my knees before the Father, from whom every family in heaven and on earth is named, that according to the riches of his glory he may grant you to be strengthened with might through his Spirit in the inner man, and that Christ may dwell in your hearts through faith; that you, being rooted and grounded in love, may have power to comprehend with all the saints what is the breadth and length and height and depth, and to know the love of Christ which surpasses knowledge, that you may be filled with all the fulness of God.

Now to him who by the power at work within us is able to do far more abundantly than all that we ask or think, to him be glory in the church and in Christ Jesus to all generations, for ever and ever. Amen.

The Unity of the Spirit [Ephesians 4:1–16]

I THEREFORE, a prisoner for the Lord, beg you to lead a life worthy of the calling to which you have been called, with all lowliness and meekness, with patience, forbearing one another in love, eager to maintain the unity of the Spirit in the bond of peace. There is one body and one Spirit, just as you were called to the one hope that belongs to your call, one Lord, one faith, one baptism, one God and Father of us all, who is above all and through all and in all. But grace was given to each of us according to the measure of Christ's gift. Therefore it is said,

"When he ascended on high he led a host of captives,
and he gave gifts to men."[1]

[d]Or *by*
[e]Or *I ask that I may not*
[1]Psalms 68:18

Oesterreichisches Archaeologisches Institut, Vienna

View of Ephesus from Bülbül Dagh

| 1 Temple of Diana | 2 Stadium | 3 Theater | 4 Market place |
| 5 Temple of Egyptian god Serapis | | 6 Arcadian Street | 7 Great gymnasium |

(In saying, "He ascended," what does it mean but that he had also descended into the lower parts of the earth? He who descended is he who also ascended far above all the heavens, that he might fill all things.) And his gifts were that some should be apostles, some prophets, some evangelists, some pastors and teachers, for the equipment of the saints, for the work of ministry, for building up the body of Christ, until we all attain to the unity of the faith and of the knowledge of the Son of God, to mature manhood, to the measure of the stature of the fulness of Christ; so that we may no longer be children, tossed to and fro and carried about with every wind of doctrine, by the cunning of men, by their craftiness in deceitful wiles. Rather, speaking the truth in love, we are to grow up in every way into him who is the head, into Christ, from whom the whole body, joined and knit together by every joint with which it is supplied, when each part is working properly, makes bodily growth and upbuilds itself in love.

The New Life in Christ [4:17–32]

Now this I affirm and testify in the Lord, that you must no longer live as the Gentiles do, in the futility of their minds; they are darkened in their understanding, alienated from the life of God because of the ignorance that is in them, due to their hardness of heart; they have become callous and have given themselves up to licentiousness, greedy to practice every kind of uncleanness. You did not so learn Christ!—assuming that you have heard about him and were taught in him, as the truth is in Jesus. Put off your old nature which belongs to your former manner of life and is corrupt through deceitful lusts, and be renewed in the spirit of your minds, and put on the new nature, created after the likeness of God in true righteousness and holiness.

Ephesus. Celsus' library, probably built in honor of the Roman senator C. Julius Celsus Polemaeanus, by his son

A. Donmez

201

"And do not get drunk with wine, for that is debauchery" (Eph. 5:18). Vintage scene on monumental Greco-Roman vase

British Museum

Therefore, putting away falsehood, let every one speak the truth with his neighbor, for we are members one of another. Be angry but do not sin; do not let the sun go down on your anger, and give no opportunity to the devil. Let the thief no longer steal, but rather let him labor, doing honest work with his hands, so that he may be able to give to those in need. Let no evil talk come out of your mouths, but only such as is good for edifying, as fits the occasion, that it may impart grace to those who hear. And do not grieve the Holy Spirit of God, in whom you were sealed for the day of redemption. Let all bitterness and wrath and anger and clamor and slander be put away from you, with all malice, and be kind to one another, tenderhearted, forgiving one another, as God in Christ forgave you.

"The whole armor of God" (Eph. 6:11). Roman soldiers, from the Altar of Ahenobarbus

Louvre

Walk as Children of Light
[Ephesians 5:1-20]

THEREFORE be imitators of God, as beloved children. And walk in love, as Christ loved us and gave himself up for us, a fragrant offering and sacrifice to God.

But immorality and all impurity or covetousness must not even be named among you, as is fitting among saints. Let there be no filthiness, nor silly talk, nor levity, which are not fitting, but instead let there be thanksgiving. Be sure of this, that no immoral or impure man, or one who is covetous (that is, an idolater), has any inheritance in the kingdom of Christ and of God. Let no one deceive you with empty words, for it is because of these things that the wrath of God comes upon the sons of disobedience. Therefore do not associate with them, for once you were darkness, but now you are light in the Lord; walk as children of light (for the fruit of light is found in all that is good and right and true), and try to learn what is pleasing to the Lord. Take no part in the unfruitful works of darkness, but instead expose them. For it is a shame even to speak of the things that they do in secret; but when anything is exposed by the light it becomes visible, for anything that becomes visible is light. Therefore it is said,

"Awake, O sleeper, and arise from the dead,
and Christ shall give you light."

Look carefully then how you walk, not as unwise men but as wise, making the most of the time, because the days are evil. Therefore do not be foolish, but understand what the will of the Lord is. And do not get drunk with wine, for that is debauchery; but be filled with the Spirit, addressing one another in psalms and hymns and spiritual songs, singing and making melody to the Lord with all your heart, always and for everything giving thanks in the name of our Lord Jesus Christ to God the Father.

Husbands and Wives [5:21-33]

Be subject to one another out of reverence for Christ. Wives, be subject to your husbands, as to the Lord. For the husband is the head of the wife as Christ is the head of the church, his body, and is himself its Savior. As the church is subject to Christ, so let wives also be subject in everything to their husbands. Husbands, love your wives, as Christ loved the church and gave himself up for her, that he might sanctify her, having cleansed her by the washing of water with the word, that he might present the church to himself in splendor, without spot or wrinkle or any such thing, that she might be holy and without blemish. Even so husbands should love their wives as their own bodies. He who loves his wife loves himself. For no man ever hates his own flesh, but nourishes and cherishes it, as Christ does the church, because we are members of his body. "For this reason a man shall leave his father and mother and be joined to his wife, and the two shall become one."[2] This is a great mystery, and I take it to mean Christ and the church; however, let each one of you love his wife as himself, and let the wife see that she respects her husband.

[2]Genesis 2:24

Obedience and Love [Ephesians 6:1-4]

CHILDREN, obey your parents in the Lord, for this is right. "Honor your father and mother"[3] (this is the first commandment with a promise), "that it may be well with you and that you may live long on the earth."[4] Fathers, do not provoke your children to anger, but bring them up in the discipline and instruction of the Lord.

Slaves and Masters [6:5-9]

Slaves, be obedient to those who are your earthly masters, with fear and trembling, in singleness of heart, as to Christ; not in the way of eye-service, as menpleasers, but as servants[f] of Christ, doing the will of God from the heart, rendering service with a good will as to the Lord and not to men, knowing that whatever good any one does, he will receive the same again from the Lord, whether he is a slave or free. Masters, do the same to them, and forbear threatening, knowing that he who is both their Master and yours is in heaven, and that there is no partiality with him.

The Whole Armor of God [6:10-20]

Finally, be strong in the Lord and in the strength of his might. Put on the whole armor of God, that you may be able to stand against the wiles of the devil. For we are not contending against flesh and blood, but against the principalities, against the powers, against the world rulers of this present darkness, against the spiritual hosts of wickedness in the heavenly places. Therefore take the whole armor of God, that you may be able to withstand in the evil day, and having done all, to stand. Stand therefore, having girded your loins with truth, and having put on the breastplate of righteousness, and having shod your feet with the equipment of the gospel of peace; above all taking the shield of faith, with which you can quench all the flaming darts of the evil one. And take the helmet of salvation, and the sword of the Spirit, which is the word of God. Pray at all times in the Spirit, with all prayer and supplication. To that end keep alert with all perseverance, making supplication for all the saints, and also for me, that utterance may be given me in opening my mouth boldly to proclaim the mystery of the gospel, for which I am an ambassador in chains; that I may declare it boldly, as I ought to speak.

Final Greetings [6:21-24]

Now that you also may know how I am and what I am doing, Tych'icus the beloved brother and faithful minister in the Lord will tell you everything. I have sent him to you for this very purpose, that you may know how we are, and that he may encourage your hearts.

Peace be to the brethren, and love with faith, from God the Father and the Lord Jesus Christ. Grace be with all who love our Lord Jesus Christ with love undying.

[f]Or slaves
[3]Exodus 20:12
[4]Deuteronomy 5:16

THE LETTER OF PAUL TO THE PHILIPPIANS

Air view of Neapolis, modern Cavalla

Greetings

[Philippians 1:1–2] Paul and Timothy, servants[a] of Christ Jesus,

To all the saints in Christ Jesus who are at Phil'ippi, with the bishops[b] and deacons:

Grace to you and peace from God our Father and the Lord Jesus Christ.

Paul's Prayer for the Philippian Christians [1:3–11]

I thank my God in all my remembrance of you, always in every prayer of mine for you all making my prayer with joy, thankful for your partnership in the gospel from the first day until now. And I am sure that he who began a good work in you will bring it to completion at the day of Jesus Christ. It is right for me to feel thus about you all, because I hold you in my heart, for you are all partakers with me of grace, both in my imprisonment and in the defense and confirmation of the gospel. For God is my witness, how I yearn for you all with the affection of Christ Jesus. And it is my prayer that your love may abound more and more, with knowledge and all discernment, so that you may approve what is excellent, and may be pure and blameless for the day of Christ, filled with the fruits of righteousness which come through Jesus Christ, to the glory and praise of God.

To Me to Live Is Christ [1:12–30]

I want you to know, brethren, that what has happened to me has really served to advance the gospel, so that it has become known throughout the whole praetor'ian guard[c] and to all the rest that my imprisonment is for Christ; and most of the brethren have been made confident in the Lord because of my imprisonment, and are much more bold to speak the word of God without fear.

Some indeed preach Christ from envy and rivalry, but others from good will. The latter do it out of love, knowing that I am put here for the defense of the gospel; the former proclaim Christ out of partisanship, not sincerely but thinking to afflict me in my imprisonment. What then? Only that in every way, whether in pretense or in truth, Christ is proclaimed; and in that I rejoice.

Yes, and I shall rejoice. For I know that through your prayers and the help of the Spirit of Jesus Christ this will turn out for my deliverance, as it is my eager expectation and hope that I shall not be at all ashamed, but that with full courage now as always Christ will be honored in my body, whether by life or by death. For to me to live is Christ, and to die is gain. If it is to be life in the flesh, that means fruitful labor for me. Yet which I shall choose I cannot tell. I am hard pressed between the two. My desire is to depart and be with Christ, for that is far better. But to remain in the flesh is more necessary on your account.

Convinced of this, I know that I shall remain and continue with you all, for your progress and joy in the faith, so that in me you may have ample cause to glory in Christ Jesus, because of my coming to you again.

Only let your manner of life be worthy of the gospel of Christ, so that whether I come and see you or am absent, I may hear of you that you stand firm in one spirit, with one mind striving side by side for the faith of the gospel, and not frightened in anything by your opponents. This is a clear omen to them of their destruction, but of your salvation, and that from God. For it has been granted to you that for the sake of Christ you should not only believe in him but also suffer for his sake, engaged in the same conflict which you saw and now hear to be mine.

Christ's Humiliation and Exaltation

[Philippians 2:1–11]

So if there is any encouragement in Christ, any incentive of love, any participation in the Spirit, any affection and sympathy, complete my joy by being of the same mind, having the same love, being in full accord and of one mind. Do nothing from selfishness or conceit, but in humility count others better than yourselves. Let each of you look not only to his own interests, but also to the interests of others. Have this mind among yourselves, which you have in Christ Jesus, who, though he was in the form of God, did not count equality with God a thing to be grasped, but emptied himself,[d] taking the form of a servant,[d] being born in the likeness of men. And being found in human form he humbled himself and became obedient unto death, even death on a cross. Therefore God has highly exalted him and bestowed on him the name which is above every name, that at the name of Jesus every knee should bow, in heaven and on earth and under the earth, and every tongue confess that Jesus Christ is Lord, to the glory of God the Father.

Shining as Lights in the World [2:12–18]

Therefore, my beloved, as you have always obeyed, so now, not only as in my presence but much more in my absence, work out your own salvation with fear and trembling; for God is at work in you, both to will and to work for his good pleasure.

Do all things without grumbling or questioning, that you may be blameless and

Bricked-up remains of the main barracks gate of the Praetorian Guard at Rome

innocent, children of God without blemish in the midst of a crooked and perverse generation, among whom you shine as lights in the world, holding fast the word of life, so that in the day of Christ I may be proud that I did not run in vain or labor in vain. Even if I am to be poured as a libation upon the sacrificial offering of your faith, I am glad and rejoice with you all. Likewise you also should be glad and rejoice with me.

Angista, believed by some to be the site outside Philippi where St. Paul preached by the riverside to Lydia and other women (Acts 16: 13)

[a]Or *slaves*
[b]Or *overseers*
[c]Greek *in the whole praetorium*

[d]Or *slave*

203

Ecole Francaise, Athens

Philippi. In the center is the ancient Roman forum on the Egnatian Way. At the upper right are the ruins of two fourth-century churches

Timothy and Epaphroditus [2:19-30]

I hope in the Lord Jesus to send Timothy to you soon, so that I may be cheered by news of you. I have no one like him, who will be genuinely anxious for your welfare. They all look after their own interests, not those of Jesus Christ. But Timothy's worth you know, how as a son with a father he has served with me in the gospel. I hope therefore to send him just as soon as I see how it will go with me; and I trust in the Lord that shortly I myself shall come also.

I have thought it necessary to send to you Epaphrodi'tus my brother and fellow worker and fellow soldier, and your messenger and minister to my need, for he has been longing for you all, and has been distressed because you heard that he was ill. Indeed he was ill, near to death. But God had mercy on him, and not only on him but on me also, lest I should have sorrow upon sorrow. I am the more eager to send him, therefore, that you may rejoice at seeing him again, and that I may be less anxious. So receive him in the Lord with all joy; and honor such men, for he nearly died for the work of Christ, risking his life to complete your service to me.

The True Righteousness
[Philippians 3:1-11]

FINALLY, my brethren, rejoice in the Lord. To write the same things to you is not irksome to me, and is safe for you. Look out for the dogs, look out for the evil-workers, look out for those who mutilate the flesh. For we are the true circum-

This mosaic from a house in Pompeii reads, "Beware of the dog"

Alinari

CAVE CANEM

cision, who worship God in spirit,^{e} and glory in Christ Jesus, and put no confidence in the flesh. Though I myself have reason for confidence in the flesh also. If any other man thinks he has reason for confidence in the flesh, I have more: circumcised on the eighth day, of the people of Israel, of the tribe of Benjamin, a Hebrew born of Hebrews; as to the law a Phar'isee, as to zeal a persecutor of the church, as to righteousness under the law blameless. But whatever gain I had, I counted as loss for the sake of Christ. Indeed I count everything as loss because of the surpassing worth of knowing Christ Jesus my Lord. For his sake I have suffered the loss of all things, and count them as refuse, in order that I may gain Christ and be found in him, not having a righteousness of my own, based on law, but that which is through faith in Christ, the righteousness from God that depends on faith; that I may know him and the power of his resurrection, and may share his sufferings, becoming like him in his death, that if possible I may attain the resurrection from the dead.

Pressing toward the Mark [3:12-16]

Not that I have already obtained this or am already perfect; but I press on to make it my own, because Christ Jesus has made me his own. Brethren, I do not consider that I have made it my own; but one thing I do, forgetting what lies behind and straining forward to what lies ahead. I press on toward the goal for the prize of the upward call of God in Christ Jesus. Let those of us who are mature be thus minded; and if in anything you are otherwise minded, God will reveal that also to you. Only let us hold true to what we have attained.

Awaiting Our Saviour [3:17-21]

Brethren, join in imitating me, and mark those who so live as you have an example in us. For many, of whom I have often told you and now tell you even with tears, live as enemies of the cross of Christ. Their end is destruction, their god is the belly, and they glory in their shame, with minds set on earthly things. But our commonwealth is in heaven, and from it we await a Savior, the Lord Jesus Christ, who will change our lowly body to be like his glorious body, by the power which enables him even to subject all things to himself.

^{e}Other ancient authorities read *worship by the Spirit of God*

Stand Firm in the Lord [Philippians 4:1-3]

THEREFORE, my brethren, whom I love and long for, my joy and crown, stand firm thus in the Lord, my beloved.

I entreat Eu-o'dia and I entreat Syn'tyche to agree in the Lord. And I ask you also, true yokefellow, help these women, for they have labored side by side with me in the gospel together with Clement and the rest of my fellow workers, whose names are in the book of life.

Rejoice in the Lord Always [4:4-7]

Rejoice in the Lord always; again I will say, Rejoice. Let all men know your forbearance. The Lord is at hand. Have no anxiety about anything, but in everything by prayer and supplication with thanksgiving let your requests be made known to God. And the peace of God, which passes all understanding, will keep your hearts and your minds in Christ Jesus.

Think about These Things [4:8-9]

Finally, brethren, whatever is true, whatever is honorable, whatever is just, whatever is pure, whatever is lovely, whatever is gracious, if there is any excellence, if there is anything worthy of praise, think about these things. What you have learned and received and heard and seen in me, do; and the God of peace will be with you.

Acknowledgment of the Philippians' Gift [4:10-20]

I rejoice in the Lord greatly that now at length you have revived your concern for me; you were indeed concerned for me, but you had no opportunity. Not that I complain of want; for I have learned, in whatever state I am, to be content. I know how to be abased, and I know how to abound; in any and all circumstances I have learned the secret of facing plenty and hunger, abundance and want. I can do all things in him who strengthens me.

Yet it was kind of you to share my trouble. And you Philip'pians yourselves know that in the beginning of the gospel, when I left Macedo'nia, no church entered into partnership with me in giving and receiving except you only; for even in Thessaloni'ca you sent me help^f once and again. Not that I seek the gift; but I seek the fruit which increases to your credit. I have received full payment, and more; I am filled, having received from Epaphrodi'tus the gifts you sent, a fragrant offering, a sacrifice acceptable and pleasing to God. And my God will supply every need of yours according to his riches in glory in Christ Jesus. To our God and Father be glory for ever and ever. Amen.

Final Greetings [4:21-23]

Greet every saint in Christ Jesus. The brethren who are with me greet you. All the saints greet you, especially those of Caesar's household.

The grace of the Lord Jesus Christ be with your spirit.

^{f}Other ancient authorities read *money for my needs*

204

← Temple of Mars Ultor (Mars the Avenger), built in Rome by Augustus to commemorate his victory at Philippi, in 42 B.C., over the murderers of Julius Caesar

→ This procession from the Altar of Peace of Augustus shows members of his household, not including slaves

Gabinetto Fotografico Nazionale, Rome

Felbermeyer

THE LETTER OF PAUL TO THE
COLOSSIANS

Greetings

[Colossians 1:1–2] Paul, an apostle of Christ Jesus by the will of God, and Timothy our brother,

To the saints and faithful brethren in Christ at Colos'sae:

Grace to you and peace from God our Father.

Sherman E. Johnson by courtesy of Zion Research Foundation

Colossae lies in a gap between hills. This view is taken from the site of Laodicea

Paul's Prayer for the Colossian Christians [1:3–14]

We always thank God, the Father of our Lord Jesus Christ, when we pray for you, because we have heard of your faith in Christ Jesus and of the love which you have for all the saints, because of the hope laid up for you in heaven. Of this you have heard before in the word of the truth, the gospel which has come to you, as indeed in the whole world it is bearing fruit and growing—so among yourselves, from the day you heard and understood the grace of God in truth, as you learned it from Ep'-aphras our beloved fellow servant. He is a faithful minister of Christ on our[a] behalf and has made known to us your love in the Spirit.

And so, from the day we heard of it, we have not ceased to pray for you, asking that you may be filled with the knowledge of his will in all spiritual wisdom and understanding, to lead a life worthy of the Lord, fully pleasing to him, bearing fruit in every good work and increasing in the knowledge of God. May you be strengthened with all power, according to his glorious might, for all endurance and patience with joy, giving thanks to the Father, who has qualified us[b] to share in the inheritance of the saints in light. He has delivered us from the dominion of darkness and transferred us to the kingdom of his beloved Son, in whom we have redemption, the forgiveness of sins.

The Fulness of God [1:15–23]

He is the image of the invisible God, the first-born of all creation; for in him all things were created, in heaven and on earth, visible and invisible, whether thrones or dominions or principalities or authorities —all things were created through him and for him. He is before all things, and in him all things hold together. He is the head of the body, the church; he is the beginning, the first-born from the dead, that in everything he might be pre-eminent. For in him all the fulness of God was pleased to dwell, and through him to reconcile to himself all things, whether on earth or in heaven, making peace by the blood of his cross.

And you, who once were estranged and hostile in mind, doing evil deeds, he has now reconciled in his body of flesh by his death, in order to present you holy and blameless and irreproachable before him, provided that you continue in the faith, stable and steadfast, not shifting from the hope of the gospel which you heard, which has been preached to every creature under heaven, and of which I, Paul, became a minister.

Paul's Ministry to the Church [1:24—2:7]

Now I rejoice in my sufferings for your sake, and in my flesh I complete what is lacking in Christ's afflictions for the sake of his body, that is, the church, of which I became a minister according to the divine office which was given to me for you, to make the word of God fully known, the mystery hidden for ages and generations[c] but now made manifest to his saints. To them God chose to make known how great among the Gentiles are the riches of the glory of this mystery, which is Christ in you, the hope of glory. Him we proclaim, warning every man and teaching every man in all wisdom, that we may present every man mature in Christ. For this I toil, striving with all the energy which he mightily inspires within me.

For I want you to know how greatly I strive for you, and for those at La'-odice'a, and for all who have not seen my face, that their hearts may be encouraged as they are knit together in love, to have all the riches of assured understanding and the knowledge of God's mystery, of Christ, in whom are hid all the treasures of wisdom and knowledge. I say this in order that no one may delude you with beguiling speech. For though I am absent in body, yet I am with you in spirit, rejoicing to see your good order and the firmness of your faith in Christ.

As therefore you received Christ Jesus the Lord, so live in him, rooted and built up in him and established in the faith, just as you were taught, abounding in thanksgiving.

Fulness of Life in Christ

[Colossians 2:8–15]

SEE to it that no one makes a prey of you by philosophy and empty deceit, according to human tradition, according to the elemental spirits of the universe, and not according to Christ. For in him the whole fulness of deity dwells bodily, and you have come to fulness of life in him, who is the head of all rule and authority. In him also you were circumcised with a circumcision made without hands, by putting off the body of flesh in the circumcision of Christ; and you were buried with him in baptism, in which you were also raised with him through faith in the working of God, who raised him from the dead. And you, who were dead in trespasses and the uncircumcision of your flesh, God made alive together with him, having forgiven us all our trespasses, having canceled the bond which stood against us with its legal demands; this he set aside, nailing it to the cross. He disarmed the principalities and powers and made a public example of them, triumphing over them in him.[d]

Seek the Things Which Are Above

[2:16–3:4]

Therefore let no one pass judgment on you in questions of food and drink or with

[a]Other ancient authorities read *your*
[b]Other ancient authorities read *you*

[c]Or *from angels and men*

[d]Or *in it* (that is, the cross)

Sherman E. Johnson by courtesy of Zion Research Foundation

Ruins of Hierapolis

Felbermeyer

Two Roman slaves being freed by their master in the presence of an official (fasces in left hand), who touches one of them with the manumission rod. Note the pileus or conical hat on the head of each slave, indicating that they are being freed. Probably first century B.C.

regard to a festival or a new moon or a sabbath. These are only a shadow of what is to come; but the substance belongs to Christ. Let no one disqualify you, insisting on self-abasement and worship of angels, taking his stand on visions, puffed up without reason by his sensuous mind, and not holding fast to the Head, from whom the whole body, nourished and knit together through its joints and ligaments, grows with a growth that is from God.

If with Christ you died to the elemental spirits of the universe, why do you live as if you still belonged to the world? Why do you submit to regulations, "Do not handle, Do not taste, Do not touch" (referring to things which all perish as they are used), according to human precepts and doctrines? These have indeed an appearance of wisdom in promoting rigor of devotion and self-abasement and severity to the body, but they are of no value in checking the indulgence of the flesh.[e]

If then you have been raised with Christ, seek the things that are above, where Christ is, seated at the right hand of God. Set your minds on things that are above, not on things that are on earth. For you have died, and your life is hid with Christ in God. When Christ who is our life appears, then you also will appear with him in glory.

The Old Life and the New

[Colossians 3:5-17]

PUT to death therefore what is earthly in you: immorality, impurity, passion,

[e]Or *are of no value, serving only to indulge the flesh*

evil desire, and covetousness, which is idolatry. On account of these the wrath of God is coming.[f] In these you once walked, when you lived in them. But now put them all away: anger, wrath, malice, slander, and foul talk from your mouth. Do not lie to one another, seeing that you have put off the old nature with its practices and have put on the new nature, which is being renewed in knowledge after the image of its creator. Here there cannot be Greek and Jew, circumcised and uncircumcised, barbarian, Scyth'ian, slave, free man, but Christ is all, and in all.

Put on then, as God's chosen ones, holy and beloved, compassion, kindness, lowliness, meekness, and patience, forbearing one another and, if one has a complaint against another, forgiving each other; as the Lord has forgiven you, so you also must forgive. And above all these put on love, which binds everything together in perfect harmony. And let the peace of Christ rule in your hearts, to which indeed you were called in the one body. And be thankful. Let the word of Christ dwell in you richly, as you teach and admonish one another in all wisdom, and as you sing psalms and hymns and spiritual songs with thankfulness in your hearts to God. And whatever you do, in word or deed, do everything in the name of the Lord Jesus, giving thanks to God the Father through him.

Social Duties of the New Life [3:18—4:6]

Wives, be subject to your husbands, as is fitting in the Lord. Husbands, love your wives, and do not be harsh with them. Children, obey your parents in everything, for this pleases the Lord. Fathers, do not provoke your children, lest they become discouraged. Slaves, obey in everything those who are your earthly masters, not with eyeservice, as menpleasers, but in singleness of heart, fearing the Lord. Whatever your task, work heartily, as serving the Lord and not men, knowing that from the Lord you will receive the inheritance as your reward; you are serving the Lord Christ. For the wrongdoer will be paid back for the wrong he has done, and there is no partiality.

Masters, treat your slaves justly and fairly, knowing that you also have a Master in heaven.

Continue steadfastly in prayer, being watchful in it with thanksgiving; and pray for us also, that God may open to us a door for the word, to declare the mystery of Christ, on account of which I am in prison, that I may make it clear, as I ought to speak.

Conduct yourselves wisely toward outsiders, making the most of the time. Let your speech always be gracious, seasoned with salt, so that you may know how you ought to answer every one.

Final Greetings [Colossians 4:7-18]

TYCH'ICUS will tell you all about my affairs; he is a beloved brother and faithful minister and fellow servant in the Lord. I have sent him to you for this very purpose, that you may know how we are and that he may encourage your hearts, and with him Ones'imus, the faithful and

[f]Other ancient authorities add *upon the sons of disobedience*

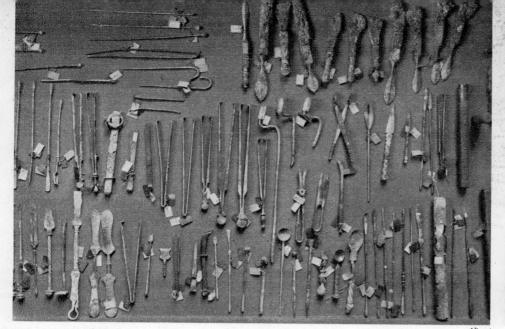
Luke was a physician. These surgical instruments from his time were found at Pompeii
Alinari

Greek Government
Athens. Air view of the Acropolis

beloved brother, who is one of yourselves. They will tell you of everything that has taken place here.

Aristar'chus my fellow prisoner greets you, and Mark the cousin of Bar'nabas (concerning whom you have received instructions—if he comes to you, receive him), and Jesus who is called Justus. These are the only men of the circumcision among my fellow workers for the kingdom of God, and they have been a comfort to me. Ep'-aphras, who is one of yourselves, a servant[g] of Christ Jesus, greets you, always remembering you earnestly in his prayers, that you may stand mature and fully assured in
[g]Or *slave*

all the will of God. For I bear him witness that he has worked hard for you and for those in La'-odice'a and in Hi-erap'olis. Luke the beloved physician and Demas greet you. Give my greetings to the brethren at La'-odice'a, and to Nympha and the church in her house. And when this letter has been read among you, have it read also in the church of the La'-odice'ans; and see that you read also the letter from La'-odice'a. And say to Archip'pus, "See that you fulfil the ministry which you have received in the Lord."

I, Paul, write this greeting with my own hand. Remember my fetters. Grace be with you.

THE FIRST LETTER OF PAUL TO THE
THESSALONIANS

S. M. Jordanidis
Salonica. Galerius, A.D. 305–311, built this arch over the Egnatian Way, traveled earlier by Paul

Greetings

[1 Thessalonians 1:1] Paul, Silva'nus, and Timothy,

To the church of the Thessalo'nians in God the Father and the Lord Jesus Christ:

Grace to you and peace.

The Thessalonians' Faith and Example
[1:2–10]

We give thanks to God always for you all, constantly mentioning you in our prayers, remembering before our God and Father your work of faith and labor of love and steadfastness of hope in our Lord Jesus Christ. For we know, brethren beloved by God, that he has chosen you; for our gospel came to you not only in word, but also in power and in the Holy Spirit and with full conviction. You know what kind of men we proved to be among you for your sake. And you became imitators of us and

of the Lord, for you received the word in much affliction, with joy inspired by the Holy Spirit; so that you became an example to all the believers in Macedo'nia and in Achai'a. For not only has the word of the Lord sounded forth from you in Macedo'nia and Achai'a, but your faith in God has gone forth everywhere, so that we need not say anything. For they themselves report concerning us what a welcome we had among you, and how you turned to God from idols, to serve a living and true God, and to wait for his Son from heaven, whom he raised from the dead, Jesus who delivers us from the wrath to come.

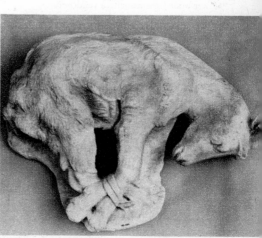
Metropolitan Museum of Art
Model of trussed-up goat ready for sacrifice

Athens. Inscription on the Temple of the Goddess Roma and Augustus. This temple, 24 feet, 6 inches in diameter, was about 100 feet east of the Parthenon. It had nine Ionic columns similar to those of the Erechtheum and was set up, as the inscription records, "by the people on the Acropolis in the time of Marathonius, priest of the Goddess Roma and Augustus Savior" (between 27 and 17 B.C.)

W. B. Dinsmoor

Paul's Ministry in Thessalonica

[1 Thessalonians 2:1–16]

FOR you yourselves know, brethren, that our visit to you was not in vain; but though we had already suffered and been shamefully treated at Phil'ippi, as you know, we had courage in our God to declare to you the gospel of God in the face of great opposition. For our appeal does not spring from error or uncleanness, nor is it made with guile; but just as we have been approved by God to be entrusted with the gospel, so we speak, not to please men, but to please God who tests our hearts. For we never used either words of flattery, as you know, or a cloak for greed, as God is witness; nor did we seek glory from men, whether from you or from others, though we might have made demands as apostles of Christ. But we were gentle[a] among you, like a nurse taking care of her children. So, being affectionately desirous of you, we were ready to share with you not only the gospel of God but also our own selves, because you had become very dear to us.

For you remember our labor and toil, brethren; we worked night and day, that we might not burden any of you, while we preached to you the gospel of God. You are witnesses, and God also, how holy and righteous and blameless was our behavior to you believers; for you know how, like a father with his children, we exhorted each one of you and encouraged you and charged you to lead a life worthy of God, who calls you into his own kingdom and glory.

And we also thank God constantly for this, that when you received the word of God which you heard from us, you accepted it not as the word of men but as what it really is, the word of God, which is at work in you believers. For you, brethren, became imitators of the churches of God in Christ Jesus which are in Jude'a; for you suffered the same things from your own countrymen as they did from the Jews, who killed both the Lord Jesus and the prophets, and drove us out, and displease God and oppose all men by hindering us from speaking to the Gentiles that they may be saved—so as always to fill up the measure of their sins. But God's wrath has come upon them at last![b]

Paul's Desire to Visit the Church Again

[2:17–3:13]

But since we were bereft of you, brethren, for a short time, in person not in heart, we endeavored the more eagerly and with great desire to see your face to face; because we wanted to come to you—I, Paul, again and again—but Satan hindered us. For what is our hope or joy or crown of boasting before our Lord Jesus at his coming? Is it not you? For you are our glory and joy.

Therefore when we could bear it no longer, we were willing to be left behind at Athens alone, and we sent Timothy, our brother and God's servant in the gospel of Christ, to establish you in your faith and to exhort you, that no one be moved by these afflictions. You yourselves know that this is to be our lot. For when we were with you, we told you beforehand that we were to suffer affliction; just as it has come to pass, and as you know. For this reason, when I could bear it no longer, I sent that I might know your faith, for fear that somehow the tempter had tempted you and that our labor would be in vain.

But now that Timothy has come to us from you, and has brought us the good news of your faith and love and reported that you always remember us kindly and long to see us, as we long to see you—for this reason, brethren, in all our distress and affliction we have been comforted about you through your faith; for now we live, if you stand fast in the Lord. For what thanksgiving can we render to God for you, for all the joy which we feel for your sake before our God, praying earnestly night and day that we may see you face to face and supply what is lacking in your faith?

Now may our God and Father himself, and our Lord Jesus, direct our way to you; and may the Lord make you increase and abound in love to one another and to all men, as we do to you, so that he may establish your hearts unblamable in holiness before our God and Father, at the coming of our Lord Jesus with all his saints.

A Life Pleasing to God

[1 Thessalonians 4:1–12]

FINALLY, brethren, we beseech and exhort you in the Lord Jesus, that as you learned from us how you ought to live and to please God, just as you are doing, you do so more and more. For you know what instructions we gave you through the Lord Jesus. For this is the will of God, your sanctification: that you abstain from immorality; that each one of you know how to take a wife for himself in holiness and honor, not in the passion of lust like heathen who do not know God; that no man transgress, and wrong his brother in this matter,[c] because the Lord is an avenger in all these things, as we solemnly forewarned you. For God has not called us for uncleanness, but in holiness. Therefore whoever disregards this, disregards not man but God, who gives his Holy Spirit to you.

But concerning love of the brethren you have no need to have any one write to you, for you yourselves have been taught by God to love one another; and indeed you do love all the brethren throughout Macedo'nia. But we exhort you, brethren, to do so more and more, to aspire to live quietly, to mind your own affairs, and to work with your

[a]Other ancient authorities read *babes*

[b]Or *completely*, or *for ever*

[c]Or *defraud his brother in business*

Reconstruction of Vardar Gate, through which Paul passed on the Egnatian Way at Thessalonica. This gate bore the inscription mentioning the Politarchs as the rulers of Thessalonica, as reported by Luke in Acts 17:6, 8

hands, as we charged you; so that you may command the respect of outsiders, and be dependent on nobody.

The Dead and the Living at the Lord's Coming [4:13–18]

But we would not have you ignorant, brethren, concerning those who are asleep, that you may not grieve as others do who have no hope. For since we believe that Jesus died and rose again, even so, through Jesus, God will bring with him those who have fallen asleep. For this we declare to you by the word of the Lord, that we who are alive, who are left until the coming of the Lord, shall not precede those who have fallen asleep. For the Lord himself will descend from heaven with a cry of command, with the archangel's call, and with the sound of the trumpet of God. And the dead in Christ will rise first; then we who are alive, who are left, shall be caught up together with them in the clouds to meet the Lord in the air; and so we shall always be with the Lord. Therefore comfort one another with these words.

Be Ready for the Lord's Coming

[1 Thessalonians 5:1–11]

BUT as to the times and the seasons, brethren, you have no need to have anything written to you. For you yourselves know well that the day of the Lord will come like a thief in the night. When people say, "There is peace and security," then sudden destruction will come upon them as travail comes upon a woman with child, and there will be no escape. But you are not in darkness, brethren, for that day to

"Those who get drunk are drunk at night" (1 Thess. 5:7). Attic red-figured cup, about 500 B.C.

Felbermeyer

surprise you like a thief. For you are all sons of light and sons of the day; we are not of the night or of darkness. So then let us not sleep, as others do, but let us keep awake and be sober. For those who sleep sleep at night, and those who get drunk are drunk at night. But, since we belong to the day, let us be sober, and put on the breastplate of faith and love, and for a helmet the hope of salvation. For God has not destined us for wrath, but to obtain salvation through our Lord Jesus Christ, who died for us so that whether we wake or sleep we might live with him. Therefore encourage one another and build one another up, just as you are doing.

Final Exhortations and Greetings

[5:12–28]

But we beseech you, brethren, to respect those who labor among you and are over you in the Lord and admonish you, and to esteem them very highly in love because of their work. Be at peace among yourselves. And we exhort you, brethren, admonish the idle, encourage the fainthearted, help the weak, be patient with them all. See that none of you repays evil for evil, but always seek to do good to one another and to all. Rejoice always, pray constantly, give thanks in all circumstances; for this is the will of God in Christ Jesus for you. Do not quench the Spirit, do not despise prophesying, but test everything; hold fast what is good, abstain from every form of evil.

May the God of peace himself sanctify you wholly; and may your spirit and soul and body be kept sound and blameless at the coming of our Lord Jesus Christ. He who calls you is faithful, and he will do it.

Brethren, pray for us.

Greet all the brethren with a holy kiss.

I adjure you by the Lord that this letter be read to all the brethren.

The grace of our Lord Jesus Christ be with you.

THE SECOND LETTER OF PAUL TO THE
THESSALONIANS

Greetings

[2 Thessalonians 1:1–2] Paul, Silva′nus, and Timothy,

To the church of the Thessalo′nians in God our Father and the Lord Jesus Christ:

Grace to you and peace from God the Father and the Lord Jesus Christ.

Time may have passed slowly for Paul, left at Athens alone. The Tower of the Winds, or Horologion, which probably contained a water clock as well as sundials, was the public timepiece in Athens

Philip Gendreau

The Judgment at Christ's Coming

[1:3–12]

We are bound to give thanks to God always for you, brethren, as is fitting, because your faith is growing abundantly, and the love of every one of you for one another is increasing. Therefore we ourselves boast of you in the churches of God for your steadfastness and faith in all your persecutions and in the afflictions which you are enduring.

This is evidence of the righteous judgment of God, that you may be made worthy of the kingdom of God, for which you are suffering—since indeed God deems it just to repay with affliction those who afflict you, and to grant rest with us to you who are afflicted, when the Lord Jesus is re-

vealed from heaven with his mighty angels in flaming fire, inflicting vengeance upon those who do not know God and upon those who do not obey the gospel of our Lord Jesus. They shall suffer the punishment of eternal destruction and exclusion from the presence of the Lord and from the glory of his might, when he comes on that day to be glorified in his saints, and to be marveled at in all who have believed, because our testimony to you was believed. To this end we always pray for you, that our God may make you worthy of his call, and may fulfil every good resolve and work of faith by his power, so that the name of our Lord Jesus may be glorified in you, and you in him, according to the grace of our God and the Lord Jesus Christ.

This bronze plaque of the city of Assos reports that the government of Assos by popular vote in A.D. 37 begs the favor of the Emperor Caligula, saying that "Every city and every nation is eager to behold the face of the God, feeling that the most delightful age for mankind is now begun. . . . We swear by the Savior and God, Caesar Augustus, and by our holy local deity, Athena, to be loyal to Gaius Caesar Augustus and all his house, to deem as friends those whom he favors and as enemies those whom he designates. With things to go well with us if we keep our oath, and the opposite if we break it"

The Man of Lawlessness

[2 Thessalonians 2:1–12]

NOW concerning the coming of our Lord Jesus Christ and our assembling to meet him, we beg you, brethren, not to be quickly shaken in mind or excited, either by spirit or by word, or by letter purporting to be from us, to the effect that the day of the Lord has come. Let no one deceive you in any way; for that day will not come, unless the rebellion comes first, and the man of lawlessness[a] is revealed, the son of perdition, who opposes and exalts himself against every so-called god or object of worship, so that he takes his seat in the temple of God, proclaiming himself to be God. Do you not remember that when I was still with you I told you this? And you know what is restraining him now so that he may be revealed in his time. For the mystery of lawlessness is already at work; only he who now restrains it will do so until he is out of the way. And then the lawless one will be revealed, and the Lord Jesus will slay him with the breath of his mouth and destroy him by his appearing and his coming. The coming of the lawless one by the activity of Satan will be with all power and with pretended signs and wonders, and with all wicked deception for those who are to perish, because they refused to love the truth and so be saved. Therefore God sends upon them a strong delusion, to make them believe what is false, so that all may be con-

[a]Other ancient authorities read sin

demned who did not believe the truth but had pleasure in unrighteousness.

Chosen to Salvation [2:13–17]

But we are bound to give thanks to God always for you, brethren beloved by the Lord, because God chose you from the beginning[b] to be saved, through sanctification by the Spirit[c] and belief in the truth. To this he called you through our gospel, so that you may obtain the glory of our Lord Jesus Christ. So then, brethren, stand firm and hold to the traditions which you were taught by us, either by word of mouth or by letter.

Now may our Lord Jesus Christ himself, and God our Father, who loved us and gave us eternal comfort and good hope through grace, comfort your hearts and establish them in every good work and word.

Pray for Us [2 Thessalonians 3:1–5]

FINALLY, brethren, pray for us, that the word of the Lord may speed on and triumph, as it did among you, and that we may be delivered from wicked and evil men; for not all have faith. But the Lord is faithful; he will strengthen you and guard you from evil.[d] And we have confidence in the Lord about you, that you are doing and will do the things which we command. May the Lord direct your hearts to the love of God and to the steadfastness of Christ.

The Obligation to Work [3:6–15]

Now we command you, brethren, in the name of our Lord Jesus Christ, that you keep away from any brother who is living in idleness and not in accord with the tradition that you received from us. For you yourselves know how you ought to imitate us; we were not idle when we were with you, we did not eat any one's bread without paying, but with toil and labor we worked night and day, that we might not burden any of you. It was not because we have not that right, but to give you in our conduct an example to imitate. For even when we were with you, we gave you this command: If any one will not work, let him not eat. For we hear that some of you are living in idleness, mere busybodies, not doing any work. Now such persons we command and exhort in the Lord Jesus Christ to do their work in quietness and to earn their own living. Brethren, do not be weary in well-doing.

If any one refuses to obey what we say in this letter, note that man, and have nothing to do with him, that he may be ashamed. Do not look on him as an enemy, but warn him as a brother.

Benediction [3:16–18]

Now may the Lord of peace himself give you peace at all times in all ways. The Lord be with you all.

I, Paul, write this greeting with my own hand. This is the mark in every letter of mine; it is the way I write. The grace of our Lord Jesus Christ be with you all.

[b]Other ancient authorities read as the first converts
[c]Or of spirit
[d]Or the evil one

Salonica (Thessalonica); looking down at the harbor from a hill

S. M. Jordanidis

"We did not eat any one's bread without paying, but with toil and labor we worked night and day, that we might not burden any of you" (2 Thess. 3:8). Weaving tent-cloth in Palestine

C. C. McCown

THE FIRST LETTER OF PAUL TO TIMOTHY

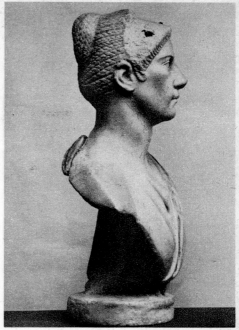

Metropolitan Museum of Art

"Not with braided hair" (1 Tim. 2:9)

Greetings

[1 Timothy 1:1–2] Paul, an apostle of Christ Jesus by command of God our Savior and of Christ Jesus our hope,

To Timothy, my true child in the faith:

Grace, mercy, and peace from God the Father and Christ Jesus our Lord.

Warning against False Doctrine [1:3–11]

As I urged you when I was going to Macedo′nia, remain at Eph′esus that you may charge certain persons not to teach any different doctrine, nor to occupy themselves with myths and endless genealogies which promote speculations rather than the divine training[a] that is in faith; whereas the aim of our charge is love that issues from a pure heart and a good conscience and sincere faith. Certain persons by swerving from these have wandered away into vain discussion, desiring to be teachers of the law, without understanding either what they are saying or the things about which they make assertions.

Now we know that the law is good, if any one uses it lawfully, understanding this, that the law is not laid down for the just but for the lawless and disobedient, for the ungodly and sinners, for the unholy and profane, for murderers of fathers and murderers of mothers, for manslayers, immoral persons, sod′omites, kidnapers, liars, perjurers, and whatever else is contrary to sound doctrine, in accordance with the glorious gospel of the blessed God with which I have been entrusted.

Paul's Thankfulness for Mercy [1:12–20]

I thank him who has given me strength for this, Christ Jesus our Lord, because he judged me faithful by appointing me to his service, though I formerly blasphemed and persecuted and insulted him; but I received mercy because I had acted ignorantly in unbelief, and the grace of our Lord overflowed for me with the faith and love that are in Christ Jesus. The saying is sure and worthy of full acceptance, that Christ Jesus came into the world to save sinners. And I am the foremost of sinners; but I received mercy for this reason, that in me, as the foremost, Jesus Christ might display his perfect patience for an example to those who were to believe in him for eternal life. To the King of ages, immortal, invisible, the only God, be honor and glory for ever and ever.[b] Amen.

This charge I commit to you, Timothy, my son, in accordance with the prophetic utterances which pointed to you, that inspired by them you may wage the good warfare, holding faith and a good conscience. By rejecting conscience, certain persons have made shipwreck of their faith, among them Hymenae′us and Alexander, whom I have delivered to Satan that they may learn not to blaspheme.

Instructions Concerning Prayer

[1 Timothy 2:1–15]

FIRST of all, then, I urge that supplications, prayers, intercessions, and thanksgivings be made for all men, for kings and all who are in high positions, that we may lead a quiet and peaceable life, godly and respectful in every way. This is good, and it is acceptable in the sight of God our Savior, who desires all men to be saved and to come to the knowledge of the truth. For there is one God, and there is one mediator between God and men, the man Christ Jesus, who gave himself as a ransom for all, the testimony to which was borne at the proper time. For this I was appointed a preacher and apostle (I am telling the truth, I am not lying), a teacher of the Gentiles in faith and truth.

I desire then that in every place the men should pray, lifting holy hands without anger or quarreling; also that women should adorn themselves modestly and sensibly in seemly apparel, not with braided hair or gold or pearls or costly attire but by good deeds, as befits women who profess religion. Let a woman learn in silence with all submissiveness. I permit no woman to teach or to have authority over men; she is to keep silent. For Adam was formed first, then Eve; and Adam was not deceived, but the woman was deceived and became a transgressor. Yet woman will be saved through bearing children,[c] if she continues[d] in faith and love and holiness, with modesty.

Qualifications of Bishops [1 Timothy 3:1–7]

THE saying is sure: If any one aspires to the office of bishop, he desires a noble task. Now a bishop must be above reproach, the husband of one wife, temperate, sensible, dignified, hospitable, an apt teacher, no drunkard, not violent but gentle, not quarrelsome, and no lover of money. He must manage his own household well, keeping his children submissive and respectful in every way; for if a man does not know how to manage his own household, how can he care for God's church? He must not be a recent convert, or he may be puffed up with conceit and fall into the condemnation of the devil;[f] moreover he must be well thought of by outsiders, or he may fall into reproach and the snare of the devil.[f]

Qualifications of Deacons [3:8–13]

Deacons likewise must be serious, not double-tongued, not addicted to much wine, not greedy for gain; they must hold the mystery of the faith with a clear conscience. And let them also be tested first; then if they prove themselves blameless let them serve as deacons. The women likewise must be serious, no slanderers, but temperate, faithful in all things. Let deacons be the husband of one wife, and let them manage their children and their households well; for those who serve well as deacons gain a good standing for themselves and also great confidence in the faith which is in Christ Jesus.

The Mystery of Our Religion [3:14–16]

I hope to come to you soon, but I am writing these instructions to you so that, if I am delayed, you may know how one ought to behave in the household of God, which is the church of the living God, the pillar and bulwark of the truth. Great indeed, we confess, is the mystery of our religion:
He[h] was manifested in the flesh,
vindicated[i] in the Spirit,
    seen by angels,
preached among the nations,
believed on in the world,
    taken up in glory.

Prediction of Apostasy [1 Timothy 4:1–5]

NOW the Spirit expressly says that in later times some will depart from the faith by giving heed to deceitful spirits and doctrines of demons, through the pretensions of liars whose consciences are seared, who forbid marriage and enjoin abstinence from foods which God created to be received with thanksgiving by those who believe and know the truth. For everything created by God is good, and nothing is to

---

[a]Or *stewardship*, or *order*
[b]Greek *to the ages of ages*

[c]Or *by the birth of the child*
[d]Greek *they continue*
[f]Or *slanderer*

[h]Greek *Who*; other ancient authorities read *God*; others, *Which*
[i]Or *justified*

211

"You shall not muzzle an ox when it is treading out the grain" (1 Tim. 5:18)

be rejected if it is received with thanksgiving; for then it is consecrated by the word of God and prayer.

A Good Minister of Jesus Christ [4:6–16]

If you put these instructions before the brethren, you will be a good minister of Christ Jesus, nourished on the words of the faith and of the good doctrine which you have followed. Have nothing to do with godless and silly myths. Train yourself in godliness; for while bodily training is of some value, godliness is of value in every way, as it holds promise for the present life and also for the life to come. The saying is sure and worthy of full acceptance. For to this end we toil and strive,[j] because we have our hope set on the living God, who is the Savior of all men, especially of those who believe.

Command and teach these things. Let no one despise your youth, but set the believers an example in speech and conduct, in love, in faith, in purity. Till I come, attend to the public reading of scripture, to preaching, to teaching. Do not neglect the gift you have, which was given you by prophetic utterance when the elders laid their hands upon you. Practice these duties, devote yourself to them, so that all may see your progress. Take heed to yourself and to your teaching; hold to that, for by so doing you will save both yourself and your hearers.

[j]Other ancient authorities read *suffer reproach*

Coin of Procurator Pontius Pilate, dated A.D. 30–31 (obverse and reverse)

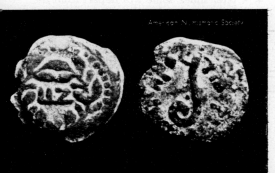

Duties toward Others [1 Timothy 5:1–6:2a]

DO not rebuke an older man but exhort him as you would a father; treat younger men like brothers, older women like mothers, younger women like sisters, in all purity.

Honor widows who are real widows. If a widow has children or grandchildren, let them first learn their religious duty to their own family and make some return to their parents; for this is acceptable in the sight of God. She who is a real widow, and is left all alone, has set her hope on God and continues in supplications and prayers night and day; whereas she who is self-indulgent is dead even while she lives. Command this, so that they may be without reproach. If any one does not provide for his relatives, and especially for his own family, he has disowned the faith and is worse than an unbeliever.

Let a widow be enrolled if she is not less than sixty years of age, having been the wife of one husband; and she must be well attested for her good deeds, as one who has brought up children, shown hospitality, washed the feet of the saints, relieved the afflicted, and devoted herself to doing good in every way. But refuse to enrol younger widows; for when they grow wanton against Christ they desire to marry, and so they incur condemnation for having violated their first pledge. Besides that, they learn to be idlers, gadding about from house to house, and not only idlers but gossips and busybodies, saying what they should not. So I would have younger widows marry, bear children, rule their households, and give the enemy no occasion to revile us. For some have already strayed after Satan. If any believing woman[l] has relatives who are widows, let her assist them; let the church not be burdened, so that it may assist those who are real widows.

Let the elders who rule well be considered worthy of double honor, especially those who labor in preaching and teaching; for the scripture says, "You shall not muzzle an ox when it is treading out the grain,"[1] and, "The laborer deserves his wages." Never admit any charge against an elder except on the evidence of two or three witnesses. As for those who persist in sin, rebuke them in the presence of all, so that the rest may stand in fear. In the presence of God and of Christ Jesus and of the elect angels I charge you to keep these rules without favor, doing nothing from partiality. Do not be hasty in the laying on of hands, nor participate in another man's sins; keep yourself pure.

No longer drink only water, but use a little wine for the sake of your stomach and your frequent ailments.

The sins of some men are conspicuous, pointing to judgment, but the sins of others appear later. So also good deeds are conspicuous; and even when they are not, they cannot remain hidden.

Let all who are under the yoke of slavery regard their masters as worthy of all honor, so that the name of God and the teaching may not be defamed. Those who have believing masters must not be disrespectful on the ground that they are brethren; rather they must serve all the

[l]Other ancient authorities read *man or woman;* others, simply *man*
[1]Deuteronomy 25:4

better since those who benefit by their service are believers and beloved.

Godliness with Contentment
[1 Timothy 6:2b–10]

TEACH and urge these duties. If any one teaches otherwise and does not agree with the sound words of our Lord Jesus Christ and the teaching which accords with godliness, he is puffed up with conceit, he knows nothing; he has a morbid craving for controversy and for disputes about words, which produce envy, dissension, slander, base suspicions, and wrangling among men who are depraved in mind and bereft of the truth, imagining that godliness is a means of gain. There is great gain in godliness with contentment; for we brought nothing into the world, and[m] we cannot take anything out of the world; but if we have food and clothing, with these we shall be content. But those who desire to be rich fall into temptation, into a snare, into many senseless and hurtful desires that plunge men into ruin and destruction. For the love of money is the root of all evils; it is through this craving that some have wandered away from the faith and pierced their hearts with many pangs.

The Good Fight of Faith [6:11–16]

But as for you, man of God, shun all this; aim at righteousness, godliness, faith, love, steadfastness, gentleness. Fight the good fight of the faith; take hold of the eternal life to which you were called when you made the good confession in the presence of many witnesses. In the presence of God who gives life to all things, and of Christ Jesus who in his testimony before Pontius Pilate made the good confession, I charge you to keep the commandment unstained and free from reproach until the appearing of our Lord Jesus Christ; and this will be made manifest at the proper time by the blessed and only Sovereign, the King of kings and Lord of lords, who alone has immortality and dwells in unapproachable light, whom no man has ever seen or can see. To him be honor and eternal dominion. Amen.

Rich in Good Deeds [6:17–19]

As for the rich in this world, charge them not to be haughty, nor to set their hopes on uncertain riches but on God who richly furnishes us with everything to enjoy. They are to do good, to be rich in good deeds, liberal and generous, thus laying up for themselves a good foundation for the future, so that they may take hold of the life which is life indeed.

Final Charge [6:20–21]

O Timothy, guard what has been entrusted to you. Avoid the godless chatter and contradictions of what is falsely called knowledge, for by professing it some have missed the mark as regards the faith.

Grace be with you.

[m]Other ancient authorities insert *it is certain that*

THE SECOND LETTER OF PAUL TO
TIMOTHY

Greetings

[2 Timothy 1:1–2] Paul, an apostle of Christ Jesus by the will of God according to the promise of the life which is in Christ Jesus,

To Timothy, my beloved child:

Grace, mercy, and peace from God the Father and Christ Jesus our Lord.

Do Not Be Ashamed [1:3–18]

I thank God whom I serve with a clear conscience, as did my fathers, when I remember you constantly in my prayers. As I remember your tears, I long night and day to see you, that I may be filled with joy. I am reminded of your sincere faith, a faith that dwelt first in your grandmother Lois and your mother Eunice and now, I am sure, dwells in you. Hence I remind you to rekindle the gift of God that is within you through the laying on of my hands; for God did not give us a spirit of timidity but a spirit of power and love and self-control.

Do not be ashamed then of testifying to our Lord, nor of me his prisoner, but take your share of suffering for the gospel in the power of God, who saved us and called us with a holy calling, not in virtue of our works but in virtue of his own purpose and the grace which he gave us in Christ Jesus ages ago, and now has manifested through the appearing of our Savior Christ Jesus, who abolished death and brought life and immortality to light through the gospel. For this gospel I was appointed a preacher and apostle and teacher, and therefore I suffer as I do. But I am not ashamed, for I know whom I have believed, and I am sure that he is able to guard until that Day what has been entrusted to me.[a] Follow the pattern of the sound words which you have heard from me, in the faith and love which are in Christ Jesus; guard the truth that has been entrusted to you by the Holy Spirit who dwells within us.

You are aware that all who are in Asia turned away from me, and among them Phygel'us and Hermog'enes. May the Lord grant mercy to the household of Onesiph'orus, for he often refreshed me; he was not ashamed of my chains, but when he arrived in Rome he searched for me eagerly and found me—may the Lord grant him to find mercy from the Lord on that Day—and you well know all the service he rendered at Eph'esus.

A Good Soldier of Jesus Christ

[2 Timothy 2:1–13]

YOU then, my son, be strong in the grace that is in Christ Jesus, and what you have heard from me before many witnesses entrust to faithful men who will be able to teach others also. Take your share of suffering as a good soldier of Christ Jesus. No soldier on service gets entangled in civilian pursuits, since his aim is to satisfy the one who enlisted him. An athlete is not crowned unless he competes according to the rules. It is the hard-working farmer who ought to have the first share of the crops. Think over what I say, for the Lord will grant you understanding in everything.

Remember Jesus Christ, risen from the dead, descended from David, as preached in my gospel, the gospel for which I am suffering and wearing fetters like a criminal. But the word of God is not fettered. Therefore I endure everything for the sake of the elect, that they also may obtain the salvation which in Christ Jesus goes with eternal glory.

The saying is sure:
If we have died with him, we shall also
    live with him;
if we endure, we shall also reign with
    him;
if we deny him, he also will deny us;
if we are faithless, he remains faith-
    ful—
for he cannot deny himself.

An Approved Workman [2:14–26]

Remind them of this, and charge them before the Lord[b] to avoid disputing about words, which does no good, but only ruins the hearers. Do your best to present yourself to God as one approved, a workman who has no need to be ashamed, rightly handling the word of truth. Avoid such godless chatter, for it will lead people into more and more ungodliness, and their talk will eat its way like gangrene. Among them are Hymenae'us and Phile'tus, who have swerved from the truth by holding that the resurrection is past already. They are upsetting the faith of some. But God's firm foundation stands, bearing this seal: "The Lord knows those who are his,"[1] and, "Let every one who names the name of the Lord depart from iniquity."

In a great house there are not only vessels of gold and silver but also of wood and earthenware, and some for noble use, some for ignoble. If any one purifies himself from what is ignoble, then he will be a vessel for noble use, consecrated and useful to the master of the house, ready for any good work. So shun youthful passions and aim at righteousness, faith, love, and peace, along with those who call upon the Lord from a pure heart. Have nothing to do with stupid, senseless controversies; you know that they breed quarrels. And the Lord's servant must not be quarrelsome but kindly to every one, an apt teacher, forbearing, correcting his opponents with gentleness. God may perhaps grant that they will repent and come to know the truth, and they may escape from the snare of the devil, after being captured by him to do his will.[c]

The Character of Man in the Last Days [2 Timothy 3:1–9]

BUT understand this, that in the last days there will come times of stress. For men will be lovers of self, lovers of money, proud, arrogant, abusive, disobedient to their parents, ungrateful, unholy, inhuman, implacable, slanderers, profligates, fierce, haters of good, treacherous, reckless, swollen with conceit, lovers of pleasure rather than lovers of God, holding the form of religion but denying the power of it. Avoid such people. For among them are those who make their way into households and capture weak women, burdened with sins and swayed by various impulses, who will listen to anybody and can never arrive at a knowledge of the truth. As Jannes and Jambres opposed Moses, so these men also oppose the truth, men of corrupt mind and counterfeit faith; but they will not get very far, for their folly will be plain to all, as was that of those two men.

[a] Or *what I have entrusted to him*

[b] Other ancient authorities read *God*

[c] Or *by him, to do his* (that is, God's) *will*
[1] *Numbers* 16:5

"It is the hard-working farmer who ought to have the first share of the crops" (2 Tim. 2:6). Titus Paconius Caledus supervises the harvest of vegetables and fruits on his farm

Alinari

In this wall painting a native of Pompeii holds a scroll, and his wife a folding wax tablet and a stylus for writing on it

Nash, Three Lions

The Abbey of the Three Fountains marks the traditional site where Paul is said to have been beheaded outside the walls of Rome

Paul's Last Charge to Timothy [3:10—4:8]

Now you have observed my teaching, my conduct, my aim in life, my faith, my patience, my love, my steadfastness, my persecutions, my sufferings, what befell me at An'tioch, at Ico'nium, and at Lystra, what persecutions I endured; yet from them all the Lord rescued me. Indeed all who desire to live a godly life in Christ Jesus will be persecuted, while evil men and imposters will go on from bad to worse, deceivers and deceived. But as for you, continue in what you have learned and have firmly believed, knowing from whom you learned it and how from childhood you have been acquainted with the sacred writings which are able to instruct you for salvation through faith in Christ Jesus. All scripture is inspired by God and[d] profitable for teaching, for reproof, for correction, and for training in righteousness, that the man of God may be complete, equipped for every good work.

I charge you in the presence of God and of Christ Jesus who is to judge the living and the dead, and by his appearing and his kingdom: preach the word, be urgent in season and out of season, convince, rebuke, and exhort, be unfailing in patience and in teaching. For the time is coming when people will not endure sound teaching, but having itching ears they will accumulate for themselves teachers to suit their own likings, and will turn away from listening to the truth and wander into myths. As for you, always be steady, endure suffering, do the work of an evangelist, fulfil your ministry.

For I am already on the point of being sacrificed; the time of my departure has come. I have fought the good fight, I have finished the race, I have kept the faith. Henceforth there is laid up for me the crown of righteousness, which the Lord, the righteous judge, will award to me on that Day, and not only to me but also to all who have loved his appearing.

Personal Instructions

[2 Timothy 4:9–18]

DO your best to come to me soon. For Demas, in love with this present world, has deserted me and gone to Thessaloni'ca; Crescens has gone to Gala'tia,[e] Titus to Dalma'tia. Luke alone is with me. Get Mark and bring him with you; for he is very useful in serving me. Tych'icus I have sent to Eph'esus. When you come, bring the cloak that I left with Carpus at Troas, also the books, and above all the parchments. Alexander the coppersmith did me great harm; the Lord will requite him for his deeds. Beware of him yourself, for he strongly opposed our message. At my first defense no one took my part; all deserted me. May it not be charged against them! But the Lord stood by me and gave me strength to proclaim the word fully, that all the Gentiles might hear it. So I was rescued from the lion's mouth. The Lord will rescue me from every evil and save me for his heavenly kingdom. To him be the glory for ever and ever. Amen.

Final Greetings [4:19–22]

Greet Prisca and Aqui'la, and the household of Onesiph'orus. Eras'tus remained at Corinth; Troph'imus I left ill at Mile'tus. Do your best to come before winter. Eubu'lus sends greetings to you, as do Pudens and Linus and Claudia and all the brethren.

The Lord be with your spirit. Grace be with you.

A. Donmez

Troy. Ancient walls of Priam's city. These walls are believed to be those of the sixth city, dating from about 1600 B.C.

Miletus. The theater

A. Donmez

---

[d]Or *Every scripture inspired by God is also*
[e]Other ancient authorities read *Gaul*

400–350 B.C.　　　**350–200 B.C.**　　　**400–350 B.C.**

Three coins of Crete showing different ideas of the Labyrinth

Gortyn, Crete. The Roman theater, with Greek laws of the fifth century B.C. inscribed on a wall

THE LETTER OF PAUL TO
TITUS

Greetings

[Titus 1:1–4] Paul, a servant[a] of God and an apostle of Jesus Christ, to further the faith of God's elect and their knowledge of the truth which accords with godliness, in hope of eternal life which God, who never lies, promised ages ago and at the proper time manifested in his word through the preaching with which I have been entrusted by command of God our Savior;

To Titus, my true child in a common faith:

Grace and peace from God the Father and Christ Jesus our Savior.

Titus' Work in Crete [1:5–16]

This is why I left you in Crete, that you might amend what was defective, and appoint elders in every town as I directed you, if any man is blameless, the husband of one wife, and his children are believers and not open to the charge of being profligate or insubordinate. For a bishop, as God's steward, must be blameless; he must not be arrogant or quick-tempered or a drunkard or violent or greedy for gain, but hospitable, a lover of goodness, master of himself, upright, holy, and self-controlled; he must hold firm to the sure word as taught, so that he may be able to give instruction in sound doctrine and also to confute those who contradict it. For there are many insubordinate men, empty talkers and deceivers, especially the circumcision party; they must be silenced, since they are upsetting whole families by teaching for base gain what they have no right to teach. One of themselves, a prophet of their own, said, "Cretans are always liars, evil beasts, lazy gluttons." This testimony is true. Therefore rebuke them sharply, that they may be sound in the faith, instead of giving heed to Jewish myths or to commands of men who reject the truth. To the pure all things are pure, but to the corrupt and unbelieving nothing is pure; their very minds and consciences are corrupted. They profess to know God, but they deny him by their deeds; they are detestable, disobedient, unfit for any good deed.

The Teaching of Sound Doctrine
[Titus 2:1–15]

BUT as for you, teach what befits sound doctrine. Bid the older men be temperate, serious, sensible, sound in faith, in love, and in steadfastness. Bid the older women likewise to be reverent in behavior, not to be slanderers or slaves to drink; they are to teach what is good, and so train the young women to love their husbands and children, to be sensible, chaste, domestic, kind, and submissive to their husbands, that the word of God may not be discredited. Likewise urge the younger men to control themselves. Show yourself in all respects a model of good deeds, and in your teaching show integrity, gravity, and sound speech that cannot be censured, so that an opponent may be put to shame, having nothing evil to say of us. Bid slaves to be submissive to their masters and to give satisfaction in every respect; they are not to be refractory, nor to pilfer, but to show entire and true fidelity, so that in everything they may adorn the doctrine of God our Savior.

For the grace of God has appeared for the salvation of all men, training us to renounce irreligion and worldly passions, and to live sober, upright, and godly lives in this world, awaiting our blessed hope, the appearing of the glory of our great God and Savior[c] Jesus Christ, who gave himself for us to redeem us from all iniquity and to purify for himself a people of his own who are zealous for good deeds.

Declare these things; exhort and reprove with all authority. Let no one disregard you.

Maintain Good Deeds [Titus 3:1–11]

REMIND them to be submissive to rulers and authorities, to be obedient, to be ready for any honest work, to speak evil of no one, to avoid quarreling, to be gentle, and to show perfect courtesy toward all men. For we ourselves were once foolish, disobedient, led astray, slaves to various passions and pleasures, passing our days in malice and envy, hated by men and hating one another; but when the goodness and loving kindness of God our Savior appeared, he saved us, not because of deeds done by us in righteousness, but in virtue of his own mercy, by the washing of regeneration and renewal in the Holy Spirit, which he poured out upon us richly through Jesus Christ our Savior, so that we might be justified by his grace and become heirs in hope of eternal life. The saying is sure.

I desire you to insist on these things, so that those who have believed in God may be careful to apply themselves to good deeds;[d] these are excellent and profitable to men. But avoid stupid controversies, genealogies, dissensions, and quarrels over the law, for they are unprofitable and futile. As for a man who is factious, after admonishing him once or twice, have nothing more to do with him, knowing that such a person is perverted and sinful; he is self-condemned.

Personal Instructions [3:12–14]

When I send Ar'temas or Tych'icus to you, do your best to come to me at Nicop'olis, for I have decided to spend the winter there. Do your best to speed Zenas the lawyer and Apol'los on their way; see that they lack nothing. And let our people learn to apply themselves to good deeds,[d] so as to help cases of urgent need, and not to be unfruitful.

Benediction [3:15]

All who are with me send greetings to you. Greet those who love us in the faith.

Grace be with you all.

[d]Or *enter honorable occupations*

Air view of Nicopolis

[a]Or *slave*

[c]Or *of the great God and our Savior*

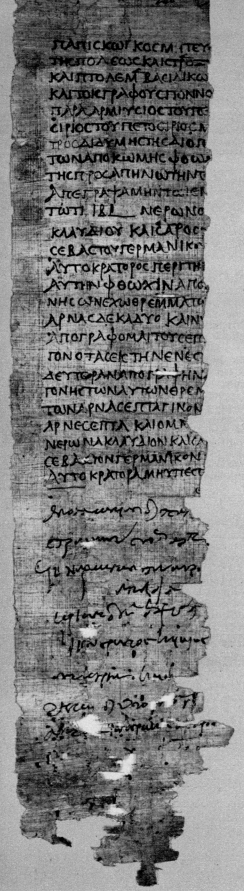

When Paul wrote a portion of one of his letters with his own hand, his handwriting was doubtless plainly distinguishable from that of his scribe. Such a contrast of book hand and cursive hand appears in this papyrus document of the first century A.D.

University Library, Cambridge

Felbermeyer

A soldier capturing a prisoner who will be sold into slavery. The costume of the prisoner shows that he came from the Parthian Empire. In Pergamum, it is reported that thirty percent of the population were slaves. In Rome slaves were not allowed to wear distinguishing marks lest they discover how numerous they were and so organize a revolt

Espérandieu

Fragment of tombstone of a quattuorvir of Nemausus (Nîmes), in southern France, who freed at least five slaves, as shown by the liberty caps at the bottom of the stone. Second half of first century A.D.

THE LETTER OF PAUL TO
PHILEMON

Greetings

[Philemon 1–3] Paul, a prisoner for Christ Jesus, and Timothy our brother,

To Phile'mon our beloved fellow worker and Ap'phia our sister and Archip'pus our fellow soldier, and the church in your house:

Grace to you and peace from God our Father and the Lord Jesus Christ.

Philemon's Love and Faith [4–7]

I thank my God always when I remember you in my prayers, because I hear of your love and of the faith which you have toward the Lord Jesus and all the saints, and I pray that the sharing of your faith may promote the knowledge of all the good that is ours in Christ. For I have derived much joy and comfort from your love, my brother, because the hearts of the saints have been refreshed through you.

Paul Pleads for Onesimus [8–22]

Accordingly, though I am bold enough in Christ to command you to do what is required, yet for love's sake I prefer to appeal to you—I, Paul, an ambassador[a] and now a prisoner also for Christ Jesus—I appeal to you for my child, Ones'imus, whose father I have become in my imprisonment. (Formerly he was useless to you, but now he is indeed useful[b] to you and to me.) I am sending him back to you, sending my very heart. I would have been glad to keep him with me, in order that he might serve me on your behalf during my imprisonment for the gospel; but I preferred to do nothing without your consent in order that your goodness might not be by compulsion but of your own free will.

Perhaps this is why he was parted from you for a while, that you might have him back for ever, no longer as a slave but more than a slave, as a beloved brother, especially to me but how much more to you, both in the flesh and in the Lord. So if you consider me your partner, receive him as you would receive me. If he has wronged you at all, or owes you anything, charge that to my account. I, Paul, write this with my own hand, I will repay it—to say nothing of your owing me even your own self. Yes, brother, I want some benefit from you in the Lord. Refresh my heart in Christ.

Confident of your obedience, I write to you, knowing that you will do even more than I say. At the same time, prepare a guest room for me, for I am hoping through your prayers to be granted to you.

Final Greetings [23–25]

Ep'aphras, my fellow prisoner in Christ Jesus, sends greetings to you, and so do Mark, Aristar'chus, Demas, and Luke, my fellow workers.

The grace of the Lord Jesus Christ be with your spirit.

[a] Or *an old man*
[b] The name Onesimus means *useful* or (compare verse 20) *beneficial*

THE LETTER TO THE
HEBREWS

God Has Spoken by His Son

[Hebrews 1:1–4] In many and various ways God spoke of old to our fathers by the prophets; but in these last days he has spoken to us by a Son, whom he appointed the heir of all things, through whom also he created the world. He reflects the glory of God and bears the very stamp of his nature, upholding the universe by his word of power. When he had made purification for sins, he sat down at the right hand of the Majesty on high, having become as much superior to angels as the name he has obtained is more excellent than theirs.

The Son Superior to Angels [1:5–14]

For to what angel did God ever say,
"Thou art my Son,
today I have begotten thee"[1]?
Or again,
"I will be to him a father,
and he shall be to me a son"[2]?
And again, when he brings the firstborn into the world, he says,
"Let all God's angels worship him."[3]
Of the angels he says,
"Who makes his angels winds,
and his servants flames of fire."[4]
But of the Son he says,
"Thy throne, O God,[a] is for ever and ever,
the righteous scepter is the scepter of thy[b] kingdom.
Thou hast loved righteousness and hated lawlessness;
therefore God, thy God, has anointed thee
with the oil of gladness beyond thy comrades."[5]
And,
"Thou, Lord, didst found the earth in the beginning,
and the heavens are the work of thy hands;
they will perish, but thou remainest;
they will all grow old like a garment,
like a mantle thou wilt roll them up,
and they will be changed.[c]
But thou art the same,
and thy years will never end."[6]
But to what angel has he ever said,
"Sit at my right hand,
till I make thy enemies
a stool for thy feet"[7]?
Are they not all ministering spirits sent forth to serve, for the sake of those who are to obtain salvation?

Such a Great Salvation [Hebrews 2:1–4]

THEREFORE we must pay the closer attention to what we have heard, lest we drift away from it. For if the message declared by angels was valid and every transgression or disobedience received a just retribution, how shall we escape if we neglect such a great salvation? It was declared at first by the Lord, and it was attested to us by those who heard him, while God also bore witness by signs and wonders and various miracles and by gifts of the Holy Spirit distributed according to his own will.

The Pioneer of Salvation [2:5–18]

For it was not to angels that God subjected the world to come, of which we are speaking. It has been testified somewhere,
"What is man that thou art mindful of him,
or the son of man, that thou carest for him?
Thou didst make him for a little while lower than the angels,
thou hast crowned him with glory and honor,[d]
putting everything in subjection under his feet."[8]
Now in putting everything in subjection to him, he left nothing outside his control. As it is, we do not yet see everything in subjection to him. But we see Jesus, who for a little while was made lower than the angels, crowned with glory and honor because of the suffering of death, so that by the grace of God he might taste death for every one.

For it was fitting that he, for whom and by whom all things exist, in bringing many sons to glory, should make the pioneer of their salvation perfect through suffering. For he who sanctifies and those who are sanctified have all one origin. That is why he is not ashamed to call them brethren, saying,
"I will proclaim thy name to my brethren,
in the midst of the congregation I will praise thee."[9]
And again,
"I will put my trust in him."[10]
And again,
"Here am I, and the children God has given me."[11]
Since therefore the children share in flesh and blood, he himself likewise partook of the same nature, that through death he might destroy him who has the power of death, that is, the devil, and deliver all those who through fear of death were sub-

University of Michigan

There are at least 35 quotations from the Old Testament in the Letter to the Hebrews. Some of these quotations, like Deut. 32:43 (Heb. 1:6), are from the Greek Septuagint rather than from the Hebrew Old Testament. This papyrus fragment of Deut. 31:21 (front) and Deut. 32:3-4 (back) dates from the second century A.D.

Gilbert Darlington

Alexandria. The great stone lighthouse, or Pharos, 445 feet tall, built after 300 B.C., was one of the Seven Wonders of the World. It guided ships to Alexandria until its fall in A.D. 1326. From a coin of Commodus

Ivan Dmitri for American Export Lines

[d] Other ancient authorities insert *and didst set him over the works of thy hands*

[a] Or *God is thy throne*
[b] Other ancient authorities read *his*
[c] Other ancient authorities add *like a garment*

[1] Psalms 2:7
[2] 2 Samuel 7:14
[3] Deuteronomy 32:43, Septuagint; Psalms 97:7
[4] Psalms 104:4
[5] Psalms 45:6–7
[6] Psalms 102:25–27
[7] Psalms 110:1
[8] Psalms 8:4–6
[9] Psalms 22:22
[10] Isaiah 8:17
[11] Isaiah 8:18

Alexandria was a city of marble when Rome was a city of brick. Except for "Pompey's Pillar," little of its ancient glory remains

Mosaic showing Alexander the Great attacking the Persian king Darius III at the battle of Issus. Alexander, the bare-headed figure on horseback at the left, charges furiously against the Persian king, who sits in his chariot at the right. This mosaic, made of bits of colored glass, is a floor pavement discovered at Pompeii in 1831. It is said to have been originally laid in Alexandria before being moved to Italy. Alexander the Great carried Greek language and culture through the entire Near and Middle East. Alexandria, the seaport in Egypt that he founded, became a great center of Greek influence and learning. Here it was that the Hebrew Old Testament began to be translated into Greek, ca. 250 to 100 B.C., beginning with the reign of Ptolemy II. This ancient Greek translation, called the Septuagint, is still the official Old Testament of the Greek Orthodox Church

Alinari

ject to lifelong bondage. For surely it is not with angels that he is concerned but with the descendants of Abraham. Therefore he had to be made like his brethren in every respect, so that he might become a merciful and faithful high priest in the service of God, to make expiation for the sins of the people. For because he himself has suffered and been tempted, he is able to help those who are tempted.

Jesus Superior to Moses

[Hebrews 3:1–6]

THEREFORE, holy brethren, who share in a heavenly call, consider Jesus, the apostle and high priest of our confession. He was faithful to him who appointed him, just as Moses also was faithful in[e] God's house. Yet Jesus has been counted worthy of as much more glory than Moses as the builder of a house has more honor than the house. (For every house is built by some one, but the builder of all things is God.) Now Moses was faithful in all God's house as a servant, to testify to the things that were to be spoken later, but Christ was faithful over God's[f] house as a son. And we are his house if we hold fast our confidence and pride in our hope.[g]

A Rest for the People of God

[3:7–4:13]

Therefore, as the Holy Spirit says,
"Today, when you hear his voice,
do not harden your hearts as in the rebellion,
on the day of testing in the wilderness,
where your fathers put me to the test
and saw my works for forty years.

Therefore I was provoked with that generation,
and said, 'They always go astray in their hearts;
they have not known my ways.'
As I swore in my wrath,
'They shall never enter my rest.' "[12]
Take care, brethren, lest there be in any of you an evil, unbelieving heart, leading you to fall away from the living God. But exhort one another every day, as long as it is called "today," that none of you may be hardened by the deceitfulness of sin. For we share in Christ, if only we hold our first confidence firm to the end, while it is said,
"Today, when you hear his voice,
do not harden your hearts as in the rebellion."[13]
Who were they that heard and yet were rebellious? Was it not all those who left Egypt under the leadership of Moses? And with whom was he provoked forty years? Was it not with those who sinned, whose bodies fell in the wilderness? And to whom did he swear that they should never enter his rest, but to those who were disobedient? So we see that they were unable to enter because of unbelief.

Therefore, while the promise of entering his rest remains, let us fear lest any of you be judged to have failed to reach it. For good news came to us just as to them; but the message which they heard did not benefit them, because it did not meet with faith in the hearers.[h] For we who have believed enter that rest, as he has said,
"As I swore in my wrath,
'They shall never enter my rest,' "[14]
although his works were finished from the foundation of the world. For he has somewhere spoken of the seventh day in this way, "And God rested on the seventh day

from all his works."[15] And again in this place he said,
"They shall never enter my rest."[16]
Since therefore it remains for some to enter it, and those who formerly received the good news failed to enter because of disobedience, again he sets a certain day, "Today," saying through David so long afterward, in the words already quoted,
"Today, when you hear his voice,
do not harden your hearts."[17]
For if Joshua had given them rest, God[i] would not speak later of another day. So then, there remains a sabbath rest for the people of God; for whoever enters God's rest also ceases from his labors as God did from his.

Let us therefore strive to enter that rest, that no one fall by the same sort of disobedience. For the word of God is living and active, sharper than any two-edged sword, piercing to the division of soul and spirit, of joints and marrow, and discerning the thoughts and intentions of the heart. And before him no creature is hidden, but all are open and laid bare to the eyes of him with whom we have to do.

Jesus the Great High Priest

[Hebrews 4:14–5:10]

SINCE then we have a great high priest who has passed through the heavens, Jesus, the Son of God, let us hold fast our confession. For we have not a high priest who is unable to sympathize with our weaknesses, but one who in every respect has been tempted as we are, yet without sinning. Let us then with confidence draw near to the throne of grace, that we may receive mercy and find grace to help in time of need.

For every high priest chosen from among men is appointed to act on behalf of men in relation to God, to offer gifts and sacrifices for sins. He can deal gently with the ignorant and wayward, since he himself is beset with weakness. Because of this he is bound to offer sacrifice for his own sins as well as for those of the people. And one does not take the honor upon himself, but he is called by God, just as Aaron was.

So also Christ did not exalt himself to be made a high priest, but was appointed by him who said to him,
"Thou art my Son,
today I have begotten thee"[18];
as he says also in another place,
"Thou art a priest for ever,
after the order of Melchiz'edek."[19]
In the days of his flesh, Jesus[j] offered up prayers and supplications, with loud cries and tears, to him who was able to save him from death, and he was heard for his godly fear. Although he was a Son, he learned obedience through what he suffered; and being made perfect he became the source of eternal salvation to all who obey him, being designated by God a high priest after the order of Melchiz'edek.

Warning against Apostasy [Hebrews 5:11–6:8]

ABOUT this we have much to say which is hard to explain, since you have become dull of hearing. For though by this time you ought to be teachers, you need

---

[e] Other ancient authorities insert *all*
[f] Greek *his*
[g] Other ancient authorities insert *firm to the end*

[h] Other manuscripts read *they were not united in faith with the hearers*
[12] Psalms 95:7–11
[13] Psalms 95:7–11
[14] Psalms 95:11

[i] Greek *he*   [j] Greek *he*
[15] Genesis 2:2
[16] Psalms 95:11
[17] Psalms 95:7–8
[18] Psalms 2:7
[19] Psalms 110:4

"You need some one to teach you again the first principles of God's word"
(Heb. 5:12). Roman bas-relief, c:a A.D. 200

Alinari

"For land . . . brings forth vegetation useful to those for whose sake it is cultivated" (Heb. 6:7)

Alice Schalek

some one to teach you again the first principles of God's word. You need milk, not solid food; for every one who lives on milk is unskilled in the word of righteousness, for he is a child. But solid food is for the mature, for those who have their faculties trained by practice to distinguish good from evil.

Therefore let us leave the elementary doctrines of Christ and go on to maturity, not laying again a foundation of repentance from dead works and of faith toward God, with instruction[k] about ablutions, the laying on of hands, the resurrection of the dead, and eternal judgment. And this we will do if God permits.[l] For it is impossible to restore again to repentance those who have once been enlightened, who have tasted the heavenly gift, and have become partakers of the Holy Spirit, and have tasted the goodness of the word of God and the powers of the age to come, if they then commit apostasy, since they crucify the Son of God on their own account and hold him up to contempt. For land which has drunk the rain that often falls upon it, and brings forth vegetation useful to those for whose sake it is cultivated, receives a blessing from God. But if it bears thorns and thistles, it is worthless and near to being cursed; its end is to be burned.

The Assurance of Hope [Hebrews 6:9–20]

THOUGH we speak thus, yet in your case, beloved, we feel sure of better things that belong to salvation. For God is not so unjust as to overlook your work and the love which you showed for his sake in serving the saints, as you still do. And we desire each one of you to show the same earnestness in realizing the full assurance of hope until the end, so that you may not be sluggish, but imitators of those who through faith and patience inherit the promises.

For when God made a promise to Abraham, since he had no one greater by whom to swear, he swore by himself, saying, "Surely I will bless you and multiply you."[20] And thus Abraham,[m] having patiently endured, obtained the promise. Men indeed swear by a greater than them-

selves, and in all their disputes an oath is final for confirmation. So when God desired to show more convincingly to the heirs of the promise the unchangeable character of his purpose, he interposed with an oath, so that through two unchangeable things, in which it is impossible that God should prove false, we who have fled for refuge might have strong encouragement to seize the hope set before us. We have this as a sure and steadfast anchor of the soul, a hope that enters into the inner shrine behind the curtain, where Jesus has gone as a forerunner on our behalf, having become a high priest for ever after the order of Melchiz'edek.

The Priestly Order of Melchizedek

[Hebrews 7:1–28]

FOR this Melchiz'edek, king of Salem, priest of the Most High God, met Abraham returning from the slaughter of the kings and blessed him; and to him Abraham apportioned a tenth part of everything. He is first, by translation of his name, king of righteousness, and then he is also king of Salem, that is, king of peace. He is without father or mother or genealogy, and has neither beginning of days nor end of life, but resembling the Son of God he continues a priest for ever.

See how great he is! Abraham the patriarch gave him a tithe of the spoils. And those descendants of Levi who receive the priestly office have a commandment in the law to take tithes from the people, that is, from their brethren, though these also are descended from Abraham. But this man who has not their genealogy received tithes from Abraham and blessed him who had the promises. It is beyond dispute that the inferior is blessed by the superior. Here tithes are received by mortal men; there, by one of whom it is testified that he lives. One might even say that Levi himself, who receives tithes, paid tithes through Abraham, for he was still in the loins of his ancestor when Melchiz'edek met him.

Now if perfection had been attainable through the Levit'ical priesthood (for under it the people received the law), what further need would there have been for another priest to arise after the order of Melchiz'edek, rather than one named after the order of Aaron? For when there is a change in the priesthood, there is necessarily a change in the law as well. For the

one of whom these things are spoken belonged to another tribe, from which no one has ever served at the altar. For it is evident that our Lord was descended from Judah, and in connection with that tribe Moses said nothing about priests.

This becomes even more evident when another priest arises in the likeness of Melchiz'edek, who has become a priest, not according to a legal requirement concerning bodily descent but by the power of an indestructible life. For it is witnessed of him,
"Thou art a priest for ever,
    after the order of Melchiz'edek."[21]
On the one hand, a former commandment is set aside because of its weakness and uselessness (for the law made nothing perfect); on the other hand, a better hope is introduced, through which we draw near to God.

And it was not without an oath. Those who formerly became priests took their office without an oath, but this one was addressed with an oath,
"The Lord has sworn
    and will not change his mind,
'Thou art a priest for ever.' "[22]
This makes Jesus the surety of a better covenant.

The former priests were many in number, because they were prevented by death from continuing in office; but he holds his priesthood permanently, because he continues for ever. Consequently he is able for all time to save those who draw near to God through him, since he always lives to make intercession for them.

For it was fitting that we should have such a high priest, holy, blameless, unstained, separated from sinners, exalted above the heavens. He has no need, like those high priests, to offer sacrifices daily, first for his own sins and then for those of the people; he did this once for all when he offered up himself. Indeed, the law appoints men in their weakness as high priests, but the word of the oath, which came later than the law, appoints a Son who has been made perfect for ever.

The High Priest of a New Covenant

[Hebrews 8:1–13]

NOW the point in what we are saying is this: we have such a high priest, one who is seated at the right hand of the

[k]Other ancient manuscripts read *of instruction*
[l]Other ancient manuscripts read *let us do this if God permits*
[m]Greek *he*
[20]*Genesis* 22:17

[21]*Psalms* 110:4
[22]*Psalms* 110:4

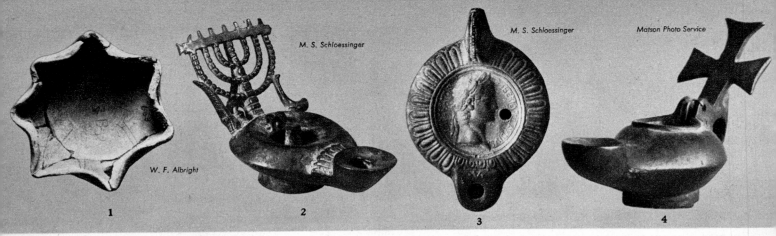

1 Seven-spouted lamp excavated at Tell Beit Mirsin; from about 1100–1000 B.C.

2 Ancient Jewish lamp with three symbols of Judaism: seven-branched candlestick (menorah), flanked by palm branch (lulab) and ceremonial horn (shofar)

3 Roman lamp bearing portrait of the Emperor Tiberius

4 Christian lamp with cross

throne of the Majesty in heaven, a minister in the sanctuary and the true tent[n] which is set up not by man but by the Lord. For every high priest is appointed to offer gifts and sacrifices; hence it is necessary for this priest also to have something to offer. Now if he were on earth, he would not be a priest at all, since there are priests who offer gifts according to the law. They serve a copy and shadow of the heavenly sanctuary; for when Moses was about to erect the tent,[n] he was instructed by God, saying, "See that you make everything according to the pattern which was shown you on the mountain."[23] But as it is, Christ[o] has obtained a ministry which is as much more excellent than the old as the covenant he mediates is better, since it is enacted on better promises. For if that first covenant had been faultless, there would have been no occasion for a second.

For he finds fault with them when he says:

"The days will come, says the Lord,
when I will establish a new covenant
with the house of Israel
and with the house of Judah;
not like the covenant that I made with
their fathers
on the day when I took them by the hand
to lead them out of the land of Egypt;
for they did not continue in my covenant,
and so I paid no heed to them, says the
Lord.
This is the covenant that I will make with
the house of Israel
after those days, says the Lord:
I will put my laws into their minds,
and write them on their hearts,
and I will be their God,
and they shall be my people.
And they shall not teach every one his
fellow
or every one his brother, saying, 'Know
the Lord,'
for all shall know me,
from the least of them to the greatest.
For I will be merciful toward their iniquities,
and I will remember their sins no
more."[24]

In speaking of a new covenant he treats the first as obsolete. And what is becoming obsolete and growing old is ready to vanish away.

The Earthly and Heavenly Sanctuaries

[Hebrews 9:1–22]

NOW even the first covenant had regulations for worship and an earthly sanctuary. For a tent[p] was prepared, the outer one, in which were the lampstand and the table and the bread of the Presence;[q] it is called the Holy Place. Behind the second curtain stood a tent[p] called the Holy of Holies, having the golden altar of incense and the ark of the covenant covered on all sides with gold, which contained a golden urn holding the manna, and Aaron's rod that budded, and the tables of the covenant; above it were the cherubim of glory overshadowing the mercy seat. Of these things we cannot now speak in detail.

These preparations having thus been made, the priests go continually into the outer tent,[p] performing their ritual duties; but into the second only the high priest goes, and he but once a year, and not without taking blood which he offers for himself and for the errors of the people. By this the Holy Spirit indicates that the way into the sanctuary is not yet opened as long as the outer tent[p] is still standing (which is symbolic for the present age). According to this arrangement, gifts and sacrifices are offered which cannot perfect the conscience of the worshipper, but deal only with food and drink and various ablutions, regulations for the body imposed until the time of reformation.

But when Christ appeared as a high priest of the good things that have come,[r] then through the greater and more perfect tent[p] (not made with hands, that is, not of this creation) he entered once for all into the Holy Place, taking[s] not the blood of goats and calves but his own blood, thus securing an eternal redemption. For if the sprinkling of defiled persons with the blood

of goats and bulls and with the ashes of a heifer sanctifies for the purification of the flesh, how much more shall the blood of Christ, who through the eternal Spirit offered himself without blemish to God, purify your[t] conscience from dead works to serve the living God.

Therefore he is the mediator of a new covenant, so that those who are called may receive the promised eternal inheritance, since a death has occurred which redeems them from the transgressions under the first covenant.[u] For where a will[u] is involved, the death of the one who made it must be established. For a will[u] takes effect only at death, since it is not in force as long as the one who made it is alive. Hence even the first covenant was not ratified without blood. For when every commandment of the law had been declared by Moses to all the people, he took the blood of calves and goats, with water and scarlet wool and hyssop, and sprinkled both the book itself and all the people, saying, "This is the blood of the covenant which God commanded you."[25] And in the same way he sprinkled with the blood both the tent[p] and all the vessels used in worship. Indeed, under the law almost everything is purified with blood, and without the shedding of blood there is no forgiveness of sins.

Sin Put Away by Christ's Sacrifice

[9:23—10:18]

Thus it was necessary for the copies of the heavenly things to be purified with these rites, but the heavenly things themselves with better sacrifices than these. For Christ has entered, not into a sanctuary made with hands, a copy of the true one, but into heaven itself, now to appear in the presence of God on our behalf. Nor was it to offer himself repeatedly, as the high priest enters the Holy Place yearly with blood not his own; for then he would have had to suffer repeatedly since the foundation of the world. But as it is, he has appeared once for all at the end of the age to

[n]Or tabernacle
[o]Greek he
[23]Exodus 25:40
[24]Jeremiah 31:31–34

[p]Or tabernacle
[q]Greek the presentation of the loaves
[r]Other manuscripts read good things to come
[s]Greek through

[t]Other manuscripts read our
[u]The Greek word here used means both covenant and will
[25]Exodus 24:8

Interior of the Temple of Solomon. The entrance is on the right, the Holy Place in the center, and the Holy of Holies with cherubim, on the left

Howard-Garber model

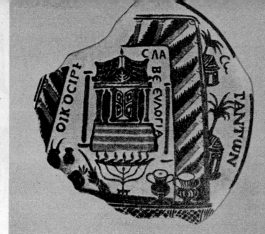

This gold-decorated glass from the Vatican, discovered in the catacombs of Rome, shows the inner court of the Temple in Jerusalem

Museo Sacro, Vatican Library

put away sin by the sacrifice of himself. And just as it is appointed for men to die once, and after that comes judgment, so Christ, having been offered once to bear the sins of many, will appear a second time, not to deal with sin but to save those who are eagerly waiting for him.

For since the law has but a shadow of the good things to come instead of the true form of these realities, it can never, by the same sacrifices which are continually offered year after year, make perfect those who draw near. Otherwise, would they not have ceased to be offered? If the worshipers had once been cleansed, they would no longer have any consciousness of sin. But in these sacrifices there is a reminder of sin year after year. For it is impossible that the blood of bulls and goats should take away sins.

Consequently, when Christ[v] came into the world, he said,

"Sacrifices and offerings thou hast not desired,
but a body hast thou prepared for me;
in burnt offerings and sin offerings thou
      hast taken no pleasure.
Then I said, 'Lo, I have come to do thy
      will, O God,'
as it is written of me in the roll of the
      book."[26]

When he said above, "Thou hast neither desired nor taken pleasure in sacrifices and offerings and burnt offerings and sin offerings" (these are offered according to the law), then he added, "Lo, I have come to do thy will." He abolishes the first in order to establish the second. And by that will we have been sanctified through the offering of the body of Jesus Christ once for all.

And every priest stands daily at his service, offering repeatedly the same sacrifices, which can never take away sins. But when Christ[w] had offered for all time a single sacrifice for sins, he sat down at the right hand of God, then to wait until his enemies should be made a stool for his feet. For by a single offering he has perfected for all time those who are sanctified. And the Holy Spirit also bears witness to us; for after saying,

"This is the covenant that I will make
      with them
after those days, says the Lord:
I will put my laws on their hearts,
      and write them on their minds,"[27]
then he adds,
"I will remember their sins and their
      misdeeds no more."[28]

Where there is forgiveness of these, there is no longer any offering for sin.

Let Us Draw Near and Hold Fast

[Hebrews 10:19–25]

THEREFORE, brethren, since we have confidence to enter the sanctuary by the blood of Jesus, by the new and living way which he opened for us through the curtain, that is, through his flesh, and since we have a great priest over the house of God, let us draw near with a true heart in full assurance of faith, with our hearts sprinkled clean from an evil conscience and our bodies washed with pure water. Let us hold fast the confession of our hope without wavering, for he who promised is faithful; and let us consider how to stir up one another to love and good works, not neglecting to meet together, as is the habit of some, but encouraging one another, and all the more as you see the Day drawing near.

Judgment for Deliberate Sin

[10:26–39]

For if we sin deliberately after receiving the knowledge of the truth, there no longer remains a sacrifice for sins, but a fearful prospect of judgment, and a fury of fire which will consume the adversaries. A man who has violated the law of Moses dies without mercy at the testimony of two or three witnesses. How much worse punishment do you think will be deserved by the man who has spurned the Son of God, and profaned the blood of the covenant by which he was sanctified, and outraged the Spirit of grace? For we know him who said, "Vengeance is mine, I will repay."[29]

And again, "The Lord will judge his people."[30] It is a fearful thing to fall into the hands of the living God.

But recall the former days when, after you were enlightened, you endured a hard struggle with sufferings, sometimes being publicly exposed to abuse and affliction, and sometimes being partners with those so treated. For you had compassion on the prisoners, and you joyfully accepted the plundering of your property, since you knew that you yourselves had a better possession and an abiding one. Therefore do not throw away your confidence, which has a great reward. For you have need of endurance, so that you may do the will of God and receive what is promised.

"For yet a little while,
and the coming one shall come and shall
      not tarry;
but my righteous one shall live by faith,
and if he shrinks back,
my soul has no pleasure in him."[31]

But we are not of those who shrink back and are destroyed, but of those who have faith and keep their souls.

Faith [Hebrews 11:1–3]

NOW faith is the assurance of things hoped for, the conviction of things not seen. For by it the men of old received divine approval. By faith we understand that the world was created by the word of God, so that what is seen was made out of things which do not appear.

Abel, Enoch and Noah [11:4–7]

By faith Abel offered to God a more acceptable sacrifice than Cain, through which he received approval as righteous, God bearing witness by accepting his gifts; he died, but through his faith he is still speaking. By faith Enoch was taken up so that he should not see death; and he was not found, because God had taken him. Now before he was taken he was attested as having pleased God. And without faith it is impossible to please him. For whoever

[v]Greek *he*
[w]Greek *this one*
[26]Psalms 40:6–8

[27]Jeremiah 31:33
[28]Jeremiah 31:34
[29]Deuteronomy 32:35

[30]Deuteronomy 32:36
[31]Habakkuk 2:3–4

221

The king whose wrath Moses braved in leading the children of Israel out of Egypt may have been Ramses II. Four colossal statues of this king are cut from the rock of Abu Simbel on the upper Nile

would draw near to God must believe that he exists and that he rewards those who seek him. By faith Noah, being warned by God concerning events as yet unseen, took heed and constructed an ark for the saving of his household; by this he condemned the world and became an heir of the righteousness which comes by faith.

Abraham and Sarah [11:8–12]

By faith Abraham obeyed when he was called to go out to a place which he was to receive as an inheritance; and he went out, not knowing where he was to go. By faith he sojourned in the land of promise, as in a foreign land, living in tents with Isaac and Jacob, heirs with him of the same promise. For he looked forward to the city which has foundations, whose builder and maker is God. By faith Sarah herself received power to conceive, even when she was past the age, since she considered him faithful who had promised. Therefore from one man, and him as good as dead, were born descendants as many as the stars of heaven and as the innumerable grains of sand by the seashore.

Strangers and Exiles [11:13–22]

These all died in faith, not having received what was promised, but having seen

Jericho. In the foreground the ruined foundations of pre-Israelite buildings dating from before the fall of the city described in the Book of Joshua

it and greeted it from afar, and having acknowledged that they were strangers and exiles on the earth. For people who speak thus make it clear that they are seeking a homeland. If they had been thinking of that land from which they had gone out, they would have had opportunity to return. But as it is, they desire a better country, that is, a heavenly one. Therefore God is not ashamed to be called their God, for he has prepared for them a city.

By faith Abraham, when he was tested, offered up Isaac, and he who had received the promises was ready to offer up his only son, of whom it was said, "Through Isaac shall your descendants be named."[32] He considered that God was able to raise men even from the dead; hence, figuratively speaking, he did receive him back. By faith Isaac invoked future blessings on Jacob and Esau. By faith Jacob, when dying, blessed each of the sons of Joseph, bowing in worship over the head of his staff. By faith Joseph, at the end of his life, made mention of the exodus of the Israelites and gave directions concerning his burial.[z]

Moses [11:23–28]

By faith Moses, when he was born, was hid for three months by his parents, because they saw that the child was beautiful; and they were not afraid of the king's edict. By faith Moses, when he was grown up, refused to be called the son of Pharaoh's daughter, choosing rather to share ill-treatment with the people of God than to enjoy the fleeting pleasures of sin. He considered abuse suffered for the Christ greater wealth than the treasures of Egypt, for he looked to the reward. By faith he left Egypt, not being afraid of the anger of the king; for he endured as seeing him who is invisible. By faith he kept the Passover and sprinkled the blood, so that the Destroyer of the first-born might not touch them.

The Israelites and Rahab [11:29–31]

By faith the people crossed the Red Sea as if on dry land; but the Egyptians, when they attempted to do the same, were drowned. By faith the walls of Jer'icho fell down after they had been encircled for

[z] Greek bones
[32] Genesis 21:12

seven days. By faith Rahab the harlot did not perish with those who were disobedient, because she had given friendly welcome to the spies.

The Judges and Prophets [11:32–40]

And what more shall I say? For time would fail me to tell of Gideon, Barak, Samson, Jephthah, of David and Samuel and the prophets—who through faith conquered kingdoms, enforced justice, received promises, stopped the mouths of lions, quenched raging fire, escaped the edge of the sword, won strength out of weakness, became mighty in war, put foreign armies to flight. Women received their dead by resurrection. Some were tortured, refusing to accept release, that they might rise again to a better life. Others suffered mocking and scourging, and even chains and imprisonment. They were stoned, they were sawn in two,[y] they were killed with the sword; they went about in skins of sheep and goats, destitute, afflicted, ill-treated—of whom the world was not worthy—wandering over deserts and mountains, and in dens and caves of the earth.

And all these, though well attested by their faith, did not receive what was promised, since God had foreseen something better for us, that apart from us they should not be made perfect.

The Discipline of the Lord

[Hebrews 12:1–11]

THEREFORE, since we are surrounded by so great a cloud of witnesses, let us also lay aside every weight, and sin which clings so closely, and let us run with perseverance the race that is set before us, looking to Jesus the pioneer and perfecter of our faith, who for the joy that was set before him endured the cross, despising the shame, and is seated at the right hand of the throne of God.

Consider him who endured from sinners such hostility against himself, so that you may not grow weary or fainthearted. In your struggle against sin you have not yet resisted to the point of shedding your blood. And have you forgotten the exhortation which addresses you as sons?—

"My son, do not regard lightly the discipline of the Lord,
nor lose courage when you are punished by him.
For the Lord disciplines him whom he loves,
and chastises every son whom he receives."[33]

It is for discipline that you have to endure. God is treating you as sons; for what son is there whom his father does not discipline? If you are left without discipline, in which all have participated, then you are illegitimate children and not sons. Besides this, we have had earthly fathers to discipline us and we respected them. Shall we not much more be subject to the Father of spirits and live? For they disciplined us for a short time at their pleasure, but he disciplines us for our good, that we may share his holiness. For the moment all discipline seems painful rather than pleasant; later it yields the peaceful fruit of righteousness to those who have been trained by it.

[y] Other manuscripts add they were tempted
[33] Proverbs 3:11–12

Warning against Rejecting God's Grace [12:12-24]

Therefore lift your drooping hands and strengthen your weak knees, and make straight paths for your feet, so that what is lame may not be put out of joint but rather be healed. Strive for peace with all men, and for the holiness without which no one will see the Lord. See to it that no one fail to obtain the grace of God; that no "root of bitterness"[34] spring up and cause trouble, and by it the many become defiled; that no one be immoral or irreligious like Esau, who sold his birthright for a single meal. For you know that afterward, when he desired to inherit the blessing, he was rejected, for he found no chance to repent, though he sought it with tears.

For you have not come to what may be touched, a blazing fire, and darkness, and gloom, and a tempest, and the sound of a trumpet, and a voice whose words made the hearers entreat that no further messages be spoken to them. For they could not endure the order that was given, "If even a beast touches the mountain, it shall be stoned."[35] Indeed, so terrifying was the sight that Moses said, "I tremble with fear."[36] But you have come to Mount Zion and to the city of the living God, the heavenly Jerusalem, and to innumerable angels in festal gathering, and to the assembly[z] of the first-born who are enrolled in heaven, and to a judge who is God of all, and to the spirits of just men made perfect, and to Jesus, the mediator of a new covenant, and to the sprinkled blood that speaks more graciously than the blood of Abel.

A Kingdom That Cannot Be Shaken

[12:25-29]

See that you do not refuse him who is speaking. For if they did not escape when they refused him who warned them on earth, much less shall we escape if we reject him who warns from heaven. His voice then shook the earth; but now he has promised, "Yet once more I will shake not only the earth but also the heaven."[37] This phrase, "Yet once more," indicates the removal of what is shaken, as of what has been made, in order that what cannot be shaken may remain. Therefore let us be grateful for receiving a kingdom that cannot be shaken, and thus let us offer to God acceptable worship, with reverence and awe; for our God is a consuming fire.

Service Well-pleasing to God

[Hebrews 13:1-19]

LET brotherly love continue. Do not neglect to show hospitality to strangers, for thereby some have entertained angels unawares. Remember those who are in prison, as though in prison with them; and those who are ill-treated, since you also are in the body. Let marriage be held in honor among all, and let the marriage bed be undefiled; for God will judge the im-

moral and adulterous. Keep your life free from love of money, and be content with what you have; for he has said, "I will never fail you nor forsake you."[38] Hence we can confidently say,

"The Lord is my helper,
I will not be afraid;
what can man do to me?"[39]

Remember your leaders, those who spoke to you the word of God; consider the outcome of their life, and imitate their faith. Jesus Christ is the same yesterday and today and for ever. Do not be led away by diverse and strange teachings; for it is well that the heart be strengthened by grace, not by foods, which have not benefited their adherents. We have an altar from which those who serve the tent[a] have no right to eat. For the bodies of those animals whose blood is brought into the sanctuary by the high priest as a sacrifice for sin are burned outside the camp. So Jesus also suffered outside the gate in order to sanctify the people through his own blood. Therefore let us go forth to him outside the camp, bearing abuse for him. For here we have no lasting city, but we seek the city which is to come. Through him then let us continually offer up a sacrifice of praise to God, that is, the fruit of lips that acknowledge his name. Do not neglect to do good and to share what you have, for such sacrifices are pleasing to God.

Obey your leaders and submit to them; for they are keeping watch over your souls, as men who will have to give account. Let them do this joyfully, and not sadly, for that would be of no advantage to you.

Pray for us, for we are sure that we have a clear conscience, desiring to act honorably in all things. I urge you the more earnestly to do this in order that I may be restored to you the sooner.

Benediction and Final Greetings

[13:20-25]

Now may the God of peace who brought again from the dead our Lord Jesus, the great shepherd of the sheep, by the blood of the eternal covenant, equip you with everything good that you may do his will, working in you[b] that which is pleasing in his sight, through Jesus Christ; to whom be glory for ever and ever. Amen.

I appeal to you, brethren, bear with my word of exhortation, for I have written to you briefly. You should understand that our brother Timothy has been released, with whom I shall see you if he comes soon. Greet all your leaders and all the saints. Those who come from Italy send you greetings. Grace be with all of you. Amen.

[b]Other ancient authorities read us

On his way to Rome, Paul may have seen Mt. Vesuvius. In A.D. 63 a ruinous earthquake destroyed many public buildings in Pompeii. Sixteen years later it was completely buried by volcanic cinders and ash during the tremendous eruption in A.D. 79

In times of danger and persecution, Christians still find courage and faith in Hebrews 11:32 to 12:29. The Roman historian Tacitus, who was not a Christian, records in his Annals (XV, 44) the persecution of the Christians under Nero in A.D. 64 as follows:

"Nero put in his own place as culprits, and punished with most ingenious cruelty, men whom the common people hated for their shameful crimes and called Christians. Christ, from whom the name was derived, had been put to death in the reign of Tiberius by the procurator Pontius Pilate. The deadly superstition, having been checked for a while, began to break out again, not only throughout Judea, where this mischief first arose, but also at Rome, where from all sides all things scandalous and shameful meet and become fashionable. Therefore, at the beginning, some were seized who made confessions; then, on their information, a vast multitude was convicted, not so much of arson as of hatred of the human race. And they were not only put to death, but subjected to insults, in that they were either dressed up in the skins of wild beasts and perished by the cruel mangling of dogs, or else put on crosses to be set on fire, and, as day declined, to be burned, being used as light by night. Nero had thrown open his gardens for that spectacle, and gave a circus play, mingling with the people dressed in a charioteer's costume or driving in a chariot. From this arose, however, toward men who were, indeed, criminals and deserving extreme penalties, sympathy, on the ground that they were destroyed not for the public good, but to satisfy the cruelty of an individual."

[z]Or *angels, and to the festal gathering and assembly*
[34]*Deuteronomy 29:18, Septuagint*
[35]*Exodus 19:12-13*
[36]*Deuteronomy 9:19*
[37]*Haggai 2:6*

[a]Or *tabernacle*
[38]*Deuteronomy 31:6, 8; Joshua 1:5*
[39]*Psalms 118:6*

PUT ON THE WHOLE ARMOR OF GOD EPH. 6:11

Augustus, seated in the center, with his left hand resting on a shield marked FELICITAS TIBERI (good fortune of Tiberius), offers an image of victory to Tiberius, standing before him in military dress. (Enlargement of head of sword-sheath below)

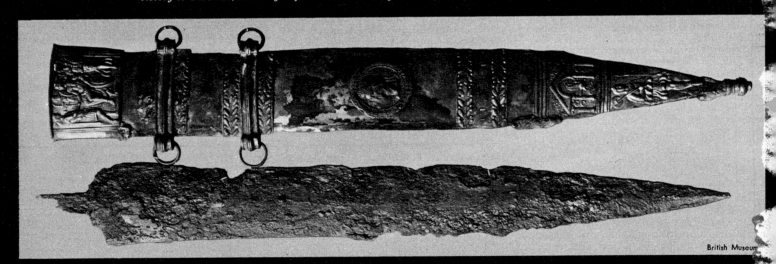

Sword sheath and Roman sword, with blade about two feet long, found at Mainz, Germany, which belonged to an officer of Drusus or Tiberius

AND TAKE . . . THE SWORD OF THE SPIRIT, WHICH IS THE WORD OF GOD EPH. 6:17

Out of Death Into Life

ISLE OF PATMOS
LOOKING DOWN ON THE HARBOR

M. Chrousaki

THE LETTERS OF JAMES, PETER, JOHN AND JUDE
AND THE REVELATION TO JOHN
REVISED STANDARD VERSION

THE DIASPORA

Circumstances dispersed the Jews to every part of the Roman Empire. This Diaspora or Dispersion helped to make possible the rapid spread of Christianity in New Testament times. It was to Jews, proselytes and Gentiles in such widely scattered communities that the general letters, such as James and 1 Peter, were addressed—the latter to people living in provinces of Asia Minor.

PROVINCES IN ASIA MINOR

PONTUS was a region on the Black Sea. A series of kings, of whom the first was Mithridates I, ruled from about 300 B.C. until the conquest by Pompey in 64 B.C. In A.D. 111 the region was joined with Bithynia to form the joint province of Bithynia and Pontus. One of the governors of this new province was Pliny the Younger, who in a letter (about A.D. 112) to the Emperor Trajan tells of the persecution of Christians in this area. There is a narrow plain along the coast, and back of that a high tableland. The native people of Pontus were called White Syrians by the Greeks, and from the sixth century B.C. on, many Greek colonies were established on the seacoast.

GALATIA was the Roman province in which were located the churches that Paul addressed in his Galatian letter. It has been described in the introduction to the illustrated book in this series containing that letter.

CAPPADOCIA lay east of Galatia and north of Cilicia. It was a mountainous region traversed by the Halys River, which flows on through Galatia and Pontus into the Black Sea. After domination by Persia and rule by native kings, Cappadocia became a Roman province in A.D. 17.

The province of ASIA extended over most of the western half of Asia Minor. Greek settlements were founded along the coast at an early time, and in the sixth century B.C. the famous Thales and other philosophers were living at Miletus. In the course of war against Antiochus the Great the Romans took possession of the region and in 189 B.C. gave it to their friend, Eumenes, king of Pergamum. In turn, in 133 B.C. his adopted son Attalus III, in order to exclude a rival, bequeathed the province back to the Romans. With such a history the province of Asia was the most thoroughly Hellenized part of all Asia Minor. It had many important cities, which were centers of Greek civilization; and when the establishment of the Roman Empire brought the benefits of peace, there was strong loyalty to Rome and disposition to worship the emperor. Native gods were also worshiped, and of these Artemis (Diana), the goddess of Ephesus, was specially prominent. In all, the province of Asia provided a remarkable meeting and mingling place for the Greek spirit and the Asian spirit.

BITHYNIA adjoined the province of Asia on the north. Mountainous and forested in large part, it has fertile valleys near the coast. The native inhabitants were immigrants from Thrace whom Herodotus calls Bithyni. The first of their leaders to have the title of king was Nicomedes I, who reigned from 278 to 250 B.C. and founded the city of Nicomedia. The last king was Nicomedes III, who willed his kingdom to the Romans in 74 B.C. Under the Romans Bithynia and Pontus were usually, for administrative purposes, combined into a single province. Next to Nicomedia the most important city of Bithynia was Nicaea, where the famous Council of A.D. 325 formulated the Nicene Creed.

PATMOS AND THE CITIES OF THE PROVINCE OF ASIA

In Revelation 1:9 John states that he was on the Island of Patmos. It was one of a group of islands known as the Sporades, lying off the coast of Asia Minor. This small volcanic island, rising to a point 800 feet above sea level, is only ten miles long and six miles broad. Although Ionian Greeks settled there at an early time, the island has often been quite deserted.

In the Book of Revelation are letters addressed to churches in seven cities of Asia. Of these, EPHESUS is described in the introduction to the illustrated Book of Acts. After the fall of Jerusalem in A.D. 70 Ephesus must have quickly risen to a place of great importance in the Christian world.

SMYRNA was an early Greek colony which was destroyed by the Lydians not long after 600 B.C. Alexander the Great planned to restore the city, and this was actually done on a new site by Antigonus (316–301 B.C.) and Lysimachus (301–281 B.C.). On some of her coins Smyrna claimed to be "first of Asia in beauty and size," and today it is still a large city. The phrase "the crown of Smyrna" seems to have been applied to the circle of public buildings on the rounded top of the hill Pagos, on the lower slopes of which the rest of the city was spread out. As early as 195 B.C. Smyrna dedicated a temple to the Goddess of Rome. The cult of the Roman emperors, however, was also established in PERGAMUM as the chief city in Asia in 29 B.C., when a temple was dedicated to Augustus and Rome by the Provincial Synod. Smyrna strove with Pergamum, and later Ephesus, for the title of the first city of Asia; and in A.D. 26 it secured

THRACIA

the sole privilege of erecting a temple to Tiberius, Livia and the Senate. Smyrna could therefore then claim the imperial title of "Temple Warden." Ephesus was not honored with this title of "Temple Warden" (Acts 19:35) until the reign of Claudius or Nero.

Coins of Pergamum are known from the fifth century B.C. Its kings were friends of the Romans; and the last of them, Attalus III, bequeathed the city and kingdom to the Roman power in 133 B.C. For a century or two the city continued as capital of the province and always remained, with Ephesus and Smyrna, one of the three great cities of imperial Asia. As indicated above, the first temple of the emperor-worship cult in Asia was built in 29 B.C. at Pergamum. Previously King Eumenes had built a great Altar of Zeus, adorned with magnificent sculptures. Behind the city there was a huge conical hill, 1,000 feet high, which in New Testament times was covered with temples to Zeus, Athena, Dionysus and Aesculapius. The emperor cult was further strengthened in Pergamum with a second temple built to Trajan, and a third in honor of Severus.

THYATIRA was on a main route leading inland into Asia. Built as a garrison city by Seleucus I, a general of Alexander the Great and the founder of the Seleucid dynasty, it was held later by the Pergamenian kings. Lying in a long and beautiful valley, Thyatira always occupied a relatively humble position. Yet some commercial importance attached to the place, particularly with regard to the manufacture of purple cloth; and in Acts 16:14 it is stated that Lydia, a seller of such goods, came from Thyatira.

SARDIS, in the Hermus valley, was on another route of travel inland from the Aegean. Prominent as capital of a powerful Lydian empire in the seventh century B.C., it was captured by Cyrus in 546 B.C. and by Antiochus the Great at the end of the third century B.C. Struck by a severe earthquake in A.D. 17, it was rebuilt rapidly with the help of Tiberius. Important industrially, Sardis was known for the manufacture of woolen stuffs and carpets. Its inhabitants were noted for luxury and licentiousness. Its patron goddess was the mother-goddess Cybele, columns of whose temple are still to be seen there.

PHILADELPHIA took its name from Attalus II Philadelphus (159–138 B.C.), who received this surname because of his loyalty to his brother Eumenes. Located in a valley tributary to that of the Hermus River, Philadelphia was on the route of the imperial post road which came from Rome by way of Troas, Pergamum and Sardis and continued to the east. In A.D. 17 the city was smitten by a severe earthquake; and several years later, according to Strabo, the inhabitants were still living outside the walls, since recurring shocks were still being felt. Its chief pagan cult was that of Dionysus, god of vegetation, especially of the vine.

LAODICEA was situated on low hills two miles south of the Lycus River and nine miles east of where that river and the Maeander come together. Trade routes from both Philadelphia and Ephesus joined here and continued toward the east. The city was probably founded by Antiochus II Theos (261–246 B.C.) and named after his wife Laodice. Lying in a fertile district, Laodicea was famous for fine wool and for large transactions in money. The Phrygian god Men was worshiped in a fine temple, adjacent to which a famous school of medicine was established. Largely destroyed by the great earthquakes of A.D. 60–61, the city was so rich it did not have to apply for an imperial subsidy.

"A wave of the sea that is driven and tossed by the wind" (Jas. 1:6)

Matson Photo Service

"Like the flower of the grass he will pass away" (Jas. 1:10).
The six-petaled flower is known today as the Star of Bethlehem

Palestine Institute

THE LETTER OF JAMES

Greetings

[James 1:1] James, a servant of God and of the Lord Jesus Christ,
To the twelve tribes in the Dispersion:
Greeting.

Joy in Trials [1:2-4]

Count it all joy, my brethren, when you meet various trials, for you know that the testing of your faith produces steadfastness. And let steadfastness have its full effect, that you may be perfect and complete, lacking in nothing.

God Gives Wisdom [1:5-8]

If any of you lacks wisdom, let him ask God, who gives to all men generously and without reproaching, and it will be given him. But let him ask in faith, with no doubting, for he who doubts is like a wave of the sea that is driven and tossed by the wind. For that person must not suppose that a double-minded man, unstable in all his ways, will receive anything from the Lord.

The Rich and the Lowly [1:9-11]

Let the lowly brother boast in his exaltation, and the rich in his humiliation, because like the flower of the grass he will pass away. For the sun rises with its scorching heat and withers the grass; its flower falls, and its beauty perishes. So will the rich man fade away in the midst of his pursuits.

Endurance of Trial [1:12-15]

Blessed is the man who endures trial, for when he has stood the test he will receive the crown of life which God has promised to those who love him. Let no one say when he is tempted, "I am tempted by God"; for God cannot be tempted with evil and he himself tempts no one; but each person is tempted when he is lured and enticed by his own desire. Then desire when it has conceived gives birth to sin; and sin when it is full-grown brings forth death.

Every Good and Perfect Gift [1:16-18]

Do not be deceived, my beloved brethren. Every good endowment and every perfect gift is from above, coming down from the Father of lights with whom there is no variation or shadow due to change.[a] Of his own will he brought us forth by the word of truth that we should be a kind of first fruits of his creatures.

Be Slow to Anger [1:19-21]

Know this, my beloved brethren. Let every man be quick to hear, slow to speak, slow to anger, for the anger of man does not work the righteousness of God. Therefore put away all filthiness and rank growth of wickedness and receive with meekness the implanted word, which is able to save your souls.

Doers of the Word [1:22-25]

But be doers of the word, and not hearers only, deceiving yourselves. For if any one is a hearer of the word and not a doer, he is like a man who observes his natural face in a mirror; for he observes himself and goes away and at once forgets what he was like. But he who looks into the perfect law, the law of liberty, and perseveres, being no hearer that forgets but a doer that acts, he shall be blessed in his doing.

Pure Religion [1:26-27]

If any one thinks he is religious, and does not bridle his tongue but deceives his heart, this man's religion is vain. Religion that is pure and undefiled before God and the Father is this: to visit orphans and widows in their affliction, and to keep oneself unstained from the world.

[a]Other ancient authorities read *variation due to a shadow of turning*

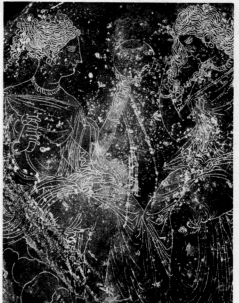

The Metropolitan Museum of Art

Part of mirror cover engraved with scene showing use of polished bronze mirror. Greek, fourth century B.C.

Bronze Roman horse-head with bridle

Walters Art Gallery

227

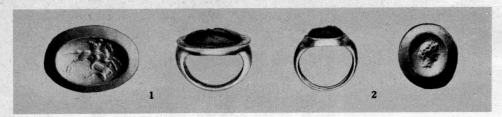

Part of a treasure found in a grave in Piraeus, Greece. (Probably early first century A.D.) (1) Gold finger ring with engraved convex garnet. Design: Greek armored rider attacking a barbarian soldier. (2) Gold finger ring with engraved convex garnet. Design: head of Dionysus. (3) Gold bracelet ending in snakes' heads. Eyes and tongues formed by beads of "mother of emerald". (4) Bracelet. Gold core decorated with beads of "mother of emerald"

Berta Segall

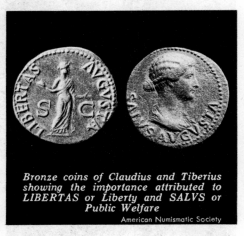

Christian Impartiality [James 2:1-7]

MY BRETHREN, show no partiality as you hold the faith of our Lord Jesus Christ, the Lord of glory. For if a man with gold rings and in fine clothing comes into your assembly, and a poor man in shabby clothing also comes in, and you pay attention to the one who wears the fine clothing and say, "Have a seat here, please," while you say to the poor man, "Stand there," or, "Sit at my feet," have you not made distinctions among yourselves, and become judges with evil thoughts? Listen, my beloved brethren. Has not God chosen those who are poor in the world to be rich in faith and heirs of the kingdom which he has promised to those who love him? But you have dishonored the poor man. Is it not the

Bronze coins of Claudius and Tiberius showing the importance attributed to LIBERTAS or Liberty and SALVS or Public Welfare

American Numismatic Society

"The ships also . . . are guided by a very small rudder" (Jas. 3:4). From monument on the Street of the Tomb. Pompeii

Felbermeyer

rich who oppress you, is it not they who drag you into court? Is it not they who blaspheme that honorable name by which you are called?

The Royal Law [2:8-13]

If you really fulfil the royal law, according to the scripture, "You shall love your neighbor as yourself,"[1] you do well. But if you show partiality, you commit sin, and are convicted by the law as transgressors. For whoever keeps the whole law but fails in one point has become guilty of all of it. For he who said, "Do not commit adultery," said also, "Do not kill."[2] If you do not commit adultery but do kill, you have become a transgressor of the law. So speak and so act as those who are to be judged under the law of liberty. For judgment is without mercy to one who has shown no mercy; yet mercy triumphs over judgment.

Faith and Works [2:14-26]

What does it profit, my brethren, if a man says he has faith but has not works? Can his faith save him? If a brother or sister is ill-clad and in lack of daily food, and one of you says to them, "Go in peace, be warmed and filled," without giving them the things needed for the body, what does it profit? So faith by itself, if it has no works, is dead.

But some one will say, "You have faith and I have works." Show me your faith apart from your works, and I by my works will show you my faith. You believe that God is one; you do well. Even the demons believe—and shudder. Do you want to be shown, you foolish fellow, that faith apart from works is barren? Was not Abraham our father justified by works, when he offered his son Isaac upon the altar? You see that faith was active along with his works, and faith was completed by works, and the scripture was fulfilled which says, "Abraham believed God, and it was reckoned to him as righteousness";[3] and he was called the friend of God. You see that a man is justified by works and not by faith alone. And in the same way was not also Rahab the harlot justified by works when she received the messengers and sent them out another way? For as the body apart from the spirit is dead, so faith apart from works is dead.

The Tongue a Little Member

[James 3:1-5]

LET NOT many of you become teachers, my brethren, for you know that we who teach shall be judged with greater strictness. For we all make many mistakes, and if any one makes no mistakes in what he says he is a perfect man, able to bridle the whole body also. If we put bits into the mouths of horses that they may obey us, we guide their whole bodies. Look at the ships also; though they are so great and are driven by strong winds, they are guided by a very small rudder wherever the will of the pilot directs. So the tongue is a little member and boasts of great things. How great a forest is set ablaze by a small fire!

[1]*Leviticus* 19:18
[2]*Exodus* 20:13-14; *Deuteronomy* 5:17-18
[3]*Genesis* 15:6

The Tongue a Fire [3:6-12]

And the tongue is a fire. The tongue is an unrighteous world among our members, staining the whole body, setting on fire the cycle of nature,[b] and set on fire by hell.[c] For every kind of beast and bird, of reptile and sea creature, can be tamed and has been tamed by humankind, but no human being can tame the tongue—a restless evil, full of deadly poison. With it we bless the Lord and Father, and with it we curse men, who are made in the likeness of God. From the same mouth come blessing and cursing. My brethren, this ought not to be so. Does a spring pour forth from the same opening fresh water and brackish? Can a fig tree, my brethren, yield olives, or a grapevine figs? No more can salt water yield fresh.

Fereday

A farmer plowing in the Holy Land

The Wisdom from Above [3:13-18]

Who is wise and understanding among you? By his good life let him show his works in the meekness of wisdom. But if you have bitter jealousy and selfish ambition in your hearts, do not boast and be false to the truth. This wisdom is not such as comes down from above, but is earthly, unspiritual, devilish. For where jealousy and selfish ambition exist, there will be disorder and every vile practice. But the wisdom from above is first pure, then peaceable, gentle, open to reason, full of mercy and good fruits, without uncertainty or insincerity. And the harvest of righteousness is sown in peace by those who make peace.

Friendship with the World

[James 4:1-10]

WHAT causes wars, and what causes fightings among you? Is it not your passions that are at war in your members? You desire and do not have; so you kill. And you covet[d] and cannot obtain; so you fight and wage war. You do not have, because you do not ask. You ask and do not receive, because you ask wrongly, to spend it on your passions. Unfaithful creatures! Do you not know that friendship with the world is enmity with God? Therefore whoever wishes to be a friend of the world makes himself an enemy of God. Or do you suppose it is in vain that the scripture says, "He yearns jealously over the spirit which he has made to dwell in us"? But he gives more grace; therefore it says, "God opposes the proud, but gives grace to the humble."[4] Submit yourselves therefore to God. Resist the devil and he will flee from you. Draw near to God and he will draw near to you. Cleanse your hands, you sinners, and purify your hearts, you men of double mind. Be wretched and mourn and weep. Let your laughter be turned to mourning and your joy to dejection. Humble yourselves before the Lord and he will exalt you.

Judging a Brother [4:11-12]

Do not speak evil against one another, brethren. He that speaks evil against a brother or judges his brother, speaks evil against the law and judges the law. But if you judge the law, you are not a doer of the law but a judge. There is one lawgiver and judge, he who is able to save and to destroy. But who are you that you judge your neighbor?

[b] Or *wheel of birth*
[c] Greek *Gehenna*
[d] Or *you kill and you covet*
[4] Proverbs 3:34

Boast Not of Tomorrow [4:13-17]

Come now, you who say, "Today or tomorrow we will go into such and such a town and spend a year there and trade and get gain"; whereas you do not know about tomorrow. What is your life? For you are a mist that appears for a little time and then vanishes. Instead you ought to say, "If the Lord wills, we shall live and we shall do this or that." As it is, you boast in your arrogance. All such boasting is evil. Whoever knows what is right to do and fails to do it, for him it is sin.

The Injustice of the Rich [James 5:1-6]

COME NOW, you rich, weep and howl for the miseries that are coming upon you. Your riches have rotted and your garments are moth-eaten. Your gold and silver have rusted, and their rust will be evidence against you and will eat your flesh like fire. You have laid up treasure[e] for the last days. Behold, the wages of the laborers who mowed your fields, which you kept back by fraud, cry out; and the cries of the harvesters have reached the ears of the Lord of hosts. You have lived on the earth in luxury and in pleasure; you have fattened your hearts in a day of slaughter. You have condemned, you have killed the righteous man; he does not resist you.

Be Patient [5:7-12]

Be patient, therefore, brethren, until the coming of the Lord. Behold, the farmer waits for the precious fruit of the earth, being patient over it until it receives the early and the late rain. You also be patient. Establish your hearts, for the coming of the Lord is at hand. Do not grumble, brethren,

[e] Or *will eat your flesh, since you have stored up fire*

Gathering the fruits of the earth

Matson Photo Service

against one another, that you may not be judged; behold, the Judge is standing at the doors. As an example of suffering and patience, brethren, take the prophets who spoke in the name of the Lord. Behold, we call those happy who were steadfast. You have heard of the steadfastness of Job, and you have seen the purpose of the Lord, how the Lord is compassionate and merciful.

But above all, my brethren, do not swear, either by heaven or by earth or with any other oath, but let your yes be yes and your no be no, that you may not fall under condemnation.

The Power of Prayer [5:13-18]

Is any one among you suffering? Let him pray. Is any cheerful? Let him sing praise. Is any among you sick? Let him call for the elders of the church, and let them pray over him, anointing him with oil in the name of the Lord; and the prayer of faith will save the sick man, and the Lord will raise him up; and if he has committed sins, he will be forgiven. Therefore confess your sins to one another, and pray for one another, that you may be healed. The prayer of a righteous man has great power in its effects. Eli'jah was a man of like nature with ourselves and he prayed fervently that it might not rain, and for three years and six months it did not rain on the earth. Then he prayed again and the heaven gave rain, and the earth brought forth its fruit.

Saving a Soul from Death [5:19-20]

My brethren, if any one among you wanders from the truth and some one brings him back, let him know that whoever brings back a sinner from the error of his way will save his soul from death and will cover a multitude of sins.

Measuring the grain

Underwood & Underwood

THE FIRST LETTER OF PETER

Greetings

[1 Peter 1:1–2] Peter, an apostle of Jesus Christ,

To the exiles of the Dispersion in Pontus, Gala′tia, Cappado′cia, Asia, and Bithyn′ia, chosen and destined by God the Father and sanctified by the Spirit for obedience to Jesus Christ and for sprinkling with his blood:

May grace and peace be multiplied to you.

Ernest Nash

Temple of Saturn on the Roman Forum, fifth century B.C., rebuilt in 42 B.C., served as the treasury of the Senate's funds. A pair of scales signified this fiscal function

Ernest Nash

Rome. First temple of Apollo, 433 B.C., rebuilt by C. Sosius, 32 B.C.

Immediately after the Apostolic Age the faith of the Christians in Bithynia was tested by the Roman authorities under Trajan, as shown in this letter of Pliny the Younger to that Emperor, ca. A.D. 112

Loeb Classical Library

A Living Hope [1:3–9]

Blessed be the God and Father of our Lord Jesus Christ! By his great mercy we have been born anew to a living hope through the resurrection of Jesus Christ from the dead, and to an inheritance which is imperishable, undefiled, and unfading, kept in heaven for you, who by God's power are guarded through faith for a salvation ready to be revealed in the last time. In this you rejoice,[a] though now for a little while you may have to suffer various trials, so that the genuineness of your faith, more precious than gold which though perishable is tested by fire, may redound to praise and glory and honor at the revelation of Jesus Christ. Without having seen[b] him you[c] love him; though you do not now see him you[c] believe in him and rejoice with unutterable and exalted joy. As the outcome of your faith you obtain the salvation of your souls.

The Inquiry of the Prophets [1:10–12]

The prophets who prophesied of the grace that was to be yours searched and inquired about this salvation; they inquired what person or time was indicated by the Spirit of Christ within them when predicting the sufferings of Christ and the subsequent glory. It was revealed to them that they were serving not themselves but you, in the things which have now been announced to you by those who preached the good news to you through the Holy Spirit sent from heaven, things into which angels long to look.

Be Holy [1:13–21]

Therefore gird up your minds, be sober, set your hope fully upon the grace that is coming to you at the revelation of Jesus Christ. As obedient children, do not be conformed to the passions of your former ignorance, but as he who called you is holy,

[a] Or *Rejoice in this*
[b] Other ancient authorities read *known*   [c] Or omit *you*

be holy yourselves in all your conduct; since it is written, "You shall be holy, for I am holy."[1] And if you invoke as Father him who judges each one impartially according to his deeds, conduct yourselves with fear throughout the time of your exile. You know that you were ransomed from the futile ways inherited from your fathers, not with perishable things such as silver or gold, but with the precious blood of Christ, like that of a lamb without blemish or spot. He was destined before the foundation of the world but was made manifest at the end of the times for your sake. Through him you have confidence in God, who raised him from the dead and gave him glory, so that your faith and hope are in God.[d]

Born Anew through God's Word [1:22–25]

Having purified your souls by your obedience to the truth for a sincere love of the brethren, love one another earnestly from the heart. You have been born anew, not of perishable seed but of imperishable, through the living and abiding word of God; for

"All flesh is like grass
and all its glory like the flower of grass.
The grass withers, and the flower falls,
but the word of the Lord abides for ever."[2]

That word is the good news which was preached to you.

Newborn Babes [1 Peter 2:1–3]

SO PUT away all malice and all guile and insincerity and envy and all slander. Like newborn babes, long for the pure spiritual milk, that by it you may grow up to salvation; for you have tasted the kindness of the Lord.

The Living Stone [2:4–8]

Come to him, to that living stone, rejected by men but in God's sight chosen and precious; and like living stones be yourselves built into a spiritual house, to be a holy priesthood, to offer spiritual sacrifices acceptable to God through Jesus Christ. For it stands in scripture:

"Behold, I am laying in Zion a stone, a cornerstone chosen and precious,
and he who believes in him will not be put to shame."[3]

To you therefore who believe, he is precious, but for those who do not believe,

"The very stone which the builders rejected
has become the head of the corner,"[4]

and

"A stone that will make men stumble, a rock that will make them fall";[5]

for they stumble because they disobey the word, as they were destined to do.

[d] Or *so that your faith is hope in God*
[1] Leviticus 11:44–45   [2] Isaiah 40:6–8
[3] Isaiah 28:16   [4] Psalms 118:22   [5] Isaiah 8:14–15

230

God's Own People [2:9–10]

But you are a chosen race, a royal priesthood, a holy nation, God's own people,[e] that you may declare the wonderful deeds of him who called you out of darkness into his marvelous light. Once you were no people but now you are God's people; once you had not received mercy but now you have received mercy.

Abstain from Fleshly Passions [2:11–12]

Beloved, I beseech you as aliens and exiles to abstain from the passions of the flesh that wage war against your soul. Maintain good conduct among the Gentiles, so that in case they speak against you as wrongdoers, they may see your good deeds and glorify God on the day of visitation.

Live as God's Servants [2:13–17]

Be subject for the Lord's sake to every human institution,[f] whether it be to the emperor as supreme, or to governors as sent by him to punish those who do wrong and to praise those who do right. For it is God's will that by doing right you should put to silence the ignorance of foolish men. Live as free men, yet without using your freedom as a pretext for evil; but live as servants of God. Honor all men. Love the brotherhood. Fear God. Honor the emperor.

The Example of Christ's Suffering [2:18–25]

Servants, be submissive to your masters with all respect, not only to the kind and gentle but also to the overbearing. For one is approved if, mindful of God, he endures pain while suffering unjustly. For what credit is it, if when you do wrong and are beaten for it you take it patiently? But if when you do right and suffer for it you take it patiently, you have God's approval. For to this you have been called, because Christ also suffered for you, leaving you an example, that you should follow in his steps. He committed no sin; no guile was found on his lips. When he was reviled, he did not revile in return; when he suffered, he did not threaten; but he trusted to him who judges justly. He himself bore our sins in his body on the tree,[g] that we might die to sin and live to righteousness. By his wounds you have been healed. For you were straying like sheep, but have now returned to the Shepherd and Guardian of your souls.

Behavior of Wives and Husbands [1 Peter 3:1–7]

LIKEWISE you wives, be submissive to your husbands, so that some, though they do not obey the word, may be won without a word by the behavior of their wives, when they see your reverent and chaste behavior. Let not yours be the outward adorning with braiding of hair, decoration of gold, and wearing of robes, but let it be the hidden person of the heart with the imperishable jewel of a gentle and quiet spirit, which in God's sight is very precious. So once the holy women who hoped in God used to adorn themselves and were submissive to their husbands, as Sarah obeyed Abraham, calling him lord. And you are now her children if you do right and let nothing terrify you.

Likewise you husbands, live considerately with your wives, bestowing honor on the woman as the weaker sex, since you are joint heirs of the grace of life, in order that your prayers may not be hindered.

Have Unity of Spirit [3:8–12]

Finally, all of you, have unity of spirit, sympathy, love of the brethren, a tender heart and a humble mind. Do not return evil for evil or reviling for reviling; but on the contrary bless, for to this you have been called, that you may obtain a blessing. For

"He that would love life
and see good days,
let him keep his tongue from evil
and his lips from speaking guile;
let him turn away from evil and do right;
let him seek peace and pursue it.
For the eyes of the Lord are upon the righteous,
and his ears are open to their prayer.
But the face of the Lord is against those that do evil."[6]

Suffering for Doing Right [3:13–22]

Now who is there to harm you if you are zealous for what is right? But even if you do suffer for righteousness' sake, you will be blessed. Have no fear of them, nor be troubled, but in your hearts reverence Christ as Lord. Always be prepared to make a defense to any one who calls you to account for the hope that is in you, yet do it with gentleness and reverence; and keep your conscience clear, so that, when you are abused, those who revile your good behavior in Christ may be put to shame. For it is better to suffer for doing right, if that should be God's will, than for doing wrong. For Christ also died[h] for sins once for all, the righteous for the unrighteous, that he might bring us to God, being put to death in the flesh but made alive in the spirit; in which he went and preached to the spirits in prison, who formerly did not obey, when God's patience waited in the days of Noah, during the building of the ark, in which a few, that is, eight persons, were saved through water. Baptism, which

Lictors were the constant attendants and guards of the Roman magistrates. They could summon offenders before the magistrates and seize, bind and scourge them as the magistrates directed

Alinari

Certificate of pagan sacrifice. In a later persecution of the Christians by the Emperor Decius, A.D. 250, many Roman citizens obtained certificates like this one, stating that they had performed sacrifices to the pagan gods:

The John Rylands Library

"To the commissioners of sacrifices from Aurelia Demos, who has no father, daughter of Helene and wife of Aurelius Irenaeus, of the Quarter of the Helleneum. It has ever been my habit to sacrifice to the gods, and now also I have in your presence, in accordance with the command, made sacrifice and libation and tasted the offering, and I beg you to certify my statement. Farewell. I, Aurelia Demos, have presented this declaration. I, Aurelius Irenaeus, wrote for her, as she is illiterate. I, Aurelius Sabinus, prytanis, saw you sacrificing. The first year of the Emperor Caesar Gaius Messius Quintus Trajanus Decius Pius Felix Augustus, Pauni 20"

[e]Greek a people for his possession
[f]Or every institution ordained for men
[g]Or carried up . . . to the tree

[h]Other ancient authorities read suffered
[6]Psalms 34:12–16

231

Paul's Photos

corresponds to this, now saves you, not as a removal of dirt from the body but as an appeal to God for a clear conscience, through the resurrection of Jesus Christ, who has gone into heaven and is at the right hand of God, with angels, authorities, and powers subject to him.

Ceasing from Sin [1 Peter 4:1-6]

SINCE therefore Christ suffered in the flesh,[i] arm yourselves with the same thought, for whoever has suffered in the flesh has ceased from sin, so as to live for the rest of the time in the flesh no longer by human passions but by the will of God. Let the time that is past suffice for doing what the Gentiles like to do, living in licentiousness, passions, drunkenness, revels, carousing, and lawless idolatry. They are surprised that you do not now join them in the same wild profligacy, and they abuse you; but they will give account to him who is ready to judge the living and the dead. For this is why the gospel was preached even to the dead, that though judged in the flesh like men, they might live in the spirit like God.

Good Stewards of God's Grace [4:7-11]

The end of all things is at hand; therefore keep sane and sober for your prayers. Above all hold unfailing your love for one another, since love covers a multitude of sins. Practice hospitality ungrudgingly to one another. As each has received a gift, employ it for one another, as good stewards of God's varied grace: whoever speaks, as one who utters oracles of God; whoever renders service, as one who renders it by the strength which God supplies; in order

[i]Other ancient authorities add *for us;* some *for you*

Ernest Nash

The great earthquake of A.D. 63 destroyed most of the public buildings of Pompeii

"Tend the flock of God" (1 Peter 5.2). To Peter, who denied him three times, Jesus said: "Feed my lambs, . . . tend my sheep, . . . feed my sheep, . . . Follow me" (John 21:16-19)

that in everything God may be glorified through Jesus Christ. To him belong glory and dominion for ever and ever. Amen.

Suffering as a Christian [4:12-19]

Beloved, do not be surprised at the fiery ordeal which comes upon you to prove you, as though something strange were happening to you. But rejoice in so far as you share Christ's sufferings, that you may also rejoice and be glad when his glory is revealed. If you are reproached for the name of Christ, you are blessed, because the spirit of glory[j] and of God rests upon you. But let none of you suffer as a murderer, or a thief, or a wrongdoer, or a mischief-maker; yet if one suffers as a Christian, let him not be ashamed, but under that name let him glorify God. For the time has come for judgment to begin with the household of God; and if it begins with us, what will be the end of those who do not obey the gospel of God? And

"If the righteous man is scarcely saved, where will the impious and sinner appear?"[7]

Therefore let those who suffer according to God's will do right and entrust their souls to a faithful Creator.

The Flock of God [1 Peter 5:1-5]

SO I exhort the elders among you, as a fellow elder and a witness of the sufferings of Christ as well as a partaker in the glory that is to be revealed. Tend the flock of God that is your charge,[k] not by constraint but willingly,[l] not for shameful gain but eagerly, not as domineering over those in your charge but being examples to the flock. And when the chief Shepherd is manifested you will obtain the unfading crown of glory. Likewise you that are younger be subject to the elders. Clothe yourselves, all of you, with humility toward one another, for "God opposes the proud, but gives grace to the humble."[8]

Humble Yourselves [5:6-11]

Humble yourselves therefore under the mighty hand of God, that in due time he may exalt you. Cast all your anxieties on him, for he cares about you. Be sober, be watchful. Your adversary the devil prowls around like a roaring lion, seeking some one to devour. Resist him, firm in your faith, knowing that the same experience of suffering is required of your brotherhood throughout the world. And after you have suffered a little while, the God of all grace, who has called you to his eternal glory in Christ, will himself restore, establish, and strengthen[m] you. To him be the dominion for ever and ever. Amen.

Final Greetings [5:12-14]

By Silva'nus, a faithful brother as I regard him, I have written briefly to you, exhorting and declaring that this is the true grace of God; stand fast in it. She who is at Babylon, who is likewise chosen, sends you greetings; and so does my son Mark. Greet one another with the kiss of love. Peace to all of you that are in Christ.

[j]Other ancient authorities insert *and of power*
[k]Other ancient authorities add *exercising the oversight*
[l]Other ancient authorities add *as God would have you*
[m]Other ancient authorities read *restore, establish, strengthen and settle*
[7]Proverbs 11:31, Septuagint   [8]Proverbs 3:34

THE SECOND LETTER OF
PETER

Greetings

[2 Peter 1:1–2] Simon Peter, a servant and apostle of Jesus Christ,

To those who have obtained a faith of equal standing with ours in the righteousness of our God and Savior Jesus Christ:[a]

May grace and peace be multiplied to you in the knowledge of God and of Jesus our Lord.

Supplement Faith with Virtue [1:3–11]

His divine power has granted to us all things that pertain to life and godliness, through the knowledge of him who called us to[b] his own glory and excellence, by which he has granted to us his precious and very great promises, that through these you may escape from the corruption that is in the world because of passion, and become partakers of the divine nature. For this very reason make every effort to supplement your faith with virtue, and virtue with knowledge, and knowledge with self-control, and self-control with steadfastness, and steadfastness with godliness, and godliness with brotherly affection, and brotherly affection with love. For if these things are yours and abound, they keep you from being ineffective or unfruitful in the knowledge of our Lord Jesus Christ. For whoever lacks these things is blind and shortsighted and has forgotten that he was cleansed from his old sins. Therefore, brethren, be the more zealous to confirm your call and election, for if you do this you will never fall; so there will be richly provided for you an entrance into the eternal kingdom of our Lord and Savior Jesus Christ.

A Reminder [1:12–15]

Therefore I intend always to remind you of these things, though you know them and are established in the truth that you have. I think it right, as long as I am in this body,[c] to arouse you by way of reminder, since I know that the putting off of my body[c] will be soon, as our Lord Jesus Christ showed me. And I will see to it that after my departure you may be able at any time to recall these things.

Eyewitnesses of His Majesty [1:16–21]

For we did not follow cleverly devised myths when we made known to you the power and coming of our Lord Jesus Christ, but we were eyewitnesses of his majesty. For when he received honor and glory from God the Father and the voice was borne to him by the Majestic Glory, "This is my beloved Son,[d] with whom I am well pleased," we heard this voice borne from heaven, for we were with him on the holy mountain. And we have the prophetic word made more sure. You will do well to pay at-tention to this as to a lamp shining in a dark place, until the day dawns and the morning star rises in your hearts. First of all you must understand this, that no prophecy of scripture is a matter of one's own interpretation, because no prophecy ever came by the impulse of man, but men moved by the Holy Spirit spoke from God.[e]

False Teachers to Arise [2 Peter 2:1–3]

BUT false prophets also arose among the people, just as there will be false teachers among you, who will secretly bring in destructive heresies, even denying the Master who bought them, bringing upon themselves swift destruction. And many will follow their licentiousness, and because of them the way of truth will be reviled. And in their greed they will exploit you with false words; from of old their condemnation has not been idle, and their destruction has not been asleep.

Unrighteous under Punishment [2:4–10a]

For if God did not spare the angels when they sinned, but cast them into hell[f] and committed them to pits of nether gloom to be kept until the judgment; if he did not spare the ancient world, but preserved Noah, a herald of righteousness, with seven other persons, when he brought a flood upon the world of the ungodly; if by turning the cities of Sodom and Gomor'rah to ashes he condemned them to extinction and made them an example to those who were to be ungodly; and if he rescued righteous Lot, greatly distressed by the licentiousness of the wicked (for by what that righteous man saw and heard as he lived among them, he was vexed in his righteous soul day after day with their lawless deeds), then the Lord knows how to rescue the godly from trial, and to keep the unrighteous under punishment until the day of judgment, and especially those who indulge in the lust of defiling passion and despise authority.

Followers in Balaam's Way [2:10b–16]

Bold and wilful, they are not afraid to revile the glorious ones, whereas angels, though greater in might and power, do not pronounce a reviling judgment upon them before the Lord. But these, like irrational animals, creatures of instinct, born to be caught and killed, reviling in matters of

The Mamertine Prison was the ancient state prison of Rome. Tradition credits parts of it to the early kings of Rome. Later tradition held that Peter and Paul were both incarcerated here

which they are ignorant, will be destroyed in the same destruction with them, suffering wrong for their wrongdoing. They count it pleasure to revel in the daytime. They are blots and blemishes, reveling in their dissipation,[g] carousing with you. They have eyes full of adultery, insatiable for sin. They entice unsteady souls. They have hearts trained in greed. Accursed children! Forsaking the right way they have gone astray; they have followed the way of Balaam, the son of Beor, who loved gain from wrongdoing, but was rebuked for his own transgression; a dumb ass spoke with human voice and restrained the prophet's madness.

[g]Other ancient authorities read love feasts

Married by his mother to Octavia when barely fifteen years old, Nero became emperor before he was seventeen. His tutors, the philosopher Seneca and the Pretorian Burrus, were displaced by Poppaea Sabina, whom he met in A.D. 58 and persuaded to divorce her husband so he could marry her. (1) Nero and his mother (Agrippina the Younger). (2) Poppaea Sabina, second wife of Nero

1   2

A.D.54–55   A.D.62–66   American Numismatic Society

[a]Or of our God and the Savior Jesus Christ
[b]Or by   [c]Greek tent
[d]Or my Son, my (or the) Beloved

[e]Other authorities read moved by the Holy Spirit holy men of God spoke   [f]Greek Tartarus

Rome: Catacomb of San Sebastian. Many Christians were buried in the catacombs of Rome. According to tradition the bones of Peter were interred for a time in the Catacomb of San Sebastian

Alinari

Slaves of Corruption [2:17-22]

These are waterless springs and mists driven by a storm; for them the nether gloom of darkness has been reserved. For, uttering loud boasts of folly, they entice with licentious passions of the flesh men who have barely escaped from those who live in error. They promise them freedom, but they themselves are slaves of corruption; for whatever overcomes a man, to that he is enslaved. For if, after they have escaped the defilements of the world through the knowledge of our Lord and Savior Jesus Christ, they are again entangled in them and overpowered, the last state has become worse for them than the first. For it would have been better for them never to have known the way of righteousness than after knowing it to turn back from the holy commandment delivered to them. It has happened to them according to the true proverb, The dog turns back to his own vomit, and the sow is washed only to wallow in the mire.

Scoffers in the Last Days [2 Peter 3:1-7]

THIS is now the second letter that I have written to you, beloved, and in both of them I have aroused your sincere mind by way of reminder; that you should remember the predictions of the holy prophets and the commandment of the Lord and Savior through your apostles. First of all you must understand this, that scoffers will come in the last days with scoffing, following their own passions and saying, "Where is the promise of his coming? For ever since the fathers fell asleep, all things have continued as they were from the beginning of creation." They deliberately ignore this fact, that by the word of God heavens existed long ago, and an earth formed out of water and by means of water, through which the world that then existed was deluged with water and perished. But by the same word the heavens and earth that now exist have been stored up for fire, being kept until the day of judgment and destruction of ungodly men.

The Coming Day of the Lord [3:8-10]

But do not ignore this one fact, beloved, that with the Lord one day is as a thousand years, and a thousand years as one day. The Lord is not slow about his promise as some count slowness, but is forbearing toward you,[h] not wishing that any should perish, but that all should reach repentance. But the day of the Lord will come like a thief, and then the heavens will pass away with a loud noise, and the elements will be dissolved with fire, and the earth and the works that are upon it will be burned up.

New Heavens and a New Earth [3:11-13]

Since all these things are thus to be dissolved, what sort of persons ought you to be in lives of holiness and godliness, waiting for and hastening[i] the coming of the day of God, because of which the heavens will be kindled and dissolved, and the elements will melt with fire! But according to his promise we wait for new heavens and a new earth in which righteousness dwells.

Grow in Grace [3:14-18]

Therefore, beloved, since you wait for these, be zealous to be found by him without spot or blemish, and at peace. And count the forbearance of our Lord as salvation. So also our beloved brother Paul wrote to you according to the wisdom given him, speaking of this as he does in all his letters. There are some things in them hard to understand, which the ignorant and unstable twist to their own destruction, as they do the other scriptures. You therefore, beloved, knowing this beforehand, beware lest you be carried away with the error of lawless men and lose your own stability. But grow in the grace and knowledge of our Lord and Savior Jesus Christ. To him be the glory both now and to the day of eternity. Amen.

[h]Other ancient authorities read *on your account*
[i]Or *earnestly desiring*

THE FIRST LETTER OF JOHN

The Word of Life

[1 John 1:1-4] That which was from the beginning, which we have heard, which we have seen with our eyes, which we have looked upon and touched with our hands, concerning the word of life—the life was made manifest, and we saw it, and testify to it, and proclaim to you the eternal life which was with the Father and was made manifest to us—that which we have seen and heard we proclaim also to you, so that you may have fellowship with us; and our fellowship is with the Father and with his Son Jesus Christ. And we are writing this that our[a] joy may be complete.

God Is Light [1:5-10]

This is the message we have heard from him and proclaim to you, that God is light and in him is no darkness at all. If we say we have fellowship with him while we walk in darkness, we lie and do not live according to the truth; but if we walk in the light, as he is in the light, we have fellowship with one another, and the blood of Jesus his Son cleanses us from all sin. If we say we have no sin, we deceive ourselves, and the truth is not in us. If we confess our sins, he is faithful and just, and will forgive our sins and cleanse us from all unrighteousness. If we say we have not sinned, we make him a liar, and his word is not in us.

[a]Other ancient authorities read *your*

Christ Our Advocate [1 John 2:1-6]

MY little children, I am writing this to you so that you may not sin; but if any one does sin, we have an advocate with the Father, Jesus Christ the righteous; and he is the expiation for our sins, and not for ours only but also for the sins of the whole world. And by this we may be sure that we know him, if we keep his commandments. He who says "I know him" but disobeys his commandments is a liar, and the truth is not in him; but whoever keeps his word, in him truly love for God is perfected. By this we may be sure that we are in him: he who says he abides in him ought to walk in the same way in which he walked.

The New Commandment [2:7-11]

Beloved, I am writing you no new commandment, but an old commandment which you had from the beginning; the old commandment is the word which you have heard. Yet I am writing you a new commandment, which is true in him and in you, because[b] the darkness is passing away and the true light is already shining. He who says he is in the light and hates his brother is in the darkness still. He who loves his brother abides in the light, and in it[c] there is no cause for stumbling. But he who hates his brother is in the darkness and walks in the darkness, and does not know where he is going, because the darkness has blinded his eyes.

[b]Or *that*
[c]Or *him*

To Whom John Writes [2:12-14]

I am writing to you, little children, because your sins are forgiven for his sake. I am writing to you, fathers, because you know him who is from the beginning. I am writing to you, young men, because you have overcome the evil one. I write to you, children, because you know the Father. I write to you, fathers, because you know him who is from the beginning. I write to you, young men, because you are strong, and the word of God abides in you, and you have overcome the evil one.

Do Not Love the World [2:15-17]

Do not love the world or the things in the world. If any one loves the world, love for the Father is not in him. For all that is in the world, the lust of the flesh and the lust of the eyes and the pride of life, is not of the Father but is of the world. And the world passes away, and the lust of it; but he who does the will of God abides for ever.

Many Antichrists [2:18-25]

Children, it is the last hour; and as you have heard that antichrist is coming, so now many antichrists have come; therefore we know that it is the last hour. They went out from us, but they were not of us; for if they had been of us, they would have continued with us; but they went out, that it might be plain that they all are not of us. But you have been anointed by the Holy One, and you all know.[d] I write to you, not because you do not know the truth, but because you know it, and know that no lie is of the truth. Who is the liar but he who denies that Jesus is the Christ? This is the antichrist, he who denies the Father and the Son. No one who denies the Son has the Father. He who confesses the Son has the Father also. Let what you heard from the beginning abide in you. If what you heard from the beginning abides in you, then you will abide in the Son and in the Father. And this is what he has promised us,[e] eternal life.

Abide in Christ [2:26-29]

I write this to you about those who would deceive you; but the anointing which you received from him abides in you, and you have no need that any one should teach you; as his anointing teaches you about everything, and is true, and is no lie, just as it has taught you, abide in him.

And now, little children, abide in him, so that when he appears we may have confidence and not shrink from him in shame at his coming. If you know that he is righteous, you may be sure that every one who does right is born of him.

Children of God [1 John 3:1-3]

SEE what love the Father has given us, that we should be called children of God; and so we are. The reason why the world does not know us is that it did not know him. Beloved, we are God's children now; it does not yet appear what we shall be, but we know that when he appears we shall be like him, for we shall see him as he is. And every one who thus hopes in him purifies himself as he is pure.

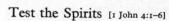

"Little children,
you are of God"
(1 John 4:4)

American Friends
Service Committee

Sin and Righteousness [3:4-10]

Every one who commits sin is guilty of lawlessness; sin is lawlessness. You know that he appeared to take away sins, and in him there is no sin. No one who abides in him sins; no one who sins has either seen him or known him. Little children, let no one deceive you. He who does right is righteous, as he is righteous. He who commits sin is of the devil; for the devil has sinned from the beginning. The reason the Son of God appeared was to destroy the works of the devil. No one born of God commits sin; for God's[f] nature abides in him, and he cannot sin because he is[g] born of God. By this it may be seen who are the children of God, and who are the children of the devil: whoever does not do right is not of God, nor he who does not love his brother.

Love One Another [3:11-18]

For this is the message which you have heard from the beginning, that we should love one another, and not be like Cain who was of the evil one and murdered his brother. And why did he murder him? Because his own deeds were evil and his brother's righteous. Do not wonder, brethren, that the world hates you. We know that we have passed out of death into life, because we love the brethren. He who does not love remains in death. Any one who hates his brother is a murderer, and you know that no murderer has eternal life abiding in him. By this we know love, that he laid down his life for us; and we ought to lay down our lives for the brethren. But if any one has the world's goods and sees his brother in need, yet closes his heart against him, how does God's love abide in him? Little children, let us not love in word or speech but in deed and in truth.

Confidence before God [3:19-24]

By this we shall know that we are of the truth, and reassure our hearts before him whenever our hearts condemn us; for God is greater than our hearts, and he knows everything. Beloved, if our hearts do not condemn us, we have confidence before God; and we receive from him whatever we ask, because we keep his commandments and do what pleases him. And this is his commandment, that we should believe in the name of his Son Jesus Christ and love one another, just as he has commanded us. All who keep his commandments abide in him, and he in them. And by this we know that he abides in us, by the Spirit which he has given us.

Test the Spirits [1 John 4:1-6]

BELOVED, do not believe every spirit, but test the spirits to see whether they are of God; for many false prophets have gone out into the world. By this you know the Spirit of God: every spirit which confesses that Jesus Christ has come in the flesh is of God, and every spirit which does not confess Jesus is not of God. This is the spirit of antichrist, of which you heard that it was coming, and now it is in the world already. Little children, you are of God, and have overcome them; for he who is in you is greater than he who is in the world. They are of the world, therefore what they say is of the world, and the world listens to them. We are of God. Whoever knows God listens to us, and he who is not of God does not listen to us. By this we know the spirit of truth and the spirit of error.

God So Loved Us [4:7-12]

Beloved, let us love one another; for love is of God, and he who loves is born of God and knows God. He who does not love does not know God; for God is love. In this the love of God was made manifest among us, that God sent his only Son into the world, so that we might live through him. In this is love, not that we loved God but that he loved us and sent his Son to be the expiation for our sins. Beloved, if so God loved us, we also ought to love one another. No man has ever seen God; if we love one another, God abides in us and his love is perfected in us.

No Fear in Love [4:13-21]

By this we know that we abide in him and he in us, because he has given us of his own Spirit. And we have seen and testify that the Father has sent his Son as the Savior of the world. Whoever confesses that Jesus is the Son of God, God abides in him, and he in God. So we know and believe the love God has for us. God is love, and he who abides in love abides in God, and God abides in him. In this is love perfected with us, that we may have confidence for the day of judgment, because as he is so are we in this world. There is no fear in love, but perfect love casts out fear. For fear has to do with punishment, and he who fears is not perfected in love. We love, because he first loved us. If any one says, "I love God," and hates his brother, he is a liar; for he who does not love his brother whom he has seen, cannot[h] love God whom he has not seen. And this commandment we have from him, that he who loves God should love his brother also.

[d]Other ancient authorities read you know everything
[e]Other ancient authorities read you

[f]Greek his
[g]Or for the offspring of God abide in him, and they cannot sin because they are

[h]Other ancient authorities read how can he

Overcoming the World [1 John 5:1-5]

EVERY one who believes that Jesus is the Christ is a child of God, and every one who loves the parent loves the child. By this we know that we love the children of God, when we love God and obey his commandments. For this is the love of God, that we keep his commandments. And his commandments are not burdensome. For whatever is born of God overcomes the world; and this is the victory that overcomes the world, our faith. Who is it that overcomes the world but he who believes that Jesus is the Son of God?

The Witness of the Spirit [5:6-12]

This is he who came by water and blood, Jesus Christ, not with the water only but with the water and the blood. And the Spirit is the witness, because the Spirit is the truth. There are three witnesses, the Spirit, the water, and the blood; and these three agree. If we receive the testimony of men, the testimony of God is greater; for this is the testimony of God that he has borne witness to his Son. He who believes in the Son of God has the testimony in himself. He who does not believe God has made him a liar, because he has not believed in the testimony that God has borne to his Son. And this is the testimony, that God gave us eternal life, and this life is in his Son. He who has the Son has life; he who has not the Son of God has not life.

Knowledge of Eternal Life [5:13-17]

I write this to you who believe in the name of the Son of God, that you may know that you have eternal life. And this is the confidence which we have in him, that if we ask anything according to his will he hears us. And if we know that he hears us in whatever we ask, we know that we have obtained the requests made of him. If any one sees his brother committing what is not a mortal sin, he will ask, and God[i] will give him life for those whose sin is not mortal. There is sin which is mortal; I do not say that one is to pray for that. All wrongdoing is sin, but there is sin which is not mortal.

The True God and Eternal Life [5:18-21]

We know that any one born of God does not sin, but He who was born of God keeps him, and the evil one does not touch him.

We know that we are of God, and the whole world is in the power of the evil one.

And we know that the Son of God has come and has given us understanding, to know him who is true; and we are in him who is true, in his Son Jesus Christ. This is the true God and eternal life. Little children, keep yourselves from idols.

[i]Greek *he*

Walters Art Gallery

Aphrodite (Venus)

J. Lane Miller

Diana (Artemis)

Metropolitan Museum of Art

Dionysus (Bacchus)

University Prints, Boston

Tyche (Fortuna) of Antioch

"Little children, keep yourselves from idols" (1 John 5:21)

Apollo

A. Donmez

Minerva

Louvre

THE SECOND LETTER OF
JOHN

Greetings

[1-3] The elder to the elect lady and her children, whom I love in the truth, and not only I but also all who know the truth, because of the truth which abides in us and will be with us for ever:

Grace, mercy, and peace will be with us, from God the Father and from Jesus Christ the Father's Son, in truth and love.

Follow Love [4-11]

I rejoiced greatly to find some of your children following the truth, just as we have been commanded by the Father. And now I beg you, lady, not as though I were writing you a new commandment, but the one we have had from the beginning, that we love one another. And this is love, that we follow his commandments; this is the commandment, as you have heard from the beginning, that you follow love. For many deceivers have gone out into the world, men who will not acknowledge the coming of Jesus Christ in the flesh; such a one is the deceiver and the antichrist. Look to yourselves, that you may not lose what you[a] have worked for, but may win a full reward. Any one who goes ahead and does not abide in the doctrine of Christ does not have God; he who abides in the doctrine has both the Father and the Son. If any one comes to you and does not bring this doctrine, do not receive him into the house or give him any greeting; for he who greets him shares his wicked work.

An Anticipated Visit [12-13]

Though I have much to write to you, I would rather not use paper and ink, but I hope to come to see you and talk with you face to face, so that our joy may be complete.

The children of your elect sister greet you.

[a]Other ancient authorities read *we*

236

THE THIRD LETTER OF JOHN

Greetings

[1-4] The elder to the beloved Gaius, whom I love in the truth.
Beloved, I pray that all may go well with you and that you may be in health; I know that it is well with your soul. For I greatly rejoiced when some of the brethren arrived and testified to the truth of your life, as indeed you do follow the truth. No greater joy can I have than this, to hear that my children follow the truth.

Service to the Brethren [5-8]

Beloved, it is a loyal thing you do when you render any service to the brethren, especially to strangers, who have testified to your love before the church. You will do well to send them on their journey as befits God's service. For they have set out for his sake and have accepted nothing from the heathen. So we ought to support such men, that we may be fellow workers in the truth.

Opposition of Diotrephes [9-10]

I have written something to the church; but Diot'rephes, who likes to put himself first, does not acknowledge my authority. So if I come, I will bring up what he is doing, prating against me with evil words. And not content with that, he refuses himself to welcome the brethren, and also stops those who want to welcome them and puts them out of the church.

Imitate Good [11-12]

Beloved, do not imitate evil but imitate good. He who does good is of God; he who does evil has not seen God. Deme'trius has testimony from every one, and from the truth itself; I testify to him too, and you know my testimony is true.

Final Greetings [13-15]

I had much to write to you, but I would rather not write with pen and ink; I hope to see you soon, and we will talk together face to face.
Peace be to you. The friends greet you. Greet the friends, every one of them.

The ruins of ancient Sodom are probably under the waters of the southern end of the Dead Sea. The name is preserved in Mt. Sdom (Jebel Usdum), a salt mountain on the southwest shore of the sea, where there are potash works

THE LETTER OF JUDE

Greetings

[1-2] Jude, a servant of Jesus Christ and brother of James,
To those who are called, beloved in God the Father and kept for Jesus Christ:
May mercy, peace, and love be multiplied to you.

Contend for the Faith [3-4]

Beloved, being very eager to write to you of our common salvation, I found it necessary to write appealing to you to contend for the faith which was once for all delivered to the saints. For admission has been secretly gained by some who long ago were designated for this condemnation, ungodly persons who pervert the grace of our God into licentiousness and deny our only Master and Lord, Jesus Christ.[a]

God's Judgment on Disobedience [5-7]

Now I desire to remind you, though you were once for all fully informed, that he[b] who saved a people out of the land of Egypt, afterward destroyed those who did not believe. And the angels that did not keep their own position but left their proper dwelling have been kept by him in eternal chains in the nether gloom until the judgment of the great day; just as Sodom and Gomor'rah and the surrounding cities, which likewise acted immorally and indulged in unnatural lust, serve as an example by undergoing a punishment of eternal fire.

False Teachers Reproved [8-13]

Yet in like manner these men in their dreamings defile the flesh, reject authority, and revile the glorious ones.[c] But when the archangel Michael, contending with the devil, disputed about the body of Moses, he did not presume to pronounce a reviling judgment upon him, but said, "The Lord rebuke you." But these men revile whatever they do not understand, and by those things that they know by instinct as irrational animals do, they are destroyed. Woe to them! For they walk in the way of Cain, and abandon themselves for the sake of gain to Balaam's error, and perish in Korah's rebellion. These are blemishes[d] on your love feasts, as they boldly carouse together, looking after themselves; waterless clouds, carried along by winds; fruitless trees in late autumn, twice dead, uprooted; wild waves of the sea, casting up the foam of their own shame; wandering stars for whom the nether gloom of darkness has been reserved for ever.

Prophecy of Enoch [14-16]

It was of these also that Enoch in the seventh generation from Adam prophesied, saying, "Behold, the Lord came with his holy myriads, to execute judgment on all, and to convict all the ungodly of all their deeds of ungodliness which they have committed in such an ungodly way, and of all the harsh things which ungodly sinners have spoken against him."[1] These are grumblers, malcontents, following their own passions, loud-mouthed boasters, flattering people to gain advantage.

Final Warnings [17-23]

But you must remember, beloved, the predictions of the apostles of our Lord Jesus Christ; they said to you, "In the last time there will be scoffers, following their own ungodly passions." It is these who set up divisions, worldly people, devoid of the Spirit. But you, beloved, build yourselves up on your most holy faith; pray in the Holy Spirit; keep yourselves in the love of God; wait for the mercy of our Lord Jesus Christ unto eternal life. And convince some, who doubt; save some, by snatching them out of the fire; on some have mercy with fear, hating even the garment spotted by the flesh.[e]

Benediction [24-25]

Now to him who is able to keep you from falling and to present you without blemish before the presence of his glory with rejoicing, to the only God, our Savior through Jesus Christ our Lord, be glory, majesty, dominion, and authority, before all time and now and for ever. Amen.

---

[a] Or *the only Master and our Lord Jesus Christ*
[b] Ancient authorities read *Jesus* or *the Lord* or *God*
[c] Greek *glories*
[d] Or *reefs*
[e] The Greek text in this sentence is uncertain at several points   [1] *Enoch* 1:9

Air view of the Isle of Patmos

The harbor of the Isle of Patmos

A seven-branched lampstand or menorah decorates this ancient oil lamp. "I saw seven golden lampstands" (Rev. 1:12)

THE REVELATION
TO JOHN
The Revelation of Jesus Christ

[Revelation 1:1-3] The revelation of Jesus Christ, which God gave him to show to his servants what must soon take place; and he made it known by sending his angel to his servant John, who bore witness to the word of God and to the testimony of Jesus Christ, even to all that he saw. Blessed is he who reads aloud the words of the prophecy, and blessed are those who hear, and who keep what is written therein; for the time is near.

Greetings to the Seven Churches [1:4-8]

John to the seven churches that are in Asia:

Grace to you and peace from him who is and who was and who is to come, and from the seven spirits who are before his throne, and from Jesus Christ the faithful witness, the first-born of the dead, and the ruler of kings on earth.

To him who loves us and has freed us from our sins by his blood and made us a kingdom, priests to his God and Father, to him be glory and dominion for ever and ever. Amen. Behold, he is coming with the clouds, and every eye will see him, every one who pierced him; and all tribes of the earth will wail on account of him. Even so. Amen. "I am the Alpha and the Ome'ga," says the Lord God, who is and who was and who is to come, the Almighty.

John Directed to Write [1:9-11]

I John, your brother, who share with you in Jesus the tribulation and the kingdom and the patient endurance, was on the island called Patmos on account of the word of God and the testimony of Jesus. I was in the Spirit on the Lord's day, and I heard behind me a loud voice like a trumpet saying, "Write what you see in a book and send it to the seven churches, to Eph'esus and to Smyrna and to Per'gamum and to Thyati'ra and to Sardis and to Philadelphia and to La'odice'a."

A Vision of the Son of Man
[1:12-16]

Then I turned to see the voice that was speaking to me, and on turning I saw seven golden lampstands, and in the midst of the lampstands one like a son of man, clothed with a long robe and with a golden girdle round his breast; his head and his hair were white as white wool, white as snow; his eyes were like a flame of fire, his feet were like burnished bronze, refined as in a furnace, and his voice was like the sound of many waters; in his right hand he held seven stars, from his mouth issued a sharp two-edged sword, and his face was like the sun shining in full strength.

The Stars and Lampstands Explained
[1:17-20]

When I saw him, I fell at his feet as though dead. But he laid his right hand upon me, saying, "Fear not, I am the first and the last, and the living one; I died, and behold, I am alive for evermore, and I have the keys of Death and Hades. Now write what you see, what is and what is to take place hereafter. As for the mystery of the seven stars which you saw in my right hand, and the seven golden lampstands, the seven stars are the angels of the seven churches and the seven lampstands are the seven churches.

238

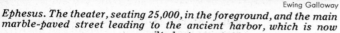

Ephesus. The theater, seating 25,000, in the foreground, and the main marble-paved street leading to the ancient harbor, which is now silted up

Ewing Galloway

Ancient agora in Smyrna

A. Donmez

To Ephesus [Revelation 2:1–7]

"TO the angel of the church in Eph'esus write: 'The words of him who holds the seven stars in his right hand, who walks among the seven golden lampstands.

"'I know your works, your toil and your patient endurance, and how you cannot bear evil men but have tested those who call themselves apostles but are not, and found them to be false; I know you are enduring patiently and bearing up for my name's sake, and you have not grown weary. But I have this against you, that you have abandoned the love you had at first. Remember then from what you have fallen, repent and do the works you did at first. If not, I will come to you and remove your lampstand from its place, unless you repent. Yet this you have, you hate the works of the Nicola'itans, which I also hate. He who has an ear, let him hear what the Spirit says to the churches. To him who conquers I will grant to eat of the tree of life, which is in the paradise of God.'

To Smyrna [2:8–11]

"And to the angel of the church in Smyrna write: 'The words of the first and the last, who died and came to life.

"'I know your tribulation and your poverty (but you are rich) and the slander of those who say that they are Jews and are not, but are a synagogue of Satan. Do not fear what you are about to suffer. Behold, the devil is about to throw some of you into prison, that you may be tested, and for ten days you will have tribulation. Be faithful unto death, and I will give you the crown of life. He who has an ear, let him hear what the Spirit says to the churches. He who conquers shall not be hurt by the second death.'

To Pergamum [2:12–17]

"And to the angel of the church in Per'gamum write: 'The words of him who has the sharp two-edged sword.

"'I know where you dwell, where Satan's throne is; you hold fast my name and you did not deny my faith even in the days of An'tipas my witness, my faithful one, who was killed among you, where Satan dwells. But I have a few things against you: you have some there who hold the teaching of Balaam, who taught Balak to put a stumbling block before the sons of Israel, that they might eat food sacrificed to idols and practice immorality. So you also have some who hold the teaching of the Nicola'itans. Repent then. If not, I will come to you soon and war against them with the sword of my mouth. He who has an ear, let him hear what the Spirit says to the churches. To him who conquers I will give some of the hidden manna, and I will give him a white stone, with a new name written on the stone which no one knows except him who receives it.'

F. K. Doerner

Statue of Demeter found in the District of the Twelve Gods in the agora, Smyrna

Ancient ascent to the Acropolis at Pergamum

F. K. Doerner

Great Altar of Zeus at Pergamum, thought by some to be the "Satan's throne" of Rev. 2:13

William A. McDonald

Ancient sarcophagus at Thyatira, now Akhisar

Modern pottery in Thyatira

Portion of Greek inscription from the sarcophagus above, the second line of which reads, "city of Thyatira"

Sardis. Ruins of Roman theater at base of hill

Sardis. Temple of Artemis

To Thyatira [2:18-29]

"And to the angel of the church in Thyati'ra write: 'The words of the Son of God, who has eyes like a flame of fire, and whose feet are like burnished bronze.

" 'I know your works, your love and faith and service and patient endurance, and that your latter works exceed the first. But I have this against you, that you tolerate the woman Jez'ebel, who calls herself a prophetess and is teaching and beguiling my servants to practice immorality and to eat food sacrificed to idols. I gave her time to repent, but she refuses to repent of her immorality. Behold, I will throw her on a sickbed, and those who commit adultery with her I will throw into great tribulation, unless they repent of her doings; and I will strike her children dead. And all the churches shall know that I am he who searches mind and heart, and I will give to each of you as your works deserve. But to the rest of you in Thyati'ra, who do not hold this teaching, who have not learned what some call the deep things of Satan, to you I say, I do not lay upon you any other burden; only hold fast what you have, until I come. He who conquers and who keeps my works until the end, I will give him power over the nations, and he shall rule them with a rod of iron, as when earthen pots are broken in pieces, even as I myself have received power from my Father; and I will give him the morning star. He who has an ear, let him hear what the Spirit says to the churches.'

To Sardis [Revelation 3:1-6]

"AND to the angel of the church in Sardis write: 'The words of him who has the seven spirits of God and the seven stars.

" 'I know your works; you have the name of being alive, and you are dead. Awake, and strengthen what remains and is on the point of death, for I have not found your works perfect in the sight of my God. Remember then what you received and heard; keep that, and repent. If you will not awake, I will come like a thief, and you will not know at what hour I will come upon you. Yet you have still a few names in Sardis, people who have not soiled their garments; and they shall walk with me in white, for they are worthy. He who conquers shall be clad thus in white garments, and I will not blot his name out of the book of life; I will confess his name before my Father and before his angels. He who has an ear, let him hear what the Spirit says to the churches.'

To Philadelphia [3:7-13]

"And to the angel of the church in Philadelphia write: 'The words of the holy one, the true one, who has the key of David, who opens and no one shall shut, who shuts and no one opens.

" 'I know your works. Behold, I have set before you an open door, which no one is able to shut; I know that you have but little power, and yet you have kept my word and have not denied my name. Behold, I will make those of the synagogue of Satan who say that they are Jews and are not, but lie —behold, I will make them come and bow down before your feet, and learn that I have loved you. Because you have kept my word of patient endurance, I will keep you from the hour of trial which is coming on the whole world, to try those who dwell upon the earth. I am coming soon; hold fast what you have, so that no one may seize your crown. He who conquers, I will make him a pillar in the temple of my God; never shall he go out of it, and I will write on him the name of my God, and the name of the city of my God, the new Jerusalem which comes down from my God out of heaven, and my own new name. He who has an ear, let him hear what the Spirit says to the churches.'

Philadelphia. Standing section of the ancient wall of Philadelphia

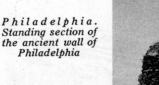

To Laodicea [3:14-22]

"And to the angel of the church in La'-odice'a write: 'The words of the Amen, the faithful and true witness, the beginning of God's creation.

" 'I know your works: you are neither cold nor hot. Would that you were cold or hot! So, because you are lukewarm, and neither cold nor hot, I will spew you out of my mouth. For you say, I am rich, I have prospered, and I need nothing; not knowing that you are wretched, pitiable, poor, blind, and naked. Therefore I counsel you to buy from me gold refined by fire, that you may be rich, and white garments to clothe you and to keep the shame of your nakedness from being seen, and salve to anoint your eyes, that you may see. Those whom I love, I reprove and chasten; so be zealous and repent. Behold, I stand at the door and knock; if any one hears my voice and opens the door, I will come in to him and eat with him, and he with me. He who conquers, I will grant him to sit with me on my throne, as I myself conquered and sat down with my Father on his throne. He who has an ear, let him hear what the Spirit says to the churches.'"

The Heavenly Throne

[Revelation 4:1-6a]

AFTER this I looked, and lo, in heaven an open door! And the first voice, which I had heard speaking to me like a trumpet, said, "Come up hither, and I will show you what must take place after this." At once I was in the Spirit, and lo, a throne stood in heaven, with one seated on the throne! And he who sat there appeared like jasper and carnelian, and round the throne was a rainbow that looked like an emerald. Round the throne were twenty-four thrones, and seated on the thrones were twenty-four elders, clad in white garments, with golden crowns upon their heads. From the throne issue flashes of lightning, and voices and peals of thunder, and before the throne burn seven torches of fire, which are the seven spirits of God; and before the throne there is as it were a sea of glass, like crystal.

The Heavenly Worship

[4:6b-11]

And round the throne, on each side of the throne, are four living creatures, full of eyes in front and behind: the first living creature like a lion, the second living creature like an ox, the third living creature with the face of a man, and the fourth living creature like a flying eagle. And the four living creatures, each of them with six wings, are full of eyes all round and within, and day and night they never cease to sing,

"Holy, holy, holy, is the Lord God Almighty,
who was and is and is to come!"

And whenever the living creatures give glory and honor and thanks to him who is seated on the throne, who lives for ever and ever, the twenty-four elders fall down before him who is seated on the throne and worship him who lives for ever and ever; they cast their crowns before the throne, singing,

"Worthy art thou, our Lord and God,
to receive glory and honor and power,
for thou didst create all things,
and by thy will they existed and were created."

Laodicea. Roman aqueduct

A. Donmez

The Scroll and Seals [Revelation 5:1-5]

AND I saw in the right hand of him who was seated on the throne a scroll written within and on the back, sealed with seven seals; and I saw a strong angel proclaiming with a loud voice, "Who is worthy to open the scroll and break its seals?" And no one in heaven or on earth or under the earth was able to open the scroll or to look into it, and I wept much that no one was found worthy to open the scroll or to look into it. Then one of the elders said to me, "Weep not; lo, the Lion of the tribe of Judah, the Root of David, has conquered, so that he can open the scroll and its seven seals."

Worthy Is the Lamb [5:6-14]

And between the throne and the four living creatures and among the elders, I saw a Lamb standing, as though it had been slain, with seven horns and with seven eyes, which are the seven spirits of God sent out into all the earth; and he went and took the scroll from the right hand of him who was seated on the throne. And when he had taken the scroll, the four living creatures and the twenty-four elders fell down before the Lamb, each holding a harp, and with golden bowls full of incense, which are the prayers of the saints; and they sang a new song, saying,

"Worthy art thou to take the scroll and to open its seals,
for thou wast slain and by thy blood didst ransom men for God
from every tribe and tongue and people and nation,
and hast made them a kingdom and priests to our God,
and they shall reign on earth."

Then I looked, and I heard around the throne and the living creatures and the elders the voice of many angels, numbering myriads of myriads and thousands of thousands, saying with a loud voice, "Worthy is the Lamb who was slain, to receive power and wealth and wisdom and might and honor and glory and blessing!" And I heard every creature in heaven and on earth and under the earth and in the sea, and all therein, saying, "To him who sits upon the throne and to the Lamb be blessing and honor and glory and might for ever and ever!" And the four living creatures said, "Amen!" and the elders fell down and worshiped.

Aramaic papyrus of fifth century B.C., tied with string and sealed with clay

Brooklyn Museum

Papyrus with seal of 116 B.C., written in Greek at Pathyris in Upper Egypt

British Museum

241

The Parthians were great horsemen and archers. This bas-relief near Persepolis shows Shapur, the victorious king of Persia, on horseback, while the Roman Emperor Valerian kneels to beg mercy, A.D. 258.

Jews and Christians alike suffered from conquest, famine, pestilence, persecution and death in the suppression of the first Jewish revolt, A.D. 66-70, by Titus, shown triumphant above

Antioch of Pisidia, ca. 93 A.D.

Antistius Rusticus, legate of the Emperor Domitian, proclaims in this edict a ceiling on the price of wheat, holding it at about twice its normal value (there then being sixteen bronze asses to a silver denarius):

"Whereas, furthermore, affirmation is made before me that previous to this long-continued and severe winter a measure of grain in the colony had cost eight or nine asses, and whereas it is most unjust that the hunger of one's own fellow citizens should be a source of profiteering for any one, I hereby forbid that the price of grain exceed a single denarius for a single measure"

(1) Sacred cart of the deified Claudius, struck by Nero; head of Claudius on obverse side. (2) Four-horse chariot of Domitian; head of Domitian on obverse

The First Seal—The Conquering Rider [Revelation 6:1-2]

NOW I saw when the Lamb opened one of the seven seals, and I heard one of the four living creatures say, as with a voice of thunder, "Come!" And I saw, and behold, a white horse, and its rider had a bow; and a crown was given to him, and he went out conquering and to conquer.

The Second Seal—Strife [6:3-4]

When he opened the second seal, I heard the second living creature say, "Come!" And out came another horse, bright red; its rider was permitted to take peace from the earth, so that men should slay one another; and he was given a great sword.

The Third Seal—Famine [6:5-6]

When he opened the third seal, I heard the third living creature say, "Come!" And I saw, and behold, a black horse, and its rider had a balance in his hand; and I heard what seemed to be a voice in the midst of the four living creatures saying, "A quart of wheat for a denarius,[a] and three quarts of barley for a denarius;[a] but do not harm oil and wine!"

The Fourth Seal—Pestilence [6:7-8]

When he opened the fourth seal, I heard the voice of the fourth living creature say, "Come!" And I saw, and behold a pale horse, and its rider's name was Death, and Hades followed him; and they were given power over a fourth of the earth, to kill with sword and with famine and with pestilence and by wild beasts of the earth.

The Fifth Seal—Persecution [6:9-11]

When he opened the fifth seal, I saw under the altar the souls of those who had been slain for the word of God and for the witness they had borne; they cried out with a loud voice, "O Sovereign Lord, holy and true, how long before thou wilt judge and avenge our blood on those who dwell upon the earth?" Then they were each given a white robe and told to rest a little longer, until the number of their fellow servants and their brethren should be complete, who were to be killed as they themselves had been.

The Sixth Seal—Cosmic Disaster [6:12-17]

When he opened the sixth seal, I looked, and behold, there was a great earthquake; and the sun became black as sackcloth, the full moon became like blood, and the stars of the sky fell to the earth as the fig tree sheds its winter fruit when shaken by a gale; the sky vanished like a scroll that is rolled up, and every mountain and island was removed from its place. Then the kings of the earth and the great men and the generals and the rich and the strong, and every one, slave and free, hid in the caves and among the rocks of the mountains, calling to the mountains and rocks, "Fall on us and hide us from the face of him who is seated on the throne, and from the wrath of the Lamb; for the great day of their wrath has come, and who can stand before it?"

[a]The denarius was worth about twenty cents

Sealing the Servants of God

[Revelation 7:1-8]

AFTER this I saw four angels standing at the four corners of the earth, holding back the four winds of the earth, that no wind might blow on earth or sea or against any tree. Then I saw another angel ascend from the rising of the sun, with the seal of the living God, and he called with a loud voice to the four angels who had been given power to harm earth and sea, saying, "Do not harm the earth or the sea or the trees, till we have sealed the servants of our God upon their foreheads." And I heard the number of the sealed, a hundred and forty-four thousand sealed, out of every tribe of the sons of Israel, twelve thousand sealed out of the tribe of Judah, twelve thousand of the tribe of Reuben, twelve thousand of the tribe of Gad, twelve thousand of the tribe of Asher, twelve thousand of the tribe of Naph'tali, twelve thousand of the tribe of Manas'seh, twelve thousand of the tribe of Sim'eon, twelve thousand of the tribe of Levi, twelve thousand of the tribe of Is'sachar, twelve thousand of the tribe of Zeb'ulun, twelve thousand of the tribe of Joseph, twelve thousand sealed out of the tribe of Benjamin.

The Multitude from the Tribulation

[7:9-17]

After this I looked, and behold, a great multitude which no man could number, from every nation, from all tribes and peoples and tongues, standing before the throne and before the Lamb, clothed in white robes, with palm branches in their hands, and crying out with a loud voice, "Salvation belongs to our God who sits upon the throne, and to the Lamb!" And all the angels stood round the throne and round the elders and the four living creatures, and they fell on their faces before the throne and worshiped God, saying, "Amen! Blessing and glory and wisdom and thanksgiving and honor and power and might be to our God for ever and ever! Amen."

Then one of the elders addressed me, saying, "Who are these, clothed in white robes, and whence have they come?" I said to him, "Sir, you know." And he said to me, "These are they who have come out of the great tribulation; they have washed their robes and made them white in the blood of the Lamb.

"Therefore are they before the throne of God,
and serve him day and night within his temple;
and he who sits upon the throne will shelter them with his presence.
They shall hunger no more, neither thirst any more;
the sun shall not strike them, nor any scorching heat.
For the Lamb in the midst of the throne will be their shepherd,
and he will guide them to springs of living water;
and God will wipe away every tear from their eyes."

The Seventh Seal—Silence

[Revelation 8:1-5]

WHEN the Lamb opened the seventh seal, there was silence in heaven for about half an hour. Then I saw the seven angels who stand before God, and seven trumpets were given to them. And another

Palestinian seal of Egyptian type about 1600 B.C., showing winged griffin

Matson Photo Service

Seal of Eliakim, steward of Jehoiachin, the next to the last king of Judah, who was carried into captivity in 597 B.C.

Athlete being crowned. Hellenistic seal from Ephesus

angel came and stood at the altar with a golden censer; and he was given much incense to mingle with the prayers of all the saints upon the golden altar before the throne; and the smoke of the incense rose with the prayers of the saints from the hand of the angel before God. Then the angel took the censer and filled it with fire from the altar and threw it on the earth; and there were peals of thunder, loud noises, flashes of lightning, and an earthquake.

The Seven Angels [8:6]

Now the seven angels who had the seven trumpets made ready to blow them.

The First Trumpet—on the Earth

[8:7]

The first angel blew his trumpet, and there followed hail and fire, mixed with blood, which fell on the earth; and a third of the earth was burnt up, and a third of the trees were burnt up, and all green grass was burnt up.

The Second Trumpet—on the Sea

[8:8-9]

The second angel blew his trumpet, and something like a great mountain, burning with fire, was thrown into the sea; and a third of the sea became blood, a third of the living creatures in the sea died, and a third of the ships were destroyed.

The Third Trumpet—on the Inland Waters [8:10-11]

The third angel blew his trumpet, and a great star fell from heaven, blazing like a torch, and it fell on a third of the rivers and on the fountains of water. The name of the star is Wormwood. A third of the waters became wormwood, and many men died of the water, because it was made bitter.

The Fourth Trumpet—on Heavenly Bodies [8:12]

The fourth angel blew his trumpet, and a third of the sun was struck, and a third of the moon, and a third of the stars, so that a third of their light was darkened; a third of the day was kept from shining, and likewise a third of the night.

An Eagle Crying Woe [8:13]

Then I looked, and I heard an eagle crying with a loud voice, as it flew in mid-heaven, "Woe, woe, woe to those who dwell on the earth, at the blasts of the other trumpets which the three angels are about to blow!"

The Fifth Trumpet—Locusts

[Revelation 9:1-6]

AND the fifth angel blew his trumpet, and I saw a star fallen from heaven to earth, and he was given the key of the shaft of the bottomless pit; he opened the shaft of the bottomless pit, and from the shaft rose smoke like the smoke of a great furnace, and the sun and the air were darkened with the smoke from the shaft. Then from the smoke came locusts on the earth, and they were given power like the power of scorpions of the earth; they were told not to harm the grass of the earth or any green growth or any tree, but only those of mankind who have not the seal of God upon their foreheads; they were allowed to torture them for five months, but not to kill them, and their torture was like the torture of a scorpion, when it stings a man. And in those days men will seek death and will not find it; they will long to die, and death will fly from them.

Description of the Locusts [9:7-11]

In appearance the locusts were like horses arrayed for battle; on their heads were what looked like crowns of gold; their faces were like human faces, their hair like women's hair, and their teeth like lions' teeth; they had scales like iron breastplates, and the noise of their wings was like the noise of many chariots with horses rushing into battle. They have tails like scorpions, and stings, and their power of hurting men for five months lies in their tails. They have as king over them the angel of the bottomless pit; his name in Hebrew is Abad'don, and in Greek he is called Apoll'yon.[b]

End of First Woe [9:12]

The first woe has passed; behold, two woes are still to come.

[b] Or *Destroyer*

This breastplate of the Emperor Augustus shows one of the proudest moments of his career. A Parthian surrenders one of the eagle standards captured from the Roman legions in the defeat of Crassus at Carrhae, (Biblical Haran), June 9, 53 B.C. Note Jupiter, Mars and other Roman gods, including Aurora with her four-horse chariot. Corbulo defeated the Parthians A.D. 59, but in A.D. 62 the Parthians disastrously defeated Paetus and the Roman legions at Rhandeia

Gallerie Musei Vaticani

Herbert Bloch

This inscription of the College of the Arval Brethren refers to the visit of Tiridates to Rome, where he received the crown of Armenia from Nero in A.D. 66. Because Nero dedicated a laurel wreath to Jupiter on this "Golden Day" in celebration of his diplomatic victory, the indicated part of the inscription decrees the following sacrifices: "[To Jupiter, a bull; to Juno,] a cow; to Minerva, a cow; to Jupiter [the Conqueror, a bull; . . . to . . .] a cow; to Peace, a cow, in front of the Arch [of Janus Geminus]," which the Emperor had closed as a symbol of peace

The Sixth Trumpet—Demonic Cavalry [9:13-19]

Then the sixth angel blew his trumpet, and I heard a voice from the four horns of the golden altar before God, saying to the sixth angel who had the trumpet, "Release the four angels who are bound at the great river Eu-phra'tes." So the four angels were released, who had been held ready for the hour, the day, the month, and the year, to kill a third of mankind. The number of the troops of cavalry was twice ten thousand times ten thousand; I heard their number. And this was how I saw the horses in my vision: the riders wore breastplates the color of fire and of sapphire[c] and of sulphur, and the heads of the horses were like lions' heads, and fire and smoke and sulphur issued from their mouths. By these three plagues a third of mankind was killed, by the fire and smoke and sulphur issuing from their mouths. For the power of the horses is in their mouths and in their tails; their tails are like serpents, with heads, and by means of them they wound.

Unrepentant Mankind [9:20-21]

The rest of mankind, who were not killed by these plagues, did not repent of the works of their hands nor give up worshiping demons and idols of gold and silver and bronze and stone and wood, which cannot either see or hear or walk; nor did they repent of their murders or their sorceries or their immorality or their thefts.

The Seven Thunders [Revelation 10:1-7]

THEN I saw another mighty angel coming down from heaven, wrapped in a cloud, with a rainbow over his head, and his face was like the sun, and his legs like pillars of fire. He had a little scroll open in his hand. And he set his right foot on the sea, and his left foot on the land, and called out with a loud voice, like a lion roaring; when he called out, the seven thunders sounded. And when the seven thunders had sounded, I was about to write, but I heard a voice from heaven saying, "Seal up what the seven thunders have said, and do not write it down." And the angel whom I saw standing on sea and land lifted up his right hand to heaven and swore by him who lives for ever and ever, who created heaven and what is in it, the earth and what is in it, and the sea and what is in it, that there should be no more delay, but that in the days of the trumpet call to be sounded by the seventh angel, the mystery of God, as he announced to his servants the prophets, should be fulfilled.

[c]Greek hyacinth

Note the four horns of this limestone altar, from the time of Solomon, found at Megiddo

Oriental Institute, University of Chicago

The golden trumpets from Herod's Temple, carried in Titus' triumphal procession after the fall of Jerusalem; from the Arch of Titus

244

Ships like this brought Vespasian, Titus and the Roman soldiers to the Holy Land

The Bitter Scroll [10:8–11]

Then the voice which I had heard from heaven spoke to me again, saying, "Go, take the scroll which is open in the hand of the angel who is standing on the sea and on the land." So I went to the angel and told him to give me the little scroll; and he said to me, "Take it and eat; it will be bitter to your stomach, but sweet as honey in your mouth." And I took the little scroll from the hand of the angel and ate it; it was sweet as honey in my mouth, but when I had eaten it my stomach was made bitter. And I was told, "You must again prophesy about many peoples and nations and tongues and kings."

The Holy City to be Trampled

[Revelation 11:1–3]

THEN I was given a measuring rod like a staff, and I was told: "Rise and measure the temple of God and the altar and those who worship there, but do not measure the court outside the temple; leave that out, for it is given over to the nations, and they will trample over the holy city for forty-two months. And I will grant my two witnesses power to prophesy for one thousand two hundred and sixty days, clothed in sackcloth."

The Two Witnesses [11:4–13]

These are the two olive trees and the two lampstands which stand before the Lord of the earth. And if any one would harm them, fire pours from their mouth and consumes their foes; if any one would harm them, thus he is doomed to be killed. They have power to shut the sky, that no rain may fall during the days of their prophesying, and they have power over the waters to turn them into blood, and to smite the earth with every plague, as often as they desire. And when they have finished their testimony, the beast that ascends from the bottomless pit will make war upon them and conquer them and kill them, and their dead bodies will lie in the street of the great city which is allegorically[d] called Sodom and Egypt, where their Lord was crucified. For three days and a half men from the peoples and tribes and tongues and nations gaze at their dead bodies and refuse to let them be placed in a tomb, and those who dwell on the earth will rejoice over them and make merry and exchange presents, because these two prophets had been a torment to those who dwell on the earth. But after the three and a half days a breath of life from God entered them, and they stood up on their feet, and great fear fell on those who saw them. Then they heard a loud voice from heaven saying to them, "Come up hither!" And in the sight of their foes they went up to heaven in a cloud. And at that hour there was a great earthquake, and a tenth of the city fell; seven thousand people were killed in the earthquake, and the rest were terrified and gave glory to the God of heaven.

[d]Greek *spiritually*

End of Second Woe [11:14]

The second woe has passed; behold, the third woe is soon to come.

The Seventh Trumpet [11:15–18]

Then the seventh angel blew his trumpet, and there were loud voices in heaven, saying, "The kingdom of the world has become the kingdom of our Lord and of his Christ, and he shall reign for ever and ever." And the twenty-four elders who sit on their thrones before God fell on their faces and worshiped God, saying,

"We give thanks to thee, Lord God Almighty, who art and who wast,
  that thou hast taken thy great power and begun to reign.
The nations raged, but thy wrath came,
  and the time for the dead to be judged,
for rewarding thy servants, the prophets and saints,
  and those who fear thy name, both small and great,
and for destroying the destroyers of the earth."

God's Temple Opened [11:19]

Then God's temple in heaven was opened, and the ark of his covenant was seen within his temple; and there were flashes of lightning, loud noises, peals of thunder, an earthquake, and heavy hail.

This wilderness of the Negev is only one of many deserts that surround the Holy Land

The Woman and the Dragon

[Revelation 12:1–6]

AND a great portent appeared in heaven, a woman clothed with the sun, with the moon under her feet, and on her head a crown of twelve stars; she was with child and she cried out in her pangs of birth, in anguish for delivery. And another portent appeared in heaven; behold, a great red dragon, with seven heads and ten horns, and seven diadems upon his heads. His tail swept down a third of the stars of heaven, and cast them to the earth. And the dragon stood before the woman who was about to bear a child, that he might devour her child

Rome. The Pantheon, built by M. Agrippa, 27 B.C., for the glorification of the family of Julius and Augustus Caesar, was dedicated to Mars and Venus, mythical ancestors of that family. After A.D. 126 Hadrian completely rebuilt the Pantheon with such durable concrete that its dome, 142 feet in diameter, still stands, with walls and roof intact, as the greatest of all Roman mausolea

Ernest Nash

when she brought it forth; she brought forth a male child, one who is to rule all the nations with a rod of iron, but her child was caught up to God and to his throne, and the woman fled into the wilderness, where she has a place prepared by God, in which to be nourished for one thousand two hundred and sixty days.

War in Heaven

[12:7–12]

Now war arose in heaven, Michael and his angels fighting against the dragon; and the dragon and his angels fought, but they were defeated and there was no longer any place for them in heaven. And the great dragon was thrown down, that ancient serpent, who is called the Devil and Satan, the deceiver of the whole world—he was thrown down to the earth, and his angels were thrown down with him. And I heard a loud voice in heaven, saying, "Now the salvation and the power and the kingdom of our God and the authority of his Christ have come, for the accuser of our brethren has been thrown down, who accuses them day and night before our God. And they have conquered him by the blood of the Lamb and by the word of their testimony, for they loved not their lives even unto death. Rejoice then, O heaven and you that dwell therein! But woe to you, O earth and sea, for the devil has come down to you in great wrath, because he knows that his time is short!"

The Dragon Pursues the Woman

[12:13–17]

And when the dragon saw that he had been thrown down to the earth, he pursued the woman who had borne the male child. But the woman was given the two wings of the great eagle that she might fly from the serpent into the wilderness, to the place where she is to be nourished for a time, and times, and half a time. The serpent poured water like a river out of his mouth after the woman, to sweep her away with the flood. But the earth came to the help of the woman, and the earth opened its mouth and swallowed the river which the dragon had poured from his mouth. Then the dragon was angry with the woman, and went off to make war on the rest of her offspring, on those who keep the commandments of God and bear testimony to Jesus. And he stood[e] on the sand of the sea.

The Beast from the Sea

[Revelation 13:1–4]

AND I saw a beast rising out of the sea, with ten horns and seven heads, with ten diadems upon its horns and a blasphemous name upon its heads. And the beast that I saw was like a leopard, its feet were like a bear's, and its mouth was like a lion's mouth. And to it the dragon gave his power and his throne and great authority. One of its heads seemed to have a mortal wound, but its mortal wound was healed, and the whole earth followed the beast with wonder. Men worshiped the dragon, for he had given his authority to the beast, and they worshiped the beast, saying, "Who is like the beast, and who can fight against it?"

[e] Other ancient authorities read *And I stood*, connecting the sentence with 13.1

War on the Saints [13:5-10]

And the beast was given a mouth uttering haughty and blasphemous words, and it was allowed to exercise authority for forty-two months; it opened its mouth to utter blasphemies against God, blaspheming his name and his dwelling, that is, those who dwell in heaven. Also it was allowed to make war on the saints and to conquer them.[f] And authority was given it over every tribe and people and tongue and nation, and all who dwell on earth will worship it, every one whose name has not been written before the foundation of the world in the book of life of the Lamb that was slain. If any one has an ear, let him hear:

If any one is to be taken captive,
    to captivity he goes;
if any one slays with the sword,
    with the sword must he be slain.
Here is a call for the endurance and faith of the saints.

The Beast from the Earth [13:11-18]

Then I saw another beast which rose out of the earth; it had two horns like a lamb and it spoke like a dragon. It exercises all the authority of the first beast in its presence, and makes the earth and its inhabitants worship the first beast, whose mortal wound was healed. It works great signs, even making fire come down from heaven to earth in the sight of men; and by the signs which it is allowed to work in the presence of the beast, it deceives those who dwell on earth, bidding them make an image for the beast which was wounded by the sword and yet lived; and it was allowed to give breath to the image of the beast so that the image of the beast should even speak, and to cause those who would not worship the image of the beast to be slain. Also it causes all, both small and great, both rich and poor, both free and slave, to be marked on the right hand or the forehead, so that no one can buy or sell unless he has the mark, that is, the name of the beast or the number of its name. This calls for wisdom: let him who has understanding reckon the number of the beast, for it is a human number, its number is six hundred and sixty-six.[g]

The New Song [Revelation 14:1-5]

THEN I looked, and lo, on Mount Zion stood the Lamb, and with him a hundred and forty-four thousand who had his name and his Father's name written on their foreheads. And I heard a voice from heaven like the sound of many waters and like the sound of loud thunder; the voice I heard was like the sound of harpers playing on their harps, and they sing a new song before the throne and before the four living creatures and before the elders. No one could learn that song except the hundred and forty-four thousand who had been redeemed from the earth. It is these who have not defiled themselves with women, for they are chaste;[h] it is these who follow the Lamb wherever he goes; these have been redeemed from mankind as first fruits for God and the Lamb, and in their mouth no lie was found, for they are spotless.

[f] Other ancient authorities omit this sentence
[g] Other ancient authorities read *six hundred and sixteen*
[h] Greek *virgins*

247

Ernest Nash

Entrance to Nero's Golden House. After the great fire, A.D. 64, that Nero blamed on the Christians, he planned and built a great palace, with gardens and a lake, running from the Palatine to the Esquiline, the central feature being an artificial lake in the valley later occupied by the Colosseum. Its grounds, believed to have included over 125 acres, extended over the Caelian Hill to the site of the Temple of Claudius, which was begun by Agrippina the Elder but destroyed by Nero. In the entrance to the vestibule was a statue of Nero 120 feet high. Nero had little time to enjoy this magnificent building, for he spent most of the years A.D. 66 to 68 in Greece and committed suicide near Rome on June 9, A.D. 68, rather than submit to arrest

Herbert Bloch   **1**   A. Deissmann   **2**   W. Schubart   **3**

(1) Original stamp of limestone, A.D. 5/6, with the name of the Emperor Augustus, used for legalizing documents. (2) Brick-stamp of Cn. Domitius Arignotus found on bricks of the Palace of Domitian on the Palatine. The sistrum, symbol of the cult of Isis, appears twice on the stamp; Domitian completely rebuilt the Temple of Isis in Rome. (3) Stamp applied on a papyrus document from Egypt, A.D. 102, shows the name of the Emperor Trajan and the crocodile-god Socnopaeus

From slab in the Cyriaca Catacomb in Rome, F. J. Doelger

In catacombs, on tombs and lamps these marks were used by early Christians:

A fish (in Greek, ΙΧΘΤΣ)
Ι = Ἰησοῦς = Jesus
Χ = Χριστός = Christ,
Θ = Θεοῦ = God's
Τ = Ὑιός = Son,
Σ = Σωτήρ = Saviour

The XP (Chi Rho)
ΧΡ[ΙΣΤΟΣ] = Christ, first two letters
The IHS
Ἰη[σοῖ]s = Jesus, first, second and sixth letters

4

1   **2**   **3**

For centuries Christians used the following designs to identify themselves to one another and on gravestones: (1) A fish and loaves (2) The Good Shepherd (3) The anchor

A Christian lamp in bronze from Scythia Minor in the museum at Turnu-Severin bears the Chi Rho (short for ΧΡ[ΙΣΤΟΣ], Christ) and the cross

F. J. Doelger

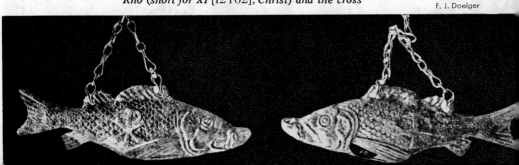

This head of Domitian is thought by some to be "the image of the beast." It was thrown from the northwest corner of the temple (erected in Ephesus by the Province of Asia to the Emperor Domitian) when his memory was officially condemned after his death in A.D. 96. This was an important event for the city of Ephesus, whose claim to be "Temple Warden" derived from this very temple

Oesterreichisches Archaeologisches Institut, Vienna

The Eternal Gospel [14:6–7]

Then I saw another angel flying in midheaven, with an eternal gospel to proclaim to those who dwell on earth, to every nation and tribe and tongue and people; and he said with a loud voice, "Fear God and give him glory, for the hour of his judgment has come; and worship him who made heaven and earth, the sea and the fountains of water."

Fallen Babylon [14:8]

Another angel, a second, followed, saying, "Fallen, fallen is Babylon the great, she who made all nations drink the wine of her impure passion."

Worshipers of the Beast [14:9–12]

And another angel, a third, followed them, saying with a loud voice, "If any one worships the beast and its image, and receives a mark on his forehead or on his hand, he also shall drink the wine of God's wrath, poured unmixed into the cup of his anger, and he shall be tormented with fire and brimstone in the presence of the holy angels and in the presence of the Lamb. And the smoke of their torment goes up for ever and ever; and they have no rest, day or night, these worshipers of the beast and its image, and whoever receives the mark of its name."

Here is a call for the endurance of the saints, those who keep the commandments of God and the faith of Jesus.

The Blessed Dead [14:13]

And I heard a voice from heaven saying, "Write this: Blessed are the dead who die in the Lord henceforth." "Blessed indeed," says the Spirit, "that they may rest from their labors, for their deeds follow them!"

The Harvest of the Earth [14:14–16]

Then I looked, and lo, a white cloud, and seated on the cloud one like a son of man, with a golden crown on his head, and a sharp sickle in his hand. And another angel came out of the temple, calling with a loud voice to him who sat upon the cloud, "Put in your sickle, and reap, for the hour to reap has come, for the harvest of the earth is fully ripe." So he who sat upon the cloud swung his sickle on the earth, and the earth was reaped.

The Wine Press of God's Wrath [14:17–20]

And another angel came out of the temple in heaven, and he too had a sharp sickle. Then another angel came out from the altar, the angel who has power over fire, and he called with a loud voice to him who had the sharp sickle, "Put in your sickle, and gather the clusters of the vine of the earth, for its grapes are ripe." So the angel swung his sickle on the earth and gathered the vintage of the earth, and threw it into the great wine press of the wrath of God; and the wine press was trodden outside the city, and blood flowed from the wine press, as high as a horse's bridle, for one thousand six hundred stadia.[i]

The Seven Last Plagues [Revelation 15:1]

THEN I saw another portent in heaven, great and wonderful, seven angels with seven plagues, which are the last, for with them the wrath of God is ended.

The Sea of Glass [15:2–4]

And I saw what appeared to be a sea of glass mingled with fire, and those who had conquered the beast and its image and the number of its name, standing beside the sea of glass with harps of God in their hands. And they sing the song of Moses, the servant of God, and the song of the Lamb, saying,

"Great and wonderful are thy deeds,
O Lord God the Almighty!
Just and true are thy ways,
O King of the ages![j]
Who shall not fear and glorify thy name,
    O Lord?
For thou alone art holy.
All nations shall come and worship thee,
for thy judgments have been revealed."

An ancient wine press. Two satyrs crush the grapes, keeping in step with the music played on the aulos (a kind of flute) by another satyr

Ernst Howard, Kultur der Antike

[i]About two hundred miles.
[j]Other ancient authorities read *the nations*

248

Air view of Megiddo. "Armageddon" is thought to be the Greek transcription of the Hebrew "Har-Magedon," which means "Mountain of Megiddo"

The mound of Megiddo, with plowmen in foreground, scene of many famous battles

The Seven Golden Bowls [15:5–8]

After this I looked, and the temple of the tent of witness in heaven was opened, and out of the temple came the seven angels with the seven plagues, robed in pure bright linen, and their breasts girded with golden girdles. And one of the four living creatures gave the seven angels seven golden bowls full of the wrath of God who lives for ever and ever; and the temple was filled with smoke from the glory of God and from his power, and no one could enter the temple until the seven plagues of the seven angels were ended.

A Voice from the Temple

[Revelation 16:1]

THEN I heard a loud voice from the temple telling the seven angels, "Go and pour out on the earth the seven bowls of the wrath of God."

First Bowl—on the Earth [16:2]

So the first angel went and poured his bowl on the earth, and foul and evil sores came upon the men who bore the mark of the beast and worshiped its image.

Second Bowl—on the Sea [16:3]

The second angel poured his bowl into the sea, and it became like the blood of a dead man, and every living thing died that was in the sea.

Third Bowl—on Rivers and Fountains

[16:4–7]

The third angel poured his bowl into the rivers and the fountains of water, and they became blood. And I heard the angel of water say,
　"Just art thou in these thy judgments,
　　thou who art and wast, O Holy One.
　For men have shed the blood of saints
　　and prophets,
　and thou hast given them blood to drink.
　　It is their due!"
And I heard the altar cry,
　"Yea, Lord God the Almighty,
　　true and just are thy judgments!"

Fourth Bowl—on the Sun

[16:8–9]

The fourth angel poured his bowl on the sun, and it was allowed to scorch men with fire; men were scorched by the fierce heat, and they cursed the name of God who had

power over these plagues, and they did not repent and give him glory.

Fifth Bowl—on the Throne of the Beast

[16:10–11]

The fifth angel poured his bowl on the throne of the beast, and its kingdom was in darkness; men gnawed their tongues in anguish and cursed the God of heaven for their pain and sores, and did not repent of their deeds.

Sixth Bowl—on the River Euphrates

[16:12–16]

The sixth angel poured his bowl on the great river Eu-phra′tes, and its water was dried up, to prepare the way for the kings from the east. And I saw, issuing from the mouth of the dragon and from the mouth of the beast and from the mouth of the false prophet, three foul spirits like frogs; for they are demoniac spirits, performing signs, who go abroad to the kings of the whole world, to assemble them for battle on the great day of God the Almighty. ("Lo, I am coming like a thief! Blessed is he who is awake, keeping his garments that he may not go naked and be seen exposed!") And they assembled them at the place which is called in Hebrew Armaged′don.

Solomon's stables at Megiddo. There was space for at least 450 horses, which were tied to the tie holes still visible in the stone posts. Note two stone mangers in the center, between the stone posts

Megiddo's water system being excavated

Augustus, 31 B.C.-A.D. 14

American Numismatic Society

Tiberius, A.D. 14–37

American Numismatic Society

Caligula, A.D. 37–41

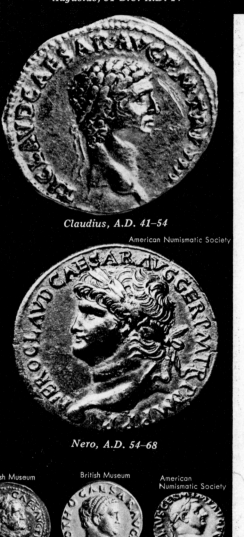

Claudius, A.D. 41–54

American Numismatic Society

Nero, A.D. 54–68

British Museum   British Museum   American Numismatic Society

Galba, Otho, Vitellius, A.D 68–69

Seventh Bowl—Poured into the Air

[16:17–21]

The seventh angel poured his bowl into the air, and a great voice came out of the temple, from the throne, saying, "It is done!" And there were flashes of lightning, loud noises, peals of thunder, and a great earthquake such as had never been since men were on the earth, so great was that earthquake. The great city was split into three parts, and the cities of the nations fell, and God remembered great Babylon, to make her drain the cup of the fury of his wrath. And every island fled away, and no mountains were to be found; and great hailstones, heavy as a hundred-weight, dropped on men from heaven, till men cursed God for the plague of the hail, so fearful was that plague.

Judgment of the Great Harlot

[Revelation 17:1–6a]

THEN one of the seven angels who had the seven bowls came and said to me, "Come, I will show you the judgment of the great harlot who is seated upon many waters, with whom the kings of the earth have committed fornication, and with the wine of whose fornication the dwellers on earth have become drunk." And he carried me away in the Spirit into a wilderness, and I saw a woman sitting on a scarlet beast which was full of blasphemous names, and it had seven heads and ten horns. The woman was arrayed in purple and scarlet, and bedecked with gold and jewels and pearls, holding in her hand a golden cup full of abominations and the impurities of her fornication; and on her forehead was written a name of mystery: "Babylon the great, mother of harlots and of earth's abominations." And I saw the woman, drunk with the blood of the saints and the blood of the martyrs of Jesus.

The Mystery of the Beast [17:6b–14]

When I saw her I marveled greatly. But the angel said to me, "Why marvel? I will tell you the mystery of the woman, and of the beast with seven heads and ten horns that carries her. The beast that you saw was, and is not, and is to ascend from the bottomless pit and go to perdition; and the dwellers on earth whose names have not been written in the book of life from the foundation of the world, will marvel to behold the beast, because it was and is not and is to come. This calls for a mind with wisdom: the seven heads are seven hills on which the woman is seated; they are also seven kings, five of whom have fallen, one is, the other has not yet come, and when he comes he must remain only a little while. As for the beast that was and is not, it is an eighth but it belongs to the seven, and it goes to perdition. And the ten horns that you saw are ten kings who have not yet received royal power, but they are to receive authority as kings for one hour, together with the beast. These are of one mind and give over their power and authority to the beast; they will make war on the Lamb, and the Lamb will conquer them, for he is Lord of lords and King of kings, and those with him are called and chosen and faithful."

The Woman a City [17:15–18]

And he said to me, "The waters that you saw, where the harlot is seated, are peoples and multitudes and nations and tongues. And the ten horns that you saw, they and the beast will hate the harlot; they will make her desolate and naked and devour her flesh and burn her up with fire, for God has put it into their hearts to carry out his purpose by being of one mind and giving over their royal power to the beast, until the words of God shall be fulfilled. And the woman that you saw is the great city which has dominion over the kings of the earth."

Vespasian, A.D. 69–79

Titus, A.D. 79–81

Domitian, A.D. 81–96

American Numismatic Society

American Numismatic Society

Felbermeyer

The Doom of Babylon [Revelation 18:1–8]

AFTER this I saw another angel coming down from heaven, having great authority; and the earth was made bright with his splendor. And he called out with a mighty voice,

"Fallen, fallen is Babylon the great!
It has become a dwelling place of demons,
a haunt of every foul spirit,
a haunt of every foul and hateful bird;
for all nations have drunk[k] the wine of
her impure passion,
and the kings of the earth have committed fornication with her,
and the merchants of the earth have
grown rich with the wealth of her
wantonness."

Then I heard another voice from heaven saying,

"Come out of her, my people,
lest you take part in her sins,
lest you share in her plagues;
for her sins are heaped high as heaven,
and God has remembered her iniquities.
Render to her as she herself has rendered,
and repay her double for her deeds;
mix a double draught for her in the cup
she mixed.
As she glorified herself and played the
wanton,
so give her a like measure of torment and
mourning.
Since in her heart she says, 'A queen I sit,
I am no widow, mourning I shall never
see,'
so shall her plagues come in a single day,
pestilence and mourning and famine,
and she shall be burned with fire;
for mighty is the Lord God who judges
her."

The Dirge over Babylon [18:9–20]

And the kings of the earth, who committed fornication and were wanton with her, will

[k] Other ancient authorities read *fallen by*

weep and wail over her when they see the smoke of her burning; they will stand far off, in fear of her torment, and say,

"Alas! alas! thou great city,
thou mighty city, Babylon!
In one hour has thy judgment come."

And the merchants of the earth weep and mourn for her, since no one buys their cargo any more, cargo of gold, silver, jewels and pearls, fine linen, purple, silk and scarlet, all kinds of scented wood, all articles of ivory, all articles of costly wood, bronze, iron and marble, cinnamon, spice, incense, myrrh, frankincense, wine, oil, fine flour and wheat, cattle and sheep, horses and chariots, and slaves, that is, human souls.

"The fruit for which thy soul longed has
gone from thee,
and all thy dainties and thy splendor are
lost to thee, never to be found again!"

The merchants of these wares, who gained wealth from her, will stand far off, in fear of her torment, weeping and mourning aloud,

"Alas, alas, for the great city
that was clothed in fine linen, in purple
and scarlet,
bedecked with gold, with jewels, and
with pearls!
In one hour all this wealth has been laid
waste."

And all shipmasters and seafaring men, sailors and all whose trade is on the sea, stood far off and cried out as they saw the smoke of her burning,

"What city was like the great city?"

And they threw dust on their heads, as they wept and mourned, crying out,

"Alas, alas, for the great city
where all who had ships at sea grew rich
by her wealth!
In one hour she has been laid waste.
Rejoice over her, O heaven,
O saints and apostles and prophets,
for God has given judgment for you
against her!"

Roman galleys, from bas-relief at Pozzuoli, probably of the time of Nero

Alinari

*Dealer in knives and sickles.
First century, Rome*

Paul's Photos

These oil merchants' jars were unearthed at Ostia, the seaport of Rome, where they were anciently covered with silt by the overflow of the River Tiber

Mosaic of Roman ship, found at Ostia

J. Lane Miller

*Roman
wine
merchant*

Rome, Fragment of tomb showing millstones worked by horses

Alinari

Song of Triumph in Heaven
[Revelation 19:1-8]

AFTER this I heard what seemed to be the mighty voice of a great multitude in heaven, crying,

"Hallelujah! Salvation and glory and power belong to our God,
for his judgments are true and just;
he has judged the great harlot who corrupted the earth with her fornication,
and he has avenged on her the blood of his servants."

Once more they cried,

"Hallelujah! The smoke from her goes up for ever and ever."

And the twenty-four elders and the four living creatures fell down and worshiped God who is seated on the throne, saying, "Amen. Hallelujah!" And from the throne came a voice crying,

"Praise our God, all you his servants, you who fear him, small and great."

Then I heard what seemed to be the voice of a great multitude, like the sound of many waters and like the sound of mighty thunderpeals, crying,

"Hallelujah! For the Lord our God the Almighty reigns.
Let us rejoice and exult and give him the glory,
for the marriage of the Lamb has come, and his Bride has made herself ready;
it was granted her to be clothed with fine linen, bright and pure"—

for the fine linen is the righteous deeds of the saints.

Silence in the Doomed City
[18:21-24]

Then a mighty angel took up a stone like a great millstone and threw it into the sea, saying,

"So shall Babylon the great city be thrown down with violence
and shall be found no more;
and the sound of harpers and minstrels, of flute players and trumpeters,
shall be heard in thee no more;
and a craftsman of any craft
shall be found in thee no more;
and the sound of the millstone
shall be heard in thee no more;
and the light of a lamp
shall shine in thee no more;
and the voice of bridegroom and bride
shall be heard in thee no more;
for thy merchants were the great men of the earth,
and all nations were deceived by thy sorcery.

And in her was found the blood of prophets and of saints,
and of all who have been slain on earth."

The Marriage Supper of the Lamb
[19:9-10]

And the angel said[1] to me, "Write this: Blessed are those who are invited to the marriage supper of the Lamb." And he said to me, "These are true words of God." Then I fell down at his feet to worship him, but he said to me, "You must not do that! I am a fellow servant with you and your brethren who hold the testimony of Jesus. Worship God." For the testimony of Jesus is the spirit of prophecy.

After Nero's death, later emperors made use of some parts of the Golden House. This room is said by some to have been the bedroom of Poppaea, wife of Nero, whom he took away from her husband Otho. Poppaea is said to have had a leading part in the murder of Nero's mother Agrippina

Alinari

The Warrior Faithful and True
[19:11-16]

Then I saw heaven opened, and behold, a white horse! He who sat upon it is called Faithful and True, and in righteousness he judges and makes war. His eyes are like a flame of fire, and on his head are many diadems; and he has a name inscribed which no one knows but himself. He is clad in a robe dipped in[m] blood, and the name by which he is called is The Word of God. And the armies of heaven, arrayed in fine linen, white and pure, followed him on white horses. From his mouth issues a sharp sword with which to smite the nations, and he will rule them with a rod of iron; he will tread the wine press of the fury of the wrath of God the Almighty. On his robe and on his thigh he has a name inscribed, King of kings and Lord of lords.

[1] Greek *he said*
[m] Other ancient authorities read *sprinkled with*

The Beast and Prophet Captured

[19:17–21]

Then I saw an angel standing in the sun, and with a loud voice he called to all the birds that fly in midheaven, "Come, gather for the great supper of God, to eat the flesh of kings, the flesh of captains, the flesh of mighty men, the flesh of horses and their riders, and the flesh of all men, both free and slave, both small and great." And I saw the beast and the kings of the earth with their armies gathered to make war against him who sits upon the horse and against his army. And the beast was captured, and with it the false prophet who in its presence had worked the signs by which he deceived those who had received the mark of the beast and those who worshiped its image. These two were thrown alive into the lake of fire that burns with brimstone. And the rest were slain by the sword of him who sits upon the horse, the sword that issues from his mouth; and all the birds were gorged with their flesh.

Satan Bound a Thousand Years

[Revelation 20:1–3]

THEN I saw an angel coming down from heaven, holding in his hand the key of the bottomless pit and a great chain. And he seized the dragon, that ancient serpent, who is the Devil and Satan, and bound him for a thousand years, and threw him into the pit, and shut it and sealed it over him, that he should deceive the nations no more, till the thousand years were ended. After that he must be loosed for a little while.

The First Resurrection [20:4–6]

Then I saw thrones, and seated on them were those to whom judgment was committed. Also I saw the souls of those who had been beheaded for their testimony to Jesus and for the word of God, and who had not worshiped the beast or its image and had not received its mark on their foreheads on their hands. They came to life, and reigned with Christ a thousand years. The rest of the dead did not come to life until the thousand years were ended. This is the first resurrection. Blessed and holy is he who shares in the first resurrection! Over such the second death has no power, but they shall be priests of God and of Christ, and they shall reign with him a thousand years.

Gog and Magog [20:7–10]

And when the thousand years are ended, Satan will be loosed from his prison and will come out to deceive the nations which are at the four corners of the earth, that is, Gog and Magog, to gather them for battle; their number is like the sand of the sea. And they marched up over the broad earth and surrounded the camp of the saints and the beloved city; but fire came down from heaven[n] and consumed them, and the devil who had deceived them was thrown into the lake of fire and brimstone where the beast and the false prophet were, and they will be tormented day and night for ever and ever.

[n]Other ancient authorities read from God, out of heaven, or out of heaven from God

Italian State Tourist Office

The Colosseum, or Flavian Amphitheater, was built on part of the grounds that Nero had used for his Golden House. In ancient times the central area was covered by a floor; below were the cages of the wild animals and the locker rooms of the gladiators. Built by Vespasian near the Arch of Titus, it seated some 45,000 people. A bronze colossus of Nero, 120 feet high, stood near by at the vestibule of Nero's Golden House, giving the Colosseum its name. This, when completed, was one of the greatest buildings in the world up to that time. It was dedicated by Titus in A.D. 80 during 100 days of elaborate and gory games

The Great White Throne [20:11–15]

Then I saw a great white throne and him who sat upon it; from his presence earth and sky fled away, and no place was found for them. And I saw the dead, great and small, standing before the throne, and books were opened. Also another book was opened, which is the book of life. And the dead were judged by what was written in the books, by what they had done. And the sea gave up the dead in it, Death and Hades gave up the dead in them, and all were judged by what they had done. Then Death and Hades were thrown into the lake of fire. This is the second death, the lake of fire; and if anyone's name was not found written in the book of life, he was thrown into the lake of fire.

The New Heaven and Earth

[Revelation 21:1–8]

THEN I saw a new heaven and a new earth; for the first heaven and the first earth had passed away, and the sea was no more. And I saw the holy city, new Jerusalem, coming down out of heaven from God, prepared as a bride adorned for her husband; and I heard a great voice from the throne saying, "Behold, the dwelling of God is with men. He will dwell with them, and they shall be his people,[o] and God himself will be with them;[p] he will wipe away every tear from their eyes, and death shall be no more, neither shall there be mourning nor crying nor pain any more, for the former things have passed away."

And he who sat upon the throne said, "Behold, I make all things new." Also he said, "Write this, for these words are trustworthy and true." And he said to me, "It is done! I am the Alpha and the Ome'ga, the beginning and the end. To the thirsty I will give water without price from the fountain of the water of life. He who conquers shall have this heritage, and I will be his God and he shall be my son. But as for the cowardly, the faithless, the polluted, as for murderers, fornicators, sorcerers, idolaters, and all liars, their lot shall be in the lake that burns with fire and brimstone, which is the second death."

[o]Other ancient authorities read peoples
[p]Other ancient authorities add and be their God

Ewing Galloway

Jerusalem. The sacred rock of Solomon's Temple

British Museum

About 539 B.C. Cyrus allowed Nehemiah and Ezra to rebuild Jerusalem. This baked-clay foundation cylinder contains Cyrus' decree granting toleration to other religions. It reads in part: "The gods who dwelt in the destroyed cities I brought back to their places and provided them with permanent abodes. I brought together all of their people and restored their habitations"

E. L. Sukenik

Third wall, started by Herod Agrippa I (A.D. 41, 44), but never completed

L. H. Vincent

Jerusalem's water supply was safeguarded by Hezekiah's Siloam tunnel, over 1,700 feet long. About 701 B.C.

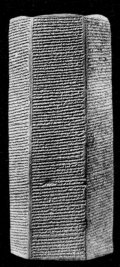

Sennacherib's clay prism reports the siege of Hezekiah in Jerusalem, 701 B.C.: "Forty-six of his strong-walled cities I besieged and took. Himself like a caged bird I shut up in Jerusalem, his royal city. Earthworks I threw up against him; the one coming out of the city gate I turned back to his misery"

Luckenbill—
Oriental Institute,
University of Chicago

This ration list shows that five years before Nebuchadnezzar destroyed the Temple of Jerusalem in 587 B.C., he was holding King Jehoiachin and five royal princes of Judah as hostages in Babylon

Ernst Weidner

The New Jerusalem [21:9-14]

Then came one of the seven angels who had the seven bowls full of the seven last plagues, and spoke to me, saying, "Come, I will show you the Bride, the wife of the Lamb." And in the Spirit he carried me away to a great, high mountain, and showed me the holy city Jerusalem coming down out of heaven from God, having the glory of God, its radiance like a most rare jewel, like a jasper, clear as crystal. It had a great, high wall, with twelve gates, and at the gates twelve angels, and on the gates the names of the twelve tribes of the sons of Israel were inscribed; on the east three gates, on the north three gates, on the south three gates, and on the west three gates. And the wall of the city had twelve foundations, and on them the twelve names of the twelve apostles of the Lamb.

The City Foursquare [21:15-21]

And he who talked to me had a measuring rod of gold to measure the city and its gates and walls. The city lies foursquare, its length the same as its breadth; and he measured the city with his rod, twelve thousand stadia;[q] its length and breadth and height are equal. He also measured its wall, a hundred and forty-four cubits by a man's measure, that is, an angel's. The wall was built of jasper, while the city was pure gold, clear as glass. The foundations of the wall of the city were adorned with every jewel; the first was jasper, the second sapphire, the third agate, the fourth

[q]About fifteen hundred miles

emerald, the fifth onyx, the sixth carnelian, the seventh chrysolite, the eighth beryl, the ninth topaz, the tenth chrysoprase, the eleventh jacinth, the twelfth amethyst. And the twelve gates were twelve pearls, each of the gates made of a single pearl, and the street of the city was pure gold, transparent as glass.

God Its Light [21:22-27]

And I saw no temple in the city, for its temple is the Lord God the Almighty and the Lamb. And the city has no need of sun or moon to shine upon it, for the glory of God is its light, and its lamp is the Lamb. By its light shall the nations walk; and the kings of the earth shall bring their glory into it, and its gates shall never be shut by day—and there shall be no night there; they shall bring into it the glory and the honor of the nations. But nothing unclean shall enter it, nor any one who practices abomination or falsehood, but only those who are written in the Lamb's book of life.

The River of the Water of Life

[Revelation 22:1-5]

THEN he showed me the river of the water of life, bright as crystal, flowing from the throne of God and of the Lamb through the middle of the street of the city; also, on either side of the river, the tree of life[r] with its twelve kinds of fruit, yielding its fruit each month; and the leaves of the

[r]Or *the Lamb. In the midst of the street of the city, and on either side of the river, was the tree of life,* etc.

Herod the Great (37 B.C.–4 B.C.) enlarged and beautified Jerusalem's walls with these huge drafted stones

Kofod Photo

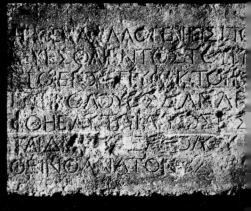

This warning notice in Greek in Herod's Temple warned Gentiles of death if they entered the inner courts

Museum of Antiquities, Istanbul

COINS OF FIRST REVOLT, A.D. 66-70

Obverse:"Shek-el of Israel"; above chalice, "Year 2." Reverse: "Jerusalem the Holy" around the stem with three flowers

JUDEA CAPTA

Judea seated under a palm tree, and Jew standing with hands bound behind his back. Titus captured Jerusalem and destroyed the Temple, A.D. 70. Coin of Titus, struck A.D. 80-81

American Numismatic Society

James Muilenburg

Letter of Bar Kochba, who led revolt A.D. 130-132, threatening Jeshua ben Gilgola with ankle irons for insubordination. "Men of Galilee" are mentioned in the fourth line

British Museum

Chosroes (Khusru) the Persian drove out the Christians, A.D. 614

Heraclius returned A.D. 629 but was driven out by the Mohammedans, A.D. 637

tree were for the healing of the nations. There shall no more be anything accursed, but the throne of God and of the Lamb shall be in it, and his servants shall worship him; they shall see his face, and his name shall be on their foreheads. And night shall be no more; they need no light of lamp or sun, for the Lord God will be their light, and they shall reign for ever and ever.

The Time Is Near [22:6-13]

And he said to me, "These words are trustworthy and true. And the Lord, the God of the spirits of the prophets, has sent his angel to show his servants what must soon take place. And behold, I am coming soon."

Blessed is he who keeps the words of the prophecy of this book.

I John am he who heard and saw these things. And when I heard and saw them, I fell down to worship at the feet of the angel who showed them to me; but he said to me, "You must not do that! I am a fellow servant with you and your brethren the prophets, and with those who keep the words of this book. Worship God."

And he said to me, "Do not seal up the words of the prophecy of this book, for the time is near. Let the evildoer still do evil, and the filthy still be filthy, and the righteous still do right, and the holy still be holy."

"Behold, I am coming soon, bringing my recompense, to repay every one for what he has done. I am the Alpha and the Ome′ga, the first and the last, the beginning and the end."

The Spirit and Bride Say, "Come" [22:14-17]

Blessed are those who wash their robes,[s] that they may have the right to the tree of life and that they may enter the city by the gates. Outside are the dogs and sorcerers and fornicators and murderers and idolaters, and every one who loves and practices falsehood.

"I Jesus have sent my angel to you with this testimony for the churches. I am the root and the offspring of David, the bright morning star."

The Spirit and the Bride say, "Come." And let him who hears say, "Come." And let him who is thirsty come, let him who desires take the water of life without price.

Come, Lord Jesus [22:18-21]

I warn every one who hears the words of the prophecy of this book: if any one adds to them, God will add to him the plagues described in this book, and if any one takes away from the words of the book of this prophecy, God will take away his share in the tree of life and in the holy city, which are described in this book.

He who testifies to these things says, "Surely I am coming soon." Amen. Come, Lord Jesus!

The grace of the Lord Jesus be with all the saints.[t] Amen.

[s]Other ancient authorities read do his commandments
[t]Other ancient authorities omit all; others omit the saints

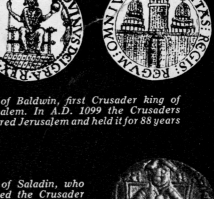

Philip Gendreau

Abd el Malik built a Moslem sanctuary, the Dome of the Rock, to cover the sacred rock of Solomon's Temple, A.D. 691

G. Schlumberger

Seal of Baldwin, first Crusader king of Jerusalem. In A.D. 1099 the Crusaders captured Jerusalem and held it for 88 years

Coin of Saladin, who crushed the Crusader army at the Horns of Hattin in A.D. 1187 and captured Jerusalem

British Museum

COINS OF SECOND REVOLT, A.D. 132-135

Obverse: Screen of the tabernacle, with Ark of the Covenant; inscription reads "Jerusalem." Reverse: Lulab and ethrog; inscription reads, "First year of the redemption of Israel"

Hadrian standing, hand raised; Judea offering incense box (?) before altar, a child before and behind her. All Jews were excluded from Aelia Capitolina, the Roman colony founded A.D. 135 on the site of Jerusalem

American Numismatic Society

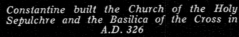

Constantine built the Church of the Holy Sepulchre and the Basilica of the Cross in A.D. 326

Alinari

Suleiman the Magnificent built the present walls that enclose the old city, A.D. 1542

Matson Photo Service

BLESSED ARE THOSE WHO HUNGER AND THIRST FOR RIGHTEOUSNESS,
FOR THEY SHALL BE SATISFIED

MATT. 5:6

CAMELS QUENCHING THEIR THIRST

Matson Photo Service

TO THE THIRSTY I WILL GIVE WATER WITHOUT PRICE FROM THE
FOUNTAIN OF THE WATER OF LIFE

REV. 21:6

SHEEP IN THE HOLY LAND

Matson Photo Service

LET HIM WHO IS THIRSTY COME, LET HIM WHO DESIRES TAKE
THE WATER OF LIFE WITHOUT PRICE

INDEX OF ILLUSTRATIONS

A

Abraham (of Ur): ziggurat, 166

Alexandria: Pharos, "Pompey's Pillar," 217

altar: Ahenobarbus, 173, 202; horns of, Megiddo, 244; Peace, 172; "Unknown God," 172; Zeus (Pergamum), 239

Angista: see Philippi

Antioch (Pisidia): preface, 130, 194; aqueduct, 197; coins, 199; Edict ca. A.D. 93, 242; sanctuary of Moon God, 196; Square of Tiberius, 144

Antioch (Syria): preface, 130; views, 142, 145, 197

Antonia, Castle of: cistern, 153. (See also Jerusalem, Praetorium)

Appian Way, 158

aqueduct: Antioch (Pisidia), 197; Claudian, 158, 173

Arab, 42, 52

Armageddon: air view, mound, Solomon's stables, water system, 249

armor: breastplate, 244; centurion, horseman, 154; Roman military standards (coin), 206; Roman soldiers, 202; Roman sword and sheath, 224

Arval Brethren inscriptions: Nov. 6, A.D. 58, 165; Mar. 28, A.D. 59, 165; Apr. 5, A.D. 59, 165; A.D. 66, 244

Asia, Province of: preface, 226

Assos: bronze plaque, 210

Athens: preface, 130; Acropolis, 207; Acropolis and Areopagus, 148; inscription on Temple Roma and Augustus, 208; Parthenon and Lycabettus, 129; rock steps of Areopagus, 148; Tower of Winds, 209

athlete: boxing, cup, with palm branch, 181; crowned, 243

Augustus: Altar of Peace, 172, 205; breastplate, 244; cameo, 143; coins, 163, 206, 250; inscription, 196; Pantheon, 246; stamp, 247; on sword sheath, 224; Temple of, at Ancyra, 198, 199; Temple of, at Pisidian Antioch, 144; Temple of Mars the Avenger, 205; Temple of Roma and Augustus, 208; Theater of Marcellus, 174; Tomb of, 163

B

Bema (Judgment seat): see Corinth

Bethany: view, 58; from Mt. of Olives, 118; road, 118

Bethel: wheat field, 17

Bethlehem: preface, 2; view, 5; Church of the Nativity, 4, 5, 69; harvest, 8; market, 69; road, 6; Shepherds' Fields, 7, 68; street scenes, 68, 69

Bethphage, 53

Bethsaida: preface, 34; air view, 78; Jordan River, 101

Bethzatha (Bethesda), Pool of: and church, 109

Bithynia: preface, 226

boat: see ship

bottles: goatskin, 40, 73

bread: eating, 80; selling, 110; making, 110, 171

bridle, 227

burdens, 15

C

Caesar: cameos, 143, 164; coins, 250. (See Augustus; Caligula; Claudius; Domitian; Nero; Tiberius; Titus; Vespasian)

Caesarea, 156

Caesarea Philippi: preface, 2; Roman bridge, 19

Caligula: bronze plaque of Assos, 210; coin, 250; obelisk, 232

camels, 167, 256

cameos: Cornucopia, 164; Gemma Augustea, 143

Cana, 102, 103

Candace, Queen of Ethiopia, 139

candles: Feast of Dedication, 117. (See also lamps)

Capernaum: preface, 34; Synagogue, 9, 39, 75

Cappadocia: preface, 226

carpenter shop, 44

catacombs: see Rome, catacombs

Cauda (Gaudho), 157

centurion: Marcus Caelius, 154

Cestius, Pyramid of, 156

chariot: four-horse, 56, 174, 242, 244

cherubim, 221

children, 20, 51, 88, 235

Christians, persecution of: Arch of Titus, 242; certificate of pagan sacrifice, 231; Circus of Gaius and Nero, 232; Eastern Roman Empire, Crusades, 255; Pliny's letter, 230; Tacitus' Annals, 223

cistern: see well

"city set on a hill," 32

Claudius: aqueduct, 158, 173; cameo, 164; coins, 163, 178, 228, 242, 250; Gallio inscription, 177; statue, 132

coins: Alexandria, 156, 217; various Asia Minor and Near Eastern, 199, 255; Corinth, 178; Crete, 215; Palestine, 90, 212, 255; Philippi, 206; Roman, 90, 157, 163, 166, 228, 233, 242, 250; Syrian, 17

Colossae: preface, 194; view 205

Colosseum, 160, 253

Corinth: preface, 130, 162; Agora (marketplace), 175, 182; Aphrodite, statue of (coin), 178; Temple of (coin), 178; canal, 187; Erastus inscription, 152; gambling counters, 178; inscription mentioning Gallio, 177; "Judgment seat" (Bema), 149, 175; Lechaeum Road, 186; Neptune, statue of (coin), 178; fountain of Peirene, 182; Peirene-watered taverns and shops, 182, 186; Roman mosaic, 181; Temple of Apollo, 149, 192; theater, 191

Crete: preface, 194; Cauda, 157; Fair Havens, 157; Labyrinth (coins), 215; Roman theater at Gortyn, 215

cup of victory, 181

Cyprus: preface, 130; view, 156; Paphos, 142

D

Damascus: preface, 130; Street called Straight, 140; wall, 140

Dead Sea, 170, 237

Dead Sea Scrolls: Isaiah, 16, 72, 119, 132; storage jar, 102

Decapolis: preface, 2; Gerasa (Gadera?), 44

deities: see gods

Derbe: preface, 194; coins, 199; mound of, 144, 196; spring, 196

Diana: coins, 199; statue, 236; Temple of, 200, 201

dog: "Beware of the dog" (Pompeii), 204

Dome of the Rock: see Jerusalem; and Solomon

Domitian: brick stamp, 247; coin, 250; head of, 248

E

The East: preface, 2

Egypt: preface, 2; hieroglyphics and gods, 132; Matariyeh, 6; Nile Delta, 6; Ramses II, 222

Ephesus: preface, 130; coins, 199; ruins of Celsus' library, 201; seal, 243; Temple of Diana, reconstruction, ruins, 200; theater and street, 150, 239

Ethiopia: Candace, Meroë pyramids, (Queen) Amanitēre, 139

F

Fair Havens, Muros and, 157

Feasts: Dedication, 117; Passover, 107; Tabernacles, 112

fig tree: early and late figs, 54; early spring, 101; mature tree, 83; ripe fruit, 23; sycamore fig, 86

fishermen with nets: casting net, 18, 38; drawing from boat, 73; large net, 127; mending, 38, 77

flowers: Lily of the Field (anemone coronaria), 11, 82; Star of Bethlehem, 12, 227

G

Galatia: preface, 194, 226; Ankara inscription and reconstruction of Temple of Augustus, 198; ruins, 199; coins, 199; Gallic chieftain (statue), 198. (See Antioch in Pisidia; also Derbe; Iconium; Lystra)

Galilee, Sea of: preface, 34; air view, Bethsaida, 78; views, 1, 43, 46, 65, 77, 111; fishing, 18, 38, 73, 77, 103; "Mensa Christi," 127; Mt. Hermon, 49, 76; Plain of Gennesaret, 47; Tabgha, 46

Gallio inscription, 177

Gennesaret, Plain of: 48; and Sea of Galilee, 47

Gerasa (Gadera?): main street, 44

Gethsemane: see Jerusalem

goats, 5, 27, 179, 195, 207, 240

goatskin bottles, 40, 73

gods, goddesses and deities: Arabian, 16, 133; Egyptian, 132, 247 (stamp); Greek, 132, 179, 183, 239; Greek and Roman, 164, 236, 244; Parthian, 133; Phrygian, 133. (See Arval Brethren inscriptions; and coins)

grain: measuring, 229; price of (inscription at Antioch), 242; grinding, 27, 50, 87; threshing, 86, 180, 189, 190. (See also harvest; millstone; plowing; seed; sickles; sower)

Greek language, 218. (See also inscriptions; and manuscripts)

H

hairdress, women's: braided hair, 211: Greco-Roman, 182

Hanukkah, 117

harvest: at Bethlehem, 8; gathering and measuring, 229; plenteous, 13; on Roman farm, 213; young wheat, "white" field, 107

"Healing of the Paralytic," 39

Hebrew: inscription, Siloam tunnel, 115. (See manuscripts)

Hebron: city, Herodian wall, cave of Machpelah, 3

The Herods (Herod Antipas, Herod Archelaus, Herod the Great): preface, 2. (See captions, 7)

Herod Agrippa I: third wall of Jerusalem, 143, 254; winter palace, 155

Herod the Great: tomb of, 7; wall and inscription, 254; warning notice from Temple, 152

Hierapolis: preface, 194; view, 206

Horns of Hattin: 10; from Plain of Gennesaret, 74

horseman, Roman, 154. (See chariot)

I

Iconium: preface, 194; coin, 199; shepherd, 196

idols: see gods and deities

"image of the beast," 248

inn, Palestinian, 6

inscriptions:
Assyrian: Sennacherib's prism, 254
Babylonian, Late: 168
Babylonian, Old: ration list, 254; Cyrus' cylinder, 254
Egyptian, 132

inscriptions (cont.)
Greek: Assos, bronze plaque, 210; Gallio, 177; Jerusalem "Libertines," 136; Jerusalem Temple, warning to Gentiles, 152, 254; Temple of Roma and Augustus, 208; Thessalonica, "Politarchs," 132; Thyatira, 240
Hebrew: Siloam tunnel, 115
Latin: Antioch, price of wheat held, 242; Arval Brethren, 132, 165, 244; Corinth, Erastus, 152; Corinth, meat market, 182; Galatia, on Temple of Augustus, 198; Lystra, 196; bronze military diploma, 180; Palatine Hill altar, 172; tombstones, 154, 167
Nabatean, 133
Phrygian, 133

J

Jacob's Well, 106

Jaffa (Joppa): market place, 47

Jebel Musa: see Mt. Sinai

Jebel Qarantal: see Mt. of Temptation

Jericho:
excavated colonnade, water basin of terraced garden, 22
excavation of Archelaus' palace, 155
Jerusalem-to-Jericho Road, 80, 81
New Testament Jericho, 52
Pre-Israelite foundations, 222

Jerusalem:
preface, 66, 130
Calvary, 30
cattle market, 105
Cenaculum, 59, 120
Church of the Holy Sepulchre: air view, 57; Easter procession, 94; entrance, 31, 63; present facade, 31, 126; steps to Chapel of the Agony, 30
Dome of the Rock, 255; from Aqsa Mosque, 54; Sacred Rock, 62, 136, 254
Garden of Gethsemane: air views, 67, 255; general views, 23, 28, 35, 53, 58, 59, 61, 84, 89, 92, 96, 117, 122
Gates, Jerusalem: Chain, 53; Damascus from inside city, 53; outside city (Sheep Gate), 108; Golden, 23; Jaffa, 21; St. Stephen's, 92, 138
Hezekiah's tunnel, 83, 254
House of Caiaphas, 28
Kidron Valley, 97; air view, 57

Jerusalem (cont.)
Mount of Olives: views, 30, 53, 58, 84, 89, 96, 97, 131; Chapel of the Ascension, 126; Church of the Lord's Prayer, 11; Garden of Gethsemane, 92; tombs on western slope, 25
pictorial history of, 254-255
Praetorium, 29, 93, 124; Lithostroton, diagram, floral piece, 125; modern structure above, 92; paving stones, 29, 93; Praetorian barracks gate, 203; staircase to Roman barracks, 61, 153
Road to Jericho: 80; sealevel sign on road, 81
Roman legion inscription, 60
Siloam, Pool of, 115; tunnel, 254
streets: 30, 105; David, 55; Via Dolorosa, 93, 94
Temple Area: air views, 57, 67, 135; ancient cistern, 73; Dome of the Rock, 54, 104; Gate of the Chain, 53; inscription warning Gentiles, 152, 254; interior court (diagram), 221; looking across to Mt. of Olives, 96; pinnacle, 9; reconstruction of interior, 221; Sacred Rock, 62, 136, 254
tomb: rock-hewn: 31, 62, 94; of Queen Helena, 63; on Mount of Olives, 25, 81
walls: 61, 89, 104; third wall of Jerusalem, 143, 254; "Wailing Wall," 56, 91, 135, 254

jewelry: rings, bracelets, 228

John the Baptist, prison site, 45

Jordan River: 36, 99; air views, 37, 71; near baptism site (?), 71; near Bethsaida, 78, 101; near Caesarea Philippi, 48; near Jericho, 8

Judea: preface, 98

Judea, wilderness of, 100; Jebel Qarantal, 37; between Jerusalem and Dead Sea, 8; Mar Saba, 35

K

kings: "seven kings," 250

knives: Roman dealer in, 251

L

lamps: bronze fish, 247; with chain, 10; with cross, 220; with menorah, 238; with menorah, lulab and shofar, 220; reddish clay, 26; Roman, 32, 220; seven-branched lampstand, 32, 91, 220; seven-spouted, 220; single-branched lampstand, 32

Laodicea: preface, 194, 226; ruins, 241

Latin: see inscriptions

law code (Hammurabi), 168

lictors, 172, 231

Lithostroton: see Jerusalem: Praetorium

lulab and ethrog, 112, 220, 255

Lydda: cloth market, 40

Lystra: preface, 194; coins, 199; mound, 145; mound and inscription, 196

M

Machaerus, ancient remains, 45

Malta: St. Paul's Bay, 156

manuscripts:
Greek: Beatty Papyrus, 60; certificate of pagan sacrifice, 231; papyrus with book and cursive hand, 216; Rylands fragment, 114; Septuagint, 217
Hebrew: Dead Sea Scrolls, Isaiah 6:8-10, 16; Isaiah 39-40, 72; Isaiah 40, 132; Isaiah 53:1, 119; scroll jar, 102; Bar Kochba letter, 255; Nash papyrus, Ten Commandments, 132
Parthian writing, 133

maps and plans:
Aegean world, 194
Ancient Rome, 162
Asia Minor, eastern, 226
Corinth, 176
Jerusalem: 95; reconstruction by Vernon, 112; Praetorium by Vincent, 125; Temple, 134
Mediterranean World, 159
Palestine: 2, 34, 66, 98; principal roads, 130

Marib: bronze statue, Temple of the Moon God, 16

markets: Bethlehem, 69; inscription from Corinth, 182; Jaffa, 47; Jerusalem, 105; Lydda, 40

marks, Christian identification, 247

Matariyeh, 6

Megiddo: air view, 249; horns of, 244; mound of, 249; plowmen, 249; stables (Solomon's), 249; water system, 249

Meroë, pyramids at, 139

Messina, Strait of, 157

Miletus: preface, 194; theater, 214

millstone; central part of rotary, 21; horse-driven, 252; rotary, 50, 87

mirror: Etruscan, 184; mirror cover, 227

Moon God, statue, Temple, 16

mosaics: Alexander and Darius III, 218; athlete, 181; *cave canem*, 204; Roman ship (Ostia), 251

Mt. Carmel, 170

Mt. Gerizim: Samaritan Passover observance on, 107

Mt. Hermon: near Caesarea Philippi, 49; from Sea of Galilee, 76

Mt. of Olives: see Jerusalem

Mt. Silpius, view from, 145

Mt. Sinai: from Jebel Musa, 113; Monastery of St. Catherine in Sinai Valley, 113; close-up of monastery, 137; Ras Safsaf, 167; shepherd and sheep, 198

Mt. Tabor: 49; from Nain, 79

Mt. of Temptation (Jebel Qarantal), 9, 37, 72

Mt. Vesuvius: see Pompeii

Muros and Fair Havens, 157

musical instruments: cithara, 184; flute (aulos), 248; flute (shepherd's), 179; horn (shofar), 10; horn (shofar) on lamp, 220; piper, 75; pipes, 14; trumpets, 244

mustard, 17

mustard tree, 43

Myra, 157

N

Nabatean: see inscriptions

Nain, 79

Nazareth: preface, 34; views, 4, 7, 36, 70, 101; carpenter shop, 44

Neapolis: air views, 146, 203

Negev, wilderness, 246

Nero: bronze statue, 253; Circus Maximus, 174; coins, 156, 157, 233, 250; Corinth Canal, 187; Golden Day, 244; Golden House, 247; inscriptions, 165; obelisk, 232; Poppaea's room, 252; Roman galleys, 251; Tacitus' Annals, 223

Nicopolis: air view, 215

Nineveh: preface, 2

O

obelisk, 232

oil jars at Ostia, 251

olive trees, 59, 92, **171**

oven, 110, 171

oxen, 42, 79, 86, 190, 219, 229; muzzled, 180, 212

P

Palestine: preface, 2, 66; inn, 6; Negev, 246; palm trees, 119; vineyard, 55; watchtower, 22. (See also plowing, Palestine)

palm branch on lamp, 220; mosaic, 181

palm trees, 6, 119

Paphos: see Cyprus

papyrus: see manuscripts and writing

Parthia: Roman breastplate, 244; Nero seeks peace (inscription), 244; soldier capturing Parthian, 216; writing, 133. (See Persia)

Patmos: preface, 226; air view, 238; harbor, 225, 238

Pergamum: preface, 226; Altar of Zeus, ancient path, 239

Persia: Alexander the Great attacking Persian King, 218; coin of Chosroes, 255; Shapur humbles Valerian, 242. (See Parthia)

Philadelphia: preface, 226; wall portion, 240

Philippi: preface, 130; air view, 147; Angista, 203; coins, 206; Roman forum, 204

phylacteries, 24

Pliny, letter to Trajan, 230

plowing: Greece, 190; Megiddo, 249; Palestine, 42, 79, 219, 229

politarchs: inscription at Thessalonica, 132; Vardar Gate, 208

Pompeii: fresco, 184; monument (Street of the Tomb), 228; mosaics, 204, 218; Mt. Vesuvius, 223; Roman road, 170, 232

Pompey's Pillar at Alexandria, 217

Pontus: preface, 226

Pool: Bethzatha, 109; Siloam, 115; Sultan, 105. (See also water supply)

pottery, 15, 17, 70, 102, 169, 240

Praetorian Guard (Rome), 203

Praetorium: see Jerusalem, Praetorium

Puteoli, 157

pyramid: Cestius, 158; Egypt, 6; Meroë, 139

R

Ramses II, statues, 222

Rhegium: Strait of Messina near Rhegium, 157

Rhodes, 151

roads, Roman: Appian Way, 158, 173; Corinth (Lechaeum Road), 186; Egnatian Way, 204, 207, 208; in Pompeii, 170; Tarsus, 141, 146

Roman Empire: preface, 130

Rome:

preface, 162

Abbey of the Three Fountains, 214

altar to "Unknown God," 172

aqueduct: Claudian, 158, 173

Rome (cont.)

Arch of Titus: 26; golden trumpets, 244; Roman soldiers, 91; Titus' four-horse chariot, 56, 242

bridge: Pons Fabricius, 166

catacombs: San Sebastian, 234

Circus Maximus, 174

Colosseum, 160, 253

Forum: 158; through Arch of Severus, 161; Basilica Julia, 163; Temple of Saturn, 230; Temple of Vesta, 163

gladiators, 174

magistrates and lictors, 172

Mamertine Prison: exterior, 158; interior, 233

Mausoleum of Augustus, 163

Nero's Golden House: entrance, 247; Poppaea's room, 252

obelisk of Circus of Gaius and Nero, 232

Pantheon, 246

Paul's Gate and pyramid of Cestius, 158

Porta Capena, 158

Praetorian barracks, 203

Servian Wall, 165

temples: Apollo, 230; Mars, 205; Saturn, 230; Vesta, 163

Theater of Marcellus, 174

Way of Victory, 163

rooftops, 79, 87, 145

S

sacrifices of animals: Altar of Ahenobarbus, 173; Arval Brethren inscriptions, 165, 244; certificate of pagan sacrifice, 231; to Dionysus, 179, 183; Suovetaurilia, 179; trussed-up goat, 207

Safed, 32

salt, 10

Samaria: preface, 98

Samaritan: Passover, 107; Scrolls of the Law, 107

sandals, 100

sarcophagus, 240

Sardis: preface, 226; Roman theater, Temple of Artemis, 240

scrolls: Dead Sea Scrolls (Isaiah), 16, 72, 119, 132; Samaritan, 107; storage jar, 102. (See writing)

sea, wave of, 227

seals: clay, 241; Egyptian, Greek, Hebrew, 243; Roman, 247

seed, sowing of: on good ground, by the wayside, on stony ground, among thorns, 64. (See also grain; sower; threshing grain)

selling: bread, 110; cloth, 185; knives and sickles, 251; salt, 10; slave, 198

Selmun Island: Statue of St. Paul, 156

Septuagint: Greek version of Old Testament, 218; papyrus fragment, 217

sepulchre, 81. (See Jerusalem, Church of the Holy Sepulchre)

Sermon on the Mount: traditional site, 10, 74

Sheba, preface, 2

Shechem: excavated mound, 106

sheep: 27, 82, 87, 107, 108, 116, 128, 139, 198, 256

Sheep Gate, Jerusalem, 108

shepherd, 68, 85, 116, 128, 196, 232

Shepherds' Fields, 7, 68

ship: Puteoli, 157; Sea of Galilee, 38, 65, 73, 77, 101, 103, 111, 127; Tyre, 151; on coins of Alexandria and Ostia, 156, 157, 217; model, 157; monument at Pompeii, 228; mosaic at Ostia, 251; Roman galley, 245, 251; sketch, 156

shofar, 10, 220

Showbread, Table of, from Arch of Titus, 91

sickles, dealer in, 251

Sidon: preface, 2; view, 41; air view, 156

Siloam, Pool of, 83, 115; inscription, 115

slaves: being freed, 206; liberty caps on tombstone, 216; sale of, 198; soldier capturing, 216; of Tiberius, 167

Smyrna: preface, 226; agora, statue of Demeter, 239

Sodom, at Dead Sea, 170, 237

soldiers:

Greek: Alexander attacking Darius III, 218

Roman: erecting trophy, 143; gravestones of centurion, horseman, 154; being paid, military diploma, 180; with shields and helmets, 202; on ship, 245

Solomon: altar at Megiddo, 244; Dome of the Rock, 54, 255; Sacred Rock, 62, 254; stables, 249; Temple, 136, 221

sower, 33, 42, 76. (See seed)

sports and games: boxing match, 181; chariot racing, 174; gambling counters (Corinth), 178; gladiators, 174; race runner (Corinth), 181; Stadium at Delphi, 193

stables at Megiddo, 249

stamp: see seals

surgical instruments, 207

swine, 13

sycamore fig tree, 86

Sychar (modern Askar), 106

synagogue, Capernaum: 9, 39; air view, 75

Syracuse, air view, 156

Syria: preface, 2

T

talent weight, 21

Tarsus: preface, 130; old Roman road, Cilician Gates, 146; Roman brick wall, 195; Roman gateway, silted-up harbor, 141

teacher and pupils bas-relief, 219

temple: see Athens; Augustus; Corinth; Diana; Ephesus; Galatia; Herod the Great; inscriptions, Greek, Latin; Jerusalem, Temple Area; Rome, temples; Sardis; Ur

Temptation, Mt. of: see Mt. of Temptation

tents: Bedouin, 188; from Trajan's column, 185

tent cloth: Cilician goats, 195; weaver and loom, 195, 210

Thessalonica (modern Salonica): preface, 130; air view, 147; Egnatian Way, 207; harbor, 210; Vardar Gate, 208

thorns: bush, 42; on Pavement, 125; wheat among thorns, 64; zizyphus spina Christi, 123

threshing grain: see grain, threshing; and oxen, muzzled

Thyatira: preface, 226; ancient sarcophagus, Greek inscription, modern pottery, 240

Tiberias on Sea of Galilee, 111

Tiberius: cameo, 143; coins, 166, 178, 228, 250; lamp, 220; slaves of, 167; Square of, 144; sword sheath, 224

Titus: Arch of, 26, 91, 244; coins, 250, 255; Colosseum, 253; destruction of Castle of Antonia, 153; triumphal chariot, 242

tomb: rock-hewn, 31, 62, 94, 157; Mausoleum of Augustus, 163; Mt. of Olives, 25; Phrygian, 133; Queen Helena, 63; tombstones, 25, 154, 167, 216

Tower of Winds, 209

treasure, found in a field, 17; in a Piraeus grave, 228

Troas (Troy): preface, 194; ancient walls, 214

Tyre: preface, 2; views, 41, 151

U

Ur: ziggurat, 166

V

veil: Greco-Roman, 182

Vespasian: coin, 250; Colosseum, 253; Corinth Canal, 187

vineyard: grape-picker, 12; grapevines, 55; pruning, 121; watchtower, 22

W

watchtower: Palestine, 22

water supply: Corinth, 182, 186; Jericho, 22; Jerusalem, 254; Megiddo, 249. (See also aqueduct; Pool; well)

weaving, 195, 210

weeds, gathering, 17

well, 15, 106, 116; cistern, 73, 153, 182; spring, 70, 102, 196. (See also Pool; water supply)

wilderness: Judea, 100; Negev, 246

wine: drinking, 209; Roman wine merchant, 251; vintage scene on vase, 202

winepress: at Ain Karem, 22; treading grapes, 248

writing: papyrus in book and cursive hand, 216; papyrus scrolls with seals, 241; wax tablet, stylus and scroll, 214. (See also inscriptions; and manuscripts)

Z

Zechariah's Pyramid, 25

ziggurat: Ur, 166